Fodor's

BRAZIL

FODOR'S TRAVEL PUBLICATIONS

NEW YORK • TORONTO
LONDON • SYDNEY • AUCKLAND

WWW.FODORS.COM

67

CONTENTS

KEY TO SYMBOLS

- Map reference
- Address
- Telephone number
- Opening times
- Admission prices
- Underground station
- Bus number
- Train station
- Ferry/boat
- Driving directions
- Tourist office
- Tours
- Guidebook
- Restaurant
- Café
- Bar
- Shop
- Number of rooms
- Air-conditioning
- Swimming pool
- Gym
- Other useful information
- ▷ Cross reference
- ★ Walk/drive start point

164
298

213
146

UNDERSTANDING BRAZIL

Understanding Brazil is an introduction to the country, its geography, economy, history and its people. Living Brazil gets under the skin of Brazil today, while The Story of Brazil takes you through the country's past.

UNDERSTANDING BRAZIL

Brazil is more of a continent than a country, both in scale (it's big enough to swallow Australia, with room left over for France and England) and in culture. Brazilians identify themselves initially by their state and then their region. Each has a well-defined personality, its own folklore and fables, its individual exuberant festivals and its own fervid mix of regional music. The many different regions of Brazil began as distant and disparate settlements on a seemingly endless coast, brought gradually together through Portuguese conquest and by the toil and sweat of several million enslaved Africans. As the Portuguese colony grew into an independent nation, the settlements and the peoples merged—both with each other, and with successive waves of immigrants from Japan, the USA and Europe—to create one of the world's most dynamic nations.

LANDSCAPE

Brazil is a vast plateau, fringed with a ragged line of serrated coastal mountains and broken by broad rivers and rugged ridges which run through its centre to culminate in a series of craggy peaks in the country's far north. When the Portuguese arrived on the powdery beaches of the coast, Brazil was a giant forest. The Mata Atlântica rainforest, next to the ocean, was lush, green and dripping with waterfalls; the central western *cerrado* (tropical savannah) was wooded and patched with savannah, waterfall-filled table-top mountains and vast wetlands; and around the myriad Amazonian rivers in the north swathed a carpet of vast rainforest green. Much has now been cut and cleared for cities. The Mata Atlântica has fared the worst, with some 90 per cent felled, but there are still extensive patches in Bahia and Rio de Janeiro states, along the São Paulo and Paraná coasts and around the spectacular Iguaçu Falls.

The little-studied *sertão*, which is made up of a uniquely Brazilian xeric scrubland forest called *caatinga*, as arid and scrubby as Australia, is pocked with smallholdings. The *cerrado* woodland and savannahs (which dip into the world's largest wetland—the Pantanal—as they stretch south towards Paraguay) exist as extensive patches in a sea of swaying soya. While the Amazon has lost more than a third of its original size, forest still stretches unbroken in every direction for more than 2,400km (1,500 miles) in its heartland.

CLIMATE

The equator crosses Brazil in the far north, running through the city of Macapá at the mouth of the Amazon. The tropic of Capricorn cuts a line across the south of the country, just north of the city of São Paulo, meaning that 90 per cent of Brazil's territory lies within the tropics. Despite this, the country's climate is surprisingly varied, with five climatic regions: equatorial, tropical, semi-arid, highland tropical and subtropical.

The Amazon states in the north all straddle the equator and thus have hot, wet and humid conditions. The tropical region lies immediately to the south and encompasses both semi-arid and highland tropical areas. The semi-arid regions are in the interior of the northeast, such as the dry and scrubby *sertão*, and also in the central west. The wet, slightly more seasonal highland regions lie along the east coast and immediately inland, north of Rio de Janeiro. South of the tropic of Capricorn, Brazil is subtropical, with a seasonal variation in climate and temperatures associated with a more Mediterranean feel. The only places in the country to receive snow lie in the highlands of the states of Santa Catarina and Rio Grande do Sul, at the southern extreme of this climatic zone.

ECONOMY

Brazil is rapidly developing as one of the world's largest agricultural and industrialized nations. According to 2009 predictions by the Economist Intelligence Unit, the country's economy will overtake that of the UK, France and Italy as early as 2011, before becoming the fifth largest in the world—in line with its physical size—in 2026. Brazil's emergent economic influence is fuelled by a combination of productivity gains and high commodity prices. Business and commerce have traditionally revolved around São Paulo, Rio and Minas Gerais states. While São Paulo remains the economic powerhouse, the agricultural states of the central west are rising to challenge Minas and Rio. The northeast remains Brazil's most economically depressed area. Currently, 22 per cent of Brazilians live below the poverty line, actually a drop from 34 per cent in 2002, although divisions between rich and poor remain some of the worst in the world. Most of the poverty is concentrated in this region.

Brazil has large deposits of oil and natural gas and is one of the largest food exporters in the world. Exports include coffee, soy beans, sugar cane, beef and cocoa. It is also the leading manufacturer of civil aircraft, after the EU and the USA, and one of the world's rising fashion and media powers. Tourism accounts for less than 1 per cent of the national economy.

POLITICS AND POLITICAL GEOGRAPHY

Brazil is a federal republic comprising 26 states, with a political system loosely based on that of the United States. Government is federal, state and municipal. The federal government sits in the capital city, Brasília. The chief of state and head of government (president) is served by a vice president and a presidentially appointed cabinet. The president and vice president are elected together by popular vote for a single four-year term. After languishing for years as a potential power, Brazil is rising in importance on the world stage, as a member of both the G20 group of industrialized nations and the emerging BRIC nations (Brazil, Russia, India and China), and with a seat on the UN security council between 2010 and the end of 2011. Dilma Rousseff was sworn in as Brazil's first female president in January 2011.

SOCIETY

Brazil is one of the world's true rainbow nations. Brazilians come from the world over, as can be seen from the faces of famous Brazilians abroad, from African-Brazilian Pelé to Japanese-Brazilian Love Fox (from cult group CSS) and blonde supermodel Gisele Bündchen. There are no proper, definitive figures for the percentages of the different racial groups in Brazil. The government has never developed a system for measuring this in the national census. However, the three major racial groups are drawn from Western Europe (principally Portuguese, Spanish, German and Italian), Africa (principally West African Yoruba people and Southwest African Bantu) and America (from myriad Native American tribal nations).

The first Europeans to arrive in great numbers were the Portuguese, who conquered and subsequently colonized the primarily Tupi-Guarani people living along the coast. Other Europeans didn't arrive until the late 19th and early 20th centuries, when they came in large numbers on government-sponsored population programmes, settling in the south and southeast. Brazil has the largest number of black people outside Africa, the ancestors of whom were brought here by the Portuguese through the largest of all the European slave trades. Other significant populations include Arabic, Japanese, Korean and Eastern European Brazilians, mostly in the south and southeast.

The official language of Brazil is Portuguese, which is spoken almost exclusively throughout the country, although Amerindian and African languages can be found in more remote areas, and other languages can still be heard from some immigrants. Brazil is the only Portuguese-speaking country in South America, giving it an instantly unique culture.

Opposite *Praia de Leao on the island of Fernando de Noronha*
Below *Coffee is one of Brazil's principal exports*
Below right *Children practising the martial art dance,* capoeira

THE REGIONS OF BRAZIL

Brazil's 26 states span half of the South American continent, covering a total area of 8,511,956sq km (3,319,663sq miles). It is a little larger than the USA, without Alaska. Each state is itself at least the size of a European country. São Paulo, for instance, is roughly the size of the United Kingdom; Sergipe, which is the smallest, is as big as Wales; Amazonas, the largest Brazilian state, covers 1,570,847sq km (612,630sq miles), making it a little larger in area than the country of Mongolia.

The states are divided into five regions *(regiões*, singular *região)*: South (Paraná, Rio Grande do Sul and Santa Catarina), Southeast (Espírito Santo, Minas Gerais, Rio de Janeiro and São Paulo), Central West (Federal District, Goiás, Mato Grosso, Mato Grosso do Sul), Northeast (Alagoas, Bahia, Ceará, Maranhão, Paraíba, Pernambuco, Piauí, Rio Grande do Norte and Sergipe) and North (Acre, Amazonas, Pará, Rondônia, Roraima and Tocantins). For this book, regions are further subdivided according to tourist highlights, as follows:

Rio de Janeiro City is Brazil's second largest city, boasting one of the most breathtaking cityscapes on the planet, pulsating nightlife and a samba-fuelled street and stadium carnival.

São Paulo City is either the largest conurbation in South America or the world—depending on whose statistics you consult—with some 20 million people crammed into a seemingly endless sea of concrete high-rise. The city is the gastronomic, fashion, cultural and nightlife capital of South America.

Rio and São Paulo States are famous for the beautiful golden beaches and jewel-like islands of the rainforest-clad Costa Verde, and the maquis-covered cape of sandy coves at Búzios. The region is dotted with interesting colonial towns and is protected by a series of national parks, rich in bird life.

The South sees Brazil at its most European. The region saw extensive German immigration in the 19th and 20th centuries and has the world's second largest bierfest. Much of the natural landscape has been cleared, but there are still spectacular forest tracts around the Iguaçu Falls and the coastal islands of northern Paraná, and there are many fine surf beaches.

Minas Gerais and Espírito Santo have lyrical landscapes, hilly colonial towns and little-visited turtle nesting beaches. Minas Gerais is Brazil's literary heartland.

Both states have extensive, if patchy, wild areas too, preserved in a series of national parks.

Bahia is African Brazil's heartland, especially the state capital, Salvador. Gorgeous coconut-palm-shaded beaches and sandy islands stretch to the north and south of Salvador, while the dry desert interior is watered by a mountain oasis in the Chapada Diamantina national park.

Recife and the Brazilian Cape is the cultural capital of northeastern Brazil and boasts the best traditional carnival in the country, rich and varied music and magnificent colonial buildings. There are beautiful beaches too—especially offshore around tiny Fernando de Noronha.

Fortaleza and the Far Northeast has a windswept coast fringed with some of South America's finest beaches, from dune-backed strands around Fortaleza, to the giant beach deserts of Maranhão. The *sertão* interior is dotted with primordial eroded mountains and ancient rock-art sites, and there are numerous colonial towns and cities, including one of the country's best-preserved, São Luis.

The Amazon is dominated by vast rivers and rainforests, which run through the region in an organic filigree of flowing water. It is home to two of the best rainforest lodges in Brazil. Towns and cities cluster along the river banks and there are few roads. Most visitors choose to visit the forest from Manaus or from the islands near Belém in the river's gaping mouth, but there are many other options: the whole of the Amazon is a region as large as Western Europe.

Right *Baia de Sancho on the lovely island of Fernando de Noronha*
Below *Looking over fashionable Ipanema in Rio de Janeiro*

The Central West still retains extensive wild tracts of gentle *cerrado* (tropical savannah) forests, and the Pantanal, the largest wetland in the world and one of the Americas' great wildlife destinations. The north of the region stretches into the Amazon.

HOW TO GET THE BEST FROM YOUR STAY

Plan for a trip to Brazil as you would a trip to the USA; the country is simply too big to cover in a single trip. One possibility is to plan for selected highlights, linked together with an air pass (available for purchase only outside Brazil) and combined with travel on the fast and efficient bus network. Or you could choose a particular region or state: Ceará or Bahia for a beach holiday; the Pantanal for wildlife; the Amazon for spectacular scenery; or Rio and São Paulo for festivals with a dash of rainforest. Getting off the beaten track will not be a problem. Even Brazil's top tourist spots are little visited by European or North American standards. There's nowhere in Brazil where tourists seem to outnumber locals or where Brazilians seem jaded by foreign travellers driving the hardest bargain. English is little spoken, even in Rio de Janeiro or Bahia, so come armed with a phrasebook and dictionary. Nor should you expect Swiss time-keeping: Life is more spontaneous than planned in Brazil.

THE BEST OF BRAZIL

RIO DE JANEIRO CITY

Carnaval (▷ 97): Watch, or even join one of the samba school or street parades in the *Mardi Gras* (Shrove Tuesday) carnival.

Corcovado (▷ 66–67): View the bays and beaches of Rio de Janeiro from the Christ statue.

Ipanema and Leblon beaches (▷ 69): Sun yourself on South America's most fashionable urban sand.

Pão de Açúcar (Sugar Loaf) (▷ 78–79): Take a cable car ride and look down on Copacabana Beach and neighbouring Ipanema from the mountain summit.

Parque Nacional da Tijuca (▷ 81): Take a guided walk through the rainforest and look out over Rio.

Reveillon (▷ 97): Join one of Rio's biggest parties, at Copacabana beach on New Year's Eve.

SÃO PAULO CITY

Cidade Jardim (▷ 128): Browse Latin America's best fashion boutiques.

Edifício Altino Arantes and Edifício Italia (▷ 112): View the city's endless Blade Runner skyline from the observation deck of either of these two towers in São Paulo's old city centre.

Museu de Arte de São Paulo (MASP) (▷ 116–117): Spend a few hours looking at examples from the finest collection of European grand master paintings in the southern hemisphere.

Parque do Ibirapuera (▷ 122–123): Wander through this city centre park, enjoying the fountains, statues and museums, or visiting the planetarium.

RIO AND SÃO PAULO STATES

Búzios (▷ 142): Swim, sunbathe, surf and snorkel on any of the town's 25 beaches that became known as a favourite destination of Brigitte Bardot.

Ilhabela and Ilha Grande (▷ 143, 144): Take light treks or a relaxing beach break on two of the Costa Verde's unspoiled islands.

Paraty (▷ 146–147): Soak up the tranquillity in this little Portuguese colonial town.

Parque Nacional Itatiaia (▷ 145): Trek through the forests of the Serra da Mantiqueira mountains.

Petrópolis (▷ 150): Visit the former Imperial city high in the Serra da Estrela mountains.

THE SOUTH

Blumenau (▷ 163): Quaff *weißbier* (Bavarian wheat beer) from traditional flagons at the world's second-largest bierfest, in October.

Foz do Iguaçu (Iguaçu Falls) (▷ 166–167): Don't miss Iguaçu, the world's mightiest and grandest waterfall, stretching for almost 3km (2 miles) and surrounded on all sides by lush subtropical forest.

Ilha de Santa Catarina (▷ 164–165): Surf and sunbathe on the beautiful island's myriad beaches.

MINAS GERAIS AND ESPÍRITO SANTO

Diamantina and Ouro Preto (▷ 186–187, 188–189): The churches and *praças* (squares) of these World Heritage Sites preserve some of the most impressive baroque art outside Europe.

Above *Colonial Portuguese buildings in Olinda*
Opposite *Sunset over Rio, viewed from Pão de Açúcar*

Parque Nacional Serra da Canastra (▷ 185): Visit one of the most rewarding bird-watching destinations in the Brazilian *cerrado* (tropical savannah).
São João del Rei and Tiradentes (▷ 190): Take the weekend narrow gauge steam train, the *Maria Fumaça*, between these pretty colonial towns.

BAHIA

Chapada Diamantina (▷ 206–207): Hike in the forests and waterfall-filled canyons of the Diamond Hills.
Morro de São Paulo (▷ 209): Relax on a salt-grain white beach on the island of Tinharé.
Reserva Particular do Patrimônio Natural Estação Veracel (▷ 211): Look for rare birds and mammals in the pristine Mata Atlântica forests near Porto Seguro.
Salvador (▷ 214–221): Stroll around the streets of this World Heritage Site, which are lined with colourful 18th-century buildings and fabulously opulent baroque and rococo churches.

RECIFE AND THE BRAZILIAN CAPE

Carnaval (▷ 263): Join Brazil's best and free simultaneous carnivals in Recife and Olinda.
Fernando de Noronha (▷ 247): Swim and dive off the glorious island beaches and explore the vast coral reefs.
Festas Juninas (▷ 263): Dance to *forró* (a fast-paced desert jig) during the lively June celebrations in Caruaru or Campina Grande.
Marechal Deodoro (▷ 248): Wander the quiet, crumbling colonial streets of this former state capital.

FORTALEZA AND THE FAR NORTHEAST

Jericoacoara (▷ 272–273): Enjoy some of the world's best kite-surfing and windsurfing on the long, flat beaches of this remote village.
Natal (▷ 278–279): Walk the castellated perimeter of the Forte dos Reis Magos.
Parque Nacional dos Lençóis Maranhenses (▷ 280–281): Take a scenic flight over the spectacular beach-dune desert.
Parque Nacional Serra da Capivara (▷ 282): Take a guided tour across the weather-worn dome-shaped mountains and visit fascinating archaeological sites.
São Luís (▷ 284–285): Wander the sleepy streets of one of Brazil's least-spoilt colonial capitals.

THE AMAZON

Analvilhanas Archipelago (▷ 298): Take a scenic flight over or a boat trip through the largest river archipelago in the world.
Belém (▷ 300–303): Dance the night away to techno-brig or carimbó-rock in one of Brazil's music capitals, or walk through its historical centre.
Cristalino Rainforest Reserve (▷ 304): Sleep in a hammock or stay in the rainforest lodge on this private reserve to enjoy unrivalled wildlife watching among stands of pristine rainforest.
Rio Branco (▷ 310): Visit the Museu da Borracha (Rubber Museum) or take an excursion to the Chico Mendes' rubber-tapper community.

THE CENTRAL WEST

Bonito (▷ 325): Visit this pretty small town, with a variety of wildlife and many outdoor activities suitable for all the family.
Brasília (▷ 326–327): See Oscar Niemeyer and Lucio Costa's functionalist fantasy Brazilian capital.
Cidade de Goiás (▷ 328): Explore the delightful town of Goiás and nearby Serra Dourada.
The Pantanal (▷ 330–331): Watch the most diverse and abundant display of wetland wildlife in the Americas.
Parque Nacional Chapada dos Veadeiros (▷ 332): Experience magical table-top mountains dripping with waterfalls and swathed in a forest of medicinal plants.

Below *Igreja de Santa Rita overlooks the harbour in Paraty*

TOP EXPERIENCES

Bring the children closer to nature at Jardim da Amazonia (▷ 329), for canoeing on the Amazon, rainforest walks and wildlife all around.

Drive along the Estrada Real (▷ 192–193), visiting some of the fine examples of Brazil's baroque churches and colonial towns.

Fly over Rio in a helicopter (▷ 96) to see all the sights in a seamless panorama, or head to Rio's Fashion Mall (▷ 93) for a rooftop photo-opportunity of the slum area of Rocinha *favela*.

Get lost in Brazilian music Enjoy some contemporary samba-funk at Rio's best small venue, the Circo Voador (▷ 94), or listen to African-Brazilian music at Carlinhos Brown's Centro de Música Negra, in Salvador (▷ 229).

Join the carnival in Rio (▷ 97), Recife (▷ 263), Salvador (▷ 231) or São Paulo (▷ 133), for a *Mardi Gras* (Shrove Tuesday) celebration with more exuberance than anywhere else on Earth.

Marvel at the falls: Experience the immensity of the Iguaçu Falls (▷ 166–167) or take a walk along the Lençóis river in the Chapada Diamantina and get close to its beautiful cascades (▷ 206–207).

Meet the locals of Brazil, some of the most welcoming people you could hope to encounter. Stay with indigenous Yawanàwá people in the relatively untouched forests near the city of Cruzeiro do Sul (▷ 310).

Pamper on the beach in Trancoso (▷ 210) or Itacaré (▷ 208) in Bahia and enjoy a relaxing stay in one of the finest small luxury hotels in South America.

Shop for traditional arts and crafts in the Mercado da Ribeira in the town of Olinda (▷ 261), bead jewellery at Belém's weekend craft market (▷ 301), or high fashion at São Paulo's exclusive Daslu store (▷ 129).

Swim, surf or kite-surf on the beaches of Cumbuco (▷ 274), near Fortaleza, or relax on the white sand beaches of Morro (▷ 209), Bahia.

Tour the Pantanal wetland (▷ 330–331), down the Transpantaneira dirt road. Visit *fazenda* ranch houses, wonder at the innumerable birds and possibly spot a jaguar or puma.

Trek in the rugged mountains of Jalapão (▷ 329), the national park of Chapada dos Veadeiros (▷ 332) or Chapada Diamantina (▷ 206–207), or explore rainforest trails at Mamirauá (▷ 308) in the Amazon.

Watch football in the world's liveliest stadium, Estadio do Maracanã (▷ 96), in Rio. Seeing a game here is an unforgettable and very noisy experience.

Watch the sunset from Corcovado (▷ 66–67) or the Sugar Loaf (▷ 78–79), in Rio.

Wildlife watch Brazil has one of the largest bird lists of any country in the world, with 1,750 species, and is also among the richest for mammals—particularly primates—as well as reptiles, amphibians and vascular plants. See many of these at Parque Nacional Itatiaia (▷ 145) or at Cristalino Rainforest Reserve (▷ 304).

Below *Primera Praia on idyllic Tinharé Island, better known as Morro de São Paulo, in Bahia State*

LIVING BRAZIL

NATURE AND WILDLIFE

Brazil is a land of natural extremes. The country is home to the world's largest river, wetland and tropical forest, and it holds the richest diversity of terrestrial plants and animals on Earth. Other tropical countries pale in comparison. For instance, while Costa Rica has four primate species, Brazil has 77, and while China has 32,200 vascular plant species (plants with a system of circulation fluids, including some ferns and seed-bearing species), Brazil has 56,215. Brazil is home to eight cat species including the magnificent jaguar, the third largest cat in the world. A fifth of all the world's birds are Brazilian and Brazil has one of the highest endemic species numbers of any country. These include some of the world's rarest birds. In addition, the country has great natural and climatic diversity, from the cool cloud forests and the coastal Mata Atlântica to the bone-dry *caatinga* scrub deserts of the *sertão* (a uniquely Brazilian biome) and the lush wetlands of the Pantanal. The centre of the country is made up of one of the most critically threatened biomes on Earth—the dry *cerrado* forests which are filled with rare medicinal plants. Despite this richness, Brazil has a very poor environmental record. Brazil has pledged to cut deforestation rates, but it is still the worst offender in the tropical world, with vast swathes of land cleared for cattle and soya. New prosperity has resulted in a series of expansionist infrastructure schemes which threaten enormous areas of forest and the livelihoods of traditional peoples.

Clockwise from above *Rocky,* caatinga *landscape in Ceara State, northeastern Brazil; aerial view of irrigated soya fields in Goiás State; feeding a Boto (pink river dolphin) in the Negro river, near Manaus, Amazonas State*

MYTHICAL AMAZONIAN BEASTS

Brazil has scores of fabled creatures (which, like Sasquatch and the Yeti, may or may not exist). The most famous and tantalizing of all is the Mapinguari. According to indigenous lore, the creature is a 2m-tall (6.5ft), shaggy-furred and foul-smelling humanoid which shuns water and, according to some, has a mouth in its chest through which it emits a guttural, terrifying roar when alarmed. American biologist David Oren has been on the trail of the Mapinguari since the 1980s and believes that the creature is a giant land sloth—a survivor of a handful of bear- and buffalo-sized creatures which thrived in South America up until the last Ice Age. Other scientists are more sceptical, saying that the Amazon has dozens of mythical inhabitants, from the Curupira (a flame-haired boy with backward facing feet) to the Yawaruna, a huge cat as big as a bull.

THE WORLD'S RAREST PARROTS

Up until the first decade of the new millennium, the *caatinga* deserts of Bahia were home to a spectacular, half-metre tall indigo parrot called Spix's macaw. Until 1990, it was believed that the last three individuals had been caught for foreign collectors by poachers. Then a single lonely male was discovered on a Bahian farm. He died in 2000, almost certainly making the species extinct in the wild.

Other giant blue Brazilian parrots seem destined to follow Spix's macaw: The world's largest parrot, the metre-tall Hyacinth macaw, saw its numbers radically reduced in the second half of the 20th century, Lear's macaw probably lives in only one site near Canudos in Bahia and the turquoise-grey Glaucous macaw is almost certainly extinct. Still, the poaching of nesting birds and other animals continues. The Brazilian government estimates that as many as 12 million animals are poached every year and the numbers of animals facing extinction in Brazil has tripled since the early 1990s.

SOYA

It is soya not logging which is the greatest cause of forest destruction in Brazil. Vast swathes of wilderness in Goiás, Tocantins, Mato Grosso and Pará have been cleared to make way for the bean, which is shipped to China or pulped for animal feed for the beef cattle of Europe. Soya is destroying the forest directly, through the felling of virgin forests for soy fields (principally in Brazil's most threatened biome, the *cerrado*), and indirectly, as soya farmers buy up cattle ranches and the cattle farmers advance into new forest areas. The lucrative soya trade has led to the paving of a road between the Central West and the Amazon, which has seen colonists from all over Brazil flood into the region, causing more deforestation. Brazil's soya lobby is the political establishment and legislation has repeatedly been flouted. The governor of the state of Mato Grosso is Blairo Maggi; the most successful soya farmer in the world. In 2003, Maggi's first year as governor, the deforestation rate in Mato Grosso more than doubled.

GIANT OTTER

One of Brazil's most extraordinary animals is the 2m-long (6.5ft) Giant Amazonian River Otter. They are found throughout South America and principally in the Orinoco, Amazon, and La Plata river systems. They live in oxbow lakes, meandering rivers and wetlands, nesting in gently sloping forested river banks, or behind river beaches with overhanging vegetation. Except for humans, they have no known predators. Yet giant otters were hunted to the brink of extinction in the 1970s, when their thick, velvety pelts were prized for fur hats and handbags. Numbers were further diminished by the release of mercury into Amazon rivers by freelance gold miners in the 1980s and 1990s. Giant otters remain rare, with an estimated 5,000 animals in the wild in South America but, thanks in part to ecotourism, their numbers are slowly recovering in one of its former strongholds, the Pantanal. Seeing a family in the wild is one of the highlights of any Brazilian wildlife excursion.

RIVER DOLPHINS

In the Amazon, teenaged girls and unfaithful wives who become unexpectedly pregnant blame it on river dolphins. According to local legend, on full moon nights male dolphins transform into handsome men in panama hats who search for a woman to seduce. They then disappear back into the river as dawn approaches. Tourists are unlikely to meet botos (or pink river dolphins) while out dancing in Manaus, but their pink dorsal fins, popping up out of the water in sluggish Amazon tributaries, are a common sight. Of the five exclusively freshwater dolphins, the 2.5m-long (8ft) Amazon bot, is the largest and the most abundant. Yet little is known about them, beyond their ability to catch fish through echo location and their gregariousness. They can often be seen schooling with another dolphin, the Tucuxi, which lives far into the Amazon system but, unlike the boto, also swims in estuaries along the South and Central American Atlantic coast.

MUSIC IN BRAZIL

Popular music is one of the highlights of a visit to Brazil. You'll hear it everywhere in an astonishing array of styles, most of which are completely unfamiliar to non-Brazilians. Be sure to include live music and plenty of time browsing through a music store in your travel itinerary. One Brazilian state alone, Pernambuco, has at least 13 different musical genres all of its own. The African-Brazilian music of Bahia, the frontiersman country music of Rio Grande do Sul and the ragtime *choro* of Rio de Janeiro are very different from each other. Taken as a whole, Brazil is a musical continent with a depth and diversity as great as the whole of Europe. Brazil's rich musical heritage comes from its geographical size and the diversity of its peoples. Africa and indigenous Brazil added their musical instruments, rhythms and chants to the bittersweet melodies of Portuguese folk music. As they grew together over the centuries, other ingredients were added: French impressionism after the founding of the Brazilian academy of arts, by Imperially commissioned French intellectuals; the popular dances of Europe as they became fashionable in Rio; ragtime, traditional jazz, bebop, the Beatles, Led Zeppelin, new wave and clubland electronica have all mixed into what is a very Brazilian musical soup.

Clockwise from above *Dancing samba to live music at the Feira de Nordestina in Rio; Caetano Veloso, one of the creators of* tropicália, *performs during the Festival de Verao in Salvador; street performance by the Olodum percussion orchestra*

THE AMAZON AND SURF GUITARRADA

The Amazon may not be the most obvious place in the world to have a vibrant surf scene, yet Belém (in the state of Pará) has been producing exciting surf music for decades. Guitarrada, as the music is known, sounds like a fusion of calypso and Dick Dale. The surf music scene is nominally inspired by the 4m-high (13ft) *Pororoca* bore wave which hurtles up the river mouth several times a year, drawing surfers from all over Brazil and, increasingly, the world. The music is undergoing a resurgence, with bands like La Pupuña playing energized, psychedelic guitarrada pop to cult audiences in Belém's waterfront bars. At weekends, huge warehouse venues throb to the sound of techno-guitarrada. A night out on the town, wearing a colourful Hawaiian surf shirt and burning lots of excess energy, is one of northern Brazil's most unmissable urban experiences.

THE GIRL FROM IPANEMA

In the late 1950s, the poet and diplomat Vinícius de Moraes and his composer friend Antônio Carlos (Tom) Jobim used to meet in one of the little *botequim* bars in Ipanema. This being Rio, they would also spend time watching the girls go by, including a teenager called Heloísa Eneida Pinto. Vinícius wrote lyrics in homage to her, and Jobim completed the music for the song: *A Garota de Ipanema (The Girl from Ipanema)*. In Brazil, this was characteristic of the *bossa nova* (new wave) of samba music fashionable at that time. When the song was then recorded in the USA by João Gilberto, his wife Astrud and saxophonist Stan Getz, it became a worldwide hit. *Bossa nova* is little played in Rio nowadays—you're much more likely to hear the city's trademark music, samba—but the bar where Tom and Vinícius originally met still stands, and is immortalized as the Garota de Ipanema bar.

RHYTHMS OF THE SAINTS

In 1990, when he came to Brazil to record the album *The Rhythm of the Saints*, Paul Simon became one of the first of a string of international musicians (who would later include Michael Jackson) to tap into the rich music scene in the country's African-Brazilian capital, Salvador. Simon recorded drums for the track *The Obvious Child* in Pelourhino and employed *batucada* drummers from the Olodum percussion orchestra as session musicians on the album. Their rhythms are indeed the rhythms of the saints, or the African-Brazilian *Orixás*, since they draw on the ritual music of *candomblé* (a spirit religion) and the music of the martial art dance, *capoeira*. There are now *afoxé* groups (often exclusively African-Brazilian parade troupes) all over the Brazilian northeast. Olodum still play on the Pelourinho in Salvador most weekends, and bands like Ilê Aiyê and Timbalada have their own musical and cultural centres.

PROTEST AND TROPICÁLIA

Brazil in the 1960s was as turbulent as Paris or Washington and much of the mixture of discontent and hope was associated with music. Intellectual young singers, like Chico Buarque from Rio de Janeiro, criticized the military regime through their traditional folk music and sambas. A generation of hip young musicians from Bahia, led by Caetano Veloso and Gilberto Gil, created a new Brazilian music called Tropicália, which embraced psychedelia, new Western musical forms and an alternative, hippy lifestyle. The spirit of the music was anti-establishment and pro self-expression. Musicians spread their message across Brazil in a series of concerts, and after one particularly enthusiastic concert in Ibirapuera Park in São Paulo, the military regime became fearful. Buarque, Veloso and Gil were exiled from the country. Other musicians who remained, like Geraldo Vandré, were tortured and new music had to pass censorship tests before it could be publicly released.

THE SCIENCE OF MANGROVE

Brazil's most famous musical martyr, and the country's counterpart to Jim Morrison or Jimi Hendrix, is Francisco de Assis França (aka Chico Science), who died in a car crash in Olinda in February 1997. This charismatic singer, songwriter and maverick cultural icon spearheaded the most influential movement in Brazilian popular music since Tropicália. It was called mangue (mangrove) beat. The movement began in the late 1980s, when Chico and two of his friends at university in Recife became disenchanted with the highly stratified arts scene in Pernambuco. Chico formed Nação Zumbi, which took Western musical forms like rock and rap and fused them with Pernambuco rhythms like *maracatu*, to create a unique, powerful musical form. Nação were joined by other bands, like Mundo Livre s/a and Mestre Ambrósio, and they inspired a roots pan-arts movement which continues to make Pernambuco one of the most vibrant and creative corners of Brazil today.

FOOTBALL AND SPORT

Brazil is patriotic about sport. Sporting events always see Brazilians beating their drums and waving their flag, and in Brazil all sport is a curiosity next to football. Offices, romances, traffic and quarrels all pause when there is an important game in the state, national or continental cups. The entire country ceases to operate during the World Cup. It has been suggested that Brazilians love football because of its level playing field. Football's strict rules guarantee that talent alone can make you rich and famous—it has certainly done so for football players like Romario, Rivaldo and Ronaldinho, all of whom came from impoverished backgrounds. Football is Brazil's greatest sporting success story. The country has won the World Cup more than any other and Brazilian players are more numerous in the FIFA all-time rankings than any others. However, Brazil's sporting prowess is far from limited to football: The country's Formula One stars come from the opposite end of the social spectrum to its footballers, and have been almost as successful. Ayrton Senna, whose life was profiled in a cinematic documentary released in 2011, was a three-time world champion and today Felipe Massa and Rubens Barrichello enjoy Formula One success. Brazilians dominate the world of jiu-jitsu and mixed martial art fighting, and also rank highly in volleyball, gymnastics and sailing.

Clockwise from above *Brazilian children grab any opportunity to emulate their footballing heroes; a mural commemorates racing driver Ayrton Senna, who was killed in 1994; Flamengo fans enjoy a match at the Maracanã stadium in Rio de Janeiro*

FOOTBALL THE DEMOCRATIZER

Football was brought to Brazil in 1894 by Englishman Charles Miller, whose name adorns a São Paulo street. He founded the Corinthians football club in São Paulo. Football was initially restricted to the wealthy; lower-class Brazilians were not welcome in competitions until the 1920s, when Rio's Vasco team was the first to field a predominantly poor and mainly black side. Vasco won the state championship. The poverty line was crossed by an African-Brazilian from the poor neighbourhood of São Cristóvão in Rio de Janeiro, called Leônidas da Silva, who became the top goal scorer in the 1938 World Cup. It was another humble African-Brazilian, Pelé, who would secure Brazil its first win in the competition 20 years later, since when Brazilian teams have won the cup four times. Pelé remains Brazil's greatest sporting hero and an international football icon.

UM MARACANAÇO

After Leônidas da Silva's performance in the 1938 World Cup, Brazil considered itself the best national team in the world and made elaborate preparations for the next World Cup, which took place in 1950. The new stadium, Maracanã, would be the largest temple to football ever constructed, and the stage for the country's inevitable triumph. Few doubted they would prevail as the other favourites were absent and Brazil was overflowing with talent. They progressed to the final four, but a shock 2–1 defeat by a weakened Uruguay team traumatized the watching 100,000 fans. The Brazilian players were vilified, sent into early retirement or never considered for the national team again. Some fans even committed suicide. A new word entered the Brazilian vocabulary—*um Maracanaço*—used to describe a footballing upset of biblical proportions.

WORLD CUP 2014

The World Cup returns to Brazil for the second time in 2014. Brazil will become the fifth country to have staged the cup twice (together with Mexico, Italy, France and Germany). While the cup will undoubtedly be a joyful occasion, Brazil faces a monumental task if it is to prepare the required infrastructure. The stadia alone in the 12 host cities are expected to cost more than £550 million and alongside these the country has pledged a high-speed rail link between São Paulo and Rio de Janeiro, and upgrades to airports costing well over £7 billion. The centrepiece of the whole tournament will be a completely refurbished and revamped Maracanã stadium, which will host the final, 64 years after the national Maracanaço tragedy. Fans and sports commentators the country over are secretly hoping that they will once more face Uruguay in the final.

AYRTON SENNA

The untimely death of Brazilian Formula One champion Ayrton Senna—in a crash in the 1994 San Marino Grand Prix—sent the country into a collective depression. He may be seventh on Formula One's all-time championship listing, but it is still hard to find a Brazilian who doesn't consider Senna the greatest driver of all time. Other international Formula One racing drivers seem to agree. In a survey carried out by the British magazine *Autosport* in 2009, 217 current and former Formula One drivers chose Senna as the greatest ever motorsport driver. However, he had his detractors. Senna was aggressive and risk-taking. British driver Jackie Stewart, also a three-time Formula One champion, once pointed out that if one totalled all the contacts made with other drivers, by all of the champions in the past, they would be fewer than the hits Senna had made in just two seasons. Senna responded by saying he was out to win. He was 34 when he died. After Senna's death the Brazilian government declared three days of national mourning in his honour.

THE GRACIES

Brazilians are famous for football, but few foreigners are aware that they are the greatest free fighters in the world. This is largely thanks to a novel system of hand-to-hand combat developed by a family of Scottish-Brazilians from the Amazon in the early 20th century. In the first decades of Japanese immigration to Brazil, local Belém boy Carlos Gracie befriended a Japanese immigrant called Mitsuyo Maeda. Maeda was a Judoka prize fighter and he taught his art to Gracie and his family. When Maeda returned to Japan, Carlos moved to Rio and founded his own jiu-jitsu school, where he and his brothers developed and perfected their own techniques, using new holds and arm locks. The school became legendary, spawning a list of champion fighters with bizarre names, including Rickson Gracie, Royler Gracie, Rillion Gracie, Carlson Gracie, and Carlos Gracie Jr. In 1992, American businessman Art Davie and Gracie scion Rorion founded the Ultimate Fighting Championship, now the leading mixed martial arts competition in the world.

CARNIVAL AND THE FESTIVAL CALENDAR

Rio de Janeiro's raucous carnival has made Brazil famous as the world capital of partying. It would be a mistake, however, to think that carnival is limited to Rio de Janeiro, or that it is Brazil's only excuse for a multi-million-people party. Carnival is a country-wide celebration taking many forms, with the biggest parties held not in Rio but in Salvador and Recife in Brazil's northeast. Every day of every year there is a festival happening somewhere in Brazil. There are big festivals in June, too. The Festas Juninas, which also take place principally in the northeast, attract crowds as large as carnival. In the north of the country, the city of São Luís and Parintins erupt into festivities for the Boi celebrations at the end of the month. Christmas and New Year see big parties too, especially in Bahia where the turn of the year is linked with important Afro-Brazilian spiritual celebrations. There are huge Easter parades in Minas Gerais. Most festivals are regional and almost all, including carnival, have a religious significance. This is often multi-layered, arising from a fusion of Christian, native Brazilian and African traditions. A few, like the November festivals in São Gabriel da Cachoeira, are purely indigenous; others, like Blumenau's bierfest, have non-Portuguese, European origins. All are, without fail, an excuse to abandon the often oppressive worries of daily life and live entirely for the present moment.

Clockwise from above *The carnival parade in Rio is world-famous for its flamboyant exuberance; Festas Juninas take place in an* arraial *(large outdoor open space) in northeastern states; New Year's Eve fireworks at Copacabana beach*

CARNIVAL NATION

Carnival is not unique to Brazil. It's a Catholic celebration that traditionally takes place around Shrove Tuesday, immediately before the beginning of the penance of Lent. Brazilian *carnaval* mixes the Portuguese Catholic celebration with African rhythms and pageantry. In Rio, the rhythm is samba: a fusion of Angolan drum patterns and European polka. In Salvador it is *afoxé*—pounded out by giant African-Brazilian drum troupes. In Pernambuco, the rhythms are *maracatu* and *frevo*. The costumed carnival troupes, or *blocos*, that march to these rhythms are derived from traditional parades conducted by African tribal nations in the Portuguese colonial era, in an effort to preserve various cultural identities. Every village, town and city in the country celebrates carnival, and there are four huge events—those mentioned above and one in São Paulo.

DESERT JIGS

The most important festivals after carnival in Brazil's northeast are the Festas Juninas, which are strongly rooted in Portuguese tradition. They officially commemorate the feast of St. John (São João), but are more a celebration of all things rural and northeastern. The main crowds gather in Campina Grande (▷ 245) and Caruaru (▷ 246), two small *sertão* towns in Paraíba and Pernambuco states respectively, to spend each weekend dancing *forró*, dressing up as yokels and eating a range of traditional dishes. These are always accompanied by Brazilian mulled wine, or *quentão*. This is drunk hot, as the festivals take place in the middle of winter, when temperatures in the *sertão* can plummet to below 20°C (70°F): icy if you're a Brazilian. Caruaru is kitted out with a full-scale caricature of a period *sertão* town, complete with a bank and a post office (which are fully functional throughout the festivities). Revellers arrive on '*forró* trains' from Recife. The festival is at its height over the weekend of, or nearest to, 23 June, St. John's day itself.

RUMBLE IN THE JUNGLE

Northern Brazil hosts the Círio de Nazaré religious processions and subsequent revelry, which take place in Belém, and the Festa do Boi Bumba, which is staged at Parintins (on an island in the middle of the Amazon). The latter is an unforgettable three days of dancing, drama and parades, as spectacular as Rio carnival. The festival is a pageant portraying the story of a couple's theft of a prize bull from a rich landowner. The song and dance spectacle takes place in a purpose-built 40,000-seat stadium called the Bumbódromo. Here, two competing teams, Caprichosos and Garantido, parade a series of vast floats surrounded by drum orchestras and scantily clad dancers. The principal characters who feature in the tale are led by the beautiful feminine spirit of the rainforest, the *cunhã-poranga*, who emerges in a burst of fireworks from the mouth of a serpent or jaguar on the most spectacular of the floats. Fans of each group, who are fiercely partisan, roar their encouragement to the two teams from the stadium throughout the proceedings.

REELING IN THE YEARS

Brazil's second biggest annual party is Reveillon, which takes place on New Year's Eve. Hundreds of thousands gather on Copacabana beach in Rio and on Avenida Paulista in São Paulo to party and watch South America's most lavish annual firework displays. There are other New Year celebrations throughout Brazil, especially in Bahia (▷ 231), where there are big parties in Porto Seguro, and in Salvador, where Barra beach is dominated by a huge stage pumping out *axé* music from the state's big stars. After midnight, devotees of the African-Brazilian spirit religion, *candomblé*, dress in white robes and light votive candles set into depressions in the sand. Next to the Igreja do Bonfim in Salvador's Boa Viagem, the party lasts until dawn when the spectacular Nosso Senhor dos Navegantes parade takes place.

WASHING THE STEPS

Bahia's most resolutely African-Brazilian festival takes place on the first or second Thursday after Epiphany, in January, at the pretty baroque church of Nosso Senhor do Bonfim (▷ 217) on the waterfront in northern Salvador. The festival begins in the early morning, when Bahian women *(Baianas)*, dressed in traditional white lace dresses and bearing flowers, congregate at the church of Nossa Senhora da Conceição da Praia, in the city's *cidade baixa* (lower city). After numbers have mounted, they lead processions of tens of thousands of pilgrims and drummers along the coast for some 10km (6 miles) to Bonfim. On arrival, they wash the steps of the church, before dancing to Bahian music until dawn. The festival is in honour of Christ as the Orixá (*candomblé* elemental spirit) Oxalá and is one of the key *candomblé* festivals of the calendar.

BRAZILIAN CUISINE

Beyond the staples of rice, beans, manioc flour and *feijoada*, food in Brazil is regional. Cooking in the south is built around the campfire barbecue and, like Argentina, is dominated by beef. Minas Gerais and Goiás are also strongly meat-orientated. The most adventurous cooking is in the far north—especially in Belém, which is rich in Amazonian fruits and exotic fish—and in Bahia, where seafood dishes like *acarajé* (deep-fried bean and shrimp fritters) and *moqueca* (a kind of stew, cooked in dendê palm oil and coconut, and spiced with chilli) abound. *Churrascarias* (spit roast meat restaurants, often all-you-can-eat) and per-kilo buffet restaurants are popular eateries, but the best food in Brazil is to be found in the fine dining restaurants in São Paulo, where Brazilian ingredients are fused with European and Japanese techniques.

Above left *Fruit for sale at the fruit and vegetable market in Ipanema*
Above right *A bowl of* feijoada, *Brazil's national dish*

FEIJOADA

Like capoeira, *candomblé* and much of its music and its carnivals, Brazil's national dish was created and developed by African-Brazilians using previous indigenous traditions. Unlike these, *feijoada* was born out of necessity. Enslaved Africans of the *engenho* sugar plantations in Brazil's northeast worked so hard that they had little time or ingredients for cooking. They grew staples on meagre plots of land: manioc roots (from which they ground a kind of coarse flour, called *farinha)*, cumin and beans *(feijões)*. These were left in a large pot, along with scraps of meat, to simmer over a slow-burning wood stove while they toiled in the fields, returning to their food after dusk. *Feijoada* was first served in restaurants, and celebrated as Brazilian, on 7 August 1833 at the Hotel Théâtre in Recife. Nowadays, it is traditionally served as Saturday lunch: a time when Brazilian families come together to eat either at home or in *feijoada* restaurants, which can be found all over the country.

FRUIT

Brazil has an astounding number of delicious fruits, particularly in the north, many of which are completely new to foreigners. Açai is a dark and highly nutritious berry from a *varzea* (seasonally flooded forest) palm tree, common in the Amazon. The berries are often served as a frozen paste, served with syrup and guaraná (a ground nut, also from the Amazon, which has stimulant effects similar to caffeine). Camu camu, another *varzea* fruit, has astonishing vitamin C content. Cacau has a delicious white, sweet flesh which pulps into a refreshing drink, as does the strangely perfumed cupuaçu. The seeds of both fruits are used to make chocolate. Other regions, most notably the *cerrado*, are home to umbu, seriguela and mangaba. These are all small pulpy fruits which produce wonderful juices. Brazil is also home to some of the world's best mangoes, papayas, bananas and custard apples, all of which come in a variety of flavours and sizes.

THE STORY OF BRAZIL

THE FIRST NATIONS

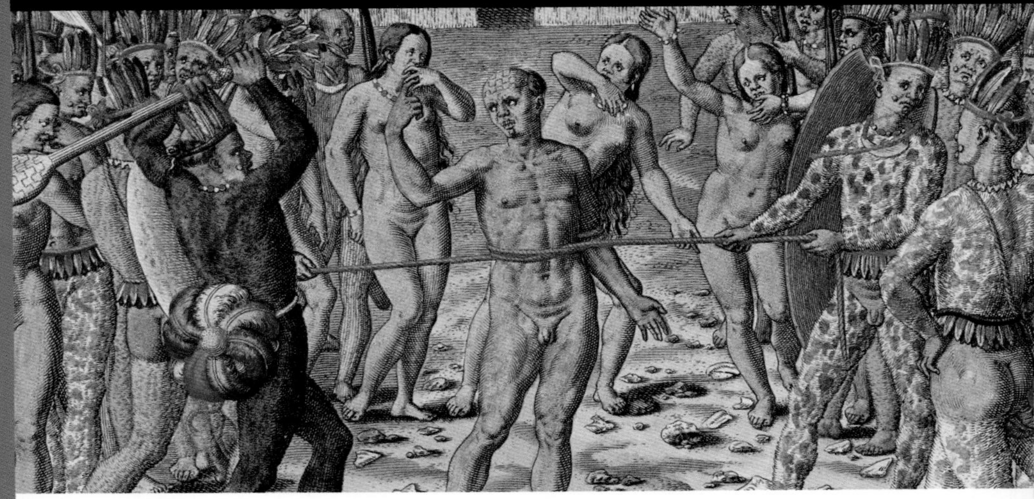

The story of the first Brazilians forms part of the larger story of the first Americans. So little is known about pre-Columbian America that archaeologists are still uncertain about who the first Americans were, when they arrived and how they did so. It is a puzzle not easily solved in an area like Brazil, where indigenous artefacts, made from perishable materials, rot quickly in the tropical climate. Few survive a generation, let alone millennia. The little known about pre-Columbian Brazil has been gleaned from a few isolated spear and arrow heads, from radiometric dating of charcoal deposits where fires once burned, and from cave paintings in the Serra da Capivara, a group of isolated hills in the dry interior of Brazil's northeast. Recent archaeological discoveries, which call into question long-established theories about the first Americans in general, appear only to have raised more questions, and divided expert opinions. However, far more is known about the native Brazilians at the time of initial contact with the Portuguese. Priests, government officials, chroniclers and explorers all left behind extensive records, as did Spanish conquistadores who journeyed through Brazil's vast interior during the 16th century, which paint a picture of life at the time through their eyes.

Clockwise from above The Execution of an Enemy by the Topinambous Indians *(1562), coloured engraving by Theodore de Bry; Francisco de Orellana named the Amazon river and founded Guayaquil in Ecuador; detail of the pre-Columbian rock drawings at Pedra Pintada, Roraima*

THE CLOVIS MODEL

Up until the 1990s, opinion on the origins of the first people in the Americas had changed little since the 19th century, when it was postulated that native Americans had arrived across the Bering Straits from Asia. The invention of radiocarbon dating in the 1950s suggested that none of the artefacts investigated up until that date, from Alaska to Tierra del Fuego, dated further back than 11,200 years. There was a preponderance of bi-facially worked flint pieces found all across the Americas but these were first found near Clovis, in New Mexico. Thus, the first Americans were named after that area and became known as the Clovis people. The Clovis hunted large and now mostly extinct mammals, like mammoths and woolly rhinos. The disappearance of these species was probably due to the success of the Clovis hunters and a catastrophic natural disaster.

CONTROVERSY FROM SOUTH AMERICA

In the 1990s, anthropologists working in South America uncovered evidence of an advanced Amazon civilization in caves near Santarém, which questioned the Clovis findings. The Pedra Pintada people were carbon dated to 11,000 years ago, making them roughly contemporary with the Clovis people. However, their tools and way of life were different. Around the same time, relics were unearthed in southern Chile—some 17,000km (10,500 miles) south of the Bering straits—which were dated to 1,100 years before the Clovis arrived in the New World. The most controversial discoveries of all came from Brazil's Serra da Capivara, where Brazilian archaeologist Niéde Guidon discovered a series of hearths. Some dated from 46,000BC, the most ancient date for human occupation in the Americas. Nowadays many archaeologists accept that there were pre-Clovis civilizations in South America. Where they came from is still open to question.

THE EARLY BRAZILIANS

Whatever were their origins, the native Brazilians that the Portuguese first encountered in 1500 were not a unified people. They were as different and diverse as the nations of Europe: peoples of various genetic and linguistic groups, engaged in constant skirmishes with each other. Some were probably descendants of the first Brazilians, others were migrants who had entered the continent from Asia, and North and Central America. Coastal Brazil, between the northeast and what is now southern São Paulo state, was in the final stages of being conquered by a wave of war-like tribes who were united only by a language, Tupi. Older nations lived in the interior, including advanced civilizations, as described in 1542 by Francisco de Orellana, the first European to navigate the Amazon: The Curucirari tribe had developed extensive agriculture and road systems, and produced fine ceramics which compared favourably with Chinese porcelain.

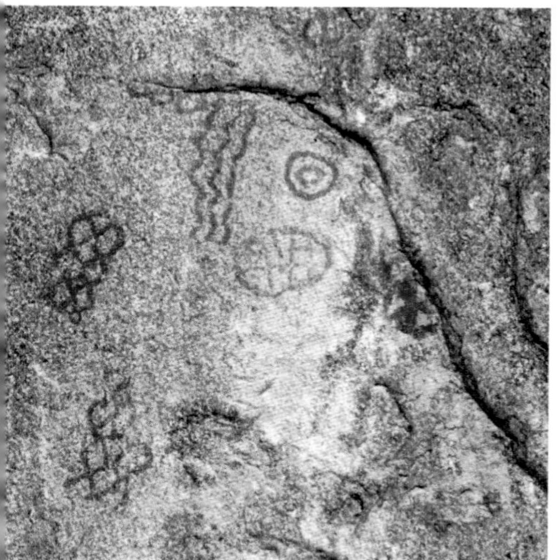

FIRST EUROPEAN CONTACT

Like the Caribbean and North America, Brazil was discovered by fluke. A minor Portuguese nobleman, Pedro Álvares Cabral, and his fleet of 13 trading ships was blown far off course on an expedition to the Indies. Far off to the west of the Azores they made first sight of land on 21 April 1500. First contact with the locals was made immediately on the beaches of what is now southern Bahia, as described by chronicler Pero Vaz de Caminha: '*...they were dark and entirely naked, with nothing to cover their private parts, and carried bows and arrows in their hands.*' After some exploration, Cabral held the first mass on Brazilian soil, planted a huge wooden cross on the shore, claimed it for Portugal and departed, leaving flagons of wine and two desperate convicts who were intended to begin intermarriage with the locals.

THE TUPI PEOPLE

The Brazilians encountered by the first Portuguese were a Tupi-speaking people called the Tupinambá. The Europeans' understanding of all native Brazilians was based almost entirely on their contact with this group. Unlike many of the indigenous Brazilians, the Tupi were a brutal people. Their tribal groups engaged in kidnapping, ritual murder and cannibalism. The latter was undertaken as an intolerable insult to the rival group, which then demanded immediate revenge. This cycle brought downfall to the Tupinambá, who readily enlisted the Europeans as allies against their enemies. As the Europeans learned of the Tupi peoples' cannibalistic practices, they used it as moral justification for the ensuing slave trade, though this made victims of many other indigenous tribes, to whom eating human flesh was anathema.

THE PORTUGUESE

The first few decades of contact were dominated by friendly banter and barter between the Portuguese and the local Brazilian indigenous people, and a trade in the Pau-Brasil dye-wood which was to give the country its name. As this trade began to grow in importance—with a substantial market developing in Europe—rivalry for early trade between Portugal and France led to the establishment of a formal colony. This was administered from various settlements or captaincies along the coast and principally from Bahia, whose capital Salvador became the first capital of the country. There was little indigenous resistance to the arrival of the Portuguese, but a great deal to the insistence that the local population should work for them (harvesting wood and planting sugar cane). Desperate for a return on their investments, far from the motherland and interpreting the edicts of their king in their favour, the Portuguese began a war against the Brazilian indigenous peoples, enslaving those conquered and using their women to people a new nation. Many of the Tupi-speaking tribes along the Atlantic coast and the isolated peoples of the Amazon basin were completely wiped out.

Clockwise from above *Benedito Calixto's painting of the landing at São Vicente in 1532; the national tree of Brazil, Pau-Brasil, gave its name to the country;* Tome de Sousa, First Governor General of Brazil, *by Margaret Dovaston (1884–1954)*

BRAZIL WOOD

Descriptions of Brazil's enormous coastal forests by Cabral's men resulted in the commissioning of a further Portuguese fleet in 1501. This was captained by Gonçalo Coelho and included Amérigo Vespucci (who would give his name to the continent) as a chronicler. The fleet made only one important discovery: a wood which produced a bright red dye of a colour popular in Europe. A trade in the wood began, depending entirely on the indigenous Brazilians. The wood became known as Pau-Brasil and the source was referred to colloquially as the land of Brasil wood, or Brasil. As the Pau-Brasil trade grew, the French became involved and the early days of peaceful barter soon degenerated into bloodshed and exploitation. The Portuguese regarded Brazil as their land—by right of papal decree—but the French saw no reason to halt a trade which was earning them money.

FIRST SETTLEMENT

By the second decade of the 16th century, the Portuguese had begun to dispatch warships to defend their interests. When this failed to stop the French trade they sent a fleet in 1530, captained by Martim Afonso de Sousa, to found a colony and formally claim the land of Pau-Brasil for Portugal. Afonso's fleet patrolled the coast for two years, destroying French ships and storehouses. In 1532 they finally settled and built their first town, at São Vicente in modern-day São Paulo state. From here, de Sousa divided the entire Brazilian coast into fourteen captaincies and awarded each to a selection of chosen subjects, or donatories. Within a decade, donatories began to harvest crops, principally sugar. The mills, or *engenhos*, required a large manual workforce and each captain was granted powers to wage war against 'troublesome' tribes. Under the pretence of crushing tribes aggressive to the colonies, the Portuguese began to ransack villages and forcibly enslave the Tupi people found there, killing all those who resisted.

THE FIRST CAPITAL

Fighting broke out throughout the donatory colonies, especially in Bahia, the largest sugar-growing area. *Engenhos* were ransacked and the Portuguese were murdered and ritually eaten. Portugal responded with increased violence. Tomé de Sousa and a fleet of ships were dispatched in 1549 to establish a capital in Brazil from which order would be imposed with an iron fist. The new colonists were made up principally of 'New Christians': Jews and Arabs forced to convert to Christianity under the threat of the Dominican-led Inquisition, including a group of firebrand Jesuits led by the charismatic Manoel de Nobrega. The Portuguese king, Joao III, gave de Sousa clear instructions—to convert the locals to Christianity, to construct more *engenhos* and to punish any Tupi people who resisted. The new capital of Portuguese Imperial Brazil was named São Salvador da Bahia de Todos os Santos (the city of the Holy Saviour of All Saints Bay). Salvador for short.

ESTABLISHING THE SLAVE TRADE

The Portuguese king's stipulations for the governance of the new colony set the course of early Brazilian history. Converted natives were captured by means of word or war and then corralled into the enormous seminary workhouses called *aldeias*, administered by the Jesuits. Although the native Brazilians were deprived of liberty and their own culture, they were afforded dignity otherwise and spared the ravages of the plantation owners. The Portuguese enslaved many of those who would not accept Christianity. The children were murdered, the women raped and forced to become prostitutes, and the men were forced to work under the lash on the plantations. Few lived longer than five years, after which they died from exhaustion or European disease. Entire nations disappeared, including the great Amazonian Curucirari and Paguana civilizations.

MEM DE SÁ AND THE FOUNDING OF RIO

The French were far more just in their treatment of the indigenous people and, as tribes throughout Brazil became increasingly hostile to the Portuguese, the Tamoio natives in the southeastern captaincy of São Vicente formed an alliance with the French. In 1555 the French founded a colony of their own, called France Antarctique, on an island in another huge Brazilian bay, Guanabara. The Portuguese responded by installing an even more ruthless governor, one of the country's fiercest soldiers, Mem de Sá. Together with his indigenous allies, the Temiminós, Mem de Sá massacred the Tamoio and the French and founded a new Portuguese settlement on Guanabara Bay, at São Sebastião de Rio de Janeiro. He also conducted a scorched-earth campaign in Bahia, burning the forests and villages that sheltered the local people, and killing all they encountered.

SUGAR AND THE SLAVE TRADE

Slave numbers soon dried up on the Brazilian coast, but the success of Brazilian sugar on European markets meant that there were more and more *engenhos* (sugar mills)—especially in Maranhão, Pará, Bahia and Pernambuco. By the mid-16th century the situation on the plantations had become critical. *Bandeirante* slaving raids were dispatched to the Brazilian interior to capture native Brazilian slaves, much to the consternation of the Jesuits who became increasingly vocal in their condemnation of the Portuguese. The slave trade was so rapacious that it had soon dispensed with all the natives that the *bandeirantes* could capture, and so Africans were imported in ever-increasing numbers from the 17th century. By the time of abolition in the late 19th century, Portugal and Republican Brazil had made some 30,000 slaving voyages transporting more than 4,650,000 Africans, mostly to Brazil. This is more than double the number of voyages undertaken (and almost double the number of Africans enslaved) by the next largest trading county, Britain, and well over ten times the number of slaves brought to the United States. The sugar-cane wealth brought by the African slaves funded magnificent churches and civic buildings displaying the first of Brazil's lavish baroque interiors.

Clockwise from above *Monument to the* Bandeirantes *in São Paulo;* Slaves in Brazil: The Terrible Torture of a Slave, *from* Journal des Voyages, *c.1865; intricate wood carvings in Igreja de São Francisco, Jacaranda, are typical of the many churches built by the Jesuits*

BLOODTHIRSTY *BANDEIRANTES*

By the early 17th century, Brazil was a century old and there were several generations whose mixed blood meant that they were neither accepted as Portuguese nor indigenous. Many became *bandeirantes*: explorers who set off barefoot into Brazil's vast forest interior in search of whatever they could find to sell. This was often indigenous people. They would travel the rivers of the interior for years at a time, finding new tribes who had never seen a foreigner. They killed the weak, old and female, and marched the remainder back to *bandeirante* towns like São Paulo, to be sold at slave markets. The *bandeirantes* also found the gold which made Brazil wealthy and their expeditions resulted in the delineation of the interior borders of modern Brazil. As such the *bandeirantes* are often regarded as heroes by many Brazilians.

RESISTANCE FROM THE JESUITS

Only Jesuits were opposed to the slave trade and the *bandeirante* raids; a number of them targetted *aldeias* (communities) in Paraguay. The orator, Father Antônio Vieira, travelled throughout Brazil denouncing the slave trade. The Jesuits became increasingly unpopular with the Portuguese. In the late 17th century a mob ransacked their college in Belém and the priests were kicked out of both Pará and Maranhão. It was the beginning of the end. Vieira died in Salvador in disgrace after a piece of vicious calumny by rival Dominicans, and the society's power and influence waned. In the 18th century the governor of Portugal, the Marquis de Pombal, persuaded the Pope to expel the Jesuits from all the Iberian colonies. The order was disbanded in 1773 by Pope Clement XIV.

THE AFRICANS

By the end of the 17th century, African slaves had become the engine that ran Brazil, working the *engenho* sugar mills and building Portuguese Brazil's burgeoning towns and cities. Most of the country's baroque churches, mansions and palaces were built and decorated by Africans, under pain of torture or death. Torture was inflicted on Africans to ensure that they did what they were told. Death was the punishment for insubordination or attempted escape. Brazil was cruel even by the brutal standards of the era, as is attested by Thomas Ewbank, an American visitor who described torture practices he had observed in northern Brazil in the 1850s: 'It is no uncommon thing to tie their hands and feet together; hoist them off the ground and beat them as near to death as possible.'

BOOM TIME

With the Tupi people quelled and Africans ensuring huge profit margins for the sugar and tobacco industry, Brazil's cities became increasingly lavish. Salvador, the Recôncavo towns (▷ 212–213), Recife (▷ 254–257) and São Luís (▷ 284–285) grew wealthy and displayed their money in handsome religious and civic buildings. Splendid churches were commissioned by religious and lay orders. Contrary to popular belief, the money for their construction did not come from the coffers in Rome. The magnificent gold-encrusted interiors of the baroque churches on Salvador's Pelourinho (▷ 214) or Recife's old Portuguese centre (Recife Antigo ▷ 255) were paid for by rich sugar and tobacco families. They competed in ostentation, commissioning the finest artists to produce works that would serve as displays to their wealth and influence. Most were carved and painted by black or mixed-race artists, prohibited from worshipping in the churches they decorated.

BIG TROUBLE WITH LITTLE HOLLAND

By the 1620s the Dutch West India Company had been formed and taken an interest in the Americas. In 1624 they dispatched a fleet of 26 ships to take Salvador and the Recôncavo (▷ 212–213) from the Portuguese. The Bahians fled and the Dutch installed their own governor in Salvador, Johan van Dorth. Their triumph was short-lived. The Portuguese returned and recaptured the city the following year, heralding a century of skirmishes. In 1629 the Dutch conquered Pernambuco, founding Dutch Recife as Mauristaad, the new capital city of the state. It was named after the governor, John Maurice of Nassau. He was enlightened by Portuguese standards, declaring religious amnesty in the city (leaving people free to practise Judaism and Islam) and encouraging the arts — Dutch painters like Frans Post (1612–1680) spent many years there. Dutch Pernambuco was formally taken back by the Portuguese in 1661.

THE GOLD RUSH, RIO AND REVOLT

Increasing prosperity in 17th-century Brazil was driven by increasing numbers of African slaves brought into the northeast to work on the *engenhos* (sugar mills). The conditions were appalling and despite punishment by torture or death many slaves fled to remote regions of the country to set up their own hidden *quilombo* communities. The most famous and successful of these was Palmares, in modern-day Alagoas state, a community led by the charismatic Zumbi, who remains an important symbolic figure for African-Brazilians to this day. The 18th century saw gold struck in the backlands of Minas Gerais, in a stream which was named Ouro Preto (black gold). This led to the establishment of a series of new towns and to the growth of the ports along the southeast coast, shifting the balance of power away from Bahia and Pernambuco to the southeast of the country, and eventually to a new capital city at Rio de Janeiro. The new towns grew as wealthy and magnificent as their predecessors in the northeast, and there was a florescence of art and architecture led by Brazilian artists like Aleijadinho. Things were not so prosperous in Lisbon. A financially crippled Portuguese empire squeezed all the precious metal and taxes they could from Brazil, resulting in widespread discontent which saw the first fruits of revolution in the campaigns of the Inconfidência Mineira in Minas Gerais, led by a group of insurgents including an army dentist called Tiradentes.

Clockwise from above *The colonial gold-mining town of Ouro Preto in Minas Gerais; Sebastião José de Carcalho e Melo, Marquis of Pombal (1699–1782); Igreja da Imperial Irmandade de Nossa Senhora da Glória do Outeiro in Rio was the favourite worshipping place of the Portuguese royal family*

PALMARES AND ZUMBI

Palmares was originally a *quilombo*: a village created by fugitive slaves. It grew to become a threat to the Portuguese later under the leadership of a charismatic African called Zumbi. He was said to be a newborn survivor of a *bandeirante* raid on Palmares, raised and educated in Recife by a priest. He was baptized, taught to read and write, and became an altar boy in his adopted father's church, whose congregation protested at his colour. At 15, he fled and by 1678 his superior education led him to become the leader of what had grown into a huge network of *quilombos*. For 14 years he headed an independent fugitive state based in Palmares, until a *bandeirante* expedition led by Domingos Jorge Velho laid waste to the town. Zumbi was tortured and killed by Jorge Velho, who carried his head around Recife before leaving it on display in front of the Carmelite church.

BLACK GOLD

It was economics and not insurrection which began to geographically shift the balance of power in Brazil. In 1695, the *bandeirantes* found gold: black gold in a little stream near the Minas Gerais town which now bears its name, Ouro Preto (▷ 188–189). In the following decades there were further discoveries throughout Minas Gerais and in towns of the Central West, notably at Pirenópolis (▷ 333) and Goiás (▷ 328). Between the last decade of the 1600s and 1750, Brazil's population more than doubled and mining overtook sugar to become Portugal's principal source of wealth. The northeastern sugar-growing heartlands of Bahia and Pernambuco rapidly found themselves on the margin of a country they had previously dominated, as new Europeans chose to arrive in Brazil at a more convenient point further south: the burgeoning port city of Rio de Janeiro.

RIO BECOMES THE NEW CAPITAL

By the mid-18th century, Portugal itself was in financial crisis, indebted to a new power with a faster, more efficient navy and larger trading Empire—Britain. Portugal turned to the Brazilian mines for a solution. She squeezed every last drop of profit from the colony through draconian taxes. Portugal's need for tight controls and efficiency meant that almost everything of value entered and left Brazil through Rio de Janeiro, further marginalizing the northeast of the country. In 1763, the Portuguese moved the vice-royalty of Brazil from Salvador to Rio, which grew rapidly. Merchants established shops and trading outlets around the modern-day Praça Quinze and churches grew in pomp and lustre. Within a few decades, Rio had established itself as the most important port and slaving centre north of the River Plate.

POMBAL'S REFORMS

In 1755 Lisbon suffered a devastating earthquake and tsunami which destroyed almost the entire city. In the aftermath, a new, modern politician took control of a still indebted Portugal. Sebastião José de Carvalho e Melo—minister of the kingdom to King José and more generally known as the Marquis of Pombal—rebuilt the city and implemented sweeping policy changes in Portugal and its colonies. Brazil's gold had been plundered and Portugal was still importing British luxury goods, while exporting little more than port wine, olive oil and cork. Pombal was the first Portuguese ruler to have a long-term vision for Brazil which concentrated not just on exploitation, but also investment. He increased the production of raw materials (introducing rice, cotton and coffee), invested in the nascent cocoa industry and increased efficiency in the *engenhos* (sugar mills). Portugal's trade with Britain turned into a surplus and Portugal was able to supply rising British demand when, from 1776, the American colonies revolted and Britain was constantly at war.

THE TEETH PULLER

Despite the Marquis of Pombal deliberately offering high-ranking posts to white Brazil-born Portuguese, the Brazilian populace still felt alienated and taxes were still high. During 1788–9, a group of young aristocratic and principally military men formed the Inconfidência Mineira, determined to rid Brazil of the Portuguese. Unusually, one member was poor: a former army dentist, Joaquim José da Silva Xavier, always known by his nickname, Tiradentes (tooth puller). After leaving the army, Tiradentes had worked extensively in the mines around Ouro Preto and seen the exploitation of native Brazilians. Trips to Rio brought him in contact with more modern ideas from Europe. Tiradentes and his fellow conspirators did little more than talk in secret, planning to found a republic based in Tiradentes' home town of São João del Rei (▷ 190). However, they were discovered by the Portuguese, arrested and—after he had assumed responsibility for the Inconfidência—Tiradentes was hung, drawn and quartered in Rio de Janeiro.

IMPERIAL BRAZIL

France had been continuously troublesome to the Portuguese in Rio since the defeat of France Antarctique in 1567, a settlement founded on the huge Guanabara Bay in front of modern-day Rio de Janeiro. In 1710 the French ransacked the city and were only expelled after Portugal agreed to pay a hefty ransom in gold and sugar. In the following decades, French pirates continuously attacked Portuguese ships on their way across the Atlantic. However, little could have prepared Rio for the momentous events to come when, fleeing from Napoleon (who threatened the whole of Iberia), the Portuguese court up and left Lisbon for Rio, escorted by a flotilla of British warships. Brazil became the new centre of the Portuguese Empire, administered from an increasingly opulent Rio de Janeiro. When the threat from Napoleon dissipated, Brazil was reluctant to relinquish its new-found power, declaring itself an independent monarchy under Emperor Dom Pedro I. Little changed for poor Brazilians, though, and the ravages of slavery continued. Discontent with the favouritism shown towards the Portuguese in court circles eventually led to pressure for a new emperor and Pedro II, the infant son of Pedro I, ascended to the throne.

Clockwise from above *A 19th-century depiction of slaves working on a coffee plantation;* Pedro I (1798–1834) Emperor of Brazil *(1825), by Henrique José da Silva; the port of Rio de Janeiro* c.1900

NAPOLEON FRIGHTENS THE PORTUGUESE

Portugal, tucked away at the far corner of Europe, had been spared the ravages of Napoleon Bonaparte during the first few years of the 19th century, but after his defeat at Trafalgar Napoleon determined to close Europe to Britain. He turned his eyes to Britain's oldest ally: the weak and ineffectual Portuguese house of Bragança. It was headed at that time by the Prince Regent, João, a shy recluse. João's ministers assured him that resistance was useless and, in November 1807, the royal family abandoned their frightened subjects and left for Brazil, under the protection of British warships. It must have been an incredible sight. Crowds thronged around the muddy docks while the entire Portuguese court and government boarded some 40 ships, carrying with them the crown jewels, royal library, carriages, horses and full retinue.

AID AND TRADE

The Portuguese arrived in Rio under the escort of the British navy, who exacted a high price for their help. Under the treaty of Methuen, signed in 1703, all of Portugal's ports were 'opened to friendly nations'. This meant the British, who held a trade monopoly, and effectively made Portugal and her colonies part of the British Empire. The Imperial Brazilian currency and banking system were managed by the British to their own advantage, with a systematic spiral of devaluation which made Brazilian goods very cheap for the English market and English goods expensive for the Portuguese. The Imperial government had to borrow money from British banks to buy British goods, which they were required to import. By the end of the 19th century, an estimated 200 million pounds sterling had left Brazil for London.

THE RECONSTRUCTION OF RIO

The Imperial capital under João VI became increasingly grand and opulent. New palaces like the Paço Imperial (▷ 82) were built to house the royal family and their 15,000 newly arrived nobleman attendants. Neoclassical administrative buildings, libraries and theatres were constructed for their places of work and entertainment. Thousands of slaves were imported to pamper them and whole neighbourhoods, built on the European model, sprang up to cater for the city's burgeoning merchant class. A city which had been a relative global backwater was soon thriving. King João loved his new homeland and capital but after Napoleon was defeated at Waterloo and the British became concerned about a possible Portuguese public revolt, he returned to Lisbon to govern Portugal itself.

INDEPENDENCE OR DEATH!

King João VI left his Byronic young son, Pedro, as Regent of Brazil. Under Pedro, Brazil and Portugal became increasingly at odds. Liberals in Lisbon were determined to return Brazil to its previous subordinate status, reneging on the political and economic equality which had come with Rio's status as the Imperial capital. In 1821, the Lisbon government formally recalled the Prince Regent to Portugal. On 9 January 1822, Dom Pedro announced that he would not be leaving Brazil. Realizing that weak Portugal was in no position to prevent Brazil's independence, Pedro wasted little time in declaring it. In September 1822, on a journey between São Paulo and Rio, he uttered his famous cry (the *Grito de Ipiranga*, ▷ 120), 'Independence or Death!', tore the Portuguese insignia off his uniform, instructed his soldiers to do the same and proclaimed, 'By the blood that flows in my veins and upon my honour, I swear to God to free Brazil.'

INDEPENDENT IMPERIAL BRAZIL

Brazil was the only country in Latin America to have a smooth transition to independence, but Pedro I ruled for only nine years. Suffering criticism and insurrection, he abandoned the country to his five-year-old son, Pedro II. By the time Pedro II came to power at the age of 15, Brazil was in the hands of a ruling oligarchy who were struggling to control a series of uprisings. Pedro did little to change Brazil. Coffee had become the country's most important export and the former *bandeirante* centre of São Paulo grew as a result. Pedro concentrated on Rio, transforming it into one of the continent's cultural centres. He also increased the already mounting pressure from Britain and domestic abolitionists on Brazil's slavers, finally breaking them in May 1888 when Brazil became the last country in the Western world to abolish slavery. His daughter, Princesa Isabel, signed the declaration (as he was away in Europe).

BRAZILIAN REPUBLIC

The abolition of slavery in 1888 made Dom Pedro II a target for wealthy landowners and military men who sought a Republican Brazil, and the emperor was eventually deposed in a quiet coup. This led to rebellions in many of the provinces, particularly Bahia, which were ruthlessly quelled by the army. The new elite of cattle ranchers and coffee growers were reluctant to employ their former slaves. Instead, they invited immigration from Europe. The economy grew rapidly but collapsed spectacularly after the Wall Street Crash of 1929, leading to an era of dictators. Getúlio Vargas dominated for much of the middle part of the 20th century. After an army coup in 1930 he became caretaker president and, but for a short break in the 1940s, remained in power for almost 25 years. His *Estado Novo* regime stamped out political opposition, nationalized the unions, installed a still-entrenched bureaucracy (which required the presentation of an identity document for even the most trivial of reasons) and became involved in numerous corruption schemes. Vargas was followed by a series of military despots propped up by the United States, who feared a Cuban-style revolution from agitators like Júlio Prestes. Brazil only emerged from authoritarian rule in the 1980s after their foreign debt had become the worst in Latin America and when international interest rates rose so sharply in 1982 that the country was no longer able to make the repayments.

Clockwise from above *Campaigners demanding direct presidential elections; US President Dwight Eisenhower with President Juscelino Kubitschek on 1 February 1960, in Rio; coffee growers were among the elite who called for a Republican Brazil*

ORDER AND PROGRESS

Abolitionism made Dom Pedro II very unpopular with the elite. By now, they were paying for much of Brazil and relied on free labour for their coffee plantations. A republican movement had been bubbling under since the 1870s and after slavery's abolition it attracted the support of the military. Eighteen months after the 1888 abolition act was passed, the army deposed Dom Pedro and declared Brazil a republic. They installed a soldier—Marechal Deodoro de Fonseca—as the first president and invented a new flag emblazoned with a new national motto, *Ordem e Progresso* (Order and Progress). A constitution created a republic of 20 states, with their own governors and powers of self-government. Literate males (who numbered around 3 per cent of the population) had the right to vote, and Church and State were separated.

BACKLAND REBELLION AND THE FIRST *FAVELAS*

In the late 1880s Brazil's marginalized ex-slaves and poor found a prophet, Antônio Conselheiro. His anti-establishment and anti-Republican views attracted thousands to his new spiritual capital of Canudos (▷ 205), in the Bahian *sertão*. By the 1890s it had become the largest town in the state after Salvador. The federal authorities sent three armies to crush it. All were defeated, until a fourth expedition of 8,000 soldiers and heavy artillery burned Canudos to the ground. Conselheiro's head was paraded around. The specially commissioned Republican army, mostly ex-slaves, was disbanded. With nowhere to go and no wage, thousands built shelters in the hills around Rio, as they had done on the hills around Canudos. These were Brazil's first slums, called *favelas* after a wild *sertão* plant.

IMMIGRATION AND DEBT

Post Canudos, Brazilian politics remained dominated by the Paulista coffee growers and the Mineira cattle ranchers, collectively known as the *café com leite* (coffee with milk) alliance. Abolitionism had left the plantations short of workers but, rather than invest in Brazilians, the racist elite invited immigration from Europe. Meanwhile, the USA was beginning to supersede Britain as the world's dominant economic power. Brazil was still exporting its agricultural products and raw materials to Europe at ever-lower prices and importing new US goods at a high rate. After the Wall Street Crash of 1929, Brazil's economy went into freefall. Coffee prices collapsed and so did the power structure of the Paulistanos. By the early 1930s, a weak government was spending a third of its budget on servicing debt.

STRONGMEN

The pre-War period saw a battle waged between two charismatic men: the communist, Prestes—who conducted a long march of the discontented through Brazil's backlands—and Getúlio Vargas, a wily populist who eventually won the political game. One of his corruption schemes caught up with him in 1954 and, faced with a hostile press and American criticism, he shot himself. Another strongman took control of the reins of power: Juscelino Kubitschek promised 50 years of economic growth in his five-year term and bankrupted the country by building Brasília (▷ 326–327) at exorbitant cost. The next president, Jânio Quadros, was left to pick up the pieces. He failed and handed the problem to João Goulart, a populist and former labour minister under Vargas. However, Goulart was deemed too left-wing by the Americans, who had him deposed by a military coup, leaving the generals in control.

THE MILITARY ERA

The new system of government saw political parties outlawed and replaced by the Aliança Renovadora Nacional (ARENA)—who were in power—and their official opposition, the Movimento Democrático Brasileiro (MDB). The puppet Congress consisted only of members of these two parties and they approved a succession of military presidents. Insurgent groups carried out a campaign of guerrilla warfare in the cities, resulting in Brazilians being forbidden to meet in groups, or dance samba. Possession of any book or document regarded as suspicious led to arrest and torture. Investment from the United States saw the economy begin to grow, as did the division between rich and poor. By 1980, the richest 10 per cent of the population were receiving 51 per cent of Brazil's GDP, with 50 per cent of the country left with only 13 per cent. Unable to control the economy, the military relinquished control.

INTO THE 21ST CENTURY

Post-dictatorship Brazil has been a turbulent place. The first elected president, Tancredo Neves, died mysteriously the night before he took office and was succeeded by José Sarney, a stooge of the landowning elite. Inflation and debt spiralled out of control and the country next elected a populist outsider, Fernando Collor de Mello, who resigned from government under a cloud of corruption which had him accused of personally pocketing millions. It took bookish sociologist and reluctant president, Fernando Henrique Cardoso, to put Brazil back on track with his economy-saving Plano Real in the 1990s. After serving his maximum two terms, Cardoso handed power to the left-wing former union leader, Luíz Inácio Lula da Silva (known as Lula), who led Brazil into new-found prosperity. Wealth is more abundant and even poorer Brazilians are beginning to notice the difference, but the divide between rich and poor is still huge and there is much corruption—both factors in rising crime and a social unrest that Dilma Rousseff, Lula's annointed successor, will need to address.

Above *Dilma Rousseff, the future president, holds a rally in October 2010 in Belo Horizonte during the elections*

CORRUPTION AND COLLOR

The first post-dictatorship president, José Sarney, singularly failed to curb Brazil's astronomical 300 per cent inflation. When Sarney's government eventually collapsed in 1989, desperate Brazilians sought a saviour from their financial troubles. They found him in the form of Fernando Collor de Mello, a silver-tongued and little-known populist from Alagoas state, with movie-star good looks. He promised Brazil an immediate curb on inflation, a return to prosperity and the impeachment of public servants on super-salaries. Ironically, it was Collor himself who was threatened with impeachment. Just two years after ascending to power he resigned under a cloud of corruption allegations and an investigation into back-handers paid to his office by lobbyists. He left government with inflation at an incredible1,500 per cent and foreign debt payments completely suspended.

THE FIREBRAND

One of the most enduring figures on the recent Brazilian political scene has been a bearded, left-wing firebrand called Luíz Inácio (Lula) da Silva. Lula was a steel-workers union leader without a tertiary education. His under-privileged upbringing endeared him to hundreds of thousands of Brazilians. Lula worked his way up through the factories to become a union leader and the founder of the left-wing PT Workers Party, as head of which he stood for president three times before eventually winning in 2002. It was the first time a member of the aristocracy had failed to win presidential office in the country's history. Fearing a surge towards Cuban-style governance, the currency plummeted once more but the panic was needless. Lula was an immensely successful and popular president, balancing economic reform with an attempt to address social ills at home, using poverty relief and a minimum wage.

ON THE MOVE

On the Move gives you detailed advice and information about the various options for travelling to Brazil before explaining the best ways to get around the country once you are there. Handy tips help you with everything from buying tickets to renting a car.

ARRIVING

ARRIVING BY AIR

Brazil is easily reachable on direct flights from the USA, Canada, South Africa and Europe and via Chile, Argentina, South Africa or the USA from Asia and the Pacific. Flights generally land in São Paulo, although Rio de Janeiro, Salvador, Manaus, Belém, Fortaleza and Recife receive flights from the USA and/or Europe. Brazil is connected to the rest of Latin America principally through Rio de Janeiro, São Paulo, Manaus, Rio Branco and Brasília. It is connected to the Guyanas through Belém, Fortaleza, Boa Vista and Macapá. Belém also receives flights from the French Caribbean.

Tickets are best value in October, November and after Carnaval (the week of Shrove Tuesday, usually in February) and at their highest in the northern hemisphere summer and the Brazilian high seasons (generally 15 December to 15 January, the Thursday before Carnaval to the Saturday after Carnaval, and 15 June to 15 August).

AIRLINES

Brazil's main national carriers are TAM, Gol, Ocean Air, Trip and Webjet. TAM has by far the most extensive international network. Most of the large European and North American carriers have flights to São Paulo, as do South African Airways. Iberian carriers, especially TAP Air Portugal, offer flights to many other Brazilian cities. Some European charter companies have seasonal flights to airports in Brazil's northeast.

AIRPORTS

» **São Paulo** has two international airports. Aeroporto Internacional de São Paulo/Guarulhos-Governador André Franco Montoro, more usually known as Guarulhos or Cumbica, lies 25km (15.5 miles) northeast of the city's downtown. There are two terminals adjacent to each other (and 10 minutes' walk apart), both of which handle international and domestic flights. There is a tourist booth on the ground floor of Terminal 1 (Mon–Fri 8am–10pm, Sat–Sun and holidays 9–9), which hands out city maps and copies of the entertainment section from the *Folha de São Paulo* newspaper, with current listings.

GETTING TO THE CITY FROM THE AIRPORT

AIRPORT	DISTANCE TO CITY	TAXIS
São Paulo Guarulhos	25km (15.5 miles)	Fixed-rate taxis charge up to R$110. Tickets are available from booths immediately outside the terminal buildings.
São Paulo Congonhas	7km (4.5 miles)	Metered taxis charge around R$30 to Jardins and R$40 to Vila Madalena.
Rio de Janeiro Tom Jobim	15km (9.5 miles)	Fixed-rate taxis charge R$50 to Copacabana or Ipanema, and R$60 to the city centre and Santa Teresa; buy a ticket at the counter. Metered taxis cost around RS$65 from Jobim to Copacabana, but beware of pirate taxis, which are unlicensed.
Rio de Janeiro Santos Dumont	In the city centre	Metered taxis charge around R$25 to Copacabana or Ipanema and R$30 to the city centre and Santa Teresa.
Salvador Luís Eduardo Magalhães	32km (20 miles)	Fixed-rate taxis charge R$60 to Barra or the Pelourinho. Tickets can be bought from the desk next to the tourist information booth.
Fortaleza Pinto Martins	10km (6 miles)	Fixed-rate taxis charge R$50 to the centre, Avenida Beira Mar or Praia do Futuro. Tickets can be bought from the booth in arrivals.
Recife Gilberto Freyre	12km (7.5 miles)	Fixed-rate taxis cost R$10 to the seafront. Tickets can be bought from the booth in arrivals.
Manaus Eduardo Gomes	10km (6 miles)	Metered taxis charge around R$50 to the centre.

There are bureaux de change and ATMs on the ground floor of both terminals, in addition to car rental offices, shops, restaurants, cafés and a pharmacy.

Aeroporto São Paulo Congonhas on Avenida Washington Luiz, 7km (4.5 miles) south of the centre, is principally a domestic airport, with a handful of international flights to Bolivia and Argentina. The twice-hourly São Paulo–Rio Santos Dumont shuttle flies from here. The airport has just one terminal, which has restaurants, shops and ATM machines on the ground floor.

» Rio is served by two airports. The Aeroporto Internacional Tom Jobim (which is also known as Galeão) lies on the Ilha do Governador, 15km (9.5 miles) north of central Rio de Janeiro and handles both international and domestic flights. The airport has two terminals. Terminal 1 handles domestic routes and Terminal 2 serves international flights. There are bureaux de change facilities in the departures area and on the first floor of international arrivals, and ATMs for major Brazilian banks. Duty-free shops are well stocked and open to arrivals as well as departures. The domestic arrivals hall in Terminal 1 has a tourist information booth (daily 6am–11pm) and there is another in the international arrivals hall in Terminal 2 (daily 6am–midnight). Both provide maps and can book hotels. Rio's other airport is Santos Dumont airport, which sits in the city centre on the shore of Guanabara Bay. It is principally used for the frequent Rio–São Paulo Congonhas air shuttle. The airport terminal has ATMs, and shops, cafés and restaurants.

» Salvador is served by Luís Eduardo Magalhães airport, 32km (20 miles) east of the centre, at Praça Gago Coutinho, São Cristóvão. Also known as Dois de Julho, it receives flights from throughout Brazil and the USA, in addition to scheduled and charter arrivals from Europe. There are ATM machines, a tourist booth (daily 8am–10pm), shops, car rental agencies and cafés on the ground floor.

» Fortaleza is served by Aeroporto Pinto Martins, at Praça Eduardo Gomes, some 10km (6 miles) south of the centre, and has flights to Lisbon,

AIRPORT CONTACTS

All airports are run by Infraero (www.infraero.gov.br).

AIRPORT	TELEPHONE	AIRPORT TOURIST INFORMATION
São Paulo Guarulhos	11 2445 2945	11 6445 2945
São Paulo Congonhas	11 5090 9000	11 5090 9000
Rio de Janeiro Tom Jobim	21 3398 5050	21 3398 4077 (Terminal 1) 21 3398 2245 (Terminal 2)
Rio de Janeiro Santos Dumont	21 3814 7070	
Salvador Luís Eduardo Magalhães	71 3204 1010	71 3450 3871
Fortaleza Pinto Martins	85 3392 1200	85 3477 1667
Recife Gilberto Freyre	81 3322 4188	81 3232 3594
Manaus Eduardo Gomes	92 3652 1120	92 3236 5154

BUS
Fast air-conditioned buses run every 30 min between Guarulhos and Congonhas, taking 45–60 min and stopping at Avenida Paulista and other points in the city centre along the way.
Fast air-conditioned buses run every 30 min between Congonhas and Guarulhos, taking 45–60 min and stopping at Avenida Paulista and other points in the city centre along the way.
There are frequent buses between Rio's two airports, the *rodoviária* bus station and the city centre. The fastest are air-conditioned and leave every 30 min (between 5am and midnight) from outside arrivals at both terminals. Cost: R$12. The bus runs on two routes. Linha 2018 via Orla da Zona Sul goes to the Terminal Alvorada bus station in Barra da Tijuca, stopping at Avenida Rio Branco in the centre, Santos Dumont airport, Flamengo, Copacabana, Ipanema, São Conrado and Barra's Avenida das Americas. Linha 2145 goes to Santos Dumont airport, calling at Avenida Rio Branco in the centre along the way. Buses can be flagged down anywhere along their route. There is also a standard Rio bus running along the 2018 line with similar frequency for a lesser fee of R$5.
See Tom Jobin bus information above.
An air- conditioned *executivo* bus connects the airport with the historic centre every 30 min, between 6am and 10pm. Cost: R$5.
Bus no 404 connects the airport to Praça José de Alencar in the centre. Cost: R$2.10. Expresso Guanabara minibuses go to and from the bus and seaside promenade . Cost: R$4.
Bus no 52 runs to the centre. Cost: R$2.10.
Airport buses run to Praça Adalberto Vale, near the cathedral in the centre of town, every 30 min between 5am and 11pm. Cost: R$2.20.

the Guyanas and major Brazilian capitals. The airport has a 24-hour tourist office, car rental booths, internet facilities, banks, bureaux de change, ATMs and restaurants.

» Recife is served by Gilberto Freyre international airport, in Guararapes, 12km (7.5 miles) from the city centre, near the hotel district of Boa Viagem. The terminal has a tourist office (daily 9–9), banks, shops, post office, car rental and restaurants.

» Manaus is served by Eduardo Gomes international airport, 10km (6 miles) north of the city centre, with flights from all of Brazil's principal cities and connections with the USA, Ecuador and Bolivia. The terminal has a tourist booth (daily 7am–11pm), ATMs, shops and cafés.

ARRIVING BY BUS

Since there are no trains or sea connections to Brazil, the only other methods of international arrival is by long-distance bus. A number of long distance bus companies link Brazil with the rest of South America, but the most convenient and common border crossings are with Argentina, Uruguay, Paraguay, Bolivia and Chile. Bear in mind, though, that journeys may take several days. Most major international bus companies in Brazil are reliable, but one of the biggest is Pluma (tel 0800 646 0300; www.pluma.com.br), which offers tickets to Argentina, Paraguay and Chile. There is a useful website, www.plataforma10.com, which allows you to book bus tickets to a range of South American countries from Argentina, Bolivia and Chile to Paraguay, Peru and Uruguay.

Border crossings are usually relatively straightforward, but do make sure you have any necessary visas and documentation as well as your passport (▷ 345).

INTERNATIONAL AIRLINES SERVING BRAZIL

AIRLINE	WEBSITE	DEPARTURE POINT	DESTINATION
Aerolíneas	www.aerolineas.com.ar	Buenos Aires	São Paulo
Aeroméxico	www.aeromexico.com	Mexico City	São Paulo
Aerosur	www.aerosur.com	Bolivian cities	São Paulo
Air Canada	www.aircanada.com	Toronto	São Paulo
Air Caraibes	www.aircaraibes.com	Cuba, Martinique, Paris	Belém
Air China	www.airchina.com	Beijing, Shanghai	São Paulo
Air Europa	www.aireuropa.com	Lisbon, Paris	Salvador
Air France	www.airfrance.com	Paris	Rio de Janeiro, São Paulo
Air Italy	www.airitaly.it	Italian cities	Fortaleza
Alitalia	www.alitalia.com	Milan	São Paulo
American Airlines	www.aa.com	US cities	Belo Horizonte, Recife, Rio de Janeiro, Salvador, São Paulo
Avianca	www.avianca.com	Bogotá	Rio de Janeiro, São Paulo
British Airways	www.britishairways.com	London	Rio de Janeiro, São Paulo
Condor	www.condor.com	Frankfurt	Recife, Salvador
Continental	www.continental.com	Newark	Rio de Janeiro, São Paulo
Copa	www.copaair.com	Havana, Panama City	Manaus, São Paulo
Delta	www.delta.com	Atlanta	Rio de Janeiro, São Paulo
Emirates	www.emirates.com	Dubai	São Paulo
GOL	www.voegol.com.br	Cordoba, Lima, Montevideo	São Paulo
Iberia	www.iberia.com	Madrid	São Paulo
KLM	www.klm.com	Amsterdam	São Paulo
Korean	www.koreanair.com	Seoul, via LA	São Paulo
LAN	www.lan.com	Lima, Santiago	Rio de Janeiro, São Paulo
Lufthansa	www.lufthansa.com	Frankfurt, Munich	São Paulo
META	www.voemeta.com	Guyanas	Belém, Boa Vista
South African	www.flysaa.com	Johannesburg	São Paulo
StarPerú	www.starperu.com	Cusco, Lima	Rio Branco
TACA	www.taca.com	Lima	São Paulo
TAM	www.tam.com.br	Asunción, Ciudad del Este, Cordoba, Frankfurt, London, Madrid, Miami, Milan, Montevideo, New York, Paris	Rio de Janeiro, São Paulo
TAP	www.flytap.com	Lisbon, Porto	Most major Brazilian airports
United	www.united.com	Chicago, Los Angeles, Miami, New York, Washington	Rio de Janeiro, São Paulo
VistaPluna	www.pluna.aero	Buenos Aires, Montevideo, Santiago	Rio de Janeiro, São Paulo

GETTING AROUND

Brazil is vast, larger than the United States, and it would take more than six hours to fly from one end of the country to the other. Nonetheless, getting around is relatively painless, though slow in the north (where there are few roads and the only alternative to flying is river transport). Buses are the principal form of terrestrial transport elsewhere, for while there are plans to develop a railway network in the southeast, trains in Brazil are almost non-existent. Distances are huge: plan journeys well ahead—especially domestic flights—as the road alternative could take literally days, even for a journey which looks relatively short on the map. To explore hidden areas of Brazil you will need to hire a car, though this should be undertaken with caution.

DOMESTIC FLIGHTS

Brazil has an extensive domestic flight network and numerous airlines, from big carriers like Gol and TAM with large, modern fleets, to smaller air-taxi firms for Bahia's offshore islands and the northern rainforest. Most of the larger towns and cities have modern airports, many of which are being refurbished in preparation for the World Cup in 2014. Prices are often very reasonable, only a little more than the equivalent bus ticket if booking well ahead over the internet or for off-peak journey times.

BUYING TICKETS

» Ticket prices within Brazil are competitive and it is often easy to obtain very good deals on the most popular routes: to Bahia and the resorts of the northeast, between São Paulo and Rio de Janeiro, or to Minas Gerais.

» Most Brazilian airline websites will not accept international credit cards, as purchases in Brazil generally have to be guaranteed by the presentation of a social security number. To avoid this problem, buy your tickets through an agency.

» Alternatively, buy an airpass before arriving in Brazil.

BRAZIL AND MERCOSUL AIRPASSES

TAM (www.tam.com.br) and Gol (www.voegol.com.br) offer a 21-day Brazil Airpass, which can only be bought outside Brazil. Prices vary according to the number of flights taken and the international airline used to arrive in Brazil. TAM also operates as part of the Mercosul Airpass, which (in addition to Brazil) is valid in Argentina, Chile, Paraguay and Uruguay using local carriers. Both passes are valid only for passengers with a return ticket to their country of international departure. Children pay a discounted rate for airpasses, and under 3s pay 10 per cent of the adult rate. Some of the carriers operate a blackout period between 15 December and 15 January, when you are unable to use your airpass.

BAGGAGE ALLOWANCES

The baggage allowance on domestic flights is not always the same as that permitted on international flights. Airlines will only allow a certain weight of luggage without a surcharge and, while airlines can be flexible, this can be as low as 20kg (44lb) in addition to two items of hand luggage weighing up to 10kg (22lb) in total. It is usually best to enquire in advance with your airline.

ROUTES

There are a handful of direct routes between the largest state capitals: São Paulo, Rio de Janeiro, Brasília, Belo Horizonte, Curitiba, Salvador and Florianópolis. Other cities are usually connected on stopping routes, comprising two or three destinations.

BRAZIL'S DOMESTIC CARRIERS

Abaeté
(Luís Eduardo Magalhães, Salvador)
tel 71 3377 3955
www.voeabaete.com.br
Flights to Morro de São Paulo and the islands of Bahia.

Addey Táxi Aéreo
(Luís Eduardo Magalhães, Salvador)
tel 71 3204 1393
www.addey.com.br
Flights to Morro de São Paulo and the islands of Bahia.

Aero Star
(Luís Eduardo Magalhães, Salvador)
www.aerostar.com.br
tel 71 3377 2555
Flights to Chapada Diamantina, Morro de São Paulo and Barra Grande, in Bahia.

Air Minas
(Tancredo Neves, Belo Horizonte)
tel 0300 210 2112
www.airminas.com.br
Destinations in Minas Gerais and São Paulo.

Avianca
(Tom Jobim, Rio de Janeiro)
tel 0800 286 6543
www.avianca.com.br
One of the largest carriers in the country with extensive routes, especially along the coast, and links throughout Latin America

Azul
(Congonhas, São Paulo)
tel 11 4003 1118
www.voeazul.com.br
Extensive routes throughout the country from its new budget airline.

GOL
(Congonhas, São Paulo)
tel 0300 789 2121
www.voegol.com.br
One of Brazil's biggest carriers, with an extensive network throughout the country.

META
(Aeroporto Internacional de Boa Vista)
tel 0300 789 5503
www.voemeta.com
Destinations in Roraima, Pará and the Guyanas.

NHT
(Aeroporto Internacional de Curitiba)
www.voenht.com.br
tel 0300 143 4343
Destinations in the interior of São Paulo and Paraná states.

Pantanal Linhas Aéreas
(Congonhas, São Paulo)
tel 0800 602 5888
www.voepantanal.com.br
Flights to the interior of São Paulo and Rio states.

Passaredo
(Aeroporto Estadual de Ribeirão Preto)
tel 0300 100 1777
www.voepassaredo.com.br
Flights throughout the northeast and central west.

Puma
(Aeroporto Internacional de Belém)
tel 0300 789 2527
www.pumaair.com.br

Flights to Belém, Macapá and São Paulo Guarulho.

Rico
(Aeroporto Internacional Eduardo Gomes, Manaus)
tel 92 3652 1164
www.voerico.com.br
Flights throughout Amazonas and Pará states.

Sete
(Aeroporto Santa Genoveva, Goiânia)
tel 62 3096 7007
www.voesete.com.br
Flights throughout the central west and north of Brazil.

TAM
(Congonhas, São Paulo)
tel 11 5582 8811
www.tam.com.br
Brazil's national carrier, with the most extensive network and international connections.

TEAM
(Santos Dumont, Rio de Janeiro)
tel 21 2117 8300
www.voeteam.com.br
Flights around Rio de Janeiro state, including to Búzios and Paraty.

TRIP
(Aeroporto Internacional de Viracopos, Campinas)
tel 0300 789 8747
www.voetrip.com.br
The principal carrier in Brazil's Amazon and central west regions, with connections to Paraná, São Paulo and cities in the northeast.

Total
(Aeroporto da Pampulha, Belo Horizonte)
www.total.com.br
tel 0300 789 8747
Routes to Porto Velho, Salvador, Brasília, São Paulo and a handful of other cities in the central west.

Varig
(Congonhas, São Paulo)
www.voegol.com.br
Brazil's once-premier carrier is recovering from bankruptcy, and has now merged with Gol.

Webjet
(Tom Jobim, Rio de Janeiro)
www.webjet.com.br
tel 21 4009 0000
Flights throughout the country.

BRAZIL'S PRINCIPAL DOMESTIC AIRPORTS

CITY	AIRPORT	ADDRESS	TELEPHONE
Aracaju	Santa Maria	Avenida Senador Júlio César Leite s/n, Atalaia	79 3212 8500
Belém	Internacional de Belém	Avenida Júlio César, Val-de-Cans	91 3210 6000
Belo Horizonte	Pampulha	Praça Bagatelle 204	31 3490 2001
	Tancredo Neves	Estrada Velha de Confins	31 3689 2700
Brasília	Internacional de Brasília	Área Especial do Lago Sul	61 3364 9000
Campo Grande	Internacional de Campo Grande	Avenida Duque de Caxias s/n	67 3368 6093
Cuiabá	Marechal Rondon	Avenida João Ponce de Arruda	65 3614 2500
Curitiba	Afonso Pena	Avenida Rocha Pombo, São José dos Pinhais	41 3381 1515
Florianópolis	Hercílio Luz	Avenida Deomício de Freitas 3393	48 3331 4000
Fortaleza	Pinto Martins	Avenida Senador Carlos Jereissati, 3000	85 3477 1200
Goiânia	Santa Genoveva	Praça Capitão Frazão 913, Setor Santa Genoveva	62 3265 1500
João Pessoa	Presidente Castro Pinto	Jardim Aeroporto, Bayeux, João Pessoa BR 101	83 3232 1200
Macapá	Internacional de Macapá	Rua Hildemar Maia s/n	96 3223 2323
Maceió	Campo dos Palmares	Rodovia BR 104, km 91	82 3214 4000
Manaus	Eduardo Gomes	Avenida Santos Dumont, 1350	92 3652 1212
Natal	Augusto Severo	Estrada do Aeroporto s/n, Parnamirim	84 3643 1811
Palmas	Palmas–Brigadeiro Lysias Rodrigues	Avenida Teotônio Segurado s/n	63 3219 3700
Porto Alegre	Internacional Salgado Filho	Avenida Severo Dullins, 90010	51 3358 2000
Porto Velho	Porto Velho	Avenida Jorge Teixeira s/n	69 3225 1339
Recife	Guararapes–Gilberto Freyre	Praça Ministro Salgado Filho s/n, Boa Viagem	81 3464 4188
Rio Branco	Rio Branco	Estrada BR-364, km 18	68 3211 1000
Rio de Janeiro	Tom Jobim	Avenida 20 de Janeiro s/n, Ilha do Governador	21 3398-5050
	Santos Dumont	Praça Senador Salgado Filho s/n	21 3814 7070
Salvador	Luís Eduardo Magalhães	Praça Gago Coutinho s/n	71 3204 1010
São Luís	Marechal Cunha Machado	Avenida dos Libaneses s/n, Tirirical	98 3217 6101
São Paulo	Guarulhos	Rodovia Hélio Schmidt s/n, Cumbica, Guarulhos	11 6445 2945
	Congonhas	Avenida Washington Luiz s/n	11 5090 9000
Teresina	Teresina	Senator Petrônio Portella	86 3225 2947
Vitória	Vitória	Avenida Fernando Ferrari s/n	27 3235 6300

For further information (in Portuguese only) and photographs see www.infraero.gov.br

MEALS AND REFRESHMENTS

» Buses stop every two to four hours for toilet breaks and snacks. A long journey (of five hours or more) will usually have at least one 30- to 45-minute meal break.

BUS STATIONS *(RODOVIÁRIAS)*

» Inter-city bus stations are called *rodoviárias*. They are often situated outside the city centres.
» Even the smallest *rodoviárias* have restaurants and snack bars. *Rodoviárias* in the larger cities—especially the state capitals—will also have banks, ATMs, shops, toilets, *guarda volume* (left-luggage stores), local bus services, information centres and large taxi ranks.
» *Rodoviárias* are the best places to buy bus tickets. Booths in the bus stations sell tickets at the cheapest prices and most take credit cards. Travel agents add on surcharges.
» Reliable bus information is hard to come by, other than from the companies themselves, inside the terminals.
» Buses usually arrive and depart in very good time. Many local buses have turnstiles, which can be inconvenient if you are carrying a large pack, but they ensure that the main area of the bus is open only to ticket holders.

BUSES

Buses are Brazil's principal form of inter-city and intra-city transport, and Brazil has a very extensive bus network. There are frequent buses from anywhere to pretty much everywhere. Inter-city buses are generally of a higher standard than their equivalent in Europe or the United States.

TYPES OF BUSES

Brazilian buses are generally fast, organized, secure and prompt. Air-conditioning can make buses cold at night, so take warm clothing. Some night buses supply blankets. There are three kinds of national bus:
» *Comum* or *Convencional*, are the slowest, cheapest and the least comfortable services, with frequent stops, often at small locations.
» *Executivo* are faster and more comfortable, and usually make no or very few stops.
» *Leito* or *Executivo Luxo* are 'executive' buses which run at night, usually between the larger towns. They have reclining seats with leg rests, toilets, and sometimes refreshments. They are the most expensive option.

BOATS

In northern Brazil, where there are very few roads but many rivers, boat travel is the only alternative to taking a plane. There are a variety of boats from fast jet launches to classic Amazon double- or triple-decker river cruisers, the most beautiful of which are made of wood.

ACCOMMODATION

Many voyages take several days, meaning that passengers have to sleep on board. Sleeping is in cabins, the most expensive of which have their own private bathrooms, or in hammocks on the open-sided decks. All accommodation is simple and meals are eaten communally.

PRINCIPAL BOAT ROUTES

JOURNEY	UPSTREAM DURATION	DOWNSTREAM DURATION	NOTE
Belém–Macapá	1 day	1 day	8 hours on a fast catamaran either way
Belém–Santarém	2 days	1 day	
Manaus–Belém	5 days	4 days	Includes several hours' stop in Santarém
Manaus–Parintins	1 day	1 day	8 hours on a fast jet boat either way
Manaus–Porto Velho	4 days	3 days	
Manaus–Santarém	2 days	1 day	
Manaus–Tefé	1 day	1 day	8 hours on a fast jet boat either way

DRIVING

Brazil is such a large country that even if travellers fly to a state or region, long distances still separate the sights. Bahia, for instance, is larger than France, and Rio de Janeiro state is only a little smaller than Great Britain. As there is almost no rail network, car hire is the only real alternative to catching a bus for exploring the many states and regions. Motorways in São Paulo, Rio and around the larger cities are of a similar standard to Europe or the USA. Many are toll roads.

BRINGING YOUR OWN CAR

Importing a car into Brazil is fraught with problems. Import duty on foreign cars is 100 per cent and the bureaucracy involved is extremely time-consuming. Shipping a car to Brazil is very expensive and cars are often held up in customs for weeks on end.

LOCAL DRIVING HABITS AND SENSIBLE PRECAUTIONS

» Brazilians drive on the right-hand side of the road.
» While legislation varies from state to state, children under 10 are generally required to use a properly installed car seat.
» Brazil has one of the worst road death rates in the world. Be wary of other drivers, especially lorries.
» Driving in Brazil is not without its dangers. Crime remains a problem, especially in cities, and rental cars are an obvious target. Keep doors locked when driving.
» If possible, avoid driving in large cities. Brazil's cities—especially São Paulo and Rio—have complicated one-way systems, often involving very large urban freeways. It is easy to get lost and, in Rio, to end up in an undesirable area.
» Keep windows wound up while driving through urban areas.
» Avoid driving at night if possible, especially in remote areas and even more so as an unaccompanied woman. Thieves look for an easy target. Bring a mobile (cell) phone with you in case your car breaks down. It can be risky to ask for help from other motorists.
» At night, it is common practice to drive slowly across red lights in urban areas, looking carefully, and you are unlikely to be prosecuted.
» Never attempt to bribe a police officer, always be courteous and be sure to observe carefully what the officers are doing if they decide to inspect the car.
» There is a zero tolerance attitude to alcohol. You must not drink a drop of alcohol and drive in Brazil.

DOCUMENTATION

Under Brazilian law all drivers are required to carry original car and personal identification documentation with you at all times. Copies of documents are not sufficient unless they are government-certified authentic copies made at a public notary *(cartorio)* and stamped with an official stamp to say that they are certified copies.
You will need:
» Driving licence. To drive in Brazil you need an international driving licence. A current national driving licence is acceptable in Brazil only if your home country is a signatory to the Vienna and Geneva conventions.
» Passport
» Rental car agreement, or car registration documents and proof of insurance.

SPEED LIMITS AND SPEED BUMPS

» Interstate highways *(Rodovias* or 'BR' roads—*Bay Airees)*: 110–120kph (68–74mph), depending on the state.
» Single lane highways: 40–100kph (25–62mph), depending on the state, municipality and locality.
» Built-up areas: 40–60kph (25–37mph), depending on the type of road and the municipality.

» Look for speed signs and be wary of speed bumps *(lombadas)*, which are steep and fierce in Brazil.
» Speeding is detected electronically using roadside and bridge-mounted cameras, and is strictly monitored. Fines vary greatly by municipality and state, but they are usually hefty (as much as R$1,000) and will be sent to the rental company. It is easy to incur a high bill without realizing it.

SIGNS, MAPS AND DIRECTIONS

» Brazil does not have a culture of map usage. It can be hard even to find a road map and they are not on sale in service stations as they are in Europe. Brazilians ask for directions. However, as almost no one speaks anything but Portuguese, this is of little use to foreigners. A map is essential and you will need to buy a road map in a large bookshop in a large city. The best are published by Quatro Rodas.
» It is important to have a knowledge of some basic Portuguese if you intend to drive yourself.
» Signs are inconsistent. Well-signposted stretches are followed by others without any signs at all.

RENTING A CAR

» Prices are higher than in Europe or the USA—expect to pay twice the rate back home per day for the equivalent hatchback or saloon.
» Car rental can be expensive in Brazil if you don't book ahead. The cheapest rate for unlimited mileage for a small car is about R$85 per day. It is cheapest to rent online, through a large company. A credit card is virtually essential for renting a car.
» Depending on the state in question, the minimum rental age is either 25 or 21. Consult your rental company website for confirmation.
» Companies working in Brazil include www.europcar.com, www.holidayautos.co.uk, www.sixt.com, www.hertz.co.uk and www.brazilcar.com.
» Check exactly what the company's insurance policy covers. It may not apply to major accidents, or 'natural' damage (such as flooding). Ask if extra cover is available. Sometimes using a credit card automatically includes insurance.
» Beware of being billed for scratches that were on the vehicle before you rented it.

BREAKDOWN

» There is little formal aid for breakdowns in Brazil beyond the rental and insurance companies. Be sure to carry a mobile phone. If your car breaks down you will need to ring the rental company. This is a good reason not to drive at night.

FUEL

» Cars run on three different forms of fuel in Brazil: petrol (gasoline), natural gas and alcohol. Through the 'powerflex' system, many cars will take two or even three forms of fuel into the same engine.
» Petrol is often contaminated with acetone or methanol, in order for petrol stations to make the largest possible profit, and engines often run inefficiently.
» Natural gas is more widely available in Brazil than in any other country in the world and can be found at most large filling stations.
» Alcohol is cheaper than petrol but less efficient. You need about 50 per cent more alcohol than regular petrol for the same distance.
» Fuel prices vary from week to week and many service stations are closed at the weekend, even in larger cities.

PARKING

» Do not leave valuables visible in the car and, in a town or city, park as close as possible to your destination.
» Car parks are usually yards, where attendants squeeze as many cars as possible into as small an area as possible, and where you are required to leave the car key. Multi-storeys are usually limited to shopping malls. Prices vary but are high in the large cities, as much R$10 per hour.
» Parking fines are sent directly to the rental company; they are not left on windscreens and you may have no idea that one has been incurred until you return home to your credit card bill. Look for parking restriction signs.
» Unofficial parking minders or street children will generally protect your car fiercely in exchange for a tip.

Below *The chart shows the distance in kilometres between cities, as the crow flies*

	Belém	Brasília	Cuiabá	Fortaleza	Manaus	Porto Alegre	Recife	Rio de Janeiro	Salvador	São Paulo
Belém		1598	1760	1152	1318	3195	1710	2480	1724	2484
Brasília	1598		878	1660	1948	1630	1620	936	1048	886
Cuiabá	1760	878		2295	1440	1694	2420	1588	1908	1332
Fortaleza	1152	1660	2295		2412	3208	655	2205	1044	2374
Manaus	1318	1948	1440	2412		3138	2870	2866	2642	2700
Porto Alegre	3195	1630	1694	3208	3138		2964	1110	2310	840
Recife	1710	1620	2420	655	2870	2964		1880	662	2126
Rio de Janeiro	2480	936	1588	2205	2866	1110	1880		1220	356
Salvador	1724	1048	1908	1044	2642	2310	662	1220		1464
São Paulo	2484	886	1332	2374	2700	840	2126	356	1464	

GETTING AROUND IN RIO DE JANEIRO

While there are big infrastructure plans for the 2014 World Cup, for now Rio remains a vast and sprawling city with chronic traffic problems and an underdeveloped public transport system. Thankfully, some tourist zones are within the small but efficient metrô network and the bus network is extensive.

METRÔ

» Although its coverage is limited, the metrô is the quickest way to get around central Rio and the main city beaches. The metrô (www.metrorio.com.br) is clean, fast and air-conditioned, and there are plans to extend it all the way to Barra da Tijuca in time for the 2014 World Cup and 2016 Olympics.

» Lihna 1 operates between the inner suburb of Tijuca (Saens Peña station) and Ipanema (Gal Osório station), via the railway station (Central), Glória and Botafogo.

» Linha 2 runs from Pavuna in the far north, through the northern suburbs and by Maracanã stadium to Central railway station, from where it runs parallel with Linha 1 to Ipanema (via Botafogo), weekdays only.

» The metrô operates Mon–Sat 5am–midnight and 7am–11pm on Sunday and holidays. Fares are R$2.80 single; multi-tickets and integrated bus/metrô tickets are also available (R$3.80–R$4).

» Buses connecting with the metrô display a blue-and-white symbol.

» Smoking is not permitted on the metrô.

BUSES

» Public buses in Rio are sometimes driven recklessly and can be a target for thieves. The *rodoviária* (central bus station) attracts thieves, so should be treated with caution, particularly at night, when taxis are a better option for getting around.

» The air-conditioned airport bus is free of these problems (▷ 39). It can be flagged down at any point and runs along Rio's main beaches.

» Buses 126, 127 or 128 run from the *rodoviária* to Ipanema and Copacabana. Bus 170 runs from the *rodoviária* to Flamengo and Botafogo. Bus journeys cost a flat rate of R$2.10.

» Rio is laid out basically on a north–south axis, so almost any bus going south with Zona Sul (South Zone) written on it will stop in Ipanema or Copacabana, and all have their destinations written on the side.

» Smoking is not permitted on buses.

TAXIS

» Taxis have red number plates with white digits (yellow with black digits for private cars). All have meters. There are two tariffs: Tariff 1 from 6am–10pm and tariff 2 from 10pm–6am and on Sundays and holidays. Tariff 2 is 25 per cent higher.

» Only use taxis with an official identification sticker on the windscreen. Don't hesitate to protest if the route is too long or the fare is too much. The fare between central Rio and Copacabana, for example, should be about R$30.

» Always try to use a taxi from a designated taxi rank or one that is called for by a hotel. These are by far the safest option. Some taxis can be hired for excursions or tours, but negotiate the price beforehand.

» Tipping is not expected by taxi drivers in Brazil.

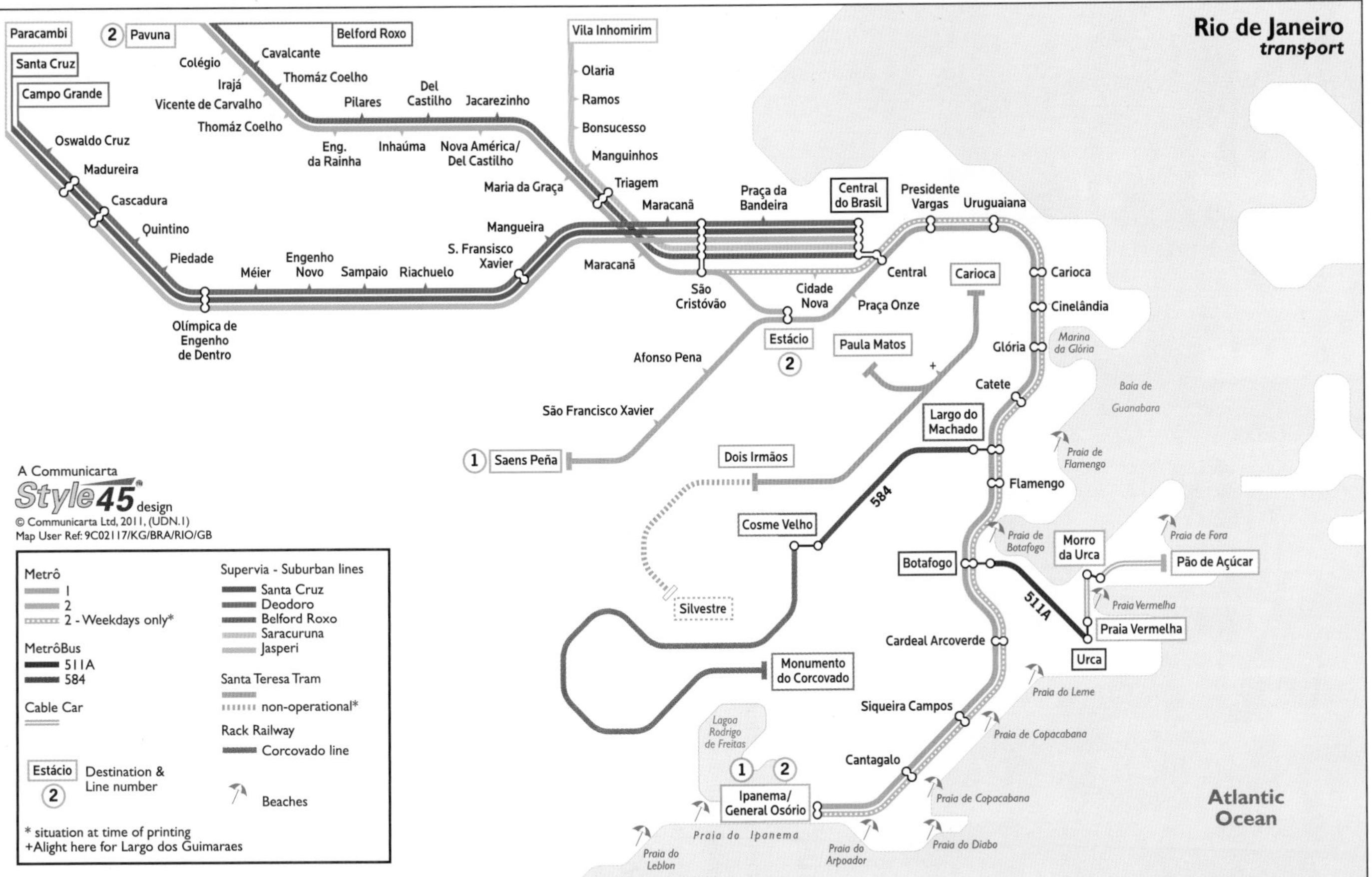

Rio de Janeiro transport
Paracambi
Santa Cruz
Campo Grande
2 Pavuna
Belford Roxo
Vila Inhomirim
Oswaldo Cruz
Madureira
Cascadura
Quintino
Piedade
Méier
Engenho Novo
Sampaio
Riachuelo
S. Fransisco Xavier
Mangueira
Olímpica de Engenho de Dentro
Colégio
Irajá
Vicente de Carvalho
Thomáz Coelho
Cavalcante
Thomáz Coelho
Pilares
Del Castilho
Jacarezinho
Eng. da Rainha
Inhaúma
Nova América/ Del Castilho
Maria da Graça
Olaria
Ramos
Bonsucesso
Manguinhos
Triagem
Maracanã
Maracanã
Praça da Bandeira
Central do Brasil
São Cristóvão
Cidade Nova
Estácio
2
Praça Onze
Central
Presidente Vargas
Uruguaiana
Carioca
Cinelândia
Glória
Catete
Largo do Machado
Flamengo
Botafogo
Cardeal Arcoverde
Siqueira Campos
Cantagalo
Ipanema/ General Osório
1 2
Afonso Pena
São Francisco Xavier
1 Saens Peña
Carioca
Paula Matos
+
Dois Irmãos
Silvestre
Cosme Velho
584
Monumento do Corcovado
Morro da Urca
Pão de Açúcar
Praia Vermelha
Urca
511A
Marina da Glória
Baía de Guanabara
Praia de Flamengo
Praia de Botafogo
Praia de Fora
Praia Vermelha
Praia do Leme
Praia de Copacabana
Praia de Copacabana
Praia do Diabo
Praia do Arpoador
Praia do Ipanema
Praia do Leblon
Lagoa Rodrigo de Freitas
Atlantic Ocean
A Communicarta Style45 design
© Communicarta Ltd, 2011, (UDN.1)
Map User Ref: 9C02117/KG/BRA/RIO/GB
Metrô
1
2
2 - Weekdays only*
MetrôBus
511A
584
Cable Car
Supervia - Suburban lines
Santa Cruz
Deodoro
Belford Roxo
Saracuruna
Jasperi
Santa Teresa Tram
non-operational*
Rack Railway
Corcovado line
Estácio 2 Destination & Line number
Beaches
* situation at time of printing
+Alight here for Largo dos Guimaraes

DRIVING

» Driving in Rio de Janeiro city is not recommended. It is very easy to get lost, which can be a hazard if a wrong turn takes you into a *favela* (slum). Traffic flow on streets changes direction according to the time of day and many Cariocas (Rio locals) drive recklessly and impatiently.

» Car rental in Rio is relatively straightforward (▷ 46). The best way to rent is from the booths in the airport, where there are English-speaking staff, if required.

» It is usual for cars not to stop at red lights after dark. Be extra vigilant.

CYCLING

» Rio is well-suited to cycling, both on- and off-road, and the city has some 74km (46 miles) of cycle paths. These run from Centro, through Zona Sul to Barra da Tijuca. Look out for aggressive drivers: cyclists are very much second-class citizens.

» There is no city cycle rental scheme, except through bicycle hire shops and a handful of hostels, most of which offer bikes for free.

» Do not cycle at night and be wary along the road between Ipanema and Barra da Tijuca. Cyclists are an easy target for thieves.

THE SANTA TERESA TRAM

» Rio de Janeiro's last remaining tram runs from near the Largo da Carioca (▷ 71) across the old aqueduct (Arcos de Lapa) to Santa Teresa (▷ 86–87)—and the junction of Ruas Progresso and Eduardo Santos or Alexandrino and Otoni.

» This is a slow route on very old, delapidated electric trams. Dozens of kids cling to the side as the vehicle ascends, and the journey is bumpy and jerky. However, the views are marvellous and the tram remains the best way to reach Santa Teresa from central Rio. The tram costs R$1. It leaves from the terminus next to the Catedral Metropólitana (▷ 63) or from Cinelândia metrô station.

ORGANIZED TOURS OF RIO

A number of the key tourist sights cannot be visited by public transport (notably Corcovado and the Christ, ▷ 66–67, and the Sugar Loaf, ▷ 78–79), but are easily reached by taxi. Taking an organized tour is a worthwhile option and there are all manner of companies offering all manner of trips:

» Rio Hiking (▷ 96) offers guided walks and light hikes throughout Rio city, including to the Pedra da Gávea boulder (▷ 90–91)—with spectacular views over the beaches and mountains—Parque Nacional da Tijuca (▷ 81), and the Corcovado Christ (tel 21 2552 9204; www.riohiking.com.br).

» Be A Local (tel 21 9643 0366; www.bealocal.com) has walking and motorbike tours around Rocinha (▷ 84)—with money going towards community projects—in addition to trips to *favela* parties at weekends and to football matches in the Maracanã stadium. Visiting a *favela* with a responsible company is an eye-opener, but avoid the larger jeep companies, which have no integration with the communities. Never enter a *favela* alone.

» Favela Adventures (http://favelatour.org) offers personalized visits on foot with local guides who live in the *favelas* (slums). It is firmly rooted in the community, in which it invests—unlike some companies that boast commitment to community-based tourism in *favelas*, but make only token donations.

» Terra Brazil (tel 21 25 43 31 85; www.terra-brazil.com) specializes in ethical tourism, offering fascinating and highly recommended tours that give a real insight into the places they visit. These include Corcovado, Rio's *favelas*, Tijuca forest and most of Rio's key sights.

» Cultural Rio (tel 21 9911 3829; www.culturalrio.com.br) has a range of tours of historical monuments, museums and key sights, conducted by Professor Carlos Roquette. There are some 200 options available, in addition to bespoke trips.

» Dehouche (tel 21 2512 3895; www.dehouche.com) provides tailor-made city tours and trips throughout Brazil for the luxury market.

» Madson Araujo offers personal tours of the city, made to order. He is a multi-lingual guide with an air-conditioned saloon car (tel 21 9395 3537; www.tourguiderio.com).

GETTING AROUND IN SÃO PAULO

São Paulo is one of the largest cities on Earth, with one of the highest densities of population. Traffic can be very slow, even though the city is cut with scores of six- to eight-lane urban highways. You would have to be suicidal to think of cycling here. Wealthy Paulistanos choose to get around by helicopter to avoid the bottlenecks and jams. Sadly, the metrô system is small and overloaded, and it is often necessary to take a taxi. Transport in the city is overseen by SP Trans. Their website (www.sptrans.com.br) has a search engine enabling visitors to plan a bus and/or metrô route across the city. It is currently only in Portuguese but is straightforward to use. *De* means 'from', *para* means 'to'.

METRÔ

» The best and cheapest way to get around São Paulo is on the underground metrô system, which is currently undergoing extensive and rapid expansion in preparation for the 2014 World Cup.

» The trains are similar to those which run on the New York subway. They are fast, clean and run on broad-gauge track, allowing for plenty of carriage space. However, they fill up quickly in rush hours (7am–10am, 4.30pm–7pm), when there are insufficient services for the heavy demand, and they are prone to unannounced and unexplained stops and cancellations. Allow plenty of time for your journey, especially at peak hours.

» The service is administered by the Companhia do Metropolitano de São Paulo—Metrô (www.metro.sp.gov.br), who have an excellent, clear website in Portuguese and English.

» There are four metro lines, with a fifth under construction. Maps are displayed only in upper concourses; there are none on the platforms and most of the maps on the internet are confusing as they incorporate the CPTM overground train routes. Each line has its own colour and directions are indicated by the name of the terminus. They are currently named and numbered as follows:

» Linha 1 Azul (Blue) runs from Tucuruvi in the north to Jabaraquara *rodoviária* in the south, via Luz, the centre and Liberdade.

» Linha 2 Verde (Green) runs from Vila Madalena to Vila Prudente, via Avenida Paulista (▷ 111) and the MASP art gallery (▷ 116–117).

» Linha 3 Vermelha (Red) runs from the Palmeiras football stadium in Barra Funda to the Corinthians football stadium in Itaquera, via the city centre.

» Linha 5 Lilás (Lilac) runs in São Paulo's far southwest, between Capão Redondo and Adolfo Pinheiro.

» Linha 4 Amarela (Yellow) is due to open in 2011 and will run between

Morumbi football stadium and Luz, via USP University at Butantã, Oscar Freire in Jardins and Avenida Paulista.

» Fares are at a flat rate of R$2.65. A combined bus and metrô ticket costs R$4.60 or R$5—useful for getting to Congonhas airport.

» A rechargeable card, Bilhete Unico, offers discounted one-way metrô travel within a limited time period. Cartão Fidelidade, a frequent traveller card, offers increasing discounts for 8, 20 or 50 journeys.

» There is no smoking permitted on the metrô.

BUSES

» São Paulo's main *rodoviária* (bus station) is at Tietê, 5km (3 miles) north of the centre (tel 11 2223 7152). If you plan to spend only a day or a few hours in the city, this is a good place to leave luggage. Left luggage costs R$10 per day per item. There are showers from R$8, clean public toilets and many restaurants. The Tietê metrô station has connections throughout the city. There are two other smaller *rodoviárias*—Barra Funda and Jabaquara—serving the São Paulo coast and Paraná and Minas Gerais states. All the *rodoviárias* are on the metrô network.

» City bus routes can be confusing for visitors and very slow in the gridlocked traffic. Avoid using buses from 7am to 10am and 4.30pm to 7pm, when the situation becomes intolerable. Nonetheless, buses are safe, clean and only crowded at peak hours. Maps of the bus routes are available at bus depots (like Anhangabaú, which is on the metrô line) and at metrô stations.

» As buses are labelled—on the sides and the fronts—with street names that mark only the start and finish of the route, it is best to plan the journey before setting off using the SP Trans website (www.sptrans.com.br).

» Bus journeys cost a flat rate of R$2.70. Pay on-board with as close as possible to the correct change. Conductors operate turnstiles.

» Smoking is not permitted on buses.

OVERGROUND URBAN TRAIN

» The train links up with the metrô and is run by the Companhia São Paulo de Trens Metropolitanos (CPTM, www.cptm.sp.gov.br). São Paulo has four stations but the only one useful for tourists is the Estação da Luz (Metrô Luz, tel 0800 550121), which receives trains from the northwest and southeast of São Paulo state and connects with the tourist train from Paranapiacaba to Rio Grande de Serra.

TAXIS

» Taxis are generally white or white and blue, with a green illuminated sign on the roof. As in Rio, all have meters. Do not get in a cab without one or without the identity of the driver clearly displayed. There are two tariffs: Tariff 1 from 6am to 10pm and tariff 2 from 10pm to 6am and on Sundays and holidays. Tariff 2 is 25 per cent higher.

» Fares start at R$4.60, with each extra kilometre costing R$1.90 (and R$0.50 for waiting time in traffic or otherwise).

» Radio taxis are easy to call—most restaurants and bars have a favourite cab company and will organize a car to pick up clients, usually within 20 minutes. Radio cabs are only slightly pricier than cabs hailed in the street.

» Use a taxi from a designated taxi rank *(ponto)* or called for by a hotel. These are by far the safest option. Some taxis can be hired for excursions or tours, but be sure to negotiate the price beforehand.

» Tipping is not expected in taxis.

DRIVING

» São Paulo is not a pleasant place in which to drive. Roads are enormous, signs poor and wrong turns can often result in a detour of many kilometres down a labyrinthine one-way system, either in gridlock or populated with impatient, speeding drivers.

» The *Guia de Quatro Rodas Ruas São Paulo* map book is an essential for any visitors planning to try their luck on the city streets.

» It is usual for cars not to stop at red lights after dark. Be extra vigilant.

» São Paulo has a zero tolerance drink-driving policy. You must not consume alcohol if you plan to drive.

» Parking is tricky. There are few spaces and few car parks outside the big shopping centres. Street parking is usually administered by unemployed Brazilians working as unofficial attendants. It is regarded as impolite and unwise not to give them a tip of at least R$2.

» The *rotatorio* rotating traffic policy means that during rush hours (7am–10am, 5pm–8pm) on designated days, certain licence-plate numbers cannot drive in greater São Paulo. Check the latest situation with your rental company.

VISITORS WITH A DISABILITY

There is some effort being made in the larger cities due to host the 2014 World Cup, but generally facilities for disabled visitors to Brazil are very poor by European or US standards. One of the best ways to visit the country is therefore with an organized tour. Problems are most acute for wheelchair users. Pavements are often crowded or in a poor state of repair. Disabled visitors must rely on the help of others. Thankfully, Brazilians are usually helpful.

BY AIR

Airports in Brazil are generally readily accessible to wheelchair users, with lifts, ramps and staff on hand to help through immigration and customs. However, it is best to arrive at least 30 minutes earlier for flights (2.5 hours before international departures, 1.5 hours before domestic flights) and ask your airline for assistance.

BY BUS, CAR AND TAXI

Very few, if any, buses in Brazil—either town or inter-city—have wheelchair access. Taxis with wheelchair access are equally few and far between, and should be requested in advance through a radio taxi firm (there are several companies in main cities, with booths at airports). Disabled drivers should bring a disabled sticker, as most shopping centres and public car parks have disabled spaces.

BY BOAT

Boat travel in the Amazon is equally difficult, for while access to the larger vessels is generally via a ramp, there are usually ribbed and rickety ladders connecting the various floors. Restaurant areas are often on decks different from the cabins. There are specialist companies providing tours for disabled visitors in the Amazon.

BY METRÔ

Rio and São Paulo metrôs have lifts and disabled chair lifts at some stations (but not all are operational).

INFORMATION

There are no federal, state or municipal government departments or agencies providing information or infrastructure for Brazil's wheelchair users or for visitors with disabilities.

» Disability Travel (www.disabilitytravel.com) is a website run by travellers in wheelchairs who research disabled travel. The site includes destination reviews, tips and useful contacts, such as lists of travel agents. The company also organizes group tours, including to the Amazon.

» The Global Access—Disabled Travel Network Site (www.globalaccessnews.com) provides travel information for 'disabled adventurers' and includes a number of reviews and tips from the public.

» The Disabled Travelers Guide (www.disabledtravelersguide.com) offers general information as well as a number of trip reports written by disabled travellers visiting countries worldwide, including Brazil.

» The Society for Accessible Travel and Hospitality (www.sath.org) holds general information.

» The Instituto Brasileiro dos Direitos da Pessoa com Deficiencia (IBDD; www.ibdd.org.br) is a large organization in Brazil, which campaigns for disabled rights. They can be contacted through the website (in Portuguese) and will respond to queries in written English.

» Turismo Adaptado (http://turismoadaptado.wordpress.com) is a Brazilian website with information about travelling as a disabled person in Brazil, in Portuguese. They will also respond to queries in written English.

» Other Brazilian organizations include the Centro da Vida Independente (www.cvi-rio.org.br).

» Operators offering holidays for travellers with disabilities include: Responsible Travel (www.responsibletravel.com), Accessible Journeys (www.accessiblejourneys.com) and Can be Done (www.canbedone.co.uk)

REGIONS

This chapter is divided into 10 regions of Brazil (▷ 8–9). Region names are for the purposes of this book only and places of interest are listed alphabetically within each region.

Brazil's Regions 54–342

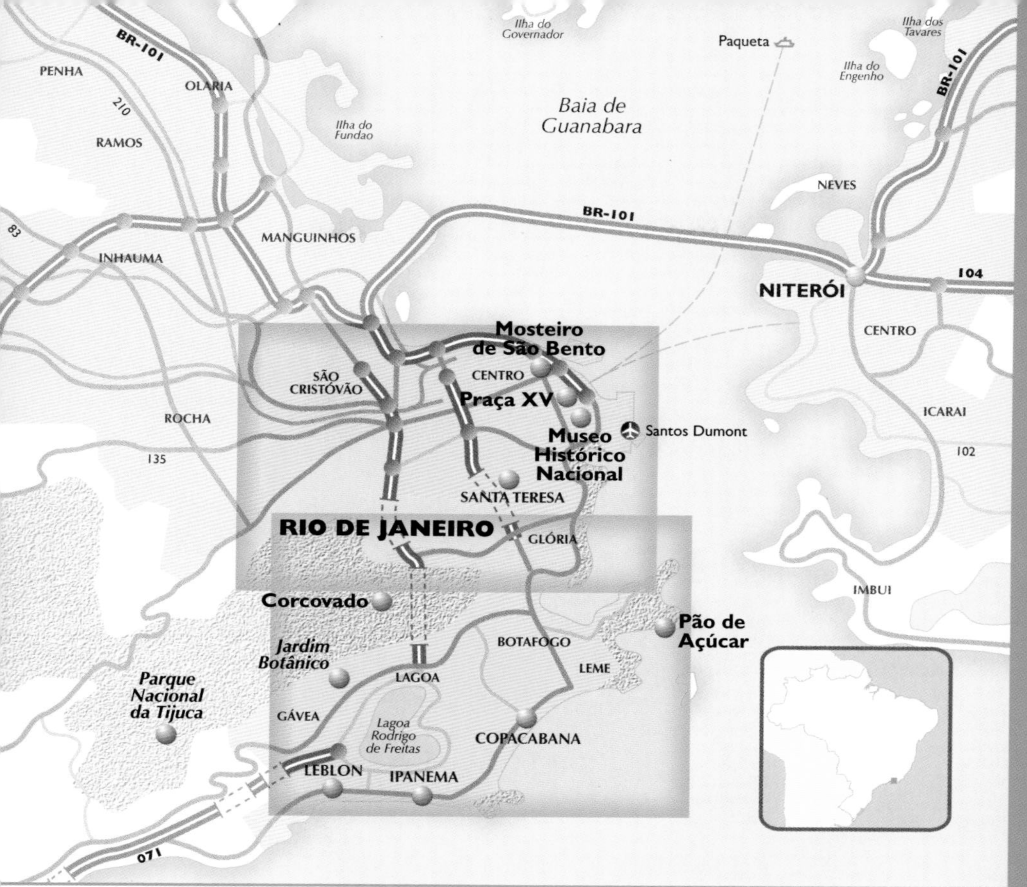

RIO DE JANEIRO CITY

Rio's locals, or as they are called by other Brazilians, the Cariocas, call their home *A Cidade Maravilhosa* (The Wonderful City). There is simply, they say, nowhere better or more beautiful on Earth. It's hard to disagree when standing on the top of the Sugar Loaf, or Corcovado, especially at the end of the day. Rainforest stretches to either side, swathing gentle sloping peaks that fall gradually to a giant, inky blue and beach-fringed, wine-glass-shaped bay. Where the bay opens to the bottle-green Atlantic, still more strands of pearly sand stretch as far as the eye can see—through Copacabana, Ipanema and São Conrado—and the city twinkles between it all in the orange and violet of the tropical twilight.

Against this beautiful backdrop, some of the world's most beautiful people play: at the huge New Year and *carnaval* (carnival) celebrations and all year round on the beaches, in the football stadia and in the plethora of samba clubs, bars and *botecos* (small streetside bars). There can be no city more enthusiastically devoted to feeling good about life than Rio. Not that the city isn't without serious problems. Grinding poverty and one of the greatest divisions between rich and poor in the world has led to high crime and, despite being chosen as a host city for the World Cup (2014) and the Olympics (2016), Rio de Janeiro remains a city where visitors have to be cautious.

Rio de Janeiro—the January River—is not, of course, a river at all. Accustomed to the immensity of South America's deltas, a Portuguese expedition that chanced upon Guanabara Bay in January 1502, mistook it for an estuary and named it in error. The city itself was founded far later, in 1565, when the Portuguese expelled a small French colony from an island in the bay (▷ 27). Its proper name is actually São Sebastião do Rio de Janeiro.

Rio was the country's capital for nearly 200 years, and the capital of the Portuguese Empire for nearly a decade. As such it has some of Brazil's best museums and galleries. Together with a lively music scene and myriad shops and boutiques, they ensure that there is plenty to do in Rio even on a rainy day.

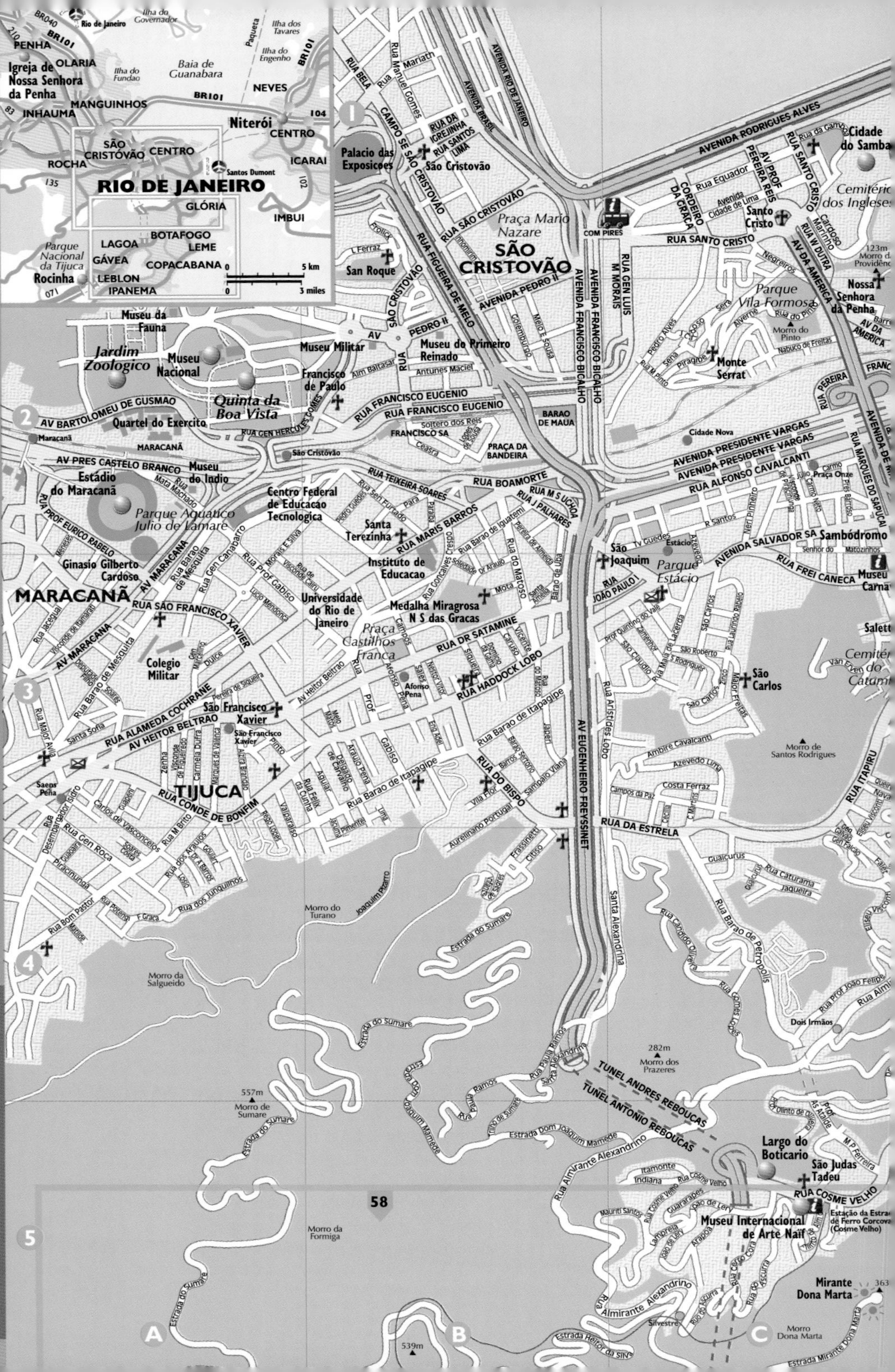

RIO DE JANEIRO
Ilha do Governador
Rio de Janeiro
Ilha dos Tavares
Paquetá
Ilha do Engenho
PENHA
OLARIA
Igreja de Nossa Senhora da Penha
Ilha do Fundão
Baía de Guanabara
BR101
NEVES
MANGUINHOS
INHAUMA
Niterói
CENTRO
SÃO CRISTÓVÃO
ROCHA
Santos Dumont
ICARAI
GLÓRIA
IMBUI
BOTAFOGO
LAGOA
LEME
Parque Nacional da Tijuca
GÁVEA
COPACABANA
Rocinha
LEBLON
IPANEMA
0 5 km
0 3 miles

SÃO CRISTOVÃO
MARACANÃ
TIJUCA
Palacio das Exposicoes
São Cristovão
San Roque
Praça Mario Nazare
Museu da Fauna
Jardim Zoologico
Museu Nacional
Quinta da Boa Vista
Museu Militar
Museu do Primeiro Reinado
Francisco de Paulo
Quartel do Exercito
Estádio do Maracanã
Museu do Indio
Parque Aquatico Julio de Lamare
Centro Federal de Educacao Tecnologica
Santa Terezinha
Instituto de Educacao
Ginasio Gilberto Cardoso
Universidade do Rio de Janeiro
Medalha Miragrosa N S das Gracas
Praça Castilhos Franca
Colegio Militar
São Francisco Xavier
Cidade do Samba
Cemitério dos Ingleses
Santo Cristo
Parque Vila Formosa
Monte Serrat
Nossa Senhora da Penha
Morro da Providência
Cidade Nova
Praça Onze
Sambódromo
São Joaquim
Parque Estácio
Museu do Carnaval
São Carlos
Morro de Santos Rodrigues
Cemitério do Catumbi
Morro do Turano
Morro da Salgueido
Morro dos Prazeres
Morro de Sumare
Morro da Formiga
Dois Irmãos
Largo do Boticario
São Judas Tadeu
Museu Internacional de Arte Naïf
Estação da Estrada de Ferro Corcovado (Cosme Velho)
Mirante Dona Marta
Morro Dona Marta
TUNEL ANDRES REBOUCAS
TUNEL ANTONIO REBOUCAS
AVENIDA RODRIGUES ALVES
AVENIDA BRASIL
AVENIDA RIO DE JANEIRO
AVENIDA PRESIDENTE VARGAS
AV EUGENHEIRO FREYSSINET
RUA DA ESTRELA
RUA CONDE DE BONFIM
RUA HADDOCK LOBO
RUA SÃO FRANCISCO XAVIER
AV MARACANA
AV BARTOLOMEU DE GUSMAO
AV PRES CASTELO BRANCO
RUA FIGUEIRA DE MELO
RUA FRANCISCO EUGENIO
RUA COSME VELHO
58

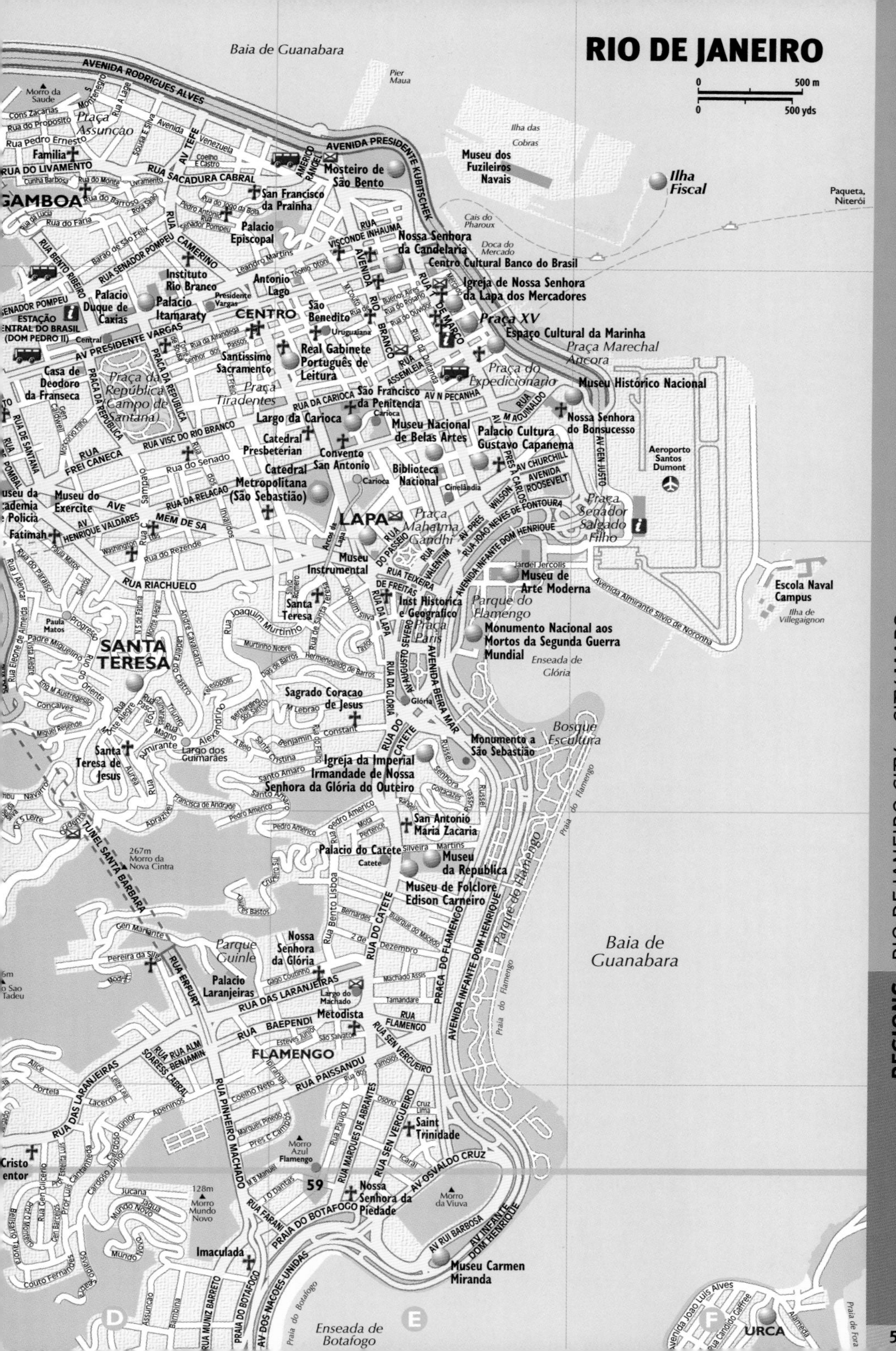
RIO DE JANEIRO
0 500 m
0 500 yds
Baia de Guanabara
Pier Maua
Ilha das Cobras
Museu dos Fuzileiros Navais
Ilha Fiscal
Paqueta, Niterói
Cais do Pharoux
Doca do Mercado
Centro Cultural Banco do Brasil
Igreja de Nossa Senhora da Lapa dos Mercadores
Praça XV
Espaço Cultural da Marinha
Praça Marechal Ancora
Praça do Expedicionário
Museu Histórico Nacional
Nossa Senhora do Bonsucesso
Aeroporto Santos Dumont
Praça Senador Salgado Filho
Escola Naval Campus
Ilha de Villegaignon
Avenida Almirante Silvio de Noronha
AVENIDA RODRIGUES ALVES
AVENIDA PRESIDENTE KUBITSCHEK
Morro da Saude
Praça Assunção
Familia
RUA DO LIVAMENTO
RUA SACADURA CABRAL
GAMBOA
Mosteiro de São Bento
San Francisco da Prainha
Palacio Episcopal
Nossa Senhora da Candelaria
Instituto Rio Branco
Antonio Lago
Palacio Duque de Caxias
Palacio Itamaraty
CENTRO
São Benedito
ESTAÇÃO CENTRAL DO BRASIL (DOM PEDRO II)
AV PRESIDENTE VARGAS
Santissimo Sacramento
Real Gabinete Português de Leitura
Casa de Deodoro da Franseca
Praça da República (Campo de Santana)
Praça Tiradentes
São Francisco da Penitencia
Largo da Carioca
Museu Nacional de Belas Artes
Palacio Cultura Gustavo Capanema
Catedral Presbeterian
Convento San Antonio
Biblioteca Nacional
Catedral Metropolitana (São Sebastião)
Museu do Exercite
LAPA
Praça Mahatma Gandhi
Museu Instrumental
Museu de Arte Moderna
Parque do Flamengo
Inst Historica e Geografico
Praça Paris
Monumento Nacional aos Mortos da Segunda Guerra Mundial
Enseada de Glória
SANTA TERESA
Santa Teresa
Sagrado Coracao de Jesus
Monumento a São Sebastião
Bosque Escultura
Santa Teresa de Jesus
Largo dos Guimarães
Igreja da Imperial Irmandade de Nossa Senhora da Glória do Outeiro
San Antonio Maria Zacaria
Palacio do Catete
Museu da Republica
Museu de Folclore Edison Carneiro
267m Morro da Nova Cintra
TUNEL SANTA BARBARA
Parque Guinle
Nossa Senhora da Glória
Palacio Laranjeiras
Largo do Machado
Metodista
FLAMENGO
Baia de Guanabara
Praia do Flamengo
Parque do Flamengo
AVENIDA INFANTE DOM HENRIQUE
PRAIA DO FLAMENGO
RUA DO CATETE
RUA DAS LARANJEIRAS
RUA PINHEIRO MACHADO
Saint Trinidade
Morro Azul Flamengo
Nossa Senhora da Piedade
Morro da Viuva
128m Morro Mundo Novo
Imaculada
Museu Carmen Miranda
PRAIA DO BOTAFOGO
AV DOS NACOES UNIDAS
Enseada de Botafogo
URCA
59
D
E
F

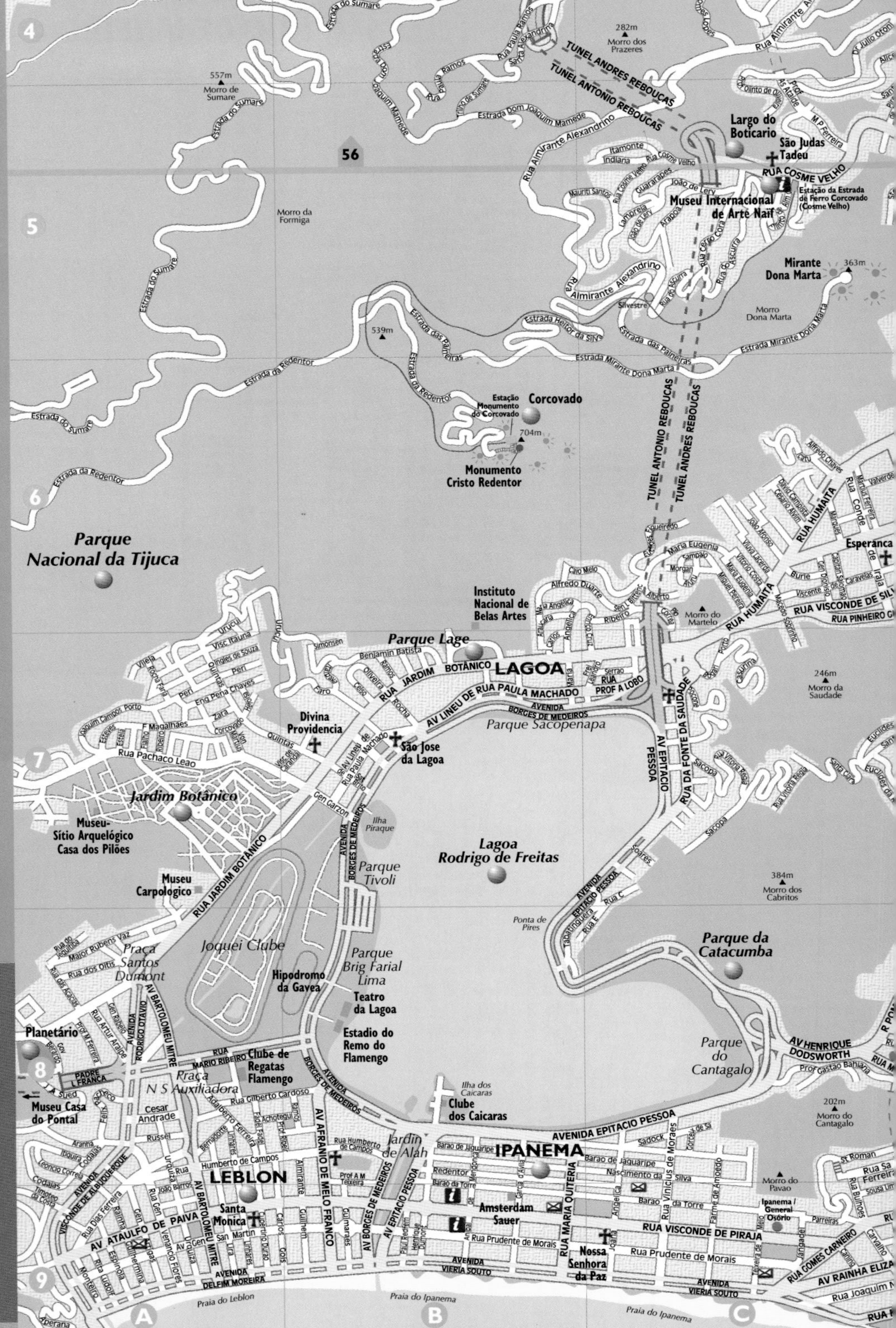

4
5
6
7
8
9
A
B
C
56
557m
Morro de Sumare
Estrada do Sumare
282m
Morro dos Prazeres
TUNEL ANDRES REBOUCAS
TUNEL ANTONIO REBOUCAS
Largo do Boticario
São Judas Tadeu
RUA COSME VELHO
Estação da Estrada de Ferro Corcovado (Cosme Velho)
Museu Internacional de Arte Naïf
Morro da Formiga
Mirante Dona Marta
363m
Morro Dona Marta
Estrada Mirante Dona Marta
Estrada das Paineiras
Estrada Heitor da Silva
Almirante Alexandrino
Rua Almirante Alexandrino
Estrada Dom Joaquim Mamede
539m
Estrada da Redentor
Estação Monumento do Corcovado
Corcovado
704m
Monumento Cristo Redentor
TUNEL ANTONIO REBOUCAS
TUNEL ANDRES REBOUCAS
Parque Nacional da Tijuca
Instituto Nacional de Belas Artes
Parque Lage
LAGOA
RUA JARDIM BOTÂNICO
RUA PROF A LOBO
AV LINEU DE RUA PAULA MACHADO
AVENIDA BORGES DE MEDEIROS
Parque Sacopenapa
Morro do Martelo
RUA HUMAITA
RUA VISCONDE DE SILVA
RUA PINHEIRO GUIMARÃES
Esperanca
246m
Morro da Saudade
Divina Providencia
São Jose da Lagoa
Rua Pachaco Leao
Jardim Botânico
Museu-Sítio Arqueológico Casa dos Pilões
Museu Carpologico
AV EPITACIO PESSOA
RUA DA FONTE DA SAUDADE
Lagoa Rodrigo de Freitas
Ilha Piraque
Parque Tivoli
384m
Morro dos Cabritos
Ponta de Pires
Parque da Catacumba
Joquei Clube
Praça Santos Dumont
Hipodromo da Gavea
Parque Brig Farial Lima
Teatro da Lagoa
Estadio do Remo do Flamengo
Planetário
Clube de Regatas Flamengo
RUA MARIO RIBEIRO
Praça N S Auxiliadora
Museu Casa do Pontal
Parque do Cantagalo
AV HENRIQUE DODSWORTH
202m
Morro do Cantagalo
Ilha dos Caicaras
Clube dos Caicaras
AVENIDA EPITACIO PESSOA
Jardim de Alah
IPANEMA
LEBLON
AV BARTOLOMEU MITRE
AV AFRANIO DE MELO FRANCO
AV BORGES DE MEDEIROS
AV EPITACIO PESSOA
RUA MARIA QUITERIA
Santa Monica
Amsterdam Sauer
Nossa Senhora da Paz
Morro do Pavao
Ipanema / General Osório
RUA VISCONDE DE PIRAJA
Rua Prudente de Morais
AV ATAULFO DE PAIVA
AVENIDA VISCONDE DE ALBUQUERQUE
AVENIDA DELFIM MOREIRA
AVENIDA VIEIRA SOUTO
RUA GOMES CARNEIRO
AV RAINHA ELIZABETH
Praia do Leblon
Praia do Ipanema

0 500 m
0 500 yds
FLAMENGO
Largo do Machado
Metodista
Tamandare
RUA DAS LARANJEIRAS
RUA BAEPENDI
RUA FLAMENGO
RUA SEN VERGUEIRO
PRAÇA DO FLAMENGO
RUA PAISSANDU
RUA PINHEIRO MACHADO
RUA MARQUES DE ABRANTES
Saint Trinidade
57
AV OSVALDO CRUZ
Morro Azul
Flamengo
Nossa Senhora da Piedade
Morro da Viuva
AV RUI BARBOSA
AV INFANTE DOM HENRIQUE
128m Morro Mundo Novo
RUA FARANI
PRAIA DO BOTAFOGO
Imaculada
Museu Carmen Miranda
Marques Olinda
AV DOS NACOES UNIDAS
Praia do Botafogo
Enseada de Botafogo
MUNIZ BARRETO
Viscente de Ouro Preto
Casa Rui Barbosa
São Inacio
RUA SÃO CLEMENTE
Museu Villa Lobos
BOTAFOGO
Botafogo
AV PASTEUR
Miranto do Pasmado
RUA VOLUNTARIOS DE PATRIA
RUA PROF A RODRIGUES
RUA DA PASSAGEM
RUA GEN SEVERIANO
AV VENCESLAU BRAS
AVENIDA PASTEUR
Universidade do Rio de Janeiro
São Joao Batista
RUA MENA BARRETO
Museu dos Teatros
RUA GEN POLIDORO
RUA ARNALDO QUINTELA
GEN G MONTEIRO
AV SAURO SODRE
Alvaro Ramos
Cemitério São João Batista
RUA REAL GRANDEZA
São João Batista
Santa Terezinha do Menino Jesus
235m Morro da Babilonia
Rua Ladeira do Leme
Gen Cardoso de Aguilar
241m Morro de Sao Joao
Cardeal Arcoverde
AVENIDA PRINCESA ISABEL
Nossa Senhora do Rosario
Gustavo Sampaio
AVENIDA ATLANTICA
Praça Alm Julio de Noronha
Morro do Urubu
Ponta do Leme
114m Morro do Leme
Praia do Leme
RUA SIQUEIRA CAMPOS
Santa Cruz
Siqueira Campos
RUA TONELERO
RUA BARATA RIBEIRO
AVENIDA NOSSA SENHORA DE COPACABANA
Praça do Lido
Copacabana
Praia de Copacabana
COPACABANA
Rua Santa Clara
CONSTANTE RAMOS
Paulo Apostolo
BOLIVAR
Museu Historico do Exercito
Forte de Copacabana
Ponta de Copacabana
Praia do Diabo
URCA
Avenida João Luis Alves
Praia da Urca
Praia de Fora
Nossa Senhora do Brasil
Avenida Portugal
218m Morro da Urca
Estação Morro da Urca
Teleférico
394m Pão de Açúcar
Estação Praia Vermelha
Praia do Vermelha
Enseada de Vermelha
D
E
F

RIO DE JANEIRO CITY STREET INDEX

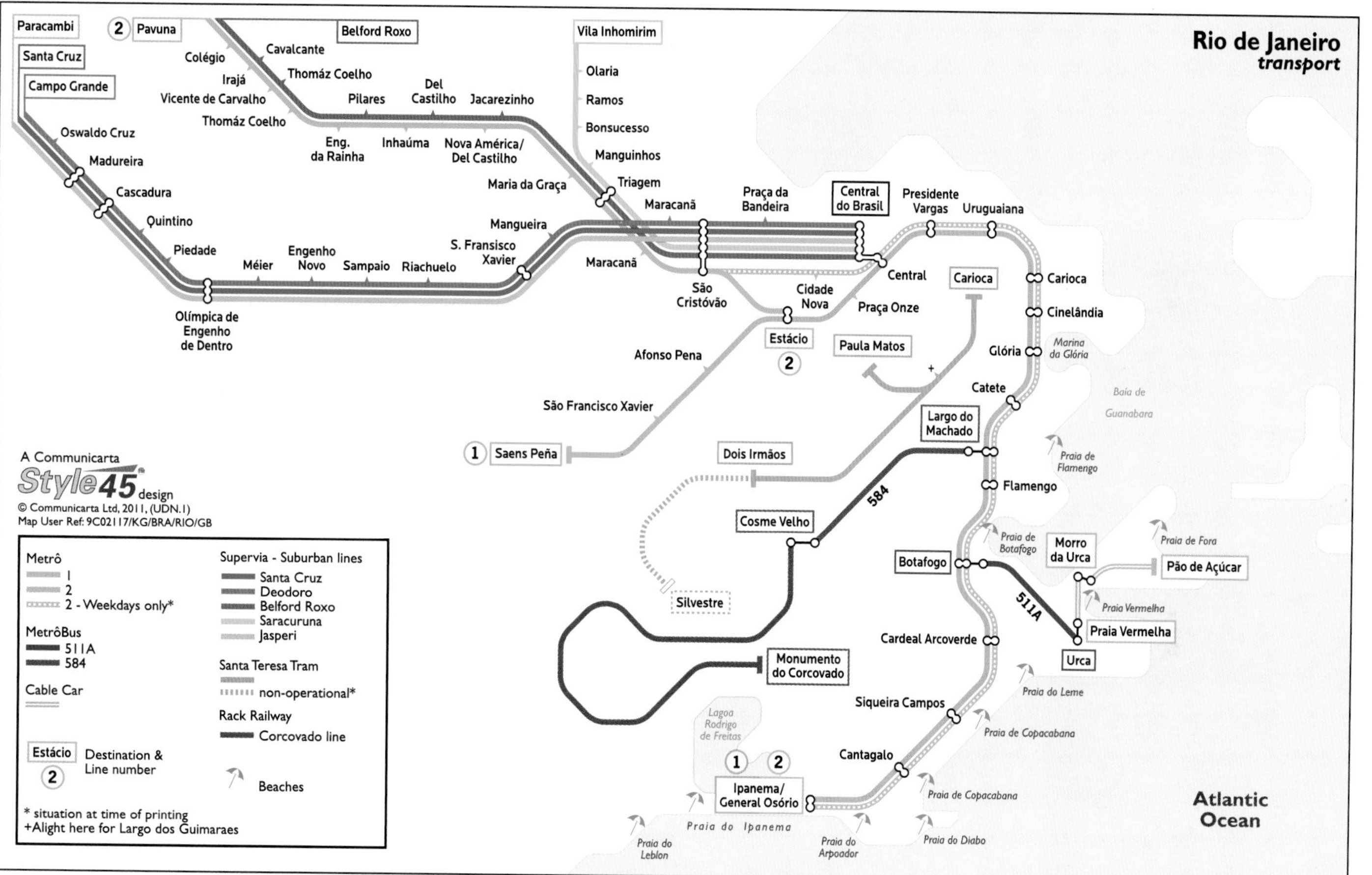

Rio de Janeiro
transport
Paracambi
Santa Cruz
Campo Grande
2 Pavuna
Belford Roxo
Vila Inhomirim
Colégio
Cavalcante
Irajá
Thomáz Coelho
Vicente de Carvalho
Thomáz Coelho
Pilares
Del Castilho
Jacarezinho
Eng. da Rainha
Inhaúma
Nova América/ Del Castilho
Maria da Graça
Olaria
Ramos
Bonsucesso
Manguinhos
Triagem
Maracanã
Oswaldo Cruz
Madureira
Cascadura
Quintino
Piedade
Méier
Engenho Novo
Sampaio
Riachuelo
S. Fransisco Xavier
Mangueira
Maracanã
Olímpica de Engenho de Dentro
Praça da Bandeira
Central do Brasil
Presidente Vargas
Uruguaiana
São Cristóvão
Cidade Nova
Central
Praça Onze
Estácio
2
Carioca
Carioca
Cinelândia
Glória
Marina da Glória
Paula Matos
Afonso Pena
São Francisco Xavier
1 Saens Peña
Catete
Baía de Guanabara
Largo do Machado
Dois Irmãos
Praia de Flamengo
Flamengo
584
Cosme Velho
Botafogo
Praia de Botafogo
Morro da Urca
Praia de Fora
Pão de Açúcar
Praia Vermelha
Praia Vermelha
511A
Urca
Silvestre
Monumento do Corcovado
Cardeal Arcoverde
Praia do Leme
Siqueira Campos
Praia de Copacabana
Lagoa Rodrigo de Freitas
Cantagalo
1 2
Ipanema/ General Osório
Praia de Copacabana
Praia do Ipanema
Praia do Leblon
Praia do Arpoador
Praia do Diabo
Atlantic Ocean
A Communicarta
Style45 design
© Communicarta Ltd, 2011, (UDN.1)
Map User Ref: 9C02117/KG/BRA/RIO/GB
Metrô
1
2
2 - Weekdays only*
MetrôBus
511A
584
Cable Car
Supervia - Suburban lines
Santa Cruz
Deodoro
Belford Roxo
Saracuruna
Jasperi
Santa Teresa Tram
non-operational*
Rack Railway
Corcovado line
Estácio 2 Destination & Line number
Beaches
* situation at time of printing
+Alight here for Largo dos Guimaraes

CANDELÁRIA

Wealthy Rio's favourite place of worship is named after a chapel that stood on the same site from 1610, built by a sailor from the Canary Islands in homage to Our Lady of Candles *(Candelária)*, who he believed had saved him from shipwreck. When it was built, the Italianate cupolas and neoclassical facade towered over its environs. Inside it is peaceful and opulent, decked out in luxurious Veronese marble—shipped from Italy at great expense—despite their being stone of equal quality in Brazil. The church is modelled on the Basílica de Estrela in Lisbon and was completed at the turn of the 18th century.

57 E1 Praça Pio X 21 2233 2324 Mon–Fri 8–4, Sat 8–12, Sun 9–1 Free Uruguaiana

CASA RUI BARBOSA

www.casaruibarbosa.gov.br

This museum is housed in the stately belle époque home of one of Brazil's most illustrious early statesmen and is a little haven of peace in the bustle of Botafogo's busy streets. The rooms contain period furniture and objects alongside some of Barbosa's belongings.

Behind is a large tropical garden with shady mango trees, heliconias and flitting hummingbirds and butterflies. On weekends there are often classical music or *bossa nova* ('new wave' jazz, ▷ 17) concerts in the main hall.

59 D6 Rua São Clemente 134, Botafogo 21 3289 4600 Tue–Fri 10–5, Sat–Sun and holidays 2–6 Adult R$3, child (under 17) R$1.50; Gardens free Botafogo

CATEDRAL METROPÓLITANA DE SÃO SEBASTIÃO

www.catedral.com.br

This towering, truncated concrete cone a few hundred metres southwest of the Convent of St. Anthony (▷ 71) was designed by a Brazilian disciple of Swiss-French Modernist architect Le Corbusier, Edgar de Oliveira da Fonseca, between 1976 and 1984. The sculptures in the cavernous and dungeon-dark church interior—illuminated by a series of vertiginous and multi-coloured stained-glass mosaic windows—are by the Italian artist, Humberto Cozzi.

The basement houses a Sacred Art Museum, which contains Dom Pedro II's throne and the golden rose awarded to Princess Isabel by Pope Leo XIII, to celebrate her signing of the Act which abolished slavery in Brazil in 1888.

57 E2 Avenida República do Chile s/n 21 2240 2669 Cathedral daily 7–5; Sacred Art Museum Tue–Thu 2–6 Cathedral free; Sacred Art Museum free Cinelândia Trams from Santa Teresa

CIDADE DO SAMBA

http://cidadedosambarj.globo.com

In 2008, Rio de Janeiro's municipal government opened this sprawling warehouse and cultural complex (the 'City of Samba') as the new home for the production wings of the city's principal samba schools. All the costumes, floats and accoutrements of the annual carnival parades for the likes of the Primeira Estação de Mangueira samba school are now made here. Visits are fascinating, showcasing the painstaking work of the thousands who work behind the scenes to make *carnaval* in Rio the most famous party in the world. Following a fire in 2011 the complex is temporarily closed. A gift shop on the site sells *carnaval* costumes, masks and souvenirs.

56 C1 Rua Rivadávia Corréa 60, Gamboa 21 2213 2503 Check website for reopening Daytime admission R$5; Show tickets including buffet dinner: adult R$190, students and over 60s R$95 Central (15-min walk) Any bus to the *rodoviária*, which is a 5-min walk to the west

Clockwise from below *A room in Museu Casa Rui Barbosa; the conical Catedral Metropólitana; the ornate interior of Igreja de Nossa Senhora da Candelária*

COPACABANA

Rio's most famous beach is the first of the Atlantic coastal beaches outside Guanabara Bay. To visitors it looks like one glorious 4km (2.5-mile) half-moon sweep of curving sand. To Cariocas it is two beaches: Copacabana comprises the southern part of the crescent, while the northern end is called Leme.

OUR LADY OF COPACABANA

The beach takes its name from a chapel which once stood on the site of the current fort at the far south of the beach. This was a sanctuary built to Our Lady of Copacabana in Bolivia, whose image was cherished by Spanish sailors travelling between Europe and Latin America in colonial times. One such sailor, shipwrecked in a storm just off Rio in the early 17th century, prayed to Our Lady of Copacabana and promised to build a chapel wherever he washed up on shore should she save him. He washed up on Copacabana beach.

EXPANSION

At that time the sands would have been completely wild and cut off from Rio de Janeiro, which was contained in Guanabara Bay by boulder mountains and forests. Settlers only arrived in earnest after the construction of a tunnel in 1891. The French actress Sarah Bernhardt made the beach popular. She was playing at a theatre in Rio in the first decade of the 20th century and spent much of her leisure time here.

THE MODERN RESORT

Copacabana exploded in population after a larger tunnel was built in the 20th century. A new road was also built, Avenida Atlântica, which is now lined with hotels and high-rise flats, including the landmark neoclassical Copacabana Palace hotel (▷ 102–103).

INFORMATION

www.rioguiaoficial.com.br
59 D8 · Avenida Princesa Isabel 183, Copacabana · 21 2541 7522 · Mon–Fri 9–6 · Cardeal Arco Verde, Siqueira Campos, Cantagalo · 119, 154, 413, 415, 455, 474; From city centre to Avenida Nossa Senhora de Copacabana

TIPS

» Do not walk on the beach at night. Although it is now lit after dark, it is still a magnet for thieves.

» On New Year's Eve, the Reveillon festival—one of the biggest in the Rio calendar—takes place on Copacabana Beach, attracting millions of party-goers who wear white and make offerings to Yemanjá, the goddess of the sea.

Above *Forte Duque de Caxias overlooks the inviting sands of Copacabana beach*

CORCOVADO

▷ 66–67.

ESPAÇO CULTURAL DA MARINHA

www.mar.mil.br

This naval museum is housed in a series of long converted colonial warehouses next to the naval wharves, just north of the city centre. It has galleries devoted to underwater archaeology and navigation, and the wharves themselves harbour a number of naval boats. They include the *Galeota do João VI*—the former royal barge, built in 1808 and which is still used for tours around the bay—a mid-20th century submarine (the *Riachuelo)* named after a battle fought by Brazil in an ignoble war against Paraguay, and a World War II warship, the *Bauru*.

57 E2 Avenida Alfredo Agache, s/n, Centro 21 2104 5592 Tue–Sun 12–5 R$10 Uruguiana Be aware that there are no restaurants nearby

ESTADIO DO MARACANÃ

Pelé scored his 1,000th goal here in 1969 and the stadium, with a capacity of 100,000, is known the world over. It is being refurbished for the 2014 World Cup, but it is possible to attend football matches in alternative stadia through a tour company. Be prepared for lots of noise and emotion if you choose to watch football in Rio.

56 A2 Rua Prof Eurico Rabelo 21 2299 2942 Daily 9–1 Admission to stadium and museum R$5 Maracanã For organized tour see www.bealocal.com No refreshments inside the stadium

IGREJA DA IMPERIAL IRMANDADE DE NOSSA SENHORA DA GLÓRIA DO OUTEIRO

www.outeirodagloria.org.br

This very Portuguese baroque church, the Church of the Imperial Brotherhood of Our Lady of Glória of Outeiro, is one of the most beautifully situated in Rio: in a stand of tropical woodland on top of a hill overlooking Glória harbour and Guanabara Bay. It was a favourite worshipping place of the Portuguese, and subsequently Brazilian, royal family. Dom Pedro II was baptized here, in a font in the octagonal nave, which is covered in some of the finest painted blue and white *azulejo* tiles in Brazil. Building on the church began in 1714, before Rio de Janeiro became the country's capital. At the time its design was as radical as any in Europe, not only for the unusual shape of the nave (which spawned imitations in Portugal) but for a concealed corridor and inner-wall passage which allowed the clergy to circulate unobserved.

57 E3 Praça Nossa Senhora da Gloria 135, Glória 21 2557 4600 Tue–Fri 9–12, 1–5, Sat–Sun 9–12 R$5 Glória

IGREJA DA NOSSA SENHORA DA LAPA DOS MERCADORES

It's easy to overlook this tiny 18th-century church, which is tucked away down a narrow alley among busy bars and shops. Its exterior is plain and modest, but the inside of the Church of Our Lady of Lapa of Merchants is a jewel, with a miniature but skilfully proportioned elliptical nave. This ascends to a delicate cupola, capped by an oval skylight and lit with a ring of spherical windows. The sacristy is adorned with some exquisitely carved statuary and as there is barely a visitor, the church is a quiet, meditative oasis of calm in the heat and hustle that is central Rio de Janeiro, just a stroll away from the busy boat harbour and the tourist sights of Praça XV (▷ 82–83). Like many of Brazil's baroque churches, Nossa Senhora da Lapa was built by a lay brotherhood and was originally smaller still. The main chapel and the tower were extended and expanded in the 19th century by Antônio de Padua e Castro, who added much of the statuary and employed a local sculptor, Antônio Alves Meira, to produce the stucco.

57 E2 Rua do Ouvidor 35, Centro 21 2509 2339 Usually Mon–Fri 8–2, but opens erratically Free Carioca

Below *The massive Estadio do Maracanã will host World Cup matches in 2014*

CORCOVADO

Cristo Redentor (Christ the Redeemer), watching over Rio from the 704m-tall (2,309ft) boulder mountain of Corcovado, has come to symbolize Brazil and was voted one of the seven wonders of the modern world in 2007 (in a poll of approximately 100 million worldwide votes, carried out by the New7Wonders Foundation). Views out from the platform which encircles the base of the figure are as breathtaking as the statue itself. They are especially magical close to sunset, when the city twinkles below and the distant hills and beaches are lit with a rich orange glow.

CREATION OF AN ICON

Brazilian civil engineer Heitor da Silva Costa won a competition to design the grand monument, launched by the city in 1921. It was inspired by Leonardo da Vinci's famous study of the human body. The statue itself was then carved from separate chunks of soapstone by the Parisian art deco sculptor Paul Landowski, who won the Prix de Rome in 1900 for a statue of David. It was carried up the mountain piece-by-piece and re-assembled. Opened to the public in 1931, the Redeemer is 30m (98ft) tall and has a tiny chapel in its base, where mass is celebrated on Sunday mornings.

REACHING THE HEIGHTS

A funicular railway—the Trem do Corcovado—runs from the Cosme Velho neighbourhood every half hour, up the steep forested slopes below Corcovado to a station close to the base of the statue itself. Escalators ascend from here to the monument. It is no longer possible to visit by road unless you join an organized tour. You can also take a 20-minute helicopter flight around Corcovado and the Sugar Loaf (▷ 78–79). Helicopters leave from the Sugar Loaf or the Lagoa Rodrigo de Freitas (▷ 96).

INFORMATION

www.corcovado.com.br

58 B6 Trem do Corcovado, Rua Cosme Velho 513, Cosme Velho 21 2558 1329 Daily 8.30–7 Adult R$36 for round-trip funicular journey and entrance to the statue, child under 5 free Largo do Machado, continuing on bus 422 or 498 south Cafés at both Corcovado and summit stations Gift shop at Corcovado station

TIPS

» Take a helicopter flight in the early morning or late afternoon for the best light.

» The ride up to the summit takes around 20 minutes, but the wait to board can be lengthy. Come early morning on weekdays for the shortest queues.

Opposite *The iconic statue of Cristo Redentor surmounts Corcovado*
Below *The view from Corcovado over Rio and the Sugar Loaf*

Above *Lagoa Rodrigo de Freitas seen from Corcovado*
Right *One of the bars in Rio Scenarium samba club in Lapa*

IGREJA DA NOSSA SENHORA DA PENHA

www.santuariopenhario.org.br
According to local myth, in the early 17th century a wealthy Portuguese, Baltasar de Abreu Cardoso, climbed the giant rock on which the Church of Our Lady of Succour is built, to survey his land. When he reached the summit he was confronted with a giant snake and in his panic he called out to the Virgin to save him. A huge lizard appeared from the bushland and killed and ate the snake. In homage, Baltasar built a small chapel on the site. The chapel became a church in the 18th century and the church is now a pilgrimage site. In October the church plays host to one of Rio de Janeiro's biggest and most traditional religious festivals, when Catholics congregate at the base of the rock, from where they crawl or walk on their knees up the 365 steps to the altar.

56 A1 (inset) Largo da Penha 19, Penha 21 2290 0942 Daily 7–6 Free Trem do Ramal train to Penha

ILHA FISCAL

The copper-green neo-Gothic folly on this island in the bay was a royal pleasure palace in the 19th century, playing host to polka dance masked balls for Rio's high society. These inspired costumed parties in the *favelas* (slums), which later developed into *carnaval*. Guided visits are co-ordinated by the Espaço Cultural da Marinha naval museum (▷ 65), which runs schooner trips to the island that take 2–3 hours.

57 F1 Accessible only on organized tours, which leave from the Espaço Cultural da Marinha (Avenida Alfredo Agache, Centro; tel 21 2233 9165; Thu–Sun at 1, 2.30, 4)

IPANEMA AND LEBLON BEACHES

▷ 69.

JARDIM BOTÂNICO

▷ 70.

LAPA

Lapa is Rio's most vibrant nightlife neighbourhood. Yet only a decade ago its shadowy streets were off-limits, even for the most streetwise Carioca. The 1920s mansions and grand old dance halls were falling to wrack and ruin. Then, the Circo Voador (▷ 94)—one of Rio's most fashionable small music venues—moved here from the Arpoador district, close to Ipanema, and it was followed by a spate of samba clubs. Nowadays, on weekend nights Ruas Mem de Sá and Lavradio throng with people. Impromptu *capoeira* and samba groups compete with the throb of *forró* music—a lively style from Brazil's northeast—and the buzz of a hundred bars. A samba club crawl here is a Rio essential. Start at the Arcos da Lapa—a 40m-high (131ft) spalted, white viaduct. Then, hop in to Comuna do Semente (for great roots samba and where the neighbourhood began, ▷ 94–95), Carioca da Gema (where Rio swings its tanned hips to samba, ▷ 94) and Rio Scenarium (▷ 95).

57 E2 Cinelândia

LAGOA RODRIGO DE FREITAS

Rio's largest lake sits between Ipanema (▷ 69) and Corcovado mountain (▷ 66–67), next to the Jardim Botânico (Botanical Garden, ▷ 70). By day, the lakeshore paths are busy with joggers and cyclists, and the water is dotted with pedal boats and canoes. At night, the *lagoa* becomes a favourite romantic spot for an ice-cold *caipirinha* (a crushed ice, fresh lime and sugar-cane spirit cocktail). Bars and restaurants fringe the lakeshore and offer views across the water to the Os Dois Irmãos mountains and to the Christ statue, high on Corcovado and illuminated in brilliant halogen white.

58 B7 Siquiera Campos

IPANEMA AND LEBLON BEACHES

The contiguous beaches of Ipanema and Leblon just to the south of Copacabana (▷ 64) are Rio de Janeiro's most fashionable stretches of sand. This is where well-dressed Rio strips off for the beach, does its beachside pull-ups and dips its tiny bikini in the water. It's also where gay and lesbian Rio lays its towel under the billowing rainbow flag which lies at the end of Rua Farme de Amoedo.

TAKE IT EASY

An afternoon here watching the girls and guys go by is an essential Rio experience. It is best accompanied by a cold coconut juice drunk straight from the shell, served at one of the myriad beachside snack bars. Views along the beaches are at their best in the late afternoon when the sky turns rosy and the setting sun silhouettes the twin peaks of Os Dois Irmãos, at the far southern end of Leblon.

HIGH STYLE BY THE BEACH

Ipanema and Leblon are also two of the city's chicest neighbourhoods. Rua Garcia d'Avila and Rua Visconde de Pirajá, in Ipanema, are lined with little boutiques stocking the best in Carioca high fashion. For culinary hotspots, Rua Dias Ferreira in Leblon is home to some of the city's most fashionable dining rooms, where kitchens are run by named chefs and where diners eat to be seen. The bar, Garota de Ipanema (Girl from Ipanema), where a passing girl inspired Tom Jobim and Vinícius de Moraes to write the *bossa nova* classic of the same name, is a five-minute walk from the beach (▷ 17).

INFORMATION

www.rioguiaoficial.com.br
Ipanema 58 B8; Leblon 58 A9
Avenida Princesa Isabel 183, Copacabana 21 2541 7522
Mon–Fri 9–6 Ipanema Gal Osório

TIPS

» Bring as little as possible to the beach and never leave items unattended. Sunshades, deck chairs, snacks and drinks are readily available.
» Waves and rip currents can be strong and the water cold.
» There is a special play area for toddlers, the Baixo Bebe (www.baixobebeleblon.com.br), at the far end of Leblon.

Below *Ipanema beach, bordered by one of Rio's most fashionable neighbourhoods*

INFORMATION

www.jbrj.gov.br

58 A7 Rua Jardim Botânico s/n 21 3874 1808 Daily 8–5 Adult R$5, child (under 7) and over 60 free 170 from the Centre, 571 from Glória and Botafogo or 572 from Copacabana and Ipanema Café Botânico in the gardens, next to the entrance

TIP

» Allow at least three hours for a visit and plan to arrive at about 2.30 on a weekday: As the air begins to cool, the light approaches its best and birds arrive from the nearby forest.

JARDIM BOTÂNICO

Rio de Janeiro's botanical gardens are among the best in South America, both as a spectacle and for what they protect and preserve. They were created in 1808 by Emperor João VI as a cool, shady retreat for the newly arrived royal family and courtiers, and as a living memory of the plants and scents of Portugal, which they had so hastily abandoned (▷ 32–33). The general public were admitted only after the establishment of the Republic in 1890.

LANDSCAPE

The gardens are in a beautiful location, huddled under Corcovado mountain (▷ 66–67) on the western side of Lagoa Rodrigo de Freitas (▷ 68). A wander through affords many different views of the Christ statue. There are 141ha (348 acres) of broad palm tree-lined avenues, winding shady paths, beds and lawns, and ponds tinkling with water from classical fountains and covered with metre-wide Amazonian Vitória Regia lillies. There's a wealth of birdlife too—some 140 species—attracted from the adjacent Tijuca forest by the numerous flowers, fruits and palm trees. Hummingbirds are particularly abundant.

ATTRACTIONS

Of more than 9,000 vascular plants and seeds, the highlights are probably the orchids and bromeliads (a family of bright tropical plants, the most well-known of which is the pineapple). There are some 1,000 species of the former in the Orquidarium, many of which come from Brazil's Atlantic coastal forests. There are museums too: The Museu Botânico has exhibitions on the conservation of Brazilian flora, while the Casa dos Pilões (a simple whitewashed cottage near the Orquidarium) was once the first gunpowder factory in Brazil. The gardens have an excellent small café, and the surrounding neighbourhood (which is also called Jardim Botânico) has many of the city's best fine-dining restaurants.

Below *The Fountain of the Muses shaded by palm trees in the botanical gardens*

LARGO DO BOTICÁRIO

This pretty little square of colonial and Imperial houses—many of them owned by painters—is named in honour of Joaquim Luiz da Silva Souto, the private pharmacist *(boticário)* to the royal family. Much of 19th-century Rio looked like this. The enclave is close to Corcovado funicular station (▷ 67) in Cosme Velho and is reachable by taxi in five minutes through the Rebouças tunnel that links the Lagoa Rodrigo de Freitas (▷ 68) with Corcovado. It is well worth visiting on the way to or from the Lagoa and the Christ statue.

56 C5 Rua Cosme Velho 822, Cosme Velho Free Largo do Machado, continuing on bus 422 or 498 south

LARGO DA CARIOCA

This long street—running between Rua da Carioca and the Metrô Carioca—which is busy with street vendors and commuters, is watched over by a cluster of beautiful colonial churches. The Igreja Convento de Santo Antônio, mostly built between 1608 and 1620, is the second oldest church in Rio (after the Mosteiro de São Bento, which was founded in 1586, although much of the building dates from later) and sits on a little hill at the Largo da Carioca. It has a beautiful sacristy decorated with *azulejos* (glazed tiles) and paintings devoted to St. Anthony (Mon–Fri 7.30–7.30, Sat 7.30–11). Next door is the newly refurbished church of the Ordem Terceira de São Francisco da Penitência, built between 1653 and 1773. It is one of the finest baroque churches in the city, with an interior covered in gold leaf (Mon–Fri 7.30–7.30, Sat 7.30–11).

Across Ruas da Carioca and 7 de Setembro, at the top of the Rua do Ouvidor in the Largo São Francisco de Paula square, is another impressive baroque church, São Francisco de Paula. Its interior has work by some of the city's most distinguished early artists, including carvings by Mestre Valentim, paintings by Vítor Meireles and murals by Manuel da Cunha (Mon–Fri 9–1). Across the Largo de São Francisco and on the corner of Rua Uruguiana and Ouvidor, is the most important African-Brazilian church in the city, the Igreja da Irmandade de Nossa Senhora do Rosário e São Benedito dos Homens Pretos, with an adjacent slavery museum (Mon–Fri 7.30–7.30, Sat 7.30–11). During the 19th century it was the site of an elaborate festival, which later contributed pageantry to carnival, recreating the coronation of the king and queen of Congo followed by processions of courtiers in fancy dress and troupes of drummers.

57 E2 Carioca, Uruguaiana Entry to churches free

MONUMENTO NACIONAL AOS MORTOS DA SEGUNDA GUERRA MUNDIAL

This striking Modernist monument to the World War II dead, comprising a long plinth watched over by a decorative twin-columned tower, sits in the middle of Burle Marx's Parque do Flamengo. It was designed by Brazilian architects Marcos Konder Neto and Hélio Ribas Marinho. The solemn stone figures on the plinth are by Alfredo Ceschiatti, who was responsible for many of the statues in Brasília. A mausoleum for some of Brazil's World War II dead sits beneath, together with a modest army museum with a small collection of medals.

57 E3 Avenida Infante Dom Henrique 75, Glória 21 2240 1333 Daily 10–4 Free Glória

Left *Igreja São Francisco da Penitência in Largo da Carioca*
Below *A building in Largo do Boticário*

INFORMATION

www.osb.org.br
57 E1 Rua Dom Gerardo 68
21 2291 7122 Daily 7–6 R$10
Uruguiana (a 10-min walk to the south)

TIPS

» Photography is not permitted in the church.
» The monastery can be reached via a winding road which leads up from Rua Dom Gerardo, just off the Praça Mauá, or via a lift, which leaves every 30 minutes from Rua Dom Gerardo 40.

Above *The fabulously ornate interior glimmers with gold*

MOSTEIRO DE SÃO BENTO

Rio de Janeiro's most opulent religious monument lies hidden in the very centre of the city, up a steep driveway and behind a sober church facade. It takes a while for eyes to adjust to the gloomy interior of the Benedictine monastery of São Bento after Rio's brilliant sunlight. When they do, they are greeted with a Catholic Aladdin's cave: a lavish display of gold and priceless art that covers the interior of the building from floor to ceiling. Burnished bleeding hearts and lacey stucco covered in gilt cluster around the nave and adjacent chapels, pendulous candelabra—by Mestre Valentim (1745–1813)—hang suspended from the high ceiling, and statues of agonized saints and cherubs encrust the walls and crowd the open spaces.

A LIFE OF DEDICATION

The church was one of the first in Rio, founded by the Benedictines in 1586, but the interior dates from Brazil's gold rush era (▷ 31). Wealthy patrons were eager to compete for social status and liberal with their donations to what were then the most important public spaces in the city, the churches. What you see today was the life work of a series of artists, many of them working alongside the Benedictine monk, Dom Domingos da Conceição. He was responsible for the best of the statuary. These include effigies of St. Benedict's sister, St. Scholastica, and of Our Lady of Monserrat, the church's patron saint, which has painted bird's eggs for eyes.

LITERARY TREASURES

The monastery library houses the most important collection of religious books in Brazil, including accounts of life in early Rio de Janeiro written by Benedictine monks. Those wishing to visit should request permission in writing from the monastery's abbot.

MUSEU DE ARTE MODERNA (MAM)

www.mamrio.com.br

Rio de Janeiro's most important modern art space is housed in a striking concrete and glass gallery, 200m (218 yards) in length and suspended on inverted v-shaped buttresses, set in expansive and shaded waterfront gardens. The building was designed in 1953 by Affonso Eduardo Reidy, who—like Oscar Niemeyer—worked with Lúcio Costa on Brazil's first significant Modernist building, the Palácio Capanema (▷ 77). Reidy's style betrays Costa's predilection for the ideas of Le Corbusier. Free of internal supporting structures and with so much glass, the gallery interior is an enormous, bright, cavernous space, much of which is taken up with temporary exhibitions by key Brazilian and international artists. These sit alongside pieces by Brazilian Modernists, like Tarsila do Amaral and Cândido Portinari, and international artists, such as American Jackson Pollock and Romanian Constantin Brâncuşi, rotated from the museum's archive of some 13,000 paintings.

57 E3 Avenida Infante Dom Henrique 85, Parque Brigadeiro Eduardo Gomes, Flamengo 21 2240 4944 Tue–Fri, 12–6, Sat–Sun and holidays, 12–7 R$8 Glória 472, 438 or 154 from Copacabana and Ipanema Buffet restaurant Gift shop

MUSEU CARMEN MIRANDA

http://carmen.miranda.nom.br/gal_museu.htm

This ungainly, concrete, pillbox-of-a-building, trapped in a small green space between the two racing tracks of an urban highway, is Rio's only testament to one of its most internationally famous daughters. The building's interior showcases a meagre collection of modest relics from her singing and acting career—a few costumes, some newspaper cuttings and magazine covers, and a handful of photos.

59 E5 Parque Brigadeiro Eduardo Gomes (in front of Avenida Rui Barbosa 560), Flamengo 21 2299 5586 Tue–Fri, 10–5, Sat–Sun 12–5 R$4 Flamengo, Largo do Machado

Above *Massive concrete buttresses support the Museu de Arte Moderna building*

MUSEU CASA DO PONTAL

www.museucasadopontal.com.br

It is difficult to reach this museum, which is tucked away on a rural road beyond the farthest reaches of Recreio dos Bandeirantes in the far south of Rio. However, those who make the effort are rewarded with one of the best collections of Brazilian folk art in the country. There are models, mechanical toys, sculptures, brightly painted effigies and other items from all over the country. The items were all produced after 1950, by more than 200 artists, and collected by a French enthusiast.

58 off A8 Estrada do Pontal 3295, Recreio dos Bandeirantes 24 2490 3278 Tue–Sun 9.30–5 Be aware that there are no restaurants nearby There is no public transport—visits must be taken with a tour company, by taxi or in a rental car

MUSEU DO FOLCLORE EDISON CARNEIRO

www.cnfcp.gov.br

This delightful small museum is a celebration of the naïve arts and crafts of rural Brazil, particularly the country's northeast. These traditional techniques grew in an era before Chinese toys and television, when many rural Brazilians lived outside the economic system, largely off the land, and made everything from their own houses and clothes to their utensils and ornaments.

The large collection is captivatingly displayed and beautifully lit. As well as toys and decorative items, it includes hundreds of carved working models of rural life: Rodeos with miniature wooden broncos bucking and throwing wooden cowboys into painted dirt, or circuses where wooden trapeze artists swing under a balsa 'big top' tent. There are several particularly exquisitely carved and moulded naïve sculptures, too, many of them transmitting great dignity and pride in a cultural tradition that is, unfortunately, slowly being eroded by a combination of economic migration and mass communication.

57 E4 Rua do Catete 181, Catete 21 2285 0441 Tue–Fri 11–6, Sat–Sun and holidays 3–6 R$5 Catete 571, 572 from Ipanema and Copacabana; 401, 406A, 434 from the centre

MUSEU HISTÓRICO NACIONAL

▷ 75.

MUSEU DO INDIO

www.museudoindio.org.br

When the Europeans arrived, Brazil was a continent of some 1,000 indigenous nations. Most were wiped out or decimated by the Portuguese and the *bandeirante* slave trade, and were it not for the work of the Villas Boas brothers after World War II, their stories and rich cultures would have been largely forgotten.

This small museum preserves about 12,000 objects from some 180 tribal nations, many of whom were befriended by the Villas Boas brothers. It has room to showcase only a few, with much of the space devoted to information panels and slide shows.

Outside is a Guaraní communal thatch house *(maloca)* and also in the museum grounds there is an excellent bookshop and an ethnological library.

59 D6 Rua das Palmeiras 55, Botafogo 21 2286 8899 Tue–Fri 9–5.30, Sat–Sun 1–5 R$8 Botafogo Bookshop

MUSEU INTERNACIONAL DE ARTE NAÏF

www.museunaif.com.br

This unprepossessing belle époque house, tucked away behind iron railings off a busy street, is easy to miss. Yet it houses one the world's largest collections of naïve art, with some 8,000 works from 130 countries. Many of the most interesting are Brazilian—the works of community artists from urban *favelas* (slums) and remote villages. They offer a fascinating window into their daily lives. The museum has a small shop selling some of the most unusual postcards in Rio de Janeiro, and is easy to visit on the way to or from Corcovado (▷ 67), as the Trêm do Corcovado funicular is within a few hundred metres.

58 C5 Rua Cosme Velho 561, Cosme Velho 21 2205 8612 Mon–Fri 1–5 R$5 Largo do Machado, continuing on bus 422 or 498 south 200m (218 yards) uphill from the Trêm do Corcovado

MUSEU NACIONAL

www.museunacional.ufrj.br

This vast and increasingly decrepit museum is set in some of the largest formal gardens in Rio de Janeiro, the Quinta da Boa Vista (▷ 84). It was once a lavish Imperial palace, but in 1889 it was inaugurated as the country's first museum. Now its frowsty rooms are home to researchers' offices and a series of galleries showcasing a miscellany of items: from dusty period furniture and the largest meteorite to fall on Brazilian soil, to mummies, dinosaur bones and classical Greek pottery. The most interesting galleries are devoted to miscellaneous Egyptian and Graeco-Roman artefacts collected by various members of the Imperial family—the Empress Dona Teresa Cristina in particular—during the 19th century. The gardens are delightful by day, with extensive ponds, shady avenues of palms and beds of vibrant tropical flowers. Be aware, however, that the gardens are unsafe after dark.

56 A2 Quinta da Boa Vista s/n, Sao Cristóvão 21 2568 8262 Tue–Sun 10–4 R$3 São Cristóvão Buffet restaurant

Above *An evocative display of indigenous culture in the Museo do Indio*

MUSEU HISTÓRICO NACIONAL

Brazil's grandest and most distinguished historical museum traces the history of the country from the pre-Columbian cave paintings of the *sertão* region, through colonial and Imperial times, to the beginning of the country's republican era in the early 20th century. Brazil's story is told through artefacts, objects, art and contemporary museum displays, showcased in a series of galleries. These are housed in a handsome Portuguese building which preserves a fragment of the first 16th-century fort, and which once functioned as the city arsenal.

THE PORTUGUESE EMPIRE

The galleries host both permanent and temporary exhibitions. The permanent exhibitions include *Portugueses no Mundo (Portuguese in the World)*, a multimedia show devoted to the remarkable achievements of Portuguese explorations. Particularly fascinating are the accounts of the early Empire, profiling routes charted by the likes of Fernão de Magalhães—Magellan (1480–1521)—and the Empire's myriad trading posts and colonies. These once stretched from Brazil to Japan and included parts of India and Sri Lanka, islands off the coast of Australia and within many of the Asian archipelagos, and trading communities or colonies in Imperial Siam, China and Africa. There are extensive exhibits detailing the history of the Portuguese within Brazil and looking at the slave trade, the sugar industry and the capture of extensive parts of the northeast by the Dutch.

THE IMPERIAL ERA AND MORE

The Memória do Estado Imperial (Memory of the Imperial State) gallery takes Brazil's story into the Imperial era—when the Portuguese set up court in Rio de Janeiro—and into subsequent independence (▷ 33). Further galleries showcase the Imperial carriage collection, an array of splendid pre-Industrial Revolution cannons, one of the largest currency collections in the world and temporary spaces housing some of the best of Rio's visiting exhibitions.

INFORMATION

www.museuhistoriconacional.com.br
57 F2 · Praça Marechal Âncora, Centro · 21 2550 9224 · Tue–Fri 10–5.30, Sat–Sun 2–6 · R$6 · Carioca · 345 from city centre or Copacabana · Good café restaurant · Gift shop

TIPS

» Allow at least a morning or afternoon for a full visit.

» The musuem can be combined with a visit to nearby Praça XV (▷ 82–83) to make a full day of activity.

Below *An impressive collection of cannons ring the Patio dos Canhoes*

MUSEU NACIONAL DE BELAS ARTES

www.mnba.gov.br

Brazil's largest and most illustrious gallery is a must for visitors interested in Brazilian art. The collection of more than 16,000 pieces include works by the majority of the country's most important pre-21st-century painters and sculptors: from the earliest colonial sketches, through the Flemish landscapes of the Dutch occupation, the bombastic war canvases of the early Republic and the anthropophagism movement which eventually created a national style in the mid-20th century.

There is a small international collection, with some important drawings, engravings and paintings by the likes of Chagall, Goya, Picasso, Tiepolo and Turner, and sculptural pieces by artists such as Rodin. Pieces from the Ashanti, Fon and Yoruba people feature in a collection of African art.

There are a number of works to look for: the Dutch-Brazilian landscapes of Frans Post (1612–80); Pedro Américo's (1843–1905) bombastic propagandist war painting *A Batalha do Avaí*; Victor Brecheret's (1894–1955) statues with their strange fusion of fascism and art deco; Di Cavalcanti's (1897–1976) bawdy celebrations of Afro-Brazilian femininity, and Cândido Portinari's (1903–62) romantic social realism in works like *Café*.

57 E2 Avenida Rio Branco 199 21 2240 0068 Tue–Fri 10–6, Sat–Sun 2–7 R$5, child under 7 R$2; free on Sun Cinelândia, Carioca

MUSEU DA REPÚBLICA

www.museudarepublica.org.br

Brazil's great dictator, Getúlio Vargas (1883–1954), met his untimely end in this stately mid-19th-century mansion house, via a self-inflicted bullet to the head after losing support from his beloved army. His suicide note read: 'I calmly take my first step on the road to eternity and I leave life to enter history'. The museum traces the story of the Republic from the first military presidents, through the turbulent years of the Great Depression and up to the rise of Vargas himself. Exhibits include the dictator's nightshirt, complete with a bullet hole in the breast. The museum has a public sitting area with televisions broadcasting the daily news and Brazilian daily papers, and is set in spacious, shady gardens which are fenced-off from the adjacent roads and offer a cool respite in the heat of the Rio day.

57 E4 Palácio do Catete, Rua do Catete 153, Catete 21 2558 6350 Tue–Sun 12–5 R$6 Catete Cafés and restaurants immediately across the road on Rua do Catete

MUSEU VILLA-LOBOS

www.museuvillalobos.org.br

This small museum occupies the former home of Latin America's most distinguished classical composer, Heitor Villa-Lobos, who died on 17 November 1959. The house is arranged as close as possible to how it would have been in Villa-Lobos's lifetime and is filled with personal objects, including instruments, scores, books and recordings.

Below *A sculpture gallery in the Museu Nacional de Belas Artes*

Villa-Lobos was a resolute Carioca—full of vibrancy—who always lived life his own way. Julian Bream, the most celebrated non-Brazilian interpreter of his guitar music, remembers him as 'larger than life, quite extraordinary. He didn't seem to be a composer. He wore loud checked shirts, smoked a cigar, and always kept the radio on, listening to the news or light music or whatever.' Villa-Lobos himself once famously remarked, 'one foot in the academy and you are changed for the worst'. His love for the traditional music of Brazil and mistrust of academic institutions did much to create the vibrant and diverse music scene which characterizes the country today. His most famous works include *Bachianas Brasileiras, Little Caipira Train, Green Mansions, Saudades das Selvas Brasileiras* and a series of *choros* (Brazil's equivalent of ragtime).

59 D6 Rua Sorocaba 200, Botafogo 21 2266 9282 Mon–Fri 10–5 Botafogo R$2; lunchtime concerts are extra, R$10–R$30

PÃO DE AÇÚCAR

▷ 78–79.

Right *Palácio do Itamaraty is surrounded by lovely gardens*
Below *Detail of the Palácio Capanema*

PALÁCIO CAPANEMA

Modern Brazilian architecture began with the construction of this government building in 1936. This block structure, elevated on plain marble pillars, was the first major Modernist building in the Americas. The Palácio was one of the very first significant buildings to be designed by the Swiss-French architect Le Corbusier and the first project which united the team of Lucio Costa, Oscar Niemeyer and Roberto Burle Marx, who would later build Brasília (▷ 326–327). The tiles inside are by the country's foremost Modernist painter, Cândido Portinari, who would also contribute to other Niemeyer buildings, including the famous Church of St. Francis in Belo Horizonte (▷ 183).

57 E2 Rua da Imprensa 16, Centro Glória, Carioca Not open to the public

PALÁCIO DO ITAMARATY

This neoclassical mansion house is set at the end of a long oblong lake and in beautiful formal gardens. It was built in 1850 for the coffee baron Francisco José da Rocha (the Count of Itamaraty) by José Maria Jacinto Rebelo (1821–71), the premier architect of his time. The palace became the first residence of the Republican presidents, before housing the Ministry of Foreign Affairs until Niemeyer's new Palácio do Itamaraty (▷ 327) opened in Brasília in 1960. Its name is Tupi for rose-coloured *(maraty)* stone *(ita)*. It now houses the Museu Histórico e Diplomático, which comprises numerous treasures—from porcelain and tapestries to sculpture, painting and jewellery—which were gathered by Brazilian diplomats or given as gifts. The map and book collection are among the best in Latin America. Be sure to visit the garden and its lush lawns, gathered around a long rectangular pond and shaded by stately palms.

57 D2 Avenida Marechal Floriano 196, Centro 21 2253 2828 Mon, Wed, Fri at 1.15, 2.15, 3.15, 4.15 Central, Presidente Vargas Free Entry only as part of a guided tour, in Portuguese

INFORMATION
59 F6 Botafogo

Above *Sugar Loaf mountain towers above the mouth of Guanabara Bay*

INTRODUCTION

The summits of Pão de Açúcar (Sugar Loaf) and its adjacent boulder mountain, Morro da Urca, offer one of the best urban views in the world: as breathtaking as those from Victoria Peak in Hong Kong or the top of Sydney's Harbour Bridge. The peaks sit on the edge of the perfect wine-glass-shaped bay of Botafogo, surrounded by the inky waters of Guanabara Bay. The long, broad white-sand sweeps of Coapacabana (▷ 64) and Ipanema (▷ 69) stretch to the south, to the twin hulking peaks of Os Dois Irmãos, and just a few kilometres to the west Christ the Redeemer stands over the entire scene, solitary on the verdant summit of Corcovado (▷ 66–67).

Pão de Açúcar's name, like other mountains in the world called Sugar Loaf, is derived from its shape, which resembles the raw sugar that used to be sold in cone shapes. The name of Rio's mountain may have a more ancient origin: The Tupi-Guarani people who lived in the region before the Portuguese conquest called high hills 'Pau-nh-açuqua'. They used them for lookouts and Pão de Açúcar would have been one of the most strategic. At 400m (1,300ft), the hill is far from the highest of Rio's coastal monolithic peaks—the Pedra da Gávea (▷ 90–91) is some 250m (820ft) higher—but it is the most strategically situated, being right at the mouth of Guanabara Bay with clear views out over the Atlantic to the north and south. It is also the most vertiginous. The first recorded non-indigenous ascent was in 1817, by a visiting English nanny, Henrietta Carstairs.

WHAT TO SEE

THE CABLE CAR RIDE

www.bondinho.com.br

Caminho aéreo (cable cars) run from a station in the suburb of Urca, which stretches around the flanks of the boulders, to the summit of Morro da Urca, with another cable car spanning the few hundred metres between that mountain and the Sugar Loaf. The views from the cars are breathtaking and the ride is a highlight of any visit to Rio. Cable cars leave every 20 minutes.

✉ Avenida Pasteur, Urca ☎ 21 2461 2700 🕐 Daily 8am–9pm; ticket office closes at 7.50 and the last car down the mountain is at 9 ✋ Adult R$22 to Morro da Urca, R$44 to continue to Pão de Açúcar, child (6–12) half price, under 6 free ☕ Café on Pão de Açúcar

WALKING UP THE MOUNTAINS

It is also possible to walk up the peaks. The Pista Claúdio Coutinho path winds its way from the neighbourhood of Urca (▷ 85), around the base of the Pão de Açúcar to the summit of the Morro de Urca (220m/722ft). It's a steep but delightful two-hour walk, which cuts across beaches before climbing through forests filled with brilliantly coloured tropical birds and tiny marmoset monkeys, eventually reaching the top of the mountain. Tour agencies offer climbed ascents of both peaks, too, such as Rio Hiking (▷ 96), Companhia da Escalada (www.companhiadaescalada.com.br) and Trilhas e Aventuras (www.trilhaseaventuras.com.br). There are routes up the mountains for both novice and experienced rock climbers.

THE SUMMITS OF THE MOUNTAINS

The views are so wonderful it is easy to spend a full day on the mountains. There are restaurants, cafés and small gift shops on top of both the Morro da Urca and Pão de Açúcar. A series of paths link them and spread out into the woodland at the summits, affording dozens of different viewpoints. The Morro da Urca has a helicopter landing pad, from where it is possible to charter a 15-minute flight out over the mountains, the adjacent beaches and the Corcovado Christ (▷ 96).

TIPS

» Rio can be hazy with traffic pollution. Come early in the day, after rain if possible, for the clearest air.

» Helicopter flights need to be booked ahead with Helisight (▷ 96) and cost from R$200 for 15 minutes.

Left *Sunset view over Rio from the heights of Pão de Açúcar*

Below *Sugar Loaf mountain offers a spectacular view of the city of Niterói, across Guanabara Bay*

PARQUE BRIGADEIRO EDUARDO GOMES

This bayside park, also known as Aterro do Flamengo, stretches along Guanabara Bay shoreline from Santos Dumont airport to the beach at Botafogo, encompassing the waterfront of Glória, Catete and Flamengo. It was designed by Brazil's most celebrated landscape architect, Roberto Burle Marx, and inaugurated in 1965. Like much of the designer's work, the park is home to many native Brazilian trees and plants. These attract many birds, making the park a delightful place for a stroll in the early morning or evening. Sights within the park include Museu de Arte Moderna (▷ 73), Museu Carmen Miranda (▷ 73) and Monumento Nacional aos Mortos da Segunda Guerra Mundial (▷ 71). The park is unsafe at night.

57 E4 Catete, Flamengo, Largo do Machado, Cinelândia, Glória

PARQUE DA CATACUMBA

www.parquedacatacumba.com.br

This small, hilly park sits just across the road from the Lagoa Rodrigo de Freitas (▷ 68), a 10-minute walk from Cantagalo metrô. It attracts few visitors and is therefore often quiet, requiring a little extra caution. Otherwise it is a delightful, woody green space decorated with sculptures by Brazilian artists like Bruno Giorgi and Alfredo Ceschiatti (who made many of the monumental statues in Brasília). It has wonderful views out over the lake and mountains from a 130m-high (425ft) lookout point, reachable via a forested trail which begins at the park gates.

58 C8 Avenida Epitácio Pessoa s/n, Lagoa Daily 8–5 Cantagalo

PARQUE LAGE

This is one of the city's prettiest and least-visited parks. It sits in the shadow of Corcovado (▷ 66–67) and is the site of a vast mansion, with an internal atrium dominated by a long rectangular pool. It looks like a film set for a gothic novel. The house and gardens were designed by the Englishman John Tyndale, for a wealthy Carioca industrialist. Today they are home to an arts and crafts school and an alfresco café sitting next to a pond of water lillies. Trails lead from the gardens to the summit of Corcovado but require a guide.

58 B7 Rua Jardim Botânico 414, Jardim Botânico 21 2538 1879 Daily 8–5 158,176 from the city centre

PARQUE NACIONAL DA TIJUCA

▷ 81.

PLANETÁRIO

www.planetariodorio.com.br

Rio's planetarium is more an astronomy complex, including a Museum of the Universe and auditorium shows in state-of-the-art theatres, showing the southern constellations. There are also thrice-weekly supervised star-gazing sessions at night through very powerful telescopes, which are very popular with local children.

58 A8 Rua Vice Governador Rubens Berardo 100, Gávea 21 2274 0046 Museum and Planetarium: Dec–Apr Tue–Fri 10–5, Sat–Sun 5–7; May–Nov Tue–Fri 3–5, Sat–Sun 5–7. Telescopes: Dec–Apr Tue–Thu 7.30am–9:30pm; May–Nov Tue–Thu 6.30am–8.30pm R$10, under 2 free 125,157 from the city centre

Left *Escola de Artes Visuais in Parque Lage*
Below *A tranquil pond in the secluded Parque da Catacumba*

PARQUE NACIONAL DA TIJUCA

Rio de Janeiro's city centre is separated from Copacabana (▷ 64) and the beaches of the Atlantic coast by a range of steep mountains, the Serra da Carioca, whose peaks include Corcovado (▷ 66–67). They are swathed in Atlantic coastal rainforest and form one of the largest urban national parks in the world, protecting some 39sq km (15sq miles) of rainforest.

FOREST OF LIFE

The forests form an important repository of Atlantic coastal species, from thousands of native and introduced vascular plants—which include endangered species of orchids—to 200 species of birds and larger mammals, including howler monkeys and Brazil's smaller felines. That they live in the centre of Rio is testament to one of the world's first conservation projects. The first Cariocas cut down much of the primary forest for firewood or sugar cane in the 16th and 17th centuries. When coffee was introduced into Rio in the late 1700s, the little forest which remained made way for plantations.

BIRTH OF THE PARK

The deforestation was so extensive that in 1861 Dom Pedro II decided that Tijuca should be replanted as an urban forest reserve. He entrusted the task to an army major, Manuel Gomes, whose six unnamed African-Brazilian slaves replanted the entire forest in 13 years.

EXPLORING TIJUCA

Myriad trails and small roads cut through Tijuca. Lookouts like the Mirante Dona Marta afford wonderful views out over the city. There are a number of waterfalls, the most spectacular of which is the Cascatinha do Taunay near the Alto da Boa Vista park entrance. Look for the tiny pink Mayrink Chapel, built in 1863, with wall panels by Cândido Portinari (1903–62).

INFORMATION

58 A6 Visitor Centre, Praça Afonso Viseu, Tijuca 21 2492 2253 Daily 8–7 Free Tours with Rio Hiking or Rio Trilhas (▷ 96)

TIPS

» Do not drive or walk through Tijuca after dark or wander away from the main sites unless you are with an organized tour or a local friend. Muggings are common.
» There is no public transport to the park.
» Within the park, Os Esquilos restaurant serves lunches (www.osesquilos.com.br; Estrada Barão E'Escragnolle, Alto da Boa Vista; tel 21 2492 2197; Tue–Sun 12–6).

Below *A panoramic view from the summit of Pico da Tijuca*

INFORMATION

57 E2 Carioca, Uruguaiana
154 from Ipanema, 484 from Copacabana, 260 from city centre

INTRODUCTION

The square of Praça XV is the heart of historical Rio. Like the rest of Brazil the city began from the sea, as a port town. The first colony was a French fort in the bay but the city began in earnest with the Portuguese settlement of São Sebastião on the mainland, near the present-day ferry port. It remained a cluster of civic buildings, watched over by a castle and a Benedictine monastery, until the Minas Gerais gold rush in the 18th century began to turn the scruffy port town wealthy.

The first area to develop was Praça XV, which became a trading centre for imported goods. The square became the centre of economic and then political life in Rio under the Portuguese. The royal family arrived on the quays here when they fled from Napoleon in 1808 (▷ 32–33) and many of the historical buildings and churches in and around the square were used by the monarchy in the Portuguese and Imperial eras. It was then known as the Largo do Carmo, but when Pedro II was deposed, the square was renamed after the date of the proclamation of the Brazilian republic—15 November 1889.

WHAT TO SEE

PAÇO IMPERIAL

www.pacoimperial.com.br

The square is dominated by the Paço Imperial—a modest colonial building in whitewash and raw stone—built in 1743 as the seat of government of the captaincy of Rio de Janeiro. When Queen Maria and her son, the Regent João, arrived in Brazil it was converted into the first Imperial palace. Today it houses offices, shops, restaurants and exhibition spaces.

Praça XV 48 21 2215 2622 Tue–Sun 12–6 R$2 Carioca

Above *Igreja de Nossa Senhora do Monte do Carmo was formerly the city's cathedral*

PALÁCIO TIRADENTES

Next to the Paço is the grander, Republican Palácio Tiradentes: an imposing neoclassical edifice named in honour of the country's first Republican martyr, Joaquim José da Silva Xavier (Tiradentes, ▷ 31) and fronted by a monumental statue of him. The building serves as the seat of the State Legislature but also contains some photographic and multimedia exhibits. Across the square to the north is the Arco de Teles arch, leading to a cobbled alley called the Travessa do Comércio. This is one of the few remnants of the city's original narrow streets, busy with bar goers drinking alfresco at tables in the early evening. Carmen Miranda lived here before embarking on her international career.

Rua Primeiro de Março s/n | Mon–Sat 10–5, Sun 12–5 | Free | Uruguaiana

IGREJA DE NOSSA SENHORA DO MONTE DO CARMO

The square is watched over by a number of churches. Before construction of the Catedral Metropólitana de São Sebastião (▷ 63), the Church of Our Lady of Mount Carmel was the city's cathedral. It looks unprepossessing from the street but inside is a fine rococo nave with beautiful ceiling panels, and walls replete with carvings by Inácio Ferreira Pinto (1765–1828), who also worked on the main chapel in the Mosteiro de São Bento (▷ 72).

Rua Primeiro de Março s/n | Mon–Fri 8–4 | Free | Uruguaiana

No photography

IGREJA DO ORDEM TERCEIRA DE NOSSA SENHORA DO MONTE DO CARMO

Next door is the Church of the Third Order of Our Lady of Mount Carmel. It's a very Portuguese church in the Pombaline style, with some beautiful gilt carvings by Mestre Valentim (1745–1813) in the nave. This most prestigious of early Carioca ecclesiastical artists was also responsible for the Chafariz do Mestre Valentim, a Mannerist drinking fountain in the square.

Rua Primeiro de Março s/n | Mon–Fri 8–4 | Free | Carioca, Uruguaiana

No photography

TIPS

» On weekdays after 6pm the pedestrianized cobbled alley, the Travessa do Comércio, becomes filled with bar tables. It makes a great spot for people-watching with a cool beer. It is deserted at the weekend.

» There are many restaurants in the Travessa do Comércio. More formal options are in the Paço Imperial.

Left *A statue of the Republican martyr Tiradentes at the entrance to the Palácio*
Below *The whitewashed facade of the 18th-century Paço Imperial*

QUINTA DA BOA VISTA AND JARDIM ZOOLÓGICO

The Quinta was the private park of the Brazilian emperors, from when the Portuguese arrived in 1808 until the proclamation of the Republic in 1889 (▷ 34). It is now the largest formal park in Rio de Janeiro's northern inner city area. Attractions include a series of lawned gardens and avenues of palms, the former Imperial palace (now the Museu Nacional ▷ 74) and, in the northeastern corner of the park, the city zoo, Jardim Zoológico.

This is a modern zoo with spacious enclosures and a collection of 2,100 animals, most of them from the Americas. They include the largest collection of New World primates on the continent, most of Brazil's felines, and threatened or endangered birds like the harpy eagle, hyacinth macaw and king vulture. The zoo operates an important captive breeding programme for endangered New World mammals, such as golden-headed and golden lion tamarins, spectacled bears and yellow-throated capuchin monkeys. There is a little zoo train that runs past the key attractions, which is a delight for children.

56 A2 · Avenida Pedro II, São Cristóvão · 21 3878 4200 · Zoo: Tue–Sun 9–4.30; Park: 7–6 · Zoo: adult R$6, child (under 1m/3ft) free · São Cristóvão · Restaurant in front of the zoo gates (www.restaurantequintaboavista.com.br)

REAL GABINETE PORTUGUÊS DE LEITURA

www.realgabinete.com.br

This lavish library is one of the many hidden architectural treasures of the city centre. The style is mock-Manueline: a late Gothic, early baroque style unique to Portugal. Among its characteristics is the use of effusive architectural ornamentation, drawing heavily on the style and decorations of Islamic art and East Indian temples, incorporating maritime elements and representations of the discoveries brought from the voyages of Vasco da Gama (1460–1524) and Pedro Álvares Cabral (1467–1520). This library is, of course, from a much later era. It was constructed around a steel frame in the 19th century, by the Portuguese architect Rafael da Silva e Castro. The library houses the largest collection of Portuguese literature outside Portugal and is decorated with statues of famous Portuguese explorers and writers.

57 E2 · Rua Luís de Camões 30, Centro · 21 2221 3138 · Mon–Fri 9–6 · Free · Carioca

ROCINHA

The bulk of Cariocas live in *favelas* (slums), like Rocinha. It straddles the hills separating two of Rio de Janeiro's richest and most exclusive neighbourhoods, Gávea and São Conrado. Many *favelas* are violent places, as the statistics attest where they are available. A British study published in 2004 found that, in the 14 years to 2002, almost 4,000 under-19-year-olds were killed by firearms in Rio— almost all in poor areas—shot in gang violence, in cross fire or by the police. This compares with 500 killed in fighting in Israel and the Palestinian territories in the same period.

Do not forget, though, that the *favelas* are also Brazil's most creative places. Samba, funk, Brazilian football and carnival all grew here. As most *favela* residents are keen to point out, they are also places where the vast majority of people are honest, everyday folk who leave for work in the morning— often in suits—and come back in the evening to a house and a family, but who simply don't have income enough to move away. According to the prestigious nationwide Fundação Getúlio Vargas university, almost 56,000 people live in Rocinha itself, though others put the figure at three times that number.

It is possible to visit, though this should never be attempted solo. A *favela* tour, however, is a safe, rewarding experience. It also supports the community and helps to break social barriers and poverty stereotypes. These can be organized at www.bealocal.com. Tours generally last around three hours and include a walk through Rocinha or another *favela*, with visits to local artists, families and community projects that are supported by the tour companies.

56 A1 (inset)

Below *Real Gabinete Português de Leitura is rich in Portuguese literature and ornamentation*

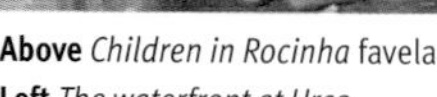

Above *Children in Rocinha* favela
Left *The waterfront at Urca*

SAMBÓDROMO

Modernist architect Oscar Niemeyer's massive samba stadium—which stretches for 0.75km (0.5 miles) and has seating for more than 75,000 people—was designed and built in fewer than six months. Completed in 1984, it is the principal venue for Rio's famous *carnaval* (carnival), which was moved from the city streets into its own designated venue in 1984. The stadium is a giant trench, with stepped terraces descending to a central street space where the principal samba schools parade. Even though it lies fallow for most of the year, it is an impressive sight, with its stark white concrete standing against the ragged *favelas* which are strewn around the surrounding hills.

You will need a ticket to get in to the Sambódromo for carnival. It is important to book in advance, preferably back home before leaving for Brazil. International tour operators charge a commission on the asking price but if you wait until you get to Rio you can't be sure of a place in the Sambódromo on the all-important nights. Tickets are either for numbered seats *(cadeiras)* or pot-luck bucket seating on the terraces *(arquibancadas)*. The grandstand seats are closest to the parade but confine you to one place, so if you are reasonably young and fit, opt for the terraces; it's far more fun to be where most people are standing up and dancing anyway. Tickets start at around R$172 , with seats in private boxes costing over R$1,720. The best days for the parades—when the famous samba schools perform—are the Sunday and the Monday of *carnaval* weekend (▷ 97). Arrive at about 7pm in time for the first procession and expect to leave at about 6am the next day.

56 C2 Rua Marquês de Sapucaí Praça Onze For more information see the Rio de Janeiro city website (www.rioguiaoficial.com.br)

SANTA TERESA

▷ 86–87.

URCA

This small, conservative military neighbourhood of quiet streets and colonial houses is huddled around the base of the Pão de Açúcar (Sugar Loaf) and Morro da Urca, and offers delightful short walks around both mountains and nearby secluded beaches. These include the Praia Vermelha and the Praia de Fora, at the foot of the Pão de Açúcar. The Pista Claúdio Coutinho walking track (▷ 79) begins between Praia Vermelha beach and the mountain, and runs along the waterfront around the foot of the rock. About 350m (380 yards) from the beginning of the path, there is a turn-off to the left for a track which winds its way up through the forest to the top of Morro da Urca, from where the cable car can be taken to the summit of the Sugar Loaf (▷ 79). Alternatively, another path, the Caminho da Costa, also runs to the summit of the Pão de Açúcar. Only one stretch, of 10m (33ft), requires climbing gear (even then, some say it is not necessary), but if you wait at the bottom of the path for a group going up, they will no doubt let you tag along. If you prefer, agencies such as Rio Hiking (▷ 96) offer guided ascents.

59 F5 Botafogo There are plenty of restaurants in the neighbourhood Pista Claúdio Coutinho starts at Praça General Tibúrcio s/n, Urca

INFORMATION

57 D3 Santa Teresa is reachable only on trams from in front of the Catedral Metropólitana or by taxi

Above *The Carmelite Convento Santa Teresa sits atop the hill*

INTRODUCTION

Santa Teresa is to Rio what Montmartre is to Paris, and clambers up a series of cobbled streets between the city centre, Botafogo and the edge of Tijuca national park (▷ 81). It's a delightful neighbourhood, with streets of stately colonial Portuguese and faux-French belle époque mansions crowning steep hills and offering magnificent views out over the city. The district was founded by Discalced Carmelite nuns, who built a convent here—in what was then the middle of a great forest—in 1750. The building still exists, on the Ladeira de Santa Teresa (number 52), but the nuns rarely leave the grounds, and the church and convent are both closed to the public. The neighbourhood gradually became a fashionable retreat for the wealthy but as the bay became more polluted in the 20th century, and the city's prosperity shifted ever farther south towards the ocean, so Santa Teresa gradually began to fall from grace. The rich left, the mansions crumbled and *favelas* appeared on the surrounding hills.

After the war Santa Teresa began a renaissance which continues to this day. Attracted by the romantic decaying architecture, wonderful views and cheap prices, writers and artists began to relocate to the neighbourhood. The Hungarian-Jewish abstract painter, Arpad Szenes and his French-Portuguese partner, fellow painter Maria Helena Vieira da Silva, lived here in the 1940s and numerous famous names form part of what is now a tight-knit artistic community. They include social realist Carlos Vergara and Modernists Waltercio Caldas and José Bechara. Many have recently opened their studios as private galleries and the neighbouhood hosts a lively annual open house arts festival, the Arte das Portas Abertas, whose dates vary from year to year (see www.artedeportasabertas.com.br for latest information).

WHAT TO SEE

CHÁCARA DO CÉU AND PARQUE DAS RUINAS

www.museuscastromaya.com.br

The most prestigious of all Santa Teresa's galleries is the Chácara do Céu, a mansion house set in wooded gardens, whose rooms preserve important works by Brazilian and European Modernists including Dalí, Monet and Matisse. The Parque das Ruinas, the shell of another mansion, sits next door to the Chácara and affords some of the best views in the neighbourhood. The two are linked together by a small bridge.

✉ Rua Murtinho Nobre 96 ☎ 21 2285 2545 ⏲ Wed–Mon 12–5 R$6 Trams from in front of the Catedral Metropólitana

LARGO DOS GUIMARÃES AND LARGO DAS NEVES

These two *largos*, or irregularly shaped *praças* (squares), surrounded by a handful of shops, bars and restaurants, form the heart of the Santa Teresa community. Locals gather here for a chat and a coffee in the morning or a cool beer at the end of the day, and the rickety trams which ride up from Lapa (▷ 68) and São Sebastião cathedral in the city centre (▷ 63) have their principal stops here. There are no specific sites of interest in either the Largo dos Guimarães or the Largo das Neves but both are great places to sit and soak up the neighbourhood's distinctive atmosphere.

Trams from in front of the Catedral Metropólitana

THE TRAM RIDE FROM THE CENTRE

The best way to reach Santa Teresa from the city centre is by tram. These rickety mid-20th century contraptions jerk their way along rails from a station next to the Catedral Metropólitana (▷ 63), across the towering white viaduct of the Arcos de Lapa and up the steep cobbled streets of Santa Teresa itself. The journey only takes about 20 minutes and the tram is invariably packed with colourful characters of all ages and social classes. Many are hangers-on—literally and precariously—clinging to the bars that run along the side of the tram.

TIP

» Santa Teresa is becoming increasingly popular as an alternative place to stay to Ipanema and the beaches. There are a number of small boutique hotels and a bed-and-breakfast homestay scheme (www.camaecafe.com), which integrates visitors with members of the local community.

Below *A tram from the city centre arrives at Largo dos Guimarães*

RIO DE JANEIRO CITY CENTRE

This walk takes in the principal historical sights in Rio de Janeiro's old city centre, including a series of fine churches. It includes a visit to the beautiful art nouveau Confeitaria Colombo coffee house.

THE WALK
Distance: 2km (1.25 miles)
Time: 3 hours including visits
Start at: Praça XV ✚ 57 E2
End at: Carioca metrô station ✚ 57 E2

HOW TO GET THERE
Buses 175, 123 run from Ipanema to Rua 1 de Março, next to Praça XV. The ferry from Niterói lands at the Praça XV ferry dock.

★ Praça XV (▷ 82–83) is a large square near the waterfront in central Rio. In the early 19th century, the *praça* was right on the waterfront and the Portuguese Royal family fleeing Napoleon disembarked here in March 1808 (▷ 32–33). British Viscount William Carr Beresford effectively ruled Portugal in their absence. The square is littered with significant colonial monuments, including a beautiful baroque fountain designed by one of Rio's first African-Brazilian artists, Mestre Valentim (1745–1813). Also in the square is the first Imperial palace, the Paço Imperial (▷ 82). The Paço now houses some of the best of the city's temporary art exhibitions, as well as offices, shops and restaurants. Walk through the Arco de Teles—an arch on the northern edge of Praça XV—into the Travessa do Comércio.

❶ This is lined with little bookshops and *botequim* bars (small, simple street bars) and is particularly lively in the early evening. Turn left at the end of the street into the Rua do Ouvidor.

❷ On the right-hand side you will find the the Igreja Nossa Senhora da Lapa dos Mercadores church (▷ 65), one of the prettiest small churches in Rio de Janeiro. The church is devoted to an image of the Virgin from near Quintela in Galicia, hidden by monks during the Moorish occupation and rediscovered by a deaf mute who is said to have been miraculously cured by the effigy. The image was worshipped by local tradesmen in an oratory which stood on the site of the present church. This building was then constructed in homage to the Virgin after the traders became prosperous and formed a lay brotherhood of Mercadores, or merchants.

Continue 100m (110 yards) along Rua do Ouvidor to the corner of Rua Primeiro de Marco. Here there are two more baroque churches.

❸ Igreja de Nossa Senhora do Monte do Carmo (▷ 83) was the city's first cathedral, where the royal family worshipped when they first came to Rio de Janeiro, and the Igreja do Ordem Terceira de Nossa Senhora do Monte do Carmo has fine gilt carving, also by Mestre Valentim.

Continue along Rua do Ouvidor, which is lined with shops, and turn left after 300m (330 yards) onto Rua Gonçalves Dias.

❹ The Confeitaria Colombo art nouveau coffee house sits on the left of the street at the corner of Rua Sete de Setembro. Stop here for a juice or a strong coffee and sweet cake. The café, which is modelled on similar grand cafés in Portugal, opened in 1894 but was expanded and refurbished with its current art nouveau flourishes between 1912 and 1918, during the early years of the coffee boom. The famous Carioca composer, Heitor Villa-Lobos, and the dictator Getúlio Vargas (▷ 35) regularly dined here.

Finish the walk on the Largo da Carioca (▷ 71), with a visit to two of the city's baroque jewels.

❺ Here are the Convento Santo Antônio and the Igreja da Ordem Terceira de São Francisco da Penitência. Both have beautiful gilt and *azulejo* tile interiors. The Convent preserves little of its colonial past but the Church of Saint Francis is one of the finest Portuguese churches in the city, with gilt ornamentation by some of the best Portuguese baroque artists to have worked in Rio de Janeiro. These included Francisco Xavier de Brito, who worked throughout Minas Gerais and who was probably Aleijadinho's teacher (▷ 189). The crossing arch is mostly his work. There is a wonderful trompe l'oeil painting on the ceiling of Saint Francis in ecstasy, painted in 1732 by Caetano da Costa Coelho, one of the first of its kind in Brazil and a precursor to the Bahian school.

Metrô Carioca lies 30m (110 yards) south of the Largo da Carioca.

WHEN TO GO

The walk is best taken in the late afternoon to early evening on a weekday, when the cafés and bars are at their liveliest.

WHERE TO EAT

Confeitaria Colombo, on the route, makes a good place for a rest and refreshment (▷ 99).

TIP

» Avoid the city centre after 8pm and on weekends, as the streets are empty, poorly lit and potentially unsafe at these times.

Above Caroicas *eating lunch on Travessa do Comércio*
Opposite *An aerial view of Praça XV de Novembro*

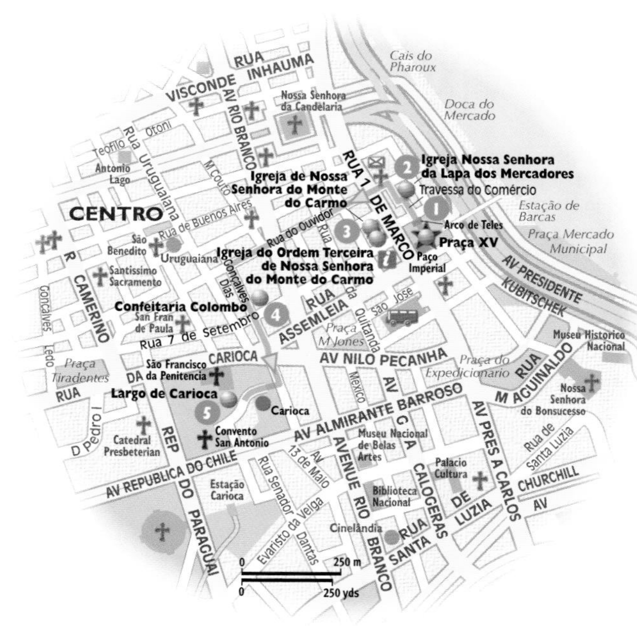

TO THE SUMMIT OF THE PEDRA DA GÁVEA IN TIJUCA NATIONAL PARK

This challenging hike involves a steep trek through rainforest to the peak of the world's largest coastal monolith: the hulking granite of Pedra da Gávea mountain. This is Rio de Janeiro's most spectacular viewpoint, with views out across Ipanema, Copacabana and the Christ high on Corcovado in one direction, and across the whole sweep of Guanabara Bay and the Atlantic as far away as Ilha Grande in the other. The climb should not be undertaken without a tour guide. This itinerary is with Rio Hiking (▷ 96).

THE WALK
Distance: 4km (2.5 miles)
Time: 5 hours
Start/end at: Hotel pick-up by tour operator

HOW TO GET THERE

The drive to the beginning of the trail takes 30 minutes from the centre of Rio or the beaches.

★ The trail begins next to the Pedra Bonita, another huge boulder mountain. Hang-gliders take off from here for flights over the forests, landing on the sand on São Conrado beach. Spectacular, if vertiginous, views off the edge offer a hint of what's to come. A narrow path runs from the Tijuca park road, cuts through *capim* grass and immediately into the forest. After a few hundred metres you will begin to see abundant birdlife.

❶ The lower reaches of the path are good areas for spotting wildlife. Palm-sized monkeys called tufted-eared marmosets are a common sight. Look out for green-headed tanagers in the lower storeys of the forest. These beautiful finch-like birds have plumage of seven different colours and appear as a brilliant flash as they fly from branch to branch. They are on the Red List of threatened and endangered species.

The path continues to climb and as it does so the forest thins and eventually disperses altogether, to give way to scrub and grassland. Vultures soar high above and the flanks of the boulder mountain appear ahead.

❷ As the forest thins the views begin. Put your sunhat on and have your camera at the ready as each turn brings a spectacular vista of forested slopes, ocean and then the city far below. The grassland areas are a good place to spot hummingbirds. These are unique to the Americas and Brazil has the greatest diversity and number of hummingbirds in the world, including the spectacular shimmering green 'emeralds' and the tiny hermits.

The trail eventually reaches the granite base of the rock. From here it's necessary to scramble up a craggy face using ropes. It's an easy 45-degree climb of about 15m (50ft). Rio Hiking has a bilingual climbing instructor who provides safety information and climbing equipment.

❸ After the climb you reach the summit of the Pedra da Gávea, with the best views in Rio: no crowds and no noise but the breeze and the distant sounds of the city some 840m (2,755ft) below.

The same trail down the mountain takes around 1.5 hours.

WHEN TO GO

Pick-ups are from the hotel early in the morning—usually between 7 and 9—as it's a long walk.

WHERE TO EAT

Rio Hiking provides food and drink for the hike.

TIPS

» Trips to the Pedra da Gávea leave only when there is an advanced booking and should be reserved at least two days in advance with Rio Hiking.

» You should bring a day backpack containing a sun hat, high-factor sun protection, insect repellent, a litre of water and any additional snacks. Ensure you wear appropriate clothing for climbing, including hiking shoes.

» Don't forget your camera to capture the amazing views, and binoculars if you are interested in trying to see more of the wildlife.

Opposite *Pedra da Gávea from the Floresta de Tijuca*

Below *A green-headed tanager, one of the species of birds that inhabit Tijuca*

SHOPPING

ANDREA SALETTO

One of the few fashionable Brazilian women's labels to come from Rio de Janeiro rather than São Paulo, Andrea Saletto sells sophisticated but sexy dresses, skirts and tops made from high-quality fabrics.

✉ Rua Nascimento Silva 244, Ipanema ☎ 21 2522 5858 🕐 Mon–Sat 10–6 🚇 Praça General Osório

ANTÔNIO BERNARDO

www.antoniobernardo.com.br

Together with São Paulo's flashy Jack Vartanian, Bernardo is Brazil's foremost jeweller. His pieces are far more understated than that of his competitors, with finely crafted work in gold and platinum, using exquisite stones. The Garcia d'Ávila shop is his flagship store but there are also outlets at Shopping Leblon (▷ 94) and São Conrado Fashion Mall (▷ 93).

✉ Rua Garcia d'Ávila 121, Ipanema ☎ 21 2512 7204 🕐 Mon–Fri 10–8, Sat 10–4 🚇 Praça General Osório

BOSSA NOVA & COMPANHIA

Copacabana's best music shop underwent a full refurbishment and expansion in 2009, turning its tired wooden floors into chic, wavy dragon's-tooth paving, installing a little music museum in the basement, and restocking with the best selection of *bossa nova* (new wave), *choro* (a Brazilian music style similar to ragtime) and Brazilian jazz in the city. The shop lies next to the Beco das Garrafas alley, where two of the creators of *bossa nova*, Tom Jobim and João Gilberto, first played together in the late 1950s (▷ 17).

✉ Rua Duvivier 37A, Copacabana ☎ 21 2295 8096 🕐 Mon–Fri 10–6, Sat 10–4 🚇 Cardeal Arcoverde

CARLOS TUFVESSON

www.carlostufvesson.com

This young designer has been one of Rio's most popular since receiving a standing ovation for his first show during Rio Fashion week in 2001. He specializes in haute couture and his dresses are famous for their strong feminine lines, which emphasize and enhance body shape.

✉ Rua Nascimento Silva 304, Ipanema ☎ 21 2523 9200 🕐 Mon–Fri 10–6 🚇 Praça General Osório

CARLOS VERGARA

www.carlosvergara.art.br

One of the city's most renowned contemporary artists has recently opened his private *atelier* (studio) to the public, showcasing his politically biting graphic art, painting and photography. The studio is worth a visit even if you aren't a collector of modern art.

✉ Rua Progresso 70, Santa Teresa ☎ 21 2508 9169 🕐 By appointment only 🚇 Praça Onze 🚌 214, 214a, from city centre; trams from in front of the Catedral Metropólitana (▷ 63)

FEIRA HIPPIE

www.feirahippieipanema.com

Since the 1960s there's been a Sunday bric-a-brac market in the large square in the heart of Ipanema, the Praça General Osório, with

Opposite *Bossa Nova & Companhia music shop in Copacabana*

hundreds of stalls selling arts and crafts, home decoration, food and clothing. The market is quiet in the early morning but by the afternoon many of the best buys have been snapped up and the stalls are unpleasantly crowded, so make this your first stop of the day. There are cafés on the square.
✉ Praça General Osório ⌚ Sun 8–6
🚇 Praça General Osório

LENNY NIEMEYER

www.lenny.com.br
Brazil's premier swimwear designer has her flagship boutique at this fashionable spot in Ipanema. She is particularly famous for her elegantly cut bikinis and one pieces and is a favourite with Brazilian supermodels and stars of TV Globo (the popular national TV channel), including Gisele Bündchen, Isabelli Fontana and Michelle Alves.
✉ Rua Garcia d'Ávila 149, Ipanema ☎ 21 2227 5537 ⌚ Mon–Fri 10–6, Sat 10–4
🚇 Praça General Osório

LIVRARIA DA TRAVESSA

www.travessa.com.br
One of the largest bookshops in the city cente, with a huge stock of books, CDs and magazines spread over several floors and a decent little coffee shop serving strong, thick espressos. The shop has plenty of English language titles and specialist interest books on Rio, as well as some of the city's more tasteful postcards. There are other branches across the city, including a large store in Ipanema.
✉ Rua 7 de Setembro 54, Centro ☎ 21 3231 8015 ⌚ Mon–Fri 9–8, Sat 9–4
🚇 Carioca ☕
✉ Rua Visconde de Pirajá 572, Ipanema
☎ 21 3205 9002 ⌚ Mon–Sat 9am–midnight, Sun 11am–midnight 🚇 Praça General Osório ☕

LOJA FLA

www.lojafla.com.br
This bustling shop in the centre of Copacabana is the place to come for Rio de Janeiro football souvenirs. Loja Fla has the largest stock of shirts, balls, boots and memorabilia devoted to the country's most popular team, Flamengo.
✉ Avenida Nossa Senhora de Copacabana 219C ☎ 21 2295 5057 ⌚ Mon–Sat 10–6
🚇 Cardeal Arcoverde

MARIA BONITA

www.mariabonita.com.br
Maria Bonita is one of the few Carioca designers not specializing in swimwear, who sell well internationally. Her sexy tops and famous jersey dresses with wrap fronts and high elasticated waists are sold in shops abroad, like Browns in New York.
✉ Rua Vinícius de Moraes 149, Ipanema
☎ 21 2287 9768 ⌚ Mon–Sat 10–6
🚇 Praça General Osório

ND

www.novodesenho.com.br
This stylish small boutique next to the MAM (Museum of Modern Art, ▷ 73) sells homeware and furniture by Brazilian artists and designers. These include established names like Carlos Vergara and Sergio Rodrigues, whose Mole chair also forms part of MAM's collection.
✉ Avenida Infante Dom Henrique 85, Glória
☎ 21 2524 2290 ⌚ Tue–Fri 12–6, Sat–Sun 12–7 🚇 Cinelândia

OSKLEN

www.osklen.com
Brazil's answer to Ralph Lauren does for surfing what that designer did for polo, producing effortlessly chic casual wear, from shirts and slacks to swimwear. Much of it has what could be referred to as an ecological theme.
✉ Rua Maria Quitéria 85, Ipanema ☎ 21 2227 2911 ⌚ Mon–Sat 10–6 🚇 Praça General Osório

RAIZ FORTE PRODUTOS DA TERRA

Brazil's indigenous people handed down a strong tradition of herbal medicine to the conquering Portuguese and modern Brazilians have a tea for almost every ailment. Here you will find many of the most popular, together with natural energy products like guaraná powder and açai pulp (▷ 22), both of which come from Amazonian plants.
✉ Avenida Ataulfo de Paiva 1160, Leblon
☎ 21 2259 0744 ⌚ Mon–Sat 10–6
🚇 Praça General Osório

RUA DO LAVRADIO ANTIQUES FAIR

This lively antiques and bric-a-brac market, held on the last Saturday of every month, is becoming Rio's equivalent of Buenos Aires' San Telmo Mercado das Antiguidades (Antiques Market). There is even live tango in the streets, alongside abundant samba.
✉ Rua do Lavradio, Lapa ⌚ Last Sat of the month, usually 10–8 🚇 Cinelândia

SALINAS

www.salinas-rio.com.br
Together with Rosa Chá and Lenny, this Rio brand produces the most highly sought-after Brazilian swimwear on the international market. They are cut for a well-toned figure, small, exquisitely made with great attention to detail, and use only the best fabrics in a variety of contemporary prints.
✉ Rua Visconde de Pirajá 547, Ipanema
☎ 21 2274 0644 ⌚ Mon–Sat 10–6
🚇 Praça General Osório
✉ São Conrado Fashion Mall ☎ 21 2422 0677 ⌚ Mon–Sat 10–6 🚌 S020 from city centre, 546 from Leblon/Ipanema

SÃO CONRADO FASHION MALL

www.scfashionmall.com.br
This shopping mall is home to many of Rio and Brazil's best designer and high-end consumer boutiques, with names like Lenny Niemeyer, Osklen, Antônio Bernardo and Rosa Chá. There are plenty of restaurants and cafés in the large food court, a cinema and rooftop views of the Rocinha *favela*. It is one of the best places in Rio to take a safe photograph of the slum.
✉ Estrada de Gávea s/n, Gavea
☎ 21 2111 4444 ⌚ Shops: Mon–Sat 10–10 (restaurants open at 11), Sun 3–9 (restaurants open at 12) 🚌 S020 from city centre, 546 from Leblon/Ipanema

SHOPPING LEBLON

www.shoppingleblon.com.br

Rio de Janeiro's newest shopping centre sits close to the beach in Leblon. Inside there are boutiques from many of the city's more exclusive retailers.

Avenida Afrânio de Melo Franco 290, Leblon 21 3138 8000 Mon–Sat 10–10, Sun 3–9 546 from São Conrado and Gávea, 2015 from city centre and Ipanema

SHOPPING RIO DESIGN

www.riodesign.com.br

This medium-sized mall on Leblon's largest shopping street originally sold only exclusive home decoration by South America's top designers. These now sit alongside sophisticated clothing boutiques (like Osklen and Verve), cafés, restaurants and bookshops—including Armazém Digital Leblon, which sells English and Portuguese books, hosts small concerts and has a little cinema.

Avenida Ataulfo de Paiva 270, Leblon 21 3206 9100 Mon–Sat 10–10, Sun 1–9 546 from São Conrado and Gávea, 2015 from city centre and Ipanema

TOCA DO VINÍCIUS

www.tocadovinicius.com.br

Rio has produced three great musical traditions: *choro*—which sounds a little like Brazilian ragtime—samba and *bossa nova*. This shop specializes in all three. The owner speaks excellent English and allows customers to listen to CDs before deciding what to buy.

Rua Vinícius de Moraes 129, Ipanema 21 2247 5227 Mon–Sat 10–6 Praça General Osório

TOULON

www.toulon.com.br

Toulon sell a wide range of fashionable casual clothing for men at what, for Brazil, are very low prices. This is one of the best places in the city to stock up on jeans with those slinky Brazilian cuts, jackets, shirts, shoes and swimwear. While we list their principal shop, they have outlets all over the city, details of which are on their website.

Rua Visconde de Pirajá 540, Ipanema 21 2239 2195 Mon–Sat 10–7 Praça General Osório

ENTERTAINMENT AND NIGHTLIFE

ACADEMIA DA CACHAÇA

www.academiadacachaca.com.br

The best *caipirinhas* (*cachaça* and fresh lime cocktails) and *cachaças* (Brazilian sugar cane spirit) are served at this delightful open-sided bar in the heart of fashionable Leblon. There are scores to choose from. Be sure to try the tangy tangerine options and the *caipira aroeira*, made with pineapple and desert chilli pepper.

Rua Conde Bernadotte 26, Leblon 21 2529 2680 Daily 12–late 546 from São Conrado and Gávea, 2015 from city centre and Ipanema

BAR DO COPA

www.bardocopa.com.br

This long, low-lit cocktail lounge next to the Copacabana Palace hotel's pool (▷ 102) is a showground for young Carioca playboys and their model consorts. However, the excellent people-watching is the only view here and there are long queues to get in.

Copacabana Palace, Avenida Atlântica 1702 21 2545 8724 Wed–Sun from 9pm Cardeal Arcoverde

BARRETO LONDRA FASANO

www.fasano.com.br

This bar is so unashamedly hip that it can be difficult to get past security on the door—unless you get there early. Big leather sofas in a windowless room are draped with the Union Jack, making this an admittedly bizarre backdrop for Rio. However, this Fasano offering makes a welcome change from some of the city's more generic drinking spots and you may just catch a glimpse of a model or rock star.

Avenida Vieira Souto, 80, Ipanema 21 3202 4000 Mon–Sat 7pm–late General Osório

BELMONTE IV

Brazil is one of the few countries in the world where bakeries play an integral part in nightlife. Cariocas come here at all hours to have a beer and eat the delicious *empanadas*—little filo pies stuffed with crabs, prawns or chicken.

Rua Jardim Botânico 617, Jardim Botânico 21 2239 1649 Fri–Sat after club hours–5am, Sun–Mon after club hours–3am 158 from city centre, 572 from Ipanema

CARIOCA DA GEMA

www.barcariocadagema.com.br

One of Rio's best samba and *choro* bars is housed in a medium-sized 18th-century town house near the Arcos de Lapa. Upstairs is a decent pizza restaurant, downstairs a bar with a tiny stage where different live acts play sets until the small hours. Come before 10pm to ensure getting a table.

Avenida Mem de Sá 79, Lapa 21 2221 0043 Mon–Sat from 9pm Admission R$20 Cinelândia

CIRCO VOADOR

www.circovoador.com.br

The first of Lapa's new wave of live music venues remains one of the best. Some of Rio's most exciting new and alternative acts play here, from Pedro Luíz e a Parede to Orquestra Imperial, and there are gigs most weekend nights which are well worth watching.

Rua dos Arcos s/n (under the arches), Lapa 21 2533 0354 Varies night to night Cinelândia 398 from city centre

CLUBE DOS DEMOCRÁTICOS

www.clubedosdemocraticos.com.br

A huge 19th-century ballroom lit by chandeliers and spotlights, and with a stage large enough for samba bands with up to 20 members. These play samba, *choro* and *forró* on weekend nights. This venue is immensely popular.

Rua da Riachuelo 91, Lapa 21 2252 4611 Mon–Sat R$20 Cinelândia 398 from city centre

COMUNA DO SEMENTE

Under the helm of co-director and jazz guitarist Yamandu Costa, the

Above *Bar Londra at the Fasano hotel in Ipanema*

pioneering club Bar do Semente underwent a full revamp in June 2009, doubling in size and launching a record label devoted to samba and *chorinho*, Brazil's equivalent of bebop. The club is now Lapa's answer to New York's Blue Note, showcasing new talent as well as classic Carioca artists like singer Elza Soares.
Rua Joaquim Silva 138, Lapa 21 2509 3591, 21 9781 2451 Tue–Thu, Sat–Sun from 8pm Glória

DA GRAÇA

A romantic *boteco* (streetside) bar on a quiet street, this place is decorated with dozens of papier-mâché and crepe flowers and models of saints. The *petiscos* (Brazilian tapas), such as gorgonzola crêpes, are delicious and there's a good range of fruit *caipirinhas*, including one that is tangy with ginger *(gengibre)*.
Rua Pacheco Leão 780, Jardim Botânico 21 2249 5484 Thu–Sun 125 from city centre and Ipanema, 409 from Guanabara Bay and city centre

DEVASSA

www.devassa.com.br
This chain of busy southern Rio de Janeiro *boteco* bars are so popular that they have succeeded in penetrating São Paulo's highly competitive nightlife scene. The secret to their success is the lively middle-class crowd and the beer which, unusually for Brazil, is brewed on site. This is one of the liveliest of all the branches, but there are others throughout the city.
Avenida Lineu de Paula Machado 696, Jardim Botânico 21 2294 2915 Daily 12–late 125 from city centre and Ipanema, 158 from Guanabara Bay and city centre

GAROTA DA GÁVEA

This bar and restaurant is another of Gávea's highly popular and informal meeting spots, off the Praça Santos Dumont. Scores of people gather here for *petiscos* (Brazilian tapas) and a cold *chopp* (draught beer) on weekend and Thursday nights.
Praça Santos Dumont 148, Gávea 21 2274 2347 Daily 11am–last client 125 from city centre and Ipanema, 158 from Guanabara Bay and city centre

HIPÓDROMO DA GÁVEA

On weekend and Thursday nights this bubbling restaurant bar, and its equivalents around the Praça Santos Dumont, fill with young middle-class Cariocas who come out to *bater o papo* (chat) and *tomar um chopp* (have a beer). Very few tourists make it here, so it's a wonderful spot to meet the locals.
Praça Santos Dumont 108, Gávea 21 2274 9720 Thu–Sun 6pm–late 125 from city centre and Ipanema, 158 from Guanabara Bay and city centre

MALA E CUIA

Lapa is filled with little *botecos* (streetside bars) and they are liveliest on weekday lunchtimes and after 9pm on Friday and Saturday. This *boteco* was once a favourite meeting spot for the composer Heitor Villa Lobos, the *choro* virtuoso Pixinguinha, and the poet Manuel Bandeira. It remains a favourite with artists and musicians today.
Praça Floriano 55, Centro 21 2240 8434 Mon–Fri 11–3.30 Cinelândia

PALAPHITA KITCH

www.palaphitakitch.com.br
These rustic log tables and chairs strewn under mock-Bedouin awnings right on the lakeshore are one of the first ports of call for Rio's romantic under-50s on a weekend night. The *caipirinhas* are strong, sweet and ice-cold and there's some live music.
Avenida Epitácio Pessoa, Quiosque 20, Lagoa 21 2227 0837 Thu–Sun 157

RIO SCENARIUM

www.rioscenarium.com.br
This is one of the larger samba clubs in Rio, with live bands playing samba standards on the ground floor, and bars and clubs on the upper levels. The club is decorated with antiques and bric-a-brac, including a 19th-century apothecary's shop, mannequins in period costume and musical instruments.
Rua Lavradio 20, Lapa 21 3147 9005 Tue–Sat from 7.30pm Admission R$30 Cinelândia

SACRILÉGIO

www.sacrilegio.com.br
This samba club sits next door to the Carioca da Gema club (▷ 94) and, like it, is housed in an 18th-century house, decorated in green and white. The live acts are excellent.
Avenida Mem de Sá 81, Lapa 21 3970 1461 Tue–Sun from 8pm R$20 Cinelândia

TEATRO ODISSÉIA

http://beta.matrizonline.com.br/teatroodisseia

Rock, reggae and funk bands play in this sweaty club near the Arcos de Lapa. Unlike most of the samba clubs, there is standing room only and the large stage at the end of the room gives something of a concert hall feel.

✉ Avenida Mem de Sá 66, Lapa ☎ 21 2226 9691, 21 2224 6367 🕐 Thu–Sun from 9pm ✋ R$20 Ⓜ Cinelândia

SPORTS AND ACTIVITIES

DELTA FLIGHT

www.deltaflight.com.br

Rio de Janeiro was built for hang-gliders, with spectacular settings, towering coastal boulder mountains for take-offs and beaches for smooth, soft landings. Most flights leave from the Pedra Bonita—a granite outcrop in Tijuca National Park (▷ 81) near São Conrado that is 700m (2,296ft) above the Atlantic—and float out over southern Rio before coming to ground at São Conrado beach. The company picks you up from the hotel and provides all equipment. Bookings are available through the internet only. Numerous other companies offer flights, including Easy Fly Rio (www.easyflyrio.com.br).

✋ From R$200 ? The total trip takes around 3 hours, depending on where you are staying in Rio, including a 30-min flight

ESTADIO DO MARACANÃ

There's no football like Brazilian football and no football crowd like a Carioca football crowd at Maracanã. It is the world's largest football stadium. The best games to see are either the local or Rio–São Paulo derbies; or, if you can get a ticket, an international game. Coming to a game without a local friend or command of Portuguese can be a daunting experience and isn't recommended, but there are a number of Rio de Janeiro tour operators who offer trips. For details of an organized tour of the stadium see www.bealocal.com. The stadium is closed for renovations for the World Cup until 2013.

✉ Rua Prof Eurico Rabelo ☎ 21 2299 2942 🕐 Stadium daily 9–1 ✋ Stadium and museum R$5; tours from R$70; match tickets from R$30 Ⓜ Maracanã

FAVELA TOURISM WORKSHOP

http://www.favelatourismworkshop.com

A visit to one of Rio's *favelas* (slums) is an educational experience, challenging preconceptions about the communities and the people who live in them. These are sensitive, guarded communities and for safety's sake as well as for respect, visits should never be made unaccompanied. Pick a tour that gives back substantially to the local community and one that does not use safari-style jeeps. These walking tours in Rocinha, with visits to the tourism workshop, offer a respectful cultural insight. They invest in the community, not just financially, but with training, unlike many tours that simply pay lip service or make very small donations. There are special rates for internet booking, minimum two people; trips are combined with visits to Corcovado, the beaches or the Botanic Gardens.

☎ Toll free in Rio 0800 282 6972, 21 7827.3024 ✋ From R$95

HELISIGHT

www.helisight.com.br

A helicopter trip over Rio is arguably the most spectacular urban flight in the world. You can see Corcovado, the Sugar Loaf, the ocean beaches, *favelas*, city skyscrapers and Maracanã stadium. Try and fly during the middle of the day when the shadows are at their shortest, so there is considerably less contrast, and set cameras to the maximum shutter speed possible to avoid blur from the rotor vibrations.

✉ Avenida Borges Medeiros, Leblon ☎ 21 2511 6455 🕐 Daily 10–6 ✋ From R$200 🚌 382 from city centre, Ipanema and Copacabana

RICO SURF

http://ricosurf.globo.com

Cariocas love to surf. The best beaches for this are out of the city, either to the east of Niterói town or south of São Conrado, at Barra da Tijuca and beyond. But surfing is also possible in Ipanema and Leblon, especially at the Arpoador. Unless you have a board you will need to rent through a school or guide. Rico Surf, in Barra, work in the Rio metropolitan area.

☎ 21 2438 1821 ✋ From R$60 per hour, including equipment rental

RIO HIKING

www.riohiking.com.br

This long-established company offer great nature walks and adventure treks (including rock climbing) throughout the city, with ascents of both Sugar Loaf and the Pedra da Gávea. They also cover destinations a little further afield, like the Serra dos Órgãos (▷ 148–149) and Itatiaia National Park (▷ 145), with single or multi-day hiking through primary rainforest abundant with wildlife. Tours begin with a hotel pick-up and bookings are internet only.

RIO TRILHAS

www.riotrilhas.com.br

Rio Trilhas offer a range of walks throughout natural Rio. One of their most popular is a half-day excursion to Corcovado, taking a little-known forest route from the baroque folly in the Parque Lage along the trail once used by Brazil's first emperor, Dom Pedro I. Tours begin with a hotel pick-up.

☎ 21 9312 342

SAVEIROS

www.saveiros.com.br

Saveiros offer a range of cruises around Guanabara Bay, taking in many of the islands and farther afield, including the open ocean and Ilha Grande (▷ 144). All include food and drink. It may be shamefully polluted but Guanabara Bay remains one of the world's largest and most beautiful urban bays. Views of Rio from the water are equally as spectaular as they are from Corcovado, especially in the early morning or late afternoon. All tours leave from the office in Glória (and adjacent marina) in the morning, usually around 9.30, and hotel pick-ups can be arranged.

Avenida Infante Dom Henrique s/n Ljs 13 & 14, Marina da Glória 21 2225 6064 Mon–Sat 10–6 Glória

SEASON SPORT

www.seasonsporttour.com

Brazil is the best in the world at beach volleyball. You can see it being played on Ipanema and Copacabana (just in front of the Copacabana Palace hotel, ▷ 102) beaches. Season Sport gives classes and the chance of a subsequent game. All gear is provided.

Rua Marquês de São Vicente 124, 507 bl. 3, Gávea 21 2529 2415 125 from city centre and Ipanema, 158 from Guanabara Bay and city centre

FOR CHILDREN

TERRA ENCANTADA

www.terraencantada.com.br

The Enchanted Land, as this theme park's name translates, is a US-style rollercoaster theme park with assorted hair-raising rides. Small by American standards, it is nonetheless one of the largest in Brazil, with one of the biggest rollercoasters in the whole of South America. The theme park lies on the outskirts of Barra da Tijuca, near Recreio dos Bandeirantes. There is no public transport; travel by taxi or rental car, or with a tour operator, such as Madson Araujo (http://tourguiderio.com; tel 21 9395 3537).

Avenida Ayrton Senna 2,800, Barra da Tijuca Tue–Sat 2–9, Sun 12–9; Jul–Aug till 10pm All entrants R$25

WATER PLANET

www.riowaterplanet.com.br

This water-based theme park, 20km (12.5 miles) from the city centre near Recreio dos Bandeirantes, offers a full day's worth of slides, swimming pools, aquatic rides and water-squirting games. There is no public transport; travel by taxi or rental car, or with a tour operator, such as Madson Araujo (http://tourguiderio.com; tel 21 9395 3537).

Estrada dos Bandeirantes, Vargem Grande 21 2428 9000 Sat–Sun 10–5; sometimes closes erratically, so check website Adult R$89, child R$44

FESTIVALS AND EVENTS

DECEMBER

REVEILLON

This New Year's Eve party is one of the biggest in the world. Several million flock to Copacabana beach to experience music from some of the city's best live bands and see spectacular fireworks spilling in waterfalls from the beachfront skyscrapers or shooting into the air from offshore boats. Other celebrations are dedicated to the *Orixá* (elemental spirit of *candomblé*, the African-Brazilian spirit religion) goddess of the sea, and devotees dressed in white make votive offerings to the beaches and launch little boats out to sea.

Avenida Princesa Isabel 183, Copacabana 21 2541 7522 Mon–Fri 9–6 119, 154, 413, 415, 455, 474 from city centre to Avenida Nossa Senhora de Copacabana Cardeal Arco Verde, Siqueira Campos, Cantagalo

FEBRUARY

DIA DE SÃO SEBASTIÃO

This festival celebrates the name day of the patron saint of Rio on 20 February, with evening processions from the Capuchinhos Church in Tijuca to the Catedral Metropólitana (▷ 63). There is also an *umbanda* (an African-Brazilian spirit religion) festival at the Caboclo Monument in Santa Teresa.

FEBRUARY–MARCH

CARNAVAL

Carnival is held for five days on the weekend before Shrove Tuesday, with extensive festivals throughout the city. These include street parades *(blocos)* and—on the Sunday and Monday nights—parades in Oscar Niemeyer's Sambódromo stadium (▷ 85). Arrive by 7pm to be in time for the first procession and expect to leave at about 6am the next day. Masquerade balls are a big part of Rio carnival too, although tickets are expensive so these are not a particularly inclusive element of the city's celebrations. Two of the most famous balls are held at the Copacabana hotel, which attracts members of Rio's high society, and at Leblon's Scala Club, a wild event that is a highlight on the gay calendar.

Sambódromo, Rua Marquês de Sapucaí Praça Onze www.rioguiaoficial.com.br is also helpful

JUNE

FESTAS JUNINAS

These rural and traditionally northeastern Brazilian festivals are increasingly big in Rio de Janeiro, where they kick off with the festival of Santo Antônio on 13 June by attending Mass and celebrations in the Largo da Carioca (▷ 71). The feast of São João (23–24 June) sees two more nights of partying throughout the city—the largest being at the Centro de Tradições Nordestinas, also known as Feira de São Cristóvão (www.feiradesaocristovao.org.br). The Festas Juninas finish with the festival of São Pedro on 29 June, with boat processions in Guanabara Bay celebrating Peter's status as the patron saint of fishermen.

OCTOBER

NOSSA SENHORA DA PENHA PILGRIMAGE

Devotees ascend the steps of this church in the northern suburb of Penha (▷ 68) throughout October, especially on Saturdays. They usually climb on their knees to pay homage to the Virgin of the Rocks and petition her for miracles.

PRICES AND SYMBOLS

The restaurants are listed alphabetically (excluding A, Al, El, La, Le and O). The prices given are the average for a two-course lunch (L) and a three-course dinner (D) for one person, without drinks. The wine price is for the least expensive bottle. All the restaurants listed accept credit cards unless otherwise stated.

For a key to the symbols, ▷ 2.

ABENÇOADO

The best tables with a view are to be found at this restaurant, 305m (1,000ft) up the Morro da Urca and reached by cable car on the way to the Sugar Loaf. It has views out over the entire city, from the iconic Christ the Redeemer statue on one side, to the beaches of Ipanema and Copacabana on the other. Choose from modern variations on comfort food like *angú* (corn meal with prawns and mushrooms) or *escondidinho* (potato and sun-dried beef pie), dusted in Minas Gerais parmesan and served on a bed of pureed cassava. The *caipirinha* cocktails and the less-alcoholic blended-fruit *batidas* are excellent. Particularly refreshing and piquant is the *caipirinha aroeira*; pineapple and chilli pepper, shaken with *cachaça* (Brazilian sugar cane spirit) and crushed ice.

✉ Morro da Urca s/n 🕐 Daily 12–2, 6–9 L R$55, D R$82, Wine R$50 Ⓜ Botafogo ❓ For cable car information (▷ 79) see www.bondinho.com.br

ADEGA FLOR DE COIMBRA

www.adegaflordecoimbra.com.br

This little restaurant in the former home of Modernist painter Cândido Portinari is one of the best traditional Portuguese restaurants in the city centre, with respectable *bacalhau* (salted cod) and a modest but decent wine list, mostly of Portuguese bottles. In the 1930s the restaurant was popular with the local left-wing intelligentsia, who would gather here to discuss and formulate political theory over a glass of chilled French wine. The crowd is now dominated by after-work suits and is particularly lively on Fridays.

✉ Rua Teotônio Regadas 34, Lapa ☎ 21 2224 4582 🕐 Daily 12–11 L R$60, D R$80, Wine R$40 Ⓜ Cinelândia 🚌 433 Vila Isabel-Leblon

ALESSANDRO E FREDERICO

www.alessandroefrederico.com.br

This fashionable café, on the busiest upmarket shopping street in the chicest corner of Ipanema, serves excellent coffee, breakfasts and brunches until late. There's a great juice bar next door.

✉ Rua Garcia d'Ávila 134, Ipanema ☎ 21 2522 5414 🕐 Daily 9am–1am L R$40, Coffee R$4 Ⓜ General Osório 🚌 572 Gloria-Leblon

ARMAZÉM DO CAFÉ

www.armazemdocafe.com.br

This traditional Portuguese café, with uniformed staff and a lush wood interior, serves more than 30 kinds of coffee, as well as snacks. You can order strong espressos, sweet American-style frothy tankards with added ingredients like chocolate and mint, and variations on Irish coffee with different liqueurs.

✉ Rua Maria Quitéria 77, Ipanema ☎ 21 2522 5039 🕐 Mon–Fri 8.30–8.30, Sat 8.30–7.30, Sun 10–7 L R$30, Coffee R$4 Ⓜ General Osório 🚌 572 Gloria-Leblon

Above *Confeitaria Colombo, an art nouveau coffee house and* boteco

BAZZAR CAFÉ

www.bazzar.com.br

This bright, airy glass-walled dining room in the Livraria da Travessa serves modern, light Italian food with a Brazilian twist. Dishes may include pumpkin risotto garnished with rocket or duck breast grilled with plantain and served with greens, spring onion and crêpes.

✉ Avenida Visconde de Pirajá 572, Ipanema ☎ 21 2249 4977 🕒 Mon–Sat 9am–11pm, Sun 12–11 L R$20, Coffee R$4 General Osório 572 Gloria-Leblon

BISTRO DO PAÇO

www.bistro.com.br

This café restaurant in the open-air central atrium of the Paço Imperial has a menu of lunches like quiches, salads, baguettes and cakes. There's a varied selection of fruit juices (mostly made from frozen fruit pulp) and excellent coffee. Between Monday and Friday the bistro serves good, inexpensive set lunches, or *Pratos Feito.*

✉ Praça XV de Novembro 48, Centro ☎ 21 2262 3613 🕒 Mon–Fri 11–8, Sat–Sun 12–7 L R$20, D R$50, Coffee R$5 Carioca

BRASSERIE EUROPA

Suits come here at lunchtime to dine in air-conditioned comfort on the excellent, tender grilled meat and fish, usually with an ice-cold draught of Warsteiner German beer. There are respectable lighter options too, especially *petiscos* (tapas-like nibbles) such as *bolinhos de bacalhau* (cod balls).

✉ Rua Senador Dantas 117 ☎ 21 2220 2656 🕒 Mon–Fri 11.30–9 L R$60, D R$60, Wine R$50 Carioca

CAFÉ DO THEATRO

www.theatromunicipal.rj.gov.br

Cariocas like to lunch here on weekdays, or to escape from the heat of Rio for a quick afternoon coffee in the cool surroundings. The coffee and cakes are excellent and there's a reasonable range of light snacks.

✉ Teatro Municipal, Praça Floriano s/n ☎ 21 2262 3935 🕒 Mon–Fri 12–3 L R$25, Coffee R$5 Cinelândia

CAIS DO ORIENTE

www.caisdooriente.com.br

The Cais is one of the grandest and most illustrious restaurants in central Rio. It is housed in the arts complex made up by the Banco do Brasil, Casa França and Post Office cultural centres. It comprises a series of distinct mock-Moorish indoor and outdoor dining areas, and the menu includes Brazilian takes on Eastern and Mediterranean dishes. Expect lots of salt and little spice in your Thai curry. The wine list has an excellent selection and there is often live music in the evening.

✉ Rua Visconde de Itaboraí 8, Centro ☎ 21 2223 2531 🕒 Tue–Sat 12–12, Sun–Mon 12–4 L R$62, D R$76, Wine R$50 Uruguaiana

CARLOTA

www.carlota.com.br

The décor is simple and elegant in the sister restaurant to Carla Pernambuco's much celebrated São Paulo dining room, with white walls and table cloths, low light and candles. The kitchen produces some of the very best Brazililian-European fusion cooking in the city, offering dishes like crispy prawns with Parma ham risotto.

✉ Rua Dias Ferreira 64, Leblon ☎ 21 2540 6821 🕒 Mon–Fri 7.30–12, Sat 1.30–5, 7.30–12, Sun 1–12 L R$70, D R$120, Wine R$60 572 Gloria-Leblon

CELEIRO

www.celeiroculinaria.com.br

Rio de Janeiro's best buffet diner serves a wealth of preprepared soups, quiches, pasta, vegetarian and meat dishes, and accompanying salads. The restaurant also has a bakery and sandwich counter.

✉ Rua Dias Ferreira 199, Leblon ☎ 21 2274 7843 🕒 Mon–Sat 11–5 L R$70, Coffee R$6 503D Botafogo-Leblon, 572 Gloria-Leblon

LE CHAMPS ELYSEES

This French restaurant close to the Santos Dumont airport is immensely popular for business lunches. Chefs Alain and Dominique Raymond have a menu of classic French dishes adapted for the Brazilian palate, such as lamb cutlets with cream sauce or prawn salad with mango and French dressing.

✉ Maison de France, 12th floor Avenida Antônio Carlos 58, Centro ☎ 21 2220 4713 🕒 Mon–Fri 12–3, 6–11 L R$60, D R$60, Wine R$40 Cinelândia

CONFEITARIA COLOMBO

www.confeitariacolombo.com.br

The ground floor of Rio's grand Portuguese art nouveau coffee house doubles up as a *boteco*. Black-tie barmen serve draught Warsteiner German beer and the *petiscos* come from the Confeitaria itself, which serves both savouries and tantalizingly sweet cakes.

✉ Rua Gonçalves Dias 32 ☎ 21 2505 1500 🕒 Mon–Fri 9–8, Sat and holidays 9.30–5; Lunch served from 11–3 only L R$30, Coffee R$6 Uruguaiana

EÇA

www.hstern.com.br/eca

Rio city centre's best business lunch is served by Frederic de Maeyer, who earned his stripes in the Michelin-starred L'Escalier du Palais Royal in Brussels and who won *Gula* magazine's New Chef of the Year in 2004. Dishes feature classical European techniques with occasional Brazilian ingredients (the parfait de gorgonzola starter is particularly popular) and the wine list is one of the best in Rio.

✉ Avenida Rio Branco 128, Centro ☎ 21 2524 2300 🕒 Mon–Fri 12–3, 7–11 L R$60, D R$60, Wine R$50 Carioca

ESPÍRITO SANTA

www.espiritosanta.com.br

Here you will find outstanding, Amazon-style cooking—strong on fish and exotic fruits and vegetables—in a simply furnished restaurant with a great view out over Santa Teresa.

✉ Rua Almirante Alexandrino 264, Santa Teresa ☎ 21 2508 7095 🕒 Mon–Wed 11.30–6, Thu–Sat 11.30–midnight, Sun 11.30–7 L R$60, D R$60, Wine R$40 214 from city centre; trams from in front of the Catedral Metropólitana (▷ 63) to the Largo dos Guimarães (▷ 87)

ESPÍRITO SANTA EMPÓRIO

www.espiritosanta.com.br

This funky 2009 opening serves Rio de Janeiro comfort food, like steaks with *farofa* (manioc flour) and Brazilian bar snacks *(petiscos)* like *empanada de adão* (filo pastries filled with beef marinated in sweet Brazilian stout ale). Cool local DJs spin Carioca funk beats on weekend nights in the third-floor club space, to a predominantly twenty- and thirty-something crowd.

Rua Lavradio 34, Centro 21 2509 5250 Mon–Tue noon–5, Wed–Sat noon–2am D R$85, Wine R$40 Cinelândia

FELLINI

www.fellini.com.br

One of the best-value pay-by-weight restaurants in Ipanema, Fellini has a large range of delicious Brazilian and international dishes, salads and quiches—all of them prepared with ultra-fresh ingredients. There are also plenty of imaginative options for vegetarians.

Rua General Urquiza 104, Leblon 21 2511 3600 Mon–Fri 11.30–4, 7.30–12, Sat–Sun 11.30–5.30, 7.30–12 L R$40, D R$60, Wine R$40 503D Botafogo-Leblon, 572 Gloria-Leblon

FORNERIA

www.laforneria.com.br

People from São Paulo look down their noses at Rio de Janeiro's pizzas and while this pizzeria cannot compare with the best of that city, chef Cândido Abreu has been serving great wood-stove Margheritas and Neapolitanas for more than 10 years, alongside house specialties like the Bufalotta (unsurprisingly, with heaps of Brazilian buffalo mozzarella).

Rua Maria Quitéria 136, Ipanema 21 2287 0335 Mon–Thu 5–1, Fri 5–2, Sun noon–1am L R$60, D R$80, Wine R$40 General Osório 572 Gloria-Leblon

GARCIA & RODRIGUES

www.garciaerodrigues.com.br

This French-owned delicatessen and lunchtime restaurant has been a popular watering hole for wealthy Cariocas for more than 10 years. They come to buy over-sweet pastries and French-style baguettes, sip frothy machiatos in the upper gallery, and preserve their wasp-like waists with light lunches and healthy snacks. The ice creams are excellent and the air-conditioned interior is a welcome respite from the heat and bustle of the shopping streets.

Avenida Ataulfo de Paiva 1251, Leblon 21 3206 4100 Sun–Thu 8am–12.30am, Fri–Sat 8am–1am L R$45, D R$45, Wine R$40 572 Gloria-Leblon

GERO

www.fasano.com.br

Star restaurateur and hotelier Rogerio Fasano's first Rio venture was this chic restaurant in the heart of fashionable Ipanema. It remains a place to be seen to dine, as much as to enjoy dining, especially in the evening, when it fills with a TV Globo crowd. The food is nevertheless excellent, with the emphasis on light, modern Italian dishes strong on fish and seafood. The long cool bar serves excellent cocktails: try the sake *caipirinhas*.

Rua Aníbal de Mendonça 157, Ipanema 21 2239 8158 Mon–Fri 12–4, 7–1, Sat noon–2am, Sun 12–12 L R$70, D R$120, Wine R$50 572 Gloria-Leblon

MARGUTTA CITTÀ

www.margutta.com.br
Chef Paolo Neroni was brought up and worked in central Italy before emigrating to Rio de Janeiro and setting-up what became an immensely popular Italian restaurant in Ipanema. His city centre restaurant opened in 2005 and has a similar menu of Italian fish dishes, pasta and risottos. These are served in a bright, airy dining room with crisp service. Like most restaurants in the centre, Margutta Città is busy, only opens at lunchtimes, and should be booked in advance.
✉ Avenida Graça Aranha 1, 2nd floor, Centro ☎ 21 2563 4091 🕐 Mon–Fri 11–4 ✋ L R$70, Wine R$40 Ⓜ Cinelândia

Above *Sawasdee Thai restaurant in the chic Leblon district*
Opposite *Porcão* churrascaria *restaurant is a meat-lover's paradise*

OUI OUI

www.restauranteouioui.com.br
Designer-dressed, arty, thirty-something Cariocas on their way to the clubs in Lapa linger over cocktails in this art deco-ish lounge and bar, and snack on surprisingly modestly priced *petiscos*—Brazilian tapas ordered in pairs—in the adjacent 1970s-inspired dining room.
✉ Rua Conde de Irajá 85, Humaitá ☎ 21 2527 3539 🕐 Tue–Sat 7–midnight ✋ Petiscos from R$18, Wine R$26 Ⓜ Botafogo 🚌 511 from Ipanema or Jardim Botânico

PORCÃO

www.porcao.com.br
Resolute carnivores should come to this cavernous *churrascaria* (spit grill) restaurant with empty stomachs. The price includes as much as you can eat and the black-tie waiters ceaselessly offer sizzling prime cuts. The salad and sushi bar has dishes suitable for traumatized vegetarians.
✉ Rua Barão da Torre 218, Ipanema ☎ 21 3389 8989 🕐 Mon–Thu 12–12, Fri–Sat noon–12.30, Sun 12–11 ✋ L R$70, D R$120, Wine R$40 Ⓜ General Osório 🚌 572 Gloria-Leblon

REPUBLIQUE

As the tricolore décor in this restaurant would suggest, the menu is inspired by France, although with a modern, fusion cuisine twist. Chef Paulo Carvalho uses conventional French techniques to produce unconventional dishes—such as a miniature strawberry tart filled with curried prawns—alongside Brazilian businessman favourites like fillet steak in garlic sauce with beans and rice. The restaurant is busiest at lunchtime.
✉ Praça da República 63, Centro ☎ 21 2532 9000 🕐 Tue–Sat 12–3, 7–11 ✋ L R$80, D R$80, Wine R$50 Ⓜ Central 🚆 Central do Brasil

SAWASDEE

www.sawasdee.com.br
Chef Marcos Sodré has been cooking Thai food à la Carioca at his restaurant by the beach on the Orla Bardot, Búzios, for some 10 years (▷ 142). His new restaurant, designed by society architect Bel Lobo, lies at the far northern end of the city's most fashionable restaurant street. More often than not, the crowd will be Ipanema 'A' list; there may be celebrities from the popular national TV station, TV Globo, and singer of the moment, Maria Rita, is a patron of this restaurant. While Sodré's cooking is light on spice by Thai standards, it bursts with flavour, especially the juicy *kung karre suparrot* (sautéed shrimps with coconut milk, pineapple and curry).
✉ Rua Dias Ferreira 571, Leblon ☎ 21 2511 0057 🕐 Mon 7–12, Tue–Thu 12–12, Fri–Sat noon–2am, Sun 12–11 ✋ L R$80, L R$80, Wine R$40 🚌 572 Gloria-Leblon

ZAZÁ BISTRÔ TROPICAL

www.zazabistro.com.br
This brightly coloured bohemian restaurant, just one block from the beach, serves North African and pan-Asian food with a Carioca twist to evening diners. The fish dishes are light and bursting with flavour, and the hippy-chic crowd always lively. Best with a partner after sundown, when the tables are lit by candles and dining in the upstairs lounge room is at its most intimate.
✉ Rua Joana Angélica 40, Ipanema ☎ 21 2247 9101 🕐 Mon–Thu 7.30–12.30, Fri–Sat 7.30–1.30 ✋ D R$120, Wine R$30 Ⓜ General Osório 🚌 572 Gloria-Leblon

ZUKA

www.zuka.com.br
Since taking over in 2006, Ludmila Soeiro has transformed what was essentially a glorified grilled meat menu into a daring fusion of Asian, Middle Eastern and Brazilian flavours. She's received numerous awards from, among others, *Veja* and *Gula* magazines—Brazil's most respected monitors of good food.
✉ Rua Dias Ferreira 233, Leblon ☎ 21 2249 7550 🕐 Mon 7pm–1am, Tue–Fri 12–4, 7–1, Sat 1–1, Sun 1–12 ✋ L R$70, D R$120, Wine R$40 🚌 503D Botafogo-Leblon, 572 Gloria-Leblon

Above *Copacabana Palace and pool*

PRICES AND SYMBOLS

Prices are the lowest and highest for a double room for one night. Breakfast is included unless noted otherwise. All the hotels listed accept credit cards unless otherwise stated. Note that rates vary widely throughout the year.

For a key to the symbols, ▷ 2.

ARPOADOR INN

www.arpoadorinn.com.br

This small hotel is in a wonderful location, right on Arpoador beach, with great views along the entire stretch of Ipanema. Rooms are plain cubes, with beds and simple furniture. The hotel offers attractive off-season special deals. There is a seafront restaurant, but this is much better for people-watching than for dining—order a coffee, then sit back and relax.

Rua Francisco Otaviano 177, Ipanema 21 2523 0060 R$215–R$300 50 General Osório

ATLANTIS COPACABANA

www.atlantishotel.com.br

The great location and low prices at this hotel more than make up for the slightly frayed, pokey rooms. The hotel is less than five minutes' walk from both Ipanema and Copacabana and boasts a tiny rooftop pool with a view. Avoid the tours proffered in the lobby, as they are overpriced.

Rua Bulhões de Carvalho 61, Arpoador 21 2521 1142 R$200–R$320 87 Rooftop General Osório

CASA AUREA

www.casaaurea.com.br

This delightful, sprawling family-run guest house sits on a quiet Santa Teresa street close to the restaurants of the Largo dos Guimarães (▷ 87). Large public areas include a spacious garden patio and open-air kitchen. Rooms vary greatly in size and décor but all are filled with bric-a-brac collected by the German-Brazilian owner. They include singles, doubles and multi-bed rooms. The staff speak English, Spanish and German.

Rua Áurea 80, Santa Teresa 21 2242 5830 R$75–R$150 14 214

Paula Matos-Castelo

COPACABANA PALACE

www.copacabanapalace.com.br

This stately art deco building right on the beach in Copacabana—with its lush carpets, chandeliers and formally suited concierges—has been a Rio icon since Fred Astaire and Ginger Rogers filmed here. Previous guests include Prince Charles and Orson Welles, and the hotel was unrivalled as the city's luxury establishment of choice until the construction of the Fasano (▷ 103) in 2007. Competition from that hotel has led to significant renovation and a new chic cocktail bar. The hotel's restaurant, Cipriani, is sister to the Cipriani restaurants in New York and Venice, and serves

some of the best Italian cuisine in the city.
Avenida Atlântica 1702, Copacabana
21 2548 7070 R$895–R$2,300, excluding breakfast 244 Outdoor Cardeal Arcoverde

DOLPHIN INN

The Dolphin is a surf home away from home: a B&B in a small terraced house whose brightly painted rooms are decorated with the bric-a-brac of a lifetime, collected by the owner—an ex-pat American-turned-Carioca surfer—both from the sea and from handicraft markets all over Brazil. The inn has a kitchen, cable TV, internet and free bottled water, and sits on a quiet, gated street less than two minutes' walk from both Ipanema and Copacabana. The Dolphin is bookable through www.bedandbreakfast.com.
Rua Bulhoes de Carvalho 480, Casa 6, Ipanema 21 9672 0025
R$170–R$240 20 Ipanema

FASANO

www.fasano.com.br
Rio de Janeiro's foremost luxury hotel has rooms overlooking the beach at Ipanema, a superb rooftop pool and bar with the best views from any hotel in the city, and public areas which are flooded with light from expanses of glass and separated by billowing Philippe Starck drapes. The Sixties London-meets-tropicália lounge bar is a popular watering hole for the Ipanema elite and the formal lobby restaurant, Fasano al Mare, serves superb light Italian-Brazilian seafood fusion cooking.
Avenida Vieira Souto 80, Ipanema
21 3202 4000 R$1,150–R$2,000
91 Rooftop
General Osório

HARMONIA

www.hostelharmonia.com
A bright little hostel in a residential house three blocks from Ipanema beach, offering three small but airy dorms and one air-conditioned double room with shared bathroom, kitchen facilities, and a lounge area decorated with stencils of Abba and the dragon's tooth paving of Copacabana. The staff speak English, Spanish, German and Swedish. You can rent surf boards and the hostel has wireless internet throughout.
Rua Barão da Torre 175, Ipanema
21 2523 4905 R$50–R$160
General Osório

IPANEMA INN

www.ipanemainn.com.br
Simple rooms with little more than a bed, cupboard space and little tables are made more attractive by good beach views from the upper storeys. It is an easy walk from the inn to the beach, and there is easy access to the best of Ipanema's shops and café restaurants.
Rua Maria Quitéria 27, Ipanema
21 2523 6092 R$212–R$330 56
503D Botafogo-Leblon, 572 Gloria-Leblon

IPANEMA PLAZA

www.ipanemaplaza.com.br
The swish marble lobby promises rooms more luxurious than the simple tile-floor and MDF apartments in this beachside tower. The best are the junior suites—some of which have views out over the lake to the Christ statue on Corcovado—and the Luxo Vista Mar rooms, with views out over Ipanema. The hotel is in an excellent location, a stroll from the sand, restaurants and shops. There is wireless internet throughout but at an extra cost.
Rua Farme de Amoedo 34, Ipanema
21 3687 2000 R$510–R$575
140 Rooftop
General Osório

IZZY RENT

www.ttabrazil.com
A great selection of apartments in Copacabana, Humaitá, Ipanema and Leblon is on offer from this company, including those with full kitchen, internet and air-conditioning, whether you are looking for something for just a couple of nights or for a longer stay. Search on the website according to your requirements.
21 2522 5768, 21 9355 7736
R$330–R$1,500

LA MAISON

www.lamaisonario.com
This 'house' is a beautiful boutique hotel that feels like a private home. Tucked away off a side street among dense greenery, its five exclusive rooms and lovely pool overlook the Cristo Redentor statue. La Maison is a discreet, stylish option for those who don't want the fuss of a large hotel, but prefer personal service.
Rua Sérgio Porto 58, Gávea 21 3205 3585 R$390–R$1,100 5 2016 Mandala-Castelo

MAMA RUISA

www.mamaruisa.com
Mama Ruisa is a self-consciously understated, tastefully decorated, discreet and charming boutique hotel in a refurbished 18th-century mansion house in Santa Teresa (▷ 86–87). There are superb, sweeping views out over the city centre and Botafogo from the rooms, the garden and pool. The seven themed rooms are named after different French cultural luminaries.
Rua Santa Cristina 132, Santa Teresa
21 2242 1281 R$680–R$810 7
Outdoor 214 Paula Matos-Castelo

MAR IPANEMA

www.maripanema.com
This central Ipanema hotel sits on one of the principal shopping streets, less than five-minutes' walk from the beach. Rooms in the upper storeys are the quietest. They are decorated very simply, with white walls, wooden floors and black and white prints of Rio. Good service includes the use of beach chairs and towels on Ipanema beach.
Rua Visconde de Pirajá 539, Ipanema
21 3875 9190 R$320–R$400 82
503D Botafogo-Leblon, 572 Gloria-Leblon

MAR PALACE

www.hotelmarpalace.com.br
The simple rooms in this 1980s tower-block hotel have been renovated to a high standard and those on the 10th floor or above have views of the Christ statue on

Corcovado. Breakfasts are generous and there is a pocket-sized pool on the roof terrace. The beach and Siqueira Campos metrô are a five-minute walk away.
✉ Avenida Nossa Senhora de Copacabana 552, Copacabana ☎ 21 2132 1500 ✋ R$230–R$250 ⓘ 103 ❋ 🏋 ≈ Rooftop 🍴 Ⓜ Siqueira Campos

MARINA PALACE

www.hoteismarina.com.br
This is one of the best of the anonymous tower hotels which crowd along the Ipanema/Leblon beachfront, both for facilities and location. It lies within walking distance of Leblon's restaurants and has spacious, bright rooms, efficient service, reasonable business services, a rooftop pool and very attractive promotional rates. The best rooms have ocean views and are on the upper floors.
✉ Rua Delfim Moreira 630, Leblon ☎ 21 2172 1000 ✋ R$340–R$465, excluding breakfast ⓘ 150 P ❋ 🏋 ≈ Rooftop 🍴 🚌 503D Botafogo-Leblon, 572 Gloria-Leblon

ORLA HOTEL

www.orlahotel.com.br
This hotel is in a superb location—in the middle of the beachfront street in Copacabana—and has wonderful views from the rooftop terrace and any of the rooms above the third floor. Rooms are modern but very small and simple, dominated by the double bed, with white walls, wood-panel floors and tiny private bathrooms. Be warned that the lifts are slow and there is often a queue for breakfast in the overly small breakfast room. There is a restaurant which serves simple dishes but is not particularly good value.
✉ Avenida Atlântica 4122, Copacabana ☎ 21 2525 2425 ✋ R$270–R$380 ⓘ 115 ❋ ≈ Rooftop 🏋 🍴 Ⓜ General Osório

PORTINARI DESIGN

www.hotelportinari.com.br
The designer touches in this fusion of boutique hotel and standard three-star establishment are more cosmetic than carefully considered. Rooms are in a run-of-the-mill Copacabana tower and have minimalist décor, functional furnishings, flat screens and WiFi.

However, service is attentive and the hotel has a small fitness centre and sauna.
✉ Rua Francisco de Sá 17, Copacabana ☎ 21 3222 8800 ✋ R$340–R$408 ⓘ 66 ❋ 🏋 🍴 Ⓜ General Osório

PRAIA IPANEMA

www.praiaipanema.com
The views from the balconies of any of the rooms above the third floor in this tower hotel are wonderful, stretching right along Ipanema beach in both directions, and it's this which justifies the high prices. The facilities themselves are of low 3-star quality, and include a restaurant serving well-presented, simple food.
✉ Avenida Vieira Souto 706, Ipanema ☎ 21 2141 4949 ✋ R$500–R$600 ⓘ 91 ❋ 🏋 ≈ Rooftop 🍴 Ⓜ General Osório

PREMIER COPACABANA

www.premier.com.br
While it's not on the beach, this tower sits very close to the metrô, offering rapid access to the Sambódromo (▷ 85) and Ipanema. The beach is a ten-minute walk away. Rooms are well-maintained, equipped with flat screen cable TVs and private bathrooms with powerful showers. The rooftop pool has views of Corcovado.

Below left *The Fasano luxury hotel overlooks Ipanema beach*
Below right *A room in one of the bed-and-breakfast establishments in Santa Teresa*

Rua Tonelero 205, Copacabana 21 3816 9090 R$200–R$300 110 Rooftop Siqueira Campos

RIO HOMESTAY

www.riohomestay.com.br

This company organizes home stays in luxurious houses owned by the city's art-minded residents, both in Santa Teresa and the fashionable beach neighbourhoods of Ipanema and Leblon. Home stays in so friendly a city offer immediate inside access to the city's social scene; there's no better way to get to know Rio than with a well-connected local. Most of the properties in Santa Teresa are reachable by tram and a number of the flats in Leblon have private parking facilities.

Rua Laurinda Santos Lobo 124, Santa Teresa 21 2225 4366 R$75–R$200 23 214 Paula Matos-Castelo

RIO HOSTEL IPANEMA

www.riohostelipanema.com

This is a small hostel in a terraced beach house, tastefully decorated with blocks of primary colour, bamboo screening and Brazilian arts and crafts. The hostel has a dormitory of between four and six beds, a double, a travel booking service and free WiFi throughout. It is close to Ipanema's Posto 9 lifeguard post.

Rua Canning Casa1, Ipanema 21 2287 2928 Dorm bed $40; Double room R$100–R$130 2 General Osório

STONE OF A BEACH HOSTEL

www.stoneofabeach.com

Party-loving young backpackers will enjoy this spacious hostel housed in one of the few old mansions still standing in Copacabana. There's a very lively bar, Bar Clandestino, which shows cult and surf films when the dance floor isn't pumping. Internet use is free and Copacabana beach is a 10-minute walk away.

Rua Barata Ribeiro 111, Copacabana 21 3209 0348 Dorm bed R$30; Double room R$130–R$150 Cardeal Arcoverde

SUN RIO

www.sunriohostel.com.br

This is much the best of a string of house-based hostels on this little avenue opposite the beach and the Pão de Açúcar, in Botafogo. Rooms and dorms are scrupulously clean, the hostel is quiet and the location excellent, less than five minutes from the metrô station and Botafogo's principal restaurants and shops.

Praia de Botafogo 462, Casa 5, Botafogo 21 2226 0461 Dorm bed R$30; Double room R$100–R$120 Botafogo

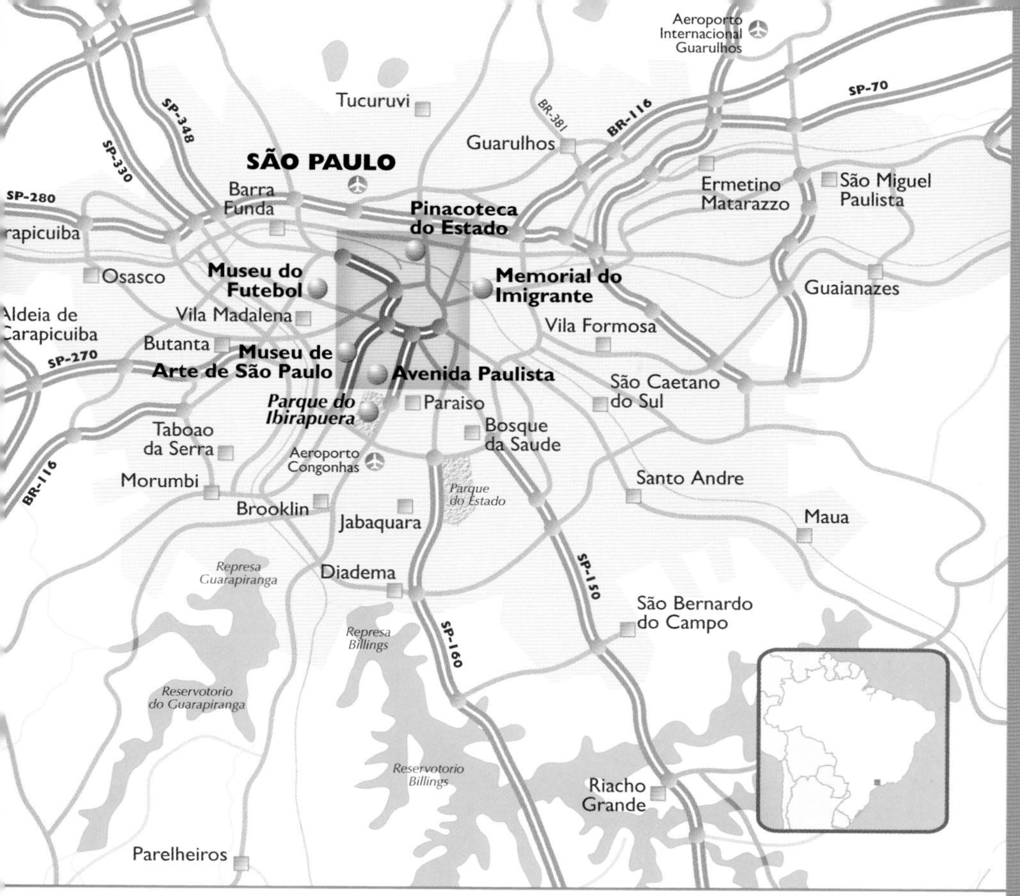

SÃO PAULO CITY

Brazil's other great metropolis is very different from Rio. There are no gorgeous balmy bays and rainforest-covered boulder mountains. São Paulo is an untidy, jagged sprawl of high-rise buildings stretching under a hot and smoggy sky to every horizon, cut by 16-lane freeways and stagnant rivers channelled into concrete gutters. São Paulo, for sure, is no beauty. Yet there are few cities as exciting or as individual.

The city sits on a high plain some 50km (30 miles) from Brazil's rainforest-shrouded Costa Verde. It began with Benedictine missionary monks in the 17th century, who hacked a trail inland and up the Serra do Mar mountains in search of indigenous converts. The remnants of their first chapel remain in the old city centre, lost in a maze of pedestrianized streets lined with museums, crumbling churches and makeshift market stalls. The imposing, modern skyscraper-lined boulevards of Avenidas Paulista, Faria Lima and Carlos Berrini stretch to the south of the old centre. This is where the city does business by day and wines, dines and dances by night in the finest and most lavish restaurants, bars and clubs south of California.

Between the museums and the business districts are a series of leafy inner city neighbourhoods, all with their own distinct identity. Jardins—the city's equivalent to London's Mayfair—is filled with chic hotels and boutiques, showcasing the best in Latin American fashion. Vila Madalena, just to the west, is younger and quirkier. Its little alleys are daubed with municipally sponsored graffiti from the same artists who painted the outside of London's Tate Modern art gallery in 2008. After dark, grungy Consolação—the new nightlife epicentre a few kilometres southwest of the old centre—jostles with thousands of young Paulistanos queuing outside a gamut of fashionable bars, lit deep velvet-red and silhouetted by heavy-set bouncers.

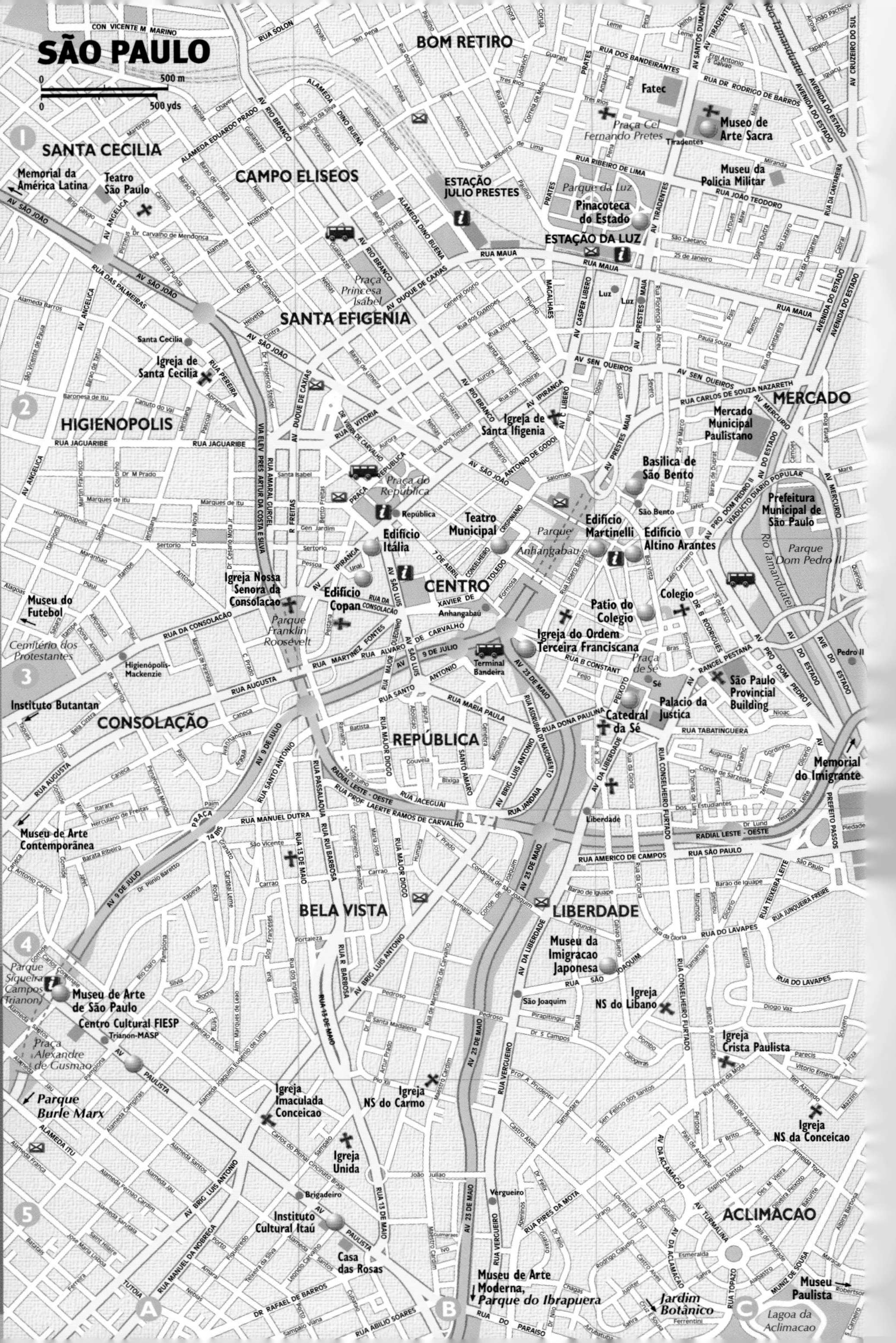

SÃO PAULO

0 500 m
0 500 yds

1
SANTA CECILIA
Memorial da América Latina
Teatro São Paulo
CAMPO ELISEOS
BOM RETIRO
ESTAÇÃO JULIO PRESTES
Fatec
Praça Cel Fernando Prestes
Museo de Arte Sacra
Museu da Policia Militar
Parque da Luz
Pinacoteca do Estado
ESTAÇÃO DA LUZ
Praça Princesa Isabel
SANTA EFIGENIA
Santa Cecilia
Igreja de Santa Cecilia
2
HIGIENOPOLIS
Igreja de Santa Ifigenia
MERCADO
Mercado Municipal Paulistano
Basilica de São Bento
Praça da República
República
Prefeitura Municipal de São Paulo
Teatro Municipal
Edifício Itália
Parque Anhangabaú
Edificio Martinelli
Edificio Altino Arantes
Parque Dom Pedro II
Rio Tamanduateí
Igreja Nossa Senora da Consolacao
Edifício Copan
CENTRO
Patio do Colegio
Colegio
Museu do Futebol
Parque Franklin Roosevelt
Igreja do Ordem Terceira Franciscana
Cemitério dos Protestantes
Higienópolis-Mackenzie
Terminal Bandeira
Praça de Sé
Sé
3
São Paulo Provincial Building
Instituto Butantan
CONSOLAÇÃO
Palacio da Justica
Catedral da Sé
REPÚBLICA
Memorial do Imigrante
Museu de Arte Contemporânea
Liberdade
BELA VISTA
LIBERDADE
4
Parque Siqueira Campos (Trianon)
Museu de Arte de São Paulo
Centro Cultural FIESP
Trianon-MASP
Museu da Imigracao Japonesa
São Joaquim
Igreja NS do Libano
Praça Alexandre de Gusmao
Igreja Crista Paulista
Parque Burle Marx
Igreja Imaculada Conceicao
Igreja NS do Carmo
Igreja NS da Conceicao
Igreja Unida
Brigadeiro
Vergueiro
5
Instituto Cultural Itaú
ACLIMACAO
Casa das Rosas
Museu de Arte Moderna, Parque do Ibrapuera
Jardim Botânico
Museu Paulista
Lagoa da Aclimacao
A
B
C

SÃO PAULO CITY STREET INDEX

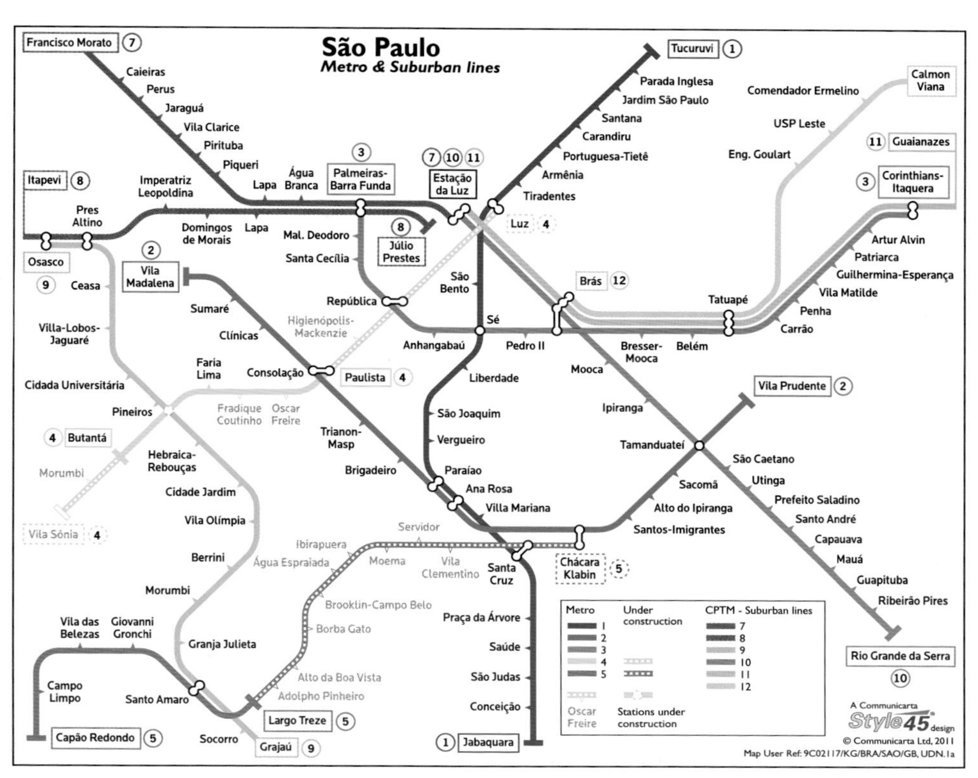

Itaú

AVENIDA PAULISTA

When Paulistanos, as the people of São Paulo city are called, compare their city with New York, they are inspired by Avenida Paulista—a long, multi-lane urban highway choked with cars and lined with towering skyscrapers. However, while New York's buildings were built by maverick business emperors with tastes for Gothic fantasy and orientalism, São Paulo's edifices are corporate and functional, impressive in scale and number more than they are architecturally. The avenue is an amazing sight, and is used as a photographic icon for the city in official publicity brochures. International tourists who come here are usually on their way merely to see MASP (▷ 116–117), which preserves the most impressive collection of European art south of the equator.

HISTORY

Until the 19th century, Paulista was fields and forest. With increasing wealth from coffee plantations and rail transport, the city rapidly began to expand and coffee barons searching for a leafy location to build their lavish mansions began to construct large houses here. By the early 20th century the avenue had become São Paulo's most desirable address and was lined with vast houses, as big as European palaces. They were in a pot-pourri of styles, reflecting the aesthetic pretensions of their owners, and ranging from neoclassical and Portuguese mock-colonial to mock-Tudor. Up until the 1950s, the street was lined with flowering tropical trees and pantile mansions. The siren of progress led to almost all of them being demolished after World War II, as was so often the case in Brazil, and by the 1960s the Avenue had lost its splendid eclectic character.

BUILDINGS OF NOTE

Only one coffee baron's mansion remains—the Casa das Rosas, a mock 19th-century French town house with a neoclassical terrace sitting in a small rose garden. The building is now a cultural centre devoted to poetry and the arts, with a display about the São Paulo poet and translator, Haroldo de Campos. There are also a handful of smaller buildings from the period on the Avenue. These include the Bank Boston building at number 800. Every December, it is tied up with ribbons to look like a cake, adorned with climbing Father Christmases. There is a small park—the Parque Tenente Siqueira Campos, which affords a tiny patch of pollution-free green, and a few other sights of note along the street: The Instituto Itaú Cultural hosts free concerts and exhibitions and is home to one of the largest currency museums in the country, the Itaú Numismática; FIESP is a state business conglomerate, with a small Centro Cultural offering free live theatre and hosting occasional art shows; and the Parque Trianon, opposite MASP, is a small area of rainforest-green lost in all the concrete. It is named in homage to the gardens of the Palace of Versailles, Paris, to which it bears no resemblance.

INFORMATION

108 A4–B5 Paraíso, Brigadeiro, Trianon-MASP

Casa das Rosas
www.casadasrosas.sp.gov.br
108 B5 Avenida Paulista 37
11 3285 6986 Tue–Fri 10–10, Sat–Sun 10–6 Free Paraíso

Instituto Itaú Cultural
www.itaucultural.org.br
108 B5 Avenida Paulista 149
11 2168 1777 Tue–Fri 10–9, Sat–Sun 10–7 Itaú Numismática currency museum R$8 Brigadeiro

Centro Cultural FIESP
www.fiesp.org.br
108 A4 Avenida Paulista 1313
11 3146 7406 Tue–Fri 10–9, Sat–Sun 10–7 Free Trianon-MASP

Parque Trianon
108 A4 Rua Peixoto Gomide at Avenida Paulista Daily 6–6 Free Trianon-MASP

TIPS

» Avenida Paulista is one of the city's most important venues for protests and celebrations. The Gay Pride march (▷ 133), city marathon (▷ 133) and New Year's Eve parties (▷ 133) take place here; the street is closed to traffic.
» The metrô is very crowded during rush hours (8–9, 5–6.30).

Opposite and above *Bustling Avenida Paulista sweeps through the city centre*

Above *The monumental Edifício Copan (left) commemorates the city's 400th anniversary*
Above right *Catedral da Sé sits on Praça da Sé, the city's largest public square*

CATEDRAL DA SÉ

This vast copper-domed church dominates the city centre's largest public square. It was designed in 1912, by Maximiliano Hell, inaugurated in the 1950s and completed with 14 spires in 2002. It is remarkable more for its size than its beauty. The exterior is a bizarre fusion of neo-Gothic and Renaissance, with a narrow nave topped by a bulbous copper-plated dome and squeezed between two enormous spires rising to 97m (318ft). The stark, rather Protestant neo-Gothic interior has space for 8,000 people. The very European stained glass was designed in Germany and Brazil, and the only obvious concessions to nationalism are the capitals, carved with Brazilian flora and fauna.

108 C3 Praça da Sé 11 3107 6832 Daily 8–7 Free Sé

EDIFÍCIO ALTINO ARANTES

This ungainly, squat homage to New York's Empire State building rises 161m (528ft) from the highest point in the city centre and has a top-floor, open-air observation platform which affords the joint-best uninterrupted views out over the sprawling city (the other notable view being from the *terraço* atop the Edifício Itália, ▷ this page). On clear days it's possible to see for 40km (25 miles). The building is more commonly known as the Edifício Banespa or Santander Cultural. Unlike the Terraço Italia, visits are free, although they are limited to five minutes, tripods are not permitted and it is not possible to visit at dusk, when the city lights twinkle to every horizon and views are at their most impressive. The building also houses a museum with a small collection of Brazilian art, including work by the Carioca social idealist, Emiliano Di Cavalcanti (1897–1976).

108 C3 Rua João Bricola 24, Sé 11 3249 7466 Mon–Fri 10–3 Free São Bento Visits are limited to 5 min and visitors need passport identification

EDIFÍCIO COPAN

www.copansp.com.br

Modernist architect Oscar Niemeyer was commissioned to design this iconic 140m-tall (459ft) concrete wave in commemoration of São Paulo's 400th birthday, in 1954. When it was finally finished in 1962 it was the largest residential building in Brazil, with 1,160 apartments and a ground floor with more than 70 shops and small businesses. Brazilian attitudes to the building are ambivalent, not least from the architect himself, who felt his original monumental vision of the building as a self-contained machine for living in had been compromised by the failure to add a theatre, massive office and gardens. Municipal authorities have used the building as a symbol of the city's modernity and prosperity, while novelist Regina Rheda described the building as being typical Niemeyer—great to photograph and lousy to live in—in her 1994 prize-winning short-story collection themed around the building, *Arca sem Noé – Histórias do Edifício Copan*.

108 B3 Avenida Ipiranga 200 República Not open to the public

EDIFÍCIO ITÁLIA AND THE TERRAÇO ITALIA

www.edificioitalia.com.br

São Paulo's other impressive city view is from the top of this giant concrete wedge next to the Edifício Copan (▷ this page). Come at dusk for the best views, when the apartment blocks and TV masts spread like dusty Lego and Meccano to every horizon, illuminated by the flash of thousands of neon signs and the light-stream of hundreds of thousands of rushing cars. The restaurant immediately below the viewing deck is remarkable only for its poor food and extortionate prices.

108 B3 Avenida Ipiranga 344, República 11 3257 6566 Daily 8–10 Viewing deck entry R$15 República Visitors need passport identification

EDIFÍCIO MARTINELLI

São Paulo's first skyscraper, which imitates apartment blocks on the Upper East Side in New York, was also the first building in South America to have more than 30 floors (it has 31 including the lobby). It was built during the Great Depression, between 1922 and 1934, and towered over the rest of the city. Locals who had never seen a skyscraper would take long detours to avoid it, believing that the building was so tall that it would collapse under its own weight.

108 C3 Avenida São João 35, Sé Anhangabaú Not open to the public

IGREJA BASILICA DE NOSSA SENHORA DE ASSUNÇÃO AND MOSTEIRO SÃO BENTO

www.mosteiro.org.br

Brazil is the only Latin American country where the Benedictine order gained a foothold in colonial times. Monks built their first church on this site in 1598, only shortly after the Jesuits had established the city, and they continue to run schools and pastoral organizations throughout the city. The current monastery church—dedicated to Our Lady of the Assumption but more often referred to simply as the monastery *(mosteiro)* by locals—is mock-medieval in style, but dating from 1914 and designed by Munich-based architect Richard Bernl. The beautifully painted Beuronese interior is by Dom Adelbert Gresnicht, a Dutch monk of the order. This style is named after techniques inspired by Eastern Orthodox iconography, developed in the late 19th century and early 20th century by Benedictines in the monastery of Beuron, in southwest Germany. The paintings in Nossa Senhora de Assunção are among the finest examples of Beuronese art in the Americas. The stained glass (and much of the statuary) is also by Dom Adelbert, with most of the windows showing scenes from the life of St. Benedict. The most beautiful, at the far end of the nave, shows Our Lady ascending to heaven, guided by the Holy Spirit in the form of a dove. The church has one of the largest organs in Brazil, which is given its own organ festival in November and December every year, when there are free recitals most lunchtimes and evenings.

108 C2 Largo São Bento, Sé 11 3328 8799 Mon–Fri 6–6, Sat–Sun 6–12, 4–6; Latin mass with Gregorian chant Sun 10am; Vespers Mon–Fri 5.25pm, Sat 5pm São Bento

IGREJA DA ORDEM TERCEIRA FRANCISCANA

This modest baroque church, hidden behind unsightly telegraph wires in a busy street, is often erroneously called 'O Convento de São Francisco' after a beautiful baroque convent that stood next door until the 1930s. This church dates from later, having an 18th-century facade facing a simple baroque interior. There are some original baroque statuary and stucco, parts of which date from the 17th century.

108 B3 Largo São Francisco 133, Sé Sé The church is currently closed, pending future restoration, and the building was condemned for its leaking roof and faulty electrics

Below *Mosteiro São Bento and its Igreja Basilica de Nossa Senhora de Assunção*

INSTITUTO BUTANTÃN

www.butantan.gov.br

Brazil is famous for its creepy-crawlies and some of the world's biggest and fiercest venomous snakes. The largest spider in the world (the bird-eating spider), which is as big as a chicken, comes from the Amazon and the *Guinness Book of Records* lists the wandering spider, which is found in São Paulo state, as the most dangerous in the world. Thankfully, the only nasty arthropods you're likely to see in São Paulo city are safely kept in pits or behind thick glass in this research institute and museum, where men in white coats milk them for their poison while kids look on in delighted horror.

108 off A3 Avenida Vital Brasil 1500 11 3726 7222 Tue–Sun 9–4 Adult R$10, child R$5, under 7 free Butantan

JARDIM BOTÂNICO

www.ibot.sp.gov.br

São Paulo's Botanical Gardens are an oasis of tropical rainforest entirely surrounded by a concrete jungle. Yet they're large enough to support wild toucans, flocks of raucous parrots and troops of howler monkeys, who roar eerily every sunset and dawn. The forest lines a series of lakes and lawns dotted with shady trees and decorative sculptures, and filled with brilliantly coloured heliconias and orchids. They are the perfect place to while away an afternoon with a stroll or a book, feeling far away from the nearby crowds. Visit on a weekday, when there's often barely another soul around.

108 off C5 Avenida Miguel Stéfano, Água Funda 11 5073 6300 Tue–Sun 9–5 Adult R$3, under 8 free São Judas

MEMORIAL DA AMÉRICA LATINA

www.memorial.org.br

This monumental complex of buildings, straddling another of São Paulo's gargantuan urban highways, was designed by Modernist architect Oscar Niemeyer in March 1989. It was built with the aim of integrating Latin American nations, culturally and politically. The memorial comprises galleries, conference spaces, a library and a parliament building, situated in huge Niemeyer concrete squares with Cyclopean scupltures (including a rather creepy open hand).

108 off A1 Avenida Mário de Andrade 664, Santa Cecilia 11 3823 4600 Tue–Fri 9–9, Sat 9–6, Sun 10–6 Free Barra Funda

MEMORIAL DO IMIGRANTE

▷ 118.

Below *Oscar Niemeyer's imposing Memorial da América Latina*

MUSEU DE ARTE CONTEMPORÂNEA (MAC)

www.mac.usp.br

Few locals know of the existence of this beautifully displayed, priceless collection of European and Latin American modern art, and even on weekends it is usually possible to have pieces by the likes of Modigliani, Picasso, Ernst and Matisse entirely to oneself. They sit alongside the best of Brazil, with work by Anita Malfatti (1889–1964), Victor Brecheret (1894–1955) and Cândido Portanari (1903–62), and three of the most important pieces by Tarsila de Amaral *(A Negra, Estrada de Ferro Central do Brasil and A Floresta)*. Amaral (1886–1973) was one of the founders of the 1930s *Antropofagia* movement (▷ 125), the first attempt to create a national artistic style. The collection is the result of a number of donations given by wealthy individuals since the early 20th century, and of prizes from São Paulo's art Biennials. It comprises some 8,000 pieces, which are rotated but which should have more gallery space when the museum moves to new facilities, closer to MAM (▷ this page), in 2011 or 2012.

108 off A4 · Rua da Reitora 160, Cidade Universitaria · 11 3091 3039 · Mon–Fri 10–6, Sat–Sun 10–4 · Free · Butantan

Right *Museu de Arte Moderna*
Below *Museu de Arte Contemporânea*

MUSEU DE ARTE MODERNA (MAM)

www.mam.org.br

As São Paulo's contemporary art museum (Museu de Arte Contemporânea, ▷ this page) showcases Modernist works, it seems fitting that its modern art museum should feature some of the best Brazilian contemporary art works. Paintings, installations and sculptures include pieces by Caetano Dias, Flàvio de Carvalho and Os Gemeos, who left their mark in late 2010 when they produced an enormous graffiti piece on the outside of the building.

The museum has a great café restaurant and a shop crammed with classy souvenirs, Brazilian art and photography books, and tasteful branded stationery.

108 off B5 · Parque do Ibirapuera, Avenida Pedro Álvares Cabral, Moema · 11 5085 1300 · Tue–Sun 10–6 · R$5.50 · Ana Rosa

MUSEU DE ARTE SACRA

www.museuartesacra.org.br

This delightful museum opposite the Pinacoteca (▷ 124–125) is often overlooked by visitors to São Paulo. Yet it is one of the finest sacred art museums in the country and a real haven from the rush of the city. The collection is housed in a large wing of one of the city's most distinguished colonial buildings, the early 19th-century Mosteiro da Luz, parts of which are still home to Conceptionist sisters. Artefacts include priceless monstrances and ecclesiastical jewellery, statuary by many of the most important Brazilian baroque masters (including Aleijadinho, Mestre Valentim and Frei Agostinho da Piedade) and by baroque master Francisco Xavier de Brito (died 1751), and painting by romantic idealist Benedito Calixto (1853–1927).

108 C1 · Avenida Tiradentes 676 · 11 3326 1373 · Adult R$5, over 60 and under 7 free · Tiradentes

MUSEU DE ARTE DE SÃO PAULO (MASP)

INFORMATION
www.masp.art.br
108 A4 Avenida Paulista 1578, Bela Vista 11 3251 5644 Tue–Sun 11–6 (except Thu 11–8); ticket office closes 30 min before closing R$15 Trianon-MASP

Above *The art museum holds renowned collections of European works*

INTRODUCTION

MASP is the most important museum in Brazil, preserving what is by far the most valuable and impressive collection of European Old Master and early Modernist paintings in the southern hemisphere. These are housed on the second floor of a striking post-modern cuboid building, by Italian architect Lina Bo Bardi, which squats on brilliant red wrap-around stilts on São Paulo's busiest commercial avenue, Avenida Paulista (▷ 111).

WHAT TO SEE

THE COLLECTION

The paintings largely reflect the taste and daring of one man: Bo Bardi's husband, Pietro Maria Bardi, an audacious, bombastic Italian naturalized as Brazilian. Bardi is surely one of the greatest art buyers of all time. Armed with money from the far-sighted media moghul, Francisco de Assis Chateaubriand Bandeira de Melo, he scouted around post World War II Europe between 1947 and 1953, and bought what are now priceless works at absurdly low prices. These include a series of 73 Degas bronzes, bought for US$45 million (today one of the pieces alone is valued at US$400 million), and Van Gogh's *The Schoolboy* and Velázquez's *Count de Olivares*, bought for a combined sum of US$80,000 and today worth in excess of US$30 million each. Rembrandts, Zurbarans, Turners, Titians, Bellinis and Raphaels followed. By the 1960s, the collection had become so important that Bardi persuaded São Paulo to build the present gallery to house it in.

The collection is extensive and, in common with many galleries worldwide, is constantly rotating as paintings are taken in and out of the archive. It can loosely be grouped by country as follows:

ITALIAN ART

The museum has 36 pre-19th-century Italian paintings. The best are Renaissance works. Seventeen date from the early Renaissance, prior to 1510, and include a run of iconographic religious works from Florence and Modena. There is a captivating portrait of St Jerome penitent in the desert by Andrea Mantegna and a Raphael resurrection. The collection also includes 10 paintings of impeccable quality covering the 150 years of Venetian painting between Bellini and Saraceni, including a magnificent Tintoretto and Titian and a Bellini Madonna and child, and a smattering of later works.

FRENCH ART AND THE PARISIAN SCHOOL

French painting dominates the MASP collection, with more than 300 works dating from the 18th century to the early 20th century. They have been masterfully assembled, with careful attention to historical unity. With a few notable exceptions (like David, Millet, Seurat and Braque) all the major artists are represented, and not just the French but those who drew influence from turn-of-the-century and early 20th-century Paris, like Van Gogh, Chagall and Picasso.

ART FROM THE IBERIAN PENINSULA AND NORTHERN EUROPE

The rest of Europe is represented with cherry-picked works from star artists. There are pieces by Dutch and Flemish artists including Holbein, Memling, Rembrandt, Bosch and Rubens, some very fine Hals and a few Franz Post Brazilian landscapes. Spanish paintings include wonderful etchings by Goya and canvases by Velázquez and El Greco. England is represented by respectable works by Constable, Gainsborough, Lawrence Reynolds and Turner.

BRAZILIAN ART

Much of MASP's national collection is archived and it cannot compare with that of Rio de Janeiro's Museu Nacional de Belas Artes (▷ 76) or the Pinacoteca (▷ 124–125). However, there are important works by Almeida Junior, Victor Brecheret, Di Cavalcanti, Tomie Ohtake and Portanari.

TIPS

» MASP is rarely crowded and you will almost always have the galleries to yourself if you visit during the week. Be aware, however, that there is no English signage, so take your phrase book if you do not speak Portuguese.

» The main galleries can be reached by lift; MASP is one of the few museums in Brazil to offer disability access.

» There is a small antiques market in the open space underneath MASP at weekends.

» The Restaurante do MASP is a good buffet restaurant (▷ 135).

Below *The light and airy galleries display the art to its best advantage*

INFORMATION

www.memorialdoimigrante.org.br
108 off C3 Rua Visconde de Parnaíba 1316, Mooca 11 2692 1866 Tue–Sun 10–5 R$6, over 60 and under 7 free Bresser

TIPS

» Tram and steam train rides operate on Sundays only. Allow an extra 30 minutes for this.
» Allow two hours for a visit, more if you go on a Sunday.
» There is an on-site café and note that picnics are not allowed in the grounds themselves.

Above *The facade of the memorial and museum*
Opposite *The main entrance to the Pacaembu stadium*

MEMORIAL DO IMIGRANTE

This memorial-come-museum is devoted to the story of European immigration into São Paulo between 1870 and 1939. It attempts to take visitors on a journey back through time and to give a real sense of what life was like for those early immigrants. The museum closed in August 2010 for a year for restoration work costing R$5 million.

PERIOD TRANSPORT

On Sundays, a 1912 tram meets visitors at Bresser metrô station, in Mooca. Trams like these plied the streets of São Paulo when the first Europeans arrived by train, from the port in Santos or from Rio. They would make their way to the Hospedaria de Imigrantes lodging house, which houses the museum today. Original locomotives and parts of the old railway station lie in the museum's grounds and it's possible to take a short steam train ride.

THE DISPLAYS

Inside the building is a series of rooms devoted to telling the story of immigrant life on the coffee plantations and in the factories of 19th- and early 20th-century São Paulo. There are replicas of rooms from a coffee *fazenda* (ranch), a simple worker's cottage, and panels and photographs profiling daily life from embarkation on the ships in Europe to the gruelling reality of the plantations in Brazil. Little is told of the hundreds of thousands of African-Brazilians who had been liberated from slavery at the time of the immigration programme (▷ 35)—and who were denied work in favour of Europeans, in what amounted to a kind of employment apartheid—but the museum is a fascinating visit nonetheless.

MUSEU DO FUTEBOL

Brazilians claim that this R$33 million museum, housed in the beautiful art deco Pacaembu Stadium, is one of the best sports museums in the world. It was inaugurated by Pelé in September 2008, who stated at the time: '*There are lots of great museums in the world: the Louvre, Madame Tussaud's, but no museum dedicated to football. I think people will be very surprised when they come here. It's very exciting.*' The museum sits in a *praça* (square) named after the Englishman who brought football to Brazil in the early 20th century, Charles Miller. Allow at least two hours to visit the museum, which is extensive.

DISPLAY GALLERIES

The World Cup, which Brazil has won more often than any other team, is the principal focus of the exhibits. One gallery is devoted to the World Cup years, profiling not just the tournament but what was happening in the world at the time and telling both stories through video footage, photographs, memorabilia and newspaper cuttings.

Another gallery profiles Brazil's greatest stars, including Garrincha, Socrates, Ronaldo (who is known as Ronaldinho or Ronaldinho Fenomeno in Brazil) and, of course, Pelé. The shirt he wore during the 1970 World Cup final—a game frequently cited as the greatest ever played—when Brazil beat Italy 4–1 to take the title for the third time, receives pride of place.

JOIN THE FUN

A third gallery is more interactive, offering visitors the chance to dribble the ball and shoot at goals. You can test your knowledge on football facts and figures, before ending your visit with an inevitable tour through a large gift shop which is well stocked with Brazilian football memorabilia.

INFORMATION

www.museudofutebol.org.br

108 off A3 Estádio do Pacaembu, Praça Charles Miller 11 3663 3848 Tue–Sun 10–5 Adult R$6, student and over 60 R$3, under 7 free. Free on Thu Clinicas (20-minute walk) Restaurants next to the museum, within the stadium

TIPS

» There is a large restaurant and sports bar next to the museum, also within Pacaembu Stadium. It serves simple dishes (chicken or meat with rice, beans and chips, and toasted sandwiches), as well as cold beer and juices. On weekend afternoons they have live music and charge a cover fee of around R$10.

» There are occasional weekend games in the football stadium. Booking is made through the individual team websites, depending on the fixture to be played.

» Team shirts are cheaper from the touts outside than from the museum shop.

Above *Display in the Museu da Imigração Japonesa*
Left *Pátio do Colégio*

MUSEU DA IMIGRAÇÃO JAPONESA

www.bunkyo.org.br

Brazil has the largest population of people of Japanese descent outside Japan. There are some 1.5 million Nikkeis or Nipo-Brasileiros in the country, the majority of them in São Paulo, Paraná and the Amazon. Over the last few decades, many have returned to Japan and there are some 300,000 or more Japanese-Brazilians, or Dekasseguis, resident there. Immigration to Brazil began on 18 June 1908, when the ship *Kasato-Maru* brought 160 families to Santos, on the coast of São Paulo. The flow reached its peak after World War I. This two-floor museum, housed in São Paulo's Japanese cultural centre, tells their story. There is a model of the *Kasato-Maru*, a replica agricultural cottage, Japanese clothing and religious items brought to Brazil, and examples of products produced in Brazil by the Japanese community. These include Brazilian sake, introduced foods which are now Brazilian staples (like soya and persimmon, which is a sweet fruit resembling a large tomato) and one of the most widely sold *cachaças* (sugar cane spirit), Ypioca.

The two countries have uniquely strong ties to this day. The museum was opened in 1978 by the then Prince and now Emperor of Japan, Akihito, as part of the 70th anniversary celebrations of Japanese immigration to Brazil.

108 C4 Rua São Joaquim 381 Third Floor, Liberdade 11 3209 5465 Tue–Sun 1.30–5.30 R$8 Liberdade There are many Japanese restaurants in the area

MUSEU DO FUTEBOL

▷ 119.

MUSEU PAULISTA (MUSEU DO IPIRANGA)

www.mp.usp.br

In 1822 a prince became an emperor here. On his way to Rio from São Paulo, which was then little more than a few buildings, Dom Pedro I shouted the *Grito de Ipiranga* (Ipiranga Cry)—'Independence or Death!' What was then a clearing next to a stream in the heart of a forest is now the inner-city suburb of Ipiranga. An enormous palace, built in 1890 in honour of Dom Pedro's *Grito*, stands at its heart, set in formal gardens. The palace is now a museum, largely devoted to the nation's history.

In reality, it houses a rather poorly kept mish-mash of exhibits ostensibly organized chronologically. These include miscellaneous pieces of colonial furniture, photographs, carriages, clothing and paintings. Pedro Américo's (1843–1905) giant canvas, *Independência ou Morte!*, depicting the young prince shouting his *Grito*, sits in the building's most handsome room of state, the Salão Nobre. The gardens follow a French renaissance style and are dotted with sculptures and monuments. These include *O Monumento à Independência*, an enormous, bombastic bronze sculpture to the nation's independence by the Italian Ettore Ximenes (1855–1926). It has a chapel in its base. Also in the grounds is the Casa do Grito—a replica of the adobe house imagined by Pedro Américo in his painting.

108 off C5 Parque da Independência s/n, Ipiranga 11 2065 8000 Tue–Sun 9–4.45 R$6; under 7 and over 60 free, and first Sun of the month free Alto do Ipiranga (20-min walk), CPTM Ipiranga (10-min walk)

PARQUE BURLE MARX

www9.prefeitura.sp.gov.br/sitesvma/100_parques

Roberto Burle Marx, who is widely considered to be South America's greatest landscape architect, was born in São Paulo in 1909. Yet aside from Ibirapuera (▷ 122–123)—which he designed with Oscar Niemeyer—these tropical gardens set in a small area of Mata Atlântica forest contain the only examples of his work in his home city. They were commissioned as the private retreat of millionaire industrialist 'Baby' Pignatari, who invited Burle Marx to fill the gardens with his sculptures. These include mirrors of water and coloured rectangular blocks decorated with abstract designs.

108 off A5 Avenida Dona Helena Pereira de Morais 200, Campo Limpo, Morumbi 11 3746 7631 Daily 7–7 R$3 Giovanni Gronchi (3km/2 miles away; taxi R$10) No refreshments available. No bicycles, skates, dogs or balls

PÁTIO DO COLÉGIO AND MUSEU PADRE ANCHIETA

www.pateocollegio.com.br

São Paulo was founded by Jesuits. On 25 January 1554 they inaugurated the Colégio de São Paulo de Piratinga on a little bluff overlooking extensive forest. That primitive wattle and daub shack, built for them by their domicile Guaraní cohorts, then became a school. That school became a church and around that church arose the city of São Paulo.

Following the edicts of the Marquês do Pombal (▷ 31) in 1760, the Jesuits were expelled from the city they founded and subsequently from Brazil, for opposing the enslavement of indigenous peoples by the São Paulo *bandeirante* slave traders. The Colégio became the seat of government of the captaincy of São Paulo, and subsequently a governors' mansion. As such, the building underwent a radical transformation in 1881. Five years later the church tower collapsed and the building, but for one piece of wall, was demolished.

When the Jesuits finally returned to São Paulo in 1954, they constructed an exact replica of their original church and college, most of which is now occupied by the Museu Padre Anchieta (named after the Jesuit priest who led the first mission). This houses, among other items, a critical painting of Anchieta's mission by Italian Albino Menghini, a 17th-century font used to baptize indigenous people, parts of the original wall, and a collection of Guaraní art and colonial relics.

108 C3 Praça Pátio do Colégio, Sé 11 3105 6899 Tue–Sun 9–5 R$5 Sé

PARQUE DO IBIRAPUERA

▷ 122–123.

PINACOTECA DO ESTADO AND ESTAÇÃO PINACOTECA

▷ 124–125.

TEATRO MUNICIPAL

www.teatromunicipal.sp.gov.br

São Paulo's grandest theatre was born of coffee baron wealth in 1911, when seeking to compete with rubber-rich Manaus (▷ 306–307) and Belém (▷ 300–303). The city built a lavish opera house and filled it with visiting European opera and ballet stars. One of the foremost Brazilian civic architects of the time, Ramos de Azevedo, was commissioned to design the building, and he built what he imagined to be a replica of the recently completed Palais Garnier, in Paris. That building's sheer size makes the bombastic Beaux Arts architecture impressive, but Ramos's building is tiny by comparison and seems like an architectural mouse that roars, with a fusion of neoclassical and Romanesque, topped with pompous baroque statues. The interior is more impressive, including a painted foyer illuminated with tall art nouveau arched windows and a beautiful concert hall, where the likes of Callas, Caruso, Toscanini, Pavlova and Nureyev have performed. The theatre continues to present artists of this calibre today.

108 B3 Praça Ramos de Azevedo, Centro 11 3223 3022 Daily 9–5 R$3 Anhangabaú

Below *The ornamented Teatro Municipal*

INFORMATION

www.parquedoibirapuera.com

108 off B5 Avenida Pedro Álvares Cabral s/n, Moema 11 5573 4180 Daily 5am–midnight Ana Rosa

INTRODUCTION

The tree-lined avenues and fountain-filled gardens of Ibirapuera Park offer one of the few green escapes from the concrete and cars in the centre of the city, and are great for a wander in the heat of the day. The park is dotted with museums, recreation spaces and architectural gems from the father of Latin American Modernism, Oscar Niemeyer.

WHAT TO SEE

NIEMEYER BUILDINGS

The most striking of the Niemeyer buildings are the wedge-shaped Auditório Ibirapuera (www.auditorioibirapuera.com.br) and the Oca, a brilliant-white dome ringed with porthole windows and sitting in the centre of a Modernist sculpture garden. The building serves as one of the city's major show rooms, especially for international exhibitions. Niemeyer's long, oblong Fundação Bienal (http://fbsp.org.br) sits opposite the Oca. São Paulo's twice-annual fashion week, and art and architecture biennials both take place here.

MUSEU AFRO-BRASIL

www.museuafrobrasil.com.br

Next to them is the Museu de Arte Moderna (MAM, ▷ 115). A covered concrete walkway leads from there to the park's largest museum, the Museu Afro-Brasil, which opened in 2004 and which has established itself as the most important centre for the study of African-Brazilian culture in Brazil outside Salvador. Museum exhibitions are devoted to the history, art, culture and music of African-Brazilian people. There are many photographs, paintings, sculptures and artefacts on display, including the hull of a slave ship, early African-Brazilian textiles and ritual items from the African-Brazilian spirit religion of *candomblé*. Displays are constantly updated and changed as the museum continues to add to its collection.

11 4004 5006 Tue–Sun 10–5 R$6

Above *The Fundação Bienal, designed by Modernist architect Oscar Niemeyer*

PLANETARIUM AND JAPANESE PAVILION

www.prefeitura.sp.gov.br/astronomia
www.parquedoibirapuera.com/pavilhao-japones.php

Less than 100m (110 yards) from the Museu is the Planetário Professor Aristóteles Orsini (tel 11 5575 5206; Fri–Sun 12–7; R$5), a newly refurbished planetarium. It features state-of-the-art Star Master equipment by Carl Zeiss, which projects star patterns onto the domed ceiling to re-create the night sky. Next to this is the Pavilhão Japonês (tel 11 5081 7296; Wed, Sat–Sun and holidays 10–12, 1–5; free), a reproduction of the Palácio Katsura, in Tokyo. It was built in Japan and re-assembled on the shore of the park's largest artificial lake, which dominates the centre of the park. The downstairs hall is an exhibition space devoted to Japanese and Japanese-Brazilian culture. Upstairs is a display of a traditional Japanese tearoom.

MORE TO SEE

STATUES AND MONUMENTS

Ibirapuera is dotted with statues and monuments. The *Monumento às Bandeiras* (Bandeiras Monument) is a brutalist art deco reminder of the *bandeirante* slave traders (▷ 28), by Brazil's foremost 20th-century sculptor, Victor Brecheret. The *bandeirantes* are associated with the city: Most expeditions left São Paulo in the 18th and early 19th century to pillage indigenous villages, search for gold and thence open up the interior of Brazil and establish the country's borders. The huge Cleopatra's needle which stands over the park near the Oca is the *Obelisco aos Herois de 32*, and is built in homage to the Paulistanos who died resisting the rise of Getúlio Vargas's *Estado Novo* regime. Above the entrance to the Sena Madureira road tunnel, which runs under Ibirapuera, is a Modernist monument to former Formula One champion Ayrton Senna, who died in a crash at the San Marino Grand Prix in 1994. Entitled *Velocidade, Alma e Emoção (Speed, Soul and Emotion)*, by Paulista artist Melinda Garcia, it is a bronze of a Formula One car on a plinth, which seems to explode into curling flame as you look at it from behind. It once had a flag in the cockpit, but this was stolen by vandals shortly after the sculpture's inauguration.

TIPS

» There are several restaurants and cafés in the park. These range from cheap stalls selling sugar cane juice and sandwiches, to buffet restaurants and chic, air-conditioned spaces like the café-restaurant in MAM.

» Bicycles can be rented in the park from vendors who operate stalls near the running track (Pista do Coopers).

» Fundação Bienal opens for exhibitions only. Tickets can be purchased at the Bienal box office on the southern side of the building.

» The Planetarium's monthly programme of events is announced on its website.

Left *Relaxing in Ibirapuera Park*
Below *Sculpture in front of the Oca*

PINACOTECA DO ESTADO AND ESTAÇÃO PINACOTECA

INFORMATION

www.pinacoteca.org.br
108 C1 Pinacoteca do Estado, Praça da Luz, Luz 11 3324 0933 Tue–Sun 10–6 Adult R$6; under 10 and over 60 free; Sat free Metrô Luz, CPTM Luz Art bookshop

Above *The neoclassical facade of the Pinacoteca dates from 1900*

INTRODUCTION

After the Museu Nacional de Belas Artes in Rio (▷ 76), the Pinacoteca holds the most distinguished collection of Brazilian art in the country. Their archive of some 5,000 works includes pieces by most of the country's major artists, from the earliest colonial times to the end of the 20th century, and all of the significant artistic movements.

These are shown in rotation in a large museum which was fully refurbished and remodelled in the mid-1990s by the Pritzker Prize-winning architect, Paulo Mendes da Rocha. Rocha completely gutted the interior of the original neoclassical building, leaving only its shell. He then filled the remaining arena with carefully positioned partitions and capped it with a translucent roof. The result is a gallery with a wonderful feeling of space and light. The gallery sits in one of the city centre's prettiest parks, the Parque da Luz. This is shaded with stately palms and decorated with ornamental ponds and sculptures.

WHAT TO SEE

THE COLLECTION

The paintings on display are grouped in galleries which combine works of historical interest (but dubious artistic pedigree) with world-class paintings and sculptures. This reflects the development of Brazilian art, climaxing in the mature and independent national styles of the 20th century. These latter works include pieces by Brazilian Modernists, including Tarsila do Amaral (1886–1973). Temporary exhibitions are held for three months on the basement floor, next to a gallery showcasing contemporary photography.

The Pinacoteca preserves some important landmark works in the history of Brazilian painting. Almeida Junior's (1850–99) *Caipira Picando Fumo* was one of the first paintings to capture everyday Brazilian life and depict the country's rich tropical light. Anita Malfatti's (1889–1964) *Tropical*—showing a peasant woman bearing a tray of exotic fruit—was one of the first examples of Brazilian Modernism. Malfatti's contemporary, Tarsila do Amaral (1886–1973), has several paintings in the Modernist section of the gallery. She drew on painting and literary styles that were not specifically European, and worked with indigenous Brazilian themes, both from the natural and ethnological world. She was one of the founders of the *Antropofagia* movement (▷ this page). Other important Brazilian artists represented include the art deco sculptor Victor Brecheret (1894–1955), Modernist muralist and social realist painter Cândido Portanari (1903–62) and abstract artist Alfredo Volpi (1896–1988).

MORE TO SEE

ESTAÇÃO PINACOTECA

The Pinacoteca's sister gallery holds the most important painting by Tarsila do Amaral, *Antropofagia* (1929). As well as being the name of a painting, *Antropofagia* was the moniker of the country's first artistic movement, named in homage to the Tupi cannibals who consumed (and were consumed by) the Portuguese. *Antropofagia* sought to do the same with European and American art. The movement's manifesto was published by Tarsila's lover Oswald de Andrade in 1928 and included the memorable third sentence: *'Tupi or not Tupi; that is the question.'*

The Estação Pinacoteca sits in the former headquarters of the Departamento Estadual de Ordem Politica e Social do Estado de São Paulo (DEOPS/SP), the military secret police. Thousands of local people were tortured and killed in the building between 1940 and 1983. The Memorial da Resistência de São Paulo museum on the ground floor tells their story through panels, documents and photographs, and demonstrates how the CIA were complicit in supporting DEOPS activities.

108 B1 · Estação Julio Prestes, Largo General Osório 66, Luz · 11 3337 0185
Tue–Sun 10–5.30 · R$6 · Luz, CPTM Luz

TIPS

» The Pinacoteca is free for all entrants on Saturday.

» There is no admission fee for the Memorial da Resistência and the Pinacoteca ticket also allows entrance into its sister gallery, so visit the Pinacoteca first to enjoy all the sights of the Estação Pinacoteca for free.

» The Pinacoteca café is a great spot for a light lunch. It serves a selection of sandwiches and pastries, together with delicious juices and coffee, and overlooks the Luz gardens.

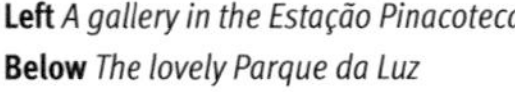

Left *A gallery in the Estação Pinacoteca*
Below *The lovely Parque da Luz*

THE CITY CENTRE

This walk includes most of the sights in São Paulo's old city centre, beginning at the huge 19th-century cathedral and finishing with a view over the megalopolis from one of its tallest buildings.

THE WALK
Distance: 4km (2.5 miles)
Time: 4 hours including visits
Start at: Praça da Sé ✚ 108 C3
End at: Praça da República ✚ 108 B2

HOW TO GET THERE
Metrô to Sé.

★ Start in the main square, outside the Catedral da Sé (▷ 112).

❶ The Praça da Sé is the largest square in central São Paulo. It is dominated by the huge early 20th-century cathedral and is always busy with street sellers and evangelists. The cathedral crypt contains the tomb of the Tupi chief, Tibiriçá, who made peace with the Jesuits and helped form the city of São Paulo.

Leave from the northeastern corner of the Praça da Sé along Rua Floriano Peixoto. Turn left after a few metres into Rua Boa Vista, crossing Rua Anchieta after about 50m (55 yards) and entering the Largo Pátio do Colégio.

❷ The Pátio do Colégio (▷ 121) includes some remnants of the monastery founded by the Jesuit Padre Anchieta in 1554, when São Paulo was still rainforest. The city grew from this site.

Cross the street from here on Rua Anchieta and turn immediately right into Rua Quinze de Novembro, continuing straight ahead until you reach the junction with Rua da Quitanda.

❸ Here you will find the Centro Cultural Banco do Brasil (www.bb.com.br). There is always an interesting art exhibition here and the building has a beautiful art deco atrium, cinema and theatre.

Continue for 100m (109 yards) along Rua Quinze de Novembro, to the corner of Rua João Bricola.

❹ The observation deck at the top of Edifício Altino Arantes (▷ 112) is the highest point in the area, offering spectacular views of the city. Visits are limited to five minutes and you will need to show your passport to enter the building.

Continue north along Rua João Bricola to the corner of Rua Boa

Opposite *Vale do Anhangabaú*
Below right *Igreja de Santo Antônio, the city's oldest church*

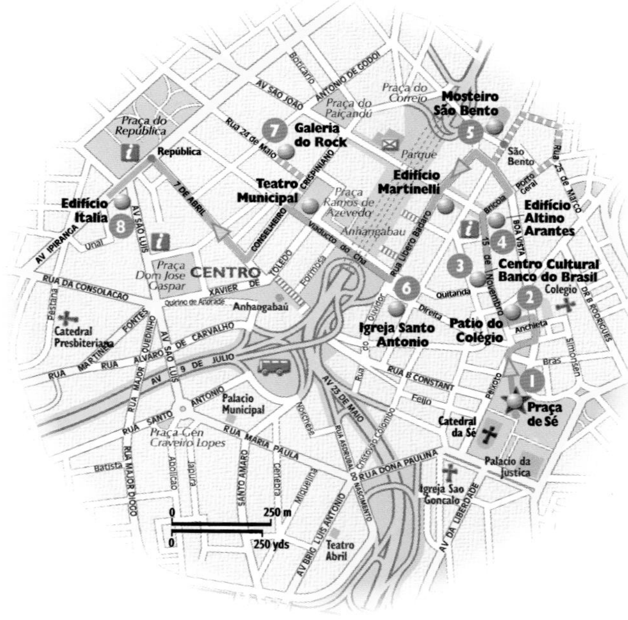

Vista, cross the street onto the Ladeira Porto Geral, one of the entrance points to the Rua 25 de Marco commercial area. Continue north on Rua Boa Vista to the Largo de São Bento.

❺ After an optional shop stop in the Rua 25 de Março (▷ 130), visit the peaceful interior of the Benedictine Mosteiro São Bento (▷ 113), which has some of the most beautiful church paintings in São Paulo.

Walk south for 500m (550 yards) along Rua Libero Badaró to the junction with Rua da Quitanda, passing the city's first skyscraper, the Edifício Martinelli (▷ 113), at Avenida São João 35.

❻ The Igreja de Santo Antônio in the Praça do Patriarca, on the corner of Rua Libero Badaró and Rua Direita, is the oldest church in the city. It dates from 1592, although much of what you see today is from reforms in 1717 and 1899. It was restored in 2005 and has a lovely tranquil interior with a modest baroque altarpiece.

Turn west and walk across the iron Viaduto do Chá for views of the Edifício Martinelli, the Vale do Anhangabaú and the Teatro Municipal (▷ 121). Turn left (south) onto Rua Conselheiro Crispiniano and the main shopping thoroughfare in this part of the city centre.

❼ If you have time, pop around the corner to one of the best places in the city to buy Brazilian music—the Galeria do Rock (Mon–Fri 7.30–7.30, Sat 7.30–6), which you can reach by turning right on Rua Conselheiro Crispiniano and immediately left onto Rua 24 de Maio. The Galeria do Rock is at No. 62.

Walk to the end of Rua Conselheiro Crispiniano and turn left onto Rua Sete de Abril, continuing 100m (109 yards) west to the Praça da República. Turn left here and walk for 100m (109 yards) to Avenida Ipiranga.

❽ The Edifício Itália (▷ 112) at Avenida Ipiranga, which overlooks Oscar Niemeyer's Edifício Copan (▷ 112) next door, is the tallest building in the city. Aim to be here for sunset for spectacular views from the Terraço Italia restaurant and viewing deck on the top floor.

Return to the Praça da República and catch a metrô at República station.

WHEN TO GO

Begin after lunch to walk off the meal, avoid the hottest part of the day and enjoy the sunset view at your destination.

WHERE TO EAT

PONTO CHIC

This corner restaurant is always busy at lunchtimes, when businessmen gather to eat São Paulo's equivalent of the hamburger, the *bauru*. The dining room is air-conditioned, offering respite from the heat of the day before you begin your walk

✉ Largo do Paissandu 27, Centro ☎ 11 3222 6528 🕘 Mon–Sat 7am–12pm 💳 From R$12 Ⓜ República

TIPS

» Check the Banco do Brasil website for details of lunchtime concerts.
» The Pátio do Colégio has a pleasant open-air café with a view out over central São Paulo. It makes a good coffee or cold juice stop.
» You will need passport identification to climb to the Edifício Itália viewing deck (admission R$15). The Terraço Italia restaurant below the deck has a cover charge of around R$10 per person for drinking even a beer or a coffee and, although the food is poor, it is worth it for the view.

SHOPPING

ANTÔNIO BERNARDO

www.antoniobernardo.com

Bernardo's largest São Paulo shop, in Jardins, has one of the most comprehensive selections of his elegant, understated gold and platinum jewellery outside the flagship Garcia d'Avila store in Rio de Janeiro (▷ 92). There are branches in other locations across the city detailed on the company website.

Rua Bela Cintra 2063, Jardins 11 3083 5622 Mon–Fri 10–8, Sat 10–5 Consolação

BENEDITO CALIXTO MARKET

www.pracabeneditocalixto.com.br

There are some 320 stalls selling bric-a-brac, antiques, vintage clothing and rare vinyl in this leafy square near Vila Madalena every Saturday throughout the year. Between 2.30 and 6.30 there's live *choro* and samba *canção* music, with extemporaneous street dancing and dozens of stalls selling a selection of food and drinks.

Praça Benedito Calixto, Pinheiros Sat 9–7 Pinheiros

BRÁS

www.alobras.com.br

Brazil's largest wholesale market proffers items of clothing by the dozen for trade buyers during the week and in smaller numbers for everyday customers on Saturdays, when the market bursts with people. There are hundreds of small shops and stalls in 55 streets, mostly selling poor quality T-shirts, jeans, children's clothes and general garments, but with the occasional bargain for those with a good eye for quality. The hunting is the fun.

Largo da Concordia, Brás 11 2694 0823 Usually Mon–Sat 8–6 Brás

CIDADE JARDIM

www.shoppingcidadejardimjhsf.com.br

A vast neoclassical edifice with a verdant tropical garden in its interior is topped with towering skyscraper apartment blocks. This shopping centre is filled with Brazilian and international names, from Carlos Miele and Osklen to Armani and Hermes. There's a members-only spa, too, a cinema and restaurants by Fasano and Kosushi.

Avenida Magalhães de Castro 12000 11 3552 1000 Mon–Sat 10–10, Sun 2–8 Berrini (from Estação da Luz station)

CONCEITO FIRMA CASA

www.conceitofirmacasa.com.br

One of the city's top homeware design stores, representing, among others, the Campana Brothers (who have had furniture shown at MOMA in New York). The wood slat *favela* (slum) chairs that first brought them international renown are now manufactured by Edra in Italy, together with their much-vaunted PVC hose and stainless steel Anemone chairs, and are unavailable here. However, this shop has a line of chairs unavailable outside Brazil.

Alameda Gabriel Monteiro da Silva 1487, Jardins 11 3068 0377 Mon–Sat 10–6 Oscar Freire

CRIS BARROS

www.crisbarros.com.br

This society fashion designer's flagship showroom opened in May 2008. It's a cavernous white cube, dominated by a wall covered with a

Opposite *Benedito Calixto is a large and lively market*

filigree of thousands of verdant, but artificial tropical vines. They perfectly offset Barros's formal womenswear collection, which mixes a range of disparate styles, from Brazilian beach to Asianesque and evening gown to girl about town.
Rua Vitório Fasano 85, Jardins 11 3082 3621 Mon–Fri 10–8, Sat 10–6 Consolação

DASLU

www.daslu.com.br
São Paulo's equivalent of New York's Barney's or London's Harrods is a temple to wanton consumerism, showcasing the best of the city's upmarket fashion under one roof. Village Daslu, which opened in early 2008, features the cream of São Paulo's young designers, including Cris Barros and Raia de Goeye dresses, the neo-nostalgic belle époque whimsy of Adriana Barra and jerseywear from exciting newcomer, Juliana Jabour. Daslu offers an exclusive lifestyle experience, ensuring that visitors can climb in and out of their air-conditioned limos confident that they need never sully the soles of their designer shoes with the outside world.
Avenida Chedid Jafet 131, Itaim Bibi 11 3841 4000 Mon–Sat 10–8 (Tue until 10) Vila Olímpia

DONA PINK

www.donapink.com.br
The flagship store of this funky young fashionista label opened in 2005, showcasing Paulistana designer Luciana Papaspyrou's light patchwork, stamped cotton and gauze party dresses, which are popular with the city's twenty- and thirty-something clubbers.
Rua Harmonia 218, Vila Madalena 11 3032 8227 Mon–Sat 10–6 Vila Madalena

DPOT

www.dpot.com.br
Modernist leather and stainless steel furniture by the best Brazilian designers, including Pritzker Prize-winning architect Paulo Mendes da Rocha, whose work includes the transformation of the Pinacoteca do Estado (▷ 124–125).
Alameda Gabriel Monteiro da Silva 1250, Jardins 11 3082 9513 Mon–Sat 10–6 Oscar Freire

ETEL INTERIORES

www.etelinteriores.com.br
Etel Carmona's chunky, rustic-chic Tucano dining tables—hewn from a vast block of sustainably sourced Amazon hardwood—sit alongside sleek, low-slung glossy hardwood *Zezinho* sideboards by designer of the moment, Isay Weinfeld (whose furnishings can be found in the Fasano hotel ▷ 136). Thankfully there are some smaller household items, including exquisite hardwood ornaments, which will easily fit in the average suitcase.
Alameda Gabriel Monteiro da Silva 1834, Jardins 11 3064 1266 Mon–Sat 10–6 Oscar Freire

FNAC

www.fnac.com.br
The large FNAC stores are Brazil's answer to Waterstones or Barnes and Noble, with the broadest and most upmarket selections of books, DVDs and CDs in the city. There are branches throughout São Paulo, but the shop on Avenida Paulista is the largest.
Avenida Paulista 901, Bela Vista 11 4003 9595 Mon–Sat 10–10, Sun 10–8 Trianon-MASP

HERCHCOVITCH

herchcovitch.uol.com.br
Alexandre Herchcovitch's cool suits and trademark skull-print shirts have walked the runways of New York, London and Paris fashion weeks. This popular designer has an enormous store in Japan, where he is something of a fashion icon, but this is his flagship outlet and it still sells more of his annual collections than any other.
Rua Haddock Lobo 1151, Jardins 11 3063 2888 Mon–Sat 10–6 Consolação

LUMINI

www.lumini.com.br
This lighting store specializes in cool shades (for lamps) and light fittings, and counts among their clients the hot architect Marcio Kogan, responsible for the exterior of the Fasano and one of the most internationally talked-about South American beach houses, the Casa du Plessis, in the exclusive Laranjeiras condominium in Rio. The store won a gold medal in 2008 from the Industrial Designers Society of America for their Super Bossa ceiling lamp, which is an energy-efficient half-moon with a shade that adjusts for light intensity operated by a simple pull mechanism.
Alameda Gabriel Monteiro Silva 1441, Jardins 11 3898 0222 Mon–Fri 9.30–7, Sat 10–2 Oscar Freire

MERCADO MUNICIPAL

www.mercadomunicipal.com.br
This gorgeous art deco covered market in the city centre was built at the height of the coffee boom and is graced with stunning stained glass windows celebrating the dignity of the worker, by Conradao Sorgenicht Filho (1869–1935). It's worth coming just for a wander through aisles bursting with produce: fresh fruit from the Amazon, salted cod from the North Sea, Brazilian parmesan and mozzarella from Minas, legs of pork and beef, juicy olives and myriad other foodstuffs. On the upper gallery are a series of restaurants offering good-value dishes of the day and giving the perfect vantage point on the hustle and bustle below.
Rua da Cantareira 306, Centro 11 3326 3401 Mon–Sat 6–6, Sun 6–4 São Bento

OLÁ

www.olaloja.com.br
Here you will find modish hand-crafted neo art nouveau decorative objects, lampshades and assorted household items crafted by a local designer, Vera Madeira.
Rua Fradique Coutinho 1340, Vila Madalena 11 3815 2549 Mon–Fri 10–7, Sat 10–6 Vila Madalena

RONALDO FRAGA

www.ronaldofraga.com

Fraga earned his design stripes at the boundary-pushing Parsons and Central Saint Martins schools in New York and London. His collection of bright natural materials for men and women combines discipline with daring, retaining a unified style across the sexes yet always surprising and delighting with its off-the-wall creativity. Clogs look like VW Beetles—and even come with little windshields—and his handmade light cotton, one-of-a-kind, off-the-shoulder *blusas devorê* tops are coveted fashion items among the young Paulistanos.

✉ Rua Aspicuelta 259, Vila Madalena ☎ 11 3816 2181 🕓 Mon–Sat 10–6 🚇 Vila Madalena

RUA 25 DE MARÇO

www.vitrine25demarco.com.br

Not all fashion in São Paulo comes at designer prices. Most Paulistanos looking for cool but affordable cuts come to this vast outdoor market, which takes up eight city blocks. Shops and stalls here offer everything from catwalk copies and counterfeit watches to Y-fronts, costume jewellery and even electronics.

✉ Rua 25 de Março, Centro ☎ 11 3227 1473 🕓 Mon–Sat 5–4 🚇 São Bento

SANTA PACIÊNCIA

www.santapaciencia.com.br

This store sells some of the prettiest children's clothes in the city, all hand made in Brazil from designs by Erika Palomino, inspired by rural France. Clothes for little boys and girls (from two-year-olds to larger children) come in tropical colours but with Provençal styling.

✉ Rua Girassol 223a, Vila Madalena ☎ 11 3814 9188 🕓 Mon–Sat 10–6 🚇 Vila Madalena

SHOPPING IBIRAPUERA

www.ibirapuera.com.br

This mid-market mall has some 400 boutiques, including many of Brazil's solid brands, like M Officer, Forum, Iodice and MOB (all fashionable for jeans), Natura and Boticário (Brazil's Body Shop equivalents) and H. Stern for jewellery.

✉ Avenida Ibirapuera 3103, Moema ☎ 11 5095 2300 🕓 Mon–Sat 10–10, Sun 2–8 🚇 Ana Rosa, with connecting bus 695V 🍴 Large food court serves expensive snacks and meals

UMA

www.uma.com.br

Raquel Davidowicz's principal boutique has rails of sleek contemporary women's blouses, skirts, dresses, and men's jeans and shirts set against low-lit, cool white walls. Her look is chic and strongly influenced by Japanese design. A popular line of dresses are made of shiny, Tricoline *elastano* that feels like a silky smooth polyester-lycra hybrid, woven like fine silk, or of organic white cotton treated to give permanent waves and crimps. There in another outlet in Jardins and a showroom in Pacaembu.

✉ Rua Girassol 273, Vila Madalena ☎ 11 3813 5559 🕓 Mon–Sat 10–6 🚇 Vila Madalena

VARTANIAN

www.jackvartanian.com

Jack Vartanian makes Brazilian jewellery at its most ostentatious, with huge chunks of precious rock set in simple gold and platinum. His upmarket bling has been touted around Hollywood red carpets by the likes of Zoe Saldana, Cameron Diaz and Demi Moore. His low-lit Jardins showroom, which looks like a giant post-modern lacquer box (with black *faux*-ebony polished wooden facing and dark, velvety carpets) offsets collections of jewellery that are available only in Brazil.

✉ Rua Haddock Lobo 1592, Jardins ☎ 11 3062 2349 🕓 Mon–Sat 10–6 🚇 Consolação

ENTERTAINMENT AND NIGHTLIFE

A MARCENARIA

www.amarcenaria.com.br

Vila Madalena's rock and Brazilian funk club is housed in a former carpenter's workshop and yard, packed with thirty-something revellers from 11pm until the early hours each weekend night.

✉ Rua Fradique Coutinho 1378, Vila Madalena ☎ 11 3032 9006 🕓 Thu–Sat 8–late 🎟 Shows from R$20 🚇 Vila Madalena

BAMBU

www.bambubrasilbar.com.br

This funky little *forró* dance bar and restaurant in the heart of Vila Madalena serves strong *caipirinhas* (sugar cane spirit and fresh lime cocktails) and northeastern campfire cooking. It has a great, informal atmosphere, upper-middle class arty crowd and live bands every weekend.

✉ Rua Purpurina 272, Vila Madalena ☎ 11 3031 2331 🕓 Thu–Sat 8–late 🚇 Vila Madalena

BARRETO

www.fasano.com.br

Heavy dark woods, choice brandies and Cuban cigars are on offer in the city's most upmarket hotel bar, to the accompaniment of live *bossa nova* (new wave) and Brazilian jazz. Barreto is on the ground floor of the Fasano hotel (▷ 136).

✉ Rua Vitorio Fasano 88, Jardins ☎ 11 3069 4369 🕓 Mon–Fri 7pm–3am, Sat 8pm–3am 🚇 Oscar Freire

BAR VOLT

www.barvolt.com.br

This long concrete room, lit by strips of multi-coloured neon and filled with a fashionable creative industry crowd, buzzes on any night of the week and is a favourite pre-club watering hole at weekends.

✉ Rua Haddock Lobo 40, Consolação ☎ 11 2936 4041 🕓 Tue, Wed 7.30pm–1am, Thu 7.30–2, Fri–Sat 7.30–3 🚇 Consolação

BOURBON STREET

www.bourbonstreet.com.br

A medium-sized show hall, with a dining area serving bar snacks and comfort food, which is cleared for dancing later in the evening, and an upper gallery with great views of the stage. It plays host to medium-sized up-and-coming São Paulo performers, like MPB singer Luciana

Above *A street market in São Paulo*
Left *Vila Madalena has many bars promoting live music*

Mello and samba-funkster Tutti Baê, alongside some international acts.
Rua dos Chanés 127, Moema 11 5095 6100 Tue–Thu & Sun 8–late, Fri–Sat 9–late; Shows usually begin at 10.30 Shows from R$15

CASA DE FRANCISCA

www.casadefrancisca.art.br

The Casa is an intimate, live music café-bar. It plays host to acts like virtuoso guitarist and composer Chico Saraíva, multi-instrumentalist Artur de Faria, or pianist Paulo Braga.
Rua José Maria Lisboa 190, off Avenida Brigadeiro Luís Antônio 11 3493 5717 Tue–Sat 8–late Brigadeiro

DIQUINTA

www.diquinta.com.br

Come here between Thursday and Saturday for some of the best small samba-funk acts on the São Paulo circuit, with names like Farofyno and Funk Como le Gusta. Located near Vila Madalena.
Rua Baumann 1435, Vila Leopoldina 11 5506 0100 Thu–Sat 8–late From R$20 Jaguaré

DRY BAR

www.drybar.com.br

The city's young and rich come to this low-lit, dark bar with walls lined with black pool-table balls, to drink from a menu of more than a dozen dry martinis and many upmarket *petiscos* (bar snacks). Make sure you dress to impress.
Rua Padre João Manuel 700, Jardins 11 3729 6653 Tue–Sat 9–2 Oscar Freire

ESCAPE

www.escapebar.com.br

One of a spate of new cocktail bars serving superb drinks in a slick modern space, which trebles up as a restaurant and an after-hours club. The crowd is resolutely middle-class professional and aged from late twenties to mid-forties.
Rua Jerônimo da Veiga 163, Itaim Bibi 11 3071 1526 Thu–Sat 8.30–late Cidade Jardim

GRAZIE A DIO

www.grazieadio.com.br

This very popular and fashionable Vila Madalena restaurant and club-bar has live music from Tuesdays to Sundays. Music tends to be up-tempo, and is played by some of the best local and visiting acts, including bands like Mombojo—the new post-Mangue Beat sensation from Recife—and Clube do Balanço, and established acts like Banda Black Rio.
Rua Girassol 67, Vila Madalena 11 3031 6568 Tue–Sun 8–late; Shows start at 10.30 R$20 Oscar Freire

MOKAI

www.mokai.com.br

This long concrete rectangle, opened in 2010, is lit by a twinkling 50sq m (550sq ft) LED ceiling. Owned by fashion impresario Amir Slama and millionaire playboy Rico Mansur, it is one of upmarket São Paulo's clubs of the moment. There is a strict door policy. Book ahead through a concierge if possible and dress in designer labels.
Rua Augusta 2805, Jardins 11 3081 3103 Thu–Sat 11–late R$80 Oscar Freire

SESC

www.sesesp.com.br

These arts centres and concert halls dotted around the city (and the country) play host to some of the most interesting medium-sized acts in Brazil. They stage formal sit-down concerts in excellent theatres with great sound systems. There is always a tempting show on somewhere—usually at SESC Pompeia or Vila Mariana—from artists like Seu Jorge, Chico Buarque and Egberto Gismonti. Check website for the nearest SESC centre.

STUDIO SP

www.studiosp.org

This great little concert hall bar is one of the best venues in the city to see up-and-coming and alternative acts, like Renato Godá (a kind of Brazilian vaudeville Tom Waits), Trash pour Quatro (who offer *bossa nova* reworkings of kitsch classics like *Material Girl*, in the spirit of Berk & The Virtual Band), Andreia Dias (who has the audience swooning with smoky, seductive electronica mixed with lilting Brazilian rhythms) or harder Mangue Beat acts like Mombojo, from Pernambuco.

Rua Augusta 591, Consolação 11 3129 7040 Tue–Sat 10–late Shows from R$20 Consolação

THE WEEK

www.theweek.com.br

One of the city's biggest and most pumping clubs attracts a mixed gay and straight crowd to its 6,000sq m (64,500sq ft) of dance floor, especially for the Saturday night Babylon party. There's even a pool in the club for when things get too steamy.

Rua Guaicurus 324, Lapa 11 3872 9966 Wed–Sat 10–late From R$30 Estação da Água Branca

SPORTS AND ACTIVITIES

B360 TRAVEL

www.b360travel.com

Private concierge duo Paula Linhares and Chris Bicalho of b360 pride themselves in providing tailor-made packages encompassing São Paulo city high-life. These can include fully prepared itineraries in hotels or private flats, the best restaurants and clubs, photo shoots with a top São Paulo fashion photographer or simply help in getting access to exclusive parties or events.

Avenida Brigadeiro Faria Lima 1713, 14th Floor 11 3038 1515 Mon–Fri 10–6 577T-10, 715M-10, 8700-10

EXERCISE IN THE PARK

www.parquedoibirapuera.com

Ibirapuera park—the most significant green space in the city centre—has a running track (Pista de Coopers) in shady woods near Portão 6. Open-air gyms with exercise machines and pull-up bars line the running track route. They are best used between 7am and dusk to ensure users' personal safety.

Avenida Pedro Álvares Cabral 11 5574 5177 Daily 5am–12pm Free Ana Rosa

FOOTBALL

São Paulo's answer to Rio's Maracanã stadium (▷ 65) is the 80,000-seater Morumbi Arena, which is home to São Paulo football club and which hosts state championships. It will be one of the stadiums used for the major World Cup matches in 2014. The best seats are in the middle-tier private boxes, which can cost up to R$120 per person for a big match.

Praça Roberto Gomes Pedrosa 1 11 3749 8000 Match tickets R$30–R$120 765A-10

FORMULA ONE

www.gpbrasil.com.br

The Brazilian Grand Prix is held in São Paulo at the Interlagos track in the far south of the city every October or November. It is difficult to imagine a noisier or more exciting spectator event. Tickets should be booked 3–6 months in advance through the race track itself.

Autodromo de Interlagos, Avenida Senador Teotonio Vilela 261 11 5041 3233 From R$300 per day Autodromo

Below *Formula One action at Interlagos*

JOCKEY CLUB
www.jockeysp.com.br
São Paulo's jockey club was founded before the coffee boom in 1875 and the city has long had a love affair with racing. The current lavish club house and track sits right on the banks of smelly Pinheiros river. Watching a race is a delight when the wind is blowing the right way.
Avenida Lineu de Paula Machado 1263, Cidade Jardim 11 2161 8300 107T-10

MATUETÉ
www.matuete.com
São Paulo's coast is fringed with beautiful beaches and islands, many of them with very comfortable boutique hotels or private homes for rental. Matueté specializes in preparing tailor-made weekend or even day breaks and they speak excellent English.
Rua Tapinas 22, 7th floor 11 3071 4515 Mon–Fri 10–6 Faria Lima

TRIP ON JEEP
www.triponjeep.com
It's hard to believe that there are wild jaguars, maned wolves and herds of deer within São Paulo's metropolitan area. Yet south of Interlagos are stretches of primary Mata Atlântica coastal rainforest, which can be reached from the city centre in just over an hour. This company specializes in wildlife trips to the area, along with longer excursions to the caves in Petar and wilderness areas on the São Paulo coast. The guides are biologists and speak excellent English.
Rua Arizona 623, Brooklin 11 5543 5281 Mon–Fri 10–6 Berrini

TROPICO
www.tropico.tur.br
Tropico organizes nature-based adventure days and weekend trips near São Paulo city, and guided walks in the rainforests of the Serra da Cantareira mountains on the edge of the city. Activities include zip-lines, canopy walking and white-water rafting. Longer excursions can be organized with plenty of notice.
11 4025 9281 Mon–Sat 8–8

FESTIVALS AND EVENTS

FEBRUARY–MARCH

CARNAVAL
www.spturis.com
On the weekend before Shrove Tuesday, samba school troupes parade in the Anhembi Sambódromo and in neighbourhoods throughout the city as part of carnival.
Avenida Olavo Fontoura 1209, Parque Anhembi, Santana 11 2226 0400
Santana

MAY–JUNE

GAY PRIDE BRAZIL
http://paradasp.wordpress.com
Taking place on Sunday in May or June, this gay, lesbian, bisexual, transvestite and transsexual parade, Parada do Orgulho Gay de Sao Paulo, has been going since 1999 and is now thought to be the biggest in the world, attracting more than 4 million people.
Avenida Paulista Linha 2 Verde

JUNE

FESTAS JUNINAS
www.spturis.com
Throughout June there are street parties, including *forró* dancing (a type of jig from the northeast) and dressing up in traditional country clothes.
Avenida Olavo Fontoura 1209, Parque Anhembi, Santana 11 2226 0400
Throughout the city

FESTA DE SÃO VITO
On 15 June, there are dances and street parties in Bela Vista neighbourhood, celebrating the name day of the patron saint of the Italian immigrants, Saint Vitus.
Avenida Olavo Fontoura 1209, Parque Anhembi, Santana 11 2226 0400
Trianon-MASP

DECEMBER

NEW YEAR'S EVE
www.spturis.com
Avenida Paulista is closed and taken over by almost a million revellers. There are firework displays and stages with live music.
Avenida Olavo Fontoura 1209, Parque Anhembi, Santana 11 2226 0400
Trianon-MASP

SÃO SILVESTRE MARATHON
www.saosilvestre.com.br
Every New Year's Eve between 2.45pm and 7pm, the streets of the city are given over to one of the largest marathons in South America. Participants run around a 15km (9 miles) circuit, cheered on by encouraging crowds.

FOR CHILDREN

JARDIM ZOOLÓGICO
www.zoologico.com.br
São Paulo's zoo is the largest in Brazil and the fourth largest in the world. It cares for around 3,200 animals, including many of the rare and endangered Brazilian species (like the harpy eagle, bush dog and maned wolf). Most of the neotropical felines (some of which are in small enclosures) and the popular international species including Bengal tigers, chimps and African elephants have homes here.
Avenida Miguel Stéfano 4241, Água Funda 11 5073 0811 Tue–Sun 9–5
Adult R$15, child (7–12) R$4.50, under 7 free Jabaquara (shuttle from metrô station to zoo R$3.20)

PLAYCENTER
www.playcenter.com.br
This rollercoaster park has been popular with Paulistano children for more than 30 years. Rides include magic roundabouts, mini-trains and, of course, those white-knuckle rollercoaster rides.
Rua Jose Gomes Falcão, Barra Funda 11 3350 0199 Tue–Sun 11–7
Adult R$48, under 10 R$29 Barra Funda Check website for sporadic closures due to special events

PRICES AND SYMBOLS

The restaurants are listed alphabetically (excluding A, Al, El, La, Le and O). The prices given are the average for a two-course lunch (L) and a three-course dinner (D) for one person, without drinks. The wine price is for the least expensive bottle. All the restaurants listed accept credit cards unless otherwise stated.

For a key to the symbols, ⊳ 2.

348 PARRILLA PORTEÑA

www.restaurante348.com.br

The best steak in São Paulo is served in an Argentinian restaurant. Porteña owner Eduardo Santaller even claims his steaks are better than those back home, as the choicest cuts are available only on export. They are prepared using only Argentinian ingredients, down to the spicy, green *chimichurri* sauce. The *ojo del bife* (prime fillet steak) cuts like brie and collapses in the mouth like flaked chocolate. The accompanying wines are equally superb, especially the 2002 Cheval dos Andes, and the dining room and garden terrace are as deliberately understated.

✉ Rua Comendador Miguel Calfat 348, Vila Olímpia ☎ 11 3849 2889 🕐 Tue–Sat 12–3, 7–11, Sun 12–3 L R$110, D R$150, Wine R$45 Ⓜ Vila Olimpia

AK DELICATESSEN

www.akdelicatessen.com.br

Former film-producer Andrea Kaufmann has two culinary obsessions—Jewish home cooking and the New York deli. She found neither in São Paulo so she opened both, in the same building. The snug upstairs eatery, decorated with foot-wide strips of retro wallpaper, offers a chic take on comfort food from all over the diaspora, including a wonderful Eastern European veal goulash with *spätzle*, pearl onions and sour cream. The downstairs deli serves the best bagels and pastrami south of the Rio Grande. Since she opened in late 2007 she has already received a gamut of top awards in Brazil, including the coveted *Folha de São Paulo* Restaurant of the Year Award, 2007.

✉ Rua Mato Grosso 450, Higienópolis ☎ 11 3231 4497 🕐 Tue–Fri 12–3, 8–12, Sat 12–4, 8–12, Sun 12–4.30 L R$40, D R$60, Wine R$40 Ⓜ Consolação

DALVA E DITO

www.dalvaedito.com.br

Dalva e Dito focuses on Brazilian home cooking, with family dishes from all over the country rendered gourmet by chef Alex Atala, such as catfish with aromatic Brazilian capim-santo and jambu leaves. Service is in a vast open-plan dining room whose back wall is a blue-and-white mosaic by Athos Bulcão (who designed the tile work in many of Oscar Niemeyer's Brasília edifices). It was the last work he undertook before his death in 2008, just six months before the restaurant opened.

✉ Rua Padre João Manoel 1115, Jardins ☎ 11 3064 6183 🕐 Mon–Fri 12–4, 5–12, Sat 12–4.30, 7–1, Sun 12–5 L R$30, D R$50, Wine R$50 Ⓜ Oscar Freire

D.O.M

www.domrestaurante.com.br

Chef Alex Atala's other Jardins restaurant (a stroll away from Dalva e Dito) has been one of the city's top restaurants since its debut in 1999 and was named one of the 50 Best in the World by Britain's *Restaurant* magazine. Dishes are fusions of European techniques and Brazilian ingredients—especially berries and fruits from the Amazon, and Brazilian river fish—all served in an open-plan dining room fronted by a long bar and a huge plate glass window, which can make diners feel like fish in an aquarium.

Above *Prêt buffet restaurant in the Museu de Arte Moderna*

✉ Rua Barão de Capanema 549, Jardim Paulista ☎ 11 3088 0761 ⌚ Mon–Fri 12–4, 5–12, Sat 12–4.30, 7–1, Sun 12–5 ✋ L R$40, D R$80, Wine R$55 Ⓜ Oscar Freire

DUI

www.duirestaurante.com.br

Bel Coelho has been causing a stir in São Paulo kitchens since she apprenticed with Laurent Suaudeau at the tender age of 17. She now runs São Paulo's current restaurant of the moment: a two-storey space with a little bar below and mezzanine restaurant above. Food is a Brazilian-Asian and light Mediterranean fusion, including dishes such as snook and octopus ceviche with guacamole foam, and grilled organic duck breast with quinoa, sauteed with leek, pesto sauce and coalhada curds.

✉ Alameda Franca 1590, Jardim Paulista ☎ 11 2649 7952 ⌚ Tue–Fri 12–3, 7–12, Sat 12–3, 7–1, Sun 12–4 ✋ L R$80, D R$110, Wine R$40 Ⓜ Oscar Freire

FASANO

www.fasano.com.br

This is the favourite dining room of São Paulo's old money elite, who sit in exquisitely designed mood-lit booths at the restaurant within the Fasano hotel (▷ 136). The menu is of classical Italian and French dishes from Salvatore Loi, who has been voted Chef of the Year by Brazil's biggest magazine, *Veja*, numerous times. The Fasano al Mare seafood tasting menu is particularly delicious.

✉ Fasano hotel, Rua Vitorio Fasano 88, Jardins ☎ 11 3069 4369 ⌚ Tue–Fri 12–3, 7–12, Sat 12–3, 7–1, Sun 12–4 ✋ L R$80, D R$120, Wine R$40 Ⓜ Oscar Freire

FIGUEIRA RUBAIYAT

www.rubaiyat.com.br

Delicious central Brazilian steaks cooked by Argentinian chef Francis Mallman. The light, bright dining room is constructed around a huge tropical fig tree. It is liveliest on Sunday lunchtimes.

✉ Rua Haddock Lobo 1738, Jardins ☎ 11 3063 3888 ⌚ Tue–Fri 12–3, 7–12, Sat 12–3, 7–1, Sun 12–4 ✋ L R$50, D R$70, Wine R$30 Ⓜ Consolação

FRAN'S CAFÉ

www.franscafe.com.br

São Paulo's answer to Starbuck's offers stronger coffee in smaller portions—made to European rather than American standards—and a menu of light eats, including toasted sandwiches and cakes.

✉ Avenida Paulista 358, Bela Vista ☎ 11 3283 5306 ⌚ Daily 7am–10.30pm ✋ Sandwiches from R$10, Coffee R$4 Ⓜ Brigadeiro ? Branches all over the city

JUN SAKAMOTO

Perhaps the best sushi in Latin America, served in an understated, modest dining room. The seats of choice are at the sushi bar itself, where the cream of the city's Japanophile gourmets sample items from the *degustation* menus.

✉ Rua Lisboa 55, Pinheiros ☎ 11 3088 6019 ⌚ Tue–Thu 7–12, Fri–Sat 7–1 ✋ D R$60, Sake R$30 Ⓜ Pinheiros

KINOSHITA

www.restaurantekinoshita.com.br

Tsuyoshi Murakami trained in the 100-year-old Ozushi restaurant in Shambashi Tokyo, ran Shubu Shubu in New York and a restaurant in Liberdade before opening his latest venture near Ibirapuera Park in early 2008. His menu features traditionally cooked, or Kappo, Japanese cuisine dotted with creative fusion dishes. Try the sumptuous tasting menu, with delights like tuna marinated in soya, ginger and garlic, served with *ponzo* sauce and garnished with *kaiware* (sprouted daikon radish seeds).

✉ Rua Jacques Félix 405, Vila Nova Conceição ☎ 11 3849 6940 ⌚ Mon–Fri 12–3, 7–12, Sat 12–4, 7–12 ✋ L R$40, D R$60, Sake R$25 Ⓜ Vila Olimpia

KOSUSHI

www.kosushi.com.br

George Yuji Koshoji seduces the city's high society with a formula of wonderful fresh ingredients and über-cool restaurant design. He has two dining rooms—one here in Itaim and another in the new Cidade Jardim shopping mall. Dishes include *sashimi anchova negra* (black smoked anchovy sashimi).

✉ Rua Viradouro 139, Itaim Bibi ☎ 11 3167 7272 ⌚ Tue–Fri 12–3, 7–12, Sat 12–4, 7–1, Sun 12–4 ✋ L R$70, D R$70, Sake R$30 🚆 Cidade Jardim ? Also at Shopping Cidade Jardim (▷ 128)

MANI

www.manimanioca.com.br

The dining room and elegant walled garden in the back patio here are a favourite eat-and-be-seen spot for São Paulo celebrities, who gaze at each other over their guava-infused terrine de foie gras with brazil nut and rum jelly, and other light Brazilian-Mediterranean fusion dishes by Catalan chef Daniel Redondo and his Brazilian partner Helena Rizzo.

✉ Rua Joaquim Antunes 210, Pinheiros ☎ 11 3085 4148 ⌚ Tue–Fri 12–3, 8–11.30, Sat 1–4, 8.30–12.30, Sun 1–3 ✋ L R$80, D R$100, Wine R$40 Ⓜ Pinheiros

PRÊT

www.mam.org.br

Ibirapuera's Museum of Modern Art (MAM ▷ 115) is home to this sumptuous lunchtime buffet restaurant, which sits in a semi-circular restaurant that is flooded with light from 3m-high (10ft) plate glass windows. The Oca sits immediately in front of the dining room, behind the sculpture garden, and the Bienal building (for Fashion Week and art shows) is less than 200m (220 yards) away.

✉ MAM, Parque Ibirapuera, Avenida Pedro Álvares Cabral ☎ 11 5574 1250 ⌚ Daily 12–6 ✋ Buffet R$40, Wine R$25 🚌 5175-10, 5178-10, 5194-10

RESTAURANTE DO MASP

www.masp.art.br

Underneath Latin America's most prestigious art gallery, MASP (▷ 116–117), is one of the city's best-value buffet restaurants. A huge array of dishes, from hearty stews and hunks of meat to veggie lasagnes and cheesy pasta, are served, sometimes to the accompaniment of live music.

✉ MASP, Avenida Paulista 1578, Bela Vista ☎ 11 3253 2829 ⌚ Tue–Sun 11.30–6.30 ✋ Buffet R$15, Coffee R$4 Ⓜ Trianon-MASP

PRICES AND SYMBOLS

Prices are the lowest and highest for a double room for one night. Breakfast is included unless noted otherwise. All the hotels listed accept credit cards unless otherwise stated. Note that rates vary widely throughout the year.

For a key to the symbols, ▷ 2.

BLUE TREE TOWERS FARIA LIMA

www.bluetree.com.br

For boutique luxury at a budget price, opt for this tall tower in the heart of one of the city's restaurant and nightlife districts. Rooms are bright and spacious, and come with boutique hotel touches (like fine bed linen). There are great views out over the skyscrapers and terracotta roofs of the city, an indoor pool, a well-equipped gym and a spa.

Avenida Brigadeiro Faria Lima 3989, Vila Olímpia 11 3896 7544 R$500–R$800 317 Indoor Faria Lima

CASAS CHARMOSAS

www.casascharmosas.com.br

Ana Carolina Salem Vanossi offers bespoke accommodation services through this private house-rental company, with properties throughout the city, including the wealthy western suburb of Morumbi near the World Cup football stadium and as far afield as the beach destinations of Angra dos Reis, Buzios and Bahia.

11 8292 0591 From R$1,200

EMILIANO

www.emiliano.com.br

Arthur Casas's stylish, minimalist hotel underwent renovation in mid-2009, adding new carpets and linens to the upper-floor suites and José Zanine Caldas armchairs to the lobby, alongside those already there by the Campana brothers and Florence Knoll. The suites are sumptuous, with leather sofas, huge flatscreen TVs, king-size beds with fine Egyptian cotton, and extensive gadgetry which controls everything in the room at the touch of a console button. The hotel has a small spa but no pool.

Rua Oscar Freire 384, Jardins 11 3069 4369 R$1,100–R$1,900 57 Oscar Freire

ESTAN PLAZA

www.estanplaza.com.br

Well-kept, if plain, small rooms are in a little tower block at a great location, close to both the restaurants of Jardins and bustle of Avenida Paulista. Rooms cost only a little more than hostel doubles, making this excellent value.

Alameda Jau 497, Jardins 11 3016 0000 R$150–R$200 120 Trianon-MASP

FASANO

www.fasano.com.br

São Paulo's finest hotel lies in the heart of Jardins and offers chic luxury. Suites come with polished wooden floors covered by rugs, and high windows flooding the rooms with ample natural light. Furnishings include leather armchairs, long hardwood commodes and generous desks, all by Latin American designer of the moment, Isay Weinfeld. The upper floors offer stunning views out over the city's twinkling skyline.

Rua Vitorio Fasano 88, Jardins 11 3069 4369 R$1,120–R$2,000 60 Indoor Oscar Freire

GRAND HYATT

http://saopaulo.grand.hyatt.com

This hotel in the heart of the new corporate district has suites large enough to play tennis in, with terraces offering views out over the city's business district. Each has

Above *The entrance to the chic Emiliano hotel in Jardins*

separate living rooms, and the hotel has the best in-house spa in the city, offering treatments like Shirodhara hot oil massage and Shiatsu.
Avenida das Nações Unidas 13301, Brooklin 11 2838 1234 R$736–R$916 485 Indoor, outdoor Morumbi

L'HOTEL PORTO BAY

www.portobay.com
This tranquil, mock-Parisian boutique hotel, with faux-Louis XVI furniture in the lobby and quiet, discreet service, lies just off Avenida Paulista. It has a series of suites organized around a central atrium and decorated with European paintings. The hotel also has a small spa.
Alameda Campinas 266, Jardins 11 2183 0500 R$850–R$1,500 75 Outdoor Trianon-MASP

IBIS PAULISTA

www.accorhotels.com.br
Quiet, safe and well-kept, this freshly built, modest, business-orientated hotel offers simple but well-kept double rooms with desks and WiFi access (extra fee). It costs only a little more than the city's backpacker hostels and is far better located.
Avenida Paulista 2355, Bela Vista 11 3523 3000 R$150 (standard price for all rooms) 236 Consolação

LANDMARK RESIDENCE

www.landmarkresidence.com.br
These 40sq m (430sq ft) apartments have lots of gaudy marble facing and saggy sofas and armchairs. The location is excellent, however, and there's a modest gym, gardens, broadband in the rooms and a small business centre.
Alameda Jaú 1607, Jardins 11 3082 8600 R$200–R$280 56 Consolação

PAULISTA GARDEN

www.paulistagardenhotel.com.br
This no-frills guest house has simple wood and whitewash rooms, and a modest breakfast of fruits, cold meats, cheese, bread rolls, tea and coffee. However, it's a 10-minute walk to both Avenida Paulista and Ibirapuera Park, and 20 minutes to the heart of Jardins. There are plenty of restaurants nearby and this is a safe area.
Alameda Lorena 21, Jardins 11 3885 8498 R$120–R$180 27 Brigadeiro

POUSADA DONA ZILAH

www.zilah.com
Rooms in this family-run guest house have space for little more than a bed and a rickety table and chair, but you'd struggle to find a better or safer location. Jardins is on the doorstep and Avenida Paulista is 10 minutes' walk away. The breakfast is generous, too, and the *pousada* has both internet and bike rental.
Alameda Franca 1621, Jardins 11 3062 1444 R$210–R$220 14 Consolação

POUSADA DOS FRANCESES

www.pousadadosfranceses.com.br
This simple hostel is 10 minutes from Avenida Paulista and offers dormitories, doubles and a range of services, including laundry, a TV room, internet and a barbecue.
Rua dos Franceses 100, Bela Vista 11 3288 1592 Dorm bed R$38; Double room R$95–R$105 14 Brigadeiro

RENAISSANCE

www.marriot.com
This tall tower hotel, designed by Ruy Ohtake, is the best business option close to the city centre. Rooms are spacious, well-appointed, modern and comfortable. Service is slick and quick, and includes 24-hour room service and WiFi in all rooms. The best restaurants in the city are on the doorstep, the hotel has a decent spa (with a sauna, steam rooms and massage), and there are superb views from the upper-storey suites.
Alameda Santos 2233, Jardins 11 3069 2233 R$800–R$1,200 65 Indoor Consolação

TIVOLI SÃO PAULO MOFARREJ

www.tivolihotels.com
The newest luxury hotel in Jardins sits in a tall tower and has a selection of plush carpeted suites and smaller rooms. The hotel sits on the crest of the hill which rises towards Avenida Paulista and rooms on the upper storeys have superb city views. The hotel has a Banyan Tree spa, large pool, business facilities, free WiFi and a well-equipped gym. Service can be patchy at times and phone calls very expensive.
Alameda Santos 1437, Jardins 11 3146 5900 R$1,000–R$1,500 220 Indoor Trianon-MASP

TRANSAMÉRICA TWENTY-FIRST CENTURY

www.transamericaflats.com.br
It may be in the heart of the most expensive area in the city but the furniture in this tower block of flats looks a little worn. Decoration may be conservative 1980s but the flats are large at 42sq m (452sq ft) and there's a gym (in need of maintenance), free WiFi and room service.
Alameda Lorena 1748, Jardins 11 3062 2666 R$225–R$310 115 Oscar Freire

UNIQUE

www.hotelunique.com.br
It's hard not to be impressed by this enormous battleship grey half moon on stilts, with porthole windows and an iron front door as big as a portcullis. Svelte staff, dressed by São Paulo's leading menswear designer, Alexandre Herchcovitz, stand in attendance and media types chat busily over thick coffee in the ground floor bar lounge. Upstairs is Skye—one of the city's bars-to-be-seen-in—with a view to rival its Los Angeles counterpart, out over a blood-red pool to leafy Jardins and the fields of crowded skyscrapers beyond. All the rooms are as slick as the exterior: ever-so-carefully-designed, decked out in light hardwood and illuminated with lights which come on at the stroke of a cable; floors in the tail-end suites curve up to meet the ceiling.
Avenida Brigadeiro Luis Antônio 4700, Ibirapuera 11 3055 4710 R$1,100–R$1,300 95 Indoor, outdoor 477U-10

COQUEIRO VERDE

RIO AND SÃO PAULO STATES

Most visitors to Rio and São Paulo states spend their time on the coast. East of Rio are the bays and surf beaches of the green forest-covered peninsula around Búzios, and the brilliant white sands around the resorts of Cabo Frio. Farther west lies the Costa Verde (Green Coast). This whole coast is romantically beautiful even by South American standards. Beach after beach—from palm-fringed coves to long swathes of talcum-fine sand—stretch along the Rio and São Paulo coast for more than 300km (186 miles). Mountains watch over them, occasionally breaking through in long spurs to plunge into the deep green Atlantic and emerge anew as chains of islands, like Ilha Grande and Ilhabela, both of them with spectacular beaches and large stretches of virgin forest. Little colonial towns like the former gold-rush ports of Paraty and São Sebastião nestle opposite them on the mainland, and the forest which shrouds them drips with waterfalls and is thick with orchids and bromeliads; in January, when the quaresma trees and flamboyant trees (also called flame trees) bloom, it bursts into brilliant reds and purples.

The Costa Verde ends just before Brazil's biggest port, Santos, an attractive colonial city which has recently undergone a major facelift. Its suburb of São Vicente was the first official Portuguese settlement. Farther west from here the coast gets still wilder, with one of the largest stretches of Atlantic coastal rainforest in South America, extending beyond Iguape and continuing through the Ilha do Cardoso island—where spectacled caiman laze on the beaches—and into Paraná.

The coastal mountains of Rio and São Paulo are swathed in forest and dotted with national parks. These include the wildlife-rich Parque Nacional Itatiaia and the Serra dos Órgãos, whose spectacular rock formations lie close to the former Imperial hill retreat of Petrópolis.

BARRETOS

www.independentes.com.br

The interior of São Paulo state is one of Brazil's great bread, beef and fruit baskets, with more arable land than Britain and a succession of small, prosperous towns which are of little interest for tourists. Barretos, in the far north of the state, is a typical town for most of the time but on 25 August every year, more than a million visitors descend on the little town for the Festa do Peão de Boiadeiro (▷ 155). This is reputedly the largest rodeo event in the world, with cowboys lassoing bullocks, riding bulls and wrestling steers. Since 1985 the event has been held in a 110ha (272-acre) park, with a stadium large enough to hold 35,000 people, designed by Modernist architect Oscar Niemeyer.

391 N14 · Rua 30 564, Centro · 17 3321 1100 · Mon–Fri 10–6 · From São Paulo

BÚZIOS

▷ 142.

CABO FRIO AND O REGIÃO DOS LAGOS

www.cabofrio.org
www.cabofrio.rj.gov.br
www.regiaodoslagos.com.br

The coastal landscape between Rio de Janeiro and Búzios is fringed with kilometres of white, talcum-fine sandy beaches, washed by powerful waves that attract surfers. Behind lie a series of brackish lakes that give the region its name: the Lake District. A strong prevailing wind and calm water means that they are among the best locations in the southeast of Brazil for wind- and kite-surfing. Offshore there are islands and capes where warm and cold currents meet, leading to an abundance of marine life and good scuba diving. The resort town of Cabo Frio is a good base for exploring the area. It and the entire region are reachable by bus or car from Rio in less than 2.5 hours.

403 R15 · Avenida do Contorno s/n, Algodoal, Cabo Frio · 22 2647 1689 · Mon–Fri 10–6 · From Rio de Janeiro

CAMPOS DO JORDÃO

www.camposdojordao.com.br

This mountain resort between Rio de Janeiro and São Paulo sits at 1,628m (5,341ft) above sea level in the Serra da Mantiqueira, in a long valley offering good walking. The climate is cold and dry in winter, and cool in summer. Minalba mineral water is produced here and there are several mineral springs in the town. One of the town districts, Abernéssia, was founded by Scotsman Robert John Reid, who created the name by Latinizing a fusion of Aberdeen and Inverness. In June and July there are classical music and dance festivals. The town's architecture is of a kitschy alpine style, with steeply gabled roofs even though the town has never seen snow.

402 P15 · Portal da Cidade (the alpine-looking gateway to the town) · Mon–Fri 10–6, Sat 10–1 · From Rio de Janeiro and São Paulo

CANANÉIA

www.cananeia.sp.gov.br

The last of southern São Paulo's small, colonial seaside towns feels lost in a time warp. Pretty colonial houses crumble, locals snooze under their hats in the main *praça* (square) and during the week it's so quiet you can hear a footstep. The town lies at the feet of the Serra do Mar mountains and sits in a natural harbour behind the sandy Ilha Comprida (▷ 143), surrounded by stretches of mangroves. People come to Cananéia for its remoteness and to take a trip to the beaches and islands. Car and passenger rafts take 10 minutes to cross the harbour to the southern reaches of Ilha Comprida. Fishing boats and launches can be chartered from the docks to the more remote islands in the Lagomar bay and to the wilderness of Ilha do Cardoso, which has some of the most pristine rainforest on the coast and whose beaches and rivers are home to 2m-long (6.5ft) spectacled caiman. Cananéia has a small and very well-maintained municipal museum (Museu Municipal de Cananéia; tel 13 3851 1753; Tue–Sun 9–6; R$1), which preserves bits of maritime miscellany and what is said to be the largest great white shark ever caught off the Brazilian coast, weighing 3.5 tonnes when caught but now considerably lighter and hanging stuffed and painted from the museum ceiling.

391 N16 · From São Paulo and Santos

Opposite *Praia Forte in Cabo Frio*
Right *The alpine-style town centre of Campos do Jordão*

INFORMATION

www.buziosturismo.com

403 R15 Portico de Búzios s/n 22 2633 6200 Daily 8–8 From Rio de Janeiro

TIP

» Book well ahead for accommodation during the carnival period (when hotel prices rise steeply)—at least three months in advance.

BÚZIOS

The pretty seaside town of Armação de Búzios nestles on a peninsula covered in diverse vegetation and fringed with dozens of long surf beaches and pretty coves. It is famous for its buzzing on-season nightlife and is particularly lively during the Christmas and New Year period, and at *carnaval* (▷ 155), when people wear fancy dress of their choice and head out in the streets to dance. Carnival in Búzios is not a spectacle, but a participatory event.

FAMOUS RETREAT

The town was a forgotten fishing community at the end of a dirt road, which had changed little since it was founded in 1740 as a whale fishery, until Brigitte Bardot visited in the 1960s. Pictures of her, walking barefoot along the beach, brought the focus of the world's press to this 'lost paradise in the tropics'. A rather tacky bronze statue of Bardot sits at the top of A Orla Bardot, the main street in town, which is more commonly known as Rua das Pedras.

INTERNATIONAL COMMUNITY

From the 1970s, wealthy Cariocas, Argentinians and hoteliers started to move to Búzios, building *pousadas* (small hotels), restaurants, bars and boutiques. As many of these businesses are foreign-owned, English, French, German and Spanish are widely spoken here.

CHOICE OF BEACHES

During the daytime, Búzios's favourite pastime is to head to one of the 25 beaches in the area. The most visited are Ossos (close to the centre and the most popular), Geribá (with strong surf and many bars and restaurants), Ferradura (a smaller surfer beach), and Ferradurinha (with waters calm enough for children). Tartaruga and João Fernandes are nestled in small coves, and Azeda and Azedinha are close to the town centre and popular with locals.

Below *Búzios still retains the appearance of a fishing village, despite its popularity*

IGUAPE AND ILHA COMPRIDA

www.guiadeiguape.com.br

This pretty little colonial town, surrounded by lush rainforest-covered hills and extensive tracts of wild mangrove wetland, sits opposite a long sandy island fronted by vast empty beaches and on the edge of two large environmentally protected areas. The Complexo Estuarino Lagunar de Iguape-Cananéia-Paranaguá stretches south towards Paraná, and to the north are the wild forests, rivers and waterfalls of the Estação Ecológico Juréia-Itatins. Both are remote, difficult to visit and require permission from park authorities. The São Paulo tour company Trip on Jeep (▷ 154) can organize bespoke trips with advance notice.

Iguape has a long history, beginning shortly after the founding of São Vicente in 1538 (▷ 27). While no buildings remain from the first 150 years of Portuguese settlement, the city centre has the largest conglomeration of Portuguese colonial architecture in São Paulo state, with stately rows of large town houses painted in warm colours, little cottages, and civic buildings sitting on a large square around the 18th-century cathedral. There are two small museums: The Museu Histórico e Arqueológico (Mon–Fri 9–11.30, 1–5.30), which was once the first gold foundry in Brazil, and the Museu de Arte Sacra (Mon–Sat 9–11.30, 1–5.30), in the 18th-century Igreja do Rosário, with a collection of 18th- and 19th-century religious artefacts.

The beaches of Ilha Comprida lie opposite the town centre, immediately across the Rio Ribeira do Iguape and a long stretch of sand flats. A pedestrian bridge spans the river but it's then 8km (5 miles) to Praia do Boqueirão Norte, the nearest beach. The sand and sea here are silty and the beach and neighbouring Viareggio are backed with holiday homes. Those further to the south are far quieter and are visited by migrating birds and nesting turtles in season.

391 N16 From Santos and São Paulo

ILHABELA

www.ilhabela.com.br

Brazil's largest coastal island is a huge mountain ridge rising steeply out of an emerald Atlantic immediately in front of the town of São Sebastião (▷ 151). The island is swathed in Mata Atlântica forest. This gets wilder as it stretches further south and is broken by clearwater streams which drop through a series of pretty waterfalls. Much of this forest is protected and is home to ocelots, marmosets and more than 200 species of birds, many of which are endemic to the region. There are also biting black flies, or *borrachudos*, particularly on the island's southern and eastern beaches, and insect repellent is essential.

Ilhabela's coastline is fringed with rocky bays, long sandy beaches and gentle coves. Those facing the shore are busiest, with almost all the island's *pousadas* located here. They stretch along Ilhabela's only paved road or sit in the villages of Perequê (where the ferry from São Sebastião arrives), Borrifos, São Pedro and Vila Ilhabela, which has a small colonial church. The Baía de Castelhanos—a 2km-long (1.25-mile) half-moon bay set in a bowl of virgin forest—lies within the Parque Estadual de Ilhabela and is considered to be the most beautiful beach in the state by many Paulistanos. The island fills up with weekenders from São Paulo from Friday night but is almost deserted during the week, particularly outside the holiday season (Dec–Jan and during carnival). There are more than 20 shipwrecks off Ilhabela, making it a popular scuba destination despite the waters being heavily fished and murky.

402 P15 Praça Vereador José Leite dos Passos 14, Barra Velha 12 3895 7259 Mon–Fri 10–6 To São Sebastião from Santos, São Paulo and Ubatuba From São Sebastião

Above *The beach at Ilhabela*

Above *Lagoa Azul on Ilha Grande is an excellent place for snorkelling*
Above left *The Museu de Arte Contemporânea in Niterói, seen from Icarai beach*

ILHA GRANDE

www.ilhagrande.com.br

Ilha Grande is a beautiful forest-covered island on the Costa Verde, fringed with more than 100 pearly beaches. There are no roads and only one tiny town, Abraão. The island remains relatively untouched by the pressures of development; the consequence of an ignoble history. In colonial times the island was an infamous pirate lair, particularly for French and British corsairs. It then became a landing post for slaves, and in the 19th century it was a leper colony. During the Vargas era and military dictatorship (▷ 35) it housed a notorious political prison—whose ruins remain—now overgrown with lianas and ferns at the end of one of the numerous trails that run across the island. Nowadays most of Ilha Grande is protected as a state park, though there is significant pressure for development from wealthy Brazilians who covet it as their own private playground.

Abraão affords easy walking access to the principal tourist beaches. Those facing the shore, like Abraãozinho (next to the town) and Palmas (a walk of one hour away) offer calm water and good swimming. Beaches like Lopes Mendes (90-minutes' walk from Abraão) are longer, broader and pounded by heavy surf. Boat excursions to reach the beaches and the Lagoa Azul (a lagoon with crystal clear water and good snorkelling) can be chartered from local fishermen in Abraão.

402 Q15 · Information booth on the docks · Thu–Sun 10–4 · To Angra do Reis and Mangaratiba from Rio de Janeiro · From Angra do Reis and Mangaratiba

NITERÓI

www.niteroi.rj.gov.br
www.neltur.com.br

Just across Guanabara Bay from Rio de Janeiro is the city of Niterói, the old capital of Rio de Janeiro state. It's much maligned by Cariocas, who joke that the best thing about Niterói is its views of Rio. While the city lacks Rio's panache and lively cultural life, its beaches are at least as beautiful, cleaner, quieter and with a series of astonishing, panoramic views of Rio across the bay huddled below Corcovado.

Niterói is an older city than Rio. When the French—under Villegagnon (1510–71) and with their indigenous Tamoio allies—established their colony on an island near modern-day Rio, the Portuguese and their allies, the Temiminós, set up camp at Niterói. The formal founding of a Portuguese settlement was here in 1573. The city was originally called Vila Real da Praia Grande. It was renamed Niterói in 1834, after the Tupi-Guarani (the first language of Brazil) for 'hidden waters', and became the capital of the province and later the state of Rio de Janeiro. The state capital moved to Rio itself in 1975, 15 years after the federal capital had moved from there to Brasília. Niterói's star attraction is Modernist architect Oscar Niemeyer's futuristic, saucer-shaped Museu de Arte Contemporânea (tel 21 2620 2481; Tue–Sun, 10–6; R$5, free on Wed). It perches dramatically on a cliff top at the end of the city beach and sits above a circular pool.

The city has numerous beaches. Icaraí, São Francisco and Charitas have wonderful views across Guanabara Bay, especially at sunset. Piratininga, Camboinhas, Itaipu and Itacoatiara are the best beaches in the city and are popular with surfers, although there can be strong rips and undertows, particularly at Itacoatiara.

403 Q15 · Estrada Leopoldo Froes 773 · 21 2710 2727 · Mon–Fri 10–6 · From the Praça XV docks, Rio de Janeiro

PARATY

▷ 146–147.

PARQUE NACIONAL DO ITATIAIA

This mountainous national park covers a series of peaks, deep ridges and gulleys in the Serra da Mantiqueira mountains, some 180km (112 miles) to the northwest of Rio de Janeiro. It offers some of the best walking and wildlife watching in the region. The park protects 30,000ha (74,100 acres) of pristine Mata Atlântica rainforest, dripping with clearwater rivers and plunging waterfalls, and an extensive area of *paramo* (high, alpine grasslands) rising to rocky crests of almost 3,000m (9,840ft). There are hikes in the park of varying length—anything from two hours to two days—running to waterfalls at Poranga or Véu de Noiva, or climbing into the mountains to the Três Picos, Agulhas Negras and the Serra das Prateleiras peaks (▷ 152–153).

GETTING TO THE PARK

Itatiaia (pronounced Eet-a-chee-ay-eeya) is a two-hour drive from Rio and three hours from São Paulo along the Dutra motorway. There are two entrances to the park. The first is via Itatiaia, from where the Estrada Parque Nacional road leads to the park visitor centre, the hotels and the trailheads for Três Picos and most of the waterfalls. The second entrance provides access to the Abrigo Rebouças lodge, which must be booked in advance for overnight stays and is the starting point for the higher peaks in the park. This is reached via BR 354, which leaves north from the town of Engenheiro Passos (the next town west of Itatiaia town on the Dutra). It is also possible to visit the park with a tour company from São Paulo or Rio (▷ 96).

FLORA

Itatiaia was Brazil's first national park. Wildlife has been protected here since the 1930s and the park is an important haven for critically endangered species listed by CITES (Convention on International Trade in Endangered Species). The abundance and diversity of wildlife results from the park's topography and the associated varied vegetation. This is stratified by altitude. The lower reaches of Itatiaia (between 800 and 1,100m/2,625 and 3,610ft) are covered with forest, ferns and flowering plants, with abundant epiphytic orchids and bromeliads. Above the rainforest, the higher reaches are covered with pines and bushes. These lead to a rocky landscape at 1,900m (6,230ft), characterized by low heath and grasses dotted with isolated trees, and many unique plants and lichens adapted to high winds and strong ultra-violet rays.

FAUNA

The park has abundant mammals. Brown capuchins and southern masked titi monkeys are common, and howler monkeys can be heard calling with their raucous roars both at dawn and in the evening. There are also agoutis, sloths, peccaries and spectacular big mammals including jaguar, tapir and puma. There are between 300 and 400 bird species, many of which are endemic, and Itatiaia is one of South America's premier bird-watching destinations. Spectacular sightings include the ultra-rare Brazilian ruby hummingbird, with emerald wings and a dazzling red chest, as well as swallow-tailed and black and gold cotingas.

INFORMATION

www.icmbio.gov.br/brasil/RJ/parna-itatiaia
402 P15 Estrada Parque Nacional 24 3352 1461 Daily 8–5 but often unmanned From Rio de Janeiro to Itatiaia town, via Resende; onward journey by taxi or local bus (▷ Tips) Dutra motorway well signposted from Rio and from Lagoa (via the Rebouças tunnel)

TIPS

» A bus from Itatiaia town, marked Hotel Simon or 504 Circular, goes to the park four times a day; coming from Resende; it may be caught at the crossroads before Itatiaia. There is only one road through the park, the Estrada Parque Nacional, on which all the hotels and the visitor centre are located.

» Through tickets back to Rio are sold at a booth in the large bar in the middle of Itatiaia main street.

» To increase your chances of seeing animals it is a good idea to hire a local guide (through one of the hotels or the visitor centre), wear muted colours and bring binoculars. Most guides do not speak English.

» The café at the visitor centre is often closed. It is best to bring your own supplies.

» Avoid coming to Itatiaia at weekends, as the park is very busy. Brazilian tourists are not wildlife enthusiasts and make a great deal of noise on the trails and around the waterfalls.

Below *Mountainous Itatiaia provides varied habitats for the abundant wildlife*

INFORMATION

www.paraty.com.br

402 P15 Largo da Pedreira 24 3371 1266 Mon–Fri 10–6, Sat–Sun 11–4 From Rio de Janeiro and São Paulo; the *rodoviária* (bus station) is 1km (0.6 miles) inland from the colonial centre

Above *Igreja de Santa Rita overlooks the fishing harbour*

INTRODUCTION

The baroque churches and little whitewashed cottages of the Portuguese colonial port town of Paraty sit between a bottle-green sea and the massive forest-clad folds of the Serra do Mar mountains. Brightly painted fishing boats bob up and down on the quay and a short launch ride away are myriad jewel-like islands and palm-shaded coves. By night the town buzzes in lively bars, and wines and dines in a number of evermore sophisticated restaurants.

Paraty was founded in the first half of the 17th century, at the beginning of the Minas Gerais gold rush. With its sheltered bays, the town was a natural choice for a port. It had been an indigenous settlement previously and Guianas Indians had cut a trail leading through the mountains and into the interior before the Portuguese arrived. This was adapted for mules and extended into southern Minas Gerais. Parts of the trail still exist, as the Caminho do Ouro, and tour operators in town can organize walking visits (www.paratyadventure.com).

The town became the chief port for the export of Minas gold in the 17th century, when its baroque churches, forts and civic buildings were constructed. In the late 19th century, the opening of the railway from the Paraíba Valley to Rio de Janeiro led to Paraty becoming isolated. The port being redundant, almost all its inhabitants left. Those that remained grew bananas, whaled or fished. While much of colonial Brazil was bulldozed in the Republican era, forgotten Paraty remained preserved as a crumbling, open-air museum until the 1950s, when it gained new recognition. It was declared a national historic monument in 1966.

WHAT TO SEE

PARATY'S COLONIAL CENTRE

Paraty has a tiny, self-contained and mostly pedestrian colonial centre jutting out into the sea. The modern town lies behind. There are no individually spectacular buildings: The town's charms lie in the conglomeration as a whole, which is unspoilt and unbroken by modern architecture. Santa Rita, the town's most photographed church, faces the bay. It was built in 1722 by freed slaves in elegant Lusitanian baroque style. The annexe houses a small Sacred Art Museum (daily 10–4; R$2) with a handful of silver monstrance and baroque statues. Nossa Senhora dos Remédios is the town's biggest church (daily 10–4). Construction began in 1787 but was not completed until 1873, when the town became rich again on coffee exports from the Paraíba Valley. The church was originally planned with two large towers, but as Paraty sits on muddy ground the architects decided that adding weight to the structure would cause subsidence, giving the present building a slightly stunted appearance. Nossa Senhora do Rosário e São Benedito, dating from 1725, was built by African-Brazilian slaves (daily 10–4). It is small and simple, but it is perhaps Paraty's most elegant church. There is a fort on the eastern edge of Paraty, across the river, with rusting cannons overlooking the bay, and the ruins of the old town gate can be seen close to the football field at the entrance to town.

MUSEUMS

The Museu de Arte e Tradições Populares (Museum of Arts and Popular Traditions; Wed–Sun 10–4; R$2) has a small display devoted to the history of the town, with replica indigenous Brazilian canoes, musical instruments, clothing from the colonial period and whaling paraphernalia. The Casa de Cadeia is the old 18th-century prison (Mon–Fri 10–4; R$2). It retains its original Portuguese iron bars and now serves as an art gallery.

TIPS

» The best way to visit the bays and islands around Paraty is to head to the docks, where fishing boats leave from around 8am whenever they are full, for morning and afternoon trips. Agencies in town also offer packages.

» In June, the town hosts the FLIP International Literary Festival (▷ 155), when world-renowned writers visit the city to present workshops and give lectures.

Below *A street in the old colonial heart of the town*

INFORMATION

www.icmbio.gov.br/parnaso
403 Q15 Avenida Rotariana s/n
21 2152 1100 Mon–Sat 10–6
R$20 To Teresópolis from Rio de Janeiro; onward transfers to the park by taxi cost around R$30

TIP

» Visits to the park can be combined with a tour of nearby Petrópolis. Companies like Roz Brazil (▷ 155) offer one- or multi-day trips, including pick-ups from Rio de Janeiro.

PARQUE NACIONAL DA SERRA DOS ÓRGÃOS

The Serra dos Órgãos lie some 100km (62 miles) northeast of the city of Rio de Janeiro and close to Petrópolis (▷ 150). They are a steep and boulder-strewn section of the long coastal ridge that stretches along the coast of Brazil between Bahia and Argentina. The Serra's rocky and vertiginous terrain made it difficult to farm or cut for firewood, and as a result it preserves an extensive area of Mata Atlântica forest and is replete with wildlife. There are fewer tourist facilities here than at Itatiaia, since access to the wilder parts of the range is more difficult. Most people access the park from Teresópolis, which is 5km (3 miles) from the park borders.

NATURAL STRUCTURES

The Serra dos Órgãos, or the Organ Mountains, are named after the bizarre tube-like rock formations which dominate the range and which resemble organ pipes. Some 11,000ha (27,170 acres) are protected as a national park, created in 1939, a little after Itatiaia. Aside from the wildlife, the park's principal draw is the precipitous boulder mountain, the Dedo de Deus (God's Finger), which rises sheer from the forest to a height of 1,692m (5,550ft). It can be seen quite clearly from the main road, a little outside the mountain town of Teresópolis. The park's highest point is the Pedra do Sino ('Bell Rock'), at 2,263m (7,423ft). A steep path winds 14km (8.5 miles) to the summit and the west face of this mountain is one of the hardest rock climbing pitches in Brazil.

WILDLIFE

The park is home to almost as many bird and mammal species as Itatiaia. These include the endangered woolly spider monkey (America's largest primate) and the very rare and endemic grey-winged cotinga. Guided tours with an expert, such as Edson Endrigo (▷ 155), will ensure you don't miss the abundance of creatures around you.

Opposite *Dedo de Deus peak*
Below *The landscapes of the park are largely untouched by human hand*

INFORMATION

www.petropolis.rj.gov.br
403 Q15 Praça da Liberdade
08000 241 516 Mon–Sat 9–8
From Rio de Janeiro

TIPS

» Petrópolis has plenty of restaurants and cafés for buying refreshments.
» A day is enough time to see the sights of Petrópolis.

Above *The neo-Gothic Alcântara cathedral holds Imperial tombs*

PETRÓPOLIS

This former Imperial hill station sits 809m (2,654ft) up in the Serra da Estrela mountains, some 68km (42 miles) north of Rio. For about 80 years it was the summer capital of Brazil; it is now a provincial city with a population of just over 300,000 people. The city was planned by Dom Pedro II (1825–91), Brazil's second and last emperor (▷ 33–34), and constructed largely by the German architect Julius Köler—which is why there is a preponderance of Teutonic architecture along the city's main avenues. It was the home of the Brazilian aviator Alberto Santos Dumont (1873–1932), who was either the second man to succeed in making a powered flight, or the first if you believe Brazilian accounts.

IMPERIAL HIGHLIGHTS

Petrópolis receives hundreds of thousands of visitors each year—almost all of them national tourists—and consequently it can be busy in high season (Dec, Jan and during carnival) and at weekends. The Museu Imperial (Imperial Palace; Tue–Sun 11–5.30; R$8) is Brazil's most visited museum. It's a modest but elegant mock-Palladian building, furnished as if the royal family had just left for the afternoon, and preserving the crown jewels. Horse-drawn carriages wait for tourists outside the front gate. Other Imperial-era sights include: the neo-Gothic Catedral de São Pedro de Alcântara (Tue–Sat 10–6; free), completed in 1925, which contains the tombs of Emperor Dom Pedro II and his wife Empress Dona Teresa Cristina; the Palácio de Cristal, designed in France as a facsimile of the crystal palaces which were popular in late 19th-century Europe, and the neoclassical Palácio Rio Negro, a former presidential mansion.

ECCENTRICITY AND INNOVATION

The Casa de Santos Dumont, his summer home (Tue–Sun 9.30–5; R$5), was designed by the aviator in 1918 to resemble an alpine chalet. It is a delightful example of a quirky inventor's house, with steps enabling visitors to ascend to the inventor's studio with only their right foot first, a rooftop observatory, a desk which converts into a bed and an alcohol-heated bathroom with what is said to have been the first heated shower in Brazil.

SANTOS

www.santos.sp.gov.br

Brazil's largest port is as beautifully situated as Rio de Janeiro, in a bay of islands and mangroves watched over by verdant mountains. It is 72km (45 miles) from São Paulo, and one of Brazil's oldest cities. The first Portuguese settlement in Brazil was made at neighbouring São Vicente in 1532 by the explorer Martim de Sousa (*c.* 1500–71), and Santos was settled shortly afterwards (São Vicente is sadly now just a suburb of Santos). By the 1580s it had grown to become an important port with some 400 houses, making it one of the largest cities in contemporaneous Brazil. The first export was sugar, grown as cane at the foot of the mountains and on the plateau, but by the 19th century Santos was exporting much of the world's coffee and was linked to São Paulo by a British-built railway line. Early 20th-century Santos was a wealthy place, with opulent coffee mansions, a smart city centre and South America's most important stock exchange, the Bolsa do Café. After the Great Depression (▷ 35), the city fell from grace and languished under a poor reputation—for pollution, yellow fever and crime—for decades.

Little changed until the late 1990s, since when Santos has undergone a renaissance. The colonial buildings have been refurbished, the bay cleaned up and trams clatter once more through the old city centre. It's a pleasant place to spend a day away from São Paulo, on the way to or from the beaches of the Costa Verde. The art deco Bolsa do Café is now a lovely museum (Mon–Sat 9–5, Sun 10–5; adult R$5, child R$2.50) devoted to telling the story of the coffee boom in Brazil and its social consequences, and there are many handsome colonial and Imperial churches. The city is also football legend Pelé's home. Though born in Minas, he played for Santos football club for almost all his life. The club stadium has a museum devoted to its glorious history and to Pelé himself (Mon–Fri 10–5; R$5).

402 P15 Largo Marquês de Monte Alegre s/n, Estação do Valongo, Centro 0800 173 887 Mon–Fri 9–5 From São Paulo and São Sebastião Bolsa do Café has a lovely café serving excellent espressos and snacks (▷ 157)

SÃO SEBASTIÃO

www.saosebastiao.sp.gov.br

São Sebastião, which sits opposite Ilhabela (▷ 143) on the São Paulo coast, is another of Brazil's colonial port towns whose few remaining colonial treasures could be lost in a malaise of concrete flats and ugly port buildings unless you know where to look. The city was settled at the end of the 16th century and some of its earliest buildings remain near the waterfront. These include the 17th-century chapel of São Gonçalo, which houses a small Museu de Arte Sacra (daily 1–5; R$2). It displays 16th-century effigies and artefacts recovered from concealed cavities in the church walls, discovered during restoration in 2003. Other sights include the town's parish church, the Igreja Matriz, an early 17th-century edifice rebuilt in 1819 (daily 9–6). There is a Museu do Naufrágio (Shipwreck Museum; Mon–Sat 10–6, Sun 10–4; R$2) near the church, exhibiting shipwrecks and the natural history of the local area. Also interesting, though not open to the public, are the Cadeia Pública (the prison), now the military police HQ, and a 17th-century mansion house, the Casa Esperança, built using whale blood and clay wattle and daub, covered over with plaster.

Head 2 or 3km (1 or 2 miles) north or south of the town to find the cleaner and more inviting beaches, including the popular surf beaches of Camburi and Maresias.

402 P15 Rua Sebastião Silvestre Neves 214, Centro 12 3891 2000 Mon–Fri 9–6 From São Paulo, Santos and Ubatuba Camburi and Maresias are reachable by bus from São Sebastião, Santos or São Paulo

UBATUBA

Aside from a single street of colonial buildings, there is little to see in Ubatuba town, but the municipality includes some of the most beautiful beaches on the Costa Verde. They range in style from the busy blue-collar stretch backed by cheap hotels at Praia Grande, and the twin half-moon bays of powdery white sand at Lázaro and Domingos Dias, to the long, deserted and forested sands of Praia da Fazenda near the fishing village of Piçinguaba. There are many waterfalls in the forests behind, which are good for bird watching.

402 P15 Praça 13 de Maio 200 12 3833 9007 Mon–Fri 9–6 A rental car is the best way to visit Ubatuba's beaches

Below *An idyllic view from the beach at Piçinguaba, near Ubatuba*

PARQUE NACIONAL DO ITATIAIA

The Trilha dos Três Picos (Três Picos Trail) is in the lower section of Itatiaia National Park. It cuts through rainforest into pine woodland, eventually reaching alpine grassland and the granite outcrops of the Três Picos. There's a good chance of seeing wildlife on the trail; especially primates and birds, for which Itatiaia is renowned.

THE WALK
Distance: 8km (5miles)
Time: 6 hours
Start/end at: Itatiaia Park Hotel

HOW TO GET THERE

The entrance to the Itatiaia National Park (▷ 145) is north of the town of Itatiaia, 180km (112 miles) west of Rio de Janeiro, on the road to São Paulo. Having arrived in Itatiaia, take the Estrada Parque Nacional road and head to Itatiaia Park Hotel, which appears on the right-hand side after 13km (8 miles), a couple of kilometres after the visitor centre. Visitors who are staying in any of the other hotels inside the national park can walk to the beginning of the trail at the Itatiaia Park Hotel.

★ The trail begins as a continuation of the hotel road, leaving the grounds of the hotel to the northeast and climbing into the forest.

❶ At the beginning of the trek there are groves of bamboo trees, which are favoured as nesting sites by colourful manakins. The vegetation then becomes progressively denser as you climb, with trees covered in bromeliads and orchids. This is a favourite area for brown capuchins and marmosets, who feed off the nuts, fruits and flowers. In places it is so narrow that hikers have to walk in single file.

Carry on the main path. For the next couple of kilometres (1.25 miles) there are no breaks in the path as it gently ascends into the heart of upper Itatiaia.

❷ This part of the mountain—between the rainforest and the upper cloud forest—is called the Serra do Palmital, named after a threatened species of palm which is illegally harvested for its delicious palm heart. This is a good area for spotting monkeys, including the woolly spider monkey, the largest neotropical primate and one of the rarest.

After a further kilometre (0.6 miles), the path forks. Keep to the left-hand fork and continue on along the larger trail.

Above *A well-prepared walker hiking one of the trails*
Left *The entrance to the national park*
Opposite *Brown-capped capuchins live in the dense vegetation of the lower slopes of the park*

❸ The rainforest now gives way to cloud forest, characterized by smaller trees and many orchids, bromeliads and other epiphytes (plants that grow on other plants and trees). Look out for cotingas (the brilliantly coloured, sparrow-sized songbirds), which are a common sight in this area.

The path climbs steeply for just under 3km (2 miles). Eventually, the forest enters a transition zone, with smaller trees and bushes, around the Rio Bonito falls.

❹ Stop for a swim in the falls, but be prepared for icy waters. In the winter months (Apr–Aug) temperatures can occasionally fall below freezing.

Leave along the path from behind the waterfall. This is an easy trail and without risks. Avoid crossing the tree trunk which blocks access to a lower trail—this is a hard route, steep and precipitous. The vegetation soon opens out into high alpine meadows, eventually reaching the Três Picos after a few hundred metres.

❺ From the Três Picos summit there are panoramic views of the Serra da Mantiqueira range, all the way to the Pico das Agulhas Negras, the highest point in the region, and all the way to the sea on very clear days.

Retrace your route to return to Itatiaia Park Hotel.

WHEN TO GO

Avoid visiting the park at weekends, when it can be very busy. It is possible to leave from Rio at around 7am, do the walk and return in a long day. Temperatures can drop below freezing between April and August, and the park can be very wet from December to February, making March and September to November the best months for a visit.

WHERE TO EAT

ITATIAIA PARK HOTEL

www.itatiaiaparkhotel.com.br

This is a huge sprawling hotel that lies at the top of the unpaved road off the main road which cuts through the park. There are superb views out over Itatiaia from its restaurant, which serves piping hot coffee for pre- and post-walk hikers.

✉ Estrada Parque Nacional, km 15 ☎ 24 3352 1230 🕒 Daily 12–3, 7–11

INFORMATION

✚ 402 P15 ℹ Estrada Parque Nacional ☎ 24 3352 1461 🕒 Daily 8–5 but often unmanned 🚌 From Rio de Janeiro to Itatiaia town, via Resende; onward journey by taxi or local bus (▷ Tips) 🚗 Dutra motorway well signposted from Rio and from Lagoa (via the Rebouças tunnel)

TIPS

» A bus from Itatiaia town, marked Hotel Simon or 504 Circular, goes to the park four times a day; coming from Resende; it may be caught at the crossroads before Itatiaia. There is only one road through the park, the Estrada Parque Nacional, on which all the hotels and the visitor centre are located.

» Through tickets back to Rio are sold at a booth in the large bar in the middle of Itatiaia main street.

» To increase your chances of seeing animals it is a good idea to hire a local guide (through one of the hotels or the visitor centre), wear muted colours and bring binoculars. Most guides do not speak English.

» The café at the visitor centre is often closed. It is best to bring your own supplies and refreshments.

» Avoid coming to Itatiaia at weekends, as the park is very busy and it can be noisy on the trails and around the waterfalls, limiting your chances of spotting wildlife.

BÚZIOS

FARM

www.farmrio.com.br

Farm has grown to be one of Brazil's most popular beach and light eveningwear shops for women. The brand was first introduced in 1997, at one of the hippie markets in Rio, and has since become renowned among twenty- and thirty-something women for its soft-as-silk cotton, bright stamps and elegant but sexy cuts. This outlet is in a small gallery of shops off the town's main thoroughfare, and there are further branches in Rio de Janeiro and throughout Brazil.

✉ Rua das Pedras 233 (aka Rua Jose Bento Ribeiro Dantas) ☎ 22 2623 7477 ⌚ Mon–Fri 10–8, Sat 10–5

LENNY

www.lenny.com.br

This is the Búzios branch of Brazil's most celebrated high-fashion bikini and swimwear brand, as worn by Gisele Bündchen, Naomi Campbell and Devon Aoki. Lenny are the most à la mode beach outfits for Búzios women, as opposed to teenagers. Branches can be found in Rio de Janeiro and throughout Brazil.

✉ Rua das Pedras 233 (aka Rua Jose Bento Ribeiro Dantas) ☎ 22 2623 3745 ⌚ Mon–Fri 10–8, Sat 10–5

TENDA

Tenda showcases many of the high-quality Brazilian beach brands which don't have their own boutiques in Búzios. Collections vary but usually include brands like the supermodels' bikini choice, Rosa Chá, and teeny bikinis for the super-slim, Blue Man.

✉ Rua das Pedras s/n (aka Rua Jose Bento Ribeiro Dantas) ☎ 22 2623 0177 ⌚ Mon–Fri 10–8, Sat 10–5

CABO FRIO

DEEP TRIP

www.deeptrip.com.br

The cape at Arraial do Cabo near Cabo Frio offers some of the best diving in southeast Brazil, with wrecks and abundant marine life attracted by the confluence of warm and cold currents. Deep Trip is the only PADI-affiliated dive operator in Arraial, with a range of courses and dive trips.

✉ Avenida Getulio Vargas, 93 Praia Grande, Arraial do Cabo ☎ 21 9942 3020 ⌚ Mon–Fri 10–5, or ring ahead ✋ From R$100 for a two tank dive ❓ Equipment and wetsuits available for hire

K-KITE

www.kkite.hpg.ig.com.br

Prevailing winds and calm water make conditions for wind- and kite-surfing ideal in the Região dos Lagos, with its salt water lakes and beaches. Board rental, tours and courses are all available.

✉ Rua da Alegria 15, Monte Alto, Arraial do Cabo ☎ 21 9351 7164 ⌚ Mon–Fri 10–5, or ring ahead ✋ From R$80 for a day, including all equipment

IGUAPE

TRIP ON JEEP

www.triponjeep.com

Access to and permission to visit the Complexo Estuarino Lagunar de Iguape-Cananéia-Paranaguá, the Estação Ecológico Juréia-Itatins, and Ilha Comprida is difficult for foreign visitors to organize. It is best achieved through an agency. Day trips or longer tours to these wilderness locations, and others closer to São Paulo city, are offered by Trip on Jeep, whose guides speak English.

✉ Rua Arizona 623, Brooklin ☎ 11 5543 5281 ⌚ Mon–Fri 10–6

ITATIAIA

RALPH SALGUEIRO

www.ecoralph.com

Trails in the Itatiaia National Park and the Serra da Mantiqueira can be bewildering to those who don't know the area and can't speak Portuguese. Guided half-day, full-day or multi-day walks are available through this

Opposite *Praia Forte in Cabo Frio is a good base for surfing*

agency and others in the locality or in Rio and São Paulo, such as Rio Hiking (▷ 96) and Trip on Jeep (▷ 154). Some also organize rock climbing.
✉ Rua Projetada 109, Vale do Ermitão, Itatiaia ☎ 24 3367 0416 🕒 Mon–Fri 10–6, or ring or email ahead

NITERÓI

SALINAS

www.salinas-rio.com.br
Jacqueline de Biase's beautifully crafted bikinis and beachwear are immensely popular with well-toned and tanned Brazilians and Americans with figures to flaunt. So much so that Salinas is the brand of choice for Victoria's Secret and is the swimwear modelled in their catalogues. Salinas is famous for its daring cuts, bright pop prints, delicate crochet and bead work, and high-quality materials. There are further shops in Rio de Janeiro and throughout Brazil.
✉ Rua Otavio Carneiro 64, Loja 104-106, Praia do Icarai ☎ 22 2610 6575 🕒 Mon–Fri 10–6, Sat 10–4

PARATY

ARMAZÉM SANTO ANTÔNIO

This small shop in a converted colonial cottage sells brightly painted model fishing boats, home décor items and decorative balloons made of papier mâché.
✉ Rua da Lapa 5 ☎ 24 3371 6542 🕒 Mon–Fri 10–8, Sat –Sun 10–4

ARTESANATO GUARANI

Look for Guarani indigenous people in Paraty. They often sell their pretty arts and crafts in the square adjacent to the Igreja Matriz. Items include bead jewellery, bows and arrows and wickerwork baskets.
✉ Praça da Matriz

GRUPO CONTADORES DE ESTÓRIAS

www.ecparaty.org.br
This adult puppet company has performed its combination of string puppetry and mime throughout the world. Shows last an hour and feature short performances from a repertoire, which includes both the poignant and the whimsical.
✉ Teatro Espaço, Rua Dona Geralda 327, Centro Histórico ☎ 24 3371 1161 🕒 Wed, Sat 9pm 🎫 R$15

PETRÓPOLIS

AVES FOTO

www.avesfoto.com.br
Brazilian birding and wildlife specialist Edson Endrigo has been running guided tours to select locations throughout Brazil for more than a decade. Scheduled or bespoke bird-watching and wildlife tours in São Paulo and Rio states could include Itatiaia, Ubatuba or the Serra dos Órgãos. Contact via the website only.

ROZ BRAZIL

http://rozbrazil.com/
British ex-pat Rosa offers one- or multi-day tours of the Imperial city and its environs in comfortable air-conditioned limousines. Optional light walking and bird watching can be included, and she also offers tours of the Serra dos Órgãos. Pick-ups are from Rio de Janeiro city or Petrópolis.
☎ 24 9257 0236

FESTIVALS AND EVENTS

FEBRUARY–MARCH

CARNAVAL

www.buziosturismo.com
www.paraty.com.br
In Búzios (▷ 142), *carnaval* is a major event, with parties and parades on the Rua das Pedras and the beaches. In Paraty (▷ 146–147) it is more folkloric, with parades in the street, a carnival queen and traditional samba dancing. In both towns, as across the country, carnival takes place annually, beginning the weekend before Shrove Tuesday and lasting a week.
ℹ Portico de Búzios s/n, Búzios ☎ 22 2633 6200 🕒 Daily 8–8 🚌 From Rio de Janeiro ℹ Largo da Pedreira, Paraty ☎ 24 3371 1266 🕒 Mon–Fri 10–6, Sat–Sun 11–4 🚌 From Rio de Janeiro and São Paulo

MARCH–MAY

FESTA DO DIVINO

www.neltur.com.br
Throughout the 40 days from Easter Sunday, a flag *(bandeira do Divino)* is progressively taken around the local municipalities of Niterói (▷ 144). The festival ends at Pentecost, with sacred and secular celebrations, including much revelry.
ℹ Estrada Leopoldo Froes 773 ☎ 21 2710 2727 🕒 Mon–Fri 10–6 ⛴ From the Praça XV docks, Rio de Janeiro

JUNE–AUGUST

FESTA LITERÁRIA INTERNACIONAL DE PARATY (FLIP)

www.flip.org.br
Workshops and lectures from renowned literary artists in the town of Paraty (▷ 146–147). Past guests have included Salman Rushdie and Maya Angelou. Most events are usually free. Tickets are available in the Flipzona tent, whose location is announced on the website each year, along with a full events listing and dates (which vary from year to year).
ℹ Largo da Pedreira ☎ 24 3371 1266 🕒 Mon–Fri 10–6, Sat–Sun 11–4 🚌 From Rio de Janeiro and São Paulo

AUGUST

FESTA DO PEÃO DE BOIADEIRO

www.guiabarretos.com
In August the little town of Barretos (▷ 141), in the interior of São Paulo state, hosts the world's biggest rodeo. There are broncos, lasso competitions and dozens of stages showcasing Brazilian and international acts, which in the past have included Mariah Carey. Most events are free. The rodeo runs for 10 days at the end of the month.
ℹ Rua 30 564, Centro ☎ 17 3321 1100 🕒 25 Aug 🚌 From São Paulo

PRICES AND SYMBOLS

The restaurants are listed alphabetically (excluding A, Al, El, La, Le and O). The prices given are the average for a two-course lunch (L) and a three-course dinner (D) for one person, without drinks. The wine price is for the least expensive bottle. Although you will find wine served in restaurants throughout Brazil, the usual drinks are bottled beer (R$5–R$8) or *caipirinhas*, the ubiquitous *cachaça* and fruit cocktails (R$8). All the restaurants listed accept credit cards unless otherwise stated.

For a key to the symbols, ⊳ 2.

BÚZIOS

BANANA LAND

Búzios's budget eating options are few and far between. This is the best of the bunch, with a big buffet set in a bright and bustling dining room. It is located in a street running parallel to the main drag, Rua das Pedras, but a block inland.

✉ Rua Manoel Turíbio de Farias 50 ☎ 22 2623 0855 ⌚ Mon–Fri 12–3, 7–11, Sat 12–3, 7–12, Sun 12–3 ✋ L R$15, D R$26

CHEZ MICHOU

www.chezmichou.com.br

An outdoor bar serving overly sweet crêpes cooked immediately to order and savoury options which are heavy on cheese and meat. It is popular for pre- and post-club fodder and very good value.

✉ Rua das Pedras 90 (aka Avenida Jose Ribeiro Dantas) ☎ 22 2623 2169 ⌚ Mon–Fri 12–3, 7–11, Sat 12–3, 7–12, Sun 12–3 ✋ L R$10, D R$20

CIGALON

This waterfront restaurant is made for romantic dining. French and Italian dishes are made with Brazilian ingredients and ultra-fresh seafood, and served at candlelit tables.

✉ Pousada do Sol, Rua das Pedras 199 (aka Avenida Jose Ribeiro Dantas) ☎ 22 2623 6284 ⌚ Daily 6pm–1am ✋ D R$60, Wine R$30

MOQUECA CAPIXABA

This restaurant is devoted to food from Rio de Janeiro's neighbour to the north, the state of Espírito Santo, which vies with Bahia in producing the finest seafood in the country. *Moquecas* are a kind of Africanized prawn or fish broth, cooked in coconut and flavoured with parsley. The owners—émigrés from Vitória—cook their *moquecas* in bright red juice from the *urucum* seed, as the locals would in Espírito Santo.

✉ Rua Manoel de Carvalho 116 ☎ 22 2623 1155 ⌚ Tue–Fri 12–3, 7–11, Sat 12–3, 7–12, Sun 12–11 ✋ L R$20, D R$40

SATYRICON

So fresh is the produce in Búzios's most illustrious seafood restaurant that it is chosen by diners while alive, from two huge aquaria in the dining room filled with lobsters, oysters and crabs. Fish are pulled from the sea and are rarely more than an afternoon old.

✉ Rua das Pedras 478 (aka Avenida Jose Ribeiro Dantas) ☎ 22 2623 2691 ⌚ Tue–Thu 5–12, Fri–Sat 5–2am, Sun 1–2am ✋ L R$50, D R$80, Wine R$30

SAWASDEE

www.sawasdee.com.br

Chef Marcos Sodré has been cooking Thai food *à la Carioca* at his restaurant by the beach on the Orla Bardot for more than a decade. His style of flavoursome Thai cooking, with spices heavily toned down for the Brazilian palate, has proved so successful that he has opened another branch of his restaurant in Rio's most fashionable restaurant street, Dias Ferreira (⊳ 101). His juicy *Kung Karre Suparrot* (sautéed shrimps with coconut milk, pineapple

Opposite *Sawasdee Thai restaurant in Búzios*

and curry seasoned with fried garlic) is a staunch favourite.
✉ Rua das Pedras 422 (aka Avenida Jose Ribeiro Dantas) ☎ 22 2623 4644 ⏲ Mon, Tue, Thu 6–12, Fri–Sat 6–1.30 ✋ D R$80, Wine R$30

CABO FRIO

PICOLINO

www.restaurantepicolino.com.br
One of the best restaurants from an undistinguished bunch in the town centre, serving fresh but simple seafood, such as Robalo à la Milenesa (hake in *farofa* flour crumbs). It has an attractive dining room in a 100-year-old building.
✉ Boulevard Canal 319 ☎ 22 2647 6222 ⏲ Mon 12–7, Tue–Sat 12–12, Sun 12–7 ✋ L R$30, D R$50, Wine R$25

CAMPOS DO JORDÃO

ARTE DA PIZZA

São Paulo state prides itself on its cheese-laden pizzas. This restaurant has won national awards for its offerings, which are light on pastry and heavy on flavour. The Napolitana is a local favourite.
✉ Avenida Frei Orestes Girardi 3549, Capivari ☎ 12 3668 6000 ⏲ Tue–Sat 12–3, 7–12, Sun 12–3 ✋ L R$20, D R$30, Wine R$30

HARRY PISEK

Campos do Jordão's love affair with all things Alpine is perpetuated in this Bavarian restaurant. The owner spent three years honing his skills in German kitchens before opening this establishment and it is considered one of the best German restaurants in the whole of Brazil. Food is traditional German fare: wurst, meatball stew, sauerkraut and apfel strudel.
✉ Avenida Pedro Paulo 857 (on the Horto Florestal road), Jardim Embaixador ☎ 12 3663 4030 ⏲ Tue–Fri 12–5, Sat–Sun 12–11 ✋ L R$20, D R$40, Wine R$30

ILHABELA

PIZZABELA

www.dellerestaurantehotel.com.br
At this hotel restaurant overlooking the water you will find excellent São Paulo-style pizza with light and fluffy pastry, delicious Portuguese *calabresa* sausage and oodles of cheese.
✉ Hotel Ilha Deck, Avenida Almirante Tamandaré 805, Itaguassu ☎ 12 3896 1489 ⏲ Mon–Fri 12–3, 7–11, Sat 12–3, 7–12, Sun 12–3 ✋ L R$26, D R$38

PARATY

BARTOLOMEU

www.bartholomeuparaty.com.br
This is the best option for meat-eaters in Paraty, with choice-cut Argentinian steaks, fresh fish and a bar serving huge *batida* cocktails (made with crushed ice, rum or vodka and soda water or lemonade).
✉ Rua Samuel Costa 176 ☎ 24 3371 5032 ⏲ Mon–Fri 12–3, 7–11, Sat 12–3, 7–12, Sun 12–3 ✋ L R$40, D R$60, Wine R$40

CATIMBAU

This romantic alfresco restaurant and bar sits over emerald-green water and between two giant boulders on a tiny island in the bay. Cooking is by local fisherman and movie-fixer Caca and his Dutch wife, Mimi, and consists of simple but very fresh seafood accompanied by an ice-cold beer or *caipirinha* (a sugar cane spirit, crushed ice and fruit cocktail).
✉ Baía de Paraty ☎ 24 3371 1847 ⏲ Thu–Sun 11–6 ✋ L R$40, Beer R$5
? Visited on request by bay tours

MERLIN O MAGO

French *cordon bleu* techniques, Brazilian ingredients and a German chef make this award-winning restaurant one of the city's best dining options. The long bar serves great cocktails and eating is by candlelight (open evenings only).
✉ Rua do Comercio 376, Centro ☎ 24 3371 2157 ⏲ Thu–Tue 7–12 ✋ DR$50, Wine R$30

PUNTO DI VINO

www.puntodivino.com.br
Neapolitan chef, Pipo, cooks the freshest seafood in town, which he catches himself. He also serves great wood-fired pizza and stocks an excellent selection of mostly Italian wines. There is live music here at weekends.
✉ Rua Marechal Deodoro 129, Centro ☎ 24 3371 1348 ⏲ Thu–Sun 12–3, 7–11 ✋ LR$30, DR$50, Wine R$30

THAI BRASIL

www.thaibrasil.com.br
Thai standards like green curry and *pad thai* are served here in an attractive dining room decorated with handicrafts and furnished with hand-painted chairs and tables. Those used to eating Thai food in Bangkok or Europe should ask for dishes to be cooked with extra chilli, as the Brazilians prefer their dishes less spicy.
✉ Rua Dona Geralda 345, Centro ☎ 24 3371 2170 ⏲ Thu–Sun 12–3, 7–11 ✋ L R$30, D R$50

VILLA VERDE

www.villaverdeparaty.com.br
A circular restaurant reminiscent of a *maloca* (indigenous Brazilian thatched roof communal house) sits here in a lovely tropical garden. It is surrounded by rainforest in a lawned area with many colourful heliconia flowers and humming birds. Dishes are light Italian in style.
✉ Estrada Paraty–Cunha km7 ☎ 24 3371 7808 ⏲ Daily 11–6 ✋ L R$50, Wine R$25

SANTOS

BOLSA DO CAFÉ

This superb little café in the Bolsa do Café museum (▷ 151) serves one of the most delicious espressos in Brazil alongside sumptuous savouries, sandwiches and snacks.
✉ Rua XV de Novembro 95, Centro ☎ 13 3213 1750 ⏲ Mon–Sat 9–5, Sun 10–5 ✋ L R$12, Coffee R$4

UBATUBA

PIZZARIA SÃO PAULO

Wood-fired pizzas are served here in a wonderful setting within a beautifully restored 18th-century building. They are cooked by a disenchanted lawyer-turned-chef who brings the authentic Italian ingredients for the gorgeous pizzas from São Paulo every weekend.
✉ Rua Doutor Esteves da Silva 26 ☎ 12 3836 1774 ⏲ Tue–Sun 12–3, 7–11 ✋ L R$20, D R$30

PRICES AND SYMBOLS

Prices are the lowest and highest for a double room for one night. Breakfast is included unless noted otherwise. All the hotels listed accept credit cards unless otherwise stated. Note that rates vary widely throughout the year.

For a key to the symbols, ▷ 2.

BÚZIOS

ABRACADABRA

www.abracadabrapousada.com.br

Rooms in this attractive mock-Mediterranean hotel gather around a pool. The best have wonderful views overlooking a bay of islands. Guests at the hotel can use the spa in the neighbouring Casas Brancas hotel (▷ this page).

✉ Alto do Humaita 13 ☎ 22 2623 1217 R$320–R$350 16 Outdoor

BRIGITTA'S

www.brigittas.com.br

This artily decorated, family-run guest house right in the town centre is where Bardot famously stayed on her visit in the 1960s. The bed she slept in is long-gone but it's possible to rent her room. It is one of just four. The guest house restaurant overlooks the water and is romantic when candlelit at night.

✉ Rua das Pedras 131 (aka Avenida Jose Ribeiro Dantas) ☎ 22 2623 6157 R$50–R$250 4

CASAS BRANCAS

www.casasbrancas.com.br

This romantic boutique hotel has a run of whitewashed rooms cascading down the hill and overlooking the bay, which wouldn't look out of place on a Greek island. The hotel has an excellent spa and one of the most intimate restaurants in Búzios, with tables in an open-sided candlelit dining area overlooking the bay.

✉ Alto do Humaita 8 ☎ 22 2623 1458 R$460–R$760 32 Outdoor

HIBISCUS BEACH

www.hibiscusbeach.com

Alice and Kevan Prior are the owners of this small hotel overlooking one of the best beaches in Búzios, Praia João Fernandes. Rooms are in spacious bungalows set in tropical gardens, with sea views from their balconies, TVs and WiFi. The *pousada* (guesthouse) has a pool, light meals available and offers help with car/buggy rentals and local excursions.

✉ Rua 1 No 22, Quadra C, Praia de João Fernandes ☎ 22 2623 6221 R$300–R$350 13 Outdoor

PRAIA DOS AMORES

www.alberguedebuzios.com.br

This International Youth Hostel Association hostel close to the *rodoviária* (bus station) and near Praia da Tartaruga beach, offers the only real budget accommodation in Búzios. There are double rooms and small air-conditioned dormitories. Both fill up quickly and it's important to book ahead.

✉ Rua das Pedras 92 (aka Avenida Jose Ribeiro Dantas) ☎ 22 2623 2422 Dorm bed R$30; double room R$80–R$140 18

VILLE BLANCHE

This guest house offers cheap tiled double rooms with fridges and en suites but no-frills. It is right in the heart of Búzios town, in a street running parallel to busy Rua das Pedras. There are also air-conditioned dormitories for up to 10 people.

✉ Rua Manoel Turibio de Farias 222 ☎ 22 2623 1201 Dorm bed R$30; double room R$130–R$180 15

CABO FRIO

POUSADA DO LEANDRO

www.pousadaleandro.com.br

This *pousada* is owned by (José) Leandro Ferreira, once a football player with Flamengo and the

Opposite *View from Casas Brancas hotel in Búzios*

Brazilian team. His trophies adorn a room next to the large pool. Rooms are modern and well-appointed, and are right next to the Praia do Forte beach.
Avenida Nilo Peçanha 333, Praia do Forte 22 2645 4658 R$175–R$400 17 Outdoor

CAMPOS DO JORDÃO

HOME GREEN HOME

www.homegreenhome.com.br
This is an ideal hotel for families or groups, with large apartment rooms having separate living areas and between one and three bedrooms. It is housed in one of the city's numerous vast mock-Alpine, steep-gabled hotels, perched on a hill overlooking a lush valley.
Rua Adolfo Torresin 800, Alto do Capivari 12 3663 2644 R$490–R$550 50

ILHABELA

REFÚGIO DAS PEDRAS

www.refugiodaspedras.com.br
This gorgeous *pousada* is set in lush forest and is fully integrated with its natural surroundings. Rooms and public areas are decked in wood and the giant granite boulders which dot the environs have been incorporated into the hotel design by architect-owner José Pinheiro, to form bathroom walls or sides to private Jacuzzis. The whole effect is extremely romantic and is for couples only; no children are permitted.
Avenida Mario Govas Jr 11495, Ponta da Sela 12 3894 1756 R$350–R$700 7 apartments Outdoor

ILHA GRANDE

ANCORADOURO

www.pousadaancoradouro.com.br
Rooms in this beachside *pousada*, a 10-minute walk east of the jetty, are plain and functional, but the location is wonderful. It sits right on the beach, with spectacular views out across the sea to the mountains of the mainland.
Rua da Praia 121 24 3361 5153 R$150–R$260 8

ITATIAIA

DONATI

www.hoteldonati.com.br
This is the best-appointed and best-situated of the dozen or so hotels inside the national park. Rooms are housed in heavy-wood Alpine-style chalets, set in tropical gardens visited by animals every night and early morning. Trails lead off from the main building into the forest and the hotel can organize accompanied walks and wildlife guides.
Estrada do Parque s/n 24 3352 1110 R$195–R$380 23 Indoor, outdoor

PARATY

BROMELIAS SPA

www.pousadabromelias.com.br
Comfortable and spacious chalet rooms are set in a hilly garden next to a rushing mountain stream. They are surrounded by lush forest, dotted with cattleya orchids and flitting with iridescent, and endangered, hummingbirds and tanagers. The hotel has an excellent spa, which is open to non-residents, and which has hot tub baths, massage and reiki treatments on offer.
Estrada para Graúna s/n 24 3371 2791 R$325–R$490 10 Outdoor

LE GITE D'INDAIATIBA

www.legitedindaiatiba.com.br
Chic chalet rooms in this French and Mineira owned and run *pousada*, a 30-minute drive from Paraty, sit eyrie-like in the lush folds of the Atlantic coastal mountains overlooking the ocean. Rooms have chunky wooden furniture, double beds covered in mosquito nets and hammocks outside. It's worth staying just for the restaurant (though this can be visited separately). Dinner here, with the sweeping views and accompanied by the music of the rainforest, is wonderful.
Estrada para Graúna s/n 24 3371 7174 R$120–R$400 5 Outdoor

HOTEL COXIXO

www.hotelcoxixo.com.br
Brazilian 1950s movie-star, Maria Della Costa, owns this charming *pousada* in the centre of Paraty's colonial centre. The best rooms are the spacious and bright upper-floor colonial suites, which are decorated with period furniture and religious artefacts. Rooms on the ground floor can be a little musty.
Rua do Comércio 362 24 3371 1460 R$200–R$350 33 Outdoor

PETRÓPOLIS

LOCANDA DELLA MIMOSA

www.locanda.com.br
This intimate *pousada* is for adults only and is situated in a neoclassical house in the mountains, a 15-minute drive from the city centre. Rooms are well-appointed and decorated with 19th-century furniture. The hotel has a spa and the price includes lunch and afternoon tea. The owner is one of the finest chefs in Brazil and guests come here to eat as much as to stay.
Alameda das Mimosas, Vale Florido 24 2233 5405 R$380–R$680 6

SOLAR DO IMPÉRIO

www.solarimperio.com.br
The most luxurious hotel in the centre of Petrópolis sits in a restored Imperial-era mansion opposite the Palácio Rio Negro. Rooms are opulent and huge, and the hotel has an excellent spa (not open to non-residents) and restaurant.
Avenida Koeler 276 24 2103 3000 R$400–R$680 24 Outdoor

UBATUBA

SOLAR DAS ÁGUAS CANTANTES

www.solardasaguascantantes.com.br
This neocolonial house sits in a palm-shaded and heliconia-filled garden near the beach. The seafood restaurant is one of the best in northern São Paulo state.
Estrada Saco da Ribeira 253, Praia do Lázaro, km 14 12 3442 0178 R$160–R$590 20 Outdoor

THE SOUTH

Southern Brazil feels very different from the rest of the country. This is the only part of the country to lie entirely outside the tropics, giving it a more European climate. Most of the people that live here are descended from Europeans who arrived in the 19th century, many of them from Germany, Italy, Eastern Europe and the Azores. The region comprises three states: Paraná is immediately south of São Paulo, and Santa Catarina and Rio Grande do Sul are on the borders of Argentina and Uruguay.

Paraná has a short but wild coastline, focused on the thickly forested Baía de Paranaguá, which—together with the tracts of forest in southern São Paulo—forms the largest stretch of Mata Atlântica (rare Atlantic rainforest) in Brazil. The interior of the state is largely agricultural apart from the Iguaçu Falls national park, which protects the rainforests around the magnificent Foz do Iguaçu, arguably the most beautiful waterfalls in the world and a must on any Brazilian itinerary.

Santa Catarina's main draw is the Ilha de Santa Catarina, a large island linked to the mainland by a bridge and fringed with some of Brazil's best beaches. The state capital, Florianópolis, lies here. The state has a number of German-speaking towns, including Blumenau, which is home to what Brazilians claim is the world's second-largest bierfest, after Munich's.

Rio Grande do Sul is *gaúcho* (cowboy) country. The people of Rio Grande do Sul are known as *gaúchos* to other Brazilians, and the herders are regularly seen in the state's traditional clothing of colourful shirts and puffy *bombacha* trousers. Most *gaúchos* are resolute carnivores and are almost as proud of their steaks as are the people of Argentina's Buenos Aires. The state capital, Porto Alegre, is the most industrialized and cosmopolitan city in the south, and tops the country's urban quality-of-life rankings. The state has good beaches nearby, fascinating ruined Jesuit missions, and stunning scenery in the Aparados da Serra national park, which lies in the Serra Gaúcha mountain range on the border with Santa Catarina state.

BLUMENAU

www.blumenau.sc.gov.br

The mock-Bavarian shopping centres with *enxaimel* exposed beams and plasterwork, American-style eateries selling huge tankards of locally brewed German ale, and its myriad wurst and sauerkraut restaurants, all make Blumenau feel like a mini-Munich transposed to Brazil. It's one of many prosperous Santa Catarina towns settled by Germans. They first arrived in 1850, 16 explorers led by the philosopher Herman Bruno Otto Blumenau. He brought them along the coast to the mouth of the Itajaí-Açu. The party made a camp on fertile ground and at a strategic bend in the river. Blumenau built a personal estate and his collaborator, Fritz Müller, turned this into a town which he named in Blumenau's honour. As the plantations flourished, so more families arrived from Germany and the village became a town with churches, schools and, eventually, a thriving textile industry.

Herman Bruno Otto Blumenau and Fritz Müller's houses still stand today as the Museu da Família Colonial, a German immigrant museum (Tue–Fri 9–5; R$2). The museum contains artefacts from the early days and period furniture, and tells the town's story in fascinating detail. There are a few other sights of note, including the German Evangelical Church and, just over 15km (9.5 miles) from the city centre, the Parque Ecológico Spitzkopf (tel 47 3336 5422; daily 7–7; R$7). This is a protected stretch of Mata Atlântica forest which covers the slopes of the 936m (3,070ft) Spitzkopf Peak, and which is cut by rushing rivers and icy waterfalls.

Blumenau has a lively Oktoberfest, which, unlike Munich's, marks the beginning of summer (rather than autumn) and which involves two weeks of revelry, with Bavarian dancing, folk music and beer.

393 M17 · Rua 15 de Novembro 420, Centro · 47 3322 6933 · Daily 9–5.30 · From Curitiba

CURITIBA

www.turismo.curitiba.pr.gov.br

Paraná's capital is famous for being a well-ordered, well-run city where the buses run on time, there is little crime and the streets are clean. It has few tourist attractions but it is a transport hub and you might stop to visit the new Museu Niemeyer: a striking Modernist building which looks like a Cyclopean eye set in white marble and which houses temporary art exhibitions. The museum sits in a park in the city centre and is easily reachable by the Linha Turismo bus from the main terminal (tel 41 3350 4400; Tue–Sun 10–6; R$4). Curitiba is also the inland terminus of the Serra Verde railway (▷ 171).

391 M16 · Rua Deputado Mário de Barros 1290 · 41 3254 6109 · Mon–Fri 8–6 · From São Paulo · Afonso Pena (Curitiba)

FLORIANÓPOLIS AND ILHA DE SANTA CATARINA

▷ 164–165.

FOZ DO IGUAÇU

▷ 166–167.

GRAMADO

www.portalgramado.com.br

The mountain village of Gramado, in Rio Grande do Sul state, is famous for its chocolate, its soaps and its fondue restaurants. Like many of Brazil's consciously quaint mountain villages it is filled with Alpine-style architecture, giving it a kitschy feel. This is accentuated in the antipodean summer, when the whole town bursts into blue and pink as millions of hydrangeas bloom. At this time of year, Gramado floods with tourists attempting to flee from the baking 40°C (104°F) heat of the plains below to the town's cool air and to shop in boutiques filled with chocolate, soap and tacky arts and crafts.

393 L18 · Avenida das Hortências 2029 · 54 3286 0220 · Daily 10–6 · From Porto Alegre

Above *Parque Vila Germanica, Blumenau*
Opposite *Museu Oscar Niemeyer, Curitiba*

FLORIANÓPOLIS AND ILHA DE SANTA CATARINA

Above *A sunset stroll along Praia Daniela at Florianópolis*

INFORMATION

www.guiafloripa.com.br
393 M17 Rua Tenente Silveira 60, Florianópolis 48 3952 7000 Daily 9–6 From airport Hercílio Luz (Florianópolis)

INTRODUCTION

Santa Catarina state's attractive modern capital, Florianópolis, straddles the mainland and the western shore of Santa Catarina Island. However, few visitors do more than pass through on their way to the beaches of the Ilha de Santa Catarina itself. In summer, when the sea is warm, these are some of the most seductive strands in the country, attracting Brazilians from far and wide.

Florianópolis—or Floripa as it is known to locals—was formally founded in 1739 by *brigadeiro* José da Silva Pais, who was appointed the first governor of the captaincy of Santa Catarina by the Portuguese crown. While there were a few ragged communities before then, it was Silva Pais who built the first forts and organized settlements, peopling them principally with sailors from the Portuguese islands of Madeira and the Azores. The first community was on the shores of the Lagoa da Conceição, in the interior of the island. The city of Florianópolis grew later with the establishment of large-scale whaling communities. There are still many Azorean villages around the island.

WHAT TO SEE

From the early days the Ilha de Santa Catarina was famous for its beauty, attracting landscape painters from all over southern Brazil, including the German-Brazilian artist Joseph Brüggemann. Its beaches and bays now attract surfers and sunbathers from all over the country. There are 42 beaches in total.

THE NORTHERN BEACHES

The beaches and coves on the northwest of the island are the busiest, offering gentle water and good swimming. The resort villages of Ponta Grossa, Jurerê, Canasvieiras and Ponta das Canas are linked together by a conurbation of condominiums and hotels which crowd behind the sand. They are very lively in summer, with a great party atmosphere. Praia do Forte, round a little cape jutting towards the shore, takes its name from the 18th-century Forte São José da Ponta Grossa (Dec–Mar daily 8–7; Apr–Nov daily 9–12, 1–5; R$4), which was built shortly after the captaincy was established and has recently been restored.

THE EASTERN BEACHES

The ocean-facing east of the island is fringed by a series of dramatic surf beaches and half-moon bays which spread north and south of the village of Barra da Lagoa. Joaquina and Mole have the best waves on the island and attract a young, middle-class, tanned and toned crowd in summer.

THE SOUTHERN BEACHES AND VILLAGES

The south of the island is dominated by the hippy-chic beach resort of Praia do Campeche, which is the resort of choice for young, single Brazilians on summer breaks. The beaches get progressively quieter to the town's southwest (▷ 172–173), rounding the southern cape of the island at another dramatically positioned fort, the Forte Nossa Senhora da Conceição, before reaching the pretty Azorean fishing village of Ribeirão da Ilha, which is famous for its bobbing fishing boats and its oysters.

MORE TO SEE

FLORIANÓPOLIS

The city itself has a pretty setting—huddled at either end of a stately suspension bridge which looks like a mini-Golden Gate—with pleasant leafy streets and a handful of decent restaurants and hotels. There is little to see in Florianópolis. The Mercado Público (Public Market) at Rua Conselheiro Mafra 255 (tel 48 3222 1259; Mon–Fri 9–6, Sat 10–2) sits in an atrium overlooked by handsome ochre-colonnaded buildings. Stalls sell tropical fruits and bric-a-brac, and there are plenty of bars and makeshift restaurants.

TIPS

» Take a bus marked *Rodoviária* (bus station) from the airport to reach the interchange if you wish to continue to other destinations on the island. For Florianópolis itself, take the *'Centro'* bus.

» The sea around Florianópolis is too cold between April and November for swimming or surfing without a wetsuit.

Below *The city of Florianópolis hugs the shoreline of the mainland and Santa Catarina island*

INFORMATION

www.fozdoiguacu.pr.gov.br
390 K16 Praça Getúlio Vargas 69, Foz do Iguaçu 45 3521 1455 Mon–Fri 8–6 Foz do Iguaçu *rodoviária* (4km/2.5 miles from city centre) Foz do Iguaçu (12km/7.5 miles from city centre)

Above *The breathtaking falls plunge 64m (210ft) on average*

INTRODUCTION

The world's mightiest and grandest waterfall is set in a bowl of verdant toucan-filled subtropical forest in the far east of Paraná state, and on the triple border of Paraguay, Argentina and Brazil. The falls are one of the few sights in the world that photos and film cannot prepare you for. They stretch for almost 3km (2 miles) and fall in a thunderous two-tier curtain from a height almost twice that of Niagara.

When the Portuguese arrived in the area—as Jesuits and as *bandeirante* slave traders—there had been indigenous people here for millennia. The Caiagangue people originally inhabited the region. The first European visitor was the Spanish conquistador, Alvaro Núñez Cabeza de Vaca, who nearly fell over the edge on his search to find a connection between the Brazilian coast and the Río de la Plata. After the expulsion of the Jesuits in the 18th century (▷ 29), the falls were largely forgotten until the area was explored by an expedition from Paraguay in 1863.

Iguaçu is an indigenous Guaraní word (meaning 'big water') and is the name of the river, rather than the falls. The Iguaçu river forms the triple international border and the falls themselves are shared between Brazil and Argentina (with Paraguay's territory beginning a few kilometres farther upstream).

WHAT TO SEE

NATIONAL PARKS

www.cataratasdoiguacu.com.br/parque.asp
www.iguazuargentina.com

The falls straddle two national parks: a Brazilian one (Parque Nacional do Iguaçu) and an Argentinian one (Parque Nacional Iguazu). Both are little explored and reachable only with a tour company (▷ 174–175), private car or taxi. Together they protect more than 130,000ha (321,000 acres) of rainforest, which are home to endangered species including jaguar.

✉ Parque Nacional do Iguaçu, Rodovia BR 469, km 18, Foz do Iguaçu ☎ 45 3521 4400
🕑 Mon–Sun 9–5 🍴
✉ Parque Nacional Iguazu, Iguazu, Misiones ☎ 54 3757 491469 🕑 Mon–Sun 9–5

GARGANTA DO DIABO (DEVIL'S THROAT)

This long waterfall-lined gorge forms the heart of Iguaçu. It is best seen from the Argentine side or from a boat in the gorge itself on the Macuco Safari tour (▷ 174), though care should be taken with personal items and electronics, as the boat passes under the falls themselves.

WALKWAYS

There are pedestrian walkways on both sides of the falls, offering spectacular vantage points. Those on the Argentinian side reach right to the lip of the Garganta do Diabo, in a series of boardwalks that are accessible on a free miniature train next to the entrance.

WILDLIFE

The falls sit on the edge of an extensive area of subtropical forest and are therefore visited by plenty of animals, especially birds. Look out for coatimundis (inquisitive, racoon-like mammals with long snouts and ringed tails), toco toucans (with their distinctive bright yellow beaks) and hand-sized, electric blue morpho butterflies, which flit in and out of the trees. Wildlife enthusiasts will also enjoy the bird park, the Parque das Aves (▷ 174), home to scores of species of rare South American (and international) birds, as well as a number of reptiles (including spectacled caiman and green anaconda). The park is set in attractive forest not far (500m/550 yards) from the entrance to the national park and can easily be visited on the way to or back from the Brazilian side of the falls.

TIPS

» As the Foz do Iguaçu is made up of 275 different but adjacent cascades, it is important to visit both the Brazilian and Argentinian sides for the best views. Borders can be crossed with minimal difficulty.

» You will need at least two days to see both sides of the falls at leisure.

Left *Toco toucan in Parque das Aves*
Below *Salto Bossetti waterfall on the Circuito Inferior (Lower Trail)*

ILHA DO MEL

www.ilhadomelonline.com

This balloon-shaped island in the wild Baía de Paranaguá is fringed with powdery white beaches and is a popular beach escape for young Paranaenses. It lies within and is surrounded by the Parque Nacional Superagüi (▷ 170). There are no roads and no cars, only a few tiny tourist towns, and the island has a laid-back, relaxed feel. The island is gradually being divided in two by the ocean, with the two halves connected only by a tiny sliver of sand. This forms two back-to-back half-moon bays at the main village of Nova Brasília, where boats arrive from Paranaguá.

Most of the hotels and guest houses are on the hilly eastern half, whose highest point is crowned with a lighthouse. The western half is flat, sandy and covered in low scrub forest. It is predominantly an ecological protection area. An 18th-century fort, the Fortaleza Nossa Senhora dos Prazeres (Fort of Our Lady of Pleasures), sits on its northern edge. There's good walking on the island. Tracks spread out from Nova Brasília, such as the Trilha de Farol (Lighthouse Trail), which is a 40-minute round-trip to the lighthouse. The Trilha Nova Brasília–Encantadas takes three hours, through forest and stretches of semi-deserted beach, taking in beautiful coastal views. Encantadas is a natural cul-de-sac, separated from Nova Brasília by impassable rocks, so take money for a taxi boat back around the Encantadas cape (fare varies; could be R$10–100). The island has good surf at Praia Grande and Praia de For, both about a 20-minute walk from the Nova Brasília jetty.

391 N16 Rua Padre Albino 45, Campo Grande, Paranaguá 41 3420 2940 Mon–Sat 10–6 From Trapiche da Rua da Praia pier on the quay in Paranaguá (daily at 3pm for Encantadas or Nova Brasília, returning the following morning at 7am (Encantadas) and 7.30am (Nova Brasília); R$24) Taxi boats also available from Paranaguá quay. There is a seasonal tourist booth sometimes open at the pier in Encantadas

Below *One of Joinville's Bavarian buildings, the railway station*

JOINVILLE

www.joinville.sc.gov.br

Santa Catarina's largest city has a substantial German population, the same bizarre Bavarian architecture as Blumenau (▷ 163) and a European feel. Germanic buildings include the railway station, built in 1906, and the Mercado Municipal (Municipal Market), with its *enxaimel* exposed beam and brickwork panelling. The Alameda Brustlein is an impressive avenue of palm trees, planted in 1873 and leading to the Museu Nacional da Imigração e Colonização (National Museum of Immigration and Colonization; www.museunacional.com.br; tel 47 3433 3736; Tue–Fri 9–5, Sat–Sun 11–5; R$2). This tells the story of immigration to the south of Brazil in much the same fashion as the Memorial do Imigrante in São Paulo (▷ 118). There is a series of well-presented information panels, with fascinating period photographs, models and a collection of objects and tools from the original German settlement. The Museu Arqueológico do Sambaqui (The Midden Archaeological Museum; tel 47 3422 5626; www.museusambaqui.sc.gov.br; Tue–Sun 9–12, 2–6) has artefacts dating back to 5,000BC, gleaned from shell middens excavated along the coast of southern Brazil.

393 M16 Avenida Herman August Lepper, 10 47 3431 3233 Mon–Fri 10–6 From all major tourist towns

MISSÕES JESUÍTICAS (JESUIT MISSIONS)

www.rotamissoes.com.br

These ruined Jesuit colleges and churches, listed as UNESCO World Heritage Sites, were set up in the 18th century to protect the indigenous Guaraní people from the *bandeirante* slave trade, and to convert them to Christianity. They lie in the extreme south of Brazil, in a region called the Real Gaúcho, the heart of cowboy country (and also in nearby Paraguay and Argentina).

The missions were the site of fierce battles between the Jesuit fathers and the slave-trading Brazilian *bandeirantes*. Slaves were

required for the sugar plantations in northern Brazil, where they were worked so hard that they had a life expectancy of only a few years. The Jesuits, under Father Antônio Vieira, campaigned fiercely against the cruelty, much to the chagrin of the colonial Portuguese, whose complaints to Lisbon were championed by the powerful Marques de Pombal. Pombal, and his French allies, had the order expelled from the Americas by the Pope, and subsequently disbanded. The missions were ransacked, the Guaraní women raped, the children murdered and the men enslaved—a story told in Roland Joffe's landmark 1986 film, *The Mission.*

The only major Jesuit ruins in Brazil are at São Miguel das Missões, 50km (30 miles) from the provincial town of Santo Ângelo in western Rio Grande do Sul. The ruined shell and adjacent tower of what was once a stately 18th-century church lie in a large lawned area in the town. At night they are illuminated and sit under a canopy of stars. It is possible to continue into Argentina from Santo Ângelo town, to visit other UNESCO protected ruins at San Ignacio Mini and Posadas. Direct buses leave Santo Ângelo for those towns, with a stop at the border for passport stamps and customs.

392 K17 São Miguel das Missões Daily 9–6 R$8 From Santo Ângelo (which is reached by bus from Porto Alegre) Very simple restaurants in São Miguel das Missões town

PARQUE NACIONAL APARADOS DA SERRA

www.guiaaparadosdaserra.com.br

This spectacular Rio Grande do Sul national park, 117km (72.5 miles) north of the state capital, Porto Alegre (▷ 170), is famous for the 8km-long (5-mile) and 720m-deep (2,360ft) Cânion de Itaimbezinho. This was formed 115 to 130 million years ago when the American and African plates were separating, and lies within the 250km-long (155-mile) Aparados da Serra mountain range, which runs through the states of Santa Catarina and Rio Grande do Sul.

The canyon offers spectacular hiking, descending through subtropical forest to unique gorge ecosytems which have adapted to the cool, dark microclimate at the bottom of Itaimbezinho. Trails pass two waterfalls, which drop 350m (1,150ft) into a dark pool in the depths of the gorge.

393 M18 No visitor centre in park From São Francisco de Paula (which is reached by bus from Joinville) Taxi from São Francisco de Paula is R$40–50 but the park is best visited with an organized tour by an agency, such as Brazil Ecojourneys (▷ 175)

PARQUE NACIONAL LAGOA DO PEIXE

www.furg.br/furg/projet/pnlpeixe

This long thin national park, east of Porto Alegre (▷ 170) and in the far south of Rio Grande do Sul state, protects a shallow brackish lake which is one of South America's premier sites for migrating water birds. Flamingos and albatrosses are among the visitors here and at the peak of migration there are literally millions of birds. The park is remote and, while access is free, there is no infrastructure, either for monitoring the wildlife or for organizing visits. The best point of entry is via the small coastal town of Mostardas. The main lake (which has the highest bird concentration) is some 20km (12.5 miles) from both Mostardas and Tavares, the other main town of the park.

393 L19 Mostardas is reachable by bus from Porto Alegre. The Mostardas–Tavares bus passes through the northern end of the park on its way to the beach Best visited with an organized tour by an agency, such as Avesfoto (▷ 175)

Above *The ruins of São Miguel das Missões Jesuit colonial church*

PARQUE NACIONAL SUPERAGÜI

www.fumtur.com.br
www.guaraquecaba.com/superagui.asp

This breathtakingly beautiful national park lies at the heart of the largest single stretch of Mata Atlântica forest in the country. It forms part of a UNESCO World Biosphere Reserve and the Nature Conservancy's Brazilian Parks in Peril Programme (www.parksinperil.org). It is contiguous with several other protected areas, both in Paraná and in neighbouring São Paulo state. Superagüi means 'the kingdom of the fish' in Tupi Guaraní. It is a fitting name for one of the largest marine nurseries in Brazil. Millions of fish and marine animals spawn and breed in the park's 33,988ha (83,950 acres) of mangrove wetlands, estuaries, mudflats and beaches—from tarpon to turtles and sea birds to sharks. The park is also a crucial repository of land species. On the myriad islands and in the stretches of mainland terra firma forest, more than half of the tree species and nearly three-quarters of its other plants are found nowhere else on Earth. There are 15 species of globally endangered birds, including the red-tailed amazon (a parrot on the 'red list' of critically endangered species, which can be seen only here and at a few coastal areas nearby), and threatened or critically endangered reptiles and mammals, including yellow-throated caiman, green turtle, jaguar, Brazilian tapir, black-faced lion tamarin, and puma.

There have been indigenous people in Superagüi for millennia, as evidenced by the 50 or so sambaqui middens that have been discovered in the park (artefacts from which can be seen in the museum in Joinville ▷ 168). While the Tupiniquin and Carijo people who inhabited the area at the time of the Portuguese conquest are long gone, there are several large Guarani villages in the forest and along the coast. These sit alongside a number of traditional fishing communities.

Visiting the park is straightforward. Boat excursions can be made from the Ilha do Mel (▷ 168), which is surrounded by the park, or from Paranaguá or Guaraqueçaba towns. Superagüi island itself sits within the national park and has a number of *pousadas* (small inns) if you wish to stay overnight.

391 N16 · Rua Padre Albino 45, Campo Grande, Paranaguá · 41 3420 2940 · Mon–Sat 10–6 · From Curitiba to Paranaguá or Guaraqueçaba · From Ilha do Mel, Paranaguá or Guaraqueçaba

Above *Black-faced lion tamarins grooming in Parque Nacional Superagüi*

PORTO ALEGRE

www.portoalegre.rs.gov.br

Rio Grande do Sul's state capital is a large modern city, watching over an expansive estuary formed by the confluence of five rivers. These spill into the second largest marine lagoon in Latin America, the Lagoa dos Patos. While the city has few sights of interest to tourists, it is one of Brazil's more pleasant capitals. It boasts more than a million trees, a rich European-Brazilian and *gaúcho* (cowboy) culture, a lively music scene, and the best restaurants and shops south of São Paulo. Porto Alegre is a good base for exploring the south of the region.

The city also hosts meetings of the World Social Forum (www.forumsocialmundial.org.br), which was launched in June 2000 at the Alternative Social Summit in Geneva. The forum is a meeting point for social movements opposed to neoliberal globalization and for expressing an alternative to the guidelines of the World Economic Forum in Davos. It is attended by more than 100,000 international delegates annually—mostly drawn from the not-for-profit and environmental world.

393 L18 · Travessa do Carmo 84, Cidade Baixa · 51 3289 1000 · Mon–Sat 10–6 · From all major tourist towns · Internacional Salgado Filho, Porto Alegre

PORTO BELO

www.portobelo.com.br

Santa Catarina state's best beaches, after the Ilha de Santa Catarina (▷ 164–165), fringe a peninsula which juts into a green Atlantic, some 60km (37 miles) north of Florianópolis. Like Búzios (▷ 142) or Porto de Galinhas (▷ 252), Porto Belo itself is a fishing village-turned-seaside resort, with a large harbour filled with bobbing fishing boats, and private yachts and motor launches. The main beaches—Praia Bombas and Praia Bombinhas—are 3 and 9km (2 and 5.5 miles) away, respectively. Both are long stretches of white-pepper fine, silky sand backed by *pousada* hotels and holiday homes. Quatro Ilhas beach—which is a 15-minute walk from Bombinhas—has good surf, and in summer there is snorkelling from floating restaurants in the rocky bay of Caixa d'Aço.

393 M17 · From Florianópolis

PRAIA DO ROSA

www.praiadorosa.com.br

This beautiful region, just over 70km (43.5 miles) south of Florianópolis, focuses on a 3.5km-long (2-mile), half-moon bay with a broad beach of fluffy white sand, sitting in preserved forests with limpid lakes. The upmarket resorts and *pousadas* in the vicinity make concerted efforts to practise sustainable tourism. They joined together in the early years of the new millennium to form a private environmental protection area (APA) devoted to the preservation of the surrounding forest and the offshore islands, which are visited by the baleia franca (southern right whale) between July and November. The Ilha do Coral and other islands offshore are good for snorkelling, and the Ilha de Papagaiao sits in a private reserve protecting 14ha (34.5 acres) of Mata Atlântica. Praia do Rosa is the only Brazilian location designated as one of the most beautiful bays in the world by the sustainable tourism NGO, Le Club des Plus Belles Baies du Monde (www.world-bays.com), which also counts Bantry Bay (Eire) and Nha Trang (Vietnam) among its members.

393 M17 From Florianópolis

SERRA DA GRACIOSA AND THE SERRA VERDE RAILWAY

The long coastal ridge which breaks into the craggy Serra dos Órgãos in Rio, and the great spurs which jut into the sea on the Costa Verde, rises dramatically in northern Paraná to form the Serra da Graciosa mountains. These are covered in primary rainforest, broken by granite rocks and cut by little trails and rivers. Much of the serra is a protected state park and the hiking and climbing here is superb.

Paraná was colonized via paths cut through the Serra da Graciosa by Brazil's indigenous people long before the arrival of the Portuguese. These were widened by the conquerors, who forced thousands of African slaves to carry river stones into the hills and turn trails into paved mule roads. These transported gold, silver, textiles and the local equivalent of tea, *herva maté* (yerba mate), between the interior of Paraná and the busy port of Paranaguá. By the late 19th century this had become one of the most important trade routes in southern Brazil and way stations had grown into prosperous villages, like Morretes and Antonina. In 1885, the trade was lucrative enough to merit the construction of a railway, the Serra Verde, which carries tourists today from Curitiba (▷ 163) to Paranaguá on one of the most spectacular mountain railway rides in South America (book in advance, ▷ 175).

393 M16 Rua Deputado Mário de Barros 1290, Curitiba 41 3254 6109 Mon–Fri 8–6 From Curitiba to Morretes and Paranaguá Daily from Curitiba to Morretes; Sundays only from Curitiba to Paranaguá

Below left *Pilgrim steps leading to the Catholic basilica in Porto Alegre*
Below *Train on the Serra Verde railway from Curitiba to Morretes*

THE UNSPOILED SOUTH OF THE ILHA DE SANTA CATARINA

This walk takes in some stunning coastal scenery in the remotest part of Santa Catarina island (▷ 164–165), cutting through the forests of the Parque Estadual da Serra do Tabuleiro, and passing a ruined Portuguese water mill. There are breaks for views and a dip in a waterfall, before arriving at a secluded beach and lighthouse on the southern tip of the island.

THE WALK
Distance: 5km (3 miles) each way
Time: 2 hours each way (or 2 hours one way and boat trip back)
Start/end at: The final stop of the Caireira da Barra do Sul bus (route 561)

HOW TO GET THERE
The bus departs from Terminal Rio Tavares, located on the SC 405, near the entrance to Praia do Campeche. Stay on the bus until the final stop.

★ The walk starts at the bus stop. A car park is located to your right. Enter and take a footpath that leads uphill, initially steeply, towards the forest. As you climb, views of the bay to the right gradually come into view.

❶ The first portion of the walk cuts through shady rainforest in the Parque Estadual da Serra do Tabuleiro. There are many bromeliads hanging in the trees, and forest birds—particularly cotingas and tanagers—are a common sight. Views to the right look northwest and from this part of the island you can see the mainland.

After a few hundred metres the path curves to the left and then flattens out again. It then begins to ascend once more, cutting its way through regenerating subtropical rainforest, thick with vines and closely packed vegetation growing over each other. Continuing for several hundred metres, the path splits in two but you can take either direction as they rejoin about 40m (44 yards) farther on. This is the highest point of the walk, 111m (364ft) above sea level. The path starts to descend, steeply at first. If the way is muddy, it's best to take the raised section of the path, where trees can be used for support if needed. Shortly afterwards you'll need to cross a stream with stepping stones, but this is easily navigable and not wide.

❷ After the stream, you'll encounter brick columns to the left of the footpath. These are from a ruined flour mill, built by the Azoreans who first settled here in the 18th century. Water turned huge stones, which crushed dried manioc (rather than wheat) into crunchy flour. This foodstuff is still eaten in Brazil today, and is known as *farofa*. It was a staple food for the country's indigenous population long before the arrival of the Portuguese.

Opposite *Praia dos Naufragados*
Right *Sculpted rocks and clear water at Praia dos Naufragados*

A farther 500m (545 yards) down the path there's a small waterfall to the left, which empties into a stream that you'll need to cross. Again, the water is shallow and large stepping stones make it easy. Follow the path as it curves to the right, although you can climb the rocks to the left to get a closer look at the waterfall.

❸ The waterfall has a small pool which is an ideal spot for a refreshing dip after the climb and descent through the forest.

Return to the path, continuing to follow it as it curves right and then left—ignore the one on the right—until it leads out of the forest and onto a beautiful wide stretch of beach.

❹ This is the Praia dos Naufragados (Shipwreck Beach), the most southerly point on the island. There are a couple of simple fish restaurants here and usually only a handful of other tourists, except in high season. It's a wonderful secluded spot for a swim and a rest, and on the beach there are no mosquitoes.

Turn right and walk along the beach towards the headland that juts out into the sea. At the end of the bay, on a hillock, is a lighthouse. There is a footpath leading to the lighthouse from the beach, although it isn't signposted. It's located above the rocks, where the vegetation begins, and is best navigated at low tide. If you prefer, you can walk on the rocks further round the edge of the bay and join the path at a later stage. As well as a lower path, you'll find another trail above it.

❺ The lower path reaches the lighthouse, while the top one leads to a set of Portuguese cannons dating from 1808. Both paths run uphill past scrubby vegetation and wild flowers, and afford stunning views over the bay below. Arriving at the lighthouse, there's a wooden viewing deck with more sweeping views.

For the return leg of the walk you can either retrace your way back to the starting location, or take a public boat round the bay on a journey that takes about 15 minutes. The boat service is only available regularly from November to March.

WHEN TO GO

The walk is best done in the early morning or late afternoon, when the light is softest.

WHERE TO EAT

The restaurants at Shipwreck Beach tend to have irregular opening times, so it is best to bring your own drink and food for a picnic.

INFORMATION

393 M17 Rua Tenente Silveira 60, Florianópolis 48 3952 7000 Daily 9–6

TIPS

» If there's been rainfall, the steep part of the walk can be difficult to navigate due to mud, so wear appropriate footwear. Hiking boots are recommended.
» Be sure to bring repellent as mosquitoes are particularly bad on the initial section of the walk.
» There is a booth to the right of the parking lot at the start of the walk, which has information about the bay boat trip. Boats run every 30 minutes (November to March) and cost R$10 per person (minimum 4 people).

FLORIANÓPOLIS AND THE ILHA DE SANTA CATARINA

BRAZIL ECOJOURNEYS

www.brazilecojourneys.com

The island provides opportunities for beach and light forest walking, paragliding and light adventure activities, which Brazil Ecojourneys (▷ 175) can arrange for you.

✉ Estrada Rozália Paulina Ferreira 1132, Armação Florianópolis ☎ 48 3389 5619

ESCOLINHA DE SURF

www.surfschoolbrazil.com

For 10 years Evandro Santos has been a professional surfer. He's been teaching locals to surf off the Ilha de Santa Catarina's eastern beaches for as long as he can remember and has recently opened up his surf school to visitors. He also rents boards.

✉ Rua Santos Reis 88, Florianópolis ☎ 48 3232 7753

SCUNA SUL

www.scunasul.com.br

This agency in Florianópolis can organize boat trips around the Ilha de Santa Catarina, with stops for snorkelling and visiting beaches.

✉ Avenida Osvaldo Rodrigues Cabral s/n, Florianópolis ☎ 48 3225 1806 🕐 Daily 10–6

FOZ DO IGUAÇU

CAMPO DE DESAFIOS

www.campodedesafios.com.br

Campo de Desafios offer white-water rafting, caving, canopy tours, rock climbing and rapelling on and around the Iguaçu river. The emphasis is on adrenaline. Trips are noisy.

✉ Rodovia das Cataratas, km 27.5, Foz do Iguacu ☎ 45 3529 6040 🕐 Daily 10–6

IGUAZU BIRDWATCHING

www.iguazubirdwatching.com.ar

The forests and national park around Iguaçu have excellent bird watching. Argentinian birder, Daniel Somay, speaks good English and knows his birds. Reserve in advance through the website.

✉ Perito Moreno 217, Iguazú, Argentina ☎ +54 3757 421 922 🕐 Mon–Fri 10–5

MACUCO SAFARI

www.macucosafari.com.br

This pricey two-hour walk, electric car and boat trip offers the chance to get up close to the base of the Iguaçu falls. The tour is only worth taking for the boat trip (there is better walking for free on the Argentinian side of the falls). Be sure to bring your own waterproof, sealable bag for cameras and clothes, as you will get completely soaked and the bags provided by the company are inadequate.

✉ Rodovia das Cataratas, km 25, Parque Nacional do Iguaçu ☎ 45 529 7976 🕐 Daily 8–6 ✋ Adult R$184, child (7–12) R$92, under 6 free

PARQUE DAS AVES

www.parquedasaves.com.br

This large aviary is home to many rare Brazilian (and international) birds, including several species of macaw, currasow and guan. These are housed in aviaries which you can walk through. There is also a butterfly house with spectacular species, including huge, iridescent morphos.

✉ Avenida das Cataratas, km 17 ☎ 45 3529 8282 🕐 Daily 8.30–5.30 ✋ R$20 ☕

ILHA DO MEL

BOAT HIRE

www.ilhadomel.com

Fishing boats can be hired in the port at either Nova Brasília or Encantadas. They can also be chartered to Superagüi island (▷ 170) from Praia da Fortaleza. Prices vary according to group sizes and time of year, and arrangements should be made directly with the boatmen.

Opposite *Walkway in Parque das Aves, Foz do Iguaçu*

Tourist booth with irregular hours on the pier at Encantadas. Nearest regular office is in Paranaguá (Rua Padre Albino 45; tel 41 3420 2940; Mon–Sat 10–6)

PARQUE NACIONAL APARADOS DA SERRA

BRAZIL ECOJOURNEYS

www.brazilecojourneys.com

This mountainous park has great hiking and wildlife watching. Brazil Ecojourneys have short and long hikes in the park and the serra, including descents into the Cânion de Itaimbezinho (▷ 169).

Estrada Rozália Paulina Ferreira 1132, Armação Florianópolis 48 3389 5619

PARQUE NACIONAL LAGOA DO PEIXE

AVESFOTO

www.avesfoto.com.br

This important waterfowl reserve is one of the key stops on the migratory passage north and south for millions of wading birds. Professional bird watcher Edson Endrigo offers trips; contact is via the website only.

PORTO ALEGRE

BAR DO GOETHE

www.bardogoethe.com.br

This bar offers the best beer in the city. There are plenty to choose from, including light draught lager *(chope)*, Bavarian wheat beer *(weissbier)* and rich dark stout *(cerveja oscura)*.

Rua 24 de Outubro 112, Moinhos de Vento 51 3222 2043 Daily 6–late

SERRA DA GRACIOSA

SERRA VERDE EXPRESS

www.serraverdeexpress.com.br

One of the great railway journeys of the world runs from Curitiba to Morretes. On Sundays it continues to Paranaguá, passing through the Serra da Graciosa (▷ 171). Try to sit on the left-hand side when descending.

Avenida Presidente Afonso Camargo 330, Estação Ferroviaria, Curitiba 41 3077 4280 Daily to Morretes, Sunday only to Paranaguá Economy ticket R$39, luxury with food R$270, child (3–12) R$189

FESTIVALS AND EVENTS

FEBRUARY–MARCH

CARNAVAL

Celebrated everywhere in the region, but particularly on the Ilha de Santa Catarina, where there are parades, dancing and general partying on the beaches. It takes place annually from the weekend before Shrove Tuesday until the end of the following weekend.

Rua Tenente Silveira 60, Florianópolis 48 3952 7000 Daily 9–6

MARCH–APRIL

FARRA DO BOI

www.farradoboi.info

Easter festivals on the Ilha de Santa Catarina include this colourful celebration, with parades and traditional music. Until 1998 it also involved the ritual slaughtering of a bull, which was then eaten. This was outlawed by federal law. Nowadays, locals celebrate by eating beef in huge quantities and dressing up in bovine costumes. Events take place annually during Holy Week throughout the island, especially in Florianópolis city and on Praia do Jurerê beach.

Rua Tenente Silveira 60, Florianópolis 48 3952 7000 Daily 9–6

AUGUST

FESTIVAL DE CINEMA DE GRAMADO

www.festivaldegramado.net

A Latin American film festival in Gramado, one of the biggest in southern Brazil, with shorts and feature films from throughout the continent. None of the films are subtitled in English so visitors will need to have Portuguese or Spanish to get the most from the showings. Dates vary from year to year but the festival usually takes place over one week from the second Friday of August.

Avenida das Hortências 2029 54 3286 0220 Daily 10–6

SEPTEMBER

SEMANA FARROUPILHA

www.semanafarroupilha.com.br

This festival takes place in Porto Alegre, usually between the second and third week of September. It is one of the largest annual celebrations of *gaúcho* (Brazilian cowboy) culture in the south, featuring parades of herdsmen in traditional dress, accompanied by huge, themed floats with *gaúcho* themes, stages with traditional *bandoneón* music, rodeos and general revelry.

Travessa do Carmo 84, Cidade Baixa, Porto Alegre 51 3289 1000 Mon–Sat 10–6

OCTOBER

OKTOBERFEST

www.oktoberfestblumenau.com.br

This bierfest, in Blumenau, is reputedly the largest outside Germany and the biggest celebration of Teutonic culture in the Americas. It includes traditional Bavarian dancing, folk music and, of course, beer drinking (usually local *weissbier*). The festival usually takes place for two weeks in mid-October. There are smaller celebrations in Joinville.

Rua 15 de Novembro 420, Centro, Blumenau 47 3322 6933 Daily 9–5.30

DECEMBER–JANUARY

BOI-DE-MAMÃO

www.boidemamaofestas.com.br

Ilha de Santa Catarina's vibrant giant puppet festival has its origins in Azorean culture. The main event is a parade with people dressed up as lavishly decorated and brilliantly coloured bulls and cows, accompanied by dancing and drum, guitar and *bandoneón*-driven bands. The parade dates vary from year to year but usually take place in mid-January and mid-June.

Rua Tenente Silveira 60, Florianópolis 48 3952 7000 Daily 9–6

PRICES AND SYMBOLS

The restaurants are listed alphabetically (excluding A, Al, El, La, Le and O). The prices given are the average for a two-course lunch (L) and a three-course dinner (D) for one person, without drinks. The wine price is for the least expensive bottle. Although you will find wine served in restaurants throughout Brazil, the usual drinks are bottled beer (R$5–R$8) or *caipirinhas*, the ubiquitous *cachaça* and fruit cocktails (R$8). All the restaurants listed accept credit cards unless otherwise stated.

For a key to the symbols, ▷ 2.

BLUMENAU

ABENDROTHAUS

A traditional German restaurant in a faux-German *enxaimel* beamed house, Abendrothaus serves only one dish—*marreco*, a traditional Bavarian oven-roasted and stuffed duck. It is immensely popular with locals, so booking ahead is essential.

✉ Rua Henrique Conrad 1194 ☎ 47 3378 1157 🕐 Sun only 11.30–3.30 ✋ L R$30, D R$30, Wine R$30

CURITIBA

BOULEVARD

Curitiba's favourite upper-end restaurant serves a mixed European menu with French, Italian and Brazilian cooking, excellent fresh fish and hearty steaks. There is also a tasting menu with *amuse-bouches* and miniature pasta, fish and meat dishes accompanied by a different wine for each dish. The dining room is smart casual, with heavy ipe-wood chairs, white linen and low lighting. An excellent wine list focuses on French, Portuguese and South American bottles.

✉ Rua Vol da Pátria 539, Centro ☎ 41 3224 8244 🕐 Mon–Fri 12–2.30, 7.30–12, Sat 7.30–12 ✋ L R$60, D R$80, Wine R$40

FLORIANÓPOLIS

ANTÔNIO'S

www.antoniosrestaurante.com.br

The large, bright open-plan dining room and bar in this mock-colonial restaurant bustles with local families, especially at weekends. They come principally for the magnificent seafood (locally caught prawns, served either grilled or breaded, are a speciality) but there are more than 80 dishes on the menu. These include pasta, grilled meats and salads, which are all served in enormous, unseasoned portions.

✉ Avenida Luíz Boiteux Piazza 2214, Cachoeira do Bom Jesus ☎ 48 3284 5736 🕐 Tue–Fri 12.30–3, 7.30–12, Sat 7.30–12, Sun 12.30–3 ✋ L R$45, D R$90, Wine R$30

CHEF FEDOCA

www.cheffedoca.com.br

Excellent fresh fish, Santa Catarina prawns and lobster, and hearty Bahian seafood dishes including Chef Fedoca's famous *moquecas* (seafood broth cooked in coconut and palm oil, seasoned with tropical herbs). He serves them light on palm oil and with generous amounts of locally caught crustaceans and prawns, large enough for two. There is also a choice of more than 30 different bottled Brazilian and German-Brazilian beers. The best tables at this waterfront restaurant are on the wooden deck, with views over the Lagoa.

✉ Rua Senador Ivo d'Aquino Neto 133, Lagoa ☎ 48 3232 0759 🕐 Dec–Mar Tue–Fri 11.30–3, 7.30–12, Sat–Sun 11.30–12; Apr–Nov Sun 11.30–6 ✋ L R$50, D R$70, Wine R$28

RANCHO AÇORIANO

www.ranchoacoriano.com

This Azorean restaurant specializes in still-wriggling Santa Catarina oysters and grilled Florianópolis prawns, both pulled from the sea literally in front of the restaurant. Fillets of fish are equally fresh and reliably include *robalo* (hake) and *garoupa* (grouper). The best tables are on the

Opposite *Fish and seafood are plentiful in Florianópolis*

restaurant's private wooden jetty, protruding into the emerald Atlantic from the rocky shoreline at Ribeirão da Ilha, near the airport.
✉ Rodovia Baldicero Filomeno 5634 ☎ 48 3337 0848 ⌚ Mon, Wed, Sun 11–11 ✋ L R$60, D R$80, Wine R$30

TOCA DA GAROUPA

www.tocadagaroupa.com.br
This long-established family-run restaurant has been voted the best for seafood in Florianópolis by Brazil's largest national magazine, *Veja*. The most popular dish is the seafood mixed grill, whose grouper, hake and assorted crustaceans and shellfish are locally caught and ultra-fresh. The large, bright open-plan dining room, decorated with flotsam and jetsam, is filled with families at weekends and busy at any time, so this isn't a great option for intimate dining.
✉ Rua Alves de Brito 178 ☎ 48 3223 1220 ⌚ Daily 12–3, 7–12 ✋ L R$65, D R$85, Wine R$40

FOZ DO IGUAÇU

BUFALO BRANCO

www.bufalobranco.com.br
Waiters in dinner jackets whisk sizzling cuts of spit roast meat from the kitchen to the hordes of chatting diners in this large and immensely popular Brazilian *churrascaria* (spit roast). There's a salad and pasta bar for those wanting to eat more than barbecued meat, and a good choice of desserts. As in most *churrascarias*, there is one price for all you can eat.
✉ Rua Rebouças 530 ☎ 45 3523 9744 ⌚ Daily 12–11 ✋ L and D R$70, Wine R$32

CHEF LOPES

www.cheflopes.com.br
Tables in this intimate and informal brasserie are flanked by a large tile-fronted bar serving ice-cold beer, *caipirinha* cocktails and a respectable selection of Argentinian wines. The menu is meat-heavy, and the plate of choice is tender fillet steak (the best in the city) served simply with rice, chips and gravy. The restaurant functions as a per-kilo (food priced by weight) buffet at lunchtime.
✉ Avenida República Argentina 632, at Rua Tarobá ☎ 45 3028 3531 ⌚ Mon–Sat 11.30–11.30 ✋ L R$20, D R$60, Wine R$30

EMPORIO DA GULA

There is a vast menu in this big and brash family restaurant in the centre of town. They offer everything from Rio Grande do Sul fillet steak to paella with Santa Catarina prawns. Brazilian staples like *feijoada* (a hearty meat and bean stew) are among the most popular choices and the restaurant is always busy with locals.
✉ Avenida Brasil 1441 ☎ 45 3521 4100 ⌚ Mon–Fri 12–3, 6.30–11, Sat 4–12, Sun 12–12 ✋ L R$20, D R$40, Wine R$25

GRAMADO

GASTHOF EDELWEISS

www.restauranteedelweiss.com.br
Gramado's favourite dish is cheese fondue made with Brazilian Emmental and Gruyere, with Swiss kirsch. This is the best place to eat it, especially if you're looking for a candlelit table for two. The restaurant also serves German dishes like *eisbein* (boiled pickled ham hock with sauerkraut) and game meat.
✉ Rua da Carriere 1119, Lago Negro, Planalto ☎ 54 3286 1861 ⌚ Daily 12–3, 7–11 ✋ L R$35, D R$60, Wine R$30

ILHA DO MEL

FIM DA TRILHA

www.fimdatrilha.com.br
Most of the island's restaurants are simple shacks serving fish, beans and rice at rickety tables. This is one of the few exceptions. Plastic tables and chairs, prettified with crochet linen tablecloths, are set out on a wooden deck next to the ochre and terracotta Fim da Trilha *pousada* (small inn). The menu comprises grilled fresh fish and crustaceans, and Spanish seafood dishes including a generous Valencian paella. There are also options for vegetarians.
✉ Prainha (Fora de Encantadas) ☎ 41 3426 9017 ⌚ Daily 12–3, 6–11 (but likely to change at whim, as most restaurants on the island) ✋ L R$20, D R$35

MAR E SOL

This simple, but very popular, spit and sawdust beachside restaurant serves big slabs of meat, fish and chicken, with accompanying beans, chips and rice to hungry post-rip curling surfers.
✉ Praia do Farol ☎ 41 3426 8021 ⌚ Daily 12–3, 6–11 ✋ L and D R$25

RECANTO DO FRANCÊS

www.recantodofrances.com.br
There's a touch of Gallic panache at this very simple *pousada* restaurant, with hearty Moroccan couscous and savoury and sweet crêpes cooked in the kitchen under the supervision of the French owner. It's a pleasant change from the island's standard beans, rice and chips options.
✉ Praia das Encantadas s/n ☎ 41 3426 9105 ⌚ Daily 12–3, 6–11 ✋ L and D R$12

JOINVILLE

CHIMARRÃO

www.chimarraochurrascaria.com.br
Chimarrão is one of the best *churrascaria* (spit roast) restaurants in Joinville, serving all-you-can-eat meat with salads and side dishes. There is a large open-plan dining room, drawing a bustling family crowd. The wine list offers a selection of more than 50 wines
✉ Rua Visconde de Taunay 343 ☎ 47 3027 7632 ⌚ Mon–Sat 11–3, 6–11, Sun 11–4 ✋ L R$40, D R$40, Wine R$30

PORTO ALEGRE

KOH PEE PEE

www.kohpeepee.com
Among the best Thai restaurants in Brazil, Koh Pee Pee has a menu that includes excellent prawns in yellow curry sauce served in a giant pineapple half. Most dishes are full of flavour but weak on chilli, as the Brazilians prefer them. The dining room is low-lit, decked out in soft colours and bamboo, and decorated with an enormous high-quality photographic print of the head of the reclining Buddha at Bangkok's Wat Pho. Koh Pee Pee is open for evening dining only.
✉ Rua Schiller 83 ☎ 51 3333 5150 ⌚ Mon–Sat 7.30–12 ✋ D R$85, Wine R$44

PRICES AND SYMBOLS

Prices are the lowest and highest for a double room for one night. Breakfast is included unless noted otherwise. All the hotels listed accept credit cards unless otherwise stated. Note that rates vary widely throughout the year.

For a key to the symbols, ▷ 2.

BLUMENAU

HERMANN

www.hotelhermann.com.br

They speak German at Hermann, as well as Spanish, Portuguese and English. Rooms are simple but sit in one of the oldest buildings in town: a handsome brick and exposed beam town house which is one of the few constructions in the city to look genuinely European.

✉ Floriano Peixoto 213 ☎ 47 3322 4370 R$80–R$480 6

CURITIBA

CURITIBA ECO-HOSTEL

www.curitibaecohostel.com.br

One of the best urban hostels in southern Brazil, set in pretty gardens and with fresh dormitories and doubles. The staff are helpful and can help organize seats on the Serra Verde trains. There are discounts for IYHA members.

✉ Rua Luiz Tramontin 1693, Campo Comprido ☎ 41 3029 1693 Dorm bed R$30; Double room R$80–R$100 20

SLAVIERO BRAZ

www.slavierohoteis.com.br

This handsome and listed 1940s mock-American deco building has more character than most of the anonymous tower block hotels in Curitiba. The rooms are spacious and refurbished, and the public areas are distinguished, if somewhat fading.

✉ Avenida Luís Xavier 67 ☎ 41 3017 1000 R$150–R$240 89

FLORIANÓPOLIS AND THE ILHA DE SANTA CATARINA

BACKPACKERS SHAREHOUSE

www.backpackersfloripa.com

This is the most popular hostel on the island, always busy with partying backpackers, so either book well ahead or avoid it if you're in search of tranquillity. Rooms are housed in a bizarre building, which is a mix of mock-Alpine, Frank Lloyd Wright and Iberian castle. It sits on a headland overlooking the beach and the owners offer surfboard rental for those brave enough to try the waves.

✉ Estrada Geral, Barra da Lagoa s/n ☎ 48 3232 7606 Dorm bed R$50; Double room R$60–R$65 6

BANGALÔS DA MOLE

www.bangalosdamole.com.br

Well-appointed, modern, small *cabanas* (double-room cabins) are perched on a headland above the beach, around a communal dining and lounge area. The best have decks with an ocean view and all share a shady waterfront garden.

✉ Rodovia Jornalista Manoel de Menezes 1005, Praia do Mole ☎ 48 3232 0723 R$100–R$200 30

PORTO INGLESES

www.portoingleses.com.br

A small family resort close to the beach, with a play area for children next to a decent pool. Rooms are simple but spacious, bright and tiled, in a four-storey concrete complex.

✉ Rua das Gaivotas 610, Praia dos Ingleses ☎ 48 3269 1414 R$340–R$550 65 Outdoor

POUSADA SÍTIO DOS TUCANOS

www.pousadasitiodostucanos.com

Large chalets in a flower-filled garden in one of the least spoilt locations on the island. The German owner is helpful and friendly and speaks many languages. The hotel organizes pick-ups and island tours, and offers a generous breakfast of fruit, pastries, cold meats and cereals.

Opposite *The belle époque Hotel das Cataratas in Foz do Iguaçu*

Estrada Geral da Costa de Dentro 2776, Pântano do Sul 48 3237 5084 R$120–R$240 14

FOZ DO IGUAÇU (BRAZIL)

BAVIERA

www.hotelbavieraiguassu.com.br

One of the many mock-Alpine hotels in this part of Brazil, with rather faded rooms that are in need of fresh paint and furnishings. However, they are good value and have satellite TV and WiFi. The hotel is also in a convenient location: on the main road and ideally situated for bars and restaurants.

Avenida Jorge Schimmelpfeng 697, Foz do Iguaçu town 45 3523 5995 R$158–R$250 23

HOSTEL NATURA

www.hostelnatura.com

This simple hostel offers some of the best value accommodation in the area and is set in attractive countryside outside Foz do Iguaçu town. Facilities include a small pool, TV lounge and a small kitchen. There's no air-conditioning in the rooms. Staff can arrange visits to the falls and other excursions. The website has directions to the hostel, with bus times and a map.

Rodovia das Cataratas, km 12.5, Remanso Grande 45 3529 6949 Dorm bed R$30; Double room R$100–R$150 12 Outdoor

HOTEL DAS CATARATAS

www.hoteldascataratas.com

This grand belle époque hotel in the Orient Express group directly overlooks the falls in the Brazilian part of the park, giving guests private access to Iguaçu when all the other visitors have left. The hotel underwent complete renovation in the new millennium and has a fine restaurant overlooking the falls, tennis courts and a tour operator. Cheapest when booked more than three weeks in advance.

Rodovia Br 469, km 32 45 2102 7000 R$755–R$1,045 195 Outdoor

FOZ DO IGUAÇU (ARGENTINA)

BOUTIQUE HOTEL DE LA FONTE

www.bhfboutiquehotel.com

This is one of the few boutique options on either side of the border, and is set in a lovely tropical garden. It has individually decorated rooms, filled with arts and crafts collected by one of the Italian owners and overlooking a tiny pool. The hotel is a real change from the tower-block options which predominate around Iguaçu. The restaurant is run by the owner, a Michelin-starred chef.

Calle 1 de Mayo y Corrientes s/n, Puerto Iguazu 3370, Argentina 549 3757 531544 US$150–US$300 8 Outdoor

ILHA DO MEL

ENSEADA DAS CONCHAS

www.pousadaenseada.com.br

Pretty rooms in beachside chalets sit in a small garden. Each has its own themed décor and the cat-loving owner prepares a big breakfast of fruits, rolls, yogurts and cereals.

Praia do Farol 41 3426 8040 R$120–R$250 4

LONG BEACH

www.lbeach.cjb.net

One of the best surfer *pousadas*, on the best surfer beach of Ilha do Mel. Spacious, airy and comfortable chalets for up to six, right on the sand. All are very simply decked out with large floor tiles and exposed brick walls, and the *pousada* offers a real surfer's breakfast, with a spread of breads, cakes, fruit, cold meats, coffee, tea and juices.

Praia Grande 41 3426 8116 R$150–R$320 10

RECANTO DA FORTALEZA

www.pousadarecantodafortaleza.com

Simple, painted wooden beach shacks, set in a garden, offer the best accommodation on the huge and lonely stretch of sand near the old Portuguese fort. Busy with young couples during high season (December to March), it is very quiet at other times and great for those seeking solitude.

Ponta do Bicho 41 3275 4455 R$120–R$230 11

RECANTO DO FRANCÊS I

www.recantodofrances.com.br

Chalets in this French-owned *pousada* are built in a shady tropical garden and painted to look like miniature Tudor mansions, each from a different French city. The *pousada* is fiercely guarded by a minuscule football-playing Yorkshire terrier. Try the fruit crêpes at breakfast, cooked by the French owner.

Praia Encantadas 41 3426 9105 R$100–R$210 8

JOINVILLE

HOTEL GERMÂNIA

www.hotelgermania.com.br

The Germânia is a big red and white concrete block near the city centre, which has a rooftop pool with views and spacious, well-appointed, business-like rooms. Each has satellite TV, WiFi and a functional work desk.

Rua Ministro Calogeras 612 47 3433 9886 R$160–R$320 30 Rooftop

PORTO BELO

PONTA DOS GANCHOS

www.pontadosganchos.com.br

This romantic resort is aimed resolutely at couples seeking solitude. Its luxury bungalows are perched on a steep rocky peninsula, overlooking a private beach and an emerald ocean. The best are the 180sq m (1,938sq ft) 'Villa Special Bungalows'. They're the kind of rooms you never want to leave, enclosed in their own subtropical gardens and with private saunas and outdoor Jacuzzis that are visible only from the fishing boats passing by almost a kilometre (0.5 miles) away on the open sea. Each has a magnificent view, out over pines and palms to a vast Atlantic horizon. The candlelit, waterfront restaurant has a menu of excellent organic Franco-Brazilian dishes.

Governador Celso Ramos, Santa Catarina 48 3262 5000 R$1,250–R$4,410 25 Indoor

MINAS GERAIS AND ESPÍRITO SANTO

The landlocked state of Minas Gerais (General Mines) is named after the gold and diamonds that were pulled from its rocky soils and rugged hills in the 18th century. They saved the Portuguese Empire from bankruptcy and made Brazil briefly rich. The legacy of this wealth can be seen today in dozens of little towns of stately colonial palaces and magnificent baroque churches. There are three towns with UNESCO World Heritage Site status here: Diamantina, in the north of the state, is the remotest and least changed—it still looks much like it did at the height of the baroque—and is surrounded by beautiful *cerrado* forest; Congonhas do Campo gathers around a spectacular baroque church famous for its lifelike statuary, chiselled by the crippled genius of Brazilian baroque, Aleijadinho (1730–1814); Ouro Preto is the largest of the towns, with an ugly modern suburb but a beautiful colonial heart, which climbs and clambers in cobblestone over a series of steep hills, containing several of the most impressive churches in the country.

The state capital, Belo Horizonte, is one of the largest cities in Brazil. While it is an inevitable transport hub, it holds little for tourists beyond an attractive garden suburb by the architectural team who built Brasília (including Oscar Niemeyer, Lucio Costa, Athos Bulcão and Cândido Portinari). Minas state does, however, have a number of natural attractions. There are several little-visited national parks, including the Serra da Canastra—which has excellent bird watching—and the Serra do Cipó, which is famous for its waterfalls.

Mineiros, as the people of the state are called, take their holidays on the beaches of neighbouring Espírito Santo, a state most foreign tourists simply pass through on their way between Rio and Bahia. There are a few sights worth a day or so's stopover: the towering Pedra Azul boulder mountain, the little capital (Vitória), which is spread behind beaches and over a bay of islands, and the small coastal town of Itaúnas, with its dune-backed beaches and wild hinterlands.

BELO HORIZONTE

www.belohorizontetur.com.br
www.turismo.mg.gov.br

The capital of Minas Gerais is the fourth largest city in Brazil, after São Paulo (▷ 106–137), Rio (▷ 54–105) and Salvador (▷ 214–221). Its skyscrapers sit on a plain ringed by mountains. Unlike the colonial towns to its north and south, Belo Horizonte is a modern city with no pre-20th-century buildings of interest. It is a pleasant place with good restaurants and bars, and a lively music scene, but most visitors are architecture buffs who come here to visit the complex of early Oscar Niemeyer buildings in the suburb of Pampulha, some 8km (5 miles) northwest of the city centre. These sit around a lake in leafy public gardens landscaped by Roberto Burle Marx and, as the project was commissioned by Juscelino Kubitschek—the president who built Brasília (▷ 326–327) in 1960—when he was governor of Minas, Pampulha is often seen as a forerunner of the Brazilian capital.

All the buildings in Pampulha are interesting for fans of Niemeyer or students of architectural history, but only one makes a visit to Pampulha worth undertaking for other tourists: the Igreja São Francisco de Assis (Tue–Sat 9–5, Sun 9–1; R$2). This is one of the Modernist architect's most celebrated constructions, built in 1942. Its arches made up of parabolic waves are fronted by a simple bell tower and it was revolutionary in its day. This was one of the first buildings in the world where concrete was moulded into organic (as opposed to rectilinear) shapes—an idea which some might say has obsessed Niemeyer ever since. His other buildings dot the lake shore: the Casa do Baile ballroom (Thu–Sun 9–7; free), one of the first projects to deploy his now-trademark snaking covered walkways; the glass and marble Museu de Arte de Pampulha (Tue–Sun 9–9; free) opposite, housing exhibitions of local artists; and the Mineirão stadium (open only for sporting events), the second largest in Brazil after Maracanã (▷ 65) and an obvious precursor to the Centro de Convenções Ulysses Guimarães in Brasília.

402 Q14 · Praça da Liberdade, s/n, Prédio Verde, Bairro Funcionários · 31 3270 8500 · Mon–Fri 9–6 · From all major tourist towns · Tancredo Neves (aka Confins), Pampulha

CONGONHAS DO CAMPO

▷ 184.

DIAMANTINA

▷ 186–187.

ITAÚNAS

www.itaunas.tur.br

This small beach town in the far north of Espírito Santo, a few kilometres from the border with Bahia, is famous for its *forró* dancing and its sand dunes. The dunes are so large that they have swallowed Itaúnas once already, in the 1970s, and the entire town had to be rebuilt from scratch. After high winds, the old church steeple can sometimes be seen poking out of the top of a dune to the town's north. The beaches near the town and the adjacent river are protected areas; the former because it is a turtle breeding ground and the latter because it preserves a small patch of one of the country's most threatened habitats, coastal heathland *(restinga)*, rich in bird life.

403 S13 · From Conceição da Barra, three to four times a day

Opposite *Niemeyer's Igreja São Francisco de Assis in Pampulha, Belo Horizonte*
Below *Colourful colonial buildings in Mariana*

MARIANA

www.mariana.org.br

It is far less celebrated today than neighbouring Ouro Preto (▷ 188–189), but Mariana is the oldest colonial town in Minas Gerais and was once the capital of the state. Nowadays Mariana feels like an Ouro Preto in miniature, without the steep hills. Here there is just one, which rises to the simple 18th-century church of São Pedro dos Clérigos (Tue–Sun 9–12, 2–4; R$2). This is a great place to begin a tour and get your bearings, with fine views over the town's small colonial centre.

The centre clusters around Praça Gomes Freire—a garden square surrounded by 18th-century town houses—and the twin churches of São Francisco de Assis (Tue–Sun 8–12, 1–5) and Nossa Senhora do Carmo (Tue–Sun 9–11.45, 2–5). The former has a ceiling by Minas's most important ecclesiastical painter, Manoel da Costa (Mestre) Athayde (1762–1830), who is buried in the church. Nossa Senhora do Carmo, which has round towers and a lozenge-shaped key window, also has paintings by the artist, though they were damaged by fire in 1999.

Mariana's third important church is the Basílica de Nossa Senhora da Assunção (Tue–Sun 8–6). It was constructed in 1760, with a late 17th-century German organ, baroque altarpieces by Francisco Xavier de Brito and a portal and font attributed to Aleijadinho (1730–1814, ▷ 184).

403 Q14 · Rua Direita 93 · 31 3558 2314 · Mon–Fri 9–6 · From Belo Horizonte and Ouro Preto

INFORMATION
402 Q14 From Belo Horizonte and Rio de Janeiro

Bom Jesus de Matosinhos
Congonhas 31 3732 1243
Chapels daily 6–5; church Tue–Sun 6–6 Free From Belo Horizonte and Ouro Preto

TIPS
» Stalls adjacent to the hill leading to the church sell soft drinks and snacks.
» Local guides in front of the church offer guided tours for R$30, but none speaks English.

CONGONHAS DO CAMPO

The tiny village of Congonhas, though often referred to as a city, is little more than a cluster of houses next to the baroque church of Bom Jesus de Matosinhos. Although beautiful in its own right, this UNESCO World Heritage-listed church is celebrated for preserving the most dynamic and impressive ensembles of statues in Latin America: Aleijadinho's 12 prophets and his *Passion of Christ*.

BOM JESUS DE MATOSINHOS

The church itself was commissioned by the diamond miner Feliciano Mendes. While on the brink of death he vowed to build a homage to 'Bom (Good) Jesus' if his life were spared. True to his word, after recovering in the 1750s, he began a church modelled on the Sanctuario de Bom Jesus in his home town of Braga, Portugal. He didn't live to see his dream realized, dying in 1765, six years before the church was completed.

IRREPRESSIBLE TALENT

'O Aleijadinho' means the little cripple. When Antônio Francisco Lisboa (1730–1814) worked at Congonhas, between 1780 and 1815, he had become so disfigured by leprosy that he had lost the use of his hands and feet. He was carried up the steep hill to the church, working until nightfall using hammers and chisels tied to the stumps that were his hands. Despite this, the soapstone statues he carved here are his masterpieces.

THE STATUES

There are two groups, from the Old and New Testaments. The Old Testament soapstone statues, of the 12 prophets, line a monumental staircase which climbs up to the church. Each is so vivid and fluid that they look as if they might step down from their plinths at any moment. Particularly impressive are Obadiah, gesturing dramatically towards heaven, Jonah, holding a scroll, and Daniel with a strange contorted lion (Aleijadinho had never seen one).

Below the prophets and stretching down the hill are seven chapels devoted to the Stations of the Cross. Polychrome statues within depict each event in lifelike detail and were painted in naturalistic colours by Mestre Athayde (1762–1830). The Crucifixion scene is particularly grizzly.

Below *View over the rooftops from Bom Jesus de Matosinhos*

OURO PRETO

▷ 188–189.

PARQUE NACIONAL DA SERRA DA CANASTRA

www.serradacanastra.com.br

This remote and expansive national park in the far southwest of Minas Gerais, near the border with Goiás state, preserves 200,000ha (494,000 acres) of pristine *cerrado* forest, savannah grassland and craggy hills dripping with rivers and streams. These form the watershed of one of the largest rivers in the Americas (and the largest to exist solely within Brazil), the Rio São Francisco. Canastra's crumbling granite peaks form part of some of the oldest rock formations on Earth and rise in a series of crumpled and crumbling escarpments to over 1,500m (4,920ft). There are many waterfalls. The most famous is the Cachoeira d'Anta, which falls through a series of rocky pools before dropping sheer for 186m (610ft) off a high escarpment. The Trilha Casca d'Anta, Canastra's most spectacular walk, leaves from in front of the waterfall to climb up the escarpment and affords views out over the stands of forest to the denuded soya pastures beyond.

The Serra is very rich in wildlife. Greater rhea (the ostrich of the Americas), maned wolf, giant armadillo and anteater are relatively common sights. This is also one of the very few places in the world where it is possible to see the critically endangered Brazilian meganser duck—most easily around the Fazenda das Pedras and in the pools above the Casca d'Anta. Other rarities include the blue-winged macaw, yellow-billed blue finch and sharp-tailed tyrant.

✚ 402 P14 ℹ Park Visitor Centre, São Roque de Minas s/n ☎ 37 3433 1195 ⏲ Daily 6–6 🚌 From Belo Horizonte

PARQUE NACIONAL SERRA DO CIPÓ

www.serradocipoturismo.com.br

This national park covers 338sq km (130sq miles) and is less than 100km (62 miles) north of Belo Horizonte. It protects some pristine areas of *cerrado*, as well as the watersheds of many of the tributaries of the São Francisco and Doce rivers. It is the easiest national park to visit from Belo Horizonte, has excellent access on paved roads and plenty of accommodation options, and lies on an alternative route to Diamantina (▷ 186–187). Like the Serra da Canastra (▷ this page) to the southwest, Cipó lies in high rugged country, the Serra do Espinhaço, which runs through the middle of northern Minas Gerais.

The park is replete with waterfalls, rare animals, birds and *cerrado* plants, like ipê trees—which bloom brilliantly between July and September—and the umbrella-shaped chuveirinho flower. May and June are good months to see puma, giant anteater and ocelot, together with maned wolf (at dawn or dusk on the quieter trails, though, as ever in Brazil, sightings are rare). The rivers are usually full at this time of year, the skies blue and many of the wild flowers in bloom. The park is a popular location for ecotourism, particularly rock climbing (▷ 194).

✚ 403 Q13 🚌 From Belo Horizonte, to Jaboticatubas or Santana do Riacho, both of which are within 10km (6 miles) of the entrance to the park

Above left *Serra da Canastra national park*
Above right *Taboleiro Falls in Serra do Cipó national park*

INFORMATION
www.diamantina.com.br
403 Q13 Praça Antônio Eulálio 53, Centro 38 3531 9527 Mon–Fri 12–5

INTRODUCTION

Minas Gerais's second World Heritage Site is less well known and less visited than either Ouro Preto (▷ 188–189) or Congonhas (▷ 184), and has fewer outstanding monuments. However, Diamantina is the best preserved and prettiest of any colonial city in Minas, and its setting, in rugged hills shrouded in *cerrado* forest, is breathtaking. The city is tiny and easily negotiable on foot. The most important sights are within easy walking distance of the main square, Praça Guerra, where there are also plenty of small cafés.

Like Minas's other colonial cities, Diamantina owes its existence and wealth to mining. In 1728, when the town was little more than a mining camp called Arraial do Tijuco, diamonds were found here. By 1750, Diamantina had handsome Portuguese houses and churches, and by the end of the century it was one of the most prosperous towns in Brazil.

WHAT TO SEE

NOSSA SENHORA DO CARMO

Diamantina's richest church was attended by the elite white community and constructed between 1760 and 1784. Inside are powerful religious paintings by José Soares de Araujo, a former bodyguard from Braga in Portugal, who turned his hand to the more delicate art of ecclesiastical painting when he settled in Diamantina. The portrait of Elijah ascending to heaven in a chariot of fire is particularly striking.

Further pictures and statues of Elijah decorate the church: panels at the rear depict him performing two miracles from the second book of Kings and a statue in one of the side altars has him brandishing a sword like the archangel Michael. Farther towards the sanctuary is a ceiling painting, of St. Simon Stock, the

Above *Festa de Nossa Senhora do Rosário dos Homens Pretos (black people) de Diamantina, held annually in October*

12th-century saint from the English county of Kent, who established the Third Carmelite order.

✉ Rua do Carmo s/n ⏲ Tue–Sun 8–12, 2–6 ✋ Adult R$3; child under 7 free

CASA DE CHICA DA SILVA

This smart town house is one block south of Nossa Senhora do Carmo and has a small collection of period furniture. It is more famous for its former owner, Francisca (Chica) da Silva, a mulatta slave (of mixed parentage) whose beauty and wit captivated one of the town's wealthiest diamond traders, João Fernandes de Oliveira, in the 1750s. Unlike most of the ex-slaves kept as mistresses or lovers by the Portuguese, Chica seems to have had all her wishes met by João. When she complained that she had never seen the sea, João built her a miniature galleon, complete with masts and sails, to use on the lake in their *fazenda* ranch house. In an era when people of mixed blood were required to avoid passing in front of white churches to prevent offence to God, Chica rose as one of the few black people to become accepted by high colonial society, for whom she threw numerous balls. She was a member of the brotherhood of Nossa Senhora do Rosário (for Africans), Merecês (for people of mixed blood) and Carmo (exclusively for whites). Despite her lover returning to Portugal, she remained popular and was buried in the church of São Francisco de Assis, a privilege traditionally reserved exclusively for whites.

✉ Praça Lobo Mesquita 266 ☎ 38 3531 2491 ⏲ Tue–Sat 12–5.30, Sun 9–12 ✋ Free

MORE TO SEE

Diamantina retains a large number of colonial buildings and some interesting little cobbled alleyways, such as Passadiço da Glória which connects the 18th-century home of the town's first bishop and a 19th-century Catholic school. The cathedral, Catedral Metropolitana de Santo Antônio (Tue–Sat 10–12, 2–6, Sun 9–2), constructed on the site of a colonial church in the 1930s, sits on an impressive square, Praça da Matriz.

TIP

» A number of pristine natural locations lie within easy reach, the most impressive of which are Biribiri (▷ 195), a former *fazenda* set in dramatic hills next to a winding black water river, and the Parque Estadual do Rio Preto, 45km (28 miles) south near the village of São Gonçalo, which is one of the best locations in Brazil for bird watching (▷ 195).

Below *Santo Antônio cathedral sits amid other fine colonial buildings*

INFORMATION

www.ouropreto.org.br
403 Q14 · Praça Tiradentes 41 (Câmara Municipal) · 31 3559 3269 · Daily 8–5 · From Belo Horizonte

Above *Terracotta rooftops of Ouro Preto*

INTRODUCTION

Salvador (▷ 214–221) may be more opulent, Olinda (▷ 250–251) more picturesque, but there is no Brazilian colonial architecture more elegant or more masterfully decorated than in this little hilly city just south of Belo Horizonte.

Ouro Preto means Black Gold, as its splendid baroque and rococo churches were built on wealth generated from tarnished nuggets pulled from the surrounding streams and hills at the turn of the 17th century. By the mid-18th century, after the gold rush, Ouro Preto was peopled by indigenous Brazilian and African slaves, adventurers from all over the country and a smattering of Portuguese noblemen. This stock produced both the city's buildings and a generation of some of Latin America's finest artists and craftsmen.

When the gold began to deplete, Ouro Preto became important for other reasons. Discontent, fostered by economic difficulties and Portugal's draconian gold taxes, resulted in the Inconfidência rebellion (▷ 31). This was led by a former dentist, Tiradentes, who is widely regarded as the father of Brazilian independence; a statue in the city's central square bears his name.

WHAT TO SEE

IGREJA DE SÃO FRANCISCO DE ASSIS

There is little ostentatious gold on show at the city's most gracious and elegant church. São Francisco's beauty lies in its lines and its craftsmanship, which are the fruit of two of Latin America's greatest ecclesiastical artists: Aleijadinho (1730–1814) and Manoel da Costa (Mestre) Athayde (1762–1830). Aleijadinho's work includes, among others, the tablet on the church's facade showing St. Francis receiving the stigmata. Athayde painted the ceiling in the nave. He also painted the scenes from the life of Abraham. Originally founded in 1766, the building was carefully restored in 2004.

Largo de Coimbra s/n · 31 3551 4661 · Tue–Sun 8–11.45, 2–5 · Adult R$8; child under 7 free

IGREJA MATRIZ DE NOSSA SENHORA DO PILAR

This church is as opulent and ornate as São Francisco de Assis is understated. Nearly half a tonne of gold and half a tonne of silver was used to gild its carved interior, and pomp and circumstance surrounded the church's inauguration in 1731, which saw grand processions of clergy and knights. The interior is largely the work of the city's other great artist, Francisco Xavier de Brito, an ex-pat Portuguese who introduced Portuguese and French baroque into Brazil and taught Aleijadinho. The gilt carving of Christ on the cross on the door-case to the *capela-mor* (apsidal chapel), and the resurrection scene on the tabernacle rank, are his finest work. He died before he could complete the church and is said to be buried somewhere inside.

Praça Mons. Castilho Barbosa s/n · 31 3551 4736 · Tue–Sun 9–11, 12–5 · Adult R$8; child under 7 free

IGREJA DE NOSSA SENHORA DA CONCEIÇÃO DE ANTÔNIO DIAS

Ouro Preto's third great church was built at the same time as the Matriz de Nossa Senhora do Pilar. While the young Aleijadinho was learning his craft alongside Francisco Xavier de Brito in that church, his architect father, Manuel Francisco Lisboa, was busy here. The building has the finest proportions of any in the city. Aside from finishing touches to the heavily gilt interior by Manuel Francisco himself, the sculptors of the elaborate interior remain largely unknown. Both Manuel and his son are buried in the church. There is a small museum devoted to Aleijadinho at the back of the church.

Praça Antônio Dias s/n · 31 3551 3282 · Tue–Sat 8.30–11.45, 1.30–4.45, Sun 12–4.45 · Adult R$5; child under 7 free

MORE TO SEE

MUSEU DA INCONFIDÊNCIA

This small museum tells the story of Tiradentes and his 'Inconfidência' revolt against the Portuguese through documents, manuscripts and paintings. These sit alongside baroque works of art by Aleijadinho, Xavier de Brito and Mestre Athayde, among others.

Praça Tiradentes s/n · Tue–Sun 12.30–6 · Adult R$5, child under 7 free

CASA DOS CONTOS

Tiradentes was imprisoned in the gloomy jail house in the basement of this imposing late 18th-century mansion house. The upper floors now house a numismatic and colonial-era furniture museum.

Rua São José 12 · Tue–Sat 12.30–5.30, Sun 9–3 · Adult R$5, child under 7 free

TIPS

» Ouro Preto is dotted with little cafés and restaurants, so drinks and other refreshments are always easy to find.

» The city centre is most easily negotiated on foot. Cabs are widespread but other public transport is virtually non-existent.

Below left *Beautiful 18th-century buildings line the cobbled streets*
Below *Igreja de São Francisco de Assis*

Above *The baroque facade of Igreja São Francisco de Assis in São João del Rei*
Opposite *Multi-hued cottages cling to the hillside in Tiradentes*

PEDRA AZUL

This 500m-high (1,640ft) dome of weather-worn blue-grey rock sticks out of the Serra Capixaba coastal mountains like a granite thumb. It is protected as a state park. Trails lead from the hotels that sit in the giant rock's shade all the way around its base. With climbing gear and written permission it is even possible to reach its summit, the views from which are almost as spectacular as the rock itself. Tiny though the forest surrounding the peak is, it nonetheless protects nesting grounds for diverse species of humming-birds and tanagers. Tufted-eared marmosets—monkeys the size of a kitten—are a common sight.

400 R12 Permission for climbing Pedra Azul must be obtained from SEAMA (Secretária de Estado do Meio Ambiente e Recursos Hídricos). Applications in written Portuguese only to Maria da Glória Brito Abaurre, SEAMA, BR 262, km 0, Pátio Porto Velho s/n, Jardim América, Cariacica, ES CEP: 29140-500 From Vitória

SÃO JOÃO DEL REI

www.saojoaodelrei.mg.gov.br

São João is less than 30km (18.5 miles) from Tiradentes (▷ this page) and it, too, has a series of beautiful churches and an attractive colonial centre. However, while Tiradentes is almost entirely given up to tourism, São João is a bustling market town.

São João's star attraction is the church of São Francisco de Assis (tel 32 3372 3110; Mon–Sat 8–5.30, Sun 9–4), one of the most impressive pieces of colonial architecture in Minas. It boasts a late Portuguese baroque curved facade, faced with an elaborately carved medallion by Francisco de Lima Cerqueira and his disciple Aniceto de Souza Lopez, dating from 1774. The church overlooks a beautiful lyre-shaped square and at sundown the shadows of the palms link together to make the instrument's strings.

There is a narrow gauge steam train to Tiradentes (▷ this page) and a small locomotive museum, the Museu Ferroviário, at the Maria Fumaça railway station (tel 32 3371 8485; museum Tue–Sun 9–11, 1–5; steam train Fri–Sun 10, 3, return 1, 5; adult R$16, child R$8). It features Pullman carriages used by Emperor Dom Pedro II and his wife when they travelled from Rio to Minas Gerais in the 19th century.

402 Q14 Avenida Tiradentes 136, Centro 32 3372 7338 Mon–Fri 9–6 From Belo Horizonte and Tiradentes

TIRADENTES

www.tiradentes.net

Tiradentes's multi-coloured Portuguese cottages and miniature baroque churches cluster around the cobbles on a series of steep, low hills around the Santo Antonio River. There's a craft shop, arty little café or gourmet restaurant on every other corner. Pretty horse-drawn carriages gather in the town's main plaza and the Maria Fumaça steam railway puffs its way towards São João del Rei at weekends (▷ this page). The tourists came here in earnest after the national TV station TV Globo staged a popular mini-series here in the 1980s. The town takes its name from the former dentist who was one of the leaders of the Inconfidência revolt (▷ 31). He was born nearby.

The city has some fine colonial buildings: The Matriz de Santo Antônio (daily 9–5), built between 1710 and 1752, has a lavish gilt interior and a carved facade which is in part attributed to Aleijadinho; the Museu Padre Toledo (tel 32 3355 1549; Tue–Fri 9–11.30, 1–4.40, Sat–Sun 9–4.40) was once the home of another of the leaders of the Inconfidência movement and is now a museum; and on the edge of town is a magnificent 18th-century baroque drinking fountain, the Chafariz de São José.

402 Q14 Rua Resende Costa 71, Centro 32 3355 1212 Daily 9–5 From São João del Rei and Belo Horizonte

VITÓRIA

www.vitoria.es.gov.br

The capital city of Espírito Santo state, with its bays, beaches and bridges, looks a little like a miniature Rio (▷ 54–105), without the towering monoliths and a sentinel Christ. Like Rio, it is dominated by a huge bay dotted with islands and fringed with sheltered coves.

The most interesting part of the city, the Vila Velha (Old Town), is reached by a fine bridge, A Terceira Ponte. Although precious few colonial buildings remain, this is one of the earliest settlements in Brazil, dating from the first half of the 16th century. The city's most impressive building, the Franciscan Mosteiro Nossa Senhora da Penha (Mon–Fri 5.30–4.45, Sun 4.30am–4.45pm) sits here on a palm-covered hill above both the bay and the simple church of Nossa Senhora do Rosário, which was built in 1551, seven years before the monastery.

403 R14 Praça Manoel Silvino Monjardim 66 27 3381 6929 Mon–Fri 9–6 From all major tourist towns Aeroporto de Vitória

ALONG THE ESTRADA REAL

This drive is a circular route, leaving from Belo Horizonte and visiting a handful of the colonial towns of southern Minas Gerais, including two UNESCO World Heritage Sites, at Congonhas do Campo and Ouro Preto. Part of the route uses the Estrada Real, now a paved highway but originally the old gold road running through to Rio. This is a long drive with plenty to see, which can be broken over two or even three days using Mariana or Ouro Preto as a hub.

THE DRIVE
Distance: 220km (136 miles)
Time: 2 days
Start/end at: Belo Horizonte

★ Belo Horizonte (▷ 183) is a large, sprawling city sitting in a bowl surrounded by craggy mountains. You may want to stay overnight here or fly in and leave direct in a rental car from Tancredo Neves (aka Confins) or Pampulha airports. The latter is more convenient and offers the chance to explore the Niemeyer buildings around Pampulha (▷ 183).

Take the BR-040 state highway south, towards Conselheiro Lafaiete and Rio de Janeiro. For the next 70km (43.5 miles) you drive on a busy two-lane highway through a landscape of rocky hills and rolling fields, until you reach a turn-off to the left signposted for the MG-443 state highway and the town of Congonhas. This takes you directly to the Estrada Real via the first of the UNESCO World Heritage Sites.

❶ Congonhas (▷ 184) is the location of the Santuário de Bom Jesus de Matosinhos church, the jewel in the crown of Minas Gerais baroque. The 18th-century basilica crowns a steep hill, reached by a cobbled path lined with chapels. These are filled with statues telling the story of the stations of the cross. A baroque staircase, watched over by statues of the 12 Old Testament prophets, then leads up to the basilica itself. The complex brings together the work of two of the most illustrious of Brazil's baroque artists, the sculptor Aleijadinho and painter Mestre Athayde.

Continue on the MG-443 (Estrada Real) for 13km (8 miles), to the village of Ouro Branco.

❷ This is one of the least visited and least spoiled of Minas's baroque mining towns, with a beautiful

Opposite *Pretty bandstand in Praça Gomes Freire, Mariana*

church and views out over southern Minas from the rocky Serra de Ouro Branco hills just outside the town. The Matriz de Santo Antônio church dates from 1717 and preserves inside a beautiful ceiling painting by Mestre Athayde.

Take the Estrada Real (MG-443) northeast from Ouro Branco for 12km (7.5 miles), to the pocket-sized village of Itatiaia, where there is another fine church. The Igreja de Santo Antônio is one of the oldest in Minas and has a carved baroque facade. Continue from here for 15km (9.5 miles) to the MG-356 road, turning right (east) towards Mariana.

❸ Mariana (▷ 183) is an enchanting small town, whose terracotta-tiled roofs huddle under rugged hills and around the winding Rio Brumado river. It is home to some of the most impressive baroque churches in Minas Gerais, including the churches of São Francisco de Assis (with paintings by Mestre Athayde) and Nossa Senhora do Carmo. There are walks in the surrounding hills, which hide many small rivers and refreshing waterfalls. The town makes an ideal stop for refreshments, or overnight stay if you prefer to break the journey. Parking is easier than in Ouro Preto and there are plenty of restaurants and hotels to choose from.

Continue to Ouro Preto, travelling west on the MG-262 road for 10km (6 miles).

❹ Ouro Preto (▷ 188–189) is the most famous of southeastern Brazil's colonial towns and another UNESCO World Heritage Site. There are enough attractions to fill a whole day here, with three spectacular churches and art by all of Minas's baroque masters. The steep cobbled streets offer delightful city walking, through *praças* decorated with ornate baroque fountains and to hilltops with sweeping views of the white and terracotta tile buildings set against the surrounding craggy hills. There is a good selection of restaurants and hotels to serve you.

Take the BR-356 west to the BR-040 and make the return journey to Belo Horizonte.

WHEN TO GO

Any time of year is good for this drive, but the bluest skies are between May and September.

WHERE TO EAT

Restaurants in Congonhas and Mariana are limited to cheap cafés, of which there are several in the town centre. Try Engenho Nôvo (▷ 198) for a cold drink to break the journey, and local specialities at lunch or dinner. If you are staying over in Mariana, the restaurant also serves as a bar in the evening. For sustenance in Ouro Preto, Casa dos Contos (▷ 199) has a buffet at lunch, and a popular menu of regional dishes in the evening.

WHERE TO STAY

POUSADA CONTOS DE MINAS
▷ 200.

POUSADA DO MONDEGO
▷ 200.

INFORMATION

Praça Tiradentes 41 (Câmara Municipal), Ouro Preto ☎ 31 3559 3269 Daily 8–5

TIPS

» Do not drive after dark in Brazil as muggings and car jackings do happen.
» Be sure to bring a road map (available only in large bookshops in the major capitals) and a phrase book (few people in rural Brazil speak English). Road maps are never sold at service stations in Brazil and are not used by most Brazilians, who rely on asking for directions.
» Buy petrol only at big brand-named service stations. Petrol in smaller service stations is often diluted with acetone, which can cause engine malfunction.

BELO HORIZONTE

ANDARILHO DA LUZ

www.andarilhodaluz.com.br

This Belo Horizonte agency offers trips throughout Minas Gerais—including the Santuário do Caraça and the Serra do Cipó—and to adventurous destinations in Brazil, including the Chapada dos Veadeiros, Serra da Capivara and the beaches of Bahia.

✉ Rua Dom Carloto Távora 88, Bairro Planalto ☎ 31 3494 2727 🕐 Mon–Fri 9–6

CINEMA SHOPPING CIDADE

www.shoppingcidade.com.br

This big shopping mall has a multiplex cinema on the top floor showing the latest international releases, in English with Portuguese subtitles. The mall itself has restaurants, pharmacies, toy shops and mid-range Brazilian fashion labels like Siberian. There are no international fashion brands.

✉ Rua Tupis 337, Centro ☎ 31 3279 1200 🕐 Mon–Sat 9–10, Sun 10–10

✋ Cinema: adult R$10–R$21, child under 11 R$5–R$10.50

GALD ECOTURISMO & AVENTURAS

www.gald.com.br

GALD offer short and multi-day trips around Minas Gerais, including the gold towns around the Estrada Real (▷ 192–193) and light adventure activities in the hills around Ouro Preto and Tiradentes (such as trail walking and rappelling). Enquiries are by internet and phone only.

☎ 31 3588 1578

MERCADO CENTRAL

www.mercadocentral.com.br

Exotic fruit, Minas cheeses, cooked meats, fish, salted cod, and arts and crafts are here in a big open market. There are also many simple bars and restaurants.

✉ Avenida Augusto de Lima 744, Centro ☎ 31 3274 9473 🕐 Mon–Sat 7–6, Sun 7–1

MINAS RADICAL

www.minasradical.com.br

This company offers a range of adventure activities at their sports centre just outside Belo Horizonte. Minas Radical's activities include paintball, abseiling, zip-lines and high-wire tree crossings.

✉ Alphaville Lagoa dos Ingleses, BR-356 km 29, Nova Lima ☎ 31 9619 6801 🕐 Mon–Fri 11–6, Sat–Sun 10–4

A OBRA

www.aobra.com.br

This low-lit smoky bar is Belo Horizonte's top alternative music venue, where you can hear the best new cutting-edge Minas acts, like Érika Machado and Babilak Ba.

✉ Rua Rio Grande do Norte 1168, Savassi ☎ 31 3215 8077 🕐 Thu–Sat 10pm–late

RONALDO FRAGA

www.ronaldofraga.com.br

Bouffant silk dresses, coolly cut jackets, daring shoes shaped like Volkswagen beetles, moon boots, satin corsets and other such over-the-top fashion from one of Brazil's most creative fashion designers. Fraga has been a big hit at São Paulo fashion week but had his beginnings in this Belo Horizonte boutique.

✉ Rua Fernades Tourinho 81, Savassi ☎ 31 3282 5379 🕐 Mon–Fri 10–6, Sat 10–5

SAFARI VIAGENS

www.safariviagens.com.br

One of the longest-established agencies in Minas Gerais, offering trips to all the main tourist destinations in the state, with day tours of Belo Horizonte (available with airport pick-up), Ouro Preto and Mariana, the Serra do Cipó, São João del Rei, Tiradentes and Diamantina. Contact is via internet only.

SANTUÁRIO DO CARAÇA

www.santuariodocaraca.com.br

This seminary in the Parque Natural do Caraça sits in an isolated patch of wild and mountainous *cerrado*. It is located some 110km (68 miles) east of Belo Horizonte, near the town of Santa Barbara, and is one of the best places in Brazil for wildlife, particularly wolves. In the 1980s, the monks began to leave food on the seminary steps for birds. It attracted maned wolves and nowadays at least four can usually be seen in the evening. Visits have become so popular that the seminary now has its own designated tourist accommodation, which must be booked in advance (▷ 201). Other endangered mammals in the park include puma, ocelot and southern masked titi monkeys, and there are self-guided trails leading into the surrounding hills, offering great long and short walks. Can be visited independently or with Andarilho da Luz (▷ 194).

✉ Santuário do Caraça, Santa Barbara
☎ 31 3837 2698

DIAMANTINA

APOCALIPSE POINT

This informal beer bar off the city's main square is one of the city's liveliest after-hours bars and dance clubs, with *sertanejo*, *forró*, *pagode* and international sounds.

✉ Praça Barão de Guaicuí 78 ☎ 38 3531 9296 🕐 Thu–Sat 8pm–late

BIRD WATCHING

The Parque Estadual do Rio Preto preserves a series of hills covered with pristine *cerrado* woodland, bursting with colourful ipê trees and abundant bird life. It sits just outside the sleepy town of São Gonçalo do Rio Preto, some 60km (37 miles) from Diamantina, which has two buses a day to São Gonçalo. There is simple accommodation available in the park. Bespoke tours can be arranged through Diamantina Travel (▷ this page).

DIAMANTINA TRAVEL

www.diamantina-travel.com.br

This small tour operator offers bespoke and itinerized trips in and around Diamantina. On the Diamantina trip, they include the pretty abandoned mill village and textile factory of Biribiri, which sits on a clearwater stream, with good swimming in deep pools and lovely light hill walks. This trip is best done in the week to avoid the crowds, and there are small cafés in Biribiri for a lunch stop. Their *cerrado* waterfall day tour includes the Cachoeira da Água Santa (Holy Water Waterfall), which falls into a dark pool in the heart of beautiful *cerrado* forest. The waterfall is said by locals to have healing properties.

✉ Rua Direita 120 sl 06, Centro
☎ 38 3531 6733 🕐 Mon–Fri 10–6
✋ From R$70

ITAÚNAS

PARQUE DE ITAÚNAS

www.guiaitaunas.com.br

Itaúnas's state park extends some 15km (9.5 miles) along the coast all the way from that town to the border with Bahia in the north. It offers the chance to take a wild nature walk without any risk of getting lost, just five-minutes' walk from the town centre. As well as 40m-high (131ft) dunes, you will pass through *restinga* bushland around the Rio Itaúnas—low grass and scrub forest which is home to numerous birds and small mammals. *Pousada* hotels and small agencies rent kayaks for a modest price for paddling inland up the river. Look for red Brocket deer, paca (which look like giant mottled guinea pigs with long legs), and, at night, grey foxes and ocelots.

Opposite *Exploring Mina da Passagem gold mine in Mariana (▷ 196)*
Below *Ipê trees colonize the* cerrado *woodland in Parque Estadual do Rio Preto*

MARIANA

MINA DA PASSAGEM

www.minasdapassagem.com.br

Mina da Passagem is the largest gold mine open to the public in the world. Visits are a real Indiana Jones experience. Nineteenth-century mine carts carry visitors deep into the passageways, whose walls yielded some 35 tonnes of gold, to a limpid clear blue underground lake. Models and display panels tell the story of the mines and of gold in Minas in general.

Estrada MG-262 31 3557 5000 Mon–Tue 9–5, Wed–Sun 9–5.30 Adult R$24, child under 7 free Taxi from Mariana R$35

OURO PRETO

ANTIGUIDADES TOLEDO

www.pousadatoledo.com.br/arte

This small boutique shop is housed in one of Ouro Preto's pretty town houses on a steep street climbing down from the old colonial centre. It sells Minas antiques, including beautiful ecclesiastical pieces and paintings.

Rua Conselheiro Quintiliano 848 31 3551 5915 Mon–Fri 10–6, Sat 10–5

TREM DA VALE

www.tremdavale.org

A 19th-century steam train runs 18km (11 miles) between the two colonial towns of Ouro Preto and Mariana, cutting through rugged hills and past rushing mountain rivers and waterfalls. There's only one train a day in each direction, a journey which lasts an hour. For the best views, sit on the right-hand side and in the back carriages. The train waits in Mariana before returning. In order to avoid a rushed visit consider staying overnight.

Praça Cesário Alvim s/n 31 3551 7705 Departs Ouro Preto Fri–Sun 10am; from Mariana 2pm Adult round trip R$35, single R$22, child (6–10) and over 60 round trip R$18, single R$11, under 5 free

MINA DO CHICO REI

This tiny mine, within walking distance of Ouro Preto, is only 1.5km (1 mile) long but it is the oldest open mine in the region and, unlike Mina da Passagem in Mariana (▷ this page), is as gloomy and inhospitable as the original 19th-century mines must have been when they were worked by slaves.

Rua Dom Silveiro 108 31 3551 1749 Daily 8–5 Adult R$10, child under 7 free

PARQUE NACIONAL SERRA DA CANASTRA

AVESFOTO

www.avesfoto.com.br

The Serra da Canastra is one of the best bird-watching destinations in the country, with threatened and endangered species including Brazilian merganser, peach-fronted parakeet and Brasília tapaculo. The Aves Foto company offers bird-watching tours with experienced professional bird-watcher, Edson

Below left *A souvenir shop in Ouro Preto*

Below *The white-eared puffbird is one of the species that inhabit the Serra da Canastra*

Endrigo. Bookings by phone and via internet only.
☎ 11 3742 8374

PARQUE NACIONAL SERRA DO CIPÓ

TRILHAS E AVENTURAS

www.trilhaseaventuras.com.br

This company have been running easy and difficult rock climbing and hill walking trips into the Serra (and throughout Brazil) for a decade, either leaving from designated points in the park or from Belo Horizonte (▷ 183).
✉ Santana do Riacho ☎ 31 3718 7014
🕑 Mon–Fri 10–6

TROPA SERRANA

http://tropa.serrana.zip.net

This family-run company offers horse-riding trips in the heart of the Serra, leaving from an 18th-century farmhouse and running along old cattle trails into wild stretches of the park. There are various packages detailed on their website. Contact them (by phone and internet only) to arrange pick-ups from Belo Horizonte or Serra do Cipó hotels.
☎ 31 3344 8986

TIRADENTES

OSCAR ARARIPE

www.oscarararipe.com.br

This is the gallery of one of the town's most respected artists, whose colourful canvases of local scenes and faux-naïve portraits have earned him more than 100 exhibitions in Brazil and Europe.
✉ Ladeira da Matriz 92 ☎ 32 3355 1148
🕑 Daily 11–4

TERRA BRAZIL

www.terra-brazil.com

This agency based in Rio offers high-quality ethical tours, in which both the environment and guides are treated with respect. Their cultural tours of the area include all the main highlights. Visitors, on both individual and tailor-made trips, visit Congonhas, taking in the sculptures by Master Aleijadinho. They can embark on a steam train trip between São João del Rei and Tiradentes, where the colonial streets and churches, as well as the surrounding countryside are explored. Finally the architectural and cultural sights of the city of Belo Horizonte are visited.
✉ Rua da Passagem 83, sala 314, Botafogo, Rio de Janeiro ☎ 21 2543 3185
🕑 Mon–Sat 9–5

VITÓRIA

AGENCIA NAUTICA CORES DO MAR

Vitória has many islands dotted in its bay and adjacent bays, including some of the most extensive stretches of mangroves of any city in Brazil. They can easily be visited on day tours with Agencia Nautica Cores do Mar.
✉ Cais do Hidroavião, Avenida Dario Lourenço de Souza, Santo Antônio ☎ 27 3222 3810 🕑 Mon–Sat 10–5

MOSTEIRO ZEN

www.mosteirozen.com.br

This Zen Buddhist monastery is on a hill some 10km (6 miles) from Vitória on the road to Linhares, and sits in extensive Mata Atlântica rainforest. On Sundays, it opens its doors to show visitors how the monks live and to allow them to explore some of the surrounding ecological trails. Those wishing to stay for longer must apply in advance to join a spiritual retreat.
✉ BR-101 to Linhares, km 217 ☎ 27 3257 3030 🕑 Sun 8–2 Free

FESTIVALS AND EVENTS

FEBRUARY–MARCH

CARNAVAL

São João del Rei and Ouro Preto have the best and liveliest carnivals in Minas Gerais. Celebrations also take place in Mariana and Diamantina. During festivities, which take place over five days and begin four days before Easter, *blocos,* or carnival groups, parade through the streets. Many of the participants are dressed in fantastic costumes. After the parades, street parties usually ensue.
ℹ Avenida Tiradentes 136, Centro, São João del Rei ☎ 32 3372 7338 🕑 Mon–Fri 9–6
ℹ Praça Tiradentes 41 (Câmara Municipal), Ouro Preto ☎ 31 3559 3269
🕑 Daily 8–5

MARCH–APRIL

HOLY WEEK

Ouro Preto celebrates Holy Week with famous traditional processions through the cobbled streets, beginning on the Thursday before Palm Sunday and culminating with a re-enactment of the crucifixion on Good Friday.
ℹ Praça Tiradentes 41 (Câmara Municipal), Ouro Preto ☎ 31 3559 3269
🕑 Daily 8–5

JULY

FESTIVAL DE INVERNO (WINTER FESTIVAL)

www.festivaldeinverno.ufop.br

Ouro Preto's University (UFMG) hosts three weeks of arts events, concerts and exhibitions by local artists from the first week of the month. There are events all over the city (advertised in the local press and in the tourist office), but they are focused on the University Campus on the outskirts of the town (taxi from the centre R$15).
ℹ Praça Tiradentes 41 (Câmara Municipal), Ouro Preto ☎ 31 3559 3269 🕑 Daily 8–5

SEPTEMBER

O DIA DAS SERESTAS

www.diamantina.com.br

Diamantina holds O Dia das Serestas, the 'Day of Serenades', on 12 September. Musicians play from the balconies of colonial buildings and along the cobbled streets. The festival is famous throughout Minas and is held in commemoration of the birthday of President Juscelino Kubitschek (▷ 35), who was born in Diamantina and who built Brasília.
ℹ Praça Antônio Eulálio 53, Centro, Diamantina ☎ 38 3531 9527 🕑 Mon–Fri 12–6

PRICES AND SYMBOLS

The restaurants are listed alphabetically (excluding A, Al, El, La, Le and O). The prices given are the average for a two-course lunch (L) and a three-course dinner (D) for one person, without drinks. The wine price is for the least expensive bottle. Although you will find wine served in restaurants throughout Brazil, the usual drinks are bottled beer (R$5–R$8) or *caipirinhas*, the ubiquitous *cachaça* and fruit cocktails (R$8). All the restaurants listed accept credit cards unless otherwise stated.

For a key to the symbols, ▷ 2.

BELO HORIZONTE

AURORA

Diners are showered with rose petals as they enter the intimate, low-lit dining room in this restaurant overlooking the Lagoa da Pampulha lake. The menu mixes Asian and Italian styles with exotic Brazilian fruits and vegetables, producing dishes like *filé ao molho de jabuticabas* (fillet steak in jabuticaba fruit sauce) and the *banquete de Buda* (coconut-encrusted prawns in Thai red curry sauce, served with coconut milk and marjoram risotto). There is also a decent wine list.

✉ Rua Expedicionário Mário Alves de Oliveira 421, São Luís ☎ 31 3498 7567 🕐 Wed, Fri 7–11, Sat 12–11, Sun 12–3 ✋ L R$30, D R$50, Wine R$30

TASTE-VIN

www.tastevin-bh.com.br

A French restaurant beloved of Mineiros for its soufflés and seafood, Taste-Vin is an intimate, formal dining room in the best part of town. The wine list has South American and European bottles.

✉ Rua Curitiba 2105, Lourdes ☎ 31 3292 5423 🕐 Tue–Thu 7.30–12, Fri–Sat 7.30–1 ✋ D R$40, Wine R$30

VECCHIO SOGNO

www.vecchiosogno.com.br

This formal Mediterranean-style restaurant, run by chef Ivo Faria who has been cooking in Belo Horizonte for more than 20 years, is popular with politicians from the nearby municipal government offices. Ivo is renowned for his excellent *degustation* (tasting) menu (which varies from month to month) and for his traditional Mediterranean dishes, which include *bacalhau* (salted cod) roasted in garlic and served with sautéed vegetables.

✉ Rua Martim de Carvalho 75, Assembléia Legislativo ☎ 31 3292 5251 🕐 Tue–Thu 12.30–12, Fri 12–2am, Sat 6–2, Sun 12–6 ✋ L R$30, D R$50, Wine R$35

XAPURI

www.restaurantexapuri.com.br

Xapuri is the best in the city for traditional Minas Gerais cooking, which has rich sauces, spit-cooked meats and unusual vegetables from the *cerrado*, like the tart yellow berry, pequi (which can only be sucked because its interior is filled with tiny, sharp spines). There is live acoustic music at weekends, usually *choro* or sung samba.

✉ Rua Mandacaru 260, Pampulha ☎ 31 3496 6198 🕐 Tue–Thu 12–11, Fri, Sat 12–12 ✋ L R$30, D R$50, Wine R$30

MARIANA

ENGENHO NÔVO

This simple restaurant with plastic chairs and tables serves local dishes and generous salads, and doubles up as a bar at night serving cold bottled beer and strong *caipirinhas* (cocktails of sugar cane spirit, crushed ice and fresh lime).

✉ Praça da Sé 26 ☎ 31 3557 5999 🕐 Tue–Sun 12–12 ✋ L R$15, D R$15, Cocktail R$8

RAMPAS

Like all restaurants in Mariana, Rampas is very simple, with a plain dining room of plastic tables and chairs. The per-kilo buffet (food

Opposite *The interior of Casa do Ouvidor which specializes in regional cuisine*

priced by weight) is one of the best in the centre of the city, though, with plenty of choice of mains and sweet sticky puddings that include delicious crème caramel *(pudim de leite)*.
✉ Praça Gomes Freire 92 ☎ 31 3557 2528 ⊙ Tue–Sun 12–11 ✋ L R$15, D R$15

OURO PRETO

BENE DA FLAUTA

www.benedaflauta.com.br
This cosy, family-run restaurant in a handsome 18th-century town house is a local favourite for traditional Minas cooking and is conveniently located in the colonial centre, next to the Igreja de São Francisco. Dishes include chicken with rice and *tutu de feijão* (refried puréed beans with manioc flour).
✉ Rua São Francisco 32 ☎ 31 3551 1036 ⊙ Mon–Fri 12–3, 7.30–11, Sat 12–5, 7.30–11, Sun 12–4 ✋ L R$20, D R$30, Wine R$32

CASA DOS CONTOS

This popular bistro has a buffet of Minas Gerais dishes and salads for lunch, and à la carte regional cooking in the evening, with meaty options like steak with red peppers, tomatoes and fried onion.
✉ Rua Camilo de Brito 21 ☎ 31 3551 5359 ⊙ Tue–Sun 12–3, 6–11 ✋ L R$20, D R$38, Wine R$30

CASA DO OUVIDOR

In one of the most upmarket Minas restaurants in the city, you will find dishes like chicken with okra, spring greens, Brazilian beans and a side dish of bacon and *farofa* (toasted manioc flour).
✉ Rua Cidade de Bobadela 42 ☎ 31 3551 2141 ⊙ Daily 11–3, 7–10 ✋ L R$40, D R$55, Wine R$30

PIACERE

www.restaurantepiacere.com.br
Reliable Italian dishes at this restaurant, in a colonial house in the centre, include various risottos and pasta handmade in the kitchen. The dining room has original 18th-century raw stone walls and an open-plan kitchen with dishes bubbling on a wood-fire stove.
✉ Rua Getúlio Vargas 241 ☎ 31 3551 4297 ⊙ Mon–Sat 7–12 ✋ D R$35, Wine R$30

SENHOR DO ROSÁRIO

www.hotelsolardorosario.com
Italian chef Luciano Boseggia commands one of the finest kitchens in the city and offers Italian dishes with a Brazilian twist. The Senhor do Rosário occupies a large dining room, whose heavy wooden tables are covered in thick white linen table cloths. The restaurant sits on the ground floor of the stately colonial Solar do Rosário hotel (▷ 201). The wine list is excellent.
✉ Rua Getúlio Vargas 270 ☎ 31 3551 5200 ⊙ Daily 12–3, 7–11 ✋ LR$ 40, D R$75, Wine R$40

SÃO JOÃO DEL REI

QUINTO DO OURO

You'll find some of the best Mineira cooking in town here, with a buffet offering a choice of dishes kept warm over a traditional Minas Gerais wood-fired stove.
✉ Praça Severiano de Resende 04 ☎ 32 3372 7577 ⊙ Mon–Fri 12–3, 6–9.30, Sat 12–3, 7.30–9.30, Sun 12–5 ✋ L R$15, D R$25, Wine R$30

RAMÓN

This excellent all-you-can-eat meat-on-a-spit restaurant, or *churrascaria*, offers generous portions of many cuts of beef, pork and poultry, and plenty of side dishes.
✉ Praça Severiano de Resende 52 ☎ 32 3372 7349 ⊙ Tue–Sat 12–3, 7.30–10, Sun 12–4 ✋ L R$35, D R$35, Wine R$34

VILLEIROS

A very popular lunchtime pay-by-weight buffet offers an enormous choice of local and pan-Brazilian dishes, like fried chicken with *farofa* (toasted manioc flour) and the national dish, *feijoada* (a stew of beans and pork or beef).
✉ Rua Jose Maria Xavier 132 ☎ 32 3372 1034 ⊙ Tue–Sat 11.30–4.30, 6.30–12, Sun 11.30–4 ✋ L R$10, D R$20

TIRADENTES

ESTALAGEM

This restaurant, sitting in a colonial cottage next to the river, has been celebrated for its hearty Minas cooking for a generation. Come with an empty stomach and with a taste for meat. The Costelas de Adão (Adam's ribs) are thankfully meaty and come with sweet potato and plantain. Other dishes include Brazilian pumpkin stuffed with jerky and Minas Gerais white curd cheese, black pepper and *taioba* fruit.
✉ Rua Min Gabriel Passos 280 ☎ 32 3355 1144 ⊙ Tue–Fri 12–4, 7–10, Sat 11.30–10, Sun 11.30–5 ✋ L R$25, D R$35, Wine R$30

QUARTIER LATIN

The kitchen in this fusion cooking restaurant is run by a Paris-trained cordon bleu chef. It offers a menu of European seafood and meat dishes cooked with Brazilian fruits, herbs and spices. Salads are made from organic vegetables grown in the garden. There is also a respectable wine list.
✉ Rua São Francisco de Paula 46, Praça da Rodoviária ☎ 32 3355 1552 ⊙ Tue–Fri 12–4, 7–11, Sat 12–11, Sun 11.30–5 ✋ L R$35, D R$70, Wine R$40

THEATRO DA VILLA

www.theatrodavilla.com.br
A lovely family-run restaurant, this place is best visited at night, when tables are laid out in the garden, overlooking a small theatre which has occasional performances. The food is excellent, mixing Italian, French and Brazilian styles and ingredients, and the wine list is equally impressive.
✉ Rua Padre Toledo 157 ☎ 32 3355 1275 ⊙ Mon–Sat 8–12 ✋ L R$30, D R$60, Wine R$40

VIRADAS DO LARGO

This restaurant vies with Estalagem (▷ this page) for the best Minas Gerais kitchen in the town. Dishes are prepared with ingredients from the restaurant's kitchen garden and served in a cosy dining room at the back of a little *praça*.
✉ Largo do Ó ☎ 32 3355 1111 ⊙ Daily 12–10 ✋ L R$30, D R$50

PRICES AND SYMBOLS
Prices are the lowest and highest for a double room for one night. Breakfast is included unless noted otherwise. All the hotels listed accept credit cards unless otherwise stated. Note that rates vary widely throughout the year.

For a key to the symbols, ▷ 2.

BELO HORIZONTE

OURO MINAS PALACE

www.ourominas.com.br
One of Belo Horizonte's plushest hotels has huge rooms fully appointed for business visitors. The top-floor suites include several for women only. Service is superior and facilities include an indoor pool, sauna and gym with personal trainers. The Palace is situated between the city centre and Pampulha.
Avenida Cristiano Machado 4001 31 3429 4001 R$460–R$630 343 Indoor

CONGONHAS

COLONIAL

www.hotelcolonialcongonhas.com.br
This hotel, which is housed in a large 18th-century town house, has an enviable location right next to the Santuário on the top of the hill. The cheapest rooms have shared bathrooms and the restaurant doubles up as a gallery for displaying local handicrafts.
Praça da Basílica 76 31 3731 1834 R$95–R$150 13

MARIANA

POUSADA CONTOS DE MINAS

www.pousadacontosdeminas.com.br
This is a small town hotel in a mock-colonial building right in the town centre. Rooms are functional but comfortable, all with en suites and air-conditioning. The quietest are numbers 13, 14 and 15, at the back of the building.
Rua Zizinha Carmello 15 31 3558 5400 R$70–R$120 32

OURO PRETO

HOTEL POUSADA SOLAR DAS LAJES

www.hotelsolardaslajes.com.br
Here you will find a small family-owned hotel with simple but elegant whitewashed rooms. They have raw stone floor tiles or polished wood floors and little window booths offering superb views of the city.
Rua Conselheiro Quintiliano 604 31 3551 1116 R$90–R$120 18

LUXOR POUSADA

www.luxorhoteis.com.br
Rooms in this converted 18th-century town house come with whitewashed walls, polished wood floors and chunky faux-colonial beds, breakfast tables and wardrobes. Large windows on the upper floors ensure plenty of natural light and the hotel restaurant (which specializes in local cooking) is decent value.
Rua Dr Alfredo Baeta 16, Praça Antônio Dias 31 3551 2244 R$265–R$460 18

POUSADA DOS BANDEIRANTES

www.hotelpousadabandeirantes.com.br
The furnishings are minimal and the whitewashed walls monastic, but rooms are well kept, service comes with warmth and courtesy and the location, right behind the Igreja de São Francisco, is hard to beat.
Rua das Mercês 167 31 3551 1996 R$80–R$120 15

POUSADA DO MONDEGO

www.mondego.com.br
This converted colonial town mansion is in a privileged location, fewer than 150m (164 yards) from the Igreja de São Francisco. Rooms are decorated with period furniture and the best have views out over the terracotta tiles of old Ouro Preto. The hotel runs a bus tour of the city, which can also be booked by non-residents.
Largo de Coimbra 38 31 3551 2040 R$300–R$700 24

Above Azulejos *(tiles) in Ouro Preto*

POUSADA SÃO FRANCISCO DE PAULA

www.pousadasaofranciscodepaula.com.br

The rooms in this small hostel near the bus station have little in them except a bed, wardrobe and a little writing desk. However, the best (on the upper floor) have views of the Igreja de São Francisco set against rugged hills and with huddles of colonial houses all around.

Rua Padre José Marcos Pena 202 31 3551 3456 Dorm bed R$30; double room R$100–R$120 18

POUSADA SOLAR DE NOSSA SENHORA DO ROSÁRIO

www.hotelsolardorosario.com.br

Another of the city's tastefully restored stately town houses, this one has a pool on the roof and a great situation in the heart of the old city. Standard rooms are small but come with en suite bathrooms. Suites are almost three times the size. All rooms on the upper floors have views over Ouro Preto and the breakfast is an enormous spread, with more than 50 items to choose from (from scrambled eggs, Minas Gerais sausages and exotic fruit, to cereals and six kinds of bread).

Avenida Getúlio Vargas 270 31 3551 5200 R$370–R$690 41 Rooftop, indoor

PARQUE NACIONAL SERRA DA CANASTRA

POUSADA MIRANTE DA CANASTRA

www.serradacanastra.com.br/pousadas/mirante.html

This rustic countryside *pousada*, a 10-minute drive from the park, offers spruce but bare rooms with hammock-strung terraces and views out over the *cerrado*. Some are large enough for groups of eight.

São Roque de Minas 37 3433 1452 R$70–R$130 14

PARQUE NACIONAL SERRA DO CIPÓ

CIPÓ VERANEIO HOTEL

www.cipoveraneiohotel.com.br

This is a very comfortable hotel on the edge of the park, with rustic air-conditioned rooms, a restaurant, its own *cachaça* (sugar cane spirit) distillery and a tour operator that offers light adventure and wildlife trips around the national park.

Rodovia MG 10, km 95 31 3718 7000 R$270–R$400 32 Outdoor

PARQUE NATURAL DO CARAÇA

SANTUÁRIO DO CARAÇA

www.santuariodocaraca.com.br

This seminary occupies an isolated site in wild and mountainous *cerrado*. It is now particularly known for its visiting maned wolves, which the monks regularly leave food out for. Rooms are functional little cells, as befitting a monastery, but the location is fabulous.

Catas Altas, Santa Barbara 31 3837 2698 R$165 35

SÃO JOÃO DEL REI

BECO DO BISPO

www.becodobispocom.br

A colonial building tucked away at the end of a tiny alley near the São Francisco church, with small but well-appointed rooms and a little pool. The hotel doesn't allow children under 12.

Beco do Bispo 93 32 3371 8844 R$210–R$325 13 Outdoor

POUSADA VILLA MAGNÓLIA

www.pousadavillamagnolia.com.br

The most upmarket hotel in São João del Rei town centre occupies this 19th-century town house a few minutes' walk from São Francisco church. It includes spacious bright rooms and a pool.

Rua Ribeiro Bastos 2 32 3373 5065 R$140–R$245 13 Outdoor

TIRADENTES

POUSADA DO ARCO IRIS

www.arcoiristiradentesmg.com.br

Rooms in this simple hotel come with little more than parquet floors and a bed but they are great value in touristy Tiradentes. The *pousada* is one of a series in a huddle of 18th-century cottages that are a five-minute walk from the town centre. It is important to book ahead at weekends, when the *pousada* is very popular.

Rua Frederico Ozanan 340 32 3355 1167 R$120–R$180 13

POUSADA DOS INCONFIDÊNTES

www.pousadadosinconfidentes.com.br

One of the most luxurious *pousadas* in the city, this has 18th-century-style spacious rooms, decorated with antique and faux-antique furnishings, the best of which have wonderful views out over the serra. They do not accept children under 12.

Rua João Rodrigues Sobrinho 91 32 3355 2135 R$500–R$700 13 Outdoor

POUSADA MARIA BONITA

www.tiradentesgerais.com.br/mariabonita

This colonial bungalow on the edge of town is great value, with simple but well-kept motel-like rooms leading to a garden with a decent-sized pool, which abuts the river. Tiradentes town centre is a 10-minute walk away.

Rua Antônio Teixeira Carvalho 134 32 3355 1227 R$140–R$180 16 Outdoor

POUSADA RICHARD ROTHE

www.pousadarichardrothe.com.br

This colonial *pousada* was originally an antiques show gallery and remains filled with period furnishings. There is a lovely pool set in a tropical garden. Breakfasts are generous and the hotel is well-situated in the centre. The *pousada* does not accept children under 12.

Rua Pedro Toledo 124 32 3355 1333 R$180–R$280 11 Outdoor

POUSO DAS GERAIS

www.pousodasgerais.com.br

Here you will find large, very comfortable duplex rooms in mock-colonial buildings next to a large pool. Furnishings are also mock-colonial, with big, solid wooden beds, lovely wrought iron headboards and worktables.

Rua dos Inconfidêntes 109 32 3355 1234 R$140–R$200 24 Outdoor

BAHIA STATE

Bahia is famous throughout Brazil for its powdery tropical beaches, vibrant African culture and the magnificent colonial architecture of its capital city, Salvador. Brazil also began in Bahia, when Portuguese caravels en route for Asia were blown far off course and ended up making landfall just south of the present day city of Porto Seguro, in the southeast.

Most visits to the state begin in Salvador, a UNESCO World Heritage Site preserving one of the largest and most impressive collections of baroque buildings in the world. The city occupies a beautiful location, straddling a peninsula at the northern mouth of the country's largest bay, the Baía de Todos os Santos. It is the centre of a unique and thriving African-Brazilian culture which has crafted Brazil's most famous cultural icons: samba, *capoeira*, and the African-Brazilian spirit religion of *candomblé*. The city boasts the largest and most raucous street carnival in Brazil.

Beaches stretch north of the capital, along the busy Coconut Coast to the state of Sergipe, less than 200km (125 miles) away. South of Salvador is the Recôncavo, the land which made Brazil rich on sugar cane and tobacco in the first centuries of the colony. It is dotted with little colonial towns, the most notable of which is Cachoeira. Farther south still are more beaches and islands: the laid-back resort island of Morro de São Paulo, the chic surf retreat of Itacaré and, in the far south, the Discovery and Whale coasts. This is the most popular beach stretch in Bahia—dotted with colonial villages like Porto Seguro, Arraial d'Ajuda and Trancoso—which have grown into fashionable resorts, justly celebrated for their long, palm-shaded beaches and the pristine rainforests which lie behind them. These remnants of the Mata Atlântica forests, which once stretched along the coast from the Amazon to Argentina, remain important repositories for rare animals and offer excellent bird watching. The Abrolhos archipelago, a short boat ride offshore, offers the best diving in Bahia and the chance to see calfing humpback whales.

The interior of the state is dotted with national parks like the Chapada Diamantina, whose table-top mountains drip with waterfalls and which offers some of the best South American trekking east of the Andes.

CANUDOS

www.canudosnet.com.br

This one-street town in the heart of the dry *sertão* desert scrubland of Bahia's vast interior marks the site of one of Latin America's most astonishing rebellions. In the 19th century, a city of robbers and bandits led by a charismatic prophet withstood the might of three Brazilian armies before being mercilessly crushed (▷ 35). Their story is told in one of the great books of early Brazilian literature, *Os Sertões* (translated into English as *Backlands: The Canudos Campaign)* by Euclides da Cunha, 1902; and in Mario Vargas Llosa's powerful 1981 publication, *La Guerra del Fin del Mundo (The War of the End of the World)*.

Modern Canudos is a sleepy place but there are a number of parks and reserves which are home to some of the rarest plants and animals in South America (including xeric bushes unique to the *sertão* and the critically endangered giant blue parrot, the lear's macaw). These include the Parque Estadual de Canudos and the Estação Biológica de Canudos, both of which protect the lear's macaw nesting sites.

398 T9 From Salvador

CARAVELAS

www.caravelasturismo.com.br

This attractive port town, sitting between long, broad beaches in the far south of Bahia, is the departure point for whale watching and dive cruises to the Abrolhos archipelago (▷ 210). Most visitors pass through the city on their way to or from the islands with barely a glance, but Caravelas has a long history, beautiful coastal wetlands and little-visited beaches. It merits an afternoon or morning's visit.

The town takes its name from the caravel ships which brought the Portuguese to Brazil. It was an important trading port in the colonial period, shipping brasil wood, sugar and then cocoa to Europe. It fell quiet after World War I, when the cocoa trade moved to Ilhéus (▷ this page). Today, its handsome late colonial and early republican buildings crumble under the strong sun and the town's economy relies almost entirely on seasonal tourism from Minas Gerais (▷ 181–201).

South of town are extensive mangrove wetlands where the Caravelas river fans out into a delta as it meets the Atlantic. There are many beaches around the town, including Iemanjá Beach, with beach bars and good surf, and Praia Ponta da Baleia to the north, which is a wild and semi-deserted beach.

401 S13 Rua Barão do Rio Branco 65 73 3297 1113 Tue–Sun 10–12, 2–6 From Porto Seguro via Eunápolis or Teixeira de Freitas (both on the BR 101 coastal highway)

CHAPADA DIAMANTINA

▷ 206–207.

ILHÉUS

www.ilheusdabahia.tur.br

The largest city on the Dendê coast is famous as the home of Brazil's most famous author after Paulo Coelho, Jorge Amado (1912–2001), who set many of his bawdy novels in the city.

Modern Ilhéus is a quiet provincial town with a big port and a scattering of interesting buildings. Visitors generally spend little time here, choosing to pass through from the airport or *rodoviária* (bus station) to the beaches of Itacaré (▷ 208), 75km (46 miles) to the north.

The city has a few historical sights worth visiting. The Igreja de São Jorge (Tue–Fri 9–12, 2–7) is a very simple and partly fortified baroque church, dating from 1556, with a small sacred art museum. Jorge Amado spent much of his early life in a house in the city centre which is now a museum, A Casa de Cultura Jorge Amado (tel 73 3634 8986; Mon–Fri 9–12, 2–6, Sat 9–1; R$5).

The Bataclã cultural centre is a former bordello and poker palace, once visited by the landowning elite (tel 73 3634 7835; daily 9–9; free). It is linked to other parts of the town by a series of secret tunnels, through which the patriarchs would escape when their wives came looking for them. The club was immortalized in 1958, in Jorge Amado's most famous novel set in Ilhéus, *Gabriela, Cravo e Canela (Gabriela, Clove and Cinnamon).*

401 S11 Avenida Itabuna 2222 (no English spoken) 73 2101 5500 Mon–Fri 10–6 From Salvador Ilhéus Jorge Amado

Opposite *Sunbathing on Praia dos Coqueiros at Trancoso (▷ 210)*

Below *Lear's macaws feeding on Licuri palm fruit, Canudos*

INFORMATION
www.guiachapadadiamantina.com.br
398 R10 From Lençóis

Above *Forests and orchards clothe the Vale de Capão*

INTRODUCTION

The Chapada Diamantina, or Diamond Hills, are a series of escarpments overflowing with waterfalls, which jut out of the arid and flat plains of the Bahian *sertão* scrubland like crumbling chocolate. They are high enough to catch warm, wet air blowing in from the Atlantic, which precipitates on the upper slopes and flows into myriad rivers that plunge and fall over the escarpments in some of the most impressive cascades in Brazil. Much of the Chapada is protected as a national park and, although it was heavily deforested up until the late 20th century, it is now recuperating. It is increasingly rich in wildlife and offers excellent bird watching.

The Chapada was home to wild animals and unperturbed indigenous Brazilians until 1732, when *bandeirante* slave traders found gold in its rivers and diamonds in its hills. A gold rush followed and, later, permanent settlement and the construction of mining towns, the largest of which was Lençóis (▷ opposite).

WHAT TO SEE

CACHOEIRA DA FUMAÇA (SMOKY FALLS)

The second tallest waterfalls in Brazil plummet 340m (115ft) from a high escarpment in the far south of the park. Their height and volume creates a wind, which blows the water vapour back up the mountain and shrouds the landscape in a curtain of fine mist that looks like smoke (hence their name). The falls can be visited on a day tour from Lençóis or as part of a longer hike. They are on private land and a fee is payable to enter. Many agencies offer trips to the park, such as Expedições H2O (▷ 227), the popular choice of budget-conscious backpackers.
 R$3

MORRO DO PAI INÁCIO (FATHER IGNATIUS'S HILL)

This table-top mountain in the far north of the national park sits at the head of a long forested valley of mountains which cuts right through the centre of the Chapada. Views from the summit are spectacular—so much so that they have become an emblem of the national park, gracing every other promotional pamphlet and poster. Access is easy; even small coaches can park in the dirt area at the hill's base, and from here it's a 20-minute walk and light scramble to the flat summit. All the agencies, including the reliable Fora da Trilha, offer trips to this peak (▷ 227). Come at sunset for the best views.

LENÇÓIS TOWN

The stone houses and steep cobbles of this pretty diamond-rush town are cradled in a green valley along the banks of a limpid mountain river (▷ 224–225). Many of the 19th-century miners' houses are now chic boutiques, bars, restaurants and *pousadas* (small hotels or inns), for Lençóis is the Chapada's tourist hub and the only real option as a place to base your stay.

398 R10 · Avenida Senhor dos Passos, s/n · 75 3334 1378 · Mon–Fri 9–5
From Salvador

THE GRUTA PRATINHA AND GRUTA AZUL (SILVER AND BLUE GROTTOES)

The Chapada is pocked with cave systems and cut by underground rivers, which form a whole series of water-filled caverns. These are two of the most accessible—lily-covered aquamarine pools, linked by an underground river through which increasing numbers of weekend visitors float on rubber tubes, leaving a light scum of dust and sun tan lotion on the surface which is sadly ever-more visible. The Grutas can only be visited as part of a tour, offered by many agencies in the area (▷ 227).

R$10

THE MARIMBUS WETLAND

The meeting of the Santo Antônio and Utinga rivers, at the eastern edge of the Chapada, forms the Marimbus wetland. It is an area of flooded forest and *pantano* wetland, rich in bird and wildlife. Marimbus is not a natural wetland. It was formed in the 19th century when the mines created so much sediment that it permanently impeded the flows of both the Santo Antônio and Utinga, causing them permanently to flood.

The wetland is best seen from a canoe and can be included as part of a day tour with any Lençóis tour operator. The best trips take a day, involve at least three or four hours in the swamp, followed by a walk to the Roncador falls, as does the Chapada Adventure agency tour (▷ 226).

TIPS

» Bring binoculars to the park. Distances are large and wildlife is hard to see close to.

» You will also need sun protection, a hat and sturdy walking shoes if you plan to visit any of the waterfalls.

» There is no disabled access anywhere in the park.

Below left *Hiking around Cachoeira da Primavera (Spring Falls)*
Below *Shops in Lençóis*

INFORMATION

www.itacare.com

401 T11 Avenida Itabuna 2222

73 2101 5500 Mon–Fri 10–6

From Ilhéus Ilhéus Jorge Amado

TIP

» There are sand fleas *(bicho de pé)* around some of the beaches in Itacaré, so be sure to use footwear when walking on trails. These creatures can easily be removed by covering the blister with petroleum jelly and then digging out the flea with a sterilized pin.

ITACARÉ AND THE PENINSULA DO MARAÚ

Itacaré grew rapidly from a fishing village into a resort town after it was discovered by surfers from São Paulo in the 1980s. They were drawn by the powerful waves on Tiririca beach but soon discovered that the little town was surrounded by dozens of other stretches of sands, from long broad strands to little bays backed by lush primary rainforest. International visitors began to arrive some 20 years later, drawn by the plush spa resorts built on the secluded beaches still farther to the south, and nowadays Itacaré is one of Bahia's principal beach towns.

BEACHES

The fishing village which sits at the heart of Itacaré is still pretty, with a bay full of boats and rows of brightly painted houses, but most visitors choose to stay on the beaches. There are dozens to choose from. Praia da Concha is the main town beach, with streets of *pousadas* and restaurants in its hinterland. Immediately to its south is Resende, running around a half-moon bay and with powdery sand and palms. It's a 10-minute walk from here to the surf beaches of Tiririca and Praia da Costa, which are still chosen as the host beaches for international tournaments. To their south is pretty Praia do Ribeira, a perfect cove sitting under forest-clad hills and washed by a little fast-flowing river. Waves are gentle and this is the best beach for families.

PENINSULA DO MARAÚ

Far wilder beaches lie to the north of Itacaré across the Rio de Contas and stretch for some 70km (43 miles) to the northern end of the Peninsula do Maraú. These include Praia do Pontal, which is about 20km (12.5 miles) long and deserted. It stretches all the way to the beaches of the Peninsula do Maraú: a longer finger of sand and *restinga* forest which separates the fierce Atlantic from the placid waters of Brazil's third largest bay, the Baía de Camamu.

Below *Coconut palms fringe sandy Resende beach*

MORRO DE SÃO PAULO

South of Salvador the Bahian coast breaks into mangrove wetlands, river mouths and forest-covered islands fringed with some of the best of the state's famous white sand beaches. The most celebrated of these is Tinharé, which is nowadays known by the name of its most famous resort, Morro de São Paulo, one of central Bahia's busiest tourist towns. It sits on a small hill at the northern tip of Tinharé island, overlooking a string of beautiful beaches shaded by coconut palms which run far to the south.

ISLAND BEACHES

Morro town has five beaches. Primeira Praia is the most built up; *pousadas* now extend so far down to the water that there is barely room left for sand. Segunda is a broad beach with plenty of accommodation and restaurants, and lively parties every night at the makeshift *palapa* (palm-thatch) beachfront bars. *Pousadas* continue in an unbroken line all the way along Terceira to the beginning of Quarta, where stays become more tranquil and *pousadas* more dissipated. The quietest beach of all, Quinta, lies far beyond Quarta. It is a 3-hour walk from town, or a 20-minute taxi ride on the only road on the island, which runs south and parallel to the sea from the beginning of Terceira Praia.

THE VILLAGE

Morro village has a few sights of interest and, as the best of the restaurants are situated here, it merits a short tour on the way to or from a meal. A small colonial *praça* (square) leads to a lighthouse and a 17th-century fort. The fort is largely a ruin but it affords great views from its broken battlements out over rusting cannons and palm fronds to the coral-fringed coast.

INFORMATION

www.morrosp.com.br

401 T11 Praça Aureliano Lima s/n 75 3652 1083 Ferries from Salvador Flights from Salvador to Morro de São Paulo airport

TIPS

» Take a boat trip round the Tinharé archipelago to see more deserted beaches and tiny fishing villages. Most hotels and *pousadas* can arrange this with local boatmen.

» Bring your own snorkel and mask. Rental prices can be steep in Morro.

» Book flights well in advance in high season (Dec–Mar) as planes are small and fill up quickly.

Above *Terceira Praia stretching into the distance*

Above *The broad, sandy beach, Praia Rio Trancoso, at Trancoso*
Right *Humpback whales frequent the seas of Parque Nacional Marinho dos Abrolhos*

PARQUE NACIONAL MARINHO DOS ABROLHOS

www.ilhasdeabrolhos.com.br

This archipelago of beach-fringed rocks off Bahia's far southern Whale Coast, near Caravelas (▷ 205), is one of Brazil's few marine national parks. It was created in 1983 to protect some of the most important coral formations in the southern Atlantic. The coral gardens and reefs around the islands may be small by Caribbean standards but they are home to around four times as many endemic coral species, including unique giant brain corals. Marine turtles are almost a guaranteed sight here and, from July to December, the seas between the islands and the coast are the best places in the Atlantic to see nursing humpback whales (▷ 226).

Abrolhos is an abbreviation of *Abre os olhos,* 'Open your eyes!' an exclamation said to have been shouted by Amérigo Vespucci when he first sighted the reef in 1503. Darwin visited the archipelago in 1830 and Jacques Cousteau studied the marine environment here in the 1970s.

401 S13 From Caravelas

PORTO SEGURO AND ARRAIAL D'AJUDA

▷ 211.

PRAIA DO FORTE AND THE BAHIA LINHA VERDE

www.costadoscoqueiros.com

Praia do Forte, which takes its name from the Castelo Garcia d'Avila—a 16th-century Portuguese fortress on the edge of town—is the best of a spread of resorts on the northern Bahia Linha Verde (also known as the Costa dos Coqueiros, or the Coconut Coast). This runs north from Salvador to the state border with Sergipe. While heavily developed, it still preserves a little of the atmosphere which first attracted tourists here in the 1970s, when it was a fishing village. The main street is traffic-free with restaurants and shops. There's a good choice of elegant *pousadas* for those who prefer to avoid the array of huge beach hotels and holiday reps. The town is the headquarters of Projeto Tamar, an NGO dedicated to preserving turtle nesting sites on Brazil's beaches. There are many nestlings in their nursery and the centre offers a fascinating insight into the biology of the marine reptiles.

Beyond Praia do Forte the Coconut Coast is lined with a combination of brash resorts like the Costa do Sauípe, forgotten villages like Mangue Seco and condominiums for weekenders from Salvador.

399 T10 Avenida ACM Daily 9–8 From Salvador

THE RECÔNCAVO

▷ 212–213.

SALVADOR

▷ 214–221.

TRANCOSO

www.trancosobahia.com.br

Bahia's best-kept beach secret of the 1990s is now a small-scale luxury resort village, replete with boutique hotels, designer shops and gourmet restaurants. It began life in Portuguese times, as a colonial church sitting on grassy makeshift square called the *quadrado*, lined with miniature bungalows. It was discovered by São Paulo hippies in the 1970s and grew in earnest in the new millennium, when Brazilian model Gisele Bündchen brought her actor boyfriend of the time, Leonardo DiCaprio, here for extended holidays.

Nowadays there are golf resorts and condos in the hills, but the town itself retains its small-scale charm. The *quadrado* is free of modern developments, no beach hotel is allowed to stand higher than two storeys and the beaches themselves are only uncomfortably crowded at the height of the season (Dec–Mar), which includes *carnaval* (▷ 231).

401 S12 From Porto Seguro

PORTO SEGURO AND ARRAIAL D'AJUDA

These two towns sit opposite each other on the banks of the Rio Buranhém, on Bahia's southern Discovery Coast. They are two of the biggest beach resorts in northeastern Brazil and tourists have been coming here since Pedro Álvares Cabral became the first European to see Brazil on Easter Day in 1500 (▷ 25).

COLONIAL PORTO SEGURO

Old Porto Seguro watches over the river and the beaches from a grassy hill shaded with palms and tropical ficus trees. It has been carefully preserved as an open-air museum. Streets of pastel-paint cottages lead to some impressive old buildings: the church of Nossa Senhora da Pena (tel 73 3288 6363; daily 9–12, 2–5); the 16th-century Casa de Câmara e Cadêia (tel 73 3288 5182; daily 9–5), once the headquarters of the Portuguese captaincy governing southern Bahia; and Brazil's oldest church, Nossa Senhora da Misericórdia (tel 73 3288 5182; Sat–Wed 9.30–1.30, 2.30–5). The church is a simple structure, with heavily fortified walls, built in 1526 to defend the first fathers against the irate indigenous Potiguar people, whose land they were requisitioning for the Portuguese crown. A simple block of marble on the grassy town square, inscribed with the Portuguese Cross, marks the point where the explorer Gonçalo Coelho formally claimed Brazil for Lisbon in 1503.

ARRAIAL D'AJUDA

While Porto Seguro has the busiest beaches with the liveliest nightlife, Arraial has the more beautiful, long broad stretches of sand backed by sandstone cliffs or shady coconut palms, which run all the way to Trancoso (▷ 210).

WILDLIFE

There are a number of protected rainforest areas, including three national parks, which are either difficult to visit or closed to the public. The 6,000ha (14,820 acres) of Estação Veracel Veracruz private reserve are equally as wild and offer superb bird watching (▷ 226). The reserve is less than 40-minutes' drive north of Porto Seguro.

INFORMATION

www.portosegurotur.com.br
www.arraialdajuda.tur.br
401 S12 · Rua Pero Vaz de Caminha 475, Centro, Porto Seguro · 73 3288 3708 · Daily 10–6 · From all major tourist towns · Aeroporto de Porto Seguro

Below *Sun worshippers on Parracho beach, Arraial d'Ajuda*

INFORMATION
398 T10 From Salvador every 30 min

INTRODUCTION

In colonial days this area, surrounding the Baía de Todos os Santos, supplied Europe with much of its sugar and Brazil with its initial flourishes of prosperity. This came at the expense of great suffering on the part of enslaved Africans, who ran and maintained the *engenho* sugar mills and cut the cane in the plantations. The legacy of this propserity and slavery are a series of delightful colonial towns with some of the richest African-Brazilian heritage in Brazil. Samba de Roda—the precursor both of the music of *capoeira* and the moves of samba—was born here, and the region remains an important centre for the spirit religion of *candomblé*.

The most interesting of the colonial towns are Cachoeira and São Felix, which face each other across the muddy brown Paraguaçu river. Between them they preserve the largest collection of baroque buildings in Bahia, after Salvador, and in the 17th and 18th centuries they ranked among the wealthiest towns in South America. It's hard to believe this today, as you could walk from one end of Cachoeira to the other end of São Felix in less than an hour, even allowing for the 10 minutes it takes to cross the river on the bridge which links them.

WHAT TO SEE

MUSEUMS

The handsome colonial Portuguese Casa da Câmara e Cadêia, on the Praça de Aclamação in Cachoeira, was the seat of Bahian government for a little under a year during the 1822 independence skirmishes against the Portuguese in Salvador. Today it houses a slavery museum with a small but shocking collection of the instruments of oppression, which ensured the survival of that institution for 350 years (tel 75 3425 1018; daily 8–12, 2–6; adult R$5, child under 10 free). The building shares a site on the main square with the Museu Regional (tel 75 3425 1123; daily 8–12, 2–6; adult R$5, child under 10 free), showcasing a poorly preserved collection of Portuguese and early Republican furniture and miscellany. The Museu da Boa Morte, also in Cachoeira, (daily 10–6; free) is a temple *(terreiro)* to *candomblé*, looked after by a society of African-Brazilian women which started as a slave sisterhood. There are effigies of Orixás (African-Brazilian spirit deities) inside.

Above *The towns of the Recôncavo became wealthy from sugar production*

IGREJA ORDEM TERCEIRA DO CARMO

The opulent exterior and interior of Cachoeira's baroque church, Igreja Ordem Terceira do Carmo, reflects the wealth which Cachoeira and São Felix enjoyed during the height of the sugar boom. The statues of Christ were imported from Macao and were probably carved by Chinese artisans, as can be seen from the marked oriental features.

✉ Praça da Aclamaçao s/n, Cachoeira 🕐 Tue–Sat 9–12, 2–5, Sun 9–12 ✋ Adult R$3, under 7 free

IGREJA MATRIZ DE NOSSA SENHORA DO ROSÁRIO

The parish church, the Igreja Matriz de Nossa Senhora do Rosário, dates from 1698 and has an interior covered with beautiful *azulejos* (glazed tiles) painted in Lisbon. The ceiling painting is by José Teófilo de Jesus, one of the most important artists of the Bahian baroque school and a pupil of José Joaquim da Rocha (*c.* 1737–1808).

✉ Rua Ana Nery s/n, Cachoeira 🕐 Tue–Sat 9–12, 2–5, Sun 9–12 ✋ Free

DANNEMANN CIGAR FACTORY

São Felix's Fabrica Dannemann produces some of Brazil's best small cigars, hand rolled by local women. The factory was founded by Geraldo Dannemann, who was born in Bremen but moved to São Felix in 1873 and achieved such success in his lifetime that he became the town's mayor.

✉ Avenida Salvador Pinto 29, São Felix ☎ 75 3438 3716 🕐 Daily 8.30–12, 1–4.30 ✋ Free

TIP

» Cigars can be purchased cheaply in the factory shop.

MORE TO SEE

PONTE PARAGUAÇU

The iron bridge linking Cachoeira and São Felix spans 300m (327 yards). It was built by the British in the 19th century, brought across by boat and reinstalled.

Below *São Felix, seen from Cachoeira, across the Paraguaçu river*

INFORMATION
401 T10 Rua das Laranjeiras 12, Pelourinho (and at the airport) 71 3321 2133 (airport office 71 3204 1444) Daily 8.30am–9pm (daily 8.30am–11pm at airport) From all major tourist towns Aeroporto Internacional Deputado Luís Eduardo Magalhães

Above *There's a relaxed atmosphere on Ondina beach*

INTRODUCTION

Bahia's capital is top of many visitors' Brazil itineraries owing to its combination of stunning colonial buildings, vibrant African-Brazilian culture and laid-back beach life. It's a city of superlatives, with the largest and liveliest street carnival in the country, its most opulent baroque church and one of the longest-established music scenes. The city is built on a succession of craggy cliffs and hills, which crest the end of a peninsula separating Brazil's largest bay, Baía de Todos os Santos, from the Atlantic. From the sea, the city appears as ranks of anonymous building-block skyscrapers but they hide the largest conglomeration of colonial buildings in Latin America. These stand preserved in the old city centre, which is a UNESCO World Heritage Site.

The city was founded in 1549 by Tomé de Sousa, acting under command from the king of Portugal to create the colony's first capital city (▷ 27). It remained Brazil's capital until 1763, when declining sugar wealth and the discovery of gold in the southeast shifted the power balance to Rio de Janeiro. However, the city remains a cultural capital. *Candomblé* and *capoeira*, the rhythm that became samba and the novels of Jorge Amado were largely developed here, as was the *tropicália* music of Caetano Veloso, Tom Zé and Gilberto Gil (▷ 17), the *batucada* beats of Olodum and Ilê Aiyê, and the *cinema novo* classics of Glauber Rocha.

Old Salvador is colloquially named after the Pelourinho, a cobbled square which lies at its heart. It comprises cobbled streets lined with Portuguese mansion houses, painted in bright primary colours and dozens of colonial churches, each more splendid than the next, but none as lavish as the Convento de São Francisco church (▷ 216), containing some of the finest baroque carving and *azulejos* (blue painted tiles) in Latin America. The area has bustling nightlife, particularly on Tuesdays and at the weekend.

Salvador is also a city of bay and ocean beaches. The bay beaches within the city itself are too polluted for swimming, but they are clean and shaded by palms on Itaparica island, immediately across the mouth of the Baía de Todos os Santos from Salvador. The city's ocean beaches get progressively cleaner the farther they get from the city centre.

WHAT TO SEE

CATEDRAL SÉ

The city's most famous colonial square is the Terreiro de Jesus (aka Praça XV de Novembro). It is surrounded by churches, the largest of which is Salvador's cathedral. It was built as a Jesuit college in the late 17th century and became the cathedral only after the demolition of the original in 1933. It has a cavernous vaulted interior, crowned with a gilt altarpiece, and its facade is modelled on the church of São Vicente de Fora in Lisbon, the burial site of the Bragança kings. Antônio Vieira—who spent much of his life trying to prevent the massacres of the indigenous peoples of Brazil by the *bandeirante* slave traders—studied, preached and spent his last days here (▷ 29). The third governor general of Brazil, Mem de Sá (1504–72, ▷ 27), who quelled the indigenous people and expelled the French from Brazil, is buried inside.

221 B2 Terreiro de Jesus s/n 71 3321 4573 Mon–Sat 8.30–11.30, 1.30–5.30 Free Latin mass with plainsong Sun, 11am

CARMELITE CHURCHES

Beyond the Pelourinho, to the north, are three impressive Carmelite churches: the Igreja do Carmo, the Igreja da Ordem Terceira do Carmo and the Convento do Carmo (which is now a hotel, ▷ 239). The Igreja do Carmo (Mon–Sat 8–12, 2–5.30, Sun 8–12; R$2) retains a beautiful painted ceiling by the freed slave, José Teófilo de Jesus. The Igreja da Ordem Terceira (Mon–Sat 8–11.30, 2–5.30, Sun 10–12; R$2) was once as rich in gilt as the Convento de São Francisco (▷ 216) but was badly damaged in a serious fire in the late 18th century. Only a few pieces of sculpture survived from the stations of the cross, masterfully carved by a mulatto slave, Francisco Xavier Chagas (aka *o Cabra*—the goat or bandit). The most impressive is also one of the grisliest pieces of baroque art south of Mexico and a monument to the transfiguration of suffering. It depicts the crucified Christ and was presumably once on a cross but Christ now lies in an antiseptic glass case, like a lab specimen. Positioned on his back in a veneer of blood and sweat (made from a mix of whale oil and tiny rubies), his body is horribly contorted in the throes of death but his face is sublimely serene.

TIPS

» Avoid walking in the historic centre after 11pm as it can be dangerous, and be careful with cameras and wallets at all times.

» Salvador is not only a good place to watch *capoeira*, it's a good place to learn it. There are many *capoeira* schools in the Forte de Santo Antônio (▷ 229).

» The best places to stay that are close to the historic centre are in the suburb of Santo Antônio.

» Maps of Salvador are on sale in the bookshops in Barra Shopping (▷ 230) and at newstands throughout the city.

» Bahians will warn you that their food is very spicy. Those used to Thai green curries or anything hotter than an Indian Dansak will find Bahian dishes mild.

» Fast boats for Itaparica and Morro de São Paulo leave from the ferry port immediately in front of the Mercado Modelo (▷ 230).

Below *Carnival procession celebrating Independence Day*

FRANCISCAN CHURCHES

The Igreja e Convento de São Francisco and the Igreja da Ordem Terceira de São Francisco are Bahia's most magnificent buildings and two of the most impressive churches in the country. They sit side by side.

Igreja e Convento de São Francisco

The Igreja de São Francisco is entered through cloisters decorated with Portuguese *azulejo* painted tiles, by the Lisbon master Bartolomeu Antunes de Jesus, and visually depict epigrams by Horace. The church itself is ostentatiously magnificent, a temple to the wealth of the rich sugar cane barons who commissioned the art, more than to the vows of poverty and charity espoused by the Franciscan order. The nave is gilded with almost a ton of pure gold and covered in paintings and statuary. These are largely the work of unknown African-Brazilian artists; their iconography is clear in the two African masks on either side of the sacristy, high up at the altar end of the nave. That the effigies they created met with some disapproval is evident from the cherubs on the walls, whose genitals have been clumsily hacked off.

221 C2 Largo do Cruzeiro de São Francisco 71 3322 6430 Mon–Sat 8–5, Sun 8–4 Adult R$4, under 7 free

Igreja da Ordem Terceira de São Francisco

The early 18th-century Igreja da Ordem Terceira de São Francisco (Church of the Third Order of St. Francis) was a plain building, until the installation of electricity in 1919 stripped away the plaster to expose an ornate Churrigueresque facade. It is one of only two examples of the baroque style in Brazil which is resolutely Spanish rather than Portuguese. The interior has ceiling paintings and panels by two of José Joaquim da Rocha's (*c.*1737–1808) students, Antônio Joaquim Franco Velasco and José Teófilo de Jesus, and also features *azulejos* of old Lisbon as it stood before it was razed to the ground by the earthquake of 1755.

221 C2 Ladeira da Ordem Terceira de São Francisco 3 71 3321 6968 Mon–Sat 8–5, Sun 8–4 Adult R$4, under 7 free

Right *Igreja e Convento de São Francisco*
Below Azulejos *decorate the entrance to the church and convent*

IGREJA DE NOSSO SENHOR DO BONFIM

This bayside late 18th-century church is one of the most important cultural sites in Brazil for the African-Brazilian spirit religion of *candomblé*. It is also the location for one of the city's most remarkable festivals, the Lavagem do Bonfim (▷ 231), which is celebrated on the third Sunday of January and dedicated to Nosso Senhor—Our Lord (Christ)—as Oxalá, the creator divinity of *candomblé*. More than a million pilgrims walk to the church from the Igreja de Nossa Senhora da Conceição da Praia, accompanied by Baianas (Bahian women, who wear traditional large swirling dresses) and troupes of drummers and musicians. When they arrive, they ritually wash the steps of the church with perfumed water. *Fitas*, little ribbons, are tied around the pilgrims' wrists by the Baianas (and by myriad touts at the appearance of a tourist at any other time). The church itself is worth visiting for its religious paintings by Joaquim Franco Velasco—especially the striking passion of Christ—and for the pretty rococo facade.

221 off B1 · Praça Senhor do Bonfim s/n · 71 3316 1673 · Tue–Sun 6–12, 2–8 · Free · 'Bonfim' bus from outside the Mercado Modelo

IGREJA DA NOSSA SENHORA DO ROSÁRIO DOS PRETOS

Halfway down Largo do Pelourinho (▷ 218) is a brilliant blue church, the Igreja da Nossa Senhora do Rosário dos Pretos. It was built by a slave brotherhood, beginning in 1704 and taking some 100 years, in the minutes of free time they had from their duties. The church remains a centre for *candomblé* and many of the statues within are worshipped as *Orixás* (spirit deities), as much as they are Catholic saints.

221 C1 · Praça José Alencar s/n, Largo do Pelourinho · 71 3241 5781 · Mon–Fri 8.30–6, Sat–Sun 8.30–3 · Free · African-Brazilian mass every Tue, 6pm

Above *Pilgrims' ribbons at Igreja de Nosso Senhor do Bonfim*

LARGO DO PELOURINHO

Although the Pelourinho lends its name colloquially to the whole complex of colonial buildings which make up Old Salvador—from the Praça Tome de Souza to Santo Antônio, more than 2km (1.25 miles) to the north—it is strictly only the cobbled square (or Largo) which sits at the bottom of Rua Alfredo Brito, just downhill from the Terreiro de Jesus. The square is named after the whipping post (pillory) where slaves were publicly humiliated for the most minor of infractions. It's beautiful as a whole, especially in the late afternoon when golden light burnishes the richly coloured buldings, and is fringed with a number of small museums and a church.

The Fundação Casa de Jorge Amado (tel 71 3321 0070; www.jorgeamado.org.br; Mon–Sat 10–6) is a glorified bookshop, masquerading as a cultural centre devoted to the famous Bahian writer. Covers of all his books decorate the walls and the novels themselves are on sale inside.

Next door is the Museu da Cidade (tel 71 3321 1967; Tue–Fri 9–6.30, Sat 1–5, Sun 9–1), with displays telling the story of the city sitting alongside African-Brazilian ritual objects. One room is devoted to the anti-slavery campaigner and romantic poet, Castro Alves (1847–71).

Less than 100m (109 yards) away is the Museu Abelardo Rodrigues (tel 71 3320 9383; Tue–Sat 1–6; adult R$5, child under 7 free), preserving the best collection of sacred art in Bahia. There is a series of tasteful, contemporary displays within a gorgeous 18th-century mansion.

221 C1

MUSEU AFRO-BRASILEIRO AND MUSEU DE ARQUEOLOGIA E ETNOLOGIA

www.ceao.ufba.br/mafro

www.mae.ufba.br

The Terreiro de Jesus is home to two of the city's best museums. The Museu Afro-Brasileiro (MAFRO) preserves some outstanding pieces of secular and ritual art. Exhibits include a gallery containing 27 2m by 3m (6.5ft by 10ft) stelae of the major *Orixás* (deities of the *candomblé* spirit religion), carved from single blocks of tropical cedar by the Brazilian-Italian artist Carybé (1911–97). The Museu de Arqueologia e Etnologia (MAE), in the basement of the same building, holds priceless indigenous artefacts and some simple exhibits on Bahian pre-historic rock paintings.

Above *Largo do Pelourinho is lined with vibrant colonial buildings*

221 B2 Prédio de Faculdade de Medicina, Terreiro de Jesus 71 3283 5540 (MAFRO); 71 3283 5530 (MAE) Mon–Fri 9–6, Sat–Sun 10–5 Entry to both museums: adult R$5, child (6–12 and over 60 R$2.50, under 7 free

PORTUGUESE CHURCHES

Opposite the cathedral (▷ 215), on the other side of the square, are two more beautiful Portuguese churches: the early 19th-century São Pedro dos Clerigos—with a rococo facade—and, next to it, the church of the baroque Ordem Terceira de São Domingos de Gusmão, which has a striking *trompe l'oeil* ceiling attributed to the most important artist of the Bahian baroque school, José Joaquim da Rocha.

221 C2 Terreiro de Jesus, Praça XV de Novembro 71 3321 9183 (São Pedro dos Clerigos); 71 3242 4185 (São Domingos de Gusmão) Mon–Sat 8.30–11.30, 1.30–5.30 Free

PRAÇA DA SÉ

The first religious buildings in the city were constructed by the Jesuits in this square, next to the Praça Tomé de Sousa (▷ this page). Until 1933, the square was dominated by one of the finest religious buildings in Brazil, the country's first cathedral. It lies immediately southwest of the present Catedral Sé (▷ 215) and was demolished to make way for a tram line which no longer operates. The *Cruz Caída (Fallen Cross)*, a sculpture by the famous Bahian artist, Mario Cravo Junior, sits on the site and commemorates its loss. On the other side of the square is the Memorial da Baiana do Acarajé (Mon–Fri 9–12, 2–6; adult R$10, under 7 free), a small museum devoted to and run by Baianas (traditionally dressed Bahian women). It traces their history and sells their food in an adjacent café.

221 B2

PRAÇA TOMÉ DE SOUSA

Salvador has its origins in this square in the city centre when governor Tomé de Sousa, and his teams of enslaved Indians and Portuguese colonists, constructed a series of administrative buildings from shell middens, mud and whale blood. None remain today but the *praça* has some eye-catching buildings. The most imposing is the French beaux arts Palácio Rio Branco, the fourth building to stand on the site of the first governor's palace. It houses government offices today. On the west side of the square is the 72m-high (236ft) art deco Lacerda lift, which runs down the cliff to the Mercado Modelo (▷ 230) and the lower part of the city, known as the Cidade Baixa. Opposite this is the late 17th-century

Below Cruz Caída, *in Praça da Sé, commemorates the country's first cathedral, demolished in 1933*

Paço Municipal, with a pretty internal courtyard. It houses municipal offices and while it is not officially open to the public it is possible to walk into the courtyard for a peek. A statue of Tomé de Sousa stands in front of the building gazing across the bay. He had been chosen by King João III himself to lead a thousand new settlers from Lisbon to Bahia to found the first Brazilian capital (▷ 27).
221 A2

MORE TO SEE

BAÍA DE TODOS OS SANTOS AND ITAPARICA ISLAND

The Baía de Todos os Santos is one of the largest bays in Latin America, extending over 1,100sq km (425sq miles). It is fringed with powder-fine beaches and dotted with little islands, many of which can be visited on day trips from Salvador. The largest of the islands, Itaparica, sits immediately opposite Salvador. It is shaped like a kidney bean, spanning 14km (9 miles) from north to south and no more than 12km (7.5 miles) from east to west. There are some fine beaches on the ocean side, and on the bay side mangrove wetlands and small river estuaries are home to kingfishers, egrets and ospreys. At weekends, the island heaves with visitors but during the week it is possible to find semi-deserted beaches. There are two small towns, Itaparica at the northern tip of the island (with a smattering of colonial and early 20th-century buildings) and Veracruz (aka Mar Grande), which is the site of little more than holiday homes. The ferry port of Bom Despacho lies between the two. The island has plenty of *pousadas* for overnight stays.
221 A1 From Salvador ferry terminal, next to the Mercado Modelo; R$4

BARRA AND THE BEACHES

The closest beach to the historic centre, with sea just about clean enough for swimming, is Barra. It has lively nightlife, many restaurants, a big air-conditioned shopping centre with a cinema (▷ 230), and hotels. It is increasingly popular as an alternative base to the city centre for foreign visitors. Salvador stretches north of here in a series of beach suburbs until it eventually peters out near the airport. The coastal road then becomes the Linha Verde (Green Line), which heads towards the Coconut Coast.

Perched on the end of Barra's beach is a lighthouse (closed to visitors but popular for sunset watching) and adjacent Portuguese fort, the Forte de Santo Antônio da Barra, which dates from the late 17th century and which is home to a maritime museum (tel 71 3264 3296; Tue–Sat 10–2, 3–6; R$6). It houses some 400 exhibits salvaged from Portuguese and Dutch ships, including the

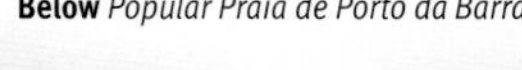
Below *Popular Praia de Porto da Barra*

Sacramento, which sank in 1688. Rio Vermelho, 5km (3 miles) to the east, has restaurants, a few hotels and the best nightlife scene outside Barra and the centre of Salvador.

221 off A3 Instituto Mauá, Praça Azevedo Fernandes 1 71 3264 4671 Mon–Fri 9–6, Sat 10–3 Air-conditioned shuttle between Barra and Rua Chile, in the city centre. Buses are marked 'Aeroporto Frescão' when leaving from the city centre, as they continue past all the Salvador beaches to the airport

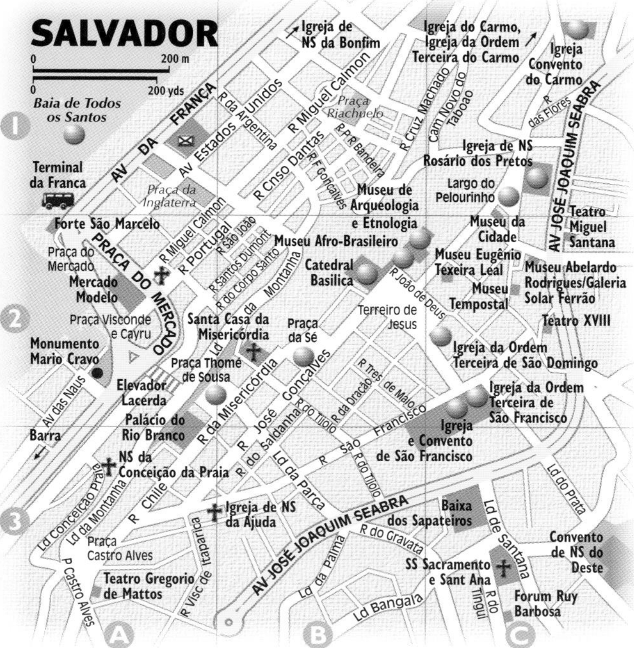

Above left *View over Baía de Todos os Santos from Praça Municipal*
Above right *Lighthouse at Barra*

THE HISTORICAL CENTRE OF SALVADOR

This walk begins in the Praça Tomé de Sousa and finishes at the bottom of Largo do Pelourinho, taking in most of the interesting sights in the historical centre and the area's exuberant urban life.

THE WALK
Distance: 1.4km (0.9 miles)
Time: 3 hours including visits
Start at: Praça Tomé de Sousa
End at: Largo do Pelourinho

HOW TO GET THERE

Buses marked Praça da Sé run to Praça Tomé de Sousa from Barra and the airport. Local bus RI or RII (marked Centro-Rodoviária-Circular) runs from the *rodoviária* (bus station) to the foot of the Lacerda public lift (which links the lower part of Salvador directly with Praça Tomé de Sousa in less than a minute. This lift is not safe after dark).

★ Start near the top of the lift in Praça Tomé de Sousa (▷ 219).

❶ Salvador began in the Praça Tomé de Sousa in March 1549, when Tomé de Sousa, the first governor general of Brazil, formally founded the city. The square is ringed on three sides with handsome buildings: the 17th-century Paço Municipal, the beaux arts Palácio Rio Branco and the elegant Lacerda lift, which was built to replace an earlier steam-powered construction. A statue of Tomé de Sousa, the city founder and first governor, stands in front of the Paço Municipal.

Leave the square from the eastern corner along the Rua da Misericórdia. Stop for a quick visit to the Santa Casa da Misericórdia complex.

❷ The Portuguese baroque church of Santa Casa da Misericórdia dates from 1774 and has a beautiful painted ceiling by Antônio Rodrigues Braga, and Portuguese painted blue and white tiles *(azulejos)* depicting colonial religious processions.

Continue along the Rua da Misericórdia to the Praça da Sé.

❸ The Praça da Sé (▷ 219) is named after Brazil's first archbishopric. The ruins of the former church ruins are celebrated with a sculpture by Mario Cravo Junior. There are magnificent views of the bay from the statue. The square is filled with food vendors and lined with cafés.

Leave the square from the eastern corner to enter another large square, the Terreiro de Jesus.

❹ The Terreiro de Jesus is the heart of colonial Salvador. It's a busy square, with impromptu *capoeira* performances, and vendors selling everything from Bahian snacks to musical instruments and arts and crafts. It is surrounded by baroque churches—most notably the Catedral Sé (▷ 215) and the church of the Ordem Terceira de São Domingos de Gusmão (▷ 219)—and colonial civic buildings, the largest of which, the Prédio da Faculdade de Medicina, houses the city's best museum, the Museu Afro-Brasileiro (▷ 218).

Walk to the far southeastern corner of the square and enter the Largo Cruzeiro de São Francisco, separated from the Terreiro de Jesus by an iconic Franciscan cross.

❺ The jewels in baroque Salvador's crown sit here. The Igreja e Convento de São Francisco (▷ 216) and the adjacent Plateresque Igreja da Ordem Terceira de São Francisco are the most famous baroque buildings in the city. Enter the first to see one of the most ostentatious displays of colonial wealth in the Americas. The painting on the wooden ceiling at the entrance to the church is by José Joaquim da Rocha.

Walk back to the Terreiro de Jesus and turn right along Rua João de Deus, the street heading northeast and downhill, at right angles to the Igreja da Ordem Terceira de São Domingos de Gusmão. Consider eating at Axego (▷ 234), which serves the best *moqueca* (seafood broth cooked in coconut and dendê oil) in the historic centre. Walk some 200m (219 yards) downhill from here to the Largo do Pelourinho. Pop into Cana Brava records (▷ 229) along the way to pick-up some traditional Bahian music.

❻ The Largo do Pelourinho (▷ 218) always bustles with activity. Here, alongside a few small museums, you will find the Fundação Casa de Jorge Amado bookshop (▷ 218) and Oficina Musical (▷ 230), which sells musical instruments and which has made *berimabaus*—Brazilian percussion instruments which resemble a stringed wooden bow—for the country's greatest players, including Naná Vasconcelos. Be sure to visit the Igreja da Nossa Senhora do Rosário dos Pretos (▷ 217), the most important church for the African-Brazilian community in the city.

WHEN TO GO

The walk is best begun in the early afternoon, thus finishing just as the low tropical sun burnishes the colonial buildings a deep orange.

WHERE TO EAT

The Praça da Sé has many cafés that make a pleasant refreshment stop, such as Coffee Shop (▷ 234), but for a hearty lunch try Axego (▷ 234) on the Rua João de Deus.

PLACE TO VISIT

SANTA CASA DA MISERICÓRDIA

✉ Rua da Misericórdia 6 🕐 Mon–Fri 9–12, 2–6 ✋ R$10

TIPS

» Look out for Oliver Santos, who does wonderful beaded hair braiding at a little stall on the Largo do Pelourinho's southeastern corner.

» Be careful with cameras and wallets at all times in the historic centre.

Opposite *Statue of Tomé de Sousa*
Below *Shops on Largo do Carmo, looking towards Largo do Pelourinho*

ALONG THE LENÇÓIS RIVER IN THE CHAPADA DIAMANTINA

This walk leaves from Lençóis town along the Lençóis river, visiting swimming holes and waterfalls. Even though all the sights lie within half an hour of the town centre, visitors during the week are few as most tourists take driven trips to the more famous landmarks farther afield. The walk offers peace, natural beauty and the chance to see birds and animals right on Lençóis's doorstep.

THE WALK
Distance: 5km (3 miles)
Time: 3–4 hours
Start/end at: On the river bank in Lençóis town

HOW TO GET THERE

Most of the hotels in the Chapada are in Lençóis and most visitors to the national park are based here. The town is tiny you can walk from one extremity to the other in 15 minutes. Lençóis can be reached by bus from Salvador.

★ The river is the town's dominant feature, lying right in the town centre.

❶ Lençóis means sheets in Portuguese and is named after the hundreds of white canvas miners' tents which formed the first settlement during the 18th-century diamond rush. From the surrounding hills they looked like white sheets, spread out along the river bank.

Hike upstream from the edge of town. A little trail follows the river bank. After 20 minutes you will reach an area of water and gravel-polished rocks. These are known as the Serrano swimming holes.

❷ These smooth rocks, surrounded by *cerrado* woodland that is filled with birds, are a perfect spot for a sunbathe and a swim. They are pocked with deep swimming pools and the river is clean and fresh, with no waterborne diseases. Some of the first diamonds in the Chapada were found in the bottoms of the pools.

Opposite *The tranquil Lençóis river*
Above *A step in the Cachoeira da Primavera*
Right *The Lençóis river in Lençóis town, near Praça Nagos*

Walk up the black rock slope on your right as you look upstream. There is a clear path running up the slope and while it splits in various places, all the trails lead to one spot, the Salão de Areias (Sand Caves), 300m (327 yards) from the riverbank.

❸ This honeycomb of little canyons, passages and caves is where local artisans collect the sand for the bottle paintings sold in Lençóis town. It's an atmospheric place, great for a little wander, and in the late afternoon the surrounding bushland is busy with hundreds of birds.

Return to the river. On the left-hand side of the water as you look upstream are two large black pipes on the river bank. These supply Lençóis with much of its water. Follow the trail that leaves behind the water pipes. You will hear the waterfalls after a few minutes.

❹ The Cachoeirinha, or little waterfall, plunges into a small dark pool off a tributary of the Lençóis river. It's another great spot for a swim. You can sit under the falls themselves for a water massage. The river's brown colour is due to tannins washed out of leaves and wood from the surrounding *cerrado* forest.

Continue 300m (327 yards) farther upstream from the Cachoeirinha falls to another rock pool, the Poço Halley (Halley Pool). There are two routes: either a rock hop and river wade or a path on the opposite bank of the river. Beyond the Poço Halley the trail cuts through some beautiful woodland surrounding a broad stretch of the river, filled with smooth, multi-coloured rocks. After 500m (545 yards) the river veers to the right and a small stream enters it from the left. Scramble up the stream bed for 300m (327 yards) to reach the impressive three-tiered Primavera (Spring) waterfall.

❺ The Cachoeira da Primavera is the most impressive waterfall within walking distance of Lençóis, plunging for some 40m (131ft) over a series of rocky escarpments into an extensive and deep plunge pool. It's a wonderful spot for a swim and a picnic.

Return to the Cachoeirinha falls along the clearly defined trail leaving from the waterfall pool. From here, follow the outward route back to Lençóis town.

WHEN TO GO

Begin the walk in the cool of the early morning, preferably around 7am, when the birds are still active and there are few tourists on the paths.

WHERE TO EAT

Bring a picnic to eat at the waterfall and a bag to collect all your rubbish, as there are no bins along the way.

TIPS

» Be sure to take a litre of water per person, a sun hat, sun protection, bathing costume, sunglasses and waterproof shoes for wading in the water. Crocs are the best option.
» Hotels and guest houses can all give information on the trails around Lençóis.

ARRAIAL D'AJUDA

AVE MARIA

www.lojaavemaria.com.br

This small lady's boutique sells pretty spring dresses in bright colours and with arty stitch work, using appliqué, embroidery and lace.

✉ Rua do Mucugê 246, Centro ☎ 73 3575 3161 🕐 Erratic opening hours

CAPOEIRA SUL DA BAHIA

www.capoeirasuldabahia.com.br

Take *capoeira* lessons with Mestre Railson, an experienced teacher, and try this Brazilian dance form with its heavy martial art influences. Mestre Railson is one of the best teachers in southern Bahia.

✉ Rua da Capoeira 57 ☎ 73 3575 2981 🕐 Contact in advance for class times

ECO PARQUE

www.arraialecoparque.com.br

Eco Water Park is a giant attraction with a giant wave pool, water slides of all descriptions and a relaxing 'Lazy River'. The water park is popular with children of all ages but is usually open only in high season (December–February).

✉ Estrada do Arraial d'Ajuda, km 4.5 ☎ 73 3575 8600 🕐 Check website, seasonal opening times vary Adult R$60, child under 12 R$30

CANUDOS

CIRO ALBANO NORTHEAST BIRDING

www.nebrazilbirding.com

The best birding guide in the northeast of Brazil offers trips around the entire region and unsurpassed specialist knowledge. He can give access to all the Lear's macaw nesting sites on a sandstone cliff in the private reserve of Estação Veracel (▷ 228).

☎ Mobile: 85 9955 5162

CARAVELAS

ABROLHOS TURISMO

www.abrolhosturismo.com.br

This company offers tours around Caravelas including boat trips: to the silt islands in the river delta with its wading birds, to the beach at Pontal do Sul with glassy waters full of shoals of fish, and to the coral reefs around the Abrolhos Archipelago. They also offer humpback whale watching between July and early December. Must be booked ahead.

✉ Praça Dr. Emílio Imbassay 8, Centro ☎ 73 3297 1149 Boats leave at 7am from the Marina Porto Abrolhos, some 5km (3 miles) north of Caravelas town centre

CHAPADA DIAMANTINA

ANITA MARTI

Anita offers wonderful therapeutic massage, shiatsu and reiki in your hotel. The treatments are perfect after a long hike.

☎ 75 9989 8328 🕐 Erratic opening hours Massage R$100

CHAPADA ADVENTURE

www.chapadaadventure.com.br

This small-scale economical tour company offers hikes, jeep-based trips throughout the national park, kayaking in the Marimbus wetlands and bespoke tours.

✉ Avenida 7 de Setembro 7, Lençóis ☎ 75 3334 2037 🕐 Mon–Sat 10–6

DIETER HERZBERG

Enjoy reiki, massage and shiatsu therapies from an experienced practitioner. Contact him by phone to arrange a treatment in your room.

☎ 75 9984 2720

Above *A* capoeira *display*

Opposite *Street performance by Olodum (▷ 229)*

EXPEDIÇÕES H2O
www.pousadadosduendes.com
This company offers some of the cheapest of the standard package trips to the tourist sights in the Chapada. Jeeps are filled with backpackers so don't expect much individual attention.
✉ Pousada dos Duendes, Rua do Pires s/n, Lençóis ☎ 75 3334 1229 🕐 Daily 9–6

EXTREME
www.extremeecoadventure.com.br
Many Brazilians love to conquer nature more than contemplate it. This company gives them the chance to leap off cliffs and canyons, rappel down waterfalls and kayak on white-water rivers. It is also one of the few companies to offer longer hikes, including a good range of 2- to 6-day walks.
✉ Avenida 7 de Setembro 15, Lençóis ☎ 75 3334 1727 🕐 Mon–Sat 10–6

FORA DA TRILHA
www.foradatrilha.com.br
This is one of the few operators to offer the Travessia Diamantina hike (with advanced notice), which takes about a week and runs the entire length of the park.
✉ Rua das Pedras 202, Lençóis ☎ 75 3334 1326, 71 8142 4369 🕐 Mon–Sat 10–6

JAQUES GAGNON
Jaques practises healing neuro-structural therapy and massage. It is great for relieving bad backs and blockages. He performs the treatment at your hotel.
☎ 75 3334 1281

LUIZ KRUG
This experienced speleologist offers serious caving and geological tours, and speaks good English. Book through Vila Serrano (▷ 237).
✉ Pousada Vila Serrano, Chapada Diamantina ☎ 75 3334 1102

NATIVOS DA CHAPADA
Noisy jaunts in the natural environment are offered by Nativos da Chapada. Activities producing maximum adrenaline include bungee jumps, waterfall rappels and zip lines.
✉ Rua Miguel Calmon 29, Lençóis ☎ 75 3334 1314 🕐 Mon–Sat 10–6

ROY FUNCH
www.fcd.org.br
This ex-pat North American is the former director of the Chapada Diamantina National Park and author of the best guidebook to the region. Roy runs walks and wildlife trips, principally from Lençóis itself.
☎ 75 3334 1305

TAMANDARÉ
This little shop sells beautiful clay figurines by renowned *sertão* artists like Zé Caboclo and tasteful rootsy home décor small enough to fit in a suitcase.
✉ Rua das Pedras s/n, Lençóis ☎ 75 3334 1207 🕐 Mon–Sat 10–6

ZAMBUMBEIRA INSTRUMENTOS
Argentinian ex-pat Jorge Fernando makes his own unique musical instruments. The range varies from twanging percussion to tiny hand-held drums, in this tiny shop on Lençóis's main street.
✉ Rua das Pedras 78, Lençóis ☎ 75 3334 1334 🕐 Erratic opening hours

ZÉ CARLOS
Enjoy a bespoke bird watching trip at various sites throughout the region with this local guide with specialist knowledge. He also speaks reasonable English. Book through Casa da Geléia (▷ 236) or Vila Serrano (▷ 237).
✉ Casa da Geléia or Vila Serrano, Chapada Diamantina ☎ 75 3334 1151, 75 3334 1486

ILHÉUS

ORBITÁ
www.orbitaexpedicoes.com.br
Scheduled and bespoke adventure trips and tours to remote regions around Itacaré, including the Peninsula do Maraú. Transfers arranged to Itacaré from Ilhéus town and airport pick-ups available. They use comfortable Land Rovers and have good English skills.
✉ Rua Marquês de Paranaguá 270 ☎ 73 3234 3250, 73 9983 6655

ITACARÉ

ITACARÉ SURF CAMP
www.itacaresurfcamp.com.br
This kid-friendly surf school runs courses from a few days to two weeks, teaching all-comers how to surf (from the absolute basics to standing up and riding high rollers). Courses take place all year round but are busiest over Christmas and New Year. They should always be booked in advance. Instructors speak good English. The company can also help organize accommodation and include all equipment and clothing in the course price.
✉ Alto da Boa Vista, 230-A (Ribeirinha) ☎ 73 9948 7727 💵 From around R$200 per person per day, including accommodation and equipment

NATIVOS

www.nativositacare.com.br

Nativos specialize in adventure sports. They arrange trips from Itacaré, with pick-ups from Ilhéus airport. Activities offered by the company include diving, white-water rafting and kayaking.

✉ Rua Pedro Longo 215, Pituba ☎ 73 3251 3503

PORTO SEGURO

AXÉ MOI

www.axemoi.com.br

In Porto's biggest dance *barraca* (beach hut), *axé* bands play their rock-influenced salsa music so loud you can feel the noise. Expect huge crowds. Facilities include a restaurant, café, bar, toilets and even a playground.

✉ Avenida Beira Mar, km 367, Praia de Taperapuã ☎ 73 3679 3237 🕑 From around 10pm ✋ R$20

ILHA DOS AQUÁRIOS

www.ilhadosaquarios.com.br

Here you will find five aquariums on an island in the river, with sharks, morays and tanks reproducing environments around Porto Seguro, from river and reef to mangroves. There's also a small orquidarium and a series of over-priced restaurants. At night, the island comes alive with gaggles of teenaged Brazilians listening to live *forró* bands, who play a Brazilian variant of country-style music, originally from the northeast.

✉ Rio Bunanhem s/n ☎ 73 3575 1031 🕑 Daily 10-6 ✋ Adult R$10, child R$5

PATAXÓ TURISMO

www.pataxoturismo.com.br

This company has been working with local indigenous Pataxó communities for some 20 years and offers visits to villages (with optional overnight stays). Money from the tours helps the local people. The company will pick you up from your hotel.

☎ 73 3288 1256

PORTO MONDO

www.portomondo.com

Porto Mondo offer great beach tours to as far south as the Whale Coast, together with kayaking on rivers near Porto Seguro, other adventure activities and the best range of local excursions on offer in Porto Seguro or Arraial d'Ajuda, including the private reserve of Estação Veracel (▷ this page). Service is excellent.

✉ Hotel Estalagem, Rua Marechal Deodoro 66 ☎ 73 3575 3686 🕑 Daily 10–6

RESERVA PARTICULAR DO PATRIMÔNIO NATURAL ESTAÇÃO VERACEL

www.veracel.com.brz

This 6,000ha (14,820 acres) of private reserve between Santa Cruz Cabrália and Porto Seguro is a haven for more than 307 bird and 40 mammals species, with rarities like harpy eagle, red-billed curassow, banded and white-winged cotingas, Brazilian tapir, jaguar and olingo. Advanced bookings only, through an agency such as Ciro Albano (▷ 226) if you don't speak Portuguese.

✉ Rodovia BR-367, km 37 ☎ 73 3166 1535, 73 8802 0161 🕑 Tue, Thu 8.30–4.30, Sat 8.30–11.30 ✋ Free

RESERVA PATAXÓ JAQUEIRA

The Pataxó are descendants of the indigenous Potiguar people, who successfully resisted the Portuguese for centuries. Their numbers were decimated and their culture almost wiped out in the 20th century. They are only now beginning to recuperate, thanks, in large part, to the initiative of this community. This Pataxó indigenous community invites tourists for day visits or overnight stays to experience their traditional way of life and learn some of their language and customs. There is a small craft shop selling beautiful ceramics, sacred incense and art. The reserve is Pataxó-owned and run. Visits are most easily made through tour operators like Pataxó Turismo or Porto Mondo (▷ this page).

✉ BR-367 Porto Seguro-Santa Cruz Cabrália 🕑 Daily 9–5 ✋ Entry to reserve R$10

TÔA TOA

www.portaltoatoa.com.br

Tôa Toa is a huge, thatched-roof *barraca* beach bar, with a big stage pumping Bahian *axé* music (which sounds like high-octane salsa mixed with rock). Expect very lively crowds in December and January, and around Carnival.

✉ Praia de Taperapuã ☎ 73 3679 1146 🕑 From around 10pm ✋ Admission R$10

PRAIA DO FORTE

CENTROTOUR

www.centrotour.com.br

Excursions around town are offered, including the Reserva Florestal da Sapiranga—a protected area of *restinga* forest and wetland just a short drive away, rich with birds and reptiles. Profits from tours help an NGO—the Associação Comunitária Desportiva, Educativa e Social do Litoral Norte (ADESLIN)—who support local poor communities and initiate recycling projects.

✉ Shopping Armazém da Vila, Avenida do Farol, Loja 19 ☎ 71 7811 0356 🕑 Daily 10–7

JÓIA RARA

This shop doubles up as an artists' studio and local jewellers can be seen crafting tasteful handmade and bespoke jewellery, using Brazilian precious stones set in silver, gold and white gold.

✉ Avenida ACM s/n ☎ 71 3676 1503 🕑 Erratic opening hours

SALVADOR

ASSOCIAÇÃO DE CAPOEIRA MESTRE BIMBA

www.capoeiramestrebimba.com.br

This school offers *capoeira* coaching in the tradition of one of the greatest practitioners, Mestre Bimba, the first master to define a system for teaching this Brazilian mix of martial art and dance. There are male and female teachers, including well-known masters like Bamba. Book ahead to arrange classes, which are bespoke and vary in size and price.

✉ Rua das Laranjeiras 1, Pelourinho ☎ 71 3322 0639 🕑 Mon–Fri 9–12, 3–8

BOTECO DO FRANÇA

www.botecodofranca.com.br

This grungy, spit and sawdust *boteco* bar, with plastic tables and chairs

Above *A party at a club in Porto Seguro*

and bottles of ice-cold beer served by rushing black-tie waiters, attracts a buzzing middle-class crowd. They come for great *batidas* (long crushed-ice, fruit and rum cocktails), *caipirinhas* and *petiscos* (tapas-like bar snacks).
✉ Rua Borges dos Reis 24-A, Rio Vermelho ☎ 73 3334 2734 🕐 Erratic opening hours

CANA BRAVA RECORDS

This great litle shop is run by a US ex-pat. It sells rare and vintage Bahian and Brazilian vinyl and CDs, with the best choice in town.
✉ Rua João de Deus 22, Pelourinho ☎ 71 3321 0536 🕐 Mon–Sat 10–6

CASA DO ILÊ AIYÊ

www.ileaiye.org.br
One of the city's most famous *batucada* (African-influenced percussion) orchestras parades at carnival. They give live performances here and at their other headquarters on the outskirts of the city in the evenings. Full details of both are on the website. There is no need to reserve in advance.
✉ Rua das Laranjeiras 16 ☎ 73 3321 4193 🕐 Mon–Sat 10–6

CASA DO OLODUM

http://olodum.uol.com.br
The Olodum *batucada* troupe found international fame playing on Paul Simon's *Rhythm of the Saints* album (1990). Their headquarters are here, in the heart of the old city centre. It includes a small gift shop selling T-shirts, CDs and other souvenirs, and a space for impromptu and scheduled performances.
✉ Rua Gregório de Matos 22 ☎ 73 3321 5010 🕐 House open daily 10–6. Performances Tue and Sun, 7pm 🖐 R$15

CENTRO DE MÚSICA NEGRA (CMN)

The International Centre for Black Music is the best venue in Salvador for African-Brazilian music, with shows from artists like Mariene de Castro and Carlinhos Brown, who runs the centre. DJs play on selected nights, from mixing desks housed in a giant space pod on stilts that towers over the colonial courtyard. Contact them for opening hours and prices of varying events.
✉ Edifício Mercado do Ouro, Rua Torquato Bahia 84, Cidade Baixa ☎ 73 3353 4333
? A down-at-heel area, so take a cab

CRAVINHO

www.ocravinho.com.br
This *cachaça* (sugar cane spirit) bar with solid wood tables is always packed with locals and tourists. *Cachaças* are served direct from barrels behind the bar and there is occasional live music.
✉ Praça 15 de Novembro 3 ☎ 73 3322 6759 🕐 Daily 11am–12

DIDARA GOYA LOPES

www.goyalopes.com.br
Shop here for dresses, kangas and tops with colourful Bahian stamps and African cuts, from a designer who has exhibited at the Glass Curtain Gallery in Chicago. There is also a branch at Lé Com Cré, in Trancoso.
✉ Rua Gregorio de Mattos, Pelourinho ☎ 73 3668 1180 🕐 Mon–Sat 10–6

ESCOLA DE CAPOEIRA ANGOLA IRMÃOS GÊMEOS

http://ecaig.blogspot.com
This *capoeira* school was founded by Mestre Curió and his student Mestra Jararaca (the first woman to earn the Mestra, or Master, title in the Capoeira Angola style). Curió learned from another legendary master, Mestre Pastinha. The school can also be found on Facebook. Contact them for current times and prices, and book ahead.
✉ Rua Gregório de Mattos 9, Pelourinho ☎ 71 3321 0396, 71 9963 3562

GRUPO CULTURAL DE CAPOEIRA ANGOLA MOÇAMBIQUE

Considered one of the best schools in the Angola tradition of *capoeira*, this place offers flexible classes and hours, making it ideal for travellers (though you should still book ahead or visit in preceding days to schedule a class). Famous teachers working here include Mestres Boca Rica and Neco, alumni of Canjiquinha and Waldemar (two of the most celebrated teachers working during the 20th century).
✉ Rua Gregório de Mattos 38, Pelourinho ☎ 71 8113 7455, 71 8811 4815, 71 3356 7640 🕐 Mon–Fri 12–2

Above *Brazilian crafts on display at a souvenir stall*

INSTITUTO DE ARTESANATO VISCONDE DE MAUÁ

www.maua.ba.gov.br

Visit this community arts shop for Pan-Bahian traditional and contemporary ceramics, carved wood, glass and silverware, lace, leather and musical instruments from an artists' co-operative. Also at Rua Gregório de Matos 27, in Salvador (tel 71 3321 5501; Mon–Fri 10–6).

✉ Largo do Porto da Barra 2, Barra ☎ 71 3264 5501 🕒 Mon–Fri 10–6

KORUNN

This thumping bar has a quieter lounge area behind a dance floor, and a stage where DJs and local rock and MPB (Musica Popular Brasileira/ Brazilian popular music) bands play.

✉ Rua Ceará 1240, Pituba ☎ 73 3248 4201 🕒 Tue–Sat from 10pm ✋ From R$15

MADRE

Madre is one of the city's swankiest electronica dance clubs, with a huge dance floor and state-of-the-art sound system. The music is cheesy European house and techno. No shorts or flip-flops are permitted.

✉ Avenida Otávio Mangabeira 2471, Boca do Rio ☎ 73 3346 0012 🕒 Wed–Sat from 10pm ✋ R$35

MERCADO MODELO

This huge covered market is next to the boat terminal for Morro de São Paulo (▷ 209). Vendors sell arts, crafts, bric-a-brac and all manner of curios, including delightful bags made out of ring-pulls which sell for hundreds of pounds in London's Knightsbridge boutiques.

✉ Praça Cairu, Cidade Baixa 🕒 Mon–Sat 9–7, Sun 9–2

MERCADO DO PEIXE

This daytime seafood market (trading from around 7am–6pm) turns into a makeshift beach bar at night, serving bottles of cold beer and bar snacks at plastic tables until around dawn.

✉ Rio Vermelho (on the beachfront opposite the Blue Tree Towers Hotel)

OFF CLUB

www.offclub.com.br

Greater Salvador's top gay club plays hard house and techno, with DJs from all over Brazil and scantily clad local go-go dancers.

✉ Rua Dias d'Ávila 33 (next to Barra lighthouse) ☎ 73 3267 6215 🕒 Tue–Sat from 10pm ✋ R$30

OFICINA DE INVESTIGAÇÃO MUSICAL (OIM)

This shop is perhaps the best place in the historical centre to buy percussion instruments, like *berimbaus* (resembling stringed wooden bows), which the owner has made for African-Brazilian musician Carlinhos Brown.

✉ Rua Alfredo Brito 24, Pelourinho ☎ 71 3322 2386 🕒 Daily 10–6

PRAÇA BECO D'ÁGUA

In this square you will find small open-air beery bars clustered around a stage with live bands, who have locals and tourists up and dancing. The Beco functions every night of the year but is busiest on Tuesdays and Thursdays to Saturdays.

✉ Praça Beco d'Água, Rua JC Rabelo, Pelourinho 🕒 Daily from 9pm ✋ Free

PRAÇA PEDRO ARCANJO

On most Saturdays locals and a handful of tourists gather here to listen to traditional Bahian *samba de roda*, from the Santo de Casa cultural band. Shows are generally free and the atmosphere is very convivial, with lively dancing both from the band and the audience.

✉ Praça Pedro Arcanjo, Pelourinho 🕒 Most Saturdays from 9pm ✋ Free

PRAÇA DO REGGAE

This square houses a complex of open-air bars, which are open every day but which are busiest on Tuesdays, when there are live reggae bands, giving locals and tourists alike an excuse to get up and dance.

✉ Largo do Pelourinho, opposite the church of Nossa Senhora do Rosário dos Pretos (▷ 217) ✋ R$8–10 cover charge per person

ROCK IN RIO

The big concert hall has one of northeast Brazil's best sound systems. The music programme is varied and DJs play between shows.

✉ Shopping Aeroclub Plaza Show, Avenida Otávio Mangabeira 6000, Boca do Rio ☎ 71 3462 8000 🕒 Wed–Sat from 10pm ✋ R$10

SHOPPING BARRA

www.shoppingbarra.com

This is the only shopping mall close to Salvador's tourist neighbourhoods. It boasts scores of mid-range women's boutiques, shoe shops, bookshops and cosmetics stores, alongside pharmacies, restaurants and travel agents. There are ATMs

and a multiplex cinema on the top floor showing international films dubbed into Portuguese. The mall is a short walk from the Barra lighthouse (▷ 220).
✉ Avenida Centenário 2992, Chame-Chame, Barra ☎ 71 2108 8288 ⌚ Mon–Sat 9–10, Sun 12–8

TATUR

www.tatur.com.br
This very professional and reliable Irish-Brazilian company has been operating in Salvador for some 20 years. They offer a broad range of tours and services in both the city and the state, including cruises in the Baía de Todos os Santos, and trips to the Recôncavo, Chapada Diamantina and other key sights.
✉ Avenida Tancredo Neves 274, Caminho das Árvores ☎ 71 3114 7900 ⌚ Mon–Fri 10–6

TRIP BRASIL

www.tripbrasil.com
Day trips from Salvador around the Recôncavo (▷ 212–213) take in Cachoiera and São Felix, a colonial *fazenda* (ranch house) for a Bahian lunch, and Dannemann cigar factory.
✉ Vila 14, Loja 50, Rua Odilon Santos 14, Rio Vermelho ☎ 71 3015 2235 ⌚ Mon–Fri 11–7

ZAUBER MULTICULTURA

This outdoor lounge and weekend psi-trance club attracts a middle-class crowd. However, it is in a down-at-heel area, so take a cab.
✉ Ladeira da Misericórdia, Edificio Taveira s/n (reachable via the street next to the Prefeitura) ☎ 73 9983 0313 ⌚ Wed–Sat from 10pm

TRANCOSO

A MARCENARIA TRANCOSO

www.marcenariatrancoso.com.br
This is a chunky, rustic-chic home décor shop by Ricardo Salem, with lovely hardwood furniture and coconut jewellery boxes in Gaudiesque organic shapes that are small enough to pack in a bag, but come at a price.
✉ Praça São João 12, Quadrado ☎ 73 3668 1023 ⌚ Erratic opening hours

LENNY

www.lenny.com.br
This designer label is the height of Brazilian beach cool, with a range of bikinis, swimsuits and post-beach apparel, all featuring fabulous prints.
✉ Praça São João, Quadrado ☎ 73 3668 1408 ⌚ Erratic opening hours

FESTIVALS AND EVENTS

JANUARY

NOSSO SENHOR DOS NAVEGANTES

This parade takes place on New Year's Eve and the following day. Effigies of Our Lady are carried through the streets near the Bonfim church in Salvador, loaded onto flower-covered boats and ferried around the waters of the Baía de Todos os Santos, next to Salvador, followed by a flotilla of small boats.
✉ Praça Senhor do Bonfim s/n
🚌 'Bonfim' bus from outside the Mercado Modelo

REVEILLON AXÉ MOI

www.reveillon-axemoi.com.br
Porto Seguro throws one of Brazil's biggest New Year's Eve parties, with *axé* music bands from Salvador playing on vast beachside sound stages and crowds of thousands gathering for the revelry.
ℹ Rua Pero Vaz de Caminha 475, Centro ☎ 73 3288 3708 ⌚ Daily 10–6 🚌 From all major tourist towns ✈ Aeroporto de Porto Seguro

LAVAGEM DO BONFIM

This festival takes place on the third Sunday in January at Salvador's Igreja de Nosso Senhor do Bonfim (▷ 217). Up to a million pilgrims gather from 9am to process from the Igreja de Nossa Senhora da Conceição da Praia, along the coast to Bonfim. They are blessed by local women dressed in traditional clothes and at the end of the procession pilgrims wash the steps of Bonfim church with perfumed water, in a purification ceremony dedicated to the creator divinity and Christ. Later, thousands dance to Bahian music until dawn.
ℹ Praça Senhor do Bonfim s/n ☎ 71 3316 1673 ⌚ Tue–Sun 6–12, 2–8 ✋ Free 🚌 'Bonfim' bus from outside the Mercado Modelo

FEBRUARY–MARCH

CARNAVAL

Salvador hosts Brazil's most raucous carnival, starting on the weekend before Shrove Tuesday and lasting for seven days. Unlike Rio de Janeiro's carnival, it is a street festival. It is dominated by the pounding rhythms of *axé* pop music (a mix of rock and salsa) and the percussive street parades of the *blocos afro* (troupes of some 200 drummers). The best night for the party is Shrove Tuesday itself, when huge floats *(trios electricos)* meet in the city-centre Praça Castro Alves for the Encontro dos Trios, playing in rotation until dawn. It is not uncommon for major stars from the Brazilian and international music scene to make surprise appearances, as Bono has in the past.

The other major centre of activity for Salvador Carnival is the beach suburb of Barra (▷ 220), frequented by the *blocos alternativos*. These include Timbalada, a drumming group formed by renowned percussionist Carlinhos Brown. It's possible to pay to join most of the parades and buy tickets for the grandstands, either through a UK tour operator or through the *blocos* themselves.
ℹ Rua das Laranjeiras 12, Pelourinho (and at the airport) ☎ 71 3321 2133 ⌚ Daily 8.30am–9pm (daily 7.30am–11pm at airport) 🚌 From all major tourist towns ✈ Aeroporto Internacional Deputado Luís Eduardo Magalhães

PRICES AND SYMBOLS

The restaurants are listed alphabetically (excluding A, Al, El, La, Le and O). The prices given are the average for a two-course lunch (L) and a three-course dinner (D) for one person, without drinks. The wine price is for the least expensive bottle. Although you will find wine served in restaurants throughout Brazil, the usual drinks are bottled beer (R$5–R$8) or *caipirinhas*, the ubiquitous *cachaça* and fruit cocktails (R$8). All the restaurants listed accept credit cards unless otherwise stated.

For a key to the symbols, ▷ 2.

ARRAIAL D'AJUDA

AIPIM

This mood-lit intimate restaurant in the heart of Arraial town serves excellent seafood and is popular with couples. The best tables sit outdoors on a terrace opening onto the garden. The dining room is decorated with nautical bric-a-brac. The cocktails are delicious, especially the *caipirinhas* and *batidas*. Aipim is open only for evening dining.

✉ Beco do Jegue 13 ☎ 73 3575 3222 🕒 Tue–Sun 6.30–12 ✋ D R$70, Wine R$35

ROSA DOS VENTOS

Ingredients for the varied and international menu are grown in this arty restaurant's kitchen garden. Specialities include fish slow-cooked in banana leaf, which is served to a lively crowd.

✉ Alameda dos Flamboyants 24 ☎ 73 3575 1271 🕒 Tue–Sun 12–3, 6.30–12 ✋ L R$65, D R$85, Wine R$40

CHAPADA DIAMANTINA

ARTISTAS DA MASSA

Wood-fired pizzas and average pasta are served in this popular restaurant in the heart of Lençóis.

✉ Rua Miguel Calmon s/n, Lençóis 🕒 Tue–Sun 11.30–3, 6.30–12 ✋ L R$20, D R$30, Wine R$30

COZINHA ABERTA SLOW FOOD

www.cozinhaaberta.com.br

This riverside restaurant serves locally sourced slow food cooked by Deborah Doitschinoff, a chef from São Paulo. The slow food movement was founded in Italy in the 1980s to preserve traditional and regional cuisine and promote farming of plants, seeds and livestock characteristic of the local ecosystem. Deborah serves delicious fusion dishes, like chicken in coconut milk with steamed prawn pasta. The restaurant is situated in an art deco house between the main square and the Canto das Aguas hotel.

✉ Rua Rui Barbosa 42, Lençóis ☎ 75 3334 1309 🕒 Daily 12.30–11 ✋ L R$35, D R$45, Wine R$40

ETNIA

Bahia likes to think that it has a taste for chilli pepper but the Thai and Indian food in this town centre restaurant is very mild by Asian or European standards. Dishes are nonetheless full of flavour and include Tom Ka Gai (chicken in coconut sauce served with jasmine, not sticky, rice). There are just five tables, all candlelit, so it is wise to book ahead when the town is busy.

✉ Rua da Baderna 111, Lençóis ☎ 75 3334 1066 🕒 Daily 12.30–3, 6.30–11 ✋ L R$35, D R$45

NECO'S

Neco's serve a set meal of dishes that were typical of those cooked by

Above *Aipim restaurant in Arraial d'Ajuda*

diamond miners during the colonial era, using *cerrado* fruits and spices. Dishes include saffron-stewed mutton with prickly pear cactus and plantain (a relative of the banana). Neco, the chef, comes from an old Chapada Diamantina family. The restaurant is open evenings only, and booking is essential.
✉ Praça Maestro Clarindo Pachêco 15, Lençóis ☎ 75 3334 1179 ⊙ Daily 6.30–11 ✋ D R$30, Wine R$35

ILHÉUS

MAROSTICA

www.marostica.com.br
The city's best Italian restaurant serves wood-fired pizzas and rather sticky pasta to a dining room packed with local families, and with tables spilling out onto the pavement.
✉ Avenida 2 de Julho 966 ☎ 75 3634 5691 ⊙ Tue–Sun 12.30–3, 6.30–11 ✋ L R$15, D R$25, Wine R$34

VESÚVIO

This Middle Eastern restaurant is housed in a handsome, Prussian-blue, early 20th-century building close to the Jorge Amado museum (▷ 205) and the cathedral, right in the centre of town. It was featured in one of the novelist's books. The tables of choice are on the pavement in front of the restaurant and there are theatrical performances on Tuesday nights.
✉ Praça Dom Eduardo ☎ 75 3634 2164 ⊙ Tue–Sun 12.30–3, 6.30–1 ✋ L R$25, D R$35

ITACARÉ

BECO DAS FLORES

www.becodasfloresitacare.com
This attractive open-air restaurant in the town centre serves large São Paulo-style wood-fired pizzas and ice-cold drinks to diners sitting at chunky wooden tables. The most popular pizzas are the Napolitano (with Brazilian buffalo mozzarella) and the Boca do Forno (with mozzarella, grated parmesan, sun-dried tomato, roasted garlic, chicken, cram cheese and rocket). Typical starters include jerky, bruschettas and *bacalhau* (dried cod) balls.
✉ Rua Lodônio Almeida 134 ☎ 75 3251 2231 ⊙ Usually daily 12.30–3, 6.30–11 ✋ L R$30, D R$45, Wine R$35

O CASARÃO AMARELO

This big yellow house overlooking the bay becomes a nightclub after hours (from around 10pm) and has a big international menu with a handful of Bahian options, including a generous seafood *moqueca* (broth seasoned with fresh vegetables and spices, cooked in coconut milk and dendê oil).
✉ Praia da Coroinha ☎ 75 9996 0599 ⊙ Usually Tue–Sun 12–2.30, 7–late ✋ L R$20, D R$30, free entry to club

LA IN

This colourful restaurant, owned by a local artist and chef, offers a mixed menu of tasty Bahian dishes. Specialities include fish in prawn sauce, baked in a banana leaf. The dining room is hung with paintings by the owner.
✉ Rua Lodônio Almeida 116 ☎ 75 3251 3054 ⊙ Usually daily 12.30–3, 6.30–11 ✋ L R$15, D R$25

MORRO DE SÃO PAULO

SABOR DA TERRA

Morro's favourite per-kilo (food priced by weight) restaurant offers a buffet at lunchtime, with a generous choice of regional and international dishes. In the evening it becomes an à la carte seafood restaurant offering regional dishes, including *moquecas* and other Bahian standards.
✉ Rua Caminho da Praia ☎ 75 3652 1156 ⊙ Erratic opening hours, usually daily 11.30–10 ✋ L R$10, D R$20

TIA DADAI

This locally owned restaurant (many are not run by islanders, who suffer high unemployment) sits on the edge of Morro's tiny colonial *praça* and serves seafood dishes, like *casquinha de siri* (baked crab in its shell), and *badejo a portuguesa* (fillet of bream in tomato and onion sauce), alongside tasty *moquecas*.
✉ Praça Aureliano Oliveira Lima ☎ 75 3652 1621 ⊙ Varies: usually daily 11.30–10 ✋ L R$20, D R$35, Wine R$28

TINHARÉ

This tiny family-run restaurant is tucked down a little alley, reachable via a series of steps running off Rua Caminho de Praia (look for the plaque). It has chunky wooden tables and a homey atmosphere, and serves some of the best traditional Bahian cooking on the island. The *bobó de camarão* (prawns cooked in a thick garlic, tomato and chilli sauce) and the *moquecas*, served in enormous portions, are popular with both locals and travellers.
✉ Rua Caminho de Praia s/n ⊙ Erratic opening hours, usually daily 11.30–10 ✋ L R$15, D R$25, Wine R$28

PORTO SEGURO

AREA

www.areagroup.com.br
The restaurant, housed in a pretty royal-blue colonial house in the old city centre and away from the beach, serves Italian-Brazilian cuisine. It is very popular with Italian tourists, who sit outside on the deck on balmy evenings to eat some of the best pasta in Porto. The gnocchi with prawns and fresh fish is a favourite.
✉ Avenida Portugal 246 ☎ 73 3288 2743 ⊙ Daily 12.30–3, 7–12 ✋ L R$35, D R$55

PORTINHA

www.portinha.com.br
Simple but fresh Bahian and pan-Brazilian food, with meat, fish and poultry dishes bubbling over a wood-fired stove, a big bar of salads, and high-calorie puddings and desserts are available in this per-kilo restaurant. It is part of a large local chain.
✉ Rua Saldanha Marinho 32 ☎ 73 3288 2743 ⊙ Daily 12–3, 6–10 ✋ L R$15, D R$30

RECANTO DO SOSSEGO

www.recantodosossego.com
The Italian chef at this alfresco restaurant right on the beach, shaded by palm thatch and cooled by a constant sea breeze, serves Italian-Brazilian fusion cooking, with dishes including *moqueca italiana* (with squid, lobster, prawns, fillets of fish, plum tomatoes and carrot).

Avenida Beira-Mar 10130, Praia do Mutá 73 3677 1266 Usually daily 12.30–3, 7–11 L R$25, D R$55, Wine R$35

PRAIA DO FORTE

O EUROPEU

This small café restaurant right on Praia do Forte's main street serves generous portions of British and Brazilian home-cooking (including a generous cooked breakfast). It is owned by an ex-pat Englishman, who also runs a little art gallery upstairs.
Avenida ACM s/n 71 3676 0232 Daily 12.30–3, 6.30–11 L R$20, D R$45, Wine R$30

SALVADOR

AMADO

www.amadobahia.com.br
Tables in this excellent Bahian seafood restaurant overlook the Baía de Todos os Santos and are particularly romantic at night, when the lights of Salvador shimmer on the water. The Bahian specialities prepared by owner and chef Edinho Enge have a gourmet twist. They include the popular prawn-stuffed squid with herb sauce and pureed mandioquinha (a native root vegetable, similar to a large salsify).
Avenida Lafayete Coutinho 660, Comércio, Campo Grande 71 3322 3520 Tue–Sat 12–3, 7–12, Sun 12–4 L R$50, D R$80, Wine R$43

AXEGO

The best *moquecas* (stews made with coconut milk) in the city are served in this second-floor restaurant, close to the Terreiro de Jesus. Come for lunch or dinner with an empty stomach and start with a *casquinha de siri* (stuffed crab shell), followed by a *moqueca* to share between two.
Rua João de Deus 1 71 3242 7481 Daily 12–3, 7–11 L R$25, D R$40, Wine R$30

BAHIACAFE

This is one of several upmarket air-conditioned cafés on the edge of the Praça da Sé, serving strong, thick Portuguese coffee and snacks.
Praça da Sé 20 71 3322 1266 Daily 12–3 Coffee and a snack R$8

BOI PRETO

www.churrascariaboipreto.com.br
Carnivores love this all-you-can-eat *churrascaria* (barbecue meat restaurant), but there is plenty on offer for non-meat eaters too, with a huge salad buffet, as well as seafood and pasta on offer. This is excellent value, but make sure you don't overdo it on the desserts and drinks which can really push up the cost of a meal. This is a bustling place, which often gets busy with tour groups, and service is efficient, if a little rushed sometimes. Enjoy live music at the weekends as you tuck into your steak. Arrive hungry and bear in mind that it is advisable to book.
Avenida Otávio Mangabeira 71 3362 8844 Daily12–5, 7–12 Buffet R$72, Wine R$35

AL CARMO

The Italian dishes in this restaurant near the Igreja do Carmo are a little stodgy. The *petiscos* (Brazilian tapas) and salads are a more reliable option, but the view out over the Baía de Todos os Santos is breathaking, especially accompanied by an ice-cold *batida*.
Rua do Carmo 66, Santo Antônio 71 3242 0232 Daily 12.30–3, 6.30–11 L R$20, D R$45

COFFEE SHOP

Brazilian Dannemann cigars sit alongside boxes from Cuba and the Dominican Republic in this air-conditioned smoking shop-cum-café. Food and drink include delicious sandwiches and strong Portuguese coffee served in china cups. Ironically, there is no smoking in the restaurant itself; cigars may be bought here but may not be enjoyed on the premises.
Praça da Sé 5 71 3322 7817 Daily 12–3 Coffee and a snack R$8

FOGO DE CHÃO PRAÇA

Salvador's most popular upmarket spit roast restaurant *(churrascaria)* is part of a large Brazilian chain and has the customary huge dining room filled with black-tie waiters whisking sizzling prime cuts in and out of the huge kitchen. A buffet bar serves salads and pasta. The prices are for all you can eat.
Rua Colombo 4, Rio Vermelho 71 3555 9292 Daily 12–3, 7–11 L R$70, D R$70, Wine R$40

LAFAYETTE

This sophisticated restaurant has a caual-chic Trancoso feel, with scatter cushions and tables dotting an outdoor deck that has a gorgeous

Below *Enjoying a meal at Axego restaurant in Salvador*

Above Moqueca da Arraia *(stingray) is a traditional Brazilian seafood stew served at Axego*

bay view. Dishes include grilled meats and poultry, and fresh fish of the day in lime sauce.
✉ Avenida Contorno 1010, Bahia Marina, Comércio, Campo Grande ☎ 71 3321 0800 ⌚ Daily 12–3, 7–1 ✋ L R$25, D R$55, Wine R$40

MAI THAI

This restaurant is in the upscale neighbourhood of Vitória, between Barra and the city centre. It sits romantically over the water of the Baía de Todos os Santos on a covered deck and is reachable by cable car from the Hotel Sol Victoria. The food is as close to Bahian as it is Thai; flavoursome, but a little heavy and underspiced by Asian standards.
✉ Avenida Sete de Setembro 2068, Hotel Sol Victoria Marina, Vitória ☎ 71 3336 7736 ⌚ Tue–Sun 6.30–12 ✋ D R$80, Wine R$40

O NILO

Middle Eastern standards are served alongside fusion dishes like *filé sultão* (lamb fillet cooked in an almond sauce and garnished with nuts) by Chef Nohad el Kadre, who learned his trade from his Lebanese parents. The dining room feels like a Dahab chill-out lounge, decorated with contemporary Middle Eastern art. Unlike most restaurants in Salvador, the menu has options for vegetarians.
✉ Rua das Laranjeiras 44 ☎ 71 3321 0073 ⌚ Daily 12–3, 7–11 ✋ L R$40, D R$60

PARAÍSO TROPICAL

The restaurant setting and the dining room are simple and unpretentious, but the food is so good that Paraíso Tropical is a regular on gourmet cooking tours from Europe. The menu includes superb *moquecas*, flavoured with organic fruits and condiments from the kitchen garden. The restaurant is a 30-minute taxi ride from the centre.
✉ Rua Edgar Loureiro 98-B, Cabula ☎ 71 3384 7464 ⌚ Tue–Sun 12–11 ✋ L R$45, D R$90

PEREIRA

The open-topped deck of this restaurant on the seafront road in Barra is a favourite spot for a sunset *caipirinha*. The food is less spectacular and includes huge cuts of steak, sticky pasta and Bahian standards, but it is possible to come just for a drink and tapas *(petiscos)*.
✉ Avenida Sete de Setembro 3959, Porto da Barra ☎ 71 3264 6464 ⌚ Daily 12–3, 7–12 ✋ L R$25, D R$40, *Petiscos* from R$7

PONTA VITAL

Chef Dom Vital's menu contains traditional recipes cooked in the Bahian Recôncavo, like spicy *acarajé* (black bean fritters) with *vatapa* (prawn paste).
✉ Rua das Laranjeiras 23, Pelourinho ☎ 71 8828 8983 ⌚ Daily 12–3, 7–11 ✋ L R$15, D R$30

RESTAURANTE-ESCOLA DO SENAC

www.ba.senac.br
There are two air-conditioned dining rooms in this centrally located catering school, serving food cooked by the students. Downstairs is a per-kilo buffet, with some 50 different plates and puddings. Upstairs is à la carte, featuring dishes like *bobó de camarão* (prawns cooked in a thick garlic, tomato and chilli sauce).
✉ Praça José Alencar 13–19, Pelourinho ☎ 71 3324 4557 ⌚ Mon–Sat 11.30–3.30 ✋ L R$15 downstairs; R$50 upstairs

SOHO

www.sohorestaurante.com.br
Salvador's celebrities and wealthy elite sip their cocktails in the long bar of this glass-fronted cube perched over the bay. Alfresco tables serve Brazilian-Japanese fusion dishes by Paulistano chef, Marcio Fushimi. The combination sushi and sashimi plates (made with locally caught fish and garnished with Brazilian fruits and spices) are particularly worth trying.
✉ Avenida Contorno 1010, Bahia Marina, Campo Grande ☎ 71 3322 4554 ⌚ Mon 12–12, Tue–Thu 12–3, 7–12, Fri–Sat 12–3, 7–1, Sun 12–4, 7–12 ✋ L R$50, D R$70, Wine R$40

TRANCOSO

O CACAU

Trancoso's favourite local restaurant serves wonderful *vatapa* (prawn, peanut and coconut pâté with dendê oil), *acarajé* (spicy black bean fritters), *caruru* (shrimp, okra and onion condiment) and seafood *moquecas* (stews made with coconut milk and dendê oil). A popular main course is fresh *camarão nativo* (local prawns).
✉ Praça São João 96, Quadrado ☎ 73 3668 1266 ⌚ Daily 12–3, 7–12 ✋ L R$40, D R$70, Wine R$30

CAPIM SANTO

www.capimsanto.com.br
Sandra Marques' garden restaurant offers one of the most romantic dining spots in Trancoso. The food and *caipirinhas* are superb. Start with a *caipisake* (made with sake) and follow it with a Bahian seafood dish like *badejo* (bass) stuffed with manioc flour and served on a bed of jack fruit and greens. Be sure to come after 8pm, when the dining room is busier.
✉ Rua do Beco, Praça São João, Quadrado ☎ 73 3668 1122 ⌚ Mon–Sat 5–11 ✋ D R$60, Wine R$30

PRICES AND SYMBOLS
Prices are the lowest and highest for a double room for one night. Breakfast is included unless noted otherwise. All the hotels listed accept credit cards unless otherwise stated. Note that rates vary widely throughout the year.

For a key to the symbols, ▷ 2.

ARRAIAL D'AJUDA

ARRAIAL HOSTEL
www.arraialdajudahostel.com.br.
This is a great value IYHA hostel. The two-storey building has an internal courtyard with a pool in a style they describe as *Greco Romano Bahiano*, with all rooms facing the pool. The hostel is central and within walking distance of the beach. Facilities include a bar, internet and good book exchange.
✉ Rua do Campo 94 ☎ 73 3575 1192 R$70–R$100 16 Outdoor

CASARÃO ALTO MUCUGÊ
www.casaraoaltomucuge.com
There are great sea views from the rooms in this farm-style hotel and a heliconia garden at the edge of a cliff overlooking the sea. There's a hot tub and a massage facility. The main house, where breakfast is served, has 19th-century décor, using a variety of objects and holy pictures. There's a pool table and a sitting room with WiFi connection. This is an altogether pleasant place to stay.
✉ Estrada Alto Mucugê s/n ☎ 73 3575 1490 R$280–R$350 8

MAITEI
www.maitei.com.br
All rooms here include sea view, air-conditioning and king-sized beds with anti-allergenic feather pillows. The decoration is rustic, including paintings by local artists. Rooms have double Jacuzzis, a minibar and flat-screen TV with cable channels. Children under 16 are excluded. The beach and town centre are within easy walking distance.
✉ Rua do Mucugê 475 ☎ 73 3575 3877 R$390–R$520 17

CARAVELAS

MARINA PORTO ABROLHOS
www.marinaportoabrolhos.com.br
Accommodation here is in homey but plain chalets, with room enough for four, clustered in a shady garden and around a pool. The hotel can organize trips around Caravelas and to the Abrolhos Archipelago (the hotel is situated at the port from where boats leave for the islands).
✉ Rua da Baleia (5km outside of town) ☎ 73 3674 1060 R$155–R$295 12 Outdoor

CHAPADA DIAMANTINA

CASA DA GELÉIA
www.casadageleia.com.br
The only hotel in Brazil which markets itself as a *pousada* and jelly house has rooms in a lovely colonial house and *cabana* chalets in a tropical garden at the Salvador entrance to town. The breakfasts are huge and include the *pousada*'s myriad home-made jams and jellies. The owner, Zé Carlos, is one of the best bird-watching guides in the Chapada (▷ 227).
✉ Rua General Viveiros 187, Lençóis ☎ 75 3334 1151 R$100–R$150 6

ESTALAGEM DE ALCINO
www.alcinoestalagem.com
This riverside *pousada* in a large, yellow 19th-century mansion is set in lush gardens. It is decorated throughout with antiques. Most rooms have shared bathrooms. Breakfast is generous and is served in the little hummingbird-filled garden next to the owner's pottery studio.
✉ Rua Gen Vivieros de Morais 139, Lençóis ☎ 75 3334 1171 R$120–R$170 7

HOTEL DE LENÇÓIS
www.hoteldelencois.com.br
Rooms are simple in this colonial building, overlooking a pool and on

Opposite *Houses in the historic centre of Arraial d'Ajuda*

the edge of the Chapada Diamantina National Park. There is little noise here but the sound of birds and staff are welcoming. There's a substantial breakfast and a restaurant serving Brazilian dishes at lunch and dinner.
Rua Altinha Alves 747, Lençóis 75 3334 1102 R$225–R$305 50 Outdoor

IYHA LENÇÓIS

www.hostelchapada.com.br
This is the best local option for backpackers. It's in a large period house at the southern end of town and boasts modern facilities, including a kitchen, laundry and a garden with hammocks. Accommodation comprises single rooms, en suite doubles and single-sex 4–6 bed dorms. The friendly staff can arrange tours, though you may find cheaper options in town.
Rua Boa Vista 121, Lençóis 75 3334 1497 Dorm bed R$25–R$45; Double room R$55–R$95 20

VILA SERRANO

www.vilaserrano.com.br
Mock-colonial bungalows are grouped around a beautifully kept garden with a central fountain. The rooms are well-fitted and modern. The friendly owners are happy to give advice on local places of interest and can arrange tours. This is one of the best places to stay in Lençóis.
Rua Alto do Bonfim 8, Lençóis 75 3334 1486 R$125–R$180 13

ILHÉUS

FAZENDA DA LAGOA

www.fazendadalagoa.com.br
This luxurious self-styled eco-hotel comprises 14 large, minimalist and modern beach bungalows designed by Cariocas Lia Siqueira and Mucki Skowronski (each are 100sq m/1,075sq ft). They are sited on a beach that is 50m (55 yards) wide and 10km (6 miles) long. To the rear is an estuary fringed by mangroves teeming with wildlife, including several species of kingfisher and heron. Ocelot can sometimes be seen in the nearby forest. It's well worth taking along binoculars (and a field guide, as the staff seem unaware of even the commonest local species). There's a tamarin sanctuary at nearby Una. Leave time to enjoy the good food and excellent *caipirinhas*.
Rodovia BA 001, Una, Ilhéus 73 3236 6046 R$200–R$750 14 Outdoor

JARDIM ATLÂNTICO

www.hoteljardimatlantico.com.br
This hotel is especially child-friendly. There's a kids club, with organized activities, and a water park. For the adults there are tennis courts, a gym, swimming pool and sauna, snooker, table tennis and the restaurant is good. The complex is set in a large tropical garden adjoining the beach. The rooms are prettily decorated and each has a mini garden. Some excursions are available.
Rodovia Ilheus-Olivenca, km 2, Jardim Atlantico, Ilhéus 73 3632 4711 R$280–R$350 55 Outdoor

ITACARÉ

ALBERGUE O PHAROL

www.albergueopharol.com.br
A reasonably priced and well-decorated hostel with plain but adequate rooms, and public areas equipped with heavy wooden furniture and lacy hammocks. There's a good choice of rooms, including private double and triple air-conditioned apartments, fan-cooled dormitories (up to six people) and a room with full disabled facilities.
Praça Santos Dumont 7, Itacaré 73 3251 2527 Dorm bed R$25–R$45; Double room R$65–R$300 14 From Ilhéus; bus stop roughly 500m (545 yards) from the hostel

MARIA FARINHA

www.mariafarinhapousada.com.br
This family-run *pousada* is centred on a traditional *oca*, a round-house as used by the local indigenous people, where the hotel has its reception and breakfast areas. The rooms, occupying a two-storey concrete building, are simply decorated. They overlook a small pool. It is a 10-minute walk to the beach. Unusually for this region, there is disabled access.
Rua Louro Amarelo 240, Conchas do Mar II, Itacaré 73 3251 3515 R$150–R$220 16 Outdoor

NAINAS

www.nainas.com.br
This bright but tranquil little place is a short walk from the beach. *Cabanas* (double-room cabins) are set in a lush garden and have white tiled floors, brightly decorated walls and colourful bedcovers. The breakfast is a smorgasbord of fresh fruits, pastries, cereals, and hot and cold dishes.
Praia da Concha 73 3251 2683 R$150–R$230 5

SAGE POINT

www.pousadasagepoint.com.br
Surf-chic is the theme here, with wood-panelled rooms decorated with driftwood articles and nautical-looking wooden beds. Cabins have terraces with hammocks overlooking the beach. Rooms vary in size so check the pictures on the website before booking. Staff can arrange tours and surf board rental. They speak English.
Praia de Tiririca 73 3251 2030 R$150–R$300 8

SÍTIO ILHA VERDE

www.ilhaverde.com.br
This hotel is distinguished by its delightful design, the bedlinen matching the warm pink and orange tones of the walls of the bungalow rooms. Even the bathrooms are designed with panache, using local craft designs influenced by the cultures of Africa and Bahia. There are lounge areas in the pleasant garden, with its heliconias and orchids, and a little pool. Families can opt for the larger *casita* (house). The breakfast is particularly good, with a huge array of fruits, cold meats, pastries and cooked dishes.
Rua Ataide Seubal 234 73 3251 2056 R$150–R$220 9 Outdoor

TXAI

www.txai.com.br.

This very luxurious hotel, with its excellent spa, comprises 40 large thatched bungalows, complete with four-poster beds and wooden sun decks. All this is set in a palm-grove on what is effectively a private beach. Although the rooms are very expensive, the staff are poorly paid. Your tips are much appreciated.

Praia de Itacarezinho 73 2627 6363 R$1,100–R$1,235 40 Outdoor

MORRO DE SÃO PAULO

AGUA VIVA

www.pousadaaguaviva.com

Agua Viva *pousada* is decorated with paintings by the owners, who are local fishermen. It's in a simple style with tiled floors and whitewashed walls. The best rooms are at the front of the building and these have small verandas.

Terceira Praia 75 3652 1217 15 R$70–R$120 8

FAROL DO MORRO

www.faroldomorro.com.br

A charming little Bahian-owned *pousada*. There is a miniature funicular railway connecting the reception area to the double-room cabins and a tiny infinity pool perched on the steep hill, all surrounding a lighthouse. The best have large windows opening out onto a glorious view of the little town and the glistening ocean.

Primeira Praia 75 3652 1036 R$250–R$350 15 Outdoor

FAZENDA VILA GUAIAMÚ

www.vilaguaiamu.com.br

The Italian owners of this farm hotel *fazenda* support an eco-tourism project which protects the Guaiamú—a species of crab—which depend on Morro's extant original mangrove forests for their survival and which inhabit a river that runs through the property. The seven *cabanas* (cabins) are sited in a garden that backs onto a little forest reserve. The hotel can arrange guided rainforest walks. The restaurant serves perhaps the best food of any hotel restaurant on the island. Massages, meditation and yoga are also available.

Terceira Praia 75 3652 1035 R$180–R$250 22

HOSTEL MORRO DE SÃO PAULO

www.hosteldomorro.com.br

This busy but competent backpacker hostel is on the outskirts of the town on the pathway leading to the spring. It offers both rooms and dorms, with a small garden and hammocks in the public areas. However, you can find cheaper air-conditioned options, instead of the basic fan-cooled rooms in this hostel, at the locally owned guest houses listed above and on the www.morro.travel website.

Rua Fonte Grande at the end of Beco dos Pássaros 75 3652 1521 Dorm bed R$30–R$56; double room R$70–R$120 10

VILA DOS ORIXÁS

www.hotelviladosorixas.com

The Vila dos Orixás, the most expensive hotel on the Praia do Encanto, is as pricey as far superior hotels in Trancoso. However, the rooms are large and in Asian beach-style, with palm-thatched concrete cabins for two that have wood floors and verandas. The location is superb, in a garden of lawn and palm-trees with a wonderful 25m (82ft) pool of deepest blue adjacent to a quiet beach. Luckily, the restaurant-bar is good for seafood and cold *caipirinhas*, as there's nowhere else to eat near by and transport by van must be booked in advance. The Vila dos Orixás is very popular with Spanish tourists.

Quinta Praia 75 3652 2055 R$300–R$375 10 Outdoor

PORTO SEGURO

HOSTEL PRAIA DE TABERAPUAN

www.portoseguroshostel.com.br

This beachside annexe of the town hostel offers doubles or plain 6-in-a-room dorms with big lockers (which can feel a little cramped), as well as a big games room and leisure area. There is internet access, a pool and tours available.

Praia deTaberapuan 73 3288 1742 R$25–R$70 20 Outdoor

POUSADA NASCENTE

http://pousadanascente.spaces.live.com

An ugly wall blocks some views here but it's only a short walk from the *pousada* to both the beach and the historic centre. Tame macaws croak benignly from their perches around the pool. The bungalows are spread around a shaded garden and the pool areas, looking towards the sea. Air-conditioned rooms are spartan but include TV and WiFi.

Estrada do Aeroporto 437, Cidade Alta 73 3288 2537 R$70–R$120 19 Outdoor

XURUPITA RESORT

www.xurupita.com

This hotel is 1km (0.6 miles) from the beach but from its hillside position there's a view of the sea. It's surrounded by Atlantic coastal forest busy with hummingbirds and tanagers at dawn. It's quiet, with no noisy music. The rectangular rooms are decorated with colourful floral murals and furnished with rather dull wicker and hardwood furniture. There's a sports centre with gym coaching, squash and tennis, and airport transfers and car rental.

Rua B 25, Taperapuã 73 2105 9500 R$350–R$450 16 Outdoor

PRAIA DO FORTE

POUSADA TIA HELENA

www.tiahelenapraiadoforte.com.br

This is a bright pinkish-purplish *pousada*, with rooms simply decked out with wooden beds and bamboo clothes racks. Helena, the lady of the house, keeps everything in order. There are reductions for three-day stays, and there are some triple and quadruple rooms, making this cheaper still for groups. What's more, a great breakfast is provided.

Alameda das Estrelas, east of Praça dos Artistas 71 3676 1198, 71 3676 1198 R$70–R$100 12

TIVOLI ECO-RESORT
www.ecoresort.com.br
This huge family resort belongs to the Portuguese Espírito Santo group. The air-conditioned rooms overlook a large pool. There's a garden filled with heliconias. Rooms are spacious and well appointed, breakfast is huge and the hotel has a state-of-the-art Thalasso spa, plus night-time entertainment. Book online or through an international agent, as it is much cheaper. The restaurant is poor.
Avenida do Farol 71 3676 4000 R$300–R$520 290 Outdoor

RECÔNCAVO

POUSADA CONVENTO DO CARMO
www.pousadadoconvento.com.br
The rather shabby old convent offers plain rooms with wooden floors and fading 17th-century furniture, a dusty chapel and a small gallery of holy pictures. Just about the only place locally, it serves a breakfast of cold meats, fruit and bread rolls, and there is a pool.
Rua Inocêncio Boaventura, Praça da Aclamação, Cachoeira 75 3425 1716 R$70– R$120 20 Outdoor

SALVADOR

ALBERGUE DAS LARANJEIRAS
www.laranjeirashostel.com.br
This is a busy (and noisy) IYHA hostel in the heart of the Pelourinho. The double rooms contain a bed, and that's about it. There are some with private bathrooms but they can be expensive at R$130 or more. You'll find better value (and possibly more sleep) in Santo Antônio. The hostel also offers internet access, tour booking services and a crêperie restaurant.
Rua Inácio Accioli 13 71 3321 1366 Dorm bed R$25–R$40; Double room R$80–R$140 15

GRANDE HOTEL DA BARRA
www.grandehoteldabarra.com.br
Built in the 1960s, this recently refurbished hotel is rather clumsy-looking. It boasts some of the largest rooms in Barra but the tiling and patent leather furniture are very standard. The best rooms are now tidy and spruced up, especially those on the top floor, which have ocean views. Unlike most hotels in Barra, the Sol has a decent-sized pool, a small gym and business facilities. Good web prices.
Avenida Sete de Setembro 3564 71 2106 8600 R$200–R$340 116 Outdoor

HOTEL ARTHEMIS
www.arthemishotel.com.br
Poorly furnished, very basic rooms but with great views for breakfast on the roof terrace (out over the Cidade Baixa and Baía de Todos os Santos to Itaparica island), so this place is better value than many of the hostels if you'd prefer a room to a dorm. Check out several rooms, though, as there is a variety of standards here.
Edifício Themis, Praça da Sé 398 R$60–R$100 21

MONTE PASCOAL PRAIA
www.montepascoal.com.br
Once again, this hotel has amazing views over the Atlantic from the rooftop pool and large windows, but is somewhat spoiled by drearily appointed tiled rooms stacked one on top of the other like boxes. Patent leather furnishings don't help. Single or double beds and flat-screen TVs are provided. However, stay here for a terrific view of the carnival (which passes right below) and the accompanying fireworks. WiFi can be used in rooms for an extra price and, unusually, there is disabled access.
Avenida Oceânica 591, Barra 71 2103 4000 R$290–R$362 80 Rooftop

PARADISE PROPERTIES BAHIA
www.pp-bahia.com
Here you will find a broad range of rental apartments, from budget accommodation cheap enough for backpackers (especially when sharing), to luxurious apartments in modern condominiums with wonderful Atlantic (and carnival) views. Most are in and around Barra and the excellent website allows for browsing by availability and online reservations. Extra services include mobile phone rental, maid service and airport pick-up.
Avenida Sete de Setembro 3743 71 3264 5588 (USA: +1 917 477 0798) R$80–R$250

Below *Largo do Pelourinho in Salvador*

PESTANA CONVENTO DO CARMO

www.pestana.com

This building is full of priceless treasures and is a UNESCO World Heritage Site. Unsurprisingly it's Salvador's grandest hotel, being a beautiful colonial convent in the historic centre of the city. The swimming pool is sited around an 18th-century fountain, and there's a spa and even a private baroque chapel. Little gilt angels watch over you in the cloister cocktail bar and the restaurants, which are beautifully decorated with *azulejos*. Service can be slow and over-elaborate at times, but the cuisine—traditional Portuguese or contemporary—can be excellent. Web discounts are usually available.

✉ Rua do Carmo 1 ☎ 71 3327 8400 (USA: +1 800 745 8883, toll free) R$510–R$700 Rooms79; Suites 11 Outdoor

PORTO FAROL

www.portofarol.com.br

Porto Farol is an enormous standardized 1990s seafront block, with a range of tiled-floor rooms fitted with laminate top wall desks and wooden breakfast tables. There's plenty of light from the big windows. The best choices are the standard and duplex apartments, with their own kitchenettes. Standard rooms are a little pokey. The best value accommodations if you are in a group are the duplex quintas, with room for 4–5 people.

✉ Rua Engenheiro Milton de Oliveira 134, Barra ☎ 71 3267 8000 R$170–R$300 39 Outdoor

POUSADA BALUARTE

www.pousadabaluarte.com

This is a small 1960s-built *pousada* (with only five guest rooms), that prides itself on its breakfast and evening meal, provided by host Zelina and her French husband. It's somewhat further from the Pelourinho than some but it's quiet, very well kept, and pleasantly decorated with local art.

✉ Ladeira do Baluarte 13, Santo Antônio Além do Carmo ☎ 71 3327 0367 R$160–R$220 15

POUSADA DO BOQUEIRÃO

www.pousadaboqueirao.com.br

This coolly elegant hotel occupies another 18th-century town house. Its open spaces and warm light has made it a favourite for filming and photo shoots, and it has some of the best views in town from the upper floor rooms. Attic rooms are quite small but great value (with shared bathroom). The hotel shop excels in local craftwork from some of the best traditional artisans.

✉ Rua Direita do Santo Antônio 48, Santo Antônio ☎ 71 3241 2262 R$90–R$270 15

POUSADA DAS FLORES

www.pflores.com.br

This *pousada* occupies a nicely fitted-out 18th-century house, 10 minutes from the Pelourinho. Rooms are fan-cooled, with optional portable air-conditioning available. Polished wooden floors are offset by bright décor in blue and yellow, and with antique wooden furniture. The smartest and largest accommodation is in the veranda suites 7, 8 and 9.

✉ Rua Dureita de Santo Antônio 442, Santo Antônio ☎ 71 3243 1836 R$180–R$250 9

POUSADA DO PILAR

www.pousadadopilar.com

Large, modern air-conditioned rooms here are furnished in dark wood and whitewash, in another converted colonial mansion house. Take an upper-floor room with a veranda for a view over the bay. Enjoy a fruit-laden breakfast served on the open-air top-floor deck, which doubles up as a bar in the evening.

✉ Rua Direita do Santo Antônio 24, Santo Antônio ☎ 71 3241 6278 R$160–R$270 12

POUSADA VILLA CARMO

www.pousadavillacarmo.com.br

Set in a beautiful colonial building, the plainly furnished but elegant fan-cooled and air-conditioned rooms are decorated with Brazilian art and ceramics chosen by the owner, Ana Luz. The rooms vary from very small to quite spacious, with the best three having balconies and views over the bay.

✉ Rua do Carmo 58, Santo Antônio ☎ 71 3241 3924 R$150–R$250 12

SOLAR DO CARMO

www.solardocarmo.com.br

Yet another converted town mansion, with a series of bland air-conditioned rooms. Again, top floor rooms are the best. Book one with a terrace so you can gaze out at the shining, glittering Baía de Todos os Santos. Breakfast on the balcony also comes with a stunning view. The owner, Flavia, provides friendly service.

✉ Rua Direita do Santo Antonio 108, Santo Antônio ☎ 71 3323 0644 R$190–R$250 10 rooms, 4 suites4

Opposite *A room in the Villa Bahia hotel in Salvador*

VILLA BAHIA

www.hotelvillabahia.com

This pleasantly unpretentious but stylish French hotel is decorated in Portuguese colonial styles from around the world, with rooms that have themes from Goa, Macau, Mozambique and Cape Verde, among others. Third-floor rooms are especially recommended for their view of the Pelourinho and the church of São Francisco. The rooftop has a Jacuzzi hot tub and tiny pool. Take care, as the surrounding streets can be dangerous after 11pm.

✉ Largo do Cruzeiro de São Francisco 16–18, Pelourinho ☎ 71 322 4271 R$400–R$550 17 Rooftop

VILLA SANTO ANTÔNIO

www.hotel-santoantonio.com

A German fashion photographer owns this Santo Antônio town house, nicely converted into a hotel. The upper-floor rooms are air-conditioned, with a shared balcony, huge French windows, queen-sized beds and views of the bay. The impressive master suite, with its lavish marble bathroom, occupies almost half a floor. Public areas are walled in rough stone with neutral decoration and comfortable furnishings.

✉ Rua Direita de Santo Antônio 130, Santo Antônio ☎ 71 3326 1270 R$250–R$350 12

TRANCOSO

MATA N'ATIVA POUSADA

www.matanativapousada.com.br

This is a delightful riverside *pousada*, where owners Daniel and Daniela show exceptional hospitality and friendliness to guests. The elegant *cabanas* (double room cabins) occupy a romantic setting in a cool and shady garden visited by numerous birds and butterflies. Daniel offers easy adventure trips—kayaking on the river or nature walking in nearby areas of *restinga* and Atlantic coastal forest—and knows all about Brazilian flora. There's also a useful collection of books on natural history in the *pousada*'s sitting area. Good English, Spanish and Italian are spoken. They provide a great breakfast and children are welcome.

✉ Estrada do Arraial, Praia dos Nativos ☎ 73 3668 1830 R$230–R$410 8

POUSADA ESTRELA D'ÁGUA

www.estreladagua.com.br

The three levels of accommodation are sited in an array of luxurious 'fishermen's shacks'. They are positioned in a long garden culminating in a large glass-fronted bar and sitting area overlooking a big, deep blue infinity pool, swaying palms and the beach. Rooms range from the Master Suite Duplex seafront—a 200sq m (2,150sq ft), two-floor *palapa* bungalow with private bamboo terraces, Jacuzzi and ocean views—to the 120sq m (1,290sq ft) Master Suite, which is similar but just one storey. There are also standard suites out back which have twins or king-sized beds. Decór is clean and minimalist. There is free WiFi throughout. The hotel is one of the few in Bahia to make efforts to practise conservational tourism by following the PNUMA UN programme for nature, installing solar power, recycling and engaging in some small welfare programmes. The restaurant opens only at night.

✉ Estrada Arraial D'Ajuda, Praia dos Nativos ☎ 73 3668 1030 R$450–R$2,080 28 Outdoor

POUSADA ETNIA

www.etniabrasil.com.br.

This chic *pousada*, owned by Andre Zanonato and Corrado Tini, has simple but elegant bungalows whose interiors have a clean Mediterranean style. They are sited in a hilly tropical forest garden, filled with brilliantly coloured birds and butterflies. At night the paths between cabins are lit by wayside lamps. There's a lush designer pool.

✉ Rua Principal 25 ☎ 73 3668 1137 R$400–R$600 8 Outdoor

E

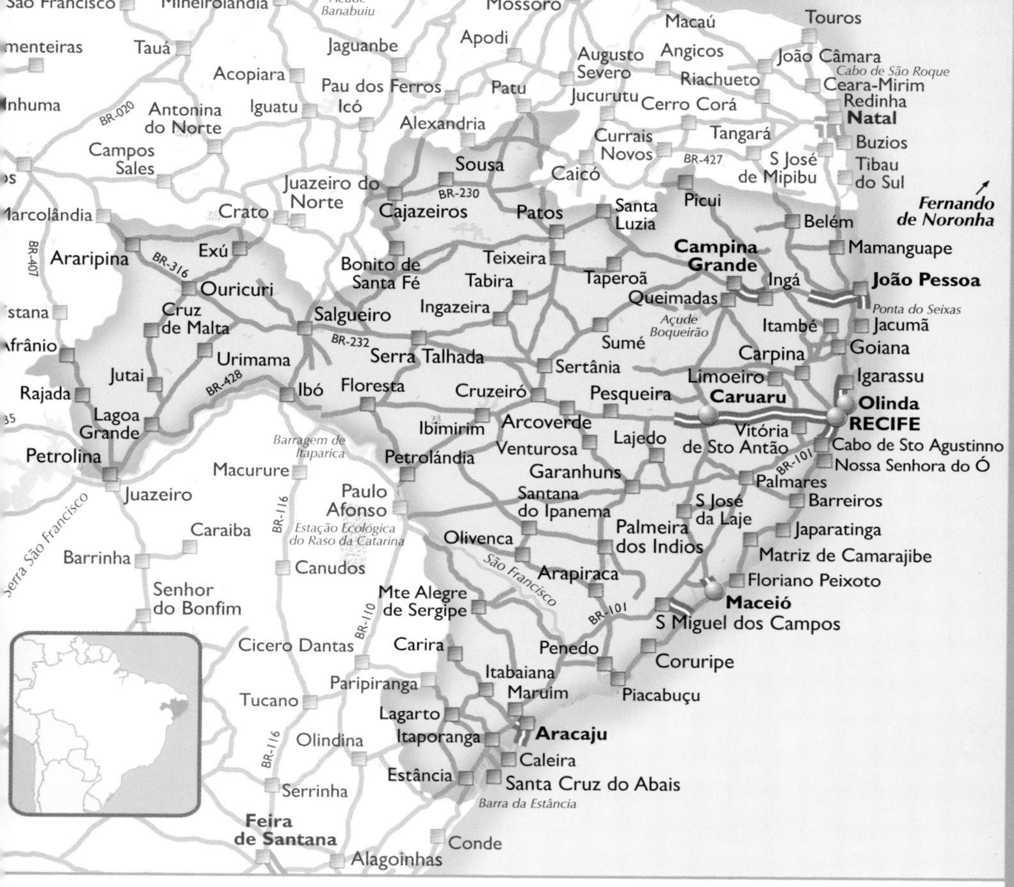

RECIFE AND THE BRAZILIAN CAPE

This region, just north of Bahia in the northeast of Brazil, is dominated by Salvador's great colonial rival, Recife. It lies in the state of Pernambuco which, like Bahia, became rich on sugar and slavery in the first centuries of the Portuguese colony. Recife and its twin city Olinda (which lies only a few kilometres away and which has the best choice of accommodation) have magnificent churches and streets of stately Portuguese buildings. Both cities also have one of the liveliest music scenes north of Rio de Janeiro and the best traditional carnival in Brazil.

Beaches stretch to the north and south of the cities and 350km (217 miles) offshore to the northeast are the jewel-like islands of the Fernando de Noronha archipelago (also in Pernambuco state), ringed with pearly beaches and set in an emerald sea. These offer some of the best scuba diving in Brazil and are protected as a marine national park. The largest island, Fernando de Noronha itself, is a UNESCO World Heritage Site.

The three other states in the region—Sergipe, Alagoas and Paraíba—are among the smallest in Brazil and often overlooked by visitors, who whisk through them on their way north or south. As a result, they retain a local integrity absent from the larger tourist centres, and can boast pretty and slowly crumbling Portuguese colonial towns like Laranjeiras, Penedo and Marechal Deodoro. Alagoas state is home to some of the most beautiful and least spoiled beaches in the northeast.

ARACAJU

www.aracaju.se.gov.br

Sergipe's state capital straddles the waters of the Rio Sergipe 327km (203 miles) north of Salvador (▷ 214–221) and the city centre is some 10km (6 miles) inland from its beaches. The city itself is a quiet, provincial place with a tawdry old centre that is best avoided, especially at night. Most visitors opt to stay on the main beach, Praia Atalaia, which is backed by an avenue of *pousadas* (small guest houses) and restaurants. This is a good base for exploring the colonial villages of São Cristóvão (▷ 252) or Laranjeiras (▷ 248), which are located near by and which can be most conveniently visited by rental car (easily organized through a *pousada)*. Other, lonelier beaches stretch north and south from Atalaia. The best of these is the 30km (18.5 miles) of sand at Atalaia Nova, on the Ilha de Santa Luzia. It lies on the north bank of the Sergipe river and is easily reached by boat from the ferry port on Avenida Rio in Aracaju. Aracaju celebrates one of the biggest out-of-season carnivals in this part of the northeast and often hosts some of the biggest bands in Brazil. In the past these have included Jota Quest and Skank.

399 U9 Travessa Baltazar Gois 86, Centro 79 3179 1932 Mon–Fri 10–6 Aeroporto de Aracaju Santa Maria From all major tourist towns To Barco Atalaia R$3

CAMPINA GRANDE

www.campinagrande.pb.gov.br

This pleasant and prosperous inland city is the second largest in the state of Paraíba, after João Pessoa (▷ this page), and is known by locals as the gateway to the dry *sertão* region. It is nestled in the gentle hills of the Serra da Borborema, 551m (1,807ft) above sea level, giving it a markedly cooler feel than the sweltering interior and humid coast. It is a good base for visiting Cariri and Ingá (▷ 253), which are around 50km (31 miles) away. The city vies with Caruaru (▷ 246), in neighbouring Pernambuco state, for the liveliest São João celebrations in Brazil. Like Caruaru, Campina Grande builds a *forró* village—as the site of *forró* dancing (a type of traditional northeastern jig) and revelry—every weekend in June (▷ 263).

Campina Grande's prosperity came from cotton. When production declined after World War II, light industry arrived, such as the only factory in the world to make Brazil's famous fashion flip-flops, Havaianas. The city has two universities and a large student population.

There are two interesting museums, sitting close to each other in the city centre. The Museu do Algodão (tel 83 3341 1039; Tue–Sat 8–12, 1–5; free) is housed in the old railway station and tells the story of the cotton industry. The Museu Histórico (tel 83 3310 6182; Tue–Sat 8–12, 1–5; R$2) sits in the old jailhouse. There are cafés and restaurants close to both.

397 U8 João Suassuna airport 83 3310 6100 Daily 9–5 Internacional de Campo Grande From João Pessoa

CARUARU

▷ 246.

FERNANDO DE NORONHA

▷ 247.

JOÃO PESSOA

www.joaopessoa.pb.gov.br

Paraíba's state capital feels like a local town. Few tourists make it here and the city sits sleepily on the banks of the sluggish Paraíba river, surrounded by stands of Mata Atlântica forest. Firstly called Filipéia, it became Parahyba in the early 18th century, after it had grown fat on sugar and was the largest city in the country after Recife and Salvador. In the 20th century it was renamed João Pessoa, after a politician who was assassinated in the 1930s.

The city centre has a few interesting colonial buildings, notably the São Francisco Cultural Centre (tel 83 3218 4505; Tue–Sun 9–12, 2–5; adult R$4, child R$2, under 7 free), which includes the Convento de Santo Antônio, built between 1589 and 1779. It is one of the most important baroque buildings in the northeast, with magnificent *azulejos* (glazed tiles painted with blue scenes) and gilt altarpieces. At night the city centre is almost deserted and most visitors stay on the beach in Tambaú or Manaira, where there are plenty of hotels and restaurants.

397 V8 Praça Amaro Ferraz Santa Rita 83 3229 1897 Mon–Fri 9–5 Presidente Castro Pinto From all major tourist towns

Opposite *Food stalls in Praça da Sé, Olinda (▷ 250–251)*
Below *Praça Anthenor Navarro in João Pessoa*

INFORMATION
www.caruaru.pe.gov.br
399 U8 From Recife

TIPS

» There are hotels in the town centre in Caruaru which should be booked well ahead for the festivals. Some tourists hire a car in Recife and commute, or take the train.

» The best places to buy Caruaru clay figurines are at the various *feiras de artesanato* (handicraft markets) dotted around the city, where they are a fraction of the price of those found in other tourist locations.

» During the Festas Juninas, the Trem do Forró train runs to Caruaru from the Marco Zero in the centre of Recife. It takes two hours and there is music and dancing all the way (▷ 263).

Above *Stalls at Feira de Sulanca, Brazil's largest street market*

CARUARU

This small *sertão* town, some 130km (80.5 miles) from Recife (▷ 254–257), is one of the folklore capitals of the northeast, with a lively arts and crafts scene, the joint largest (with Campina Grande, ▷ 245) and most traditional June festivities (Festas Juninas, ▷ 263), and the most famous Easter pageant in Brazil, at Nova Jerusalem in the village of Fazenda Nova (▷ 263).

LOCAL FRICTION

The town's celebrated rivalry with Campina Grande, across the border in Paraíba state, began over a title—O Capital do Agreste (Capital of the Agrarian Northeast)—with the two cities competing for agricultural economic supremacy like rival football teams do for league supremacy. Locals are fiercely loyal to their city's potato and tomato-driven wealth, become visibly angry when unfavourable comparisons are made with Campina Grande and even shun the use of fashionable Havaianas (made in Campina Grande) in favour of rival flip-flop brands. The town has a long agricultural past. It grew from a big cattle farm owned by Captain José Rodrigues de Jesus, prospered exporting fruit and vegetables to Recife and, in 1895, underwent an economic boom with the arrival of the railways. This saw the construction of most of the handsome early Republican buildings gathered around the leafy central *praça* (square).

MARKETS

Nowadays the town is famous throughout Brazil for its local *ferias*, or markets, which were originally devoted to foodstuffs but which now also sell arts and crafts. The most famous is the Feira da Sulanca, held in the city centre on Tuesdays, with some 10,000 stalls and 40,000 visitors. Many of the clay figurines and wooden models sold in tourist shops in Brazil are produced in Caruaru. The best work, by local artisans like Zé Caboclo and Mestre Vitalino, are becoming increasingly valuable collectors' items.

FERNANDO DE NORONHA

This tiny archipelago, some 350km (217 miles) off the Brazilian coast, feel like Hebridean islands transposed into the tropics. Volcanic rocks as ancient and cracked as those found on Scotland's Isle of Mull form ocean-worn sea caves and crumbling headlands, between which are swathes of glorious sandy beaches. The sea is as emerald as the ocean around the Scottish isles, and equally as rich in marine life, but Noronha is close to the equator, making the water here much warmer, inviting and superb for scuba diving (▷ 260).

HISTORY

Noronha was first sighted in 1503 by the chronicler, Amérigo Vespucci (after whom the Americas were named, ▷ 26). They were a pirate lair during the early years of the Spanish and Portuguese colonies, being permanently settled by the Portuguese in the early 18th century. There is only one inhabited island, Fernando de Noronha itself; its satellites are little more than rocks poking out of the ocean. The Forte dos Remédios fort and the little baroque church of Nossa Senhora dos Remédios in the island's only town, Vila dos Remédios, date from this period. In World War II, Noronha was a US air base and afterwards a political prison for those who dared oppose Getúlio Vargas and the subsequent military regime (▷ 35). Many were tortured and murdered here.

ECOLOGY

The main island is a UNESCO World Heritage Site and a marine national park. Visitor numbers are restricted in order to prevent degradation but Noronha is not the ecological paradise it seems. Almost all of the native vegetation was chopped down in the 19th century, when a giant native rodent was wiped out and linseed, feral cats and dogs, goats, rats, mice, tegu lizards and cavies were introduced. These continue to damage bird and turtle nesting sites and native vegetation. Birds such as sooty tern, masked booby, white-tailed tropicbird and the endemic Noronha eared dove, or arribaçã, cling to life here. The most spectacular larger animals are the marine turtles (which nest on most of the islands' beaches) and the spinner dolphins, which live in the bays (especially Baía do Sancho).

INFORMATION

www.noronha.com.br
397 W6 inset Vila dos Remédios
81 3619 1378 Mon–Fri 10–6
From Recife or Natal (45 min); book ahead as visitor numbers are restricted

TIPS

» Allow two to three days for a visit to the island. It is small enough to be circumnavigated in a boat in less than three hours, but you will need time to soak up the atmosphere. There are *pousadas* throughout Noronha.
» Scuba trips can be arranged in Vila dos Remédios (▷ 260). Snorkel hire can be expensive, though, so bring your own.
» There is a hefty environment tax levied on visitors, starting at R$36 per day and rising with the length of stay.

Below *Baía do Sancho, looking towards Dois Irmãos*

LARANJEIRAS

www.laranjeiras.se.gov.br

This village of terracotta-tiled roofs, whitewashed cottages and colonial churches sits in gently undulating green hills, 23km (14 miles) from Aracaju (▷ 245). A tiny settlement was founded in 1594 but began to develop in earnest from 1701, when the Jesuits founded a chapel (A Capela de Santo Antônio) and a residence (O Retiro). Both buildings survive as national heritage buildings but can only be visited if arranged two days in advance. The church of Nossa Senhora da Conceição is equally interesting and easier to access, though it doesn't have fixed opening hours. It was the last church built by the Jesuits in the state and has a beautifully carved door frame and tranquil interior. There are a number of other religious buildings worth seeing but it is the village as a whole which is the main attraction, with its timeless sleepy feel and complete lack of tourists.

399 U9 Rua Sagrado Coração Jesus 90, Centro 79 3281 1054 Mon–Fri 10–6 From Aracaju

MACEIÓ

▷ 249.

MARECHAL DEODORO

www.marechaldeodoro.al.gov.br

The former capital of Alagoas state is another of the sleepy and unspoiled colonial towns which sit between Bahia and Pernambuco. It is situated on the shore of one of the large lakes which gives Alagoas its name, some 22km (13.5 miles) south of the current capital, Maceió (▷ 249). The town takes its name from its most famous citizen, Marechal Manuel Deodoro da Fonseca, the fierce and generously whiskered army marshall who became Brazil's first president after the deposition of Dom Pedro II on 15 November 1889 (▷ 35). Before his ascendance, the settlement was known simply as Cidade de Alagoas. The town has a forgotten feel; its beautiful churches crumble, the paint on its pretty 18th-century town houses peels and, when there are no cars passing, its streets are so quiet you could hear a mouse trot. The house where Deodoro grew up is now a small museum, the Museu Marechal Deodoro (daily 8–5; free), which is worth visiting for the insight it gives into life in 19th-century Brazil. The town is also celebrated for its macramé lace and for its musicians, including fiddle-player Nelson da Rabeca. One of the best beaches in the area, Praia do Francês, lies a few kilometres east of Marechal and you can visit both locations on a full- or half-day trip from Maceió.

399 U9 Rua Boa Vista 453, Centro 82 3315 5700 Mon–Fri 10–6 From Maceió

OLINDA

▷ 250–251.

PENEDO

Like Marechal Deodoro (▷ this page), Penedo is a preserved—if slowly decaying—colonial town. While tourists tramp the cobbles of Ouro Preto (▷ 188–189) and Paraty (▷ 146–147), they are rare in this old river port town in Alagoas state. Yet the town's site, on a curve of the blue Rio São Francisco, is as impressive as its colonial churches.

Penedo grew rich in the 17th century from the Minas gold and diamond trade. Bullion and stones were transported down the Rio São Francisco from Bahia and Minas on twin-masted *saveiro* yachts, still occasionally seen on the river today. The town's splendid churches all date from this period. They include Nossa Senhora da Corrente (Tue–Sun 8–5)—with a richly gilded nave and altarpiece, and paintings by the Pernambucan Portuguese artist, Libório Lázaro Lial—and the church of Nossa Senhora dos Anjos (Tue–Fri 8–11, 2–5, Sat–Sun 8–11). This has Portuguese-baroque filigree flourishes and a painting of God the Father watching over the world, surrounded by the three Brazilian races (indigenous, black and white).

399 U9 Avenida Floriano Peixoto 127, Centro 82 3551 2727 Mon–Fri 10–5 From Maceió and Aracaju

MACEIÓ

While having no individual sights of significant interest, the capital of Alagoas state is one of Brazil's most attractive coastal cities, with beautiful clean beaches, safe streets and a tiny colonial centre. Some of the best beaches in the northeast—long, fine white strands of sand under groves of coconut palms—lie a short drive or bus ride away, as does the sleepy former capital of Marechal Deodoro (▷ 248).

NOTABLE BUILDINGS

Maceió's old centre is filled with Portuguese colonial and Republican beaux arts and art deco buildings, and is small enough to walk around in less than an hour. Streets radiate from the main square, the Praça dos Martírios, around which early Maceió's most important buildings congregate. They include the Palácio do Governo and the 19th-century church of Bom Jesus dos Mártires, which is covered in Portuguese *azulejo* tiles.

MUSEUMS

On the same square as the town's ungainly cathedral, the Praça Dom Pedro II, is the Museu de Artes Pierre Chalita (tel 82 3223 4298; Mon–Fri 8–12, 2–5.30; adult R$3, child under 7 free), which houses more than 3,000 colonial paintings, pieces of silverware and furniture. It also includes a gallery showcasing Brazilian Modernist painters, including the founder of the *antropofagia* movement, Tarsila do Amaral (▷ 125). The city's other interesting museum is the Museu Théo Brandão (tel 82 3221 2651; Tue–Fri 9–5, Sat–Sun 2–5; R$2), which is devoted to northeastern popular culture, exhibiting some of the best ceramic pieces by traditional artists like Mestre Vitalino from Caruaru (▷ 246) and anthropomorphic models by local artist, Júlio Rufino.

BEACHES

Maceió is most famous for its beaches, which are washed by an impossibly aquamarine Atlantic. They include Trapiche and Avenida in front of the city, Pajuçara (which houses budget accommodation and a nightly crafts market), and Ponta Verde and Jatiúca, with clean sand, the best hotels and a pretty esplanade lined with cafés and restaurants.

INFORMATION

www.turismo.al.gov.br
399 U9 Rua Boa Vista 453, Centro 82 3315 5700 Mon–Fri 10–6 From all major tourist towns Campo dos Palmares

TIPS

» There are plenty of cafés and restaurants in the historical centre of town, ideal for cold juices and a break from the heat of the day.
» The city beaches of Trapiche and Avenida are too polluted for bathing; head for the cleaner sands of Jatiúca if you intend to spend any significant time on the shore.

Above *Pajuçara beach*
Opposite *Sunset over the church of Nossa Senhora da Corrente and the São Francisco river in Penedo*

INFORMATION

www.olinda.pe.gov.br

399 V8 Largo do Amparo 81 3439 9434 Mon–Fri 10–6 From all major tourist towns; the Rio Doce bus, number 891, runs between Recife and Olinda

Above *Nightlife in Praça da Sé*

INTRODUCTION

The cobbled streets and colourful houses of this delightful UNESCO-listed colonial city clamber over a series of hills next to the tropical Atlantic, a few kilometres north of Recife (▷ 254–257). It's a delightful place to wander around and a safer and more salubrious base for exploring the region than Recife. There are art galleries and arts and crafts shops in many of the colonial houses, and myriad magnificent colonial buildings and churches. The best way to see Olinda is on foot as the centre is compact and easily walkable in a long afternoon.

The city was founded in 1535, when the Portuguese captain of the Imperial donatory of Pernambuco declared: *'Oh, linda situação para se erguer una cidadela!' ('Oh, what a beautiful location to build a city!').* Like neighbouring Recife, Olinda grew wealthy through the sugar trade, resulting in the construction of opulent civic buildings and Jesuit and Franciscan colleges. In 1630, the city was overthrown and burnt by the Dutch, who made their capital of Mauritsstadt on the mangrove-swathed islands in Recife. When the Portuguese reconquered Pernambuco, they refurbished and rebuilt Olinda. The city became the capital of the state for a brief period from 1827.

WHAT TO SEE

BASILICA E MOSTEIRO DE SÃO BENTO

This monastery and church was founded in 1582 by Benedictine monks, burned by the Dutch in 1631 and subsequently restored in 1761. It is the site of Brazil's first law school and where slavery in Brazil was first abolished. The church has one of Brazil's most magnificent interiors, dominated by a towering tropical cedar altarpiece covered in gilt. There are fine carvings and paintings throughout.

Rua São Bento 81 3429 3288 Mon–Fri 8.30–11.30, 2.30–5; Mass Sat 6.30am and 6pm, Sun 10am with Gregorian chant Free

CATEDRAL BASILICA IGREJA DA SÉ

The best views in Olinda are from the cathedral, which sits high on a hill, overlooking the entire town and a sweep of beaches that lead to the distant skyscrapers of Recife. The church itself dates from 1540 but has undergone many changes and retains little of its original baroque finery. The great liberation theologian, Helder Camara, is buried inside.

Alto da Sé s/n · Mon–Fri 8–12, 2–5 · Free

IGREJA E CONVENTO FRANCISCANO DE NOSSA SENHORA DAS NEVES

The first Franciscan convent in Brazil lies hidden behind a discreet facade, tucked away on a small street near the cathedral. It is one of the most magnificent complexes of baroque buildings in the northeast. The Franciscans began construction of the buildings, which comprise the convent, the church of Nossa Senhora das Neves and the chapels of São Roque and St. Anne, in 1585. The convent cloisters and church are covered with beautiful blue and white Portuguese *azulejo* tiles, and the church and chapels have some exquisitely carved statues and paintings of the Holy Family.

Rua de São Francisco 280 · 81 3429 0517 · Mon–Fri 7–12, 2–5 · Adult R$4, child under 7 free

MORE TO SEE

MUSEU DO MAMULENGO

Olinda is famous for the giant puppets *(mamulengos)* which are marched through the streets during carnival. There are around 1,000 in this large museum, some of them more than 200 years old. The majority are caricatures of famous local figures, mostly politicians, musicians and celebrities.

Rua do Amparo 59 · 81 3429 6214 · Tue–Fri 8–5, Sat–Sun 10–5 · Free

MERCADO RIBEIRA

Olinda's bustling arts and crafts market sells clay figurines from Caruaru (▷ 246), small *mamulengo* masks, carnival costumes and *frevo* (a local dance and music style) umbrellas. It was once a slave market.

Rua Bernardo Vieira de Melo s/n · Daily 6am–midnight

OLINDA'S BEACHES

While they are immensely popular at weekends with locals, the town beaches are too dirty for swimming. For cleaner waters head north just 16km (10 miles) to Pau Amarelo, where there is a small semi-ruined Dutch fort and a Saturday night craft fair on the beachfront from 6pm.

TIPS

» Be extra vigilant with cameras and valuables during carnival in Olinda; pick-pocketing is common.

» Book accommodation for Olinda carnival at least three months in advance.

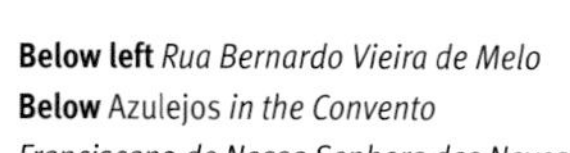

Below left *Rua Bernardo Vieira de Melo*
Below Azulejos *in the Convento Franciscano de Nossa Senhora das Neves*

PONTA DO SEIXAS

www.joaopessoa.pb.gov.br

This shallow-curving and forested cape on the southern outskirts of João Pessoa (▷ 245) is the most easterly point in the Americas. This fact is commemorated by a modest black and white lighthouse, called the Farol do Cabo Branco, shaped like a triangular prism. Some of Paraíba's best beaches are nearby. These include the urbanized Cabo Branco, a little to the north of the cape itself, Ponta do Seixas at the cape and Penha immediately to its south (which has a church where devotees make indulgences to the saints).

399 V8 Praça Amaro Ferraz Santa Rita, João Pessoa 83 3229 1897 Mon–Fri 9–5 From João Pessoa Presidente Castro Pinto (João Pessoa)

PORTO DE GALINHAS

www.portodegalinhas.tur.br

Pernambuco's busiest beach resort encircles this small fishing town, 60km (37 miles) south of Recife (▷ 254–257). The name Porto de Galinhas (Chicken Port) refers to its links to slave smuggling, as the code for a new shipment was 'the chickens have arrived'. Many died in transportation. The modern village was visited only by hippies from Recife and the southeast, until it was discovered by Brazilian television in the 1990s and resorts began to breed rapidly along the long coconut-fringed coast. The town itself now bristles with tourist shops, restaurants and cafés, and hundreds of touts offering trips on traditional *jangada* sailboats to the dead coral reefs which form natural pools a kilometre or so offshore.

399 V8 Rua da Esperança s/n 81 3552 1728 Daily 11–6 From Recife

RECIFE

▷ 254–257.

RIO SÃO FRANCISCO

www.caninde.se.gov.br

The São Francisco is the largest river to both originate and terminate in Brazil, the fourth longest in South America and the 20th longest on Earth. Amérigo Vespucci (▷ 26) passed the mouth of the river, in modern Sergipe and Alagoas states, in 1502. The indigenous name for the river at that time was Opará. The river drains an area of 630,000sq km (242,000sq miles) and is the only waterway to cut through the dry *sertão* region. It has long been a symbol of hope for the people that eke out a living in these hostile backlands. The Brazilian government has vote-winning, but scientifically misguided, plans to drain it and irrigate huge swathes of inland Bahia, Minas and the northeast. The flow of the São Francisco is already diminished by huge hydroelectric dams but for now it is still possible to take boat trips on the lower portions of the river along a series of magnificent Xingó Canyons (▷ 262).

399 T9

SÃO CRISTÓVÃO

Brazil's fourth oldest town, and Sergipe's first, sits perched on a hill 17km (10.5 miles) southwest of Aracaju (▷ 245). It is one of Latin America's colonial gems, yet few tourists make it here and visitors

Left *Farol de Cabo Branco lighthouse at Ponta do Seixas*

Below *Porto de Galinhas beach, Pernambuco*

are likely to have the town almost completely to themselves. It was founded by Cristóvão de Barros in 1590, and it seems to have changed little since its glory days in the 18th century. The city has a long and often troubled history. In 1637 it was invaded by the Dutch during their take-over of Pernambuco state. They left the town in semi-ruins when they were eventually expelled by the Portuguese in 1645. São Cristóvão was the capital of Sergipe state until it was replaced by Aracaju in 1855, after which time the town fell into sleepy doldrums.

There are few modern buildings and the tranquil and little tourist-tramped old centre is awash with whitewash, terracotta tiles thickly painted yellow, blue door frames and green window shutters. Some have elaborate Moorish balconies. Praça São Francisco in the centre of the town was granted UNESCO World Heritage status in 2010. The square is surrounded by historical buildings; these include some of the finest early Portuguese colonial buildings in northeast Brazil. The Santa Casa da Misericórdia and adjacent church and convent of São Francisco (Praça São Francisco s/n; Tue–Fri 10–12, 2–4, sporadic opening at weekends) are two of the most impressive baroque buildings in the town. The church (1693) has beautiful rococo stucco work and fine *azulejos*, with a simple white baroque interior and *trompe l'oeil* ceiling. It is also home to a sacred art museum. The Convento do Carmo (Praça do Carmo s/n; Tue–Fri 10–12, 2–4, sporadic opening at weekends), which dates from 1699, sits in the upper part of the city and has an impressive carved doorway and a classic whitewashed baroque pediment with lavish florid decoration. There is a museum of votive offerings in the convent (free), with hundreds of petitions. Other buildings worth looking out for include the churches of Nossa Senhora da Vitória, Nossa Senhora do Rosário dos Homens Pretos and the Mosteiro São Bento, all with impressive facades but currently closed to the public.

The town makes a pleasant half-day trip from Aracaju and visits here can be combined with trips to Laranjeiras (▷ 248).

399 U10 Travessa Baltazar Gois 86, Centro, Aracaju 79 3179 1932 Mon–Fri 10–6 Aeroporto de Aracaju Santa Maria From Aracaju

SOUSA, CARIRI AND INGÁ

www.cmsousa.pb.gov.br

The interior of Paraíba state is dotted with pre-Columbian and prehistoric sites. At Sousa, petroglyphs and dinosaur footprints have been found, the latter fossilized in Jurassic river mud. At Cariri, giant wind and rain-sculpted boulders once used as caves by a *sertão* hermit are daubed with ancient rock art, and at nearby Ingá, archaeologists have unearthed a 25m-long (82ft) boulder covered with mysterious petroglyph inscriptions, dated to 8000BC. All can be visited on tours with Natal operator Manary (▷ 260) or, with more difficulty, on public transport. Cariri and Ingá lie close to Campina Grande (▷ 245), in Paraíba. Sousa is 300km (186 miles) to the northwest.

Sousa 396 T7; Cariri 399 U8; Ingá 399 V8 From Campina Grande

Above *Petroglyphs at Ingá, dating from 8000BC*

RECIFE

INTRODUCTION

Together with Salvador (▷ 114–121), Recife is the cultural and economic capital of northeastern Brazil, and one of the most important cities in the country. It has some magnificent baroque buildings from the 17th- and 18th-century sugar boom, a very lively music scene, captivating traditional folklore and one of the most authentic carnivals in the country (▷ 263). The city takes its name from the coral reefs *(recifes)* that lie off its shore.

The old Portuguese capital of Pernambuco state was at neighbouring Olinda (▷ 250–251). However, when the Dutch came and conquered Pernambuco in 1630, they burnt Olinda and built their own capital on the mangrove-fringed islands below. Dutch Recife covered a series of islands in the Capibaribe estuary, which form the modern-day neighbourhoods of Recife Antigo, Santo Antônio and Boa Vista. These are the focus of Recife's famous nightlife today, and of the Recife carnival. When the Portuguese reconquered Pernambuco, they settled in Recife as well as Olinda, further expanding the city and building some of the most striking churches and civic palaces in the country. Little remains of the original Dutch capital, except a line of remodelled tall houses on the banks of the river in Boa Vista and the massive Forte do Brum, at the northern end of Recife Antigo (Old Recife) island.

INFORMATION

www.recife.pe.gov.br

+ 399 V8 **i** Praça Artur Oscar ☎ 81 3425 1700 ◷ Mon–Sat 10–5 🚌 From all major tourist towns; the Rio Doce bus, number 891, runs between Recife and Olinda ✈ Guararapes

WHAT TO SEE

RECIFE ANTIGO

This grid of handsome colonial and Republican streets overlooking the Atlantic is the spiritual heart of Recife. Many of the city's famous bars lie here and most of the city's carnival action takes place around the Marco Zero, an open space which is named after a plaque marking the official centre of both Recife Antigo and the city as a whole. Forte do Brum (tel 81 3224 8492; Tue–Fri 9–6, Sat–Sun 1–5; free), the old Dutch fort from which Recife grew, lies at the northern end of the island. At the other end is the Kahal Zur Israel Synagogue (tel 81 3224 2128; Tue–Fri 10–12, 2–5; R$4), originally built in 1637 under Dutch rule (when the 'New Christians', who were Jews and Muslims forced to convert under the Inquisition, were given freedom to worship). It was the first synagogue in the Americas. When the Portuguese returned they expelled the Jews, many of whom left for Suriname, and destroyed the building. The synagogue was rebuilt in the 20th century.

+ Forte do Brum 257 C1; Kahal Zur Israel Synagogue 257 C2

CONCATEDRAL DE SÃO PEDRO DO CLÉRIGOS

This imposing baroque church, sitting behind one of central Recife's busiest public squares, dates from 1728. It is made up of two massive towers astride a typical Portuguese baroque facade, with an elaborately carved door and window frames. Behind is an unusual octagonal nave. The interior is surprisingly plain, as the nave was stripped of its original decoration (but for two gilt pulpits and a *trompe l'oeil* painting by the Pernambuco artist, João de Deus Sepúlveda) in the 19th century.

+ 257 B3 ✉ Rua São Pedro s/n, Santo Antônio ☎ 81 3224 2954 ◷ Mon–Fri 8–11, 2–5, Sat–Sun 8–5 ✋ Free

CAPELA DOURADA

The Capela Dourada, or Golden Chapel, is Recife's most lavish piece of baroque architecture. The chapel was built in 1697 by a wealthy lay brotherhood, the Ordem Terceira de São Francisco de Assis, and is covered almost entirely in gold leaf and decorated with fine baroque carvings and paintings. The chapel is

Opposite *The Palace of Justice on Praça da Republica*

TIPS

» Last entry to the Instituto Ricardo Brennand is at 4.30, half an hour before it closes, but you should allow at least 90 minutes for a visit.

» Be careful swimming on Recife's beaches, especially at Boa Viagem, where there have been shark attacks.

» Olinda is a better place to stay over and is close enough to be used as a base for visiting Recife. Recife's hotels are scruffy and the city can be dangerous at night.

» As well as being Brazil's most colourful and traditional large carnival, all the events are free in Recife and Olinda.

part of a complex that also includes the Igreja São Francisco and the convent of Santo Antônio.

257 B2 Rua do Imperador s/n, Santo Antônio 81 3224 0530 Mon–Fri, Sun 8–11, 2–5 R$2

INSTITUTO RICARDO BRENNAND

www.institutoricardobrennand.org.br

This fake Norman castle, complete with moat and castellated walls, houses the priceless art, armour and document collection of a scion of the wealthy Brennand family. Paintings include the largest conglomeration of Dutch-Brazilian landscapes in the world, mostly by Franz Post (1612–80). There are hundreds of suits of armour (including some for dogs and children), magnificent Toledo swords, and antique books and manuscripts from Dutch and early Portuguese colonial Pernambuco.

257 off A2 Alameda Antônio Brennand, Várzea 81 2121 0352 Tue–Sun 1–5 R$5; free on Tue

OFICINA BRENNAND

www.brennand.com.br

This surreal fantasy garden and ceramic museum showcases the work of Latin America's most celebrated Modernist ceramic artist, Francisco Brennand (cousin to Ricardo Brennand, ▷ this page). Ceramic snakes emerge wriggling from lawns, serried ranks of egrets look down from towering walls over formal fountains and ponds designed by Burle Marx (▷ 121), and in the gallery itself there are hundreds of pieces by the artist. The museum has a good air-conditioned restaurant and gift shop.

257 off D2 Propriedade Santos Cosme e Damião s/n, Várzea 81 3271 2466 Mon–Thu 8–5, Fri 8–4 Adult R$10, child under 7 free

Below *Concatedral de São Pedro do Clérigos in Pátio de São Pedro*

BOA VIAGEM

The long urban strip of sand of Boa Viagem beach stretches for 7km (4 miles). Lined by towering buildings, including hulking international hotels, the sands are filled with sunbathers and beach sellers. The coastal reef protects the beach and gives rise to calm water. There has been some local environmental damage caused when a new port was constructed.

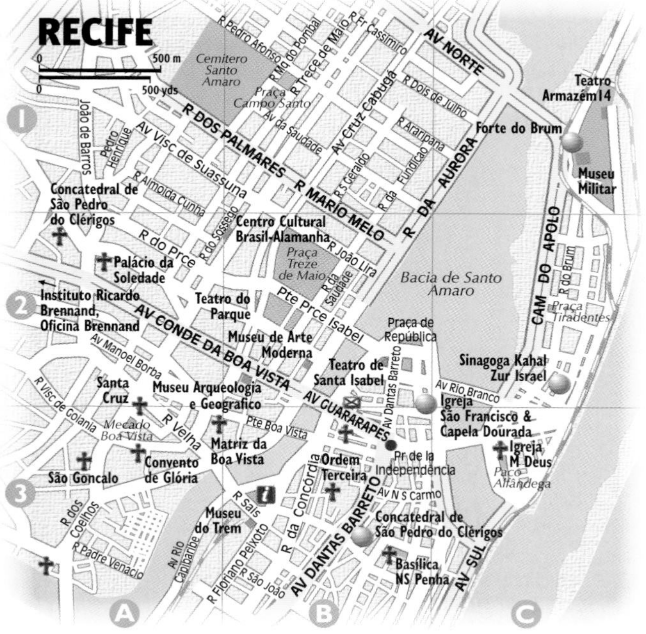

Above left *Sculpture garden and fountain at Oficina Brennand*
Above right *Cloisters at Capela da Ordem Terceira de São Francisco de Assis*

ALONG THE NORONHA BEACHES

This walk takes in the most spectacular beaches on Fernando de Noronha's north shore. It begins at the beach of Cacimba do Padre and ends in the little colonial town of Vila dos Remédios. It requires some scrambling over rocks and rock pools in the open sun but has great opportunities for a swim to cool down.

THE WALK
Distance: 3.5km (2.2 miles)
Time: 3–4 hours with stops for a swim
Start at: Praia Cacimba do Padre
End at: Vila dos Remédios town

HOW TO GET THERE

Take a taxi to a trail leading down to Praia Cacimba do Padre, or a trail from adjacent Baía do Sancho.

★ Start on the beach at Cacimba do Padre and walk east to its far end, where there are a series of rock pools which are perfect for a paddle. Look out for sand dollars (a kind of sea urchin) along the way.

❶ Praia da Cacimba do Padre is one of Brazil's most magnificent beaches. It stretches for 900m (980 yards) as a broad expanse of talcum powder-fine sand which squeaks when you walk across it. International surf championships are held here every summer, when waves reach up to 5m (16.5ft) high. Two tiny, pyramid islands, Os Dois Irmãos, watch over its western end.

At the end of the beach is a rocky headland. A trail leads up through the forest here. Climb for spectacular views over Cacimba do Padre to the west and the hook-shaped Morro do Pico to the east. When you have taken in the scenery, clamber down to the next beach.

❷ Praia do Bode has gentler waves than Cacimba do Padre and is a good spot for a swim. Continue east along the beach to reach another headland and clamber over here for the next beach. Look for noddies and boobies, sea birds which roost and nest on the island.

❸ This next beach is Praia do Americano, which has gentle waves and soft sand. US marines were based here in World War II, giving the beach its name. At low tide it's possible to walk round the rocks from here to the neighbouring beach to the east, Praia do Boldró. Exposed reefs on this latter beach form rock pools at low tide, large enough to swim in. At high tide the surf is good.

The trail climbs from the eastern end of Boldró, through more scrubby forest and around the base of the

Morro do Pico. Look out for the endangered Noronha vireo—a tiny pale-breasted bird—and the jay-like Noronha elaenia in the trees; they are two of the island's three endemic bird species (the third being the Noronha eared dove). There are more wonderful views east and west at the top of the path.

❹ The next beach is Praia da Conceição, which presents another swimming opportunity as waters are usually calm. A large rock called Pião sticks out of the beach with a distinctive narrow base and flat top. There are more natural swimming pools here at low tide at the far eastern end of the beach.

Climb over the next headland to the final beaches, Praia do Meio and the adjacent Praia do Cachorro. The latter offers some of the best swimming, as waves are broken by offshore reefs. A trail leads inland from either beach to Vila dos Remédios. Visit the old Portuguese fort on the hill, Forte dos Remédios (▷ 247), which doubled-up as a prison during the dictatorship, and the tiny church of Nossa Senhora dos Remédios (▷ 247), before having a cold juice or beer at a café in town.

Opposite *The sun sets behind Pião on Praia da Conceição*
Right *Baía do Sancho lies next to Praia da Cacimba do Padre*
Below *Lovely Praia da Cacimba do Padre, where the walk starts*

WHEN TO GO

Noronha is beautiful at any time and at its greenest between March and May.

WHERE TO EAT

CACIMBA BISTRO

Grilled fish or meat and ice-cold beer and juices.
✉ Praça Eurico Dutra 9, Vila dos Remédios ☎ 81 3619 1200 🕔 Daily 10–5

INFORMATION

www.noronha.com.br
✚ 397 W6 inset ℹ Vila dos Remédios
☎ 81 3619 1378 🕔 Mon–Fri 10–6
✈ From Recife or Natal (45 min); book ahead as visitor numbers are restricted

TIPS

» Crocs or sturdy beach sandals are ideal footwear for this walk, and be sure to bring sun cream and a beach hat, as well as swimwear and a towel if you want to take advantage of the fantastic calm waters.
» Carry at least a litre of water and a snack with you, as there is nowhere to buy either along the way.

CARIRI

MANARY

www.caririecotours.com.br

This excellent company has been taking eco/cultural tours around the *sertão* and especially to Sousa and Cariri for over a decade. Their emphasis is geological and archaeological. Trips in jeeps or small buses (depending on numbers) are well-organized and comfortable.

✉ Rua Francisco Gurgel, Ponta Negra Beach, Natal ☎ 84 9928 0198

FERNANDO DE NORONHA

AGUAS CLARAS

www.aguasclaras-fn.com.br

Fernando de Noronha has some of the best diving in the south Atlantic. There are extensive coral reefs around the islands and the opportunity for drift and wreck diving. Turtles are abundant here and there is a large colony of spinner dolphins living off the island's north coast. The Aguas Claras company has been organizing dive trips for many years and instructors are PADI gold members.

✉ Vila dos Remédios s/n ☎ 84 3206 4354 🕑 Usually Mon–Sun 10–6

MACEIÓ

DEL (JOSE DOS SANTOS FILHO)

This excellent tour guide has tours along the coast and to the colonial towns, including Marechal Deodoro (▷ 248). Del has a good command of English and is very knowledgeable about northeastern traditions.

☎ 82 3241 4966 or 82 8859 34079 (mobile)

LAMPIÃO

This exuberant seafront dance bar has live *forró* music every night from a band dressed in traditional *sertão* outfits. Music includes *forró* standards from the great mestre Luíz Gonzaga and more modern *forró* pop. There are *petiscos* (tapas-like snacks) and comfort food available (chicken/fish/meat and beans and rice), alongside bottles of cold beer served in coolers.

✉ Avenida Alvaro Otacílio 47, Praia de Jatiúca ☎ 82 3325 4376 🕑 Tue–Sun 6–late 🎟 R$5 after 9pm

MAIKAI

www.maikaimaceio.com.br

Maceió's biggest club plays popular regional music with live bands on a high stage. At weekends there are crowds of thousands. The music is mostly energetic Bahian *axé* pop.

✉ Rua Engenheiro Paulo B Nogueira, quadra 14 ☎ 82 3305 4400 🕑 Tue–Sat 6–late 🎟 Admission R$20

OLINDA

BODEGA DO VEIO

There is live regional music here from Thursday to Sunday every week. Saturday nights are occasionally hosted by famous local fiddle player, Mestre Salustiano. The rum and fruit *caipirinha* cocktails are strong and cold, and the bar serves *petiscos* and simple food.

✉ Rua do Amparo 212 ☎ 81 3429 0185 🕑 Thu–Sun 7–12

Opposite *Scuba diving at Fernando de Noronha*

CASA DA RABECA

www.casadarabeca.com.br

This simple bar and adjacent concert hall nestled in forest on the outskirts of Olinda is the best place in the city to hear traditional local bands. It was founded by one of the most influential roots musicians in Pernambuco, Mestre Salustiano, who hosts shows most weekend nights. Music is predominantly traditional *forró (forró pé-de-serra)*—a bouncy two-step jig played on fiddles and accordion. Dancing is exuberant and acrobatic. The bar offers choice *petiscos*, including fried chicken in Pernambuco herbs, and roasted *sertão* goat.

✉ Rua Curupira 340, Cidade Tabajara, Olinda ☎ 81 3437 7207 🕐 Sat 9–late, Sun 5–12 💳 R$10–R$20

CHEVROLET HALL

www.chevrolethall.wcms.com.br

Recife and Olinda's premier concert hall hosts big international and national acts most weekends. In the past they have included the Cranberries and Bahian superstars Ivete Sangalo and Chiclete com Banana. Crowds are huge and very lively. Booking ahead is essential.

✉ Armazém Central Complexo de Salgadinho, Avenida Pan Nordestina 314, Santa Tereza, Olinda ☎ 81 3429 4467

MERCADO DA RIBEIRA

This lively local covered market on the road between Olinda and Recife has dozens of stalls selling everything from tropical fruits—like mangoes and papayas—to arts, crafts and musical intstruments. Adjacent souvenir shops proffer similar fare and some even sell *mamelucos* (giant street puppets).

✉ Rua Bernardo Vieira de Melo 🕐 Daily 9–6

PRETO VELHO

There are great views from the plastic tables at this simple bar on the hill near the cathedral. Locals come to drink an ice-cold bottle of beer and, on weekend nights, to dance to regional music from established Olinda and Recife artists such as Mestre Salustiano.

✉ Rua Bispo Coutinho 681 ☎ 81 9927 1474 🕐 Tue–Sun 6–12

PORTO DE GALINHAS

BIROSCA DA CACHAÇA

www.biroscadacachaca.com.br

This dance bar near the beach is extremely popular with young singles. Shows range from local and international DJs spinning Brazilian and European club music, to a selection of live bands.

✉ Rua Beijupirá 5, Porto de Galinhas ☎ 81 3552 2699 🕐 Tue–Sun 8–late 💳 R$10–R$20

CHICKEN CLUB

Beachside *forró* and strong *caipirinhas* make this one of the most popular bars in Porto de Galinhas. Things hot up from around 9pm on any night in the summer and are at their liveliest on weekends when students from Recife overflow onto the sand.

✉ Avenida Beira Mar s/n 🕐 Dec–Mar daily 1–12; Apr–Nov Tue–Sun 6–12

RECIFE

ARMAZÉM 14

This small concert venue is played by the best of the mangue beat (▷ 17) and new alternative Pernambuco acts. There are live bands on most weekends and in the past the cream of Recife rock have starred here, including Nação Zumbi, Mundo Livre s/a and newcomers Mombojo.

✉ Avenida Alfredo Lisboa s/n, Cais do Porto, Recife Antigo ☎ 81 3424 5613 🕐 Fri–Sun from 8pm, depending on the show

AUDITÓRIO DOS DIARIOS ASSOCIADOS

This small concert hall in the suburb of Santo Amaro hosts a variety of shows, from classical concerts to cutting-edge contemporary music. The latter includes the Projeto Vitrine arts festival (usually June–July), whose acts have included bands like Grupo Taquara, celebrated for mixing classical music virtuosity and northeastern Brazilian rhythms.

✉ Rua do Veiga 600, Santo Amaro ☎ 81 3320 2020 🕐 Usually 7–12, depending on the show ❓ Taxis cost around R$20 from Recife city centre

BORATCHO

www.boratcho.com.br

This Mexican bar is decorated with art by local artists and has been hosting great Recife bands for nearly a decade.

✉ Galeria Joana Darc, Pina ☎ 81 3327 1168 🕐 Thu–Sat 7–late

BURBURINHO

This spit-and-sawdust bar tucked into a crumbling house in old Recife town has been at the cutting edge of breaking new local bands for more than a decade. There's always an interesting act playing on a Friday and Saturday night, and a lively crowd of locals sipping bottled beer and snacking on *petiscos,* which include delicious *bolinhos de bacalhau* (salted cod balls).

✉ Rua Tomazina 106, Recife Antigo ☎ 81 3224 5854 🕐 Thu–Sat 7–late

CENTRAL

www.centralrecife.com.br

One of the most sophisticated drinking spots in terms of atmosphere and clientele in Recife, with cold beer, decent food and occasional live bands.

✉ Rua Mamede Simões 144, Boa Vista ☎ 81 3222 7622 🕐 Mon–Sat 8–12

CINE PASTEL AND SHOPPING BOA VISTA

www.shoppingboavista.com.br

This multiplex cinema is the closest to Recife's city centre and shows Brazilian and international major release films. Most are dubbed into Portuguese (marked DUB, for *dublado)*. Films shown in English are marked LEG *(legendas*, with subtitles). It is within an air-conditioned shopping mall.

✉ Rua do Giriquiti 48 ☎ 81 3423 5666 🕐 Shopping mall open Mon–Sat 9–10, Sun 12–8 (doors close after the last film finishes, around midnight)

CINE AND SHOPPING TACARUNA

www.shoppingtacaruna.com.br
This state of the art multiplex on the top floor of Recife's plushest shopping mall shows the latest international blockbusters on huge modern screens. Many releases are shown in English with subtitles. Films shown in English are marked LEG *(legendas*, with subtitles), those dubbed into Portuguese are marked DUB *(dublado*, dubbed).
Avenida Governador Agamenon Magalhães 153, Santo Amaro 81 3412 6000 Shopping mall open Mon–Sat 9–10, Sun 12–8 (doors close after the last film finishes, around midnight)

CLUBE PORTUGUÊS

www.clubeportuguesdorecife.com.br
This sports hall doubles up as a medium-sized concert venue at weekends and always has an interesting billing of classy Brazilian and Latin American acts. These have included performers like reggae singer Edson Gomes and Mexican crooner Maite Perroni. There are sporting events too, including handball matches, table tennis and floor hockey.
Avenida Rosa e Silva 172, Graças 81 3231 5400 Thu–Sat 7–12

DEPOIS DANCING BAR

Live bands are followed by local DJs in this very popular club. There are three areas: a whisky bar serving cold beers and Jack Daniels, and two dance halls with live bands or DJs.
Avenida Rio Branco 66 81 3424 7451 Thu–Sun 9–late R$10

DOWNTOWN PUB

www.downtownpub.com.br
This mock-British pub heaves with Pernambuco teenagers at weekends, who come to listen to rowdy, newly-breaking local twenty-something bands playing regional rock. Tables spill into the street, and drinks and food are limited to bottled beer and toasted sandwiches.
Rua Vigário Tenório 105, Recife Antigo 81 3424 5731 Wed–Sat 9–1am, Sun 9–12 R$20

NOX

www.clubnox.com.br
This mood-lit, faux-Ibiza dance club has a thumping sound system. National and international DJs play on weekend nights in the only space in Recife for those craving European dance music. The main floor has space for almost 500 and the upstairs lounge offers bar snacks by local celebrity chef Douglas Van Der Ley.
Avenida Domingos Ferreira 2422, Boa Viagem 81 3326 8836 Thu–Sat 9–late R$30

TREM DO FORRÓ

www.tremdoforro.com.br
Every June, during the Festas Juninas, this designated Festa de São João train and associated tour leaves for Caruaru (▷ 246) from the Marco Zero (▷ 255) in the centre of Recife. There is *forró* music and dancing within the train for the entire two-hour journey and the wagons are all painted in garish festival colours. Few foreign tourists climb on board. The tour is bookable only through the tour operator, Serrambi.
Serrambi, Rua da Amizade 38, Graças 81 3423 5000 Jun only, usually Mon–Fri 10–6 R$15 Tours include a pick-up from the hotel on request. Consult the website or contact Serrambi for annual variations in timetable

UK PUB

www.ukpub.com.br
Since the pioneers of mangue beat fused British new wave with local rhythms in the 1980s (▷ 17), Recife has had a love affair with the UK. This vibrant city-centre bar is a homage to London pubs, with draught beer on tap (none of it ale), a happy hour (usually from 7pm) and bar snacks (Brazilian *petiscos*, like cod balls). There's live music or DJs at weekends and a crowd aged from 18 to 30-something.
Rua Francisco da Cunha 165, Boa Viagem 81 3465 1088 Daily 7–12 Admission R$20 (for shows)

RIO SÃO FRANCISCO

BARCOS COMPLEXO DO XINGÓ

Boats for trips to the Xingó Canyons (▷ 252) leave from the quayside of the tiny *sertão* town of Canindé de São Francisco in northwestern Sergipe. They take you to the deserted white sand beaches at the river's mouth near Penedo in Alagoas. The tours cannot be booked in advance, so it's just a question of arriving and jumping on board. Trip lengths vary according to the destination—from an hour to the canyons, to three hours if you include the beaches.
Cais do Canindé s/n

Below *Street performers on Rua da Moeda in Recife*

FESTIVALS AND EVENTS

FEBRUARY–MARCH

CARNAVAL

www.carnavaldorecife.com.br
http://carnaval.olinda.pe.gov.br
The most traditional and least touristy street carnivals in Brazil take place in the twin cities of Recife and Olinda, both of which are entirely free and commence, as all *Mardi Gras* carnivals, on the weekend before Shrove Tuesday.

Recife's carnival takes place in Recife Antigo (Old Recife). On the Friday, in the streets around the Pátio de São Pedro, there are spectacular *maracatú* parades, with troupes of up to 100 drummers and *blocos* (groups dressed in colourful costumes and swirling white dresses). Naná Vasconcelos, the great Recife percussionist, opens *carnaval*. Next morning there is a huge Cock of the Dawn parade (Galo da Madrugada), which is said by locals to be the largest street gathering in the world. Despite its name, this usually begins at around 10am. Floats with many of the most famous stars—like Lenine, Alceu Valença and Eddie—pass through the teeming crowds. Carnival shows continue until dawn on stages dotted around Old Recife for the next five nights.

In Olinda, there are parades and parties on the steep cobbled streets between pretty 18th-century houses and opulent churches overlooking the shimmering Atlantic. Troupes of acrobatic *frevo* dancers, twirling umbrellas, wander through the throng playing and dancing with effortless gymnastic flexibility, between the costumed crowds and parades of giant puppets. Local people form costumed groups, or *blocos*, which you can join as they pass. These *blocos* include O Homem da Meianoite and Elefantes. The streets of Olinda become very crowded and all the accommodation is booked up. Be prepared to base yourself in Recife and travel in (by bus and taxi) each day.

MARCH–APRIL

SEMANA SANTA

www.novajerusalem.com.br
Caruaru celebrates Semana Santa (Holy Week) on Good Friday by staging Brazil's most famous Easter pageant—a re-enactment of the trial and crucifixion of Christ—at the village of Nova Jerusalem, near the town of Fazenda Nova. TV Globo soap-opera stars often appear as the key players.

APRIL

PRO-ROCK FESTIVAL

www.reciferock.com.br
Recife hosts a celebration of rock, hip-hop and mangue beat (▷ 17) at the Centro de Convenções, Complexo de Salgadinho and other venues. Dates for the festival vary (and are published on the website) but it usually takes place over the second or third weekend in April.

JUNE

FESTAS JUNINAS

According to the people of the Paraíba, the Festas Juninas in Campina Grande (▷ 245) are the biggest in the world, though Pernambucans claim this for their city, Caruaru (▷ 246). They construct a designated and purpose-built *forró* village each year, and host huge stages with performances by *forró* pop bands.

Caruaru competes enthusiastically with Campina Grande to host the largest and most exuberant Festas Juninas, with a similar and equally enticing mix of traditional and contemporary *forró* bands. The whole town is illuminated with flashing lights and revellers in hicky costumes arrive in huge numbers from Recife on the Trem do Forró (▷ 262).

In Recife, the Festas Juninas mean big celebrations for the whole month all over the city, especially on the final weekend of June. This coincides with the Festa de São João (the Feast of St. John). There is much dancing, especially to *forró*, a great number of processions and general revelry.

JULY

FESTA DA NOSSA SENHORA DO CARMO

For the week of 11–16 July, Recife commemorates the saint's day of the patron saint of the city with dances and celebrations in the old city centre. Processions led by costumed *frevo* dancers leave from the Marco Zero (▷ 255), accompanied by troupes of drummers, and the whole city uses the *festa* as an excuse to party.

OCTOBER

RECIFOLIA

www.recifolia.com.br
Recife sees a repetition of *carnaval* over a whole weekend; dates vary, see website for details.

NOVEMBER–MARCH

SURF CHAMPIONSHIPS

Various international surf championships are held at Praia Cacimba do Padre, Fernando de Noronha. They are usually between November and March, when waves reach up to 5m (16.5ft) high.

DECEMBER

IEMANJÁ

Recife holds one of the biggest *candomblé/umbanda* festivals of the year during the week of 1–8 December. Most of the events are open to devotees of the African-Brazilian spirit religions only, and there is little for tourists, but you will see groups of women dressed in white walking throughout the city, and presenting votive offerings on the beaches of Boa Viagem to the south of the centre. These usually take place at sunset and dawn.

EATING

PRICES AND SYMBOLS

The restaurants are listed alphabetically (excluding A, Al, El, La, Le and O). The prices given are the average for a two-course lunch (L) and a three-course dinner (D) for one person, without drinks. The wine price is for the least expensive bottle. Although you will find wine served in restaurants throughout Brazil, the usual drinks are bottled beer (R$5–R$8) or *caipirinhas*, the ubiquitous *cachaça* and fruit cocktails (R$8). All the restaurants listed accept credit cards unless otherwise stated.

For a key to the symbols, ⊳ 2.

ARACAJU

CANTINA D'ITALIA

www.cantinaditalia.com.br

This Italian restaurant offers a menu of pasta and risottos, and crispy wood-fired pizzas. However, the expensive cars parked outside attest to it being the most popular Italian in town, as well as being a fashionable beachside spot for sunset. The best tables and views are on the top deck.

Avenida Santos Dumont s/n 79 3243 3184 Tue–Sun 12–3, 7–11 L R$20, D R$30, Wine R$34

CARIRI

www.cariri-se.com.br

There are several lively bar-restaurants on this beachfront strip. Cariri has a great kitchen, offering regional favourites like *frango caipira* (chicken cooked in a tomato and onion sauce) or *moqueca de camarão* (prawn broth cooked in coconut milk and dendê oil, and seasoned with herbs). There's live *forró* music Tuesdays to Saturdays.

Avenida Santos Dumont 243 79 3243 1379 Tue–Sat 12–3, 7–11 L R$15, D R$25, Wine R$28

CAMPINA GRANDE

SAPORE D'ITALIA

www.saporeditalia.net

This pizzeria serves great Margaritas and Napolitanas in Campina Grande and is very popular with local families. The restaurant has a delivery service to hotels and homes.

Rua Santo Antônio 74 83 3341 5859 Daily 6–11 D R$35, Wine R$40

MACEIÓ

AKUABA

www.akuaba.com.br

This brightly decorated restaurant, whose walls are hung with traditional northeast Brazilian arts and crafts, serves delicious African-Brazilian cooking. Dishes include Bahian favourites like *moqueca de camarão*, with prawns.

Rua Ferroviário Manuel Gonçalves Filho 6, Mangabeiras 82 3325 6199 Tue–Sun 12–3, 6–11 L R$15, D R$40, Wine R$35

BARRICA'S

www.barricaspizzaria.com.br

This beachfront bar attracts everyone from courting couples to families, who come for the huge menu of wood-fired pizzas, pastas, grilled and fried meat, seafood and pan-fried fish. There is live music at the bar every weekend.

Avenida Álvaro Calheiros 354, Ponta Verde 82 3327 0909 Daily 12–3, 6–11 L R$20, D R$35, Wine R$ 30

DIVINA GULA

www.divinagula.com.br

This fine regional restaurant is run by portly Algoan chef André Generoso. The walls of the big open-plan dining room are plastered with photos of celebrities like ZeZe di Camargo and Vanessa da Mata sampling dishes from the huge menu. This includes everything from roast suckling pig and chicken cooked in passion fruit sauce, to *tutu de feijão Mineira* (mashed beans with Minas Gerais sausage, beef shank, rice and plantain). One portion is often big enough for two people.

Rua Engenheiro Paulo B. Nogueira 85 82 3235 1016 Tue–Sun 12–3, 7–12 L R$40, D R$70, Wine R$36

Opposite *Diners in Oficina do Sabor restaurant in Olinda*

KHARRUF

This Arabic restaurant, on the most chic street corner on fashionable Jatiúca beach, serves Middle Eastern *petisco* snacks, like *kibe* (deep-fried spicy meatballs) and falafel, alongside hearty main courses. Many dishes use lamb from the owner's farm.
✉ Avenida Álvaro Octacílio 6595, Praia de Jatiúca ☎ 82 3355 2323 🕐 Tue–Sun 12–3, 7–12 🖐 L R$50, D R$65

LUA CHEIA

This beachside restaurant has a huge dining area overlooking the Atlantic and serves regional dishes made with fresh, locally sourced ingredients, including Alagoas kid encrusted with *sertão* herbs and duck breast in pepper sauce.
✉ Rodovia AL-101 Norte, km14, Garça Torta ☎ 82 3355 1186 🕐 Tue–Sun 12–3, 7–12 🖐 L R$50, D R$65, Wine R$45

WANCHAKO

www.wanchako.com.br
Lima's gourmet scene arrived in Brazil with this kitchen, run by Peruvian ex-pat Jose Bert and his Alagoas wife, Simone. Food is Andean and Nipo-Peruvian, featuring dishes like prawn with pumpkin tarts, green banana and spinach, alongside Peruvian standards like ceviche (fish pickled in citrus and spices). Drinks include delicious pisco sours.
✉ Rua São Francisco de Assis 93, Jatiúca ☎ 82 3377 6024 🕐 Mon–Thu 7–12.30, Fri 12–4, 7–12.30, Sat 7–12 🖐 L R$50, D R$90, Wine R$40

OLINDA

OFICINA DO SABOR

www.oficinadosabor.com
Chef Cesar Santos has been wooing locals to his colourful dining room and alfresco terrace with an ocean view for almost 20 years. They come for traditional Lusitanian dishes like *bacalhau* (salted codfish), Pernambuco catch of the day cooked in ginger sauce, and surubim catfish in passion fruit soubise with sautéed sweet potato and rice. The restaurant has won more awards than any in Olinda, including 10 coveted *Veja* magazine awards.
✉ Rua do Amparo 355 ☎ 81 3429 3331 🕐 Tue–Fri 12–4, 6–12, Sat 12–1am, Sun 12–5 🖐 L R$60, D R$70, Wine R$45

XINXIM DA BAIANA

Pumping Bahian music and northeastern sounds from a 1960s jukebox accompany plates of steaming *moqueca* (Bahian stew) and Bahian bar *petiscos* (Brazilian tapas) in this popular restaurant, which is always packed with locals of all ages, from families with toddlers to elderly couples. On Wednesday nights, from 9pm, there is *forró* dancing.
✉ Praça do Carmo 742, Carmo ☎ 81 8634 3330 🕐 Tue–Sun 12–3, 7–12 🖐 L R$30, D R$50

PORTO DE GALINHAS

BEIJUPIRÁ

www.beijupira.com.br
The resort's most romantic restaurant serves ultra-fresh seafood al fresco at candlelit tables. Most dishes are flavoured with *beijupirá*—a *sertão* and *cerrado* herb—and mix seafood with Brazilian fruits like the sharp pitanga.
✉ Rua Beijupirá, Beira Mar ☎ 81 3552 2354 🕐 Daily 12–3, 7–12 🖐 L R$50, D R$90, Wine R$40

RECIFE

É

www.egastronomia.com.br
Chef Douglas Van Der Ley serves classic French dishes with a Brazilian twist, with plates like fillet steak with foie gras, accompanied by sweet potato purée and cheese tartlet. The sumptuous dining room has warm colours, lounge music and low light. Be sure to try something from the dessert menu, which changes, literally, daily.
✉ Rua do Atlantico 147, Pina ☎ 81 3325 9323 🕐 Tue–Sat 8–1.30am 🖐 D R$90, Wine R$40

LEITE

This Portuguese-Brazilian fusion restaurant is one of the oldest in the country and has been serving Portuguese standards like *bacalhau* (smoked cod) since 1882. These sit alongside juicy king prawns fried in garlic butter, served with cream cheese sauce and Brazil nut rice. It is frequently voted the best in the city but only opens for lunch.
✉ Praça Joaquim Nabuco 147/53, near the Casa de Cultura, Santo Antônio ☎ 81 3224 7977 🕐 Tue–Fri, Sun 11.30–4 🖐 L R$60, Wine R$35

LA MAISON

La Maison is a fondue restaurant in a low-lit basement with a kitschy, 1970s illicit feel. Appropriately cheesy and good fun, with rosé wine and peach melba on the menu.
✉ Avenida Boa Viagem 618 ☎ 81 3325 1158 🕐 Tue–Sat 12–3, 7–11, Sun 12–4 🖐 L R$30, D R$50, Wine R$40

PARRAXAXÁ

www.parraxaxa.com.br
This lively local alfresco restaurant, near the beach in Boa Viagem, serves regional dishes like tapioca pancakes (savoury pancakes made with crushed manioc grain), *carne do sol* (Brazilian jerky) and stuffed duck breast. At lunchtime, the restaurant serves a good-value buffet and in the evenings it is à la carte. Staff are dressed like *sertão* cowboys and *forró* blasts out of the sound system or from bands on the stage.
✉ Rua Baltazar Pereira 32, Boa Viagem ☎ 81 3463 7874 🕐 Mon–Thu 11.30–10, Fri 11.30–11, Sat 6am–11pm, Sun 6am–10pm 🖐 L R$15, D R$50

PONTE NOVA

www.restaurantepontenova.com.br
This smart dining room is decked out in warm hardwood and with tables draped in heavy cotton tablecloths. Chef Joca Pontes is one of the best in the city. He was awarded Recife chef of the year for two years running by *Veja* magazine (2007, 2008). His specialities include smoke-perfumed duck breast with tamarind honey and Madeira sauce, and kid cooked in stout beer.
✉ Rua do Cupim 172, Graças ☎ 81 3327 7226 🕐 Mon–Thu 12–3, 7.30–11.30, Fri 12–3, 7.30–1, Sat 7.30–1 🖐 R $70, D R$90, Wine R$40

PRICES AND SYMBOLS
Prices are the lowest and highest for a double room for one night. Breakfast is included unless noted otherwise. All the hotels listed accept credit cards unless otherwise stated. Note that rates vary widely throughout the year.

For a key to the symbols, ▷ 2.

ARACAJU

CELI PRAIA

www.celihotel.com.br

This is, strictly speaking, a business hotel and it looks it; it could almost be an office block. Rooms are large, modern and comfortable, with balconies and internet access. Services include a gym, 24-hour business centre, pool, sauna and one of the best restaurants on the beach. There are good online rates.

Avenida Oceânica 500, Praia Atlaia 79 2107 8000 R$250–R$400 93 Outdoor

CARUARU

GRANDE HOTEL SÃO VICENTE DE PAULO

www.grandehotelcaruaru.com.br

This is a large business-like hotel in the centre of town. It has a range of suites and apartments, pleasantly decorated with fresh checked bedcovers and cool wall colours. Services include air-conditioning, laundry, garage, bar, large restaurant, pool and TV.

Avenida Rio Branco 365 81 372 5011 R$200–R$300 81 Outdoor

FERNANDO DE NORONHA

ECO-POUSADA TEJU-AÇU

www.pousadateju.com.br

This small boutique hotel, a five-minute stroll from Boldró beach, is one of the few on the island to attempt to practise eco-tourism. The extensive decking and each of the *cabanas* (double-room cabins, which overlook a jewel-like pool and the ocean) are made from sustainably harvested timber, water is recycled and sewage is treated. The hotel can organize your flights to and from the island, in addition to excursions and boat trips around Fernando de Noronha during your stay.

Estrada da Alamoa, Boldró 81 3619 1277 R$850–R$1,100 12 Outdoor

MACEIÓ

CASA GRANDE DA PRAIA

www.hotelcasagrandedapraia.com.br

Staff here are friendly and they serve a good breakfast. Some of the beds are a bit musty and spongy, so do check first. You'll find the best rooms in the upper floor annexe overlooking a small garden. It is near the beach.

Rua Jangadeiros Alagoanas 1528, Pajuçara 82 3231 3332 R$100–R$190 23

IYHA ALAGAMAR HOSTEL

A scarcity of hostels in Maceió means that it can be hard to get a room here; you'll need to book two months in advance for Christmas, New Year and Carnival, and about a week in advance in low season (Apr–Nov). The hostel always requires a 50 per cent up-front deposit into their bank account. The rooms are shabby and institutional. The mattresses are covered with plastic. Dorms are single-sex; lower floors are musty.

Rua Pref Abdon Arroxelas 327 82 3231 2246 Dorm bed R$30; double room R$80–R$150 14

PONTA VERDE PRAIA

www.hotelpontaverde.com.br

This is a large multi-storey hotel in an optimum beach setting, with easy access to dance clubs and restaurants to the north, and Praia Pajuçara to the west. The range of air-conditioned rooms are all well-appointed and comfortable, with

Opposite *A room in Hotel 7 Colinas, Olinda*

international TV and WiFi. The best on the upper floors have wonderful sweeping views out over the sea. They provide a gorgeously arranged buffet breakfast.
✉ Avenida Álvaro Otacílio 2933, Ponta Verde ☎ 82 2121 0040 R$375–R$550 203 Rooftop

POUSADA ESTALAGEM

www.pousadaestalagem.com.br
Sited in a quiet back street above a photo shop, this *pousada* includes several nice, bright flats with cooking facilities. Some have space for up to six in one room, making this a possible choice for group bookings.
✉ Rua Engenheiro Demócrito Sarmento Barroca 70 ☎ 82 3327 6088 R$120–R$180 8

RITZ PRAIA

www.ritzpraia.com.br
This recently refurbished high-rise is a block from the beach. Rooms are airy and brightly furnished with good views from the top. The pool on the sun deck is about the size of a double bed.
✉ Rua Eng Mário de Gusmão 1300, Laranjeiras, Ponta Verde ☎ 82 2121 4600 R$180–R$210 53 Rooftop

MARECHAL DEODORO AND PRAIA DO FRANCÊS

POUSADA BOUGAINVILLE E RESTAURANT CHEZ PATRICK

Here you will find a pretty little *pousada* set in gardens brightened by bougainvillea and heliconia blooms, right on the beach. It has a range of simply furnished, well-maintained rooms, all with air-conditioning and TVs showing international channels. They are gathered around a small pool. The hotel restaurant serves seafood and simple French dishes.
✉ Rua Sargaço 3, Praia do Francês ☎ 82 3260 1251 R$80–R$150 12 Outdoor

PENEDO

POUSADA COLONIAL

This *pousada* is in a converted colonial building with creaky wooden floors and huge rooms, the best of which have views out over the river. All the bedrooms are fan-cooled but for the suites. Reception staff are friendly and efficient.
✉ Praça 12 de Abril 21, 5-min walk from the bus station ☎ 82 3551 2355 R$80–R$120 14

OLINDA

HOTEL 7 COLINAS

www.hotel7colinas.com.br
Rooms in this low-key hotel are gathered around a gorgeous, sculpted deep-blue pool and set in tropical gardens shaded by giant fig trees and busy with colourful hummingbirds and tanagers. Rooms and public areas are decorated with pieces by local artists (including Francisco Brennand, ▷ 256) and tiny marmoset monkeys visit the alfresco breakfast area every morning.
✉ Ladeira de Sao Francisco 307 ☎ 81 3439 6055 R$230–R$350 44 Outdoor

OLINDA HOSTEL

www.alberguedeolinda.com.br
IYHA youth hostel in a concrete house near Olinda's ramshackle beach. It has fan-cooled dorms and doubles, all sparsely furnished at a basic level. The lobby is decorated with rustic artwork. The hostel has a tropical garden, TV room, and a shady area with hammocks.
✉ Rua do Sol 233 ☎ 81 3429 1592 Dorm bed R$30; double room R$100–R$120 34 Outdoor
Discount for IYHA members

POUSADA PETER

www.pousadapeter.com.br
The Pousada Peter advertises itself as being a prime spot for watching the Olinda Carnival, as its terraces overlook one of the main streets along the procession's route. Rooms are rather small but the lounge is spacious and decorated with Pernambuco crafts and colourful artwork. Breakfast is served on the terrace overlooking distant Recife and the postage stamp-sized pool.
✉ Rua do Amparo 215 ☎ 81 3439 2171 R$100–R$280 13 Outdoor

POUSADA DOS QUATRO CANTOS

www.pousada4cantos.com.br
This *pousada* is a large converted townhouse with a little walled garden, terraces and smallish pool. The rooms and suites are decorated in warm brown shades with Pernambuco arts and crafts, and furnished mostly with antiques. Breakfast includes local specialities and the service is friendly and helpful.
✉ Rua Prudente de Morais 441 ☎ 81 3429 0220 R$98–R$280 15 Outdoor

PORTO DE GALINHAS

IYHA POUSADA A CASA BRANCA

www.pousadaacasabranca.com.br
Olinda's newest hostel is housed in a scrupulously clean, well-kept, modern building and offers a range of air-conditioned doubles and fan-cooled dorms. It's about a 10-minute walk from the beach. To get there from the seafront, take a right off Rua Beijupira opposite Rua Carauna, and walk inland for 400m (436 yards). The *pousada* is in a square 150m (164 yards) before the Estrada Maracaipe.
✉ Praça 18 ☎ 81 3552 1808 Dorm bed R$30; double room R$90–R$150 14

RECIFE

POUSADA VILLA BOA VISTA

www.pousadavillaboavista.com.br
This is a brightly coloured modern hotel. Rooms are comfortable, with bathrooms with showers, set around a courtyard. It is quiet, safe and a five-minute taxi ride from the centre.
✉ Rua Miguel Couto 81, Boa Vista ☎ 81 3223 0666 R$119–R$180 30

RECIFE PALACE

www.lucsimhoteis.com.br
A comfortable business hotel with a decent restaurant, this sits right on the beach at Boa Viagem. Views from the top-floor rooms are marvellous. All rooms have work areas, king-sized beds and marble bathrooms. The hotel has a small spa and sauna.
✉ Rua da Aurora 225, Boa Vista ☎ 81 3231 1200 R$140–R$260 297 Rooftop

FORTALEZA AND THE FAR NORTHEAST

This region comprises the states of Rio Grande do Norte, Ceará, Piauí and Maranhão, which include large expanses of little-visited semi-arid interior and a beautiful delta-strewn coastline. Brazil's far northeastern coast is sunny, dry and cooled by an almost constant ocean wind, which has blown sand from the beaches and sandstone cliffs into huge seafront dunes over millions of years. These are so large in the state of Maranhão that they form a coastal desert, the Lençóis Maranhenses, a large area of which is protected as a national park. Other dunes rise behind the long, broad beaches and the fishing villages—like Punta Negra (the most northern of the Rota do Sol beaches that lie on Rio Grande do Norte's eastern shores), Genipabu, and Jericoacoara—which have grown over the last decade to become international resort towns. The wind- and kite-surfing here ranks with the best in the world.

The region has large cities too: vibrant Fortaleza, which is famous for its weekday nightlife, sleepy Natal, and the colonial city of São Luís, which sits on the edge of a vast estuary and which is replete with fine Portuguese buildings. The city is one of two World Heritage Sites in the region. The other is the Parque Nacional da Serra da Capivara, whose dome-like hills and forgotten canyons are covered in rock art, and continue to spark debate among archaeologists. It is one of many protected park areas and reserves in this region of Brazil, which sits in the vast *sertão* hinterland of the far northeast—a landscape which extends through the entire centre of the country and which resembles the Australian outback in appearance, vegetation and scale. Distances between sights in the desert-like interior are huge, and are best visited as part of an organized tour. It is not a good place to run out of fuel or water.

ALCÂNTARA

This little-visited colonial city is on the banks of the muddy Rio Bacanga, across the water and some 22km (13.5 miles) from the Maranhão state capital, São Luís (⊳ 284–285). It is delightful for a half-day wander. It preserves one of the largest and least modified groups of 17th- and 18th-century colonial buildings in Brazil, and—together with São Luís—is a National Heritage Site.

SUGAR SLAVES

The town grew wealthy as the preferred retreat of sugar cane barons. The crop was initially harvested by enslaved natives captured from the Amazon and later by West African slaves. Entire Amazon civilizations were wiped out to feed the plantations of Pará and Maranhão, and are known only from early accounts by conquistadores like Francisco de Orellana (⊳ 25). Thousands of Africans have given Alcântara and São Luís a distinctive culture and cuisine, with *cacuriá* dancing (from which *lambada* is derived), the *candomblé* spirit religion and spicy food.

HISTORICAL SIGHTS

The town clusters around a pretty grassy square called the Praça da Matriz, which retains a slave whipping post at its centre. Almost 50 of the city's few hundred houses are protected by the federal heritage bureau, IPHAN, and many have been restored. On the square, the Museu Histórico (daily 9–2; free) preserves some fine *azulejos* (painted and glazed tiles) and curios, including a bed which was built especially for a scheduled visit by the Emperor, Dom Pedro. It was never slept in, since the visit was cancelled. Another small museum, the Casa Histórica (Mon–Fri 10–4; free), has some 18th-century English furniture and porcelain imported by the Alcântara aristocracy. There is a ruined fort on the southern edges of town and a number of churches, including the 17th-century Igreja de Nossa Senhora do Carmo (Mon–Fri 8–1, 2–6, Sat–Sun 9–2), with a finely carved rococo interior.

INFORMATION

www.turismo.ma.gov.br
395 Q5 Rua Portugal 165, São Luís 98 3231 0822 Mon–Fri 9–6
From São Luís

TIPS

» There are plenty of cheap restaurants around the main square in Alcântara and the town has a handful of very simple guest houses for those wishing to stay overnight.

» Come during the week if you can, when the town is almost entirely free of tourists and you will have its sleepy streets very nearly to yourself.

Above *The ruins of São Mathias church on Praça da Matriz*
Opposite *A Renaissance town house in ruins on Rua da Amargura*

BEBERIBE AND THE MORRO BRANCO BEACHES

This small provincial town, 80km (50 miles) southeast of the largest city in the region, Fortaleza (▷ 274–275), is the access point for a string of lovely beaches. These include Morro Branco, just a few kilometres from the town, which is backed by striated, ochre and red sandstone cliffs and has beautiful views. There is a small fishing village-turned-beach resort here, with *pousadas* (small inns), holiday homes and little sailing boats dragged up onto the beach. This village and others in the entire Beberibe municipality are famous throughout the country for their bottled sand paintings, made with dirt from the cliffs and beaches, and sold by tourist shops and vendors in the town. Beaches stretch farther south and include Praia das Fontes, Praia Uruaú and Fortim, getting quieter the further south you go.

✝ 396 T6 ℹ Avenida General Afonso Albuquerque Lima, Fortaleza ☎ 85 3101 4688 ⊙ Mon–Fri 10–6 🚌 From Fortaleza

CANOA QUEBRADA

www.portalcanoaquebrada.com.br

Eastern Ceará's most popular small beach resort clambers over rugged and multi-coloured sandstone cliffs, 170km (105 miles) southeast of Fortaleza. Like Trancoso (▷ 210) and Jericoacoara (▷ 272–273), it was a little fishing village until it was discovered by São Paulo hippies in the 1970s, and subsequently by big Brazilian package tour operators. Canoa's small-town, under-the-stars feel has long gone now. Big resorts stretch to the east and west, and the village streets burst with tourists in high season (Dec–New Year and two weeks preceding carnival). Nightlife is vibrant—many beach-side shacks double up as *forró* bars at night with music and dancing—and extemporaneous tour operators in town offer all manner of adventure activities, such as sand boarding, windsurfing and kite-surfing (on the Jaguaribe estuary, ▷ 288), as well as the buggy rides which have degraded many of the dune ecosystems.

✝ 397 U6 ℹ Avenida General Afonso Albuquerque Lima, Fortaleza ☎ 85 3101 4688 ⊙ Mon–Fri 10–5 🚌 From Fortaleza

DELTA DO PARNAÍBA

The Delta do Parnaíba, which separates Parnaíba town (▷ 273) in Piauí state from Tutóia, in Maranhão, is huge. It is dotted with beach-fringed islands, lined with mangroves, and sparsely populated with fishing communities which have changed little in a hundred years. It is remote, difficult to access and stunningly beautiful. Wildlife is abundant, with hundreds of species of birds, including the rufous crab-hawk and scarlet ibis, both of which are on the Red List of endangered species. These live alongside larger mammals, such as manatee, jaguar and puma. The delta is little studied, however, and the area has never been properly explored by serious ornithologists. Travel here is only possible on a tour (▷ 289) and is most easily conducted as part of a journey between the Lençóis Maranhenses (▷ 280–281) and Jericoacoara (▷ below) or Fortaleza.

✝ 395 S5 ℹ Rua Dr Oscar Clark 575, Parnaíba ☎ 86 3321 1532 ⊙ Mon–Fri 9–5

FORTALEZA

▷ 274–275.

JERICOACOARA

After Canoa Quebrada (▷ this page) had lost its charm to over-development, São Paulo's beatniks

Above left *The red sandstone cliffs between Beberibe and Morro Branco*
Above right *Bringing home the catch at Canoa Quebrada*
Opposite *Kite-surfer at Jericoacoara*

discovered this fishing village in Ceará state in the 1980s. It is in a spectacular setting at the end of a gentle cape, surrounded by glorious beaches, towering dunes and broken, ocean-worn rocks. Beaches close to Jeri (as it is often referred to) offer superb kite-surfing and windsurfing, and there is good walking and cycling along the long flat sands. There are no streets, only sand trails, and the village can only be reached by four-wheel drive jeeps from nearby Jijoca (▷ 288–289). Difficulty of access has afforded Jericoacoara more protection from the ravages of development than Canoa Quebrada, but there are nonetheless problems. These are principally from Italian-owned hotels which have been built right onto the sand, bypassing the local environmental regulations with *braggadocio*. An influx of European tourists has seen property prices rise so high that families who have lived here for generations are forced out of the market. Visitors concerned about preserving this beautiful location can do much to help by choosing local tour operators and hotels, and sustainable practitioners.

396 S5 · Avenida General Afonso Albuquerque Lima, Fortaleza · 85 3101 4688 · Mon–Fri 10–6 · From Fortaleza to Jijoca. Some hotels in Jericoacoara can organize minivan transport direct from Fortaleza to Jericoacoara itself

JUAZEIRO DO NORTE

www.juazeiro.ce.gov.br

Few tourists make it to this provincial capital deep in the southern Ceará *sertão* dryland but it's a fascinating place for those intrigued by Brazilian religious folklore. Juazeiro was home to one of the *sertão's* cult figures—Padre Cícero (Romão Batista)—who ranks alongside the wayfaring prophet Antônio Conselheiro (▷ 35) in mythological importance in the northeast. Cícero, who had long championed the rights of Juazeiro's late 19th-century poor, was hailed as a saint after a consecrated host he passed to a woman at mass reportedly bled in her mouth. A giant statue of Cícero watches over the modern town like a standing Buddha. There is also a museum devoted to the priest in the town (tel 88 3511 4487; Mon–Fri 8–6; free) and Juazeiro has grown to become the most important pilgrimage site in northeastern Brazil.

396 T7 · From Fortaleza

NATAL

▷ 278–279.

PARNAÍBA

www.parnaiba.pi.gov.br

Parnaíba, in the state of Piauí, is a pleasant provincial town on the banks of the Parnaíba river, where foreign tourists are as rare as polar bears and greeted with the same mix of puzzlement and curiosity. At the town's heart is a small but perfectly formed and newly restored colonial centre, which can be walked around in less than half an hour and which has some decent hotels and restaurants. The combination of an attractive riverside setting, sleepy charm and local authenticity make Parnaíba a good place to break a journey between Fortaleza (▷ 274–275) and São Luís (▷ 284–285).

There are beaches and other attractions nearby. The Pedra do Sal is a palm-shaded and sheltered lagoon 12km (7.5 miles) from the town with beaches and good, safe swimming. Coqueiro is a rustic fishing village, with rock pools to explore and a broad strand of sand. Boats leave for the wilds of the Delta do Parnaíba (▷ 272) from the Porto das Barcas, 8km (5 miles) from the colonial centre of Parnaíba.

395 S5 · Rua Dr Oscar Clark 575 · 86 3321 1532 · Mon–Fri 9–6 · From Fortaleza, São Luís and Teresina

INFORMATION

396 T6 Avenida General Afonso Albuquerque Lima 85 3101 4688 Mon–Fri 10–6 From all major tourist towns Pinto Martins

TIPS

» Iracema is the best area to dine in Fortaleza, where there are many restaurants and bars.

» The local football team (Fortaleza Esporte Clube) will receive a new home ground after Fortaleza has built a new stadium to host matches in the 2014 World Cup. For details on their games and how to attend them see the club website (www.fortalezaec.net).

Opposite *Statues overlooked by high-rises at Iracema*

Below *O Ponte dos Ingleses pier stretches into the ocean from the promenade*

FORTALEZA

The skyscraper flats and *forró* (northeastern music and dance) bars of Ceará's state capital bask under an impossibly blue sky, behind a series of gorgeous white-sand beaches. It's the largest city in northeastern Brazil after Salvador, but it feels like a small town; which indeed it was until the mid-19th century, when it grew through the cotton trade with Europe. It has no sights of significant historical interest but it does have seawater which rarely drops below 20°C (52°F), and cheap flights from Europe ensure a steady trickle of tourists.

PRAIA DE IRACEMA

Most visitors head to the beaches. Closest to the centre is the former port of Iracema, with the old port of Fortaleza behind it. The beach bears the name of a romantic novel (and its heroine), by local 19th-century author, José de Alencar. It begins at the 19th-century Ponte dos Ingleses (English Bridge). This was built by the British Civil engineering firm, Norton Griffiths and Company, in 1921 as a commercial jetty for the port but was never completed due to lack of funds, and re-opened instead as a promenade pier. Many of the city's lively nightlife spots, including the Dragão do Mar centre (▷ 288) lie just behind and the beachfront is busy with restaurants and *pousadas* (small inns).

TIME FOR A DIP

Swimming is much better at Praia de Meireles, which is shaded by coconut palms and towering hotels, and which hosts a weekend night market selling Ceará lace among other arts and crafts. Praia do Futuro, 8km (5 miles) southeast of Iracema, is the most popular bathing beach and has lively nightlife on Thursday nights.

OTHER BEACHES

There are numerous other beaches to the east and west of Fortaleza, including what is said to be the world's best location for kite-surfing, Cumbuco, some 33km (20.5 miles) west of Iracema. Here there are many foreign-owned hotels and condominiums. Fortaleza is also home to the Parque Ecológico do Rio Cocó (▷ 276).

PARQUE ECOLÓGICO DO RIO COCÓ

www.parquevivo.ufc.br

This conservation area within the city limits of Fortaleza (▷ 274–275) lies 2km (1.25 miles) behind both Meireles and Futuro beaches and protects 1,312ha (3,240 acres) of a threatened and uniquely South American coastal scrub forest called *restinga*, alongside coastal wetland and savannah. It is a haven for wildlife within the city—particularly for birds and small mammals—but has suffered from pollution in the last few decades and from the impact of heavy building programmes which bypassed municipal environmental legislation in an alleged corruption scheme. The park spans the margins of the Rio Cocó and is cut by forested trails and bridges. It is the largest area of forest in the city, never closed and a peaceful place during the day, but it is dangerous at night, despite the police station within its confines.

396 T6 (within Fortaleza) Reachable only by taxi

PARQUE ESTADUAL MATA DA PIPA

www.pipa.com.br/santuarioecologico

Bird watchers come to this 300ha (741-acre) state park, also known as Santuário Ecológico de Pipa, on a cape to the north of Pipa beach (▷ 283) in Rio Grande do Norte state. It is an old *fazenda* (a farm, ironically owned by one of the country's greatest environmental villains, responsible for the Itaipu dam) and one of the few surviving patches of endangered Mata Atlântica forest in this part of northeastern Brazil. A series of well-signposted trails run through the reserve and to the clifftops at its edge, which afford views out over the bays and beaches of Pipa and Tibaú do Sul (▷ 283), which are less than a 40-minute walk away.

There are four forest walks, all of them taking less than an hour. The Jacú trail—named after the turkey-like guans which are a common sight on the path—leads to the park's highest point, where a fire tower offers a panoramic view of the canopy. The Boa trail winds through the forest to a small pool where paca and agouti (large and long-legged muntjak-like rodents) come to drink. The Maiden path runs along the clifftop and the Peroba trail runs through arches of verdant peroba and pororoca bushes to Madeiro Point at the end of the cape, with views north to Tabatinga Point and south to Cabo Verde Point. Be sure to take binoculars and a camera.

397 V7 Daily 9–5 R$5 Taxis from Pipa beach

PARQUE NACIONAL CHAPADA DAS MESAS

www.carolinanet.com.br

This 160,000ha (395,200-acre) national park is in the far south of Maranhão state, near the city of Carolina. It protects a series of table-top mountains, dripping with dozens of beautiful waterfalls and situated in closed canopy *cerrado* forests filled with maned wolf and puma. Access is difficult but well worth the effort, as tourists are few and far between and the park offers a real sense of virgin wilderness within what is Brazil's most critically threatened biome. There are dozens of mountains, sitting in a huge plain covered entirely with low forest and so far from any major urban centres that the air is clean enough to see for over 40km (25 miles).

Waterfalls within the park include the three-tiered Cachoeira da Pedra Caída (35km/22 miles north of Carolina), the Cachoeira do Itapecuru (32km/20 miles from Carolina) where two cascades plunge into a single inky pool, and the Cachoeira São Romão (70km/43 miles from Carolina) , a roaring curtain of water more than 100m (328ft) wide. Like so many of Brazil's natural sights, all are threatened by a hydroelectric project.

Below *A male blue dacnis, as found in Parque Estadual Mata da Pipa*

Above *Some of the unique rock formations in Sete Cidades national park*
Above right *The cable car to Ubajara cave in Parque Nacional de Ubajara*

398 P7 Secretaria de Turismo Esportes e Meio Ambiente, Rua Duque de Caxias 522, Centro, Carolina 99 3531 8378 Mon–Fri 9–6 From São Luis to Carolina There are no rental car agencies in Carolina. The only access to the park is via taxi

PARQUE NACIONAL DOS LENÇOIS MARANHENSES

▷ 280–281.

PARQUE NACIONAL SERRA DA CAPIVARA

▷ 282.

PARQUE NACIONAL DAS SETE CIDADES

www.piemtur.pi.gov.br

This national park covers 6,221ha (15,366 acres) and is 190km (118 miles) northeast of Teresina (▷ 283). It is the most accessible of all the outback parks that dot the seemingly endless desert interiors of Piauí and Maranhão states. It protects seven strangely eroded sets of low table-hills—the 'Sete Cidades' (Seven Cities) of the park's name. These can all be visited in a day as the park's diameter is only 12km (7.5 miles). The summit of each hill affords a different view and at both dawn and sunset the whole eerie landscape is illuminated with a rich golden light. During the week there are rarely any other visitors and the atmosphere is magical. Some of the rocks and canyons are daubed with naturalistic art and symbols, which have been dated as 5,000 to 10,000 years old.

There are numerous little rivers in the park and 22 springs, attracting wildlife from the surrounding *caatinga* scrubland, including white-tailed deer, paca, six-banded armadillo and more than 100 bird species.

395 S6 Centro de Convenções, Rua Acre s/n, Teresina 86 3221 7100 Mon–Fri 9–5 The only access to the park is via taxi

PARQUE NACIONAL DE UBAJARA

www.portalubajara.com.br

There is good day hiking and light caving in this protected area 3km (2 miles) from the town of Ubajara, between Fortaleza (▷ 274–275) and Teresina (▷ 283). This is the smallest of Brazil's federally protected national parks and was founded to protect a spectacular cave system and 563ha (1,390 acres) of semi-arid highland *caatinga* landscape. A short cable-car ride or a 6km-long (3.75-mile) trail brings visitors from the park entrance and through the scrubland (which is filled with rare birds) to the Ubajara cave mouth, perched on the side of the range's steep escarpment. There are 15 chambers inside, extending into the hill for many kilometres, but only a few are open to visitors. All are illuminated and filled from ceiling to floor with flowstones and massive stalactites and stalagmites. Visits are conducted by guides whose services seem to consist of comparing the rock formations to animals, rather than providing scientific information.

Further trails lead around the caves to viewpoints on the summit of the table-top mountains, and lush rivers form waterfalls. These include the Cachoeira do Boi Morto (13km/8 miles from Ubajara town) and the Cachoeira da Floresta, which sits on a private reserve that has a little snack bar for drinks and sandwiches.

396 S6 Sede do Parque, Estrada de Telferico s/n, Ubajara 85 3272 1600 Tue–Sun 8–5 R$5 (including cable-car ride)

INFORMATION
397 V7 Rua Mossoró 359, Tirol 84 3232 2470 Mon–Fri 10–5 From all major tourist towns Augusto Severo

INTRODUCTION

The capital of the state of Rio Grande do Norte sits on a peninsula formed by the Atlantic to the east and the broad estuary of the Rio Potengi to the west. Long, broad and dune-backed beaches stretch to the north and south and draw thousands of European tourists during the Brazilian winter. The city is building a big new international airport in anticipation of far larger arrivals for the World Cup in 2014, and subsequent years.

On Twelfth Night 1598, the Portuguese began building a fort on the peninsula, which they called the Forte dos Reis Magos, after the Three Wise Men or Mage Kings *(Reis Magos)* who arrived in Bethlehem twelve days after Christ's birth. On 25 December 1599, Portuguese priests said mass on the beach at the tip of the peninsula, which was christened Natal (Christmas) in the day's honour, and later gave its name to the village which grew up around the fort.

WHAT TO SEE

O FORTE DOS REIS MAGOS

That first fort still stands today, at the point where the Potengi disgorges its muddy flow into the sea. It is built as a five pointed star, a standard formation used by the Portuguese at forts like Almeida, along the homeland frontier with Spain. A castellated walkway leads around its entire perimeter for almost 800m (872 yards). The original piece of lioz stone used in the 16th century to mark Natal's Praia do Marco beach as Portuguese crown territory sits in the armoury. It bears the cross and shield of the Portuguese coat of arms. In the old quarters of the donatory captain there is a collection of colonial knick-knacks and in the dungeon there are some grim instruments of Renaissance torture, including a hole in the floor where prisoners were chained and gradually drowned by the rising tide.

Praia do Forte s/n 84 3202 9006 Daily 8–4 Adult R$5, under 7 free

Above *Boats on dune-backed Genipabu beach*

GENIPABU

This little beach resort immediately across the Potengi from Natal is one of the most photographed locations on the northeastern coast. An enormous dune, 60m (197ft) in height, sweeps in a gentle curve down to a crescent beach which is capped with a thatched roof restaurant, poised to catch the rays of the setting sun. New arrivals in the resort are greeted by beach buggy touts, who offer over-priced adrenaline rush rides on the dunes, a practice which has led to the destruction of hundreds of delicate fixed dune ecosystems in the northeast. The area around Genipabu is ostensibly a protected area and can be enjoyed equally well on foot, or even camel (▷ 289), and the view of the sunset on camel-back is magical, with only the sound of the waves and wind to disturb the music of VW beetle engines as buggies whizz past the caravanserai every five minutes.

From Natal *rodoviária* (Avenida Capitao Moreira Gouveia 1237; tel 84 3232 7310)

PONTA NEGRA AND THE ROTA DO SOL

South of Natal town, dune-backed beaches stretch almost unbroken to the Lagoa Guarairas at Tibaú do Sul (▷ 283), some 80km (50 miles) to the south, along a stretch of coastline marketed as the Rota do Sol (the Path of the Sun). The most famous beach on the Rota do Sol—and one of the most popular beaches in the northeast—is Ponta Negra, 6km (3.75 miles) south of Natal city centre. It is packed with regimented ranks of small hotels, *pousadas* (small inns) and condominiums, and has an iconic 40m-high (130ft) dune at its far southern end. Beyond the condominiums of Búzios, 20km (12.5 miles) south of Ponta Negra, the beaches get steadily quieter.

From Natal *rodoviária* (Avenida Capitao Moreira Gouveia 1237; tel 84 3232 7310)

TIPS

» Visit Genipabu on a weekday for a semblance of serenity.

» Ponta Negra can be unsafe and unsavoury after dark; avoid the beach and stick to the main path.

Below *The belle époque Teatro Alberto Mananhão in Natal*

PARQUE NACIONAL DOS LENÇÓIS MARANHENSES

INFORMATION

www.parquelencois.com.br
395 R5 Rua Portugal 165, São Luís 98 3231 0822 Mon–Fri 10–5
To Barreirinhas from São Luís

Above *Aerial view of the extensive white sand dunes*

INTRODUCTION

Northeastern Brazil's dunes become so extensive in the state of Maranhão that they form a beachside sahara of shifting sand, which runs northwest from the Delta do Parnaíba (▷ 272) for some 140km (87 miles) along the coast and 50km (31 miles) inland. From the air, the dunes look so white that they resemble wrinkled bedlinen: hence their name, the Maranhão Sheets. The Parque Nacional Lençóis Maranhenses, which forms a protected portion of the Lençóis, covers an area of 1,550sq km (596sq miles). Between December and June, the dunes are broken by blue and green freshwater lakes, which provide a breathtaking contrast with the brilliant-white sand.

The town of Barreirinhas, on the banks of the Rio Preguiças, makes the best base for a visit. While the views are magnificent, there is more to see than scenery. The Lençóis are a repository of endangered species, including Amazonian manatee, leatherback and green turtles, puma, jaguar and spectacled caiman. The lakes have been little-studied by scientists, but they protect unique species like the South American lungfish, which cocoon themselves in moist mud in the dry season, emerging during the summer rains. Migratory birds like the lesser yellowlegs winter here when it gets too chilly in Alaska, and hundreds of xeric vascular plants (plants with their own water system), sedges and grasses are endemic to the dunes. Unfortunately there are no guides working in the park who can unlock these secrets, as tourism here still concentrates on adventure activities and sightseeing.

WHAT TO SEE

GRANDES LENÇÓIS

The Lençóis are divided into two regions, separated by the Rio Preguiças. The protected area lies across the western shore of the river and is known as Grandes (big) Lençóis. Access is from the low-key tourist town of Barreirinhas, where tour operators, such as Ecodunas (▷ 289), offer walks in the park and scenic flights.

PEQUENOS LENÇÓIS

The unprotected stretches of the Lençóis run east to the Delta do Parnaíba and are known as Pequenos (little) Lençóis. They are far less visited and can be accessed along the Rio Preguiças from Barreirinhas. Beach drive expeditions from Barreirinhas to Jericoacoara (▷ 272–273) or Parnaíba (▷ 273) pass through the Pequenos Lençóis.

SAND DUNES

It is possible to make hiking tours and thrilling jeeps rides over the sand dunes with accredited guides and reputable companies such as Terra Brazil (▷ 197).

LAGOONS

The area's spectacular lagoons are spread over a large area, with some as large as enormous lakes. Lagoa Bonita and Lagoa Azul near Barreirinhas are easily accessible, while Lagoa da Gaivota (Seagull Lagoon) is more than 60km (37 miles) away, but well worth a visit (contact local travel agencies).

MORE TO SEE

COASTAL TOWNS

The course of the Rio Preguiças is broken with tiny hamlets, where it is possible to really get away from it all and either sleep out under the stars in a hammock under an open-sided *palapa* (thatched roof; ▷ 286), or take a room in a beachside hotel. These settlements include Vassouras (which is little more than a house at the base of a dune), Mandacaru (with a lighthouse and a few arts and crafts shops) and Caburé, a little resort on a huge and windy Atlantic beach.

TIPS

» The Lençóis are becoming increasingly polluted by wind-blown plastic bags, which are not disposed of properly in Maranhão. Refuse plastic bags in shops where possible.

» Be careful of broken glass, especially in Caburé where rubbish is buried rather than collected.

Left *A shopkeeper in Barreirinhas*
Below *Fisherman on the Rio Preguiças*

PARQUE NACIONAL SERRA DA CAPIVARA

This remote 130,000ha (321,100 acres) of national park land is some 500km (310 miles) south of Teresina (▷ 283), in the hot heart of the *sertão*. It is another of the northeast's UNESCO World Heritage Sites. It preserves a series of bizarre honeycombed, dome-shaped mountains surrounded by patchy *cerrado* and scrubby *caatinga* vegetation, and is cut by deep gorges and canyons which are so narrow they are barely ever illuminated by the torrid tropical sun.

ARCHAEOLOGICAL DEBATE

Archaeologists came here in the 1970s to investigate more than 30,000 cave paintings, petroglyphs and the remains of settlements which cover canyon and escarpment walls. Some of these have been controversially dated as 45,000 years old by Brazilian archaeologist, Niède Guidon. These findings have been disputed by non-Brazilian archaeologists as false positives arising from mistakenly dating natural charcoal as man-made charcoal. Another Brazilian archaeologist, Walter Neves, discovered that 12,000-year-old skulls discovered at Pedra Furada (a location in the Serra) showed features that were non-Mongoloid. This challenges the theory that the first Americans migrated from Asia across the Bering Straits. The skull dimensions and facial features matched most closely to those of the native people of Australia and Melanesia.

VISITS

Some 400 archaeological sites have since been identified in the Serra, 22 of which are open to tourists and accessible on boardwalks and paths. Tours are conducted by trained guides from the Fundação Museu do Homem Americano (Fumdham, which is the museum charting the history of the first Americans), at nearby São Raimundo Nonato. Whatever their age and whomever the artists, the paintings are fascinating: the representation of everyday activities of an ancient pre-Columbian people, their festivities, hunting and sexual conduct.

INFORMATION

www.fumdham.org.br

385 R8 Fundação Museu do Homem Americano, Centro Cultural Sérgio Motta, Bairro Campestre 89 3582 1612 Tue–Sun 9–5 Park admission and tour R$20 Access is by tour only

TIPS

» There is no disabled access to the park. Tours involve at least an hour of walking in rocky terrain, so bring walking shoes.

» It can be very hot and dry at any time of year. Bring bottled water, sun protection and a broad-rimmed hat.

Below *Visitors admire the clusters of rock art at the Toca do Boqueiro site*

SÃO LUÍS

▷ 284–285.

TERESINA

www.teresina.pi.gov.br

The capital of the state of Piauí is a desert city, which vies with the central west's Corumbá (▷ 328) and Cuiabá (▷ 328) as the hottest place in Brazil. In the baking summer months it's not unusual for the temperature to go above 45°C (113°F) in the middle of the day. Thankfully, it cools by some 15–20°C (60–70°F) at night.

While there's little in Teresina to draw tourists, the city is an inevitable transit point for those heading from Maranhão state to the Serra da Capivara (▷ 282) and is the best place to break a journey. It sprawls around the banks of the sluggish Rio Poti in a flat grid of streets, shaded by abundant trees and lined with attractive 19th-century and early-Republican terracotta-roofed buildings. The city was founded in the 18th century as a waystation for the cotton and cattle trade, when it was known as the Vila do Poti. It was renamed in honour of the Empress of Brazil and wife of Dom Pedro II, Teresa Cristina, who had supported moving the state capital from Oreias.

There are a handful of buildings worth seeing in passing. The Palácio de Karnak (tel 86 3221 9820; Mon–Sat 8–6; free), just west of Praça Frei Serafim, is a grand neoclassical edifice set in pretty gardens landscaped by Roberto Burle Marx. It has been the governor's palace since 1926 and is now the state legislature. Inside is a collection of period furniture and artefacts, and a rare set of lithographs of the Middle East from 1839. These are by the Scottish artist David Roberts, famous for his depictions of unexcavated temples throughout the Middle East and, most notably, in Egypt. These presumably gave the palace its name (after the Egyptian temple site of Karnak). Visits to the interior of the Palácio are free, but by prior appointment only. The Casa da Cultura (tel 86 3215 7849; Mon–Fri 8–7, Sat 9–1, Sun 1–4; free) tells the story of Teresina through the lives of its glitterati, who include the journalist Carlos Castelo Branco and the photographer Jose de Medeiros. It also hosts concerts and exhibitions.

There is a colourful morning market called the troca-troca which still, in part, functions on a medieval barter system. Where the Poti meets the Parnaíba river, there is a pretty wooded park, the Parque Encontro dos Rios (tel 86 3217 5020; daily 8–6; free). Canoes are available for hire.

385 R6 Rua Tersandro Paz 2129
86 3221 4096 Mon–Fri 10–5
From São Luís Teresina

Above *Beach life at Tibaú do Sul*

TIBAÚ DO SUL AND PRAIA DA PIPA

www.tibaudosul.com.br

Tibaú do Sul is some 80km (50 miles) south of Natal (▷ 278–279), in Rio Grande do Norte state. It still retains some of its sleepy, fishing-village atmosphere, despite being situated on the Rota do Sul coast (▷ 279), on one of the most popular stretches of beach in the northeast. It retains its cobbled streets and has bobbing boats in the big, brackish (and manatee-filled) Lagoa Guarairas. It has lovely views from its situation high on a bluff between surf beaches. The town is close to a whole series of beaches, running south towards the state border with Paraíba. The most popular of these by far is Praia da Pipa, backed by high sandstone cliffs and washed by a balmy sea. The resort village which has grown up behind it is more developed than Tibaú do Sul and is famous for its laid-back daytime feel and its frenetic high-season nightlife. There are many *pousadas* (small inns) and fine restaurants between Tibaú do Sul and Pipa, as well as a nature reserve, the Parque Estadual Mata da Pipa.

397 V7 Rua Mossoró 359, Tirol, Natal 84 3232 2470 Mon–Fri 10–6
To Tibaú do Sul and Pipa from Natal

SÃO LUÍS

INFORMATION

395 Q5 Rua Portugal 165 98 3231 0822 Mon–Fri 10–5 From all major tourist towns Marechal Cunha Machado

Above *Rua da Estrela is colourful whatever the weather*

INTRODUCTION

Maranhão's state capital is the least visited and least spoilt colonial Portuguese city in Brazil's northeast. Its churches, while not as lavish as Recife's (▷ 254–257), are in more salubrious surroundings, as there has been extensive refurbishment and renovation in the city centre in recent years. The customary Brazilian building-block high-rise apartments cluster around the muddy beaches, rather than around the old centre, and many of its town houses and Portuguese mansions are covered in fine blue and white *azulejo* (traditionally painted and glazed) tiles. São Luís has an African-Brazilian culture as distinctive as Salvador's (▷ 214–221), albeit on a far smaller scale. It has its own regional music, dances and annual festivities, which are as alive and well in the second decade of the new millennium as they were before the television age.

The city was the only state capital in Brazil not to have been founded or named by the Portuguese. The French got here first, in 1612, and named their unprepossessing little fort after St. Louis IX of France. Somehow tiny Portugal succeeded in removing them, just as it had unseated the colony of France Antarctique in 16th-century Rio de Janeiro (▷ 27). The Portuguese built their own port here, planted sugar and enslaved legions of indigenous people. São Luís got rich, spread across the bay to Alcântara (▷ 271) and prospered, until the British began to grow sugar more efficiently in the Caribbean in the 18th century. Modern São Luís is the capital of Brazil's poorest state, having its greatest social divide, and is largely owned and run as the demesne of the powerful Sarney family .

WHAT TO SEE

CATEDRAL DA SÉ

The great Jesuit orator, Antônio Vieira (▷ 29), delivered his anti-slavery hellfire sermons in the churches of Maranhão in 1653 and was kicked out of São Luís city for his impudence, precipitating the disbanding of the Jesuit order. One such church is the Catedral da Sé; an imposing neoclassical edifice with a plain interior, mostly dating from the early 20th century.

✉ Praça Dom Pedro II, s/n ☎ 89 3222 7380 🕑 Daily 8–7 ✋ Free

PALÁCIO DOS LEÕES

This stately palace on old São Luís's main avenue retains parts of the original French fort in its walls. It was expanded by the Portuguese after they conquered the city in 1615. The palace was the seat of state government in the early republic and is now part musuem, part government offices. Visitors are given felt shoes so as not to scuff the jacaranda wood floors as they walk through rooms—furnished like a minor European stately home—with chairs, tables and ornaments from Portugal, France and England, and monumental paintings by Vitor Meirelles (1832–1903).

✉ Avenida Dom Pedro II s/n ☎ 89 3214 8638 🕑 Mon, Wed, Fri 3–6 ✋ R$8

MORE TO SEE

There are other churches worthy of a visit. Nossa Senhora do Carmo (tel 98 3222 6104; daily 7–11.15, 2.30–6) was built in 1627 and has a sumptuous filigreed early rococo facade. The Igreja do Desterro (daily 8–11.30, 3–6.30), which has a beautiful foliated pediment, stands on the site of the first religious building in the city, a humble hermitage. It has been rebuilt twice: once in 1648 after it was gutted by the invading Dutch and again in 1839, by the African-Brazilian devotee, José Lé, who rebuilt it from the ground up with the help of friends after it fell into serious disrepair.

TIPS

» Try and be in São Luís for the lively Bumba-Meu-Boi celebrations in June (▷ 289).

» To see the best of the old civic buildings, walk down Rua Portugal and Rua do Giz, in the old city centre.

» The old colonial centre is the best place to find cafés and restaurants.

Left *Participants in the Bumba-Meu-Boi festival, celebrated in June*

Below *Buildings near the Convento*

FROM BARREIRINHAS TO JERICOACOARA

This spectacular beach tour, by boat and jeep, crosses the Lençóis and the Delta do Parnaíba before navigating east through extensive dune systems in Ceará state and ending at the beach town of Jericoacoara. The scenery along the way is desolate in parts, exuberant in others and invariably magnificent. The journey as a whole is much the most interesting way of travelling overland between Maranhão and Ceará states.

THE DRIVE
Distance: 400km (248 miles)
Time: 3 days
Start at: Barreirinhas 395 R5
End at: Jericoacoara 395 S5

HOW TO GET THERE

The journey can only be undertaken with an experienced local tour operator (this bespoke itinerary is with Ecodunas, ▷ 289) and should on no account be attempted alone. It is easy to get lost in the Lençóis Maranhenses and there is no rescue and recovery. There are buses from São Luís to the start town of Barreirinhas, where there is accommodation, and Ecodunas will pick you up from your hotel.

★ Barreirinhas (▷ 280) is a small town huddled under a dune on the edge of the Parque Nacional dos Lençóis Maranhenses (▷ 280–281). It is the most convenient base for visiting the national park. The Ecodunas offices lie here at Rua Inácio Lins 164. The first part of the tour comprises a boat journey towards the ocean along the lovely Rio Preguiças.

❶ Look out for Amazon and ringed kingfishers along the riverbank, and brown capuchin monkeys congregating in the trees.

The boat stops for lunch at the tiny settlement of Vassouras.

❷ Vassouras consists of little more than a house, which doubles up as a restaurant and makeshift, hotel. The hotel has no beds, just space for hammocks, but sits under a 70m-high (229ft) dune, with superb views from the top. There is no shade, so bring a sun hat if you wish to climb to the top as it is blazing hot at any time of year.

The boat continues to the beach town of Caburé where there is an optional overnight stop.

❸ Caburé (▷ 281) sits on a tiny spit less than a kilometre wide, fronted by an enormous beach which stretches for more than 80km (50 miles) in

Left *The mouth of the Rio Preguiças*
Above *Sculpted dunes in Lençóis Maranhenses national park*
Opposite *The vehicle and passenger ferry which crosses the Rio Preguiças*

either direction. Sunsets from the shore are particularly beautiful. Atlantic waves are fierce and there are strong currents, so swimming is best in the Rio Preguiças immediately behind the village.

The journey continues east from Caburé to Tutoía town, with a five-hour jeep ride through the spectacular Pequenos Lençóis. It is rare to see anyone on the first part of this extensive stretch along vast beaches and below towering dunes. Lunch is taken at the riverside town of Paulino Neves. From here it's a two-hour drive to Tutoía, for boats across the Delta do Parnaíba.

❹ The river Parnaíba flows 1,700km (1,054 miles) through the *sertão* of Maranhão and Piauí states to spread into one of the largest deltas in South America (▷ 272), formed by an accident of coastal geography more than the power of the river itself. There are more than 70 islands along the fractured coast that makes the river mouth so huge, some of them large enough for several villages. The scenery, beaches and islands are breathtaking.

The four-hour boat ride through the mouth of the Delta brings you to Parnaíba town, which sits a few kilometres from its river port. This is another good spot to make an overnight stop.

❺ Parnaíba (▷ 273) is a delightful small port town with a pocket-sized 18th-century centre. It grew prosperous on the cotton, cattle and mineral trades. There are restaurants near the river serving simple food, should you choose to eat outside your designated hotel.

Jeeps leave the next morning for Camocim, on the PL210 highway. This is the least interesting and quickest part of the journey. At Camocim a roll-on-roll-off ferry takes ten cars at a time across the river to Coreaú. It is a two-hour journey from here through broken dunes and along beaches to Jericoacoara (▷ 272–273). From the tour end, you can arrange transport on to the Ceará state capital at Fortaleza (▷ 274–275), where there are onward air and bus connections throughout Brazil for the rest of your stay.

WHEN TO GO

The journey is best undertaken between July and December, when the dune lakes are full in the Lençóis Maranhenses.

WHERE TO EAT

The locations visited en route are very small and restaurant choice is minimal. Most establishments outside Parnaíba and Barreirinhas will only serve one dish, usually fish. Ecodunas will be happy to find restaurants for you along your journey. Before you leave you may enjoy Barlavento Carlão (▷ 290), in Barreirinhas, and Na Casa Dela (▷ 291) could provide a romantic meal to end your trip in Jericoacoara.

TIPS

» Although spectacular, the journey is rough and dusty, and while Ecodunas use air-conditioned four-wheel drive cars, ferries and boat rides can be uncomfortable (and at times a little hair-raising).

» Bring bottled water, a sun hat, a mosquito net for the smaller hotels, plenty of sun protection and anti-diarrhoea tablets.

» If you intend to include this journey as part of a longer Brazil trip, do not use standard suitcases. Wheels can get clogged with sand and bulky suitcases with handles are impractical. Rucksacks are a better option.

CANOA QUEBRADA

KITE FLAT WATER

www.brasilkiteflatwater.com

One of the larger and best-organized of the Canoa Quebrada kite schools, who can arrange packages of tuition and equipment hire, including accommodation and transfers from Fortaleza.

✉ Rua Dragão do Mar ☎ 85 9604 4953

KITESURF UNIVERSITY

www.ikubrasil.com

One of a number of very small local operators renting kites and boards, and offering kite-surf instruction. Guides speak several European languages, including English, Spanish and Italian.

✉ Rua Principal s/n

FORTALEZA

BIRDING NORTH EAST BRAZIL

www.nebrazilbirding.com

Ciro Albano is considered to be the most experienced bird-watching guide in the northeast of Brazil, offering bespoke and scheduled trips to the Serra de Baturité and the other mountains around Fortaleza, as well as locations further afield like Canudos (▷ 205) and southern Bahia (▷ 202–241).

☎ 85 9955 5162

CEARÁ SAVEIRO

Yacht and *jangada* (raft) trips from Praia de Mucuripe, around the beaches and offshore reefs in Fortaleza. There are stops for snorkelling and for exploring the different beaches.

✉ Avenida Beira Mar 4293 ☎ 85 3263 1085

DRAGÃO DO MAR

www.dragaodomar.org.br

This big cultural and entertainment centre, set 400m (436 yards) behind the beach, has live music most nights and there are numerous small bars and restaurants. It is the best spot in the city for experiencing traditional nightlife.

✉ Dragão do Mar 81, Praia de Iracema ☎ 85 3488 8600

O PIRATA

www.pirata.com.br

The liveliest of Praia do Iracema's numerous night spots, which hosts a famous Monday night with live regional *forró* music and other Brazilian bands.

✉ Rua dos Tabajaras 325, Iracema ☎ 85 4011 6161

TEATRO JOSÉ DE ALENCAR

www.secult.ce.gov.br

This magnificent theatre in the eclectic style is surrounded by Burle Marx Gardens. At the centre of the city's cultural life, it showcases a variety of performances from theatre to dance and music, both contemporary and classical from Brazil and around the world.

✉ Praça do José Alencar ☎ 85 3101 2583

JERICOACOARA

ASSOCIAÇÃO DE BUGUEIROS (ABJ)

This is the Jericoacoara beach buggy company, who use local drivers for their tours and thus ensure

Opposite *Kite-surfing at Canoa Quebrada*

that money goes back into the community.
✉ Rua Principal s/n ☎ 88 3669 2284

ASSOCIAÇÃO DOS CAVALEIROS DE JERICOACOARA
For a change from a beach buggy, try a guided horse-riding trip around the town from the Jericoacoara Equestrian Association. You can ride along the beaches to the Pedra Furada and visit the nearby lakes and dunes.
✉ Rua das Dunas at Rua Nova Jeri, next to the sunset dune ☎ 88 8801 6871; pedromenezes76@hotmail.com

VILA KALANGO
This is not just a hotel (▷ 293) but also offers wind- and kite-surf packages to Jericoacoara, staying at the Vila in the town or at their sister hotel, Rancho do Peixe, on the kite and windsurf beach of Praia da Preá.

NATAL

CENTRO DE TURISMO
www.centrodeturismonatal.com
This big shop, housed in an old prison, has an impressive choice of handicrafts and local art sold from various stalls.
✉ Rua Aderbal de Figueiredo 980, off Rua Gen Cordeiro, Petrópolis ☎ 84 3212 2267
🕑 Sun–Wed 9–7, Thu 9–10pm

CENTRO MUNICIPAL DE ARTESANATO
This artisan centre sells local arts and crafts, including the famous sand-in-bottle pictures made from material gathered from the cliffs and beaches.
✉ Avenida Presidnete Café Filho, Praia dos Artistas 🕑 Daily 10–10

DROMEDUNAS
www.dromedunas.com.br
Cleide Gomes and Philippe Landry offer dromedary rides on the dunes above Genipabu. Walks last around half an hour and they make a far more peaceful alternative to buzzing dune buggies. You will find them on Genipabu beach.
✋ R$30 for a 30-min ride

FESTIVALS AND EVENTS

JUNE

BUMBA-MEU-BOI
This very lively traditional festival, with roots in indigenous Brazil, West Africa and pagan Portugal, takes place throughout June. It is rich with symbolic meaning on dozens of levels and is the largest festival in this part of northeastern Brazil. Celebrations not only herald the coming of the rain and the imminent harvest, but also tell the story of the death and resurrection of a legendary ox—a metaphor for the cycles in farming life. There are street bands and parades, particularly in front of São João and São Benedito churches in São Luís, and dances somewhere in the city almost every night in June. There are also a whole string of smaller, related festivals elsewhere. The largest celebrations are during the weekend closest to 28 June.
ℹ Rua Portugal 165, São Luís ☎ 98 3231 0822 🕑 Mon–Fri 10–5

MANARY
www.caririecotours.com.br
Well-organized and comfortable trips to the Serra da Capivara and other destinations in the northeastern *sertão*, from a long-established company specializing in archaeological and geological tours.
✉ Rua Francisco Gurgel, Ponta Negra Beach ☎ 84 9928 0198

PARNAÍBA

DELTA DO RIO PARNAÍBA
www.deltadorioparnaiba.com.br
This Parnaíba-based company offer boat trips into the delta and to other locations in Piauí and Maranhão states. Prices depend on group numbers and destinations.
✉ Porto das Barcas 13 ☎ 86 3321 1969

PARQUE NACIONAL LENÇOIS MARANHENSES

ECODUNAS
www.ecodunas.tur.br
This company offers the best-run trips into the Lençóis Maranhenses (▷ 280–281), from light morning trips to three-week expeditions. Excursions are bespoke and should be booked at least two weeks in advance. They also run multi-day transfers to Jericoacoara (▷ 286–287), with sleeping in *palapa* thatch huts, and to the interior of Piauí.
✉ Rua Inácio Lins 164, Centro Barreirinhas ☎ 11 9902 9149, 11 4654 1200

PARQUE NACIONAL SERRA DA CAPIVARA

TRILHAS DA CAPIVARA
For guided visits in the park, with trail walks and archaeological walks to rock art sites, the company uses FUMDHAM guides (▷ 282) and can organize transfers from hotels in the region. Bring water and a snack.
☎ 89 3582 1294; trilhascapivara@uol.com.br

SÃO LUÍS

ANTIGAMENTE
Crowds gather at this restaurant and after-hours bar, and at the neighbouring Armazen Estrela, to hear live music at weekends from 6pm. It is so popular that the clientele spill out onto the adjacent square.
✉ Rua da Estrela 220 ☎ 98 3232 3964

PHYLIPI
Phylipi is an excellent guide, who speaks fluent English and French. He offers architectural trips around São Luís and Alcântara, and walking tours of the historical centre.
☎ 98 8118 1710; phylipi@hotmail.com

REGGAE BAR DO PORTO
São Luís is famous for its live Brazilian reggae and this is one of the most established live music bars. It gets very busy at weekends and there is no admission fee.
✉ Rua do Portugal 49 ☎ 98 3232 1115

PRICES AND SYMBOLS

The restaurants are listed alphabetically (excluding A, Al, El, La, Le and O). The prices given are the average for a two-course lunch (L) and a three-course dinner (D) for one person, without drinks. The wine price is for the least expensive bottle. Although you will find wine served in restaurants throughout Brazil, the usual drinks are bottled beer (R$5–R$8) or *caipirinhas*, the ubiquitous *cachaça* and fruit cocktails (R$8). All the restaurants listed accept credit cards unless otherwise stated.

For a key to the symbols, ▻ 2.

BARREIRINHAS

BARLAVENTO CARLÃO

The best restaurant in town, serving good river and marine fish in exotic fruit sauces, *carne do sol* (meat jerky) and delicious fresh fruit juices. Meals are served in an attractive dining room and on an alfresco deck overlooking the river.

✉ Avenida Beira Rio s/n ☎ 98 3349 0627 🕐 Daily 12–3, 6.30–11 L R$25, D R$35

FORTALEZA

RESTAURANTE DO SUIÇO

It's well worth heading a few blocks inland to eat the superior wood-fired pizzas in this atmospheric open-sided restaurant. The bar serves good cocktails and cheap, very cold beer. There's always a lively crowd, with many European ex-pats.

✉ Rua Antônio Augusto and José Agustinho, Praia de Iracema 🕐 Daily 12–3, 6.30–11 L R$25, D R$40, Wine R$40

ROMAGNA MIA

Owned by an Italian, this restaurant is excellent for fresh seafood (especially the king prawns in garlic), pasta and thin-crust pizza. Guests sit in a vine-shaded garden tiled with mock-Copacabana dragon's-tooth paving.

✉ Rua Joaquim Alves 160 🕐 Tue–Sat 12–3, 6.30–11 L R$20, D R$30

SANTA CLARA CAFÉ ORGÂNICO

www.santaclara.com.br

This cosy little café, a few metres from Iracema beach at the Dragão do Mar complex, serves delicious organic coffees, juices and cold drinks, plus sandwiches and desserts, including sweet, sticky *pudim de leite* (crème caramel). Find the Santa Clara café at the end of the red girder walkway, or upstairs, depending on which way you go.

✉ Rua Dragão do Mar 81, Praia de Iracema 🕐 Mon–Sat 7–4 L R$15

SOBRE O MAR

www.sobreomardiracema.com.br

This is a great place to watch the sunset over the pier, drinking a delicious icy *batida* cocktail or a *vodka com abacaxi* (vodka with pineapple). For the children, a *petit gateau* with chocolate sauce is difficult to beat but you may prefer to choose a different venue for your main course.

✉ Rua dos Tremembés 2 ☎ 85 3219 6999 🕐 Tue–Sun 12–3, 6–11 L R$25, D R$45, Wine R$35

Above *Succulent seafood from Fortaleza*

JERICOACOARA

BISTROGONOFF

As you'd guess from the name, this restaurant specializes in stroganoffs but also has a good choice of other meat dishes, fish and pasta. The Paulista owners ensure a friendly atmosphere. The venue is popular in the evenings so maybe book ahead.
✉ Beco do Guaxelo 60 ☎ 88 3669 2220 ⌚ Daily 12–3, 7–11 ✋ L R$15, D R$25 ? Closes sporadically Mar–Jul and Aug–Sep

NA CASA DELA

There's an intimate and romantic setting here, the tables set out on sand under palm trees. Waitresses wear brilliantly coloured regional dress and the food displays the best of northeastern Brazilian and Bahian cuisine. Try delicious sun-dried meat with onions, manioc flour, rice and puréed squash, washed down with a cold *Bohemia* beer.
✉ Rua Principal s/n ☎ 88 3669 2024 ⌚ Daily 12–3, 7–11 ✋ L R$25, D R$40, Wine R$30 ? Closes sporadically Mar–Jul and Aug–Sep

NATAL

CHAPLIN

This restaurant is part of a leisure complex that includes a bar, English pub and a nightclub. Traditional seafood is the principal menu option, with fillets of hake or grouper grilled or fried lightly in flour and served with beans and rice.
✉ Avenida Pres Café Filho 27, Praia dos Artistas ☎ 84 3236 3696 ⌚ Daily 12–3, 6–12 ✋ L R$30, D R$40

ESTAÇÃO TREM DE MINAS

This is a posh self-service restaurant serving lunch and dinner with a mix of meaty central Brazilian standards, including *tutu de feijão* (refried beans with garlic, served with manioc flour) and Brazilian sausages served with mashed squash. There's live music at night and cocktails on the terrace, where you can choose from 40 brands of *cachaça* (sugar cane rum).
✉ Avenida Pres Café Filho 197, Praia do Meio ☎ 84 3202 2099 ⌚ Daily 12–3, 6–12 ✋ L R$30, D R$40

PARNAÍBA

LA BARCA

Here you will find Brazilian standards and decent river and marine fish dishes, including fillets of freshly caught hake and tarpon. They are served in an airy dining room overlooking the river, east of the colonial centre.
✉ Avenida Nações Unidas 200 ☎ 86 3322 2825 ⌚ Tue–Sat 12–3, 6.30–11, Sun 12–4 ✋ L R$20, D R$30

SÃO LUÍS

ANTIGAMENTE

This is a cheerful restaurant serving standard Portuguese and Brazilian dishes, including fish such as snook and yellow fish and pizza. The décor is bright with colourful bottles and local art. It's bustling at the weekends with live bands and an enthusiastic crowd of all ages.
✉ Rua da Estrela 220 ☎ 98 3232 3964 ⌚ Tue–Sat 12–3, 7–12, Sun 12–4 ✋ L R$20, D R$30

ARMAZÉM DA ESTRELA

On the top floor here is a classy fine-dining restaurant, offering French-Brazilian dishes as well as international standards (like steak Diane). Try the partridge in *cajá* fruit sauce. Downstairs there's a great little *botequin* (street bar), where you can get excellent *petisco* (tapas-like) snacks. The ambience is cool, in a brick and stone room with Romanesque arches. There is live traditional and eclectic music, from samba to choro, at weekends .
✉ Rua da Estrela 401 ☎ 98 3254 1274 ⌚ Mon–Sat 11–midnight ✋ L R$25, D R$35

PADARIA FRANCÊS VALÉRY

This modest little bakery is the place to go for scrumptious cakes, faux-French éclairs, quiches, tropical fruit juices and coffee, combined with all the usual Brazilian friendliness.
✉ Rua do Giz (28 de Julho) 164 ⌚ Mon–Fri 6–4 ✋ L R$10

PAPAGAIO AMARELO

Superb fish and regional dishes stand out here in an imaginative and varied menu. It is another bustling venue, especially at the weekend, like the neighbouring Antigamente (▷ this page), in this busy street. There's good live music here too.
✉ Rua da Estrela 210 ☎ 98 3221 3855 ⌚ Tue–Sat 12–3, 7–12, Sun 12–4 ✋ L R$30, D R$45, Wine R$45

TERESINA

CAMARÃO DO ELIAS

Camarão do Elias is considered to be the city's best fish restaurant, serving a mix of regional and Bahian dishes, including *moqueca de camarão* (a traditional prawn broth made with coconut milk and spices).
✉ Avenida Pedro Almeida 457 ☎ 86 3232 5025 ⌚ Tue–Sat 7.30pm–1am, Sun 11–4 ✋ L R$30, D R$40

FAVORITOS COMIDAS TÍPICAS

This home-style and welcoming restaurant in the city centre serves regional specialities, including *carne do sol* (jerky) accompanied by rice and kale.
✉ Rua Angelica 1059 ☎ 86 3232 2121 ⌚ Mon–Sat 12–3, 6–12, Sun 12–3 ✋ L R$20, D R$40, Wine R$40

TIBAÚ DO SUL AND PIPA

CAMAMO BEIJUPIRÁ

This fine restaurant specializes in a variety of fusion dishes which are served by chef/owner Tadeu Lubambo. The interior has an exotic candlelit ambience where the air is scented with cinnamon and vanilla. There is an excellent wine list. Reservations are essential so ring the day before.
✉ Tibaú do Sul, access via RN-003 ☎ 84 3246 4195 ⌚ Daily 8pm–1.30am ✋ D R$60, Wine R$40

TOCA DA CORUJA

www.tocadacoruja.com.br
Superlative and beautifully presented regional food is served in a romantic tropical garden setting. Dishes include prawns served with wild rice and the wine list is one of the best in Pipa.
✉ Avenida Baia dos Golfinhos, Pipa ☎ 84 3246 2226 ⌚ Daily 7.30–midnight ✋ D R$50, Wine R$40

PRICES AND SYMBOLS

Prices are the lowest and highest for a double room for one night. Breakfast is included unless noted otherwise. All the hotels listed accept credit cards unless otherwise stated. Note that rates vary widely throughout the year.

For a key to the symbols, ▷ 2.

BARREIRINHAS

POUSADA BELO HORIZONTE

www.bhmirante.com.br

Situated near the central square, this decent hotel includes friendly service from the owner, Albino. Rooms are well-kept, tiled and whitewashed. The quietest are at the front. Enjoy a pleasant rooftop breakfast. There is a sister *pousada* in Caburé (▷ 281).

✉ Avenida Joaquim Soeiro de Carvalho 245 ☎ 98 3499 0054 R$70–R$120 21

CANOA QUEBRADA

POUSADA LATITUDE

www.pousadalatitude.com.br

This *pousada* consists of spacious, air-conditioned, two-storey bungalows in a large complex off the main street. They are not particularly interesting but with decent service.

✉ Rua Dragão do Mar (Broadway) ☎ 88 3241 7041 R$90–R$150 18 Outdoor

POUSADA OÁSIS DO REI

www.pousadaoasisdorei.com.br

This *pousada* has simple rooms around a pool in a little garden, with polished concrete or tiled floors; some have sea views and some have bed space for three or four. All have little terraces slung with hammocks. The *pousada* is basic in style and facilities but has free WiFi. Children under six stay for free.

✉ Rua Nascer do Sol 112 ☎ 88 3421 7081 R$100–R$180 14 Outdoor

POUSADA VIA LÁCTEA

www.pousadavialactea.com

The chunky brick building here may not be beautiful, but the views are and the beach is only roughly 50m (55 yards) away. English is spoken and tours can be organized. The proprietors allow camping in the lawned back garden.

✉ Just off Rua Dragão do Mar (Broadway) R$100–R$180; camping R$10–R$20 10 P

FORTALEZA

POUSADA SALINAS

www.pousadasalinas.com.br

A pleasant but very basic *pousada*, with clean unadorned rooms that have air-conditioning, TVs, fridges and parking. It is located just across from the sea. There is some English spoken by staff and the simple breakfast is self-service.

✉ Avenida Zezé Diogo 3300, Praia do Futuro ☎ 85 3234 3626 R$80–R$140 19 P

POUSADA DO SUIÇO

www.pension-vom-schweizer.com.br

Situated in a very private, quiet street, this Swiss-run *pousada* includes a choice of rooms, some with kitchens and air-conditioning, including TVs and fridges. The owner changes cash and traveller's cheques and offers an airport pick-up for R$75. Rooms must be reserved in advance between mid-October and February.

✉ Rua Antônia Augusto 141, Iracema ☎ 85 3219 3873 R$80–R$135 33

SEARA PRAIA

www.hotelseara.com.br

Here you will find an upmarket hotel with top facilities, including a pool, gym and cyber café. It is 30 per cent cheaper between April and October. The hotel has a very good restaurant serving French cuisine .

✉ Avenida Beira Mar 3080, Meireles ☎ 85 4011 2200 R$267–R$321 217 Outdoor

Opposite *Pousada Portas da Amazônia*

JERICOACOARA

POUSADA NOVA ERA

www.novaerapousada.com.br

This pretty little *pousada* fewer than five-minutes' walk from the beach offers a selection of bright rooms and chalets. They sit in an Italianate garden here, shaded by numerous trees and coloured with tropical flowers. There is room for five in the larger cabins, making this an economical option for groups. It is Italian-owned.

Rua do Forró s/n 88 3669 2056 R$180–R$220 18

POUSADA ZÉ BENTO

This good-value hotel has small, tiled rooms with white walls and little bathrooms off a small, palm shaded and sandy garden annexe. Tours can be organized by the friendly staff and it is locally owned.

Rua São Francisco s/n 88 3669 2006 R$60–R$100 12

POUSADA ZÉ PATINHA

www.sandjeri.com.br

Simple, air-conditioned or fan-cooled plain white rooms are available here in two parallel corridors. There are no outside windows so rooms overlook the corridor, but they remain cool and quiet all day and the beach is 200m (218 yards) from the front door. Beds have decent mattresses. The hotel is locally owned.

Rua São Francisco s/n 88 3669 2081 R$60–R$100 16

VILA KALANGO

www.vilakalango.com.br

Local artwork decorates rooms in stilt house cabins set in a tree-filled garden, behind the beach. There are mosquito nets, and some rooms are air-conditioned. The garden has a pool and bar area, there is a decent restaurant and excellent facilities for kite-surfers and windsurfers. The Vila has a sister hotel, Rancho do Peixe, on Praia da Preá. Shuttle buses are provided on request to and from Fortaleza for arrival and departure (a five-hour drive).

Rua do Ibama s/n 88 3669 2289 R$305–R$535 24 Outdoor

NATAL

HOTEL E POUSADA O TEMPO E O VENTO

www.otempoeovento.com.br

This small terracotta and whitewash hotel is a block back from the beach, with a range of air-conditioned rooms gathered around a pool. The *luxo* rooms are by far the best. The cheaper ones have a fan only. Low season discounts are available.

Rua Elias Barros 66 84 3219 2526 R$100–R$160 22 Outdoor

IYHA LUA CHEIA

www.luacheia.com.br

This is one of the best youth hostels in Brazil. It occupies a mock-castle with a medieval-style Taverna Pub in the basement. It is IYHA affiliated, and the low prices per person include breakfast. Even the website is fun!

Rua Dr Manoel Augusto Bezerra de Araújo 500 84 3236 3696 Dorm bed R$30; double room R$96– R$120 (discount for students and members) 26

OCEAN PALACE

www.oceanpalace.com.br

The 5-star rating here ensures large, comfortable suites, and also smaller, pokier family rooms and a string of bungalows lined up near the beach. Public areas include a lovely ocean-front pool and terrace, plus tennis court, spa and children's play area. There's a relaxed and friendly atmosphere, too. The hotel is huge, however, and would not be the choice for those looking for beachside boutique intimacy.

Via Costeira, km 11, near Ponta Negra 84 3220 4144 R$530– R$750 305 Outdoor P

SÃO LUÍS

POUSADA PORTAS DA AMAZÔNIA

www.portasdaamazonia.com.br

This *pousada* in the centre of town has been beautifully converted from the original colonial mansion. Rooms are coolly elegant with wooden floors. Breakfast is served in the shade of the garden. There's an on-site pizzeria for evening meals. Internet access is available.

Rua do Giz 129 98 3222 9937 R$139–R$209 29

QUALITY GRAND SÃO LUÍS HOTEL

www.atlanticahotels.com.br

This is a splendid 1960s hotel. Rooms have writing desks and plain, functional furniture, but the best of them have sea views. There are business facilities, pool and gym.

Praça Dom Pedro II 299 98 2109 3500 R$209–R$230 211 Outdoor

TERESINA

RIO POTY

www.riopoty.com

One of the better options in town, Rio Poty provides spacious, bright rooms with bathrooms in a concrete block overlooking a big swimming pool. It's probably more suitable for business needs than for a family holiday.

Avenida Mcal Castelo Branco 555, Ilhota 86 4009 4009 R$215–R$390 54 Outdoor

TIBAÚ DO SUL AND PIPA

PONTA DO MADEIRO

www.pontadomadeiro.com.br

This place provides very comfortable and spacious air-conditioned chalets with striking local interior design. There's a beautiful pool with a bar and spectacular views over the Praia do Madeiro. Service is excellent and there is a good restaurant.

Avenida Antonio Florencia 2695 (midway between Tibaú do Sol and Pipa) 84 3246 4220 R$348–R$610 40 Outdoor

TOCA DA CORUJA

www.tocadacoruja.com.br

This is a superb luxury hotel. It offers a range of chalets, set in forested gardens next to Pipa beach. The pool is beautiful and the restaurant top-ranking.

Praia da Pipa 84 3246 2226 R$480–R$1,400 23 Outdoor

THE AMAZON

Brazil's Amazonian territory makes up almost half the country and is larger than Western Europe. It's not all forest. Brazil's highest mountain—the Pico da Neblina, at 3,014m (9,886ft)—is in the Amazon and there are extensive areas of savannah, islands with fluffy white sand beaches and cities of more than a million people: Manaus and Belém. Nor is the Amazon a single river. Most of South America's rain and Andean meltwater flows into the Amazon through thousands of tributaries. These rise and fall by up to 40m (131ft) annually to flood hundreds of thousands of square kilometres of forest and create unique seasonally inundated biomes, called *varzea* and *igapó*.

The forest is being chopped at a depressing rate—for soya, cattle and logs—and flooded for vast hydroelectric dams. However, vast swathes remain primeval and undisturbed, in areas never paddled through, or trod, even by an indigenous foot. Access to the Amazon is through the capital cities of one of the eight Brazilian states which comprise the region: principally through Manaus (capital of Amazonas), Belém (capital of Pará) and Rio Branco (capital of Acre).

Manaus and Belém are large cities. The former sits on the Rio Negro and is surrounded by dozens of rainforest lodges. It is also the departure point for the town of Parintins and its Boi Bumba festival, the Amazon equivalent of the Rio carnival. Belém has less infrastructure but is a more interesting city in its own right. It boasts vibrant culture, the best music scene in northern Brazil and a beautiful colonial centre, sitting in the mouth of the river next to the magnificent island of Marajó.

Rio Branco, in Acre state in the far west of Brazil, offers the chance to really get off the beaten track. There are well-organized tours to remote indigenous villages and some of the best eco-lodges in the region. There are other options too, such as Boa Vista in the remote and far-northern state of Roraima, and the superb lodges in the Mamirauá and Cristalino reserves.

AMAPÁ

www.setur.ap.gov.br

This small state sits sandwiched between the northern bank of the Amazon, the Atlantic Ocean and French Guiana. The equator passes straight through its capital city of Macapá. It is a quiet, provincial town, huddled on the riverbank behind a spalted 17th-century Portuguese fort, the Forte de São José do Macapá, with the savannahs and forests of the Amazon at its back. Tourism in Amapá is in its infancy and the few international visitors who venture here are mostly French, on their way overland from Cayenne to the beaches and islands near Belém. Macapá attracts increasing numbers of surfers, who gather at the myriad mouths of the Amazon (particularly the Aguari) to catch the pororoca bore wave, which occurs several times a year. This is one of the largest tidal bores in the world, reaching a height of 4m (13ft) and a speed of up to 21kph (13mph).

379 M3 Avenida Binga Uchôa 29, Macapá 96 3212 5335 Mon–Fri 10–6 International routes from Cayenne, in French Guiana River boats from Belém and Santarém Internacional de Macapá There is a tourist office at the airport which opens only for flight arrivals

THE AMAZON AROUND MANAUS

▷ 298–299.

BELÉM

▷ 300–303.

BELTERRA AND FORDLÂNDIA

www.santarem.pa.gov.br

Henry Ford bought land at Santarém, near the mouth of the Tapajós, in 1934. He built these two rubber plantation towns and filled them with workers, hoping that they would supply the Ford Motor Company with all the rubber they needed for car tyres. By 1940, plantations around the towns were flourishing and the *seringueiro* rubber tappers were paid wages which allowed them financial freedom. They were also given Detroit-style accommodation, a free hospital and medical inspections, a cinema, sports clubs, and even an ice machine. This was in sharp contrast to the contemporaneous Brazilian practice, under which they were enslaved by both debt and the whip. However, the cities had died a few years later, after the neat rows of rubber plants were attacked by voracious Amazon parasites. The *seringueiros* neglected the neat rows of Detroit houses, ignored the American cinema and sports club, and lived off their week's pay for months, refusing to work until the money had run out. Medical supplies were stolen and sold on the black market, and Ford, far from raising productivity with his Detroit methods, actually lowered it. Fordlândia produced less rubber than tapping wild forest trees. After losing US$30 million, he sold the towns to the Brazilian government, who turned Fordlândia and Belterra into an agricultural research station.

Belterra 378 K5; Fordlândia 383 K5 Rua Floriano Peixoto 777, Santarém 93 3523 2434 Mon–Fri 10–5 From Cuiabá River boats to Santarém from Belém, Macapá, Manaus, and destinations throughout the Amazon Aeroporto de Santarém

BOA VISTA AND RORAIMA STATE

www.boavista.rr.gov.br

Brazil's most northern state, Roraima, lies on the borders of both Venezuela and Guyana; it's closer to Miami than it is to São Paulo. The capital, Boa Vista, is uneventful, small and modern, laid out in a grid on the banks of the pretty Rio Branco and surrounded by Amazonian savannah. It lies within easy access of both Venezuela and Guyana, and visiting the Angel Falls, the Gran Sabana or the Rupununi in those countries is straightforward. Agencies in Boa Vista organize trips, as well as tours to the table-top mountain of Mount Roraima, which marks the convergence of all three countries, and to the upper Rio Branco and the Serra do Tepequém mountains.

377 G2 Rua Coronel Pinto 267, Boa Vista 95 2121 2525 Mon–Fri 9–6 From Manaus, Guyana and Venezuela Boa Vista International border crossings: Guyana (Lethem), Venezuela (Santa Elena)

Opposite *Teatro Amazonas opera house in Manaus (▷ 307)*

Below *Marco Zero, the line of the equator, in Macapá*

INFORMATION

382 H5 (Manaus) Rua da Instalação 70, Manaus 92 3633 7955 Mon–Fri 10–6 From Boa Vista River boats from Santarém and destinations throughout the Amazon Eduardo Gomes (Manaus) There is a tourist booth at the airport (Mon–Fri 10–8) and another next to the Teatro Amazonas (▷ 307) in Manaus city centre (daily 10–6)

Above *The Anavilhanas Islands on the Rio Negro in the Amazon forest near Manaus*

INTRODUCTION

Manaus lies at the confluence of the Solimões and Negro rivers. After they join they become the Amazon river, at least for Brazilians. It is particularly beautiful around Manaus. The dark tea-coloured Negro is lined with white-sand beaches and the Solimões runs into an endless series of lily-covered lakes and floating islands. *Igarapés*, or creeks, run into the forest from both river systems, and jungle lodges, museums and private homes lie secreted in their depths. Others float on the water, rising and falling with the annual floods.

WHAT TO SEE

ANAVILHANAS ARCHIPELAGO

The world's largest river archipelago—comprising hundreds of forested islands and *igarapés*—begins some 90km (56 miles) upstream of Manaus, near the town of Novo Airão. At dusk, thousands of swallows rush in to the islands to roost just as thousands of bats leave for their night hunt. Rio Negro safari cruises, like those offered by Amazon Clipper and Amazon Gero Tours (▷ 315), almost always visit the Anavilhanas, and it is possible to swim with dolphins here.

LAGO MAMORI

This large lake, which is fed by a river and which runs into hundreds of small creeks and areas of flooded forest, is home to a number of riverine communities involved in homestay ecotourism projects. The farther reaches of the lake back onto unspoiled Amazonian forest and make a good area for seeing primates and birds, like hoatzins.

The lake can be visited with Amazon Gero tours (▷ 315).

MEETING OF THE WATERS

The waters of the black Rio Negro and cappuccino-coloured Solimões run side by side for more than 20km (12.5 miles) before gradually merging to form the Amazon. The sight of two rivers flowing together but apart is striking, particularly when a pink river dolphin pops out of the gentle waves.

MUSEU SERINGAL

A 25-minute boat ride from Ponta Negra Beach in Manaus will take you to the end of a little *igarapé* creek. Hidden behind a beach there is this full-scale reproduction of an early 20th-century rubber-tapping mansion house. It is accurate to the last detail, with serf quarters, a factory and a shop selling authentic products and balls of raw rubber. It was built for the 2002 Portuguese film, *A Selva*. A guided tour here is fascinating; ask to be taken round by one of the former rubber tappers and for them to tell the story of their experiences under debt peonage, which enslaved Brazilians up until the 1970s.

Igarapé São João, 15km (9.5 miles) north of Manaus up the Rio Negro · 92 3234 8755 · Tue–Sun 8–4 · R$3, including tour · R$15 round trip on a private launch from the Tropical Manaus Hotel (▷ 321)

PARQUE ECOLÓGICO DE JANAUARI

This 9,000ha (22,230-acre) reserve is like a giant Amazon theme park, geared up to receive large numbers of tourists. Most of the animals you'll see are tame and are owned by vendors and shopkeepers who operate around the lake in the park. Most visitors hoping to see the wild Amazon find the tame scrub forest in the park and the captured animals disappointing but it is easy to visit on a day tour from Manaus with any of the larger operators, such as Amazon Explorers (www.amazonexplorers.com.br).

Daily 10–6

TIPS

» The Anavilhanas, Lago Mamori and Parque Ecológico de Janauari can only be visited as part of a jungle tour.

» Taxi boats can be taken to the Museu Seringal from Ponta Negra beach for around R$15.

» There are many rainforest lodges on both rivers (▷ 319–320). The Negro has far fewer insects and less wildlife; the Solimões has more of both, including mosquitoes.

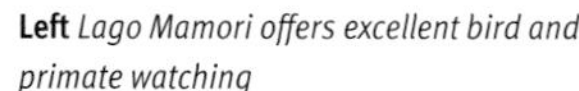

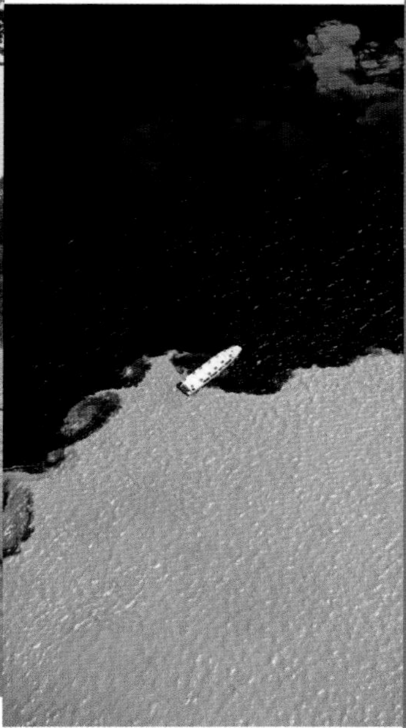

Left *Lago Mamori offers excellent bird and primate watching*
Below *Meeting of the waters of the Amazon and Negro rivers near Manaus*

Above *Boats moored in Belém harbour*

INFORMATION

www.paraturismo.pa.gov.br

394 N4 Praça Waldemar Henrique s/n 91 3224 9493 Mon–Fri 10–6 From São Luís and all major tourist towns River boats from Macapá and Santarém Internacional de Belém

INTRODUCTION

Belém's isolation and a long, glorious past (beginning in 1616 and including a period as South America's wealthiest city) have left it with a unique heritage. Its colonial centre is the most extensive and impressive of any Brazilian city north of Recife, with many fine civic palaces and Portuguese churches. The city's Nazaré festival (▷ 316) is one of the country's largest and most colourful, and Belém has had a rich and creative arts scene since colonial times. This is most obvious today in the music; with its ears to the Caribbean and Europe, as well as its African and indigenous roots, Belém has produced a sound all its own. Calypso-tinged surf guitar music, high-octane *lambada* reggae and psychedelic *Luso* rap-rock explode from dozens of great little bars and giant heaving clubs on weekends, making it one of the most exuberant nightlife scenes in Brazil.

The city sits on the edge of wilderness. From an aeroplane it first appears on the horizon as a distant cityscape of serrated concrete spires, sitting in a vast expanse of Amazon forest with meandering brown rivers and inky swamps, and dotted with beach-fringed islands, many of which are low-key resorts.

WHAT TO SEE

BASÍLICA DE NOSSA SENHORA DE NAZARÉ

www.ciriodenazare.com.br

This huge Romanesque cathedral is the most important pilgrimage site in northern Brazil and the most magnificent 20th-century church in the country. It was built with money from rubber wealth. Its newly restored interior is lined with twin arcades supported by decorated Corinthian marble columns. They lead to a brilliantly coloured altarpiece housing the effigy of Our Lady of Nazareth. A small museum showcases pieces from the Círio de Nazaré festival, which is celebrated every October and which sees millions of pilgrims process through the city.

301 off C3 Praça Justo Chermont, Avenida Magalhães Barata Mon–Sat 5–11.30, 2–8, Sun 5.45–11.30, 2.30–8 Free

THE COLONIAL CENTRE

The eggshell blue and ochre mansions, spalted forts, baroque spires and terracotta roofs of old Belém cluster around the docks to form the city centre. It's a delightful place to explore, though the torrid and humid climate makes an air-conditioned taxi a necessity for walks of longer than five minutes in the heat of the day. Start in the Praça da República, watched over by the gorgeous neoclassical, early 20th-century Teatro da Paz opera house (Tue–Fri 9–6; R$6). Visit the 17th-century Forte do Castelo Portuguese fort and archaeological museum (tel 91 3223 0041; daily 8–11pm; R$4), and finish at the Estação das Docas (www.estacaodasdocas.com.br), tastefully restored old warehouses on the quay with wonderful views over the Guajará Bay.

MERCADO VER-O-PESO

There's no market like Ver-o-Peso anywhere. It is the old Portuguese market built on the docks, housing stalls offering everything from black-magic remedies to fried tapioca, indigenous arts and crafts, and sisal sacks of forest-fresh Brazil nuts. Under the covered section, there are hundreds of alien tropical fruits and river fish as big as a man, with barbel moustaches and soapy skin.

301 A2 Boulevard Castilhos França 27, Campina 91 3212 0549 Daily 5am–9pm

MORE TO SEE

THE ISLANDS

There are myriad islands in the Guajará Bay and in the network of rivers that separate Belém from Macapá, which is 330km (205 miles) away across the mouth of the Amazon. The largest, Marajó (▷ 305) is a little larger than Denmark. Others, like Mosqueiro and Cotijuba, which are both fringed with lovely beaches, are similar in size to the British Channel Islands and can be visited in a day or as a weekend trip (▷ 314).

TIPS

» Be sure to be in Belém on a weekend night to enjoy some of the best nightlife north of Rio and São Paulo.

» Belém has some of the best cooking in the country. Local dishes include *takaka no tucupi* (shrimp and jambu leaves cooked in manioc juice).

» The Estação das Docas is a great place to relax in one of the air-conditioned restaurants, which serve ice-cold juices as you enjoy the views.

» Be vigilant for pick-pockets around Ver-o-Peso.

Overleaf *The beautiful altar of the Basílica de Nossa Senhora de Nazaré, Belém*

INFORMATION

www.cristalinolodge.com.br
383 K8 Alta Floresta, Mato Grosso
66 3512 7100 From Alta Floresta
Alta Floresta

TIPS

» Be sure to book rooms as far in advance as possible—a year in advance is recommended by the lodge.

» The lodge will pick up from the airport and can organize internal flights, given a month's notice.

» Bring insect repellent, a torch (flashlight) and light long-sleeved clothes and trousers which will dry quickly.

CRISTALINO RAINFOREST RESERVE

The southern Amazon includes a variety of diversified habitats where flora and fauna thrive, and there is an astonishing richness of biodiversity. Cristalino Rainforest Reserve, on the Cristalino river in the north of Mato Grosso state, is one of the best locations on the planet for wildlife enthusiasts. It offers superb guided visits to pristine rainforest, comfortable accommodation and excellent wildlife-watching facilities. Visits here are one of the highlights of a trip to Brazil.

ECO-RESERVE

Cristalino is a private reserve the size of Manhattan island, with a rainforest lodge at its heart (▷ 319), accesssed via the small Mato Grosso town of Alta Floresta. It abuts the 184,940ha (456,800 acres) of Cristalino State Park—itself connected to other protected areas—to form a huge conservation corridor in the southern Amazon. The lodge here is a model for ecotourism best practice, fulfilling all four of the key conservational tourism criteria: conserving natural resources and biodiversity, conducting environmental education activities with the local community (leading to employment), practising responsible ecotourism (with recycling, water treatment, small group sizes and excellent guiding) and funding a research foundation.

WILDLIFE IN ABUNDANCE

Cristalino has so far recorded 600 bird species, with new ones added almost monthly. This amounts to half of the avifauna in the Amazon and a third of all species found in Brazil. There is an abundance of mammals, especially the Brazilian tapir and giant river—you may even be extremely fortunate to see a jaguar or puma—alongside very rare or endemic species like bush dogs, red-nosed bearded saki monkey and the white-whiskered spider monkey.

These animals can be spotted on trail walks, boat trips on the river or from the lodge's enormous birding tower, which offers viewing in and above the forest canopy. There is also a hide next to a clay lick for seeing tapir, peccary and, rarely, big cats. Scopes and binoculars are available and there is an excellent small library of field guides. The canoe trips on the Cristalino river complement the educational programmes, providing unique opportunities to interact with nature in this amazing environment.

Below *Canoeing at Cristalino Jungle Lodge*

FLORESTA NACIONAL DO TAPAJÓS

www.paraturismo.pa.gov.br

This large rainforest reserve on the banks of blue Tapajós river, some 120km (75 miles) south of Santarém (▷ 311) is home to myriad riverine communities who eke a living from fishing, and harvesting Brazil nuts and rubber. Agencies and guides in Santarém, such as Gil Serique (▷ 316), offer trips to visit both them and the surrounding forest. Animals have largely been hunted-out close to the water's edge, but the forest still retains stands of towering kapok and Brazil nut trees.

✚ 378 K5 ℹ Rua Floriano Peixoto 777, Santarém ☎ 93 3523 2434 ⏲ Mon–Fri 10–5

ILHA DE MAIANDEUA AND VILA DO ALGODOAL

www.algodoal.com.br
www.paraturismo.pa.gov.br

This sandy island washed by brackish, opaque water from the mingling of the Amazonian rivers and the Atlantic has become a small-scale beatnik resort popular with Europeans, particularly French weekenders from the French Guianan capital, Cayenne. The island sits in a partially protected reserve, reached by a three-hour bus journey and short ferry ride from Belém (▷ 300–301). There is nothing to do here but sunbathe, swim and stroll around the dune-backed beaches. The main town of Algodoal—which has effectively given its name to the island—is little more than a single sandy street with a few very simple restaurants, bars and *pousadas*. Donkey carts connect it with the island's other beaches, many of which also have *pousadas*.

✚ 394 P4 ℹ Praça Waldemar Henrique s/n, Belém ☎ 91 3224 9493 ⏲ Mon–Fri 10–6 🚌 From Belém ⛴ Ferry from Belém

ILHA DO MARAJÓ

www.paraturismo.pa.gov.br

Marajó is a richly forested island of shifting sands and muddy rivulets sitting in the mouth of the river Amazon—between Macapá (▷ 297) and Belém (▷ 300–301)—coloured by flocks of scarlet ibis and snowy egrets. Marajó is made entirely of silt and sand brought downstream by the great river and dumped at the mouth of the Atlantic. Its size is testimony to the river's power. It is 2km (1.25 miles) deep and covers an area roughly the size of Costa Rica (48,000sq km/18,450sq miles).

The island is highly fertile and much of the region around the main settlements of Soure, Salvaterra and Cahoeira do Arari have become ranch lands, famed for Brazilian buffalo mozzarella. Buffalo were introduced to Marajó by the Jesuits, and some have reverted to a life in the wild, living in the flooded grasslands that permeate the island's eastern half. They are also used as a means of transport; Marajó's police patrol the island on buffalo-back. The western portion of the island is covered in some of the Amazon's densest and most handsome forest, enormous tracts of which are unexplored. Marajó is fringed by broad beaches, washed by an ocean of greeny-blue freshwater. Little archer fish play in the waves, and in the thousands of square kilometres of mangroves stretching around and behind, shrimp, fish fry and crabs thrive, helping to create an ecosystem that supports large colonies of waterfowl. Scarlet and wood ibis, southern lapwing, ash-throated crake, roseate spoonbill and sooty barbthroat can all be found in Marajó's wetlands.

✚ 379 N4 ℹ Praça Waldemar Henrique s/n, Belém ☎ 91 3224 9493 ⏲ Mon–Fri 10–5 ⛴ River boats from Belém and Macapá

Above *View of the Tapajós river through the rainforest at Floresta Nacional do Tapajós*

INFORMATION

382 H5 · Rua da Instalação 70, Manaus · 92 3633 7955 · Mon–Fri 10–5 · From Boa Vista · River boats from Santarém and destinations throughout the Amazon · Eduardo Gomes · There is a tourist booth at the airport (Mon–Fri 10–7) and another next to the Teatro Amazonas (daily 10–6)

Above *Aerial view of Manaus city*

INTRODUCTION

In the last 20 years Manaus has gone from seedy port town to the bustling modern state capital of Amazonas. Its splendid rubber-boom mansions and palaces have been refurbished, its streets cleaned up and many of the fetid *favelas* (slums) which filled its *igarapés* (river creeks) have been remodelled as parks lined with attractive, if simple, social housing. As it prepares for the World Cup in 2014, Manaus is becoming an increasingly pleasant city and a destination in its own right, rather than being merely a jumping-off point for the jungle lodges which dot its forest environs.

Manaus is named after the Manaós, an Amazon tribe long extinguished. Though what you see today is the product of the 19th-century rubber boom, the city was built on the trade in 'Red Gold', as the Portuguese called captured natives. When the Portuguese built the first small fort, Barra, here in 1669, the stone was brought laboriously up river by slaves. The fort they helped to build soon became the headquarters of upper Amazon and Rio Negro *bandeirante* expeditions (▷ 28). Their activities are the reason why there are so few tribes living along the margins of the Amazon and Rio Negro.

In a few decades Barra went from a few hundred straw huts to the re-christened metropolis of Manaus. Commercial shipping routes connected the city with New York and Liverpool, bringing rubber out and European fineries in. The wealth was founded on slavery. Tribes like the Bora, Andoke and Huitoto were rounded up by militia hired by rubber barons and forcibly settled in labour camps, with names like El Encanto (The Delightful Place). On the Putamayo, all but 8,000 of the 50,000 natives that once lived in the region were killed and each ton of rubber cost seven human lives.

WHAT TO SEE

CENTRO CULTURAL DOS POVOS DA AMAZÔNIA

www.ccpa.am.gov.br

This large cultural complex devoted to the indigenous peoples of the Amazon houses a series of rooms showcasing artefacts (including splendid headdresses, ritual clothing and weapons) with adjacent explanatory displays in Portuguese and passable English. Outside are two *malocas* (indigenous communal homes) built by Desano and Yanomami people, and a play area for the kids.

✉ Praça Francisco Pereira da Silva s/n, Bola da Suframa ☎ 92 2125 5300 🕑 Tue–Sat 10–5 ✋ R$8

PALACETE PROVINCIAL

This elegant late 19th-century civic palace and former police station sits in front of a pretty tropical garden square in the city centre. It houses six small museums and a lovely air-conditioned café. The most interesting is the Pinacoteca do Estado, an art gallery showcasing work by important Brazilian painters, including Oscar Ramos, Moacir Andrade and Roberto Burle Marx. The Museu de Numismática has Brazilian and international coins and notes, the Museu Tiradentes tells the story of assorted Brazilian military campaigns, and the Museu de Arqueologia has a tiny handful of fascinating pre-Columbian Amazon relics. The Museu da Imagem e do Som has a small cinema and also offers free internet and a DVD library. In the basement there is an archaeological research centre and laboratory.

✉ Praça Heliorodo Balbi s/n ☎ 92 3635 5832 🕑 Tue–Fri 9–5, Sat 10–7, Sun 4–9 ✋ Free ☕

TEATRO AMAZONAS

This massive, Italianate opera house—topped with a cupola decorated with a mosaic in the colours of the Brazilian flag—was the crowning glory of the rubber boom. Its interior is equally lavish, with a ballroom of polished rainforest wood and an elaborately painted ceiling. There is also a concert hall featuring a *trompe l'oeil* ceiling and masks in homage to Shakespeare, Mozart, Verdi and Molière adorning the walls.

✉ Rua Tapajós s/n, Praça São Sebastião ☎ 92 3232 1768 🕑 Daily 9–5 ✋ Tour R$5.70

? Tickets for concerts are available only at the theatre box office, with payment in cash

TIPS

» There are tours of the Teatro Amazonas interior, but it's best seen during a concert; they take place frequently.

» There are cafés in the Praça São Sebastião square, next to the Teatro, which sell cold juices, coffees and beers until around 10pm nightly.

» Do not walk around the dock areas in Manaus after dark. They are not safe.

Below left *The elegant interior of Teatro Amazonas opera house*

Below *Ticuna ritual puppets in the Centro Cultural dos Povos da Amazônia*

MAMIRAUÁ

www.mamiraua.org.br

This reserve of 1.25 million hectares (3.1 million acres) is 631km (391 miles) upstream from Manaus, near the town of Tefé. It is one of the largest areas of protected rainforest on the planet. It preserves *varzea*, terra firma forest, rivers and lakes, which form a triangular area between the Solimões and Japurá rivers. The riverine communities who live here cooperate and participate in the running of the reserve. Part of the project involves sustainable tourism, which is conducted through a tourist headquarters in a location on the southern edge of the protected area. There is abundant wildlife here, including the endangered white uakari monkey—with shaggy fur and a bright red face—harpy eagle and five species of macaw.

Stays should be for a minimum of three days and two nights to get a sense of what there is to see at Mamirauá, and to make the long boat trip (or 45-minute flight) from Manaus to Tefé and the subsequent 60-minute speedboat transfer to the lodge worthwhile. Accommodation is at the floating Uakari lodge (▷ 320), which is situated in a bend in a blackwater river near a series of huge ox-bow lakes. Days are spent exploring these lakes—which are rich in wildlife—taking short walks through terra firma forest and visiting riverine villages within the park. Guiding is excellent and conducted by local people and resident biologists, all of whom speak some English. It is advisable to bring binoculars as wildlife in the Amazon is always tricky to see and is often high in the tree canopy on the edge of lakes and riverbanks. Book visits at least two weeks in advance.

376 E5 ☎ 97 3343 4672, 97 3343 4160 River boats from Manaus to Tefé ✈ Aeroporto de Tefé ? Mamirauá include a speedboat pick-up from Tefé in the price

MANAUS

▷ 306–307.

MONTE ALEGRE

www.paraturismo.pa.gov.br

This tiny town in Pará state is perched on a bluff overlooking the Amazon, between Santarém (▷ 311) and Belém (▷ 300–301). It helped to change history in the Americas in the 1990s, when a Brazilian team led by Anna C. Roosevelt—granddaughter of Teddy, and one of a very few archaeologists who considered the Amazon worthwhile excavating—unearthed evidence of a sedentary Amazon civilization, based in caves near the town. These Pedra Pintada Indians had been living off the rainforest as many as 11,000 years ago, making them roughly contemporary with, or only a little later than, what were then thought to be the first Americans, the North-American Clovis people (▷ 24). However, the Pedra Pintada were very different from Clovis. Even at this early stage, they lived more like the Tupi people who met the first conquistadores—foraging in the forest, making use of plants and animals, making rock tools and crafting triangular, and distinctly un-Clovis, spear points. They were also artists; the Pedra Pintada caves are named after their painted walls. There is no formal infrastructure in Monte Alegre, but visits to the caves and the marshland and seasonally flooded lakes can be organized through the handful of *pousadas* (inns) in town.

378 L4 River boats from Santarém and destinations throughout the Amazon

Above *Uakari floating lodge in Mamirauá sustainable development reserve*

ÓBIDOS

www.obidos.com.br

Before the Andes existed, the Amazon river system drained into the Pacific, on the other side of the South American continent. When the mountains rose, the rivers flooded to form a huge inland freshwater sea. Óbidos town marks the point where that sea eventually burst through the Guyana shield to drain into the Atlantic and form the Amazon River system. It is the narrowest and deepest point on the river. The Amazon is only 2km (1.25 miles) wide here, narrower than it is at Iquitos (over 2,500km/1,550 miles upstream). The town itself is a tiny sleepy place, with little to see but the river and the 17th-century Forte Pauxis, which has a solitary Portuguese cannon. There are a few very simple guest houses near the docks.

378 K4 River boats from Santarém and destinations throughout the Amazon

PARINTINS

www.parintins.com

This tiny town—sitting on the Ilha dos Tupinambás island in the midst of an archipelago between Manaus (▷ 306–307) and Santarém (▷ 311)—hosts one of Brazil's biggest parties, the Festa do Boi Bumba (▷ 316), on the weekend between 24 June and the end of the month each year. It is a spectacle which rivals *carnaval* in Bahia or Rio, and like them it is an explosion of jubilation from the poor and indigenous of mixed-race Brazil. For the rest of the year the town is quiet, and has little else to draw visitors.

378 J5 River boats from Manaus and Santarém Aeroporto Júlio Belém (Parintins)

PORTO VELHO

www.portovelho.ro.gov.br

The capital of Rondônia state is a big, industrial city on the Amazon's biggest tributary, the Rio Madeira, with little to offer the tourist. While there are beautiful stretches of forest to the north, there is no infrastructure. Porto Velho's relative prosperity comes from logging, cattle ranching and one of the world's biggest civil engineering projects—the construction of two huge twin hydroelectric dams—which have swollen the population and brought in new money. Buildings in the pocket-sized 19th-century city centre are being renovated and by 2012 steam trains will run along a section of the old Madeira–Mamoré railway, through a large riverside park dotted with sizeable Vitória Regia lily ponds and overlooking the Rio Madeira.

381 F7 From all major tourist towns River boats from Manaus Porto Velho

PRESIDENTE FIGUEIREDO

This small rainforest resort, around 200km (124 miles) from Manaus on BR 174, is a popular getaway for the Manaus middle-class. Few foreigners ever visit and little English is spoken. Though it is crowded at weekends, in the week it can be pretty quiet. The main attractions are the numerous beautiful waterfalls, natural swimming pools, and underground rivers and caves, all of which can be visited with a guide (such as Cristina de Assis ▷ 315). Numerous threatened and endangered bird species live here, including Guianan cock of the rock. Presidente Figueiredo can easily be visited in a day trip from Manaus.

377 H4 Rua da Instalação 70, Manaus 92 3633 7955 Mon–Fri 10–6 From Manaus Eduardo Gomes (Manaus) There is a tourist booth at the airport (Mon–Fri 10–8) and another next to the Teatro Amazonas (▷ 307) in Manaus city centre (daily 10–6)

Below *Santuario Falls in Presidente Figueiredo rainforest reserve*

RIO BRANCO AND ACRE STATE

Acre state and its capital, Rio Branco, are closer to the Pacific than to Rio de Janeiro. The state has much to offer: 82 per cent of its territory is covered with primary forest and it has some of the most exciting ethno-tourism projects in South America. The recent opening of fast road routes and cheap flights between Rio Branco and Peru's Cusco has made Acre the easiest state in Brazil to visit as part of a multi-destination South American holiday.

TOWN SIGHTS

Rio Branco is a clean, well-maintained and orderly provincial city. It has the highest percentage of cycleways of any city in Brazil, some attractive green spaces and a lively waterfront promenade, the Mercado Velho, which buzzes with bar life in the evenings, especially at weekends. Attractions within the city include the Museu da Borracha (tel 68 3223 1202; Tue–Fri 8–6, Sat–Sun 4–9; free), which tells the story of the Acre rubber trade, and the Casa Povos da Floresta (tel 68 3224 5667; Wed–Fri 8–6, Sat–Sun 4–9; free), with artefacts and arts and crafts from the state's indigenous people.

FARTHER AFIELD

Expeditions leaving from the city enable tourists to stay with indigenous Yanawa people in the pristine forests in the far west of the state, near the city of Cruzeiro do Sul. Here, primary Amazon forest rises gently towards the Andes in a series of craggy mountain ranges, including that of the spectacular Serra do Divisor national park on the border with Peru. South of Rio Branco, easily visitable en route to the Peruvian and Bolivian borders, is the Chico Mendes' rubber-tapper community ecotourism project at Xapuri. The forests here are pristine and full of wildlife, and the tourism infrastructure excellent; with comfortable accommodation in a series of rustic houses. All of these excursions are best made with an agency, such as Maanaim (▷ 316).

INFORMATION

381 D8 Estádio, Avenida Chico Mendes, Rio Branco 68 3201 3024, 68 3223 3998 Mon–Fri 10–6 From Porto Velho and towns within Bolivia and Peru Internacional de Rio Branco There is also a tourist booth in town on Avenida Getúlio Vargas 91, Praça dos Povos da Floresta

TIP

» Regular flights to Cusco (for Machu Picchu), in addition to new bus connections and fast border processing, make Acre easy to visit as an excursion from Peru, or vice versa.

Below *Brazil nut trees in Acre state*

SALINÓPOLIS

www.salinas.tur.br

This resort lies 223km (138 miles) from Belém (▷ 300–301), on Pará's Atlantic coast at the farthest outreaches of the Amazon delta. It has squeaky clean, dune-backed and broad sandy beaches, which stretch for tens of kilometres around a central bay. They are washed by a clean, slightly brackish sea, are very popular with weekenders from Belém and have lively nightlife during the high season (July), when there is live *brega* and *forró* at the *barracas* (beach bars).

Atalaia, an island opposite the resort, is quieter and fringed with even better beaches. It is easily reached by taxi boat.

394 P4 Praça Waldemar Henrique s/n, Belém 91 3224 9493 Mon–Fri 10–6 From Belém

SANTARÉM AND ALTER DO CHÃO

www.santarem.pa.gov.br

The provincial Amazon port town of Santarém sits at the confluence of the brown Amazon and brilliant blue Tapajós rivers, at the far end of the soya highway which drains the continent-sized plantations of central Brazil. Almost all of their harvest is consumed by a gigantic Cargill soya plant at Santarém's industrial port. It is the only town between Manaus and Belém with any tourism infrastructure beyond cheap hotels and restaurants. Tour operators in Santarém offer trips to the Floresta Nacional do Tapajós reserve (▷ 305) and the old Henry Ford rubber-boom plantation towns of Fordlândia and Belterra (▷ 297).

While much has been degraded, there are still beautiful stretches of forest and river near Santarém. The Tapajós is only a minor tributary of the great river, but it carries more water than the Mississippi and is 30km (18.5 miles) wide at Santarém, giving the city a maritime feel. Farther upstream, towards Itaituba, it is lined with a series of beautiful beaches, the most attractive being Alter do Chão, a stunning strip of white sand sticking into the Tapajós river. It is a 45-minute drive to the south of Santarém and easily visited by taxi or with a tour operator. There are many small restaurants here and the beach is a popular excursion destination from the city.

Santarém has a long history. European Santarém began life as a Jesuit mission in 1661, later becoming an assembly town used for the 'settlement' of indigenous peoples, who became slaves. In the 18th century, the town became a popular base for European naturalists. Henry Bates spent several years here in the 1850s researching and writing *A Naturalist on the River Amazon*. It was even settled, for a short while, by a few hundred confederate refugees from the American Civil War. Most packed up and went home when the cotton plantations failed, but a few stayed, and their English surnames survive today in modern Santarém. Henry Wickham, the Englishman who supplanted the Brazilian rubber trade with his plantations in Malaysia, tested his ideas in Santarém in 1876, such as planting and cultivating trees in rows. When his Malaysian plantations were successful, he burst Brazil's rubber bubble.

In 1922, torrential rain washed tons of mud off the streets of Santarém, exposing stone tools and fragments of pottery that had lain buried for millennia. The ceramics were as fine as anything that had been found in the Americas. We still know very little about the civilization that produced them.

378 K4 Rua Floriano Peixoto 777 93 3523 2434 Mon–Fri 10–5 From all major tourist towns River boats from Belém, Macapá and Manaus Aeroporto de Santarém

Above *Alter do Chão white sand beach bordering the Tapajós river*

BELÉM'S COLONIAL CENTRE

This walk takes in the principal sights of Belém's colonial centre, the recently renovated docks and its famous morning market. Be sure to watch your belongings as pick-pockets operate around the market.

THE WALK
Distance: 2km (1.4 miles)
Time: 3 hours including visits
Start at: Mercado Ver-o-Peso
End at: Teatro da Paz, Praça da Republica

HOW TO GET THERE
Travel by taxi or on foot to Ver-o-Peso market.

★ Aim to arrive at the quayside before 7.30am, when the morning is still relatively cool and there is plenty of activity in the market. Wander at will through the market buildings.

❶ Literally meaning 'see the weight', Ver-o-Peso market (▷ 301) is one of the most unusual and colourful markets in Brazil. It is housed in a series of small iron buildings on the quayside and comprises stalls selling everything from giant river fish to herbal remedies and souvenirs. It is at its busiest in the early mornings.

Be sure to walk into and around the fish market, where fish as heavy as a human lie on white-tile slabs next to baskets of piranhas and bizarre armour-plated catfish. Head for the northern part of the market.

❷ Here you can breakfast on buttered tapioca pancakes sweetened with coconut milk and Amazon honey at one of the food stalls. These manioc meal pancakes have been eaten in Amazonia for thousands of years. Wash it down with an energy-enhancing, indigo açai or a tangy cupuaçu juice.

Walk southwest past the market, towards the Forte do Castelo (▷ 301) and turn left on Rua Doutor Malcher, where you will see the city's cathedral.

❸ The imposing, brilliant white facade of the Catedral Metropolitana de Belém hides a splendid neoclassical interior bedecked in marble and with a series of chapels secreted behind colonnades. It is worth visiting for the exuberant ceiling paintings by the Italian artist

Domenico de Angelis and Giuseppe Capranesi, who became famous for his work on the Teatro Amazonas in Manaus (▷ 307). Few visitors to the Amazon realize that the artists first came to the region at the invitation of Dom Antonio de Macedo Costa, the bishop of Pará in 1882—to completely renovate the cathedral's interior and paint the auditorium in Belém's Teatro da Paz, only to see it destroyed in an accident a few decades later. The cathedral itself is 18th century—work began on the building in 1748 and was finished in 1782.

Retrace your steps to the Forte do Castelo, less than 50m (55 yards) in front of the church on the riverbank.

❹ There has been a fort in Belém since the 18th century. This building dates largely from 1878, when the original buildings were completely reconstructed. It houses an interesting, air-conditioned archaeological museum showcasing indigenous artefacts found in Belém and on the Ilha do Marajó (▷ 305). There are excellent views across the river and Ver-o-Peso from the ramparts of the fort.

Walk through the busy heart of commercial Belém along Rua João Alfredo, which becomes Rua Santo Antônio after four blocks. Turn right onto Avenida Presidente Vargas and walk for 250m (273 yards) to the Praça da Republica. This stretch can be covered in a few minutes in a taxi if the Amazon heat is too oppressive. The Praça da República is a large, leafy square which hosts one of the best handicraft markets in the north of Brazil at weekends. The Teatro da Paz sits at its eastern end.

❺ The Teatro da Paz (▷ 301), a neoclassical opera house, was built when Belém became rich during the rubber boom. It is one of the largest and most lavish theatres in South America, with beautiful ceiling and wall paintings in both the concert hall and the ballroom.

There are many taxi stands around the Praça, to return you to your starting point or to take you to the Estação das Docas.

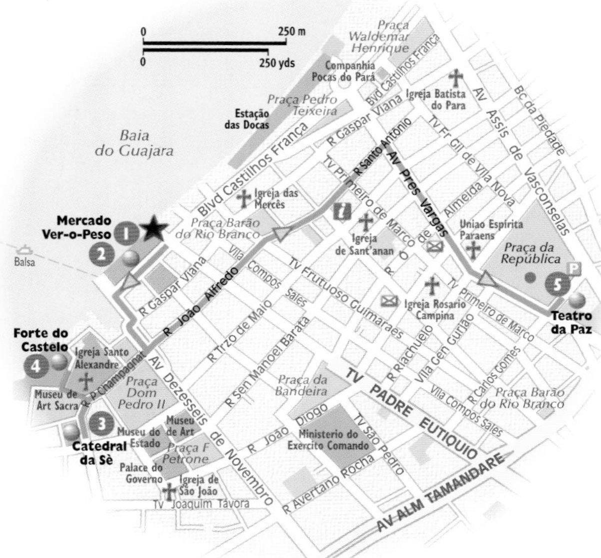

WHEN TO GO

To see the market at its best and avoid the worst heat of the day, start early and have breakfast on the way.

WHERE TO EAT

Stop at the Ver-o-Peso market or the Estação das Docas, which has many air-conditioned restaurants. At the end of the walk, the restaurant in the Hilton on the northwestern corner of the Praça da Republica serves cold drinks and snacks all day.

PLACE TO VISIT

CATEDRAL METROPOLITANA

✉ Praça Frei Caetano Brandão s/n 🕐 Mon 3–4, Tue–Fri 8–11, 3.30–6 ✋ Free

TIP

» Ná Figueiredo's shop (▷ 314) in the Estação das Docas is one of the best places in northern Brazil to buy CDs of local music. It also sells great T-shirts, skirts, jeans and accessories.

Opposite *Avenida Presidente Vargas*
Below *Preparing açai at Ver-o-Peso market*

BELÉM

AMAZON STAR

www.amazonstar.com.br

This company has been offering river cruises around Belém and the nearby Amazon islands on comfortable river boats for almost 20 years. They also have trips to Marajó (▷ 305), and longer cruises to Santarém (▷ 311).

✉ Rua Henrique Gurjão 208 ☎ 91 3241 8624

BAR DO GILSON

This lovely, intimate bar is situated in a covered courtyard and is decorated with arty black and white photography, and paintings by local artists. It hosts live *chorinho* music, a kind of Brazilian ragtime, on weekend nights. Gilson himself often plays mandolin in the band.

✉ Travessa Padre Eutíquio 3172 ☎ 91 3272 1306 🕐 Tue–Sat 10am–1am

CARROUSEL

This enormous warehouse club has live *aparelhagem* parties at weekends attended by thousands. *Aparelhagem* music is a kind of fast-paced techno with twanging Belém *guitarrada* guitars, played by DJs on sound stages that look like space-shop consoles from the film *Barbarella*.

✉ Avenida Amirante Barroso at Antônio Baena 🕐 Fri–Sat 10pm–3am

FEIRA DE ARTESANATO

Every weekend sees an arts and crafts market in Belém's principal square, Praça da República. Stalls here sell distinctive seed and bead jewellery, wicker baskets and ornaments, hammocks and other arts and crafts.

✉ Praça da República 🕐 Sun 7–4

MORMAÇO

www.mormaco.net

This dockside warehouse on the riverside is one of the best places in the city to hear cutting-edge live Belém bands, playing local rhythms like *carimbó*, infused with reggae, rap and rock.

✉ Passagem Carneiro da Rocha s/n, Mangal das Garças, Arsenal ☎ 91 3223 9892 🕐 Fri–Sat 10pm–4am

NÁ FIGUEIREDO

www.nafigueredo.com.br

This great little arty fashion boutique (which also has a branch in the Estação das Docas complex on the waterfront) has one of the best selections of local CDs in north Brazil.

✉ Avenida Gentil Bittencourt 449, Nazaré ☎ 91 3224 8948 🕐 Mon–Fri 10–6, Sat 10–5

A PORORÓ

Every Friday and Saturday this aircraft hangar-sized club heaves with thousands who come to dance to furiously fast techno *brega* sung by duets in spangly skirts and satin suits—an absolute Belém institution.

✉ Avenida Senador Lemos 3316, Sacramenta ☎ 91 3233 7631 🕐 Fri–Sat 10pm–4am

SÃO MATEUS

A buzzing street bar where a few hundred of Belém's middle-class gather on weekend evenings to listen to local rock. There are softer sounds on week nights. Good bar snacks *(petiscos)*, cocktails (like the *caipirinhas* made with rum and fruit) and very cold beer are all served.

✉ Rua Joaquim Lopes Bastos 314 ☎ 91 3245 1612 🕐 Tue–Sun 7.30–12

Above *Band in Estação das Docas, Belém*

BOA VISTA

RORAIMA ADVENTURES

www.roraima-brasil.com.br

One of the most reputable adventure travel companies in northern Brazil, offering treks up Mount Roraima (▷ 297), hikes in Tepequem and the Serra Grande mountains, and other wilderness destinations in Amazonas and Roraima states.

✉ Rua Coronel Pinto 86 sl. 106, Edifício Manoel Nabuco, Centro ☎ 95 3624 9611, 95 9115 4171 (mobile) 🕐 Mon–Fri 10–5

MANAUS

AMAZON ANTÔNIO TOURS

www.antonio-jungletours.com

This company can provide good-value rainforest tours on a very pretty blackwater river 200km (124 miles) northeast of Manaus, parts of which are wild, and other parts of which are home to riverine communities.

✉ Rua Lauro Cavalcante 231 ☎ 92 3234 1294 🕐 Daily 10–5

AMAZON CLIPPER

www.amazonclipper.com.br

The best of the wildlife river cruises are with this long-standing company, who take small boats on a range of trips up the Rio Negro and Amazon, with knowledgeable wildlife guides. Booking is done through the website.

☎ 96 3656 1246

AMAZON GERO TOURS

www.amazongerotours.com

This well-established company, with more than a decade of experience with international tourists, offers homestays and community visits to the riverine people near Lago Mamori (▷ 298) and volunteer tourism alongside the standard rainforest adventure trips. Trips include rainforest camping, jungle lodge tours, river boat cruises and river boat rides to the Anavilhanas islands (▷ 298), and swimming with pink dolphins. Pick-ups at the airport are available.

✉ Rua 10 de Julho 679 ☎ 92 3232 4755, 92 9983 6273 🕐 Daily 10–5

Right *Traditional crafts are abundant in Ver-o-Peso market, Belém*

CENTRAL DE ARTESANATO BRANCO E SILVA

This small shopping arcade is lined with arts and crafts shops, many of whose proprietors can be watched as they work on site.

✉ Rua Recife 1999 ☎ 92 3642 5458 🕐 Mon–Sat 10–6

CRISTINA DE ASSIS

Cristina is an English-speaking guide who can give cultural tours of the city and sights like the Museu Seringal (▷ 299), as well as tours to swim with dolphins in the Anavilhanas (▷ 298; these need to be organized at least a week in advance) and to Presidente Figueiredo (▷ 309).

☎ 92 9114 2556; amazonflower@bol.com.br

DJALMA OLIVEIRA

Take a nightlife tour of Manaus's vibrant clubs, or just use the private car hire (which is far better value than with a cab if you are going to make several stays).

✉ Rua 10 de Julho 679 ☎ 92 9112 3942; djalmatour@hotmail.com

ECOSHOP

www.ecoshop.com.br

This centrally located boutique gallery sells indigenous crafts from all over the Amazon, with Yanomami and Tikuna wicker-work baskets, Wai Wai necklaces and Baniwa ritual items.

✉ Largo de São Sebastião ☎ 92 3234 8870 🕐 Mon–Sat 10–5 ❓ Also at the Amazonas Shopping Mall (tel 92 3642 2026; Mon–Sat 9–9, Sun 10–4)

GALERIA AMAZONICA

www.galeriamazonica.org.br

This big gallery, devoted to arts and crafts made by the Waimiri Atroari indigenous people of northern Amazonas state, sits right opposite the Teatro Amazonas (▷ 307). It is one of the best places for buying indigenous art in Brazil.

✉ Rua Costa Azevedo 272, Largo do Teatro ☎ 92 3233 4521 🕐 Daily 10–6

GERALDO MESQUITA HOUSEBOAT CRUISES

Cruises around Manaus and the Lago Mamori (▷ 298) in gorgeous converted traditional wooden river boats, some of which are more than 40 years old. There are many options, from day trips with accommodation onshore to cruises of several days in more remote areas.

☎ 92 3232 4755; reservasgero@hotmail.com

PEDRO NETO

This adventure tour specialist offers light adventure trips and wildlife walks in the INPA rainforest reserve (a large area of extensive forest on the edge of Manaus, to which Pedro has privileged access). Alternatively, you can choose to take a trip to Presidente Figueiredo (▷ 309) for trail-walking to waterfalls, abseiling and bird watching.

☎ 92 8831 1011; pedroffneto@hotmail.com

Below *An Amazon river boat arrives at Manaus*

FESTIVALS AND EVENTS

FEBRUARY–MARCH

CARNAVAL

The biggest celebrations of the Brazilian calendar see huge parades in the *sambódromo* in the city of Manaus (▷ 306–307), which was built in imitation of Rio's (▷ 97) but is three time as large. Frenetic partying lasts for five days.

JUNE

FESTA DO BOI BUMBA

www.boibumba.com

Northern Brazil's most exuberant party is held in Parintins (▷ 309) every year over a weekend between 24 June and the end of the month. It sees two competing schools—Garantido and Caprichosos—enact a folk legend for some six hours nightly on each of the three days (there is general 24-hour partying for the rest of the weekend). This is the same story as the Bumba-Meu-Boi festival in Maranhão (▷ 289), albeit with some Amazonian additions. It recounts the triumphant victory of a caboclo slave and his beautiful wife, Catirina, over their cruel and greedy landowner through a colourful pageant danced all night in the purpose-built Bumbódromo stadium. Some 40,000–60,000 frenetically dancing spectators cheer them on and they are judged winners according to their dance, music and costume. The huge floats take a year to make.

FESTIVAL DO AMAZONAS

Cultural events, including art exhibitions, theatre performances and sporting events, in addition to live music and dancing throughout the city of Manaus (▷ 306–307). Specific dates vary from year to year.

OCTOBER

CÍRIO DE NAZARÉ

www.ciriodenazare.com.br

One of the biggest celebrations in Brazil, and the largest in northern Brazil, sees millions of visitors (but relatively few foreigners) arrive in Belém (▷ 300–301). There are huge candlelit processions through the colonial centre of the city, followed by much music, dancing and general revelry. The festival takes place on the second Sunday in October.

PORTO VELHO

ARTESANATO INDIGENA KARITIANA

This shop is owned by the Karitiana indigenous people and run by them as a cooperative. It sells beads, earrings and necklaces, ritual items and weapons.

✉ Rua Rui Barbosa 1407, between José Camacho and Calama ☎ 69 3229 7591 🕐 Daily 8–12, 2–5

RIO BRANCO AND ACRE

MAANAIM

www.maanaim-amazonia.com

Maanaim organizes visits to Ashaninka, Yawanawa and other indigenous communities throughout Acre, to the beautiful Serra do Divisor national park on the Peruvian border and to the Serengal Cachoeira Chico Mendes rainforest reserve in Xapuri (▷ 310). This company is well-organized and extremely friendly and welcoming.

✉ Rua Colômbia 39, Bairro Bosque ☎ 68 3223 3232 🕐 Mon–Fri 10–5

SANTARÉM

GIL SERIQUE

www.gilserique.com

Santarém's most experienced tour guide offers trips to the Tapajós National Forest (▷ 311), to stay with riverine communities and to visit the Maica wetlands east of Santarém (▷ 311), which have spectacular birdlife. The guides speak good English and all have huge enthusiasm for their subject.

✉ Rua Adriano Pimentel 80 ☎ 93 9124 7584

PRICES AND SYMBOLS

The restaurants are listed alphabetically (excluding A, Al, El, La, Le and O). The prices given are the average for a two-course lunch (L) and a three-course dinner (D) for one person, without drinks. The wine price is for the least expensive bottle. Although you will find wine served in restaurants throughout Brazil, the usual drinks are bottled beer (R$5–R$8) or *caipirinhas*, the ubiquitous *cachaça* and fruit cocktails (R$8). All the restaurants listed accept credit cards unless otherwise stated.

For a key to the symbols, ▷ 2.

BELÉM

BOTECO DAS ONZE

This handsome colonial building by the riverside is Belém high society's favourite spot to come for dinner. It has live regional and Brazilian music most nights and a series of dining rooms which lead to an open-air patio and a beautiful view over the river. Dishes include river fish such as *tambaqui* (a delicious Amazonian fish) with mango and black beans.

✉ Praça FC Brandão s/n ☎ 91 3224 8599 🕑 Mon 6–12, Tue–Sun 12pm–1am 🖑 L R$30, D R$50, Wine R$35

CANTINA ITALIANA

Claudia Luzi runs the kitchen at Belém's best Italian in this modest, air-conditioned restaurant close to the Palacete Principal. She creates *Luso*-Tuscan fusion dishes, such as *bacalhau* (salted cod) risotto, and rich pasta dishes like four cheese lasagne. Hotel delivery is available.

✉ Travessa Benjamin Constant 1401 ☎ 91 225 2033 🕑 Tue–Sat 11.30–3.30, 7.30–10 🖑 L R$ 25, D R$40, Wine R$30

CHURRASCARIA RODEIO

www.rodeiogrill.com.br

Cuts of pork, beef, chicken, sausages and river fish are presented here alongside a huge choice of buffet dishes, all for a set price. You'll have to take a short taxi ride to get here.

✉ Avenida Augusto Montenegro, km 4 ☎ 91 3323 8800 🕑 Daily 11.30–3, 7.30–12 🖑 L and D R$40, Wine R$42

CHURRASCARIA TUCURUVI

www.churrascariatucuruvi.com.br

This big open-plan dining room, housed in a warehouse-like building, is one of the most popular *churrascaria* spit-roast restaurants in Belém. There are fish, sushi and salads available alongside the customary cuts of meat that are charged at a fixed price.

✉ Travessa Benjamin Constant 1843, Nazaré ☎ 91 3235 0341 🕑 Daily 11.30–3, 7.30–12 🖑 L and D R$40, Wine R$35

LÁ EM CASA

www.laemcasa.com

This self-service buffet restaurant, with à la carte options, serves regional specialities like *tacacá no tucupi*—a delicious acrid soup with prawns, cooked with mouth-numbing jambo leaves. It is within the air-conditioned confines of the Estação das Docas complex (▷ 301), with pleasant views out over the river.

✉ Avenida Boulevard Castillio França, Estação das Docas s/n ☎ 91 3212 5588 🕑 Daily 12–12 🖑 L R$30, D R$40, Wine R$40

MANJAR DAS GARÇAS

Watch the scarlet ibis fly across the river as you eat the vast lunches or pile your plate from the evening buffet at this restaurant sitting over the water on the outskirts of the city. The weekend buffet has some 30 regional dishes to choose from.

✉ Praça Carniero da Rocha s/n, Arsenal da Marinha, Mangaldas Garças ☎ 91 3242 1056 🕑 Tue–Thu 12–4, 8–12, Fri–Sat 12–4, 8–2, Sun 11–6 🖑 L R$35, D R$55, Wine R$30

BOA VISTA

PEIXADA TROPICAL

A large variety of fresh river fish straight from the market is prepared simply at this alfresco riverside restaurant. Portions are filling so you may want to share.

✉ Rua Pedro Rodrigues at Ajuricaba ☎ 95 224 6040 🕑 🖑 L R$25, Wine R$25

Above *Boteco das Onze in Belém*

MACAPÁ

CANTINHO BAIANO

In a favourite stretch of the river for restaurants, this very simple place overlooking the water is a ten-minute walk south of the fort. They serve excellent river fish, including fried or grilled *tambaqui* ribs.
Avenida Beira-Rio 1 96 3223 4153 Mon–Sat 11.30–2.30, 6.30–11 L R$20, D R$30

MANAUS

BANZEIRO

www.restaurantebanzeiro.com.br
Manaus's most upmarket new restaurant takes northern Brazilian cooking and gives it a French twist. Dishes include *costela de tambaqui* (ribs of the *tambaqui* fish, one of the most delicious Amazonian fishes) with salad and fried plantain, and Amazon river fish steak with butter, capers, prawns, sage and mushrooms. It's around 20 minutes by cab from the centre.
Rua Libertador 102, Nossa Senhora das Graças 92 3234 1621 Daily 11.30–3, Mon–Sat 7–11.30 L R$40, D R$60, Wine R$40

BÚFALO

www.churrascariabufalo.com.br
Central Manaus's most popular spit-roast *churrascaria* comprises a big dining room with linen-covered tables spreading out from a central buffet counter. They serve sushi, pasta, salads and desserts, all of which are in addition to the cuts of sizzling meat whisked out of the kitchen by rushing waiters for a fixed price.
Avenida Joaquim Nabuco 628 92 3633 3733 Daily 11.30–3, 7.30–12 L and D R$80, Wine R$45

FIORENTINA

The most traditional Italian restaurant in the city serves very cheese-heavy vegetarian dishes and pastas, and at weekends there are generous *feijoadas* (meat and bean stews), with prices reduced by half on Sundays. Dishes are served with mugs of wine.
Rua José Paranaguá 44, Praça da Polícia 92 3232 1295 Mon–Sat 11.30–3, 7.30–12 L R$30, D R$40, Wine R$30

HIMAWARI

This restaurant, with simple, contemporary decor, overlooking the Praça São Sebastião and the cathedral, serves Japanese food, some of it made with local river fish. This is one of the few local restaurants open on Sunday night.
Rua 10 de Julho 618, opposite Teatro Amazonas 92 3233 2208 Tue–Sun 11.30–2, 6.30–10 L R$20, D R$35, Wine R$45

PORTO VELHO

CAFÉ MADEIRA

Particularly at sunset, this popular restaurant, which sits overlooking the Madeira river, is a wonderful place to enjoy an icy *chopp* draught beer and a *petisco* bar snack. Main courses include steak, river fish and chicken fillets with rice and coco beans.
Major Amarantes at Carlos Gomes, on the riverfront 69 3229 1193 Daily 11.30–2, 5.30–10 L R$15, D R$25

MYOSHI

www.myoshi.com.br
Myoshi is the place to go if you want really good Japanese and Oriental food. It has a large, air-conditioned and open-plan dining room that serves an evening sushi and sashimi buffet. You can also enjoy Brazilian fusion options, such as salmon and cream cheese sushi *tucumã*—made with an Amazon river fish—and a dessert of banana and chocolate sushi. It's a 15-minute taxi ride from the centre but they will deliver.
Avenida Amazonas 1280, Bairro NS das Graças 68 3224 4600 Daily 11.30–2.30, 6.30–11 L R$30, D R$50, Wine R$45

RIO BRANCO

AFA

www.afabistro.com.br
The best-value per-kilo restaurant in the city serves a wide choice of dishes, from *tambaqui* river fish stew, lentils, spit-roast beef, and decent salads, to a range of very sweet puddings. There are plenty of options for vegetarians here, too.
Rua Franco Ribeiro 108 68 3224 1396 Daily 11–3 L R$20

ELCIO

At this traditional restaurant you'll taste superb fish *moquecas* here—as good as anything you'll find in Espírito Santo or Bahia—which are fish stews in a rich coconut sauce, flavoured with an Amazon leaf, *xicoria*, and fresh coriander. Here they are accompanied with rice, *pirão* (manioc puree), *farofa* and delicious chilli and tucupi sauce. They serve two to three people.
Avenida Ceará 2513 68 3226 1629 Daily 11.30–3, 6.30–10 L R$20, D R$35

MATA NATIVA

Try spicy *moqueca de tambaqui* (Bahian spicy coconut soup with *tambaqui* river fish) or *galinha caipira*, herb-coated chicken served with *pirão* (manioc puree) and *vatapa* (prawn paste), in this roadside garden restaurant. It's on the road to Sena Madureira, some 6km (3.75 miles) from the centre. Plates are big enough for four people. This place is very popular at weekends.
Estrada Via Verde 1971, km 2 68 3221 3004 Mon–Sat 9–3, 7–10 L R$20, D R$40

SANTARÉM

MASCOTE

This simple, waterside fish restaurant serves great fried or grilled *tambaqui* and *pacu* (two fine Amazonian river fish) and a variety of ice creams flavoured with Amazon fruits, like cupucacu and camu camu, which has the highest vitamin C content of any fruit in the world.
Praça do Pescador 10 91 3523 2844 Mon–Sat 11.30–3, 7.30–11 L R$15, D R$25, Wine R$35

SABOR CASEIRO

This city-centre restaurant with basic decor specializes in dishes from northern Brazil, including mouth-numbing *tacaca* soups (made from the juice of raw manioc) and fried river fish, alongside the usual chicken or meat with rice, beans and chips.
Rua Floriano Peixoto 521 91 3522 5111 Mon–Sat 11.30–3, 7.30–11 L R$20, D R$35

PRICES AND SYMBOLS

Prices are the lowest and highest for a double room for one night. Breakfast is included unless noted otherwise. All the hotels listed accept credit cards unless otherwise stated. Note that rates vary widely throughout the year.

For a key to the symbols, ▷ 2.

AMAZONIAN LODGES

Lodges are usually only available as part of a package booking with an agency or guide. These include transfers to the site, since most are very remote and inaccessible by public transport, on poorly surfaced roads or only reachable by boat. Rates are all inclusive of food (and non-alcoholic drinks) and usually negotiable at time of booking, depending on party size and the length of stay rather than the time of year. (See also Jardim da Amazonia, ▷ 341.)

AMAZON ANTÔNIO LODGE

This is a thatched-roof wooden lodge with plain, fan-cooled wooden rooms and an observation tower, set in a beautiful location overlooking a broad curve in the river Urubu. Accommodation has to be booked as part of an all-inclusive package through Amazon Antônio Tours (▷ 315). It is very popular with backpackers and one of the best bottom-range options in the region.

✉ On river Urubu 200km (124 miles) from Manaus 🖐 R$200–R$300 🛈 12

AMAZON ECOPARK LODGE

www.amazonecopark.com.br

This comfortable lodge in a private reserve, only 40 minutes from the airport, is the best location close to the city. It sits on a small white-sand creek on a stretch of secondary forest that is cut by many creeks and rivers. An island in front is a sanctuary for rescued primates, with white uakari, capuchins and many curious coatis. The park makes a real effort to practise sustainable tourism and is run in partnership with the Living Rainforest Foundation.

✉ Igarapé do Tarumã, 20km (12.5 miles) from Manaus ☎ 92 2547 7742, 92 9146 0594 🖐 R$200–R$300 🛈 64 ⛴ 15 min from Manaus by boat

AMAZON LODGE

This is one of the simpler lodges, on the Lago do Juma, near Mamori (▷ 298). There are 12 basic apartments, with fan-cooled rooms, cold showers and a restaurant with mosquito netting. The lodge can only be visited on an organized tour with an operator like Amazon Gero Tours (▷ 315), or a guide like Cristina de Assis (▷ 315).

✉ Lago do Juma, 80km (50 miles) from Manaus ☎ 92 656 3878 🖐 R$200–R$300 🛈 15

CABANA TACHI

This simple, rustic community-owned lodge is run in partnership with Amazon Gero Tours (▷ 315). It's part of a pioneering project which sees money and resources returning to the community. Set in one of the most pristine stretches of forest in the region, it's good for wildlife watching.

✉ Mamori 🖐 R$200–R$300 🛈 8

CRISTALINO JUNGLE LODGE

www.cristalinolodge.com.br

The Cristalino Jungle Lodge, at the Cristalino Rainforest Reserve (▷ 304), has a range of rooms. The private bungalows are very comfortable: stylish *luxe* tile-roofed wooden chalets with windows for walls, thick double beds, bathrooms with solar-powered hot water showers, separate living areas with sofas and hammock-slung terraces. Standard rooms are simpler, in concrete cabins with tiled floors, double or twin beds and bathrooms. The cabins are set out in a forest glade dotted with fruit trees.

✉ Alta Floresta, Mato Grosso ☎ 66 3512 7100 🖐 R$505–R$620 🛈 28

Above *Bungalow at Cristalino Jungle Lodge*

MAMORI JUNGLE LODGE
You get the best deal here with a designated package from Amazon Gero Tours (▷ 315). It's one of the more comfortable lodges in Parana do Araça on the Lago Mamori (▷ 298). There are smart wooden chalets housing suites of individual rooms, which come furnished with double or single beds complete with mosquito nets.
✉ Lake Mamori, 60km (37 miles) south of Manaus 🖐 R$300–R$350 ⓘ 10

POUSADA ECOLOGICA
This comfortable *pousada* overlooks a small river and is situated in the Chico Mendes reserve in Xapuri (▷ 310). It includes a series of very comfortable wooden *cabanas*, with air-conditioned suites and dorms that have an open-sided public dining and lounge area. Day or night safari walks are R$15, bookable through Maanaim (▷ 316).
✉ Serengal Cachoeira, Ramal do Cachoeira, Xapuri ☎ 68 9984 4738 🖐 R$120–R$300 ⓘ 14

POUSADA UAKARI
www.uakarilodge.com.br
This (together with Cristalino Jungle Lodge ▷ 319) is the best lodge for wildlife, guiding and ecotouristic practice in the Brazilian Amazon. The lodge comprises ten suites of rooms with a spacious 25sq m (30sq yards), floating on the river in the heart of the Mamirauá reserve (▷ 308). Tours and guiding are excellent.
✉ Speedboat transfers provided from Tefé, 660km (410 miles) north of Manaus ☎ 97 3343 4672, 97 3343 4160 🖐 R$350–R$500 ⓘ 10

ZEQUINHA LODGE
Zequinha is a basic lodge, with very simple wooden fan-cooled rooms and one air-conditioned suite in a round *maloca* (indigenous Brazilian communal house) 100m (109 yards) from a bluff overlooking the Lago Mamori (▷ 298). This lodge is best booked through Amazon Gero Tours (▷ 315).
✉ Lake Mamori, 60km (37 miles) south of Manaus 🖐 R$180–R$220 ⓘ Communal sleeping areas and 2 rooms

BELÉM

ITAOCA BELÉM
www.hotelitaoca.com.br
The Itaoca is an efficient place with bright but old-fashioned and very plainly furnished air-conditioned rooms, which have writing desks and private bathrooms. They provide a decent breakfast. You're advised to book on the upper floors if possible, as the lower rooms can be plagued by street noise.
✉ Avenida Presidente Vargas 132 ☎ 91 4009 2400 🖐 R$120–R$240 ⓘ 49 ❄

MACHADO'S PLAZA
www.machadosplazahotel.com.br
This boutique hotel boasts airy, tastefully decorated air-conditioned rooms with cream or bright orange walls and beds with bright counterpanes. The hotel has a small business centre, plunge pool and a pleasant breakfast area.
✉ Rua Henrique Gurjão 200 ☎ 91 4008 9800 🖐 R$220–R$420 ⓘ 36 ❄

LE MASSILIA
www.massilia.com.br
This French-owned boutique hotel has smart duplexes and plain doubles with dark brick walls, all overlooking a little pool and garden deck. The restaurant serves excellent French cuisine and there's a tasty French breakfast to start your day.
✉ Rua Henrique Gurjão 236 ☎ 91 3224 2834 🖐 R$110–R$180 ⓘ 20 ❄ 🏊 Outdoor 🍴

BOA VISTA

AIPANA PLAZA
www.aipanaplaza.com.br
The best hotel in town has rooms gathered around a large pool with a sun deck, set in palm tree-shaded gardens. Rooms are modern and feature cream walls with abstract art, and dark floor tiles.
✉ Joaquim Nabuco 53, Praça do Centro Cívico ☎ 95 3224 4116 🖐 R$165–R$220 ⓘ 87 🏊 Outdoor

ILHA DO MARAJÓ

CASARÃO DA AMAZÔNIA
www.amazzonia.info
The Casarão was the only colonial mansion in Soure town and was falling down until the first decade of the new millennium, when Italian owner, Giancarlo, refurbished it in mock-palladian style and painted it light blue. He's installed a lovely sculpted pool and a reasonable

Below *A wooden chalet bedroom in Mamori Jungle Lodge*

wood-fired pizza restaurant and re-opened it as a hotel. It's now the best in town.
4° Rua 626, Soure 91 3741 2222 R$200–R$350 24 Outdoor Packages including Marajó tours are available

MACAPÁ

CETA ECOTEL

www.ecotel.com.br.
This *pousada* hotel has cabins set in a private section of rainforest and gardens filled with palm trees that are home to sloths and capuchin monkeys. It is a 20-minute cab ride from Macapá's city centre. There are guided walks which take you into the surrounding forest.
Rua do Matodouro 640, Fazendinha 96 3277 3396 R$210–R$620 20

MANAUS

DEZ DE JULHO

www.hoteldezdejulho.com
This hotel is the best economical option in the old city centre for those travelling on a budget, who would prefer not to stay in a backpacker-filled hostel. The rooms are simple but very clean; some have air-conditioning and hot water. There's a laundry, two tour operators and efficient, English-speaking staff.
Rua 10 de Julho 679 92 3232 6280 R$90–R$95 69 Outdoor

HOSTEL MANAUS

www.hostelmanaus.com
The town's IYHA hostel sits in one of Manaus's old republican-era buildings around 10 minutes' walk from the Praça São Sebastião. It's Australian-run and includes good-value dormitories and private rooms. There are views of the city from the upper floors and the place is always busy with backpackers, making it a good place for finding a jungle tour to join up with. This hostel is not to be confused with a non-HI hostel in the city using a similar name.
Rua Lauro Cavalcante 231 92 3233 4545 Dorm bed R$30; double room R$55–R$65 18

TAJ MAHAL HOTEL

www.grupotajmahal.com.br
This tower hotel has wonderful views out over Manaus from the upper storeys, and a rather old-fashioned top-floor revolving restaurant (come for a *caipirinha* cocktail only). Facilities include a tour agency and a spa, but the bedrooms are in need of some refurbishment.
Avenida Getúlio Vargas 741 92 3627 3737 R$280–R$460 170 Outdoor

TROPICAL BUSINESS

www.tropicalhotel.com.br
As you might guess from the name, this is the business companion to the Tropical and just a few doors away. The rooms are some of the best appointed and most modern in the city and offer superb views over Ponta Negra beach from the upper floors. The hotel has the best business facilities in the city.
Avenida Coronel Teixeira 1320 92 2123 3000 R$350–R$550 255 Outdoor

TROPICAL MANAUS HOTEL

www.tropicalmanaus.com.br
This 5-star hotel in Ponta Negra is popular with tour groups and sits in its own semi-forested parkland with its own Rio Negro jetty, private beach, tennis courts and a large pool. Rooms are large but in need of a refresh of décor. They lie along seemingly endless corridors and there are several restaurants, including a decent *churrascaria*. Service can be slow.
Avenida Coronel Teixeira 1320, Ponta Negra 92 3659 5000 R$500–R$700 69 Outdoor

PORTO VELHO

SAMAUMA

This is by far the best mid-range option in the city centre, with brick annexes of cosy, comfortable and air-conditioned rooms. All have international TV and private bathrooms. There is free WiFi in all areas, breakfast and friendly, welcoming staff. The restaurant is popular locally.
Rua Dom Pedro II 1038 69 3224 5300; hotelsamauma@hotmail.com R$150–R$220 21

RIO BRANCO

IMPERADOR GALVEZ

The Imperador Galvez offers two annexes of comfortable, quiet and modern rooms gathered around a large pool. There's international flat-screen TV and free WiFi. Breakfasts are enormous and will last all the way through until the evening.
Rua Santa Inés 401 68 3223 7027 R$200–R$250 42 Outdoor

INACIO PALACE

www.irmaospinheiro.com.br
The Inacio Palace was refurbished in early 2010, receiving fresh light peach décor, bathrooms with granite basins and new tiles, and functional work desks. Rooms are bright and spacious. The hotel has free WiFi, serves a generous breakfast and has English-speaking staff. There's a *churrascaria* restaurant next door.
Rua Rui Barbosa 450–69 69 3214 7100 R$165–R$250 54 Indoor

TERRA VERDE

www.terraverdehotel.com.br
The nicest of Terra Verde's suites include two flat-screens and separate living and sleeping areas. The rooms are well fitted, with air-conditioning. There's a pool, and free WiFi throughout. Breakfast is a simple, self-service affair. This is one of the best hotels in the city.
Rua Marechal Deodoro 221 69 3213 6000 R$180–R$220 34 Outdoor

SANTARÉM

SANDIS

www.hotelsandis.com.br
The best rooms in this 2008-opening hotel are large, bare, modern tile-floored white rooms with DVD players, 34-inch TVs and dining tables. The cheaper options are cosier and have a double and a single bed, making them good value for families.
Rua Floriano Peixoto, 609 93 2101 2700 R$130–R$150 39

THE CENTRAL WEST

Brazil's enormous centre is covered not with rainforest but with *cerrado*—a sparse, woody forest of flowering trees and medicinal plants broken by savannah grasslands. It is the country's most critically threatened habitat, cleared for cattle ranching and, increasingly, for soya. It's also the best biome in South America for spotting wildlife, which makes it home to a series of national parks: the Chapada dos Veadeiros (a table-top mountain range cut by hundreds of waterfalls and rivers), the savannah grasslands of Parque Nacional das Emas and, in the south of the region, the Pantanal. All are UNESCO World Heritage Sites. The Pantanal is the largest wetland area in the world and is the highlight of any wildlife trip to Brazil, with birds, reptiles and mammals occurring here in spectacular numbers. A visit to the Pantanal can be combined with a trip to the rainforest without having to travel too far. In the far north of Mato Grosso state, the *cerrado* merges with the Amazon and here lie two of the best rainforest lodges in Brazil—Cristalino Jungle Lodge (▷ 304) and Jardim da Amazonia—both in private reserves.

Brazil's capital city, Brasília, also lies in the Central West. The capital was moved here from Rio in 1960, when a team led by the Modernist architect Oscar Niemeyer and the urban designer Lucio Costa built a Jetson-age concrete city from nothing in the middle of what was nowhere, in four years. Its monumental buildings are protected as a World Heritage Site. Older cities lie dotted around the region: cobbled, colonial Pirenópolis; wistful, timeless Cidade de Goiás (which is one of the best-preserved colonial towns in South America, and is another World Heritage Site) and torrid Cuiabá and Corumbá (the Pantanal gateways lying at the north and south of the wetland).

BONITO

This small town is hidden in the shallow Bodoquena hills, south of the Pantanal (▷ 330–331) in Mato Grosso do Sul state. It was 'discovered' by the popular TV channel, TV Globo, in 1993 and has been popular with Brazilian families every August since. It's perfect for the family palate, with a whole series of attractions—each offering about one or two hours' enjoyment—easy access to cafés and a central town with hotels, restaurants and bars.

RIVERS AND WILDLIFE

Bonito became famous for its clearwater rivers, filled with fish, broken by gentle waterfalls and set in pretty *cerrado* forest filled with brown capuchin monkeys, agouti and paca (both a kind of rodent). There are many such rivers, including the Rio Sucuri, the Rio da Prata and the Rio Formoso, which forms a big natural pool at the Parque Ecológico Baía Bonita (Aquário Natural, ▷ 336). Forest walks around the Sucuri river offer good opportunities to see wildlife, as plenty of birds, large rodents and primates appear when visitor numbers are low.

CAVES AND FEATURES

The surrounding hills are pocked with deep caves, a number of which are filled with deep-blue reflective pools. These include the Abismo Anhumas, full of stalactites and stalagmites. The Vigilante e Cortina is a 1.8m-high (6ft) finger of apparently melting rock, standing sentinel in front of a wall dripping with slender stalactites and flowstones. The Gruta da Lagoa Azul is a 50m-long (164ft) blue pool pierced by shafts of sunlight and surrounded by 25ha (62 acres) of beautiful *cerrado*.

As well as the attractions, there are plenty of light adventure activities, like zip-lining, tree-top walking courses, rafting in rubber dinghies and snorkelling, all with proper safety measures and great fun even for very small children. All of these activities, and the caves, can be enjoyed with a local tour agency, such as Explore Pantanal (▷ 337).

INFORMATION

www.portalbonito.com.br

390 J14 Praça Rachid Jauli

67 3255 1449 Daily 10–6

From Campo Grande and Miranda

Internacional de Campo Grande

TIPS

» Most of the attractions in Bonito have small cafés on-site serving snacks and refreshments.

» Use T-shirts for sun protection when snorkelling, as sun cream damages the water.

Above *Stalactites in Gruta da Lagoa Azul*
Opposite *Characins or piraputangas in a river near Bonito*

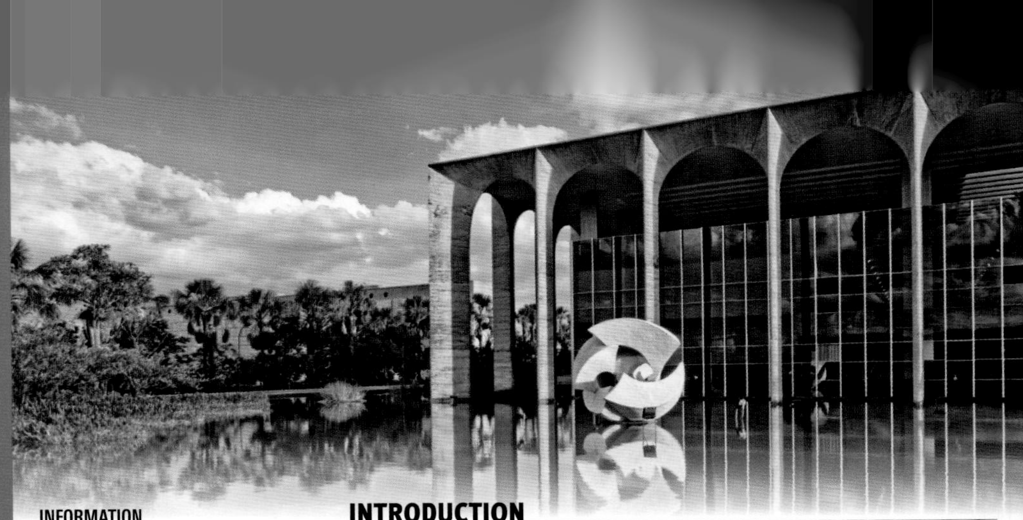

INFORMATION

www.setur.df.gov.br
389 N11 SDC Eixo Monumental, Lote 5, Centro de Convenções Ulysses Guimarães Ala Sul, 1 Andar 61 3214 2742 Daily 8–12, 2–5 From all major tourist towns Internacional de Brasília

Above *Palácio do Itamaraty, designed by Oscar Niemeyer*

INTRODUCTION

Brasília was a project powered by the indefatigable will of one man. Plans to build a new capital in the centre of the country had been drawn up as early as 1822, but it took Juscelino Kubitschek (▷ 35), Brazil's self-proclaimed great modernizer—whose famous election-winning catchphrase was 'fifty years in five'—to turn the dream into reality. His capital was rushed through from start to finish within his presidential term of office (1956–1961). The blueprint was cleared by Congress in 1956. Work began the following year and by the time American President Eisenhower laid the cornerstone of the US embassy in February 1960, accompanied by a great media fanfare, the new capital was largely complete.

Kubitschek's dream was realized by the urban planner Lucio Costa, architect Oscar Niemeyer, landscape-architect Roberto Burle Marx and the civil engineer Israel Pinheiro. Ceramic artist Athos Bulcão added the iconic Modernist *azulejo* tiles which adorn many of the buildings. The backbreaking work was done by hundreds of thousands of migrant workers from the northeast, called *candangos*, temporarily housed in purpose-built worker cities like Tagautinga. Kubitschek broke Brazil with his city. He left the treasury bankrupt, all its credit lines exhausted and exposed the country to a military coup (▷ 35).

Lucio Costa's vision of Modernity was built on the architectural precepts of Le Corbusier (▷ 77), where buildings and cities were machines for life. Citizens in Brasília are filed by occupation into dedicated work and residential zones, numbered like computer code.

The result is a strange city, full of bombastic monumental buildings but without any neighbourhoods, pavements (sidewalks) or recreational communal spaces. In other words, it is great to photograph but more difficult to live in.

WHAT TO SEE

PRAÇA DOS TRÊS PODERES

This enormous square lies at one end of the main avenue of Brasília, the Eixo Monumental. It is the heart of federal government, flanked by the 'three powers' which give it its name: the Judiciary, the Presidency and the Congress. The most famous of the buildings make up the Congresso Nacional (Mon–Fri 9–11.30, 3.30–4.30, Sat–Sun 10–2; free), comprising a dome (which sits over the Senate) and an inverted dome (over the Chamber of Deputies). The domes are balanced by the twin towers of the Executive, which hover over them. The formal tension between these buildings was intended by Niemeyer to symbolize the tension and harmony of government itself. Watching over the Congress from the other side of the square are the seats of the other two branches of power: the presidential offices of the Palácio do Planalto (Mon–Fri 3–5; free) and the Supremo Tribunal Federal, the Supreme Court headquarters (not open to the public).

PALÁCIO DO ITAMARATY AND PALÁCIO DA JUSTICA

Immediately below this group of buildings and next to Congress are the Palácio do Itamaraty (Mon–Fri 3–5, Sat–Sun 10–3; free) and the Ministry of Justice, with artificial cascades falling from its facade (Palácio da Justiça; Mon–Fri 9–11, 3–5; free). Itamaraty is particularly elegant. Its Modernist columns rise from a lily pond to form smooth arches, conveying all the sense of weightlessness of a European cathedral chancel. Inside is a vast hall displaying some fine sculpture and paintings. Notable are Pedro Américo's *O Grito de Ipiranga*, depicting the moment when Dom Pedro dramatically shouted his declaration of Brazilian Independence (▷ 33), and Jean-Baptiste Debret's painting of his subsequent coronation. There are also works by the important Brazilian Modernists Candido Portinari, Alfredo Volpi and Pedro Correia de Araújo. The building takes its name from that of the same name in Rio de Janeiro (▷ 77).

327 B3

CATEDRAL METROPOLITANA NOSSA SENHORA APARECIDA

Niemeyer's crown-of-thorns cathedral sits a few hundred metres west of the Praça dos Três Poderes (▷ 326). It is most beautiful from within. The 16 soaring curved pillars spread like fingers, and between them are a series of glass windows in a fluid greens, blues, yellows and whites. These windows, and the pale marble of the interior, infuse the building with a soothing transcendent light. The altarpiece—over which sculptures of the archangels are suspended—was given by Pope Paul VI, who also blessed the metal cross sitting on top of the building. The trance-like statues of the evangelists outside the cathedral are by the Mineiro sculptor Alfredo Ceschiatti, who also sculpted blind *Justice* in the Praça dos Três Poderes and the archangels within the church.

327 B2 Eixo Monumental Mon 8–5, Tue–Fri 8–6, Sat 8–5 Free

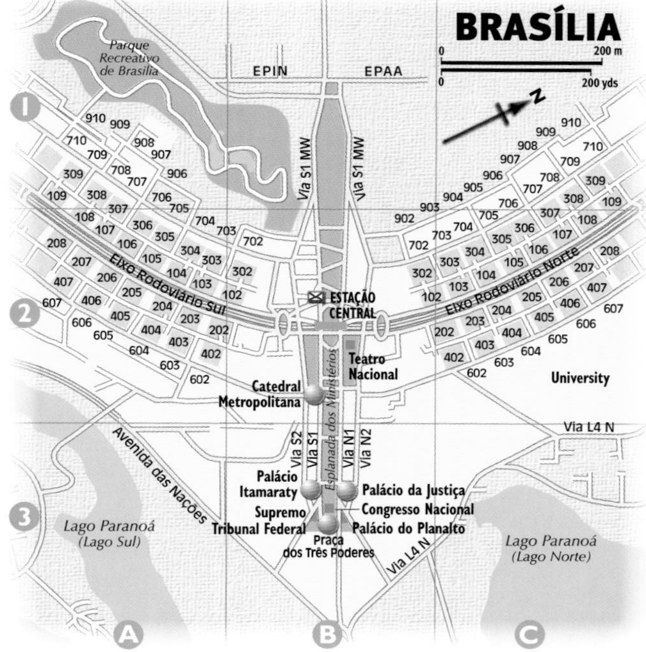

TIPS

» There is very limited disabled access, even in this relatively modern capital city.

» There are ralatively few pavements in Brasília. The best way to get around is by taxi; buses are very crowded and pick-pocketing is common.

» Brasília can be extremely hot in the middle of the day between November and April. Be sure to carry a sun hat, bottled water and sun screen.

» Next to the cathedral are two more Niemeyer buildings, which opened much more recently, in 2007: the Museu Nacional (a space-age dome whose entrance is reached by a sinuous runway; Mon 8–5, Tue–Fri 8–6, Sat 8–5; free) and the Biblioteca Nacional, a 122m-long (400ft) white wedge, faced with a concrete Mashrabiya screen and watching over a series of inky pools (Mon 8–5, Tue–Fri 8–6, Sat 8–5; free).

Below *Detail of Niemeyer's Catedral Metropolitana Nossa Senhora Aparecida*

CIDADE DE GOIÁS

www.cidadedegoias.com.br

Although it is a UNESCO World Heritage Site, Cidade de Goiás, which is referred to simply as Goiás by locals, remains little known outside its home state. Yet this is a delightful little town nestled at the feet of rugged hills and bathed in golden light for almost the whole year round. It sits astride a rushing mountain stream which spills out of the Serra Dourado mountains. Handsome 18th-century town houses watch over pretty cobbled streets and tranquil *praças* (squares). There are timeless local markets and many handsome churches decorated by the celebrated Goiás sculptor, José Joaquim da Veiga Valle. There is also a museum which displays his work, the Museu de Arte Sacra (tel 62 3371 1207; Tue–Fri 8–5; R$4), in the town's most beautiful church, the Igreja da Boa Morte.

It is possible to trek in the nearby Serra Dourado (the Golden Mountain Range), which is cut by clearwater rivers running over pretty waterfalls. Tour companies in the town offer trips to the waterfalls and *cerrado* forests which lie here, and which are still hunted by maned wolf and the occasional puma.

388 M11 Praça da Bandeira 1, Centro 62 3371 1996 Mon–Fri 10–5 From Brasília, via Goiânia Santa Genoveva (Goiânia)

Above *Colonial buildings on the waterfront of Corumbá*

CORUMBÁ

www.corumba.com.br

Brazil's joint hottest city (with Teresina ▷ 283 and Cuiabá ▷ this page) swelters on the banks of the Paraguai river in the heart of the southern Pantanal (▷ 330–331). It is on the western edge of Brazil; Bolivia lies just across the river, and Paraguay a little over 100km (62 miles) downstream. Corumbá is the most attractive city in a region dominated by large, spread-out cities and tiny cowboy villages, and the only one to have an old Portuguese colonial centre. This comprises a small street of brightly painted houses overlooking the River Paraguai, and a harbour of bobbing fishing boats. It is a particularly pleasant spot to while away a few hours at sunset.

The city has a long and bloody history. The Forte Junqueira (tel 67 3231 5828; daily 9–11, 1.30–4; free), built within the city limits, was a base during the 19th-century Paraguayan war and was the second fort built in Corumbá. The first defended the Portuguese against the fearsome Guiacurú Indians, who were finally only defeated by trickery. Most were later massacred, but a few survive as the modern-day Kadiweu. Corumbá is a good alternative base to Campo Grande or Miranda (▷ 331) for visits to the southern Pantanal, which lies literally on the doorstep. Many Mato Grosso do Sul tour agencies (such as Explore Pantanal ▷ 337) have sub-offices or agents here and those that don't can organize hotel pick-ups. The streets near the bus station are unsafe after dark.

390 J13 Rua XV de Novembro 659, Centro 67 3231 2886 Mon–Fri 10–5 From Miranda, Campo Grande and other major tourist towns Aeroporto Internacional de Corumbá

CUIABÁ

www.cuiaba.mt.gov.br

The prosperous state capital of Mato Grosso offers little to attract visitors in its own right, but is an important transport hub. Tours for the northern Pantanal, the Chapada dos Guimarães mountains (▷ 329), Nobres (▷ 329) and Jardim da Amazonia (▷ 329) all leave from here (▷ 336–337), as do most of the flights for the Alta Floresta (for Cristalino Jungle Lodge, ▷ 319). There are a few sights to while away any waiting hours. The Museu do Marechal Rondon (tel 65 3615 8489; Tue–Fri 9–11, 2–6; R$2) holds some important ritual head-dresses and ceramics collected from Pantanal indigenous people, including the Kadiweu and Bororo. The hulking concrete cathedral (built after the demolition of the original baroque edifice, which was founded in the 18th-century gold rush) contains some fine statuary by the Goiás artist José Joaquim da Veiga Valle (Mon–Fri 10–12, 2–5, Sat 10–12, 2–4, Sun 10–12; free).

390 J13 Rua Engenheiro Ricardo Franco 365 65 3613 9300 Daily 9–5 From all major tourist towns Marechal Rondon (Cuiabá)

ILHA DO BANANAL

http://turismo.to.gov.br

The Ilha do Bananal, in the state of Tocantins, is the largest island within a river in the world. It is smaller than the Ilha do Marajó (▷ 305) but Marajó is partly within the Atlantic, while Bananal lies more than 1,000km (620 miles) from the sea, in the Araguaia river. The island is wild, with huge anaconda- and caiman-filled swamps, and extensive stands of *cerrado* and gallery forest. At its southern fringes there are a number of indigenous villages which are off-limits to tourists. It has been preserved partly by its remoteness and visits are difficult, only possible through an operator in Palmas, the capital of Tocantins state (such as Korubo Expedições).

388 M9 Avenida NS 6 Avse 33, Palmas 63 3218 5023 Mon–Fri 10–5 From all major tourist towns Aeroporto Regional de Palmas

JALAPÃO

http://turismo.to.gov.br

The eastern frontier of Tocantins state, bordering the states of Bahia, Piauí and Maranhão, is made up of huge and little-explored *cerrado* and *caatinga* wilderness of craggy table-top mountains, vast plains and miniature dune deserts. There are only a few villages here and abundant wildlife, including maned wolf, banded anteater and lear's macaw. Visits are easily organized through tour operators (▷ 336–337). If possible, avoid travelling to the region with Brazilian groups, as they tend to be very noisy and seeing animals is therefore far more difficult.

385 P9 Avenida NS 6, Avse 33, Palmas 63 3218 5023 Mon–Fri 10–5 From all major tourist towns Aeroporto Regional de Palmas

JARDIM DA AMAZONIA

www.jdamazonia.com.br

Lost in the vast sea of soya that covers much of the northern part of Mato Grosso state—planted to feed the beef cattle of Europe and the soy sauce bottles of Beijing—is an idyllic private rainforest reserve. It is a magical place, focused on a converted farmhouse at a bend in a broad river, surrounded by tropical gardens which effortlessly merge with the towering forest. The Jardim offers some of the most comfortable stays in the Amazon and is one of the best places in the region to which you can safely bring children (▷ 341). Activities at Jardim da Amazonia include canoeing on the river, rainforest walks and wildlife watching. Jaguar, puma, anaconda and giant otter are abundant here, capybara graze on the garden lawns at twilight and a tapir comes to steal cashew fruits from trees near the rooms in the dead of night. Book at least three days in advance, with a reputable agency such as Pantanal Nature (▷ 337).

387 J10 Rodovia MT-10, km 88, São José do Rio Claro, Mato Grosso 66 3386 1221 The reserve's location, far from any public transport, makes travel there without an agency both difficult and inadvisable

NOBRES

www.nobres.mt.gov.br

Tourism is in its infancy in this tiny town, some 100km (62 miles) north of the Chapada dos Guimarães (▷ this page) in Mato Grosso state. It sits in low hills, encompassed by *cerrado* and savannah that are filled with bird and animal life. Like Bonito, the surrounding landscape is cut by stunning clearwater rivers and is home to impressive caves and rock formations. The most beautiful of the rivers include the Rio Triste and Estivado, both of which are glassy-clear and filled with piarucu, piraputanga and dourado fish, and freshwater stingrays. Visits to the attractions around Nobres can only be conducted with a tour agency from Cuiabá, such as Pantanal Nature (▷ 337).

387 J10 Rua Engenheiro Ricardo Franco 365, Cuiabá 65 3613 9300 Daily 9–6 From Cuiabá Marechal Rondon (Cuiabá)

PANTANAL

▷ 330–331.

PARQUE NACIONAL CHAPADA DOS GUIMARÃES

www.chapadadosguimaraes.com.br

At 500 million years, these honey-coloured tablelands and escarpments, 68km (42 miles) northeast of Cuiabá (▷ 328), are among the oldest rock formations in the world. Their high *cerrado* forests, savannahs and pasturelands are visited by international ornithological tours as they offer abundant birdlife close to the Pantanal (▷ 330–331). There is good day walking to caves, small stands of forest and look-outs with wonderful sweeping views. The little town which shares its name with the Chapada has numerous small *pousadas*, shops and cafés, as well as spiritual centres devoted to the cult of the UFO. As the (disputed) geodesic centre of the continent, the tablelands ostensibly emit magnetic waves attractive to aliens and are said to be strong enough to reduce the speed of a car—a phenomenon which could also be attributed to steep hills and rocky dirt roads. The principal highway (BR 251) runs down the lip of the Chapada, offering magnificent views over the Mato Grosso plains. There are also numerous lovely waterfalls, the most famous and tallest of which are the Véu de Noiva, or Bridal Veil falls.

387 J11 Rua Engenheiro Ricardo Franco 365, Cuiabá 65 3613 9300 Daily 9–5 From Cuiabá to Chapada dos Guimarães town Marechal Rondon (Cuiabá)

PARQUE NACIONAL DA CHAPADA DOS VEADEIROS

▷ 332.

PARQUE NACIONAL DAS EMAS

www.parquenacionaldasemas.com.br

The BBC filmed much of their *cerrado* forest footage for the landmark Andes to Amazon wildlife series in this remote national park in southern Goiás state. Its low grasslands and xeric forests are one of the best places in the country to see maned wolf and the smaller wild cats like jaguarundi and oncilla. As there are relatively few visitors, you will usually have trips in the park to yourself. Visits to the park can be organized through hotels in Chapadão do Céu, or through an international wildlife package with tour operators such as the Pantanal Bird Club (▷ 337). It is also possible to charter a taxi in Chapadão do Céu for around R$60 per hour.

388 L12 Avenida Ema, Quadra 51 s/n, Chapadão do Céu 64 3634 1228 From Goiânia to Chapadão do Céu

INFORMATION

www.pantanalms.tur.br

387 J12 Parque dos Poderes, Bloco 12, Campo Grande 67 3318 5000 Mon–Fri 10–5 Rua Engenheiro Ricardo Franco 365, Cuiabá 65 3613 9300 Daily 9–6 Rua XV de Novembro 659, Centro, Corumbá 67 3231 2886 Mon–Fri 10–5 From all the major tourist towns of Brazil, to Campo Grande and Cuiabá. Connections can then be made to Bonito, Corumbá, Miranda and Porto Jofre Internacional de Campo Grande, Marechal Rondon (Cuiabá) and Aeroporto Internacional de Corumbá

Above *Sunrise in the Pantanal near Miranda town*

INTRODUCTION

The Pantanal covers much of Mato Grosso do Sul and southern Mato Grosso states, and stretches into Paraguay and Bolivia. It is the world's largest wetland and the best place in Brazil for seeing wildlife because it doesn't have the dense vegetation of the jungle. While the bird species count is not as high as the Mata Atlântica (▷ 6) or the Amazon (▷ 294–321), the numbers of birds that gather here at the end of the dry season (late Sep–early Oct) beggar belief. Herons, storks, ibises and countless other waterfowl wade in the shallow pools that pock the Pantanal, and in the gutters that line the various dirt roads. Rhea stride slowly through the grasslands, the air is thick with flycatchers and hummingbirds, and a raptor sits on every other fence post. There are plenty of large mammals too, from innumerable capybara, through tapir, giant anteater and armadillo, to maned wolf, jaguar, puma, ocelot and all five of Brazil's smaller cat species.

The Pantanal concentrates such large numbers of animals because of its abundant shallow fresh water and its variety of habitats. These include swampland, savannah grasslands, *cerrado* forest, *igapó* and *varzea* (seasonally flooded forests on blackwater and brownwater rivers, respectively) and gallery forests of a kind only found elsewhere in the Amazon to the north. All are flooded in the wet season (Oct–Mar), when nutrient-rich water drains from the Brazilian shield via a series of sluggish rivers, into the vast flat-bottomed bowl which comprises the Pantanal. Algae and waterplants bloom and zooplankton breed profusely, providing ample food for fish and rodents, which are in turn preyed upon by larger animals.

WHAT TO SEE

ESTRADA PARQUE

This dirt road runs north from the BR-262 to Corumbá (▷ 328). It cuts through some of the southern Pantanal's wildest country and is the access road for many small *fazenda* ranch houses, many of which are open to tourists (▷ 341–342).

ESTRADA TRANSPANTANEIRA

The northern Pantanal counterpart to the Estrada Parque (▷ 330) runs south from the Mato Grosso BR-70 highway to the town of Porto Jofre (▷ this page), and is just a few hours drive from Cuiabá city (▷ 328). It is lined with *fazenda* ranch houses, bisected by small rivers and teeming with wildlife in the dry season. It is possible to take a self-drive tour of the Transpantaneira, but *fazendas* should be booked in advance and prices are usually cheaper organized as a package from Cuiabá, with an operator like Pantanal Nature (▷ 337).

NHECOLANDIA

Just east of the Estrada Parque (▷ 330), the landscape is a flat area of seasonal lakes, patchy forest and open grasslands, cut by large rivers including the Negro and Taquari. Many of the backpacker tours running out of Campo Grande and Corumbá (▷ 328) visit here on their camping safaris. A series of *fazendas* along the rivers offer more comfortable accommodation (▷ 341–342).

PORTO JOFRE

This small Mato Grosso town, sitting on the banks of a tributary of the Paraguai river at the end of the Transpantaneira (▷ this page), is one of the best places in South America for seeing wild jaguars. They gather on riverbank beaches at dawn in the dry season and can usually be found by local Pantaneiro guides, like Joel Souza (▷ 336–337).

From Cuiabá

MORE TO SEE

MIRANDA

This pocket-sized Pantanal town has a lively festival every autumn, the Festa do Homem Pantaneiro (▷ 337). It is surrounded by numerous *fazenda* ranch houses, many of which offer tourist accommodation and wildlife trips (▷ 341–342). The town is also the terminus of the newly revitalized Trem do Pantanal train (▷ 337), which runs from Mato Grosso do Sul's state capital, Campo Grande, across parts of the southern Pantanal.

Rodoviária, Estrada BR262 s/n Daily 10–6

TIPS

» Visiting the Pantanal is easiest with a tour operator from one of the towns or cities (▷ 337). Book ahead and arrange for airport transport. Touts descend on arriving tourists at the airports and bus stations in Campo Grande and Cuiabá, but the tours offered tend to be cut-price, with poor guiding and accommodation.

» Trips to the Mato Grosso Pantanal can be combined with visits to the Mato Grosso Amazon (▷ 304), Nobres (▷ 329) and the Chapada dos Guimarães (▷ 329).

» Trips to the Mato Grosso do Sul Pantanal can be combined with visits to Bonito (▷ 325).

» Bring a good pair of binoculars to the Pantanal. They will greatly enhance your enjoyment of the wetlands.

Below *A jabiru stork, one of the many waterfowl that inhabit the Pantanal*

PARQUE NACIONAL DA CHAPADA DOS VEADEIROS

This range of table-top mountains cut by broad rivers encloses one of the largest protected areas of *cerrado* in the interior of Brazil and one of the world's oldest and most diverse tropical ecosystems. It lies in the north of Goiás state, on the border with Tocantins, and can easily be visited en route between that state and Brasília (▷ 326–327). The landscape here is magical. While the Amazon is mostly closed forest, with vibrant rich greens and browns, the colours in the Chapada are crepuscular, the forests spaced out and bushy, and separated by rushing waterfalls, glassy rivers and meadows that are filled with medicinal plants and dotted with stands of buriti palm.

PROTECTED SPECIES

Together with Emas (▷ 329), the Chapada dos Veadeiros is a UNESCO World Heritage Site. Between them, these national parks contain more than 60 per cent of all the flowering plants, and just under 80 per cent of all the vertebrate species, known to exist in the *cerrado*. With the exception of the giant otter (▷ 15), all of the *cerrado's* endangered large mammals occur in the Chapada and Emas. In the Chapada, they include giant anteater, puma, jaguar, giant armadillo and maned wolf. There are many rare small mammals and birds, some of which are endemic to the region, such as the cone-billed tanager and the rufous-capped spinetail.

VISITING THE PARK

There are two towns in the Chapada which serve as gateways to the park, and to the numerous waterfalls, rivers and forests which surround it: Alto Paraíso de Goiás (with the bulk of the *pousadas*, restaurants and tour operators) and smaller, prettier São Jorge. Like the town of Chapada dos Guimarães (▷ 329), Alto Paraíso is a spiritual centre, with many new-age shops and therapists offering treatments like reiki and Ayurvedic massage.

INFORMATION

www.chapada.com
www.altoparaiso.com
389 N10 · Avenida Ary Valadão, Alto Paraíso · 62 3446 1201 · Park daily 8–5 · Entrance fee R$5 · From Brasília to Alto Paraíso and São Jorge · No overnight visits

TIPS

» There are only 450 visitors allowed in the park at any one time and only with an accredited guide, so be sure to book ahead with an agency, such as Alternativas (▷ 336).

» Bring bottled water and a sun hat when trekking in the park.

Below *Table-top mountains and* cerrado *are characteristic of the national park*

PIRENÓPOLIS

This delightful and well-preserved little gold-rush town, settled in rocky hills with abundant waterfalls, lies just 140km (87 miles) from Brasília and can easily be visited as an overnight stop from that city. Rows of pastel-paint Portuguese cottages rise through its cobbled streets to stately churches and small *praças* (squares). There are abundant comfortable guest houses and *pousadas*, and many good restaurants.

NOTABLE BUILDINGS

The principal pleasure in Pirenópolis is to wander its pretty streets; there are no individually spectacular monuments. In the town centre is a delightful small art deco theatre, the Teatro de Pirenópolis (tel 62 3331 2029) and many churches. Nossa Senhora do Carmo is the town's simplest but also its prettiest (Wed–Sun 11–5; free). It sits next to the river opposite Rua Rosário and was constructed in 1750 as a private chapel for the family of the wealthy miner Luciano Nunes Teixeira. It has a modest baroque interior and functions as a small sacred art museum, preserving a handful of ecclesiastical pieces from colonial churches which no longer stand in the city. The parish church, Nossa Senhora do Rosário, is the largest in the town and had a magnificent baroque interior until 2002, when it was consumed by fire (Mon, Thu–Sun 7–11, 1–5; R$1).

FOREST RESERVE

Just over 12km (7.5 miles) from Pirenópolis is the Santuário de Vida Silvestre Vagafogo (tel 62 3335 8515; www.vagafogo.com.br; daily 9–5), a private family-run reserve in *cerrado* woodland. Aside from offering the most delicious afternoon teas in Goiás state—made with home-produced drinks, jams and bread—the owner, Evandro, has set up a small ecotourism project.

INFORMATION

www.pirenopolis.tur.br
388 N11 Rua do Bonfim, Pirenópolis 62 3331 2633 Mon–Fri 10–5 From Brasília Internacional de Brasília

TIP

» Pirenópolis hosts one of the most colourful festivals in central Brazil, the Festa do Divino (▷ 337).

Above *Participants in the Festo do Divino Espírito Santo make their way towards the town centre*

A PANTANAL SAFARI

This journey down the Estrada Transpantaneira dirt road is best conducted as a bespoke journey with a tour operator. It takes in three of the best Pantanal *fazendas* and can be continued to Porto Jofre if desired, which is the best place in the northern Pantanal for seeing jaguars.

THE TOUR
Distance: 300km (186 miles)
Time: 3–4 days
Start/end at: Cuiabá

★ Cuiabá (▷ 328), the capital of Mato Grosso state, is the capital of the far Central West and an important transport hub. It will be one of Brazil's World Cup cities in 2014. All the northern Pantanal tour agencies are based here, including Pantanal Nature (▷ 337). Arrive in Cuiabá by bus from any of the major tourist towns of the region, or fly to the town's airport, Marechal Rondon.

The first part of the journey leaves Cuiabá on the BR-70 interstate highway to Rondônia and Acre. The road is asphalted for 100km (62 miles) before a turn-off onto the MT-60 Transpantaneira dirt road at the small town of Poconé.

❶ Poconé is a small gold-rush town, founded in 1777 by the Portuguese fortune-hunter Luiz de Albuquerque de Melo Pereira e Cáceres. It marks the beginning of the Pantanal.

The Estrada Transpantaneira begins here and runs south for 150km (93 miles).

❷ The Transpantaneira (▷ 331) is itself a great location for wildlife spotting, especially at the end of September, in the hour before and after dawn or dusk. Huge flocks of egrets, roseate spoonbills and wood storks descend on the roadside gullies, mingling with jabiru storks and capped herons. Capybara cross the road in groups of up to 20, together with greater rhea, marsh deer and the occasional anaconda. The scores of creeks, which the road crosses on rickety wooden bridges, are filled with spectacled caiman. Birding from this road can produce over 100 species in a single day.

Drive 25km (15.5 miles) south, crossing the Rio Bento Gomes to the Araras Lodge. This is the first overnight stop.

❸ Araras Lodge (▷ 341) is one of the best lodges on the Transpantaneira. A path leads from the lodge buildings to an area of swamp land immediately to the north. This is full of caiman and waterfowl. A walkway leads out across it to a large tree with a viewing platform built high in the crown of the branches. At dusk and dawn this is one of the best spots for birds and wildlife watching in the northern Pantanal.

The next day, leave early for the Pouso Alegre, next door.

❹ The long driveway at the Pouso Alegre (▷ 342) is lined with trees nested by various species of parakeets, toucan and jabiru storks, and lined with ponds where hundreds of caiman bask in the sun. Hyacinth macaws congregate in the trees in front of the *pousada* every afternoon after 4pm and it is possible to rent horses here and go for guided rides through the *pousada*'s extensive grounds.

Continue along the Transpantaneira for another 20km (12.5 miles), to the Rio Clarinho *pousada* on the right-hand side of the road.

❺ The Pousada Fazenda Rio Clarinho (▷ 342) sits on the Rio Claro river. It is lined with beautiful gallery forest—which is home to large bands of peccary (a pig-like mammal)—and the trees around the site hide rare birds like agami heron. Accommodation at the *pousada* is simple but comfortable and it is possible to stay here or return to sleep at Araras Lodge.

The journey can be continued to Porto Jofre, another 100km (62 miles) to the south, or return to Cuiabá.

WHEN TO GO

The wildlife is most prolific here at the end of the dry season (during August and September is ideal), when there may still be rain but the flood waters have receded and the precipitation is not great enough to make travel difficult.

WHERE TO EAT

All the *fazendas* visited on this tour will provide your meals but accommodation should be booked in advance.

INFORMATION

Rua Engenheiro Ricardo Franco 365, Cuiabá ☎ 65 3613 9300 🕐 Daily 9–6

TIPS

» It is essential to bring good binoculars to the Pantanal to make the most of your wildlife-spotting opportunities. Sun cream and appropriate clothing are also essential, and if you want to see the dawn displays, you may want to bring an alarm clock.
» It is not advisable to visit the Pantanal during the hottest part of the year (Nov–Dec), or during the peak of the wet season (Feb–Mar), when floods make roads impassable and can reach dangerous levels.
» Mosquitoes can be a pest during the wetter months (Sep–Apr). Insect repellent is available at pharmacies in Cuiabá.

Opposite *Tourists enjoying a safari*
Left *Capybara can be seen from the Transpantaneira*
Below *Cattle ranchers in the Pantanal*

BONITO

AQUÁRIO NATURAL

This clearwater river lagoon, filled with fish, is the easiest snorkelling spot in Bonito. The water barely moves and the Aquário provide lifejackets, masks and snorkels, making this one of the best options in Bonito for children. As with all other attractions in Bonito, visits must be organized through a tour operator, like Explore Pantanal (▷ 337).

✉ Estrada para Jardim, km 8, and then 5.5km (3.5 miles) of dirt road 🕐 Daily 9–6 Adult R$125, including lunch, child (under 7) R$115

BRASÍLIA

BRASÍLIA CITY TOUR

www.brasiliacitytour.com.br

These comfortable tour buses leave from the Brasília Shopping centre and Torre de TV (TV Tower), at the eastern end of the Eixo Monumental (▷ 326). They call at around 20 key city sights, including the Palácio do Itamaraty, Palácio da Justiça, Catedral and Congresso Nacional.

☎ 61 9298 9416 🕐 Mon–Wed 10.30, 2, 4, 7, Thu–Sun 10.30, 12, 1.30, 3, 4.30, 7 Adult R$25, child (6–12) R$15, under 6 free ? From Brasília Shopping and Torre de TV (except Mon, from Brasília Shopping only)

CLUBE DE CHORO

www.clubedechoro.com.br

This club, housed in a bunker-like building designed by Niemeyer, is devoted to one of Rio de Janeiro's most traditional music genres, *choro*. This is one of the best locations in the country to hear the music, which sounds a little like ragtime played on guitars, mandolins and woodwind.

✉ SDC, Quadra 3, Bloco G ☎ 61 3327 0494 🕐 Wed–Sat 9–late Shows from R$10

PRESMIC TURISMO

www.presmic.com.br

This company can arrange full-day, half-day and night-time architectural tours of Brasília. Book ahead for English-speaking guides and stipulate if you want to see any of the more modern Niemeyer museums, like the Museu Nacional and the Biblioteca Nacional (▷ 327).

✉ SHS, Quadra 1, Bloco A, Loja 35 ☎ 61 3233 0115 🕐 Mon–Sat 10–5

CHAPADA DOS VEADEIROS

ALTERNATIVAS

www.alternativas.tur.br

Alternativas are the best of the Chapada tour operators, with excellent tours in and outside the park and a broad range of adventure activities. This is one of the few tour operators in the region owned and run by locals.

✉ Avenida Ary Valadão Filho 1331, Alto Paraíso ☎ 62 3446 1000

ECOROTAS

www.ecorotas.com.br

This company offers the least strenuous tours of the Chapada, including van trips to the principal sights outside the park and short gentle walks within the park itself.

✉ Rua das Nascentes 129, Alto Paraíso ☎ 62 3446 1820 🕐 Daily 9–5

TRAVESSIA

www.travessia.tur.br

Treks in and around the national park are offered, with a large choice of adventure activities. Experienced instructors run excursions including rappelling and canyoning.

✉ Avenida Ary Rua Valadão Filho 979, Alto Paraíso ☎ 62 3446 1595

PANTANAL: NORTH

ECOVERDE TOURS

www.ecoverdetours.com.br

Expect no-frills on these backpacker tours of the Pantanal. The owner, Joel Souza, has many years guiding

Opposite *An excursion by canoe is one way to see the Pantanal*

experience, knows his birds and beasts and speaks good English, but other guides in his employ are not always of the same standard. However, there is no better option in Cuiabá for a budget trip.
✉ Rua Pedro Celestino 391, Centro, Cuiabá ☎ 65 9638 1614, 65 3624 1386

PANTANAL BIRD CLUB

www.pantanalbirdclub.org
This Peruvian and Argentinian company runs professional bird-watching tours throughout the Central West of Brazil, using excellent birding guides and visiting the more touristy areas, like the Chapada dos Guimarães (▷ 329) and the Transpantaneira (▷ 331), in addition to less accessible locations like Emas National Park (▷ 329). Contact is through the website and email (birdclub@gmail.com).

PANTANAL NATURE

www.pantanalnature.com.br
Well-organized trips are run to the northern Pantanal, Nobres (▷ 329), the Chapada dos Guimarães (▷ 329) and Pousada Jardim da Amazônia (▷ 341). Guiding is excellent and the company is the best option for wildlife enthusiasts.
✉ Rua Campo Grande 487, Cuiabá ☎ 65 3322 0203

FESTIVALS AND EVENTS

FEBRUARY

FESTA DE NOSSA SENHORA DE CANDELÁRIA

This festival, in honour of the patron saint of Corumbá (▷ 328), takes place on 2 February each year, with parades, dances and much revelry. All shops and businesses, except hotels and restaurants, are closed.
ℹ Rua XV de Novembro 659, Centro ☎ 67 3231 2886 🕒 Mon–Fri 10–5

MAY–JUNE

FESTA DO DIVINO ESPÍRITO SANTO

This is one of the most colourful festivals in central Brazil, in the city of Pirenópolis (▷ 333). It entails religious processions, battles between Moors and Christians, and a cowboy parade *(cavalgada)* which runs out over the *cerrado* of Goiás to many other villages. It is held 50 days after Easter, over the weekend of Pentecost Sunday.
ℹ Rua do Bonfim, Pirenópolis ☎ 62 3331 2633 🕒 Mon–Fri 10–5

JUNE

FESTA DO ARRAIAL DO BANHO DE SÃO JOÃO

On 24 Jun, Corumbá (▷ 328) celebrates with processions during the day, stalls of meaty food, loud fireworks and the ritual baptism of an effigy of St John in the Rio Paraguai.
ℹ Rua XV de Novembro 659, Centro ☎ 67 3231 2886 🕒 Mon–Fri 10–5

OCTOBER

FESTIVAL PANTANAL DAS ÁGUAS

At this festival in mid October, which is also in Corumbá, there are more parades of giant *mameluco* puppets—similar to those found in Olinda (▷ 250–251)—and everybody douses each other in water, which is great in the 40°C (104°F) heat, unless you are carrying a camera. It is Brazil's equivalent of Thailand's Songkran festival.
ℹ Rua XV de Novembro 659, Centro ☎ 67 3231 2886 🕒 Mon–Fri 10–5

OCTOBER–NOVEMBER

FESTA DO HOMEM PANTANEIRO

In a celebration of the Pantanal way of life, Miranda hosts this lively festival. There are four days of rodeos, lassoes, cowboys in leather and stetsons, cheesy country music and prize bulls, all held in a purpose-built arena.

PANTANAL: SOUTH

EXPLORE PANTANAL

www.explorepantanal.com
The best tours in southern Pantanal are offered by this company, run by a Kadiwèu indigenous guide. This is the only agency within easy reach of Bonito that speaks English and has many years of experience. It is also one of the few companies which includes visits to indigenous villages alongside their wildlife tours, and puts money back into the communities. There are many tours to choose from—such as visiting the Gruta Lagoa Azul (▷ 325) or Abismo Anhumas (▷ 325)—and bespoke options. Try floating down the Rio Sucuri and then walking near by, or light rapid-running in inflatable dinghies down the Rio Formoso (both near Bonito).
✉ Rua Dr Alexandre 305, Miranda ☎ 67 3242 4310, 67 9292 3342

TREM DO PANTANAL

www.serraverdeexpress.com.br
This tourist-designated diesel train takes 11 hours to make the trip of 220km (136 miles) across the Pantanal between Campo Grande and Miranda, including a two-hour stop for lunch in the tiny town of Aquidauana and other breaks at stations to buy indigenous arts and crafts or snacks. There's little to see along the way, just miles of flat wetland broken by trees or pasture, but the journey is more comfortable and leisurely than taking the bus.
✉ Estação Ferroviaria s/n ☎ 67 3384 6755 🕒 Sat–Sun only 💳 R$39–R$800 (for a private cabin for eight people) bookable only through tour operators (▷ this page)

PIRENÓPOLIS

PADILHA ECOTURISMO

www.padilhaecoturismo.pirenopolis.tur.br
This small operator, run by local Paulo Padilha, can organize transfers from Brasília to Pirenópolis, hotel reservations, trekking, rafting and sightseeing around Pirenópolis.
☎ 62 3331 2998

EATING

PRICES AND SYMBOLS

The restaurants are listed alphabetically (excluding A, Al, El, La, Le and O). The prices given are the average for a two-course lunch (L) and a three-course dinner (D) for one person, without drinks. The wine price is for the least expensive bottle. Although you will find wine served in restaurants throughout Brazil, the usual drinks are bottled beer (R$5–R$8) or *caipirinhas*, the ubiquitous *cachaça* and fruit cocktails (R$8). All the restaurants listed accept credit cards unless otherwise stated.

For a key to the symbols, ▷ 2.

ALTO PARAÍSO DE GOIÁS

OCA LILA

This mock-indigenous round house is on a quiet back street in Alto Paraíso. It serves a good-value lunchtime buffet of vegetarian fare, including lentil bakes, *cerrado* stews (like soya meat with pungent *pequi* fruit) and salads. In the evening it reverts to à la carte pizzas and vegetarian dishes.
✉ Avenida Joao Bernardes Rabelo 449 ☎ 62 3446 1006 ⌚ Mon–Sun 12–4.30, 6.30–12 ✋ L R$20, D R$35, Wine R$35

BONITO

CANTINHO DO PEIXE

This popular restaurant in the centre of Bonito is celebrated for its regional river fish dishes, like *pintado* catfish cooked in a sauce made from brilliant red *urucum* berries. Food is served in a large, open-sided dining room.
✉ Rua 32 de Março 1918 ☎ 67 3255 3381 ⌚ Mon–Sat 11–3, 6–11 ✋ L R$25, D R$40, Wine R$30

BRASÍLIA

ALICE

www.restaurantealice.com.br

Restaurant Alice is recommended by *Veja* magazine—Brazil's equivalent of the USA weekly, *Newsweek*—voted as their best restaurant in the city several times. Food is modern Brazilian-French in technique, with Brazilian ingredients and dishes like fillet of fish served in a light *moqueca* sauce (with coconut milk and herbs) and served on a bed of rice. The wine list is excellent. It's situated in Brasilia's most prestigious neighbourhood, Lago Sul, about 8km (5 miles) from the city centre.
✉ SHIS, QI 17 Comércio Local, Edifício Fashion Park , Lago Sul ☎ 61 3248 7743 ⌚ Tue–Sat 12–3, 8–12, Sun 12–4 ✋ L R$60, D R$80, Wine R$40

AQUAVIT

www.restauranteaquavit.com

Danish architect-turned-chef, Simon Lau Cederholm, fuses architectural and gastronomic style in this Modernist dining room, perched in a glass cube on the side of his home and watching over Paranoá lake. The dinner to go for is the once-a-year Babette's Feast Banquet—an ingredient-by-ingredient reproduction of the meal in Gabriel Axel's 1987 Academy Award-winning film of the same name—from (sustainably sourced) turtle soup to roast quail. Thankfully many of the dishes are available à la carte at other times.
✉ Mansões do Lago Norte , ML 12, Conjunto 1, Casa 5 ☎ 61 3369 2301 ⌚ Wed–Sat 8.30pm–2am ✋ D R$90, Wine R$40

O CONVENTO

www.oconvento.com.br

This restaurant offers modern Brazilian cooking, with dishes like grilled duck breast in passion fruit and spice sauce, served with new potatoes and sautéed apple. Food is served in a large dining room decorated with antiques and arts and crafts. There's live jazz and *choro* music on Thursdays.
✉ SHIS, Quadra I9, Conjunto 9, Casa 4 ☎ 61 3443 3104 ⌚ Tue–Thu12–3.30,

Above *A classic* caipirinha *makes a good accompaniment to Brazilian dishes*

8–12, Fri–Sat 12–3.30, 8–1, Sun 12–4 L R$45, D R$70, Wine R$35

O ESPANHOL

The Central West's finest Spanish restaurant hosts the city's annual Spanish festival in November. For the rest of the year it serves reliable Castillian and Andalucian standards, including paella, to a mixed crowd of politicians and businessmen.
Avenida W3 Sul, Quadra 404, Bloco C, Loja 7 61 3224 2002 Daily 12–12 L R$30, D R$40, Wine R$30

LE FRANÇAIS

This popular French bistro serves classic and modern Franco-Brazilian fusion dishes, making use of *cerrado* fruits and vegetables. The dining room is formal, with faux-Louis XVII chairs with buttoned cushioning, heavy linen tablecloths and silver plate cutlery. The restaurant has a 40-bottle wine list and is another *Veja* magazine favourite, voted their best French restaurant in the city in 2003.
Avenida W3 Sul, Quadra 404, Bloco B, Loja 27 61 3225 4583 Mon–Sat 11.30–3, 6.30–11 L R$55, D R$70, Wine R$45

OCA DA TRIBO

Dutch Cordon Bleu chef Gabriel Fleijsman provides a buffet of meat stews and organic chicken with wholegrain rice, in addition to plenty of vegetarian options in this wholefood restaurant. The communal house is decorated with artefacts from the Xingu.
SCES, Trecho 2, opposite Agepol 61 3226 9880 Tue–Fri 12–3, Sat 12–4 L R$60, Wine R$35

PATÚ ANÚ

www.patuanu.com.br
Tables in Lucas Fernandes Arteaga's dining room are the most coveted in the city, so book well ahead. Arteaga earned his stripes in the Michelin 3-star Martín Berasategui in San Sebastian and his delectable *degustation*-only menu fuses molecular gastronomy with Latin panache, offering dishes like duck in tucupi sauce with crispy *farofa* (manioc flour) and mandioquinha (a Brazilian root vegetable like a large salsify). The restaurant itself is equally delightful, tucked away in *cerrado* forest on the city's northern outskirts, with sweeping views of the distant city twinkling in Paranoá lake.
SMLN, Trecho 12, Conjunto 1, Casa 7 61 3369 2788 Mon–Sat 8.30pm–2am D R$90, Wine R$400

PIANTELLA

Brasília's political movers and shakers have been cutting deals over prime cuts of meat for decades in this big, bright marble dining room flooded with natural light from huge glass windows. The wine and drinks list is excellent and the black-tie service crisp and formal.
SCLS 202, Bloco A, Loja 34 61 3224 9408 Tues–Sat 12–4, 7–1.30, Sun 12–5 L R$60, D R$80, Wine R$40

PORCÃO

www.porcao.com.br
The Brasília branch of Brazil's favourite top-of-the-range *churrascaria* chain has a piano bar and a large veranda. As ever, meat is served in all-you-can-eat quantities by black-tie waiters who whisk around the big open-plan dining room.
Sector de Clubes Sul , Trecho 2, Conjunto 35, Rest 3 61 3223 2002 Mon–Thu 12–12, Fri–Sat noon–12.30am, Sun 12–11 L and D R$86, Wine R$45

ZUU AZDZ

www.zuuazdz.com.br
Mara Alcamim's swish, glass-sided dining room opened in 2006 and is a favourite courting spot for society couples. The menu here is Brazilian fusion, having a flirtation with molecular gastronomy. There are lots of meat and chicken options, and daring side dishes like chantilly cream infused with hot wasabi.
210 Sul, Bloco C, Loja 38 61 3244 1039 Mon–Fri 12–5, 7–12, Sat 7–1 L R$60, D R$90, Wine R$45

CIDADE DE GOIÁS

FLOR DO IPÊ

Tables in this restaurant are set in a beautiful garden with views of the river and the serra. The Goiânian food is the best in town, with a huge choice of hearty stews and roasts, many of them flavoured with *cerrado* herbs and spices.
Praça da Boa Vista 32, at the end of the road leading across the bridge from the centre 62 3372 1113 Mon–Fri 11.30–3, 6.30–10.30, Sat 11.30–3, 6.30–11, Sun 12–4 L R$30, D R$45, Wine R$40

CUIABÁ

CHOPPÃO

www.choppao.com.br
This well-established restaurant is, after more than 30 years, a local institution. They serve enormous portions of tasty comfort food, from grilled meats with beans and rice to thick chicken soup. You will find a lively atmosphere at all times of the day and night.
Praça 8 de Abril 65 3623 9101 Tue–Fri 12–3, 6.30–11, Sat 12–3, 6.30–1 L R$25, D R$35, Wine R$35

GETÚLIO

Even the locals sometimes complain of the heat in torrid Cuiabá, so this restaurant is a welcome air-conditioned haven. They provide very good food, meat dishes being a speciality. The pizzas are also reliable and wood-fired, and it's all served by black-tie waiters. There's a buffet lunch on Sundays. The live music (upstairs on Friday and Saturday evenings) is played by well-known Brazilian performers.
Avenida Getúlio Vargas 1147, at São Sebastião 65 3264 9992 Tue–Fri 12–3, 6.30–11, Sat 12–3, 6.30–1 L R$35, D R$45, Wine R$45

PIRENÓPOLIS

CAFFÈ TARSIA

www.caffetarsia.com.br
An excellent menu of Mediterranean dishes, Goiás food and steaks makes this place one of the most popular choices on a colonial street lined with a dozen restaurants. Sample the great *caipirinhas* (*cachaça* cane rum, crushed ice and fruit cocktails).
Rua do Rosário 34 62 3331 1274 Mon–Fri 12–3, 6.30–11, Sat 12–3, 6.30–12 L R$30, D R$50, Wine R$30

PRICES AND SYMBOLS

Prices are the lowest and highest for a double room for one night. Breakfast is included unless noted otherwise. All the hotels listed accept credit cards unless otherwise stated. Note that rates vary widely throughout the year.

For a key to the symbols, ▷ 2.

BONITO

POUSADA OLHO D'ÁGUA

www.pousadaolhodagua.com.br

This is a comfortable *pousada* (guest house) offering extras like horse-riding and bike rental (for a fee). The cabins are either air-conditioned or fan-cooled and are set in an orchard next to a small lake. There's solar-powered hot water and decent food (including the dishes made from vegetable garden produce).

Rodovia Três Morros, km 1, Zona Rural 67 3255 1430 20 R$180–R$280

TAPERA

www.taperahotel.com.br

You may need to provide your own transport to get to this simple *pousada* 10km (6 miles) from the town centre on the road to Jardim. However, you'll find a quiet, cool and breezy location with fine views and spacious, bright, airy and comfortable rooms. There is also a generous buffet breakfast of fruit, cold meat, pastries, juices and coffee.

Estrada Ilha do Padre, km 10 67 3255 1700 46 R$135–R$190 Outdoor

BRASÍLIA

CASABLANCA

www.casablancabrasilia.com.br

A hotel block designed in homage to Niemeyer's Modernist style has Gothic arches echoing his Palácio do Itamaraty (▷ 327). The rooms are newly refurbished but are still spartan shells that have standard catalogue furniture. The best, on the upper floors, are the freshest and bightest.

SHN, Quadra 3, Bloco A 61 3328 8586 58 R$280–R$350

KUBITSCHEK PLAZA

www.plazabrasilia.com.br

This tall tower is popular with the business community. It has modern, no-nonsense rooms with plenty of workspace and good facilities, broadband access in each room, and there's a pool, sauna and gym.

SHN, Quadra 2, Bloco E 61 3329 3333 264 R$400–R$550 Rooftop

NACIONAL

www.hotelnacional.com.br

When Brasília was in its infancy, this enormous skyscraper hotel was the place to stay in Brasilia. Nowadays the rooms seem old-fashioned and the décor tired, but the panoramic views from the upper floors are superb. There are several restaurants in the complex, a small music hall (which is almost always deserted) and a sauna.

SHS, Quadra 1, Bloco A 61 3321 7575 347 R$175–R$440 Outdoor

EL PILAR

www.elpilar.com.br

This small, locally owned and run hotel has plain but well-kept fan-cooled and air-conditioned rooms with tiled floors and private bathrooms. Avoid those below street level as they collect car fumes.

SHN, Quadra 3, Bloco F 61 3533 5900 64 R$170–R$220

ROYAL TULIP ALVORADA

www.royaltulipbrasiliaalvorada.com

This is one of the largest hotels in the country, with 395 rooms spread around a brilliant red horseshoe designed by Unique Hotel (▷ 137) architect Ruy Ohtake. They include a variety of luxurious suites and cater mostly for visiting businessmen and politicians. There are all the expected facilities in profusion: several swimming pools, tennis courts, spa, gym and sauna. The most interesting

Opposite *Lobby of the Royal Tulip Alvorada hotel in Brasília*

accommodation is in the upper-floor suites, which were refurbished recently with Niemeyer sketches, new carpets and fresh bedding. The restaurants are adequate but pricey, so eat elsewhere.
SHN, Trecho 1, Conjunto 1B, Bloco C 70800 200 61 3424 7000 395 R$400–R$540 Outdoor

CHAPADA DOS GUIMARÃES

POUSADA PENHASCO

www.penhasco.com.br
This mini resort, made up of a series of breeze-block chalets with terracotta roofs, sits on the edge of one of the Chapada's towering sandstone cliffs, affording sweeping views out over the plains below. The hotel is great for families, with children's play areas, several natural and artificial swimming pools (one with a waterslide), tennis courts and the opportunity to organize tours around the Chapada.
Avenida Penhasco s/n, Bom Clima 65 3301 1555 53 R$225–R$400 Outdoor, indoor

CHAPADA DOS VEADEIROS

CASA DAS FLORES

www.pousadacasadasflores.com.br
Only candlelight illuminates the rooms in this pleasant, rustic and romantic little *pousada*, so bring a torch for reading any later than 6pm. There's a sauna, pool and the decent attached restaurant serves a bountiful breakfast of fruit, rolls, cut meat, cheeses and juices, but with little competition locally in this price bracket, it feels somewhat expensive.
Vila de São Jorge, Alto Paraiso 62 3455 1055, 62 3455 1049 R$257–R$357 (inclusive of breakfast, lunch and dinner) Outdoor

POUSADA CASA ROSA

This pretty little guest house has chalets and rooms in mock-colonial annexes, gathered in a garden filled with tropical flowers. The hotel staff are friendly and accommodating and the breakfast is one of the best in Alto Paraíso, with a spread of pastries, tropical fruit, cold meat, cheeses, and tea, coffee and juices.
Rua Gumercindo Barbosa s/n, Alto Paraíso 62 3446 1319 24 R$130–R$170 Outdoor

CAMPO GRANDE

JANDAIA

www.jandaia.com.br
This tall tower in the heart of the city centre has very comfortable business-like rooms. They include solid and spacious work areas, WiFi, marble en suites and views out over the city from the top floor.
Rua Barão do Rio Branco 1271 67 3316 7700 140 R$265–R$380 Outdoor

CIDADE DE GOIÁS

CASA DA PONTE

Rooms in this art deco building, set next to the bridge and overlooking the Rio Vermelho, are small but well-maintained. Those on the upper floors come with air-conditioning, and views over the river and colonial terracotta of the town.
Rua Moretti Foggia, Lote 1 62 3371 4467 38 R$50–R$80

FAZENDA MANDUZANZAN

www.manduzanzan.com.br
Lost in the *cerrado* near the region's prettiest waterfalls, this mini-*fazenda* provides sauna, horse-riding and spring-water swimming pools. Lunch is included in the price and rooms are housed in mock-colonial chalets with terracotta tiled roofs and whitewashed walls.
On the road to Cachoeira das Andorinhas, km 8 62 9982 3373 16 R$270–R$345 Outdoor

CORUMBÁ

NACIONAL PALACE

www.hnacional.com.br
This big concrete block in the middle of Corumbá has modern, well-appointed but simple rooms, with wooden facing, cream painted walls and little balconies overlooking an outdoor pool. Buffet breakfasts are generous, with hot food—including bacon and eggs—sitting alongside the usual breads, pastries, fruit, coffee and juices.
Rua América 936, Centro 67 3234 6000 134 R$180–R$220 Outdoor

CUIABÁ

AMAZON PLAZA

www.hotelamazon.com.br
This modern business-orientated hotel sits in easy walking distance of a string of restaurants in the city centre, and has spacious, well-appointed rooms. They contain king-sized beds and WiFi, and look over a central pool.
Avenida Getúlio Vargas 65 2121 2000 84 R$220–R$280 Outdoor

JARDIM DA AMAZONIA

www.jdamazonia.com.br
The Jardim reserve (▷ 329) has some of the most comfortable rooms in the Amazon, with large colourful en-suites decorated with Brazilian arts and crafts, and all with big French windows leading to balconies that have views over the tropical garden. All have air-conditioning, cable TV and huge beds. It is bookable as part of a package with Pantanal Nature (▷ 337).
Rodovia MT-10, km 88, São José do Rio Claro, Mato Grosso 66 3386 1221 R$350–R$550 7

PANTANAL: NORTH

ARARAS LODGE

www.araraslodge.com.br
This is one of the most comfortable places to stay on the Transpantaneira dirt road (▷ 331), with 19 modern and well-appointed air-conditioned rooms. There's good food, a pool and plenty of wildlife in the adjacent stretch of swampland and gallery forest, which is reachable on a wooden walkway. The lodge can be visited on organized tours but should be requested well in advance as it is popular with European tour groups.
Transpantaneira, km 32, Pocone 65 3682 2800 19 R$420–R$560 (inclusive of breakfast, lunch and dinner) Outdoor

POUSADA FAZENDA RIO CLARINHO

This simple rustic farmhouse with whitewashed walls and terracotta roofs offers very plain, Spartan rooms with little more than a bed, mosquito net and wooden wardrobe. There is also dormitory sleeping in hammocks. The *pousada* sits next to the Rio Clarinho, which is home to rare agami herons, families of giant river otters and peccaries.
✉ Transpantaneira, km 40 ⓘ 20 R$200–R$300 (inclusive of breakfast, lunch and dinner) 🍴 ? Bookable only through Pantanal Nature (▷ 337)

POUSO ALEGRE

www.pousalegre.com.br
Rooms in this *pousada* are rustic, with little more than whitewash and a wooden (mosquito net-swathed) double bed, but the environs teem with caiman, capybara and an astonishing number of birds, especially on the morning horseback trail. The remote ox-bow lake is particularly good for waterfowl (including agami and zigzag herons). Proper birding guides can be provided with advance notice and the lodge can be visited on an organized tour.
✉ Transpantaneira, km 36 ☎ 65 3626 1545 ⓘ 13 R$350–R$400 (inclusive of breakfast, lunch and dinner) 🍴

PANTANAL: SOUTH

CACIMBA DE PEDRA

www.cacimbadepedra.com.br
The caiman farm and adjacent guest house sit in a patch of deciduous forest with many horse and walking trails. These lead to a series of small lakes, filled with caiman and anaconda. Rooms are plain, in a modern annexe and all with little more than a TV, bed and worktable, but they are scrupulously clean and sit in front of an inviting pool. There is a hyacinth macaw nest on the farm and tapir sightings are common in the grounds at night.
✉ Estrada Agachi, Aquidauana ☎ 67 9982 4655 ⓘ 11 R$250–R$350 (inclusive of breakfast, lunch and dinner) Outdoor 🍴

FAZENDA BARRANCO ALTO

www.fazendabarrancoalto.com.br
A working ranch in the heart of Nhecolandia (▷ 331), this dates from the early 1900s. It sits on a curve in the Rio Negro surrounded by *cerrado* and gallery forests and is accessed via the Estrada Parque (▷ 330). Specialist wildlife guides can be booked, given at least a month's notice.
✉ Caixa Postal 109, Aquidauana ☎ 67 3241 4047 ⓘ 5 R$720–R$800 (inclusive of breakfast, lunch and dinner) Outdoor 🍴

FAZENDA SAN FRANCISCO

www.fazendasanfrancisco.tur.br
This working cattle ranch near Miranda (▷ 331) is one of the best places in the southern Pantanal to see carnivores. The farm allows jaguars to kill limited numbers of cattle and tags the big cats to know their whereabouts. A night truck ride provides a good chance of seeing wildlife. Accommodation is simple in rustic air-conditioned cabins, around a pool in a garden filled with rheas.
✉ Fazenda San Francisco turn-off from BR-262, 30km (18.5 miles) west of Miranda ☎ 67 3242 3333 ⓘ 10 R$380–R$440 (inclusive of breakfast, lunch and dinner) Outdoor 🍴

PARQUE NACIONAL DAS EMAS

FAZENDA SANTA AMÉLIA

The cattle and soya bean ranch here runs wildlife tours through the property's paltry remnant *cerrado* forest but can organize transfers to the genuine wilds at nearby Emas. Rooms are in comfortable modern chalets with cable TV. They have en suite bathrooms with granite basins and powerful showers.
✉ Estrada Serranópolis, Chapadão do Céu ☎ 64 3634 1380 ⓘ 10 R$180–R$250 (inclusive of breakfast, lunch and dinner) Outdoor 🍴

PIRENÓPOLIS

CASA GRANDE

www.casagrandepousada.com.br
A grand old colonial mansion in the heart of Pirenópolis, this hotel has a small tropical garden visited by dozens of hummingbirds in the late afternoon and early morning. Rooms are plain and simple but public areas are decorated with antique furniture.
✉ Rua Aurora 41 ☎ 62 3331 1758 ⓘ 24 R$110–R$195 Outdoor

O CASARÃO

www.ocasarao.pirenopolis.tur.br
This private house and *pousada*, set in lovely heliconia-filled gardens in the town centre, is decorated throughout with chunky period furniture. Rooms have four-poster beds equipped with mosquito nets and they sit next to a little pool. Service is excellent and the *pousada* can arrange tours and transfers.
✉ Rua Direita 79 ☎ 62 3331 2662 ⓘ 11 R$150–R$210 Outdoor

POUSADA ARVOREDO

www.arvoredo.tur.br
A pleasantly quiet little *pousada* nestles in a little wood just outside the town centre. Clean, modest fan-cooled rooms have polished tile floors, whitewashed walls, little wooden side tables and beds covered in colourful counterpanes. They gather around a small pool and there are rate discounts on weekdays.
✉ Avenida Abércio Ramos, Qd 07, Lt 15 ☎ 62 3331 3479 ⓘ 14 R$95–R$200 Outdoor

Below *A bedroom in Fazenda San Francisco, Pantanal South*

PRACTICALITIES

Practicalities gives you all the important practical information you will need during your visit from money matters to emergency phone numbers.

WEATHER

CLIMATE AND WHEN TO GO

Climatically Brazil is a year-round destination but you should consider the particular weather for the regions you intend to visit before making your travel plans.

In the southeast (Rio de Janeiro, Espírito Santo, Minas Gerais and São Paulo) precipitation is at its highest in the Brazilian summer from December to February. These are also the warmest months. Cold fronts sweeping in from the south Atlantic can cause a drop in temperature of as much as 10°C (18°F).

In Bahia and the northeast summer is dry, sunny and hot. Temperatures can reach as high as 35°C (95°F) in the midday sun. Winter in the northeast is the wet season (months vary according to the subregion, ▷ 6 Climate). This is usually characterized by rain and sun within the same day, but it can occasionally rain non-stop for many days at a time.

In the Amazon, the rainy season also depends on location, but it runs roughly from mid-December to mid-May, and the dry season is from June to early December. Temperatures don't change much in equatorial climates and, even though it does rain more in the rainy season, it is also true that many plants produce fruits and flowers, which attract birds and primates.

Summer is the best time to travel to the subtropical south (Paraná, Santa Catarina and Rio Grande do Sul) as during the winter (June to August) parts of the region can experience frost and even snow. In areas of higher altitude, over 2,500m (8,200ft) in the mountain ranges of Serra da Mantiqueira or inland Rio Grande do Sul, temperatures between June and September can drop to well below freezing.

During the rainy season in the Pantanal and the central west (between December and March), downpours are intense, the temperature is high, and most of the Pantanal gets flooded. It is not the ideal period to travel. The dry season in the Pantanal is from July to September, though July is also Brazilian school holiday month. Alternatively, there are the intermediate seasons.

WEATHER REPORTS

The BBC has an excellent international weather forecast website (www.bbc.co.uk/weather). Many other local news network stations provide international weather such as CNN (http://weather.edition.cnn.com). For a specialized website with temperatures given in Fahrenheit go to www.weather.com or www.accuweather.com. If you are fluent in Portuguese you could try www.climatempo.com.br.

TIME

Brazil has four time zones. Mainland Brazil east of Cuiabá is three hours behind Greenwich Mean Time (GMT). This comprises most of Brazil visited by international tourists, including all the states of the south and southeast, Bahia and Ceará. Fernando de Nornha island, in Pernambuco state east of the Brazilian cape is two

RIO

TEMPERATURE

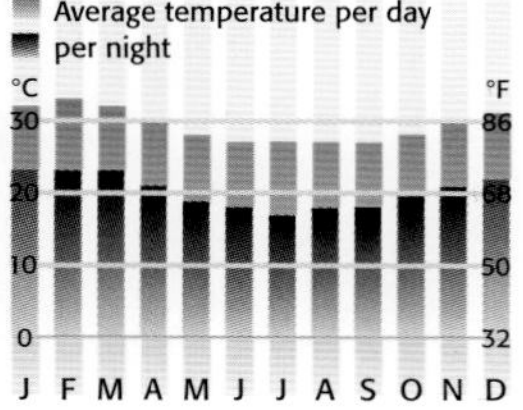

RAINFALL

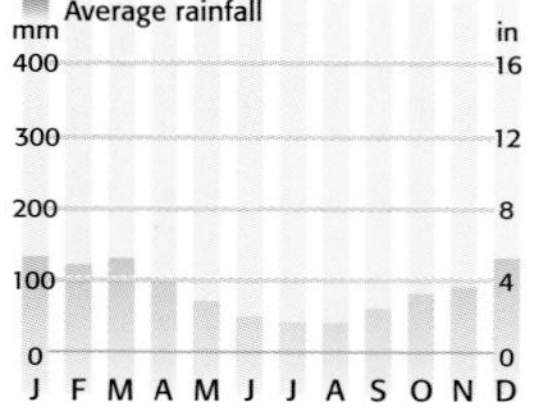

RECIFE

TEMPERATURE

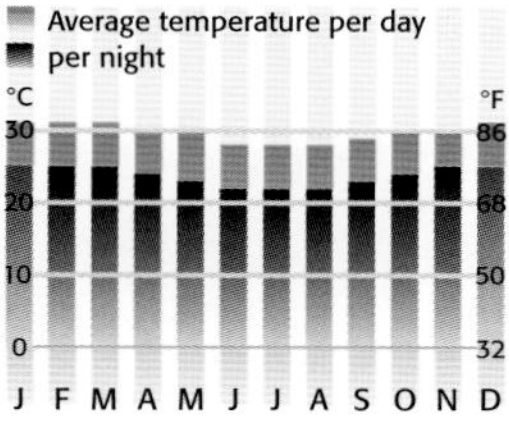

RAINFALL

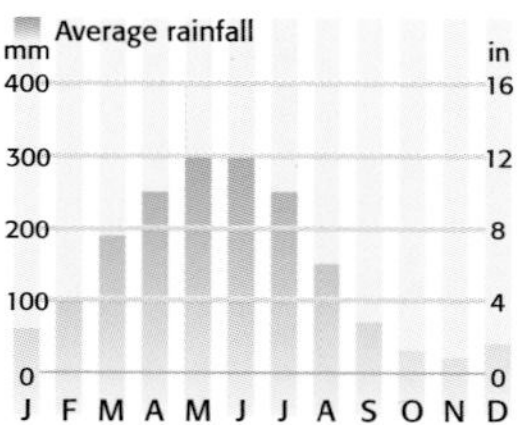

BELÉM

TEMPERATURE

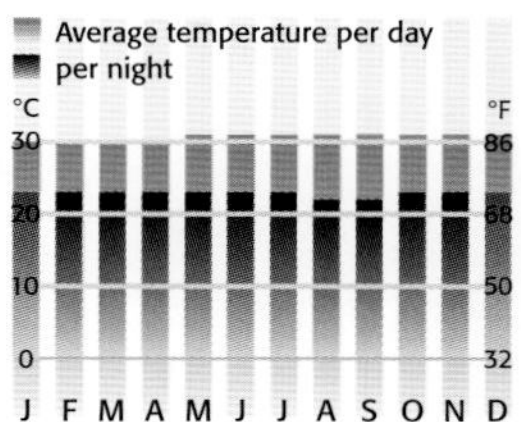

RAINFALL

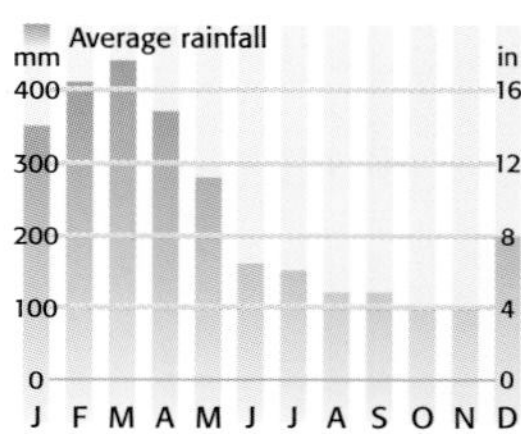

hours behind GMT. East of Acre and west of Cuiabá are four hours behind GMT. This area is made up of all the Amazon states except Amapá, as well as Mato Grosso and Mato Grosso do Sul. Acre and a small section of Amazonas state are five hours behind GMT.

DOCUMENTS

PASSPORTS AND VISAS

As a general rule, Brazil requests visas based on the principle of reciprocity of treatment given to Brazilian citizens. Please check with the Brazilian Consulate in your region. All visitors need a passport valid for six months.

Citizens of the European Union and Switzerland, Mercosul countries, some Caribbean and Central American countries, Malaysia, Thailand, Israel and some African countries do not require visas to visit Brazil. US, Australian, Indian, Canadian, Chinese and New Zealand citizens require visas. The situation can change at any time so check with the Brazilian consulate for the latest information. On arrival visitors are issued with a form which must be filled out in black ink and subsequently a 90-day entry pass, which can be extended to up to 180 days at any Polícia Federal station in the country. The form must be kept with the passport for the duration of the stay and presented on leaving. Loss will incur long delays and a fine. Passports must be produced on demand at the request of a police officer. A photocopy will often suffice. Brazilian nationals must enter and leave Brazil with their Brazilian passport only.

Those requiring a visa are prohibited to engage in business, work, or academic activities in Brazil and first arrival in Brazil must take place within 90 days from the date the visa was issued. A visa is good for multiple entries within the duration of the visa.

Visa applications for US citizens

Visas must be completed online before being printed out. Passports need a validity of six months and with at least two adjacent blank visa pages available for the visa stamp (excluding the pages reserved for amendments and endorsements). Applicants need to submit one recent 5cm x 5cm (2in x 2in) passport-type photograph of the applicant, front view and showing entire face, on a white background. Snapshots, computer pictures and picture photocopies are not accepted. In addition, you need to present a printout of your itinerary, or a photocopy of your round-trip ticket or e-ticket, or a signed letter by the travel agency, addressed to the Brazilian Consulate, attesting to the acquisition of the ticket and confirming round-trip bookings.

The notarization of documents issued in the US must be performed by a notary public within the jurisdiction of the Brazilian Consulate. Visas for US citizens cost US$140 in January 2011.

IDENTIFICATION

You are required to carry ID with you at all times in Brazil. Police can ask to see ID on a whim and many public buildings will allow entry only on presentation of a recognized document. Visitors should carry with them some photo identification, such as passport or driving licence at all times, or a photocopy of such a document formally validated and stamped by the Brazilian consulate or a notary fiscal validated by a Brazilian consulate.

Drivers should always carry their valid driver's licence and passport and all the car documents. These

CUSTOMS

What you can bring into the country duty free:

Tourist baggage is admitted into Brazil under a regime of temporary admittance, whereby the visitor's baggage is exempt from customs duties for a determined period of time, provided that the goods are withdrawn from Brazil before the term of this period. This period of time is set by the customs officer in accordance with the visitor's period of regular stay in Brazil, which is determined by the immigration officer at the point of entry and is usually 2–3 months.

On arrival, all visitors must present a *Declaração de Bagagem Acompanhada – DBA* (Accompanied Baggage Declaration) form. These are distributed on in-coming flights and are available in the immigration section at Brazilian international airports. The form stipulates that the following are goods to declare: animals, plants, seeds, foodstuffs and medication subject to health inspection, weapons and ammunition; goods subject to temporary admittance (these vary year from year but generally include any item worth over US$3,000); commercial or industrial samples or goods intended for commercial or industrial use; valuables (cash, cheques or traveller's cheques) worth over R$10,000 (or equivalent in foreign currency); other goods, where the traveller wishes to get proof of their admittance into Brazil.

Goods destined for consumption within Brazil (including gifts) are subject to an overall limit of US$500 (when the traveller enters Brazil by air or sea) or US$150 (when the traveller enters Brazil by land, river or lake) per person. Goods in excess of the stipulated amount are subject to customs duties, calculated at the rate of 50 per cent of their value. Books, leaflets, periodicals, as well as clothes and other garment articles, toilet articles and footwear intended for the traveller's personal use are exempt from customs duties. Goods purchased at a duty free shop in Brazil upon arrival are exempt from customs duties up to an overall limit of US$500 per person.

What you cannot bring into the country duty free:

Goods whose quantity, nature or variety demonstrates importation or exportation for commercial or industrial purposes.

Automobiles, motorcycles, scooters, bicycles with an engine, rolling houses and other land automotive vehicles; aircraft; boats of all kinds, jet skis and similar, and ship engines; cigarettes and liquor made in Brazil, destined to be sold abroad; liquor, tobacco and similar manufactured products, when the traveller is less than 18 years old; goods purchased in duty free shops upon the traveller's arrival in Brazil above the value of US$500.

need to be presented to police on request. Failure to do so can result in very steep fines or even arrest.

YELLOW FEVER CERTIFICATES

All visitors to Brazil need a yellow fever vaccination certificate, if they have travelled within the previous 90 days to any of the following countries: Angola, Bolivia, Benin, Burkina Faso, Cameroon, Colombia, Democratic Republic of Congo, Ecuador, French Guiana, Gabon, Ghana, Gambia, Republic of Guinea, Liberia, Nigeria, Peru, Sierra Leone, Sudan or Venezuela.

A yellow fever vaccination is also advisable if travelling to any of the following states in Brazil: Acre, Amapá, Amazonas, Goiás, Maranhão, Mato Grosso, Mato Grosso do Sul, Pará, Rondônia, Roraima, Tocantins, or the Federal District (Brasília).

BRAZILIAN EMBASSIES AND CONSULATES ABROAD

AUSTRALIA

General Consulate of Brazil in Sydney
L17 St. Martins Tower, 31 Market Street, Sydney NSW 2000
tel (00612) 9267-4414/15
http://sydney.itamaraty.gov.br

CANADA

General Consulate of Brazil in Montreal
1 Westmount Square, Suite 1700, Montreal, Quebec, H3Z 2P9
tel (001514) 499-0968/69/70
www.consbrasmontreal.org

UNITED KINGDOM

Consulate General of Brazil in London
3 Vere Street, London W1G 0DG
tel (0044) (20) 7659 1550
www.consbraslondres.com

UNITED STATES OF AMERICA

General Consulate of Brazil in Chicago
401 North Michigan Avenue - Suite 1850, Chicago, Illinois 60611
tel (001312) 464-0244/5/6/7
www.brazilconsulatechicago.org

General Consulate of Brazil in Los Angeles
8484 Wilshire Boulevard - Suites 711/730, Beverly Hills, California 90.211
tel (001213) 651-2664
www.brazilian-consulate.org

General Consulate of Brazil in New York
1185 Avenue of the Americas, 21st Floor, New York, NY 10036
tel (001917) 777-7777
www.brazilny.org

MONEY

BEFORE YOU GO

Take a little cash in the form of US dollars to Brazil and debit cards—ideally one MasterCard/American Express and one Visa, and a credit card as back-up. US dollars are easy to exchange in banks or larger hotels, though rates can be poor. Traveller's cheques are not a good option as they incur up to US$20 commission per transaction. Many banks change a minimum of US$300 cash or US$500 traveller's cheques. The euro and pound sterling have a far poorer exchange rate.

Be sure to advise your bank that you are travelling as cards are often automatically blocked on unadvised withdrawals from Brazil.

THE REAL

The Brazilian unit of currency is the real (R$ Reais) divided into 100 centavos. Notes in circulation are in denominations of 100, 50, 10, 5, 2 and 1 real (the latter of which is becoming increasingly rare). Coins are in denominations of 1 real and 50, 25, 10, 5 and 1 centavos. Cash sums in excess of US$10,000 must be declared on entering Brazil. Residents may only take out the equivalent of US$4,000.

WITHDRAWING MONEY

Automatic Teller Machines (ATMs) are widespread in Brazil. They offer the cheapest and most convenient way of withdrawing money and generally the best rates of exchange. They are usually closed after 9.30pm in large cities. The best banks for international cards are Bradesco, HSBC and Banco24Horas. A handful of Banco do Brasil branches accept international cards. ATMs should be used with care after dark, particularly outside shopping malls, airports and bus stations.

CREDIT CARDS

Credit cards are widely used. Diners Club, MasterCard, Visa and American Express are accepted.

WIRING MONEY

Money sent to Brazil through transfers is normally paid out in Brazilian currency, so do not have more money sent out than you need for your stay. It can take as much as four weeks to clear the bureaucracy.

DISCOUNTS

Senior citizens (aged over 60), students with a valid international student identity card and children aged under 10 can often get discounts on admission charges to museums and attractions.

TIPPING

Tipping is not customary in Brazil, but is always appreciated, especially in hotels where cleaning and menial staff are often very poorly paid. Most restaurants add a 10 per cent service charge. Where tipping is voluntary, 10 per cent is fine.

HEALTH

Private health care in Brazil is excellent, with modern facilities and well-trained doctors. Private dentistry is excellent and cheaper than its equivalent in Europe or the US. There is a public system too, but it is severely overstretched and under-funded. The best way to find a hospital is through the hotel concierge, a tour operator or tourist office. Pharmacies *(farmácias)* are widespread and can be found even in the smallest towns.

Many medicines can be purchased over the counter, including some antibiotics. If you are taking regular medication, be sure to bring the pharmaceutical name of your medicine with you to Brazil as brand names can differ. Dengue fever is the principal serious viral disease in Brazil. Bacterial diseases include traveller's diarrhoea, bacillic dysentery and tuberculosis (TB). Parasitic diseases include Chagas disease (trypanosomiasis) and minor infections like cutaneous larva migrans *(bicho geografico)* and chiggers *(bicho do pé)*.

Tap water in Brazil is not generally safe to drink, so buy bottled water.

IMMUNIZATIONS

Visit a GP or travel clinic at least six weeks before leaving for Brazil to find out up-to-the-minute information on vaccinations and general health risks for Brazil. It is a good idea to take out travel insurance, know your own blood group, and if you suffer a long-term condition such as diabetes or epilepsy make sure someone knows or that you have a Medic Alert bracelet/necklace with this information on it. At the date of publication, the following immunizations were recommended for Brazil: **hepatitis A and B, typhoid** (for travellers visiting non-urban areas), **yellow fever** (for those visiting anywhere in north or northwest Brazil and mandatory for anyone arriving from a yellow fever infected country), **rabies** (for travellers anticipating exposure to wild animals, including bats), **measles, mumps, rubella** (MMR) and **tetanus-diphtheria**. While there is malaria in Brazil, the risk of malaria transmission outside the Amazon regions is negligible or non-existent.

DISEASES IN BRAZIL

» **Yellow fever** is a potentially fatal viral infection transmitted by mosquitoes. In mild cases the symptoms are similar to influenza, but serious cases develop a high temperature and may have a series of after-effects, such as internal bleeding, kidney failure and meningitis. A classic feature of yellow fever is hepatitis, which is the reason for the yellow colouring of the skin (jaundice) and the name of the disease. There is yellow fever in the Amazon and central west and some parts of Rio Grande do Sul and São Paulo.

» **Chagas disease** (American trypanosomiasis) is caused by a protozoal parasite related to the parasite that causes sleeping sickness in Africa. Chagas occurs in rural areas in Brazil where it is transmitted by a blood-sucking bug *(Panstrongylus megistus)*, which looks like a large bed bug—dark with a red striped pattern around the edges of the abdomen—ranging in length from 10mm to 25mm (0.5–1 inch). They hide during the day and emerge at night to feed while the victim sleeps. Unlike mosquitoes they bite for a protracted period—up to half an hour. The wound itself is painless but it leaves an itchy red bump. The faeces transmit the Chagas infection. Initial symptoms of Chagas disease involve local swelling, with fever, tiredness and enlargement of lymph glands, spleen and liver. Look for the insects before sleeping, kill them and be sure to sleep under a mosquito net.

» **Dengue fever** is transmitted by a group of viruses spread by fast-flying, black-and-white mosquitoes that bite during the day. Dengue is widespread in coastal regions, in both rural and suburban environments. It has flu-like symptoms—high fever, weakness, headaches and nausea. It usually occurs in two phases. The first is characterized by a fever and a skin rash. This generally clears up after a few days to return in a milder form a few days later and then finally disappear altogether. In some cases dengue can be more severe. There is no specific treatment for dengue beyond drinking plenty of fluids and resting. Painkillers based on paracetamol (Tylenol in Brazil) should be used as aspirin, ibuprofen and dorflex can increase the risk of haemorrhage. Those who are severely affected should

HEALTHY FLYING

» Visitors to Brazil may be concerned about the effect of long-haul flights on their health. The most widely publicized concern is deep vein thrombosis, or DVT. DVT is the forming of a blood clot in the body's deep veins, particularly in the legs. The clot can move around the bloodstream and could be fatal. Flying increases the likelihood of DVT because passengers are often seated in a cramped position for long periods of time and may become dehydrated.

» Those most at risk include the elderly, pregnant women and those using the contraceptive pill, smokers and the overweight. If you are at increased risk of DVT see your doctor before departing.

» To minimize risk: drink water (not alcohol); don't stay immobile for hours at a time; stretch and exercise your legs periodically; wear elastic flight socks, which support veins and reduce the chances of a clot forming.

EXERCISES

1. Ankle Rotations Lift feet off the floor. Draw a circle with the toes, moving one foot clockwise and the other counterclockwise.

2. Calf Stretches Start with heel on the floor and point foot upwards as high as you can. Then lift heels high keeping balls of feet on the floor.

3. Knee Lifts Lift leg with knee bent while contracting your thigh muscle. Then straighten leg pressing foot flat to the floor.

be taken to hospital. Although it may take a number of weeks, most people recover fully without further problems.

» **Hepatitis** is a symptomatic description for an infection which causes an inflammation of the liver. Viral causes of the disease can be acquired anywhere in the world. The most obvious symptom is jaundice—yellowing of the skin and the whites of your eyes. Hepatitis A is spread through contaminated water. Hepatitis B is spread through blood and unprotected sexual intercourse. Pre-travel hepatitis vaccines are the best prevention.

» **Rabies** *(raiva)* is rare in Brazil where it is transmitted by bats, monkeys and foxes. The virus attacks the nervous system and is excreted later in the saliva. Only one in six people who have been bitten by a rabid animal develops symptoms—even if they have not been treated. But rabies is nonetheless very dangerous. There is a vaccine and, if you've been bitten, there's every chance that you can be treated before the symptoms develop as between three weeks and three months can pass between infection and the onset of symptoms (incubation period), though in individual instances it may be as much as several years.

» **Typhoid** is spread by poor sanitation (unwashed hands, or seepage from cesspits to drinking water or shower water sources). Typhoid is an intestinal infection which can spread into the bloodstream and attack the white blood cells. Symptoms begin with a slowly rising temperature with a headache and cough, often nosebleeds and some abdominal pain. This is followed by collapse and a very high fever (up to 40°C/104°F), diarrhoea, and often spots on the chest. Typhoid is easily treatable with antibiotics. There is also a vaccine.

OTHER TROPICAL INFECTIONS

Cutaneous larva migrans *(bicho geográfico)* is a skin infection by a nematodal worm whose larvae are found in animal faeces. It is characterized by an itchy moving spot which leaves a red trail. It is easily treated with Thiabendazole cream or Albendazole tablets (both available in pharmacies in Brazil). Jiggers/chiggers/chigoe fleas *(bicho do pé)* are burrowing fleas that enter the skin—usually of the feet under the nails where they lay eggs which form cysts with a little black head, before hatching into hundreds of little babies. They are easily treated, by covering the cyst with Vaseline for a day and then gouging it out with a sterile needle. There are also small (harvest) mites called chiggers, which bite humans—these are harmless and unrelated.

DIARRHOEA AND INTESTINAL UPSET

The better restaurants in Brazil have good sanitation so diarrhoea is usually no more than an occasional nuisance born of unfamiliar diet. The best remedy is rest and plenty of fluids taken with rehydration sachets (Dioralyte or in Brazil Hidrafix or *solução sal açúcar)*. If symptoms persist beyond 10 days it is best to consult a doctor.

THE SUN

Even when there's a cooling sea breeze or cloud cover Brazil's sun is formidable. Cover up well and apply plenty of sunscreen. It's widely available in Brazil but the higher protection factors (30 or above) are exorbitantly expensive. For light skin it is important to use a high-factor sunscreen (30–50) with UVA and UVB protection. However, even the darkest skin will burn in Brazil.

VENOMOUS ANIMALS

Brazil has the world's deadliest spider. Brazilian wandering spiders or Brazilian Huntsmen *(aranhas armadeiras)* are responsible for more human deaths than any other spider. These big, hand-sized, fast-moving nocturnal hunters like to roost in dead leaves, sheds and wood piles and are extremely aggressive when disturbed. However, the risk they pose is negligible.

The story for snakes is similar. Brazil has some nasty forest vipers—the Bushmaster *(Surucucu)* is the largest and most powerful venomous snake in the new world, and the Fer de Lance *(Jararaca)* is aggressive and highly venomous. However, bites from both snakes are very rare and venom is not always administered by the reptiles.

Those who are unfortunate enough to be bitten by a venomous animal should try to photograph the culprit and then seek medical attention as quickly as possible. Limbs should be immobilized with a bandage or a splint and get the patient to lie still. Slashing the bite area and trying to suck out the poison is not advisable.

HEALTH INFORMATION AND WEBSITES

Blood Care Foundation
www.bloodcare.org.uk
An NGO that will dispatch certified non-infected blood of the right type to the hospital/clinic where you are being treated.

Centers for Disease Control and Prevention
www.cdc.gov
Useful US site with good advice, tips and up-to-date disease maps.

fitfortravel
www.fitfortravel.nhs.uk
General information, vaccine requirements and travel advice for travellers from the UK to Brazil.

Medic Alert
www.medicalalert.co.uk
Produces bracelets and necklaces for those with medical problems.

NetDoctor
www.netdoctor.co.uk
General health advice site with a useful section on travel and an 'ask the expert' interactive chat forum.

World Health Organization (WHO)
www.who.int
Lists the latest outbreaks and vaccination recommendations.

BASICS

CHILDREN

Brazilians adore children, and they are generally welcome and well attended to. Children are allowed to run around pretty much everywhere and are not expected to keep quiet or be miniature adults. Even expensive restaurants provide children's seats and most have children's menus, and often crayons and paper to keep them happy.

» Many hotels offer a discount family rate, don't charge for children under 5 and can provide an extra bed for a double room, either free of charge or for a very small fee.

» A handful of the more exclusive beach resorts do not accept children. If you are planning to stay in such a hotel it is best to enquire ahead.

» Children under 3 generally travel for 10 per cent of the full fare on internal flights and for 70 per cent until 12 years old.

» Prices on buses depend on whether the child will occupy a seat or a lap. Laps are free and if there are spare seats after the bus has departed the child can sit on one of those for free.

» Transport can involve long waits in *rodoviárias* (bus stations), but there are generally restaurants and plenty of places to sit down.

» While it is best to bring medication for motion sickness (such as Kwells) with you from home, Dramin—which comes in dropper bottles—is available in Brazil.

» Baby food and nappies (diapers) are widely available, but large-sized nappies can be very hard to come by, especially outside the cities.

» High protection sunscreen is expensive in Brazil, so bring a large bottle from home.

» You may also wish to bring a favourite formula milk.

ELECTRICITY

The power supply in Brazil is generally 110V 60 cycles AC, but in some cities and areas 220V 60 cycles AC is used. Plugs are two pin and either round (European) or flat (US). Most sockets will take both types.

LAUNDRY

There are laundromats *(lavanderias)* in all large towns and cities. Very few are self-service. You leave your laundry at the *lavanderia* and come to collect it later. *Lavanderias* are generally less than half the price of a hotel laundry service.

MEASUREMENTS

Brazil has officially adopted the metric system as standard: millimetres, centimetres, metres, kilometres; grams, kilograms and tonnes; millilitres, centilitres and litres. Fuel is sold in litres.

PUBLIC TOILETS

Public toilets are non-existent in Brazil outside shopping malls, museums, airports and bus stations. They are called *banheiros* or *lavabos*. It is often acceptable to use restrooms in chain restaurants, bars and venues for a small fee.

SMOKING

In Brazil, smoking is forbidden in all enclosed public spaces. In restaurants there should be a non-smoking section but in reality most restaurants place non-smoking tables side by side with tables for smokers.

CONVERSION CHART

From	To	Multiply by
Inches	Centimetres	2.54
Centimetres	Inches	0.3937
Feet	Metres	0.3048
Metres	Feet	3.2810
Yards	Metres	0.9144
Metres	Yards	1.0940
Miles	Kilometres	1.6090
Kilometres	Miles	0.6214
Acres	Hectares	0.4047
Hectares	Acres	2.4710
Gallons	Litres	4.5460
Litres	Gallons	0.2200
Ounces	Grams	28.35
Grams	Ounces	0.0353
Pounds	Grams	453.6
Grams	Pounds	0.0022
Pounds	Kilograms	0.4536
Kilograms	Pounds	2.205
Tons	Tonnes	1.0160
Tonnes	Tons	0.9842

Anti-smoking legislation was introduced in the state of São Paulo in 2009. Establishments violating the law can be hit with a hefty fine of a maximum of R$1,500.

TRAVELLERS WITH DISABILITIES

Facilities for travellers with disabilities are almost non-existent in Brazil (▷ 52). Access ramps and special facilities on public transportation and taxis are rare. Sidewalks are often in a poor state of repair or crowded with street vendors requiring passers-by to brave the passing traffic. Disabled toilets are usually present in airports, bus stations and large public buildings in principal centres.

YOUTH DISCOUNTS

» Full-time students can buy an international student ID card (ISIC). This can be used widely in Brazil for discounted admission to museums and attractions. It offers no discount for travel.
» Under 27s can buy an International Youth Travel Card which has similar benefits.
» Hostelling International is a membership organization which gives its members discounts at some 4,000 youth hostels in more than 80 countries. There are many members in Brazil. It also helps with discounts on hostel-organized tours, concessions on some entertainment during your travels, reduced price admission to certain museums and cultural centres, and reductions on selected travel services. Membership can be purchased at any HI Youth Hostel Association office or from approved outlets. You will need ID and two passport photographs. For more information see www.hihostels.com.

SAFETY

EMERGENCIES

Emergency phone numbers in Brazil vary from state to state and according to the service in question. In Rio de Janeiro, for example city numbers are as follows: Fire Department *(Bombeiros)* 193, Police *(Polícia)* 190, Ambulance *(Ambulância)* 192. Little to no English is spoken.

Police emergencies can also be reported through the Tourist Police, who exist only in Rio de Janeiro at Avenida Afrânio de Melo Franco 159 (tel 021 3399 7170) and who speak some English. Hotel staff should be able to help in an emergency if they speak English.

TRAVEL INSURANCE

Visitors to Brazil are strongly advised to take out travel insurance. Robberies and snatch thefts are widespread, and ambulances take patients without health insurance to public hospitals where service and conditions are often worse than you may be used to. Be sure to report any crimes to the police at a police station *(delegacia de policia)* and ask for a printed accident report *(Boletim de Ocorrência* or BO).

For medical emergencies in Brazil always call the insurance hotline on your travel insurance policy.

SAFETY IN CITIES

Brazil's big cities have very high rates of violent crime, but most violence is restricted to the *favelas* (slums) where the violence is literally as bad as a low-scale civil war. You should never enter a *favela* unless accompanied by workers from NGOs, tour groups or other people who know the local residents well and are accepted by the community.

PRECAUTIONS

» Dress down in Brazil; wear a cheap, plastic, digital watch and be extremely discreet about showing any jewellery.
» Before you leave your hotel, ask advice from the hotel staff about which places are and are not considered safe, and be vigilant especially after dark.
» Keep cash in different places about your person. Money belts are useful and cash can also be hidden in bandages or shoes.
» Keep luggage in front of you at buses and railway stations.
» Consider taking a taxi at night and when travelling with luggage.

MUGGINGS

Mugging can take place anywhere, but is most common on dark beaches at night and on quiet streets. Take few valuables with you and keep to safe areas. If you are mugged never panic, and hand over your valuables without hesitation or conflict. It is very rare for a tourist to be hurt during a robbery in Brazil.

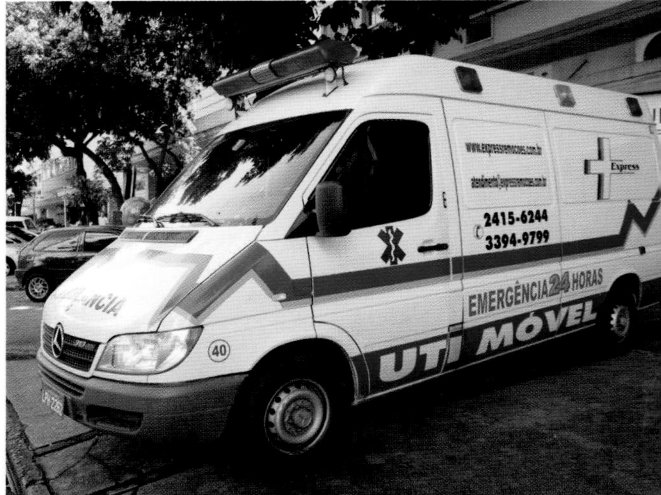

'GOOD NIGHT CINDERELLA'

A cocktail of drugs called *Boa Noite Cinderela* (Good Night Cinderella) has been used in robberies and sexual assaults in Brazil. Not all the perpetrators are Brazilian. The cocktail comprises one or several of Flunitrazepam (Rohypnol), Ketamine and Gamma-hydroxybutryate (GHB). All are colourless (although official Roche Rohypnol had a blue dye added post 1998). These drugs are added to drinks bought by a 'friend'—usually on the beach, at carnival or parties, or even in a hotel room from an invited or solicited guest. Symptoms begin with drowsiness, slurring of speech and general muscular grogginess. It's easy to mistake the initial signs for drunkenness. The eventual sleep can last up to 24 hours. To avoid being drugged you should always purchase your own drinks or accept only sealed bottles and keep them within sight.

POLICE

Brazilian police are not always trustworthy and can be very tough with criminals. The Polícia Federal handle all federal law duties, including immigration. They include the Polícia Federal Rodoviária. The Polícia Militar are the state street police force. They are not the same as the Military Police. The Polícia Civil are also state controlled and conduct detective investigations. There are other forces too, including the Guarda Municipal, the Tourist Police (see above) and special divisions like Choque and Bope.

EMBASSIES AND CONSULATES IN BRAZIL

AUSTRALIA

Australian Embassy
SES Quadra 801, Conjunto K, Lote 7, Brasilia
tel 61 3226 3111
www.brazil.embassy.gov.au

CANADA

Canadian Embassy Brasília
Avenida das Nações Quadra 803, Lote 16, Brasília, 70410-900
tel 61 3424 5400

Canadian Consulate General Rio de Janiero
Avenida Atlântica 1130 5th Floor, Atlântica Business Center, Copacabana, Rio de Janiero
tel 21 2543 3004

IRELAND

Irish Embassy Brasília
SHIS QL Conjunto, 05 Casa, 09 Lago Sul, Brasília, 71630-255
tel 061 3248 8800; www.embassyofireland.org.br

Irish Consulate in São Paulo
Al. Joaquim Eugênio de Lima, 447
São Paulo, 01403 001
tel (11) 3147 7788; www.embassyofireland.org.br

NEW ZEALAND

New Zealand Embassy
SHIS QI 09 conj. 16 casa 01, Brasília-DF 71625-160,
tel 61 3248 9900; www.nzembassy.com/brazil

UNITED KINGDOM

British Embassy, Setor de Embaixadas Sul
Quadra 801, Lote 8, Brasília, 70408-900,
tel 61 3329 2300
http://ukinbrazil.fco.gov.uk/en

British Honorary Consulate
Avenida Estados Unidos 18-B, 8° Andar-Comércio, Edificio Estados Unidos, Salvador, 40010-020
tel 71 3243 7399
http://ukinbrazil.fco.gov.uk/en

British Consulate-General
Praia do Flamengo 284/2 andar,
Rio de Janeiro RJ, 22210-030
tel 21 2555 9600
http://ukinbrazil.fco.gov.uk/en

British Consulate-General
Rua Ferreira de Araujo 741 – 2 Andar, Pinheiros
São Paulo, 05428-002
tel 11 3094 2700
http://ukinbrazil.fco.gov.uk/en

USA

US Embassy
SES – Avenida das Nações, Quadra 801 Lote 03, Brasilia, DF, 70403-900,
tel 61 3312 7000
http://brasilia.usembassy.gov/

São Paulo Consulate General
Rua Henri Dunant 500, Chácara Santo Antônio, São Paulo, 04709 110
http://brasilia.usembassy.gov/

Rio de Janeiro Consulate
Avenida Presidente Wilson 147, Castelo, Rio de Janeiro, 20030-020
tel 21 3823 2000
http://brasilia.usembassy.gov/

Recife Consulate
Rua Gonçalves Maia 163, Boa Vista, Recife, Pernambuco, 50070-060
tel 81 3416 3050
http://brasilia.usembassy.gov/

COMMUNICATION

Internet use is widespread in Brazil. In early 2010 there were more than 72 million users—almost 40 per cent of the population and some 10 million broadband subscribers. This makes Brazil seventh in the world in terms of internet usage. ADSL is the access technology of choice, accounting for 84 per cent of the country's broadband market.

MOBILE PHONES

Mobile (cell) phones are ubiquitous in Brazil. Coverage is excellent even in many remote areas. But prices are among the highest in the world in real terms and you will need a Brazilian social security number (CPF) to buy a SIM card. The best way to circumvent this problem is to ask a friend or member of staff to buy one for you. SIM cards are available at most newsstands for between R$5 and R$10.

MAKING A PHONE CALL

When making a call in Brazil you will need to dial a 2-digit telephone company code prior to the area code for all calls. A call to São Paulo, for example, from any other municipality begins with the code of your chosen phone company (e.g. 31 for Telemar) followed by 11 for São Paulo, then the 8-digit number of the subscriber. The same is true for international calls where 00 is followed by the operator code and then the country code and number. The most common operator codes are Embratel (021), Telefônica (015) and Telemar (031).

TELEPHONE BOOTHS

Orelhões ('big ears') are also ubiquitous. Look for big, green, ear-shaped fibreglass mouldings on the street. In some places these have other distinctive shapes—parrots in the Amazon or jabiru storks in the Pantanal. To use the telephone you will need a pre-paid phone card *(cartão telefônico)*, available from newsstands, post offices and some pharmacies. The cards cost around R$7 for 40 units and R$12 for 90 units. International phone cards *(cartões telefônicos internacionais)* are increasingly available in tourist areas and are often sold at hostels.

MAIL

Postal services in Brazil are blighted by frequent strikes. Air mail should take about seven days to or from Britain or the US. To avoid queues and obtain higher denomination stamps go to the designated stamp desk *(selos)* at the post office. Look for the distinctive yellow and blue Correios sign.

Post offices sell cardboard boxes for sending packages internally and abroad. Rates and rules for sending vary from post office to post office, even within the same town, and staff often seem to make up the price on the spot. The quickest service is by SEDEX.

INTERNATIONAL DIALLING CODES	
Australia	00 61
Belgium	00 32
Canada	00 1
France	00 33
Germany	00 49
Greece	00 30
Ireland	00 353
Netherlands	00 31
New Zealand	00 64
Spain	00 34
Sweden	00 46
UK	00 44
USA	00 1

OPENING TIMES

» Brazilians tend not to be good timekeepers and opening hours are flexible throughout the country.
» Banks are generally open weekdays between 10am and 4pm.
» Post Office opening hours vary considerably, but they are usually open from 8am to 5pm. Some branches open on Saturdays.
» Shop hours also vary. Street shops are generally open Monday to Saturday 9am to 6pm. Shopping malls open Monday to Thursday 10am to 10pm, Friday and Saturday 10am to 11pm, and Sundays noon to 8pm.
» Bars are open all hours. Many function as café-restaurants during the day.
» Brazilians do not take siestas.

PUBLIC HOLIDAYS

Public holidays *(feriados públicos)* vary year by year and state by state. Federal holidays for 2012 as follows:

1 Jan – Sunday – New Year's Day
20–21 Feb – Monday and Tuesday – Carnaval
6 Apr – Friday – Paixão de Cristo (Good Friday)
21 Apr – Saturday – Dia de Tiradentes (Tiradentes Day)
1 May – Tuesday – Dia do Trabalho (Labour Day)
7 Jun – Thursday – Corpus Christi
7 Sep – Friday – Dia da Independência (Independence Day)
12 Oct – Friday – Nossa Sra. Aparecida (Our Lady Aparecida, patroness of Brazil)
2 Nov – Friday – Dia de Finados (Day of the Dead)
15 Nov – Thursday – Proclamação da República (Proclamation of the Republic)
25 Dec – Tuesday – Natal (Christmas Day)

MEDIA

NEWSPAPERS AND MAGAZINES

Media in Brazil were built on the US model. There is no national newspaper, only national news magazines and the market, especially for television, is dominated by huge corporations.

The main Rio papers are *O Jornal do Brasil* (www.jb.com.br), *O Globo* (www.oglobo.com.br) and *Jornal do Commércio* (www. jornaldocommercio.com.br). In São Paulo, they are *O Estado de São Paulo*, (www. estado.com.br), *Folha de São Paulo* (www.folha.uol.com. br) and *O Diário de São Paulo* (www. diariosp.com.br). Around the country, the major cities have their own local press. Foreign-language newspapers are restricted to *The Brazilian Post* (http://wn.com/brazil).

There are many weekly news magazines. The largest is *Veja* (veja. abril.com.br); others include *Istoé* (www.istoe.com.br) and *Epoca* (http://revistaepoca.globo.com).

MAPS

Tourist office maps are often not to scale and do not even mark individual streets. Finding a proper street map in Brazil is a challenge: They are few and far between and Brazilian streets often have a colloquial name as well as an official one.

Quatro Rodas (quatrorodas.abril. com.br) publish the best maps in Brazil but do not cover all the cities. Quatro Rodas maps and map books are available in large bookshops, airport bookshops and some newsstands but are not available outside Brazil, nor are reliable street maps of anywhere in the country.

Google maps cover Brazil and are usually the best option.

TELEVISION

Nationwide television channels are Globo, based in Rio de Janeiro, and Record and Bandeirantes, based in São Paulo. Rede Amazônica operates in the northern region. Scheduling revolves around light entertainment, soap operas, sensationalist news and football.

RADIO

Brazil has many community radio stations. International broadcasters such as BBC World Service (www. bbc.co.uk/worldservice) and Voice of America (www.voanews.com) are available. Compact or miniature portables are recommended, with digital tuning and a full range of shortwave bands, as well as FM, long and medium wave.

FILMS AND BOOKS

A basic understanding of Brazil, its history, politics and culture will greatly enhance your visit. These books are an enjoyable read and will help you scratch beneath the surface of Brazil. Very few works of Brazilian fiction have been well translated into English.

BRAZILIAN FICTION

» *Dom Casmurro* by Joaquim Maria Machado de Assis is a biting satirical novel from Brazil's greatest 19th-century writer.

» *Iracema* by Cearense José de Alencar is a romantic story of the love of an indigenous girl and a Portuguese man: the Brazilian *Last of the Mohicans*.

» *Os Sertões (Rebellion in the Backlands)* by Euclides da Cunha chronicles the Canudos war and is the first book critically to expose the two Brazils of master and ex-slave, which persist to this day, and the brutality which preserves them.

» *The War of the End of the World* by Mario Vargas Llosa is an epic account of the Canudos campaign.

» *Grande Sertão: Veredas* by João Guimarães Rosa is the country's greatest modern novel, set in Minas Gerais *sertão*.

» *O Povo Brasileiro (The Brazilians)* by Darcy Ribeiro is an exploration of the Brazilian national character from one of the country's most distinguished anthropologists.

» *Gabriela: Clove and Cinnamon* by Jorge Amado is a bawdy romp set in a 1920s Ilhéus populated by colourful Bahian characters.

» *A Republica dos Sonhos* by Nélida Piñon is the story of a Galician family moving to Brazil.

» *Relato de um certo Oriente (A Certain Orient)* by Milton Hatoum tells of the experiences of a Lebanese family moving to Manaus in the 19th century.

» *Inferno* by Patrícia Melo is a gritty tale of life in the *favela*.

HISTORY AND CULTURE

» *Red Gold, Amazon Frontier* and *Die if You Must* by John Hemming are the best histories of Brazil, told from the perspective of the indigenous people. They are extremely well researched, scholarly and very readable.

» In *The Brazilians* by Joseph Page, each chapter is an illuminating, well-researched essay on Brazilian whims and idiosyncrasies.

FILMS

Brazilian film began in earnest with the Cinema Novo movement in the 1950s and 1960s with directors like Glauber Rocha and Nelson Pereira dos Santos. Oswaldo Massaini's *O Pagador de Promessas (The Keeper of Promises)* became the first Brazilian film to be nominated for an Oscar and won the Palme d'Or at Cannes. But it suffered under the dictatorship and only re-emerged in the 1990s when *O Quatrilho* by Fábio Barreto, which told the story of two Italian immigrant couples in Rio Grande do Sul in the early 20th century, was also nominated for an Oscar.

The 1990s also saw the rise of two new directors. Walter Salles earned another Oscar nomination for his poignant road movie, *Central Station (Central do Brasil)*, while Fernando Meirelles created a new genre of gritty *favela* films with his stunningly shot and edited *Cidade de Deus (City of God)*. This was followed in 2007 by another award-winning film set in the *favelas*, *Elite Squad (Tropa de Elite)*.

TOURIST OFFICES

There are no federal tourist offices within Brazil outside of Brasília. State and federal tourist offices are listed in the Regions section.

There are tourist offices *(secretarias do turismo)* and information posts throughout the country. Most have little to offer international tourists. Some have limited information and English may not always be spoken.

STATE TOURISM OFFICES

ACRE

Secretaria de Estado de Turismo - SETUR/AC
Av. Getúlio Vargas 233, 4° andar, Centro, Rio Branco, 69900-160
tel 68 3224 3727/4535 3223/3998
www.ac.gov.br

ALAGOAS

Secretaria de Estado do Turismo - SETUR -
Rua Boa Vista 453, Centro, Maceió, 57020-110
tel 82 3315 5703
www.turismo.al.gov.br

AMAPÁ

Secretaria de Estado do Turismo - SETUR/AP
Rua Independência 29, Centro, Macapá, 68900-090
tel 96 3212 5326/5327
www.setur.ap.gov.br

AMAZONAS

Empresa Estadual de Turismo - AMAZONASTUR
Rua Saldanha Marinho 321, Centro, Manaus, 69010-040
tel 92 2123 3800/2123 3803
www.amazonastur.am.gov.br

BAHIA

Secretaria de Turismo do Estado da Bahia - SETUR/BA
Avenida Tancredo Neves 776 - 8°, Pituba, Salvador, 41820- 904
tel 71 3116 4093/4130
www.setur.ba.gov.br

CEARÁ

Secretaria Estadual de Turismo - SETUR/CE - Centro Administrativo Gov. Virgílio Távora Ed. SEPLAN Térreo
Fortaleza, 60839-900
tel 85 3101 4688
www.ceara.gov.br

DISTRITO FEDERAL

Secretaria de Turismo do Distrito Federal - SETUR/DF - SCN
Quadra 4, Bloco B, Sala 502, Brasília, 70714-906
tel 61 3429 7600
www.brasiliatur.df.gov.br

ESPÍRITO SANTO

Secretaria de Estado do Turismo - SETUR/ES
Rua Amélia da Cunha Ornelas No. 89, Bento Ferreira, Vitória ES, 29050-620
tel 27 3380 2221; www.es.gov.br

GOIÁS

Secretaria de Turismo de Goiânia - AGETUR/GO
Centro de Cultura e Convenções R-30 Esq. c/ R-04 s/n Bloco A, Piso Mezanino, Goiânia,74015-900
tel 62 3201 8100/8117
www.agetur.go.gov.br

MARANHÃO

Secretaria de Estado do Turismo
Rua Portugal 165, Centro, São Luís, 65010-480
tel 98 3231 0822
www.turismo.ma.gov.br

MINAS GERAIS

Secretaria de Estado do Turismo de Minas Gerais - SETUR/MG
Praça da Liberdade, s/n°, Prédio Verde, 2° andar - Funcionários, Belo Horizonte MG, 30140-110 -
tel 31 3270 8501
www.turminas.ma.gov.br

MATO GROSSO

Secretaria de Estado de Desenvolvimento do Turismo - SEDTUR/MT
Centro Político Administrativo, Térreo, Cuiabá, 78050-970
tel 65 3613 9340/9313
www.sedtur.mt.gov.br

MATO GROSSO DO SUL

Secretaria de Estado de Desenv. Agrário, Prod., Ind., Com. e Turismo - SEPROTUR
Pq. dos Poderes, Bl. 12, Campo Grande 79031-902
tel 67 3318 5000; www.seprotur.ms.gov.br

PARÁ

Companhia Paraense de Turismo - PARATUR/PA
Praça Maestro Waldemar Henrique, s/n, Centro, Belém, 66040-000
tel 91 3212 0575/3210 6330
www.paraturismo.pa.gov.br

PARAÍBA

Secretaria de Estado do Turismo e Desenvolvimento Econômico - SETDE/PB
Avenida João da Mata, s/n°, Bloco 2, 1° andar, Centro Admin, João Pessoa, 58015-020
tel 83 3218 4400/3218 4401
www.setde.pb.gov.br

PARANÁ

Paraná Turismo - PARANATUR/PR
Rua Deputado Mário de Barros, 1290, 3° andar, Centro, Curitiba, 80530-913
tel 41 3313 3500/3506/3313
www.cidadao.pr.gov.br

PERNAMBUCO

Secretaria de Turismo - SETUR/PE
Complexo Viário Vice-Governador Barreto Guimarães, s/n, Salgadinho, Olinda, 53111-970
tel 81 3427 8115/8215
www2.setur.pe.gov.br

PIAUÍ

Empresa de Turismo do Piauí - PIEMTUR/PI
Rua Acre, s/n Centro de Convenções, Teresina, 64001-650
tel 86 3221 7100/3222 6254
www.piemtur.pi.gov.br

RIO DE JANEIRO

Secretaria de Estado de Turismo, Esporte e Lazer do Rio de Janeiro - SETE/RJ
R. México, 125, 8° andar, Centro, Rio de Janeiro, 200040-000
tel 21 2299 3070/3076/3100
www.turisrio.rj.gov.br

RIO GRANDE DO NORTE

Secretaria de Estado do Turismo do Rio Grande do Norte - SETUR/RN
Rua Mossoró 359, Petrópolis, Natal, 59020-100
tel 84 3232 2518; www.rn.gov.br

RIO GRANDE DO SUL

Secretaria de Estado do Turismo - SETUR/RS
Avenida Borges de Medeiros 1501, 10° andar, Porto Alegre, 90119-900
tel 51 3228 5400/5427
www.turismo.rs.gov.br

STATE TOURISM OFFICES CONTINUED

RONDÔNIA

Superitendência Estadual de Turismo - SETUR/RO
Avenida 7 de setembro 237, Prédio do relógio, Centro, Porto Velho, 78900-005
tel 69 3216 5973
www.setur.ro.gov.br

RORAIMA

Departamento Estadual de Turismo de Roraima - DETUR
Rua Coronel Pinto 241, Bairro Centro, 69301-150
tel 95 2121 2561/ 3623 2365
www.rr.gov.br

SANTA CATARINA

Secretaria de Turismo, Cultura e Esportes - SETUR/SC
Rua Eduardo Gonçalves D' Avila 303, B. Itacorubi, Florianópolis, 88034-496
tel 48 3212 1901
www.sol.sc.gov.br

SERGIPE

Empresa Sergipana de Turismo S/A - EMSETUR/SE
Travessa Baltazar Góes 86, Ed. Estado de Sergipe 11º andar, Aracaju, 49009-900
tel 79 3179 1937
www.turismosergipe.net

SÃO PAULO

Secretaria do Esporte e Turismo - SET/SP
Praça Antônio Prado 09, Centro, São Paulo, 01010-904
tel 11 3241 5822
www.saopaulo.sp.gov.br

TOCANTINS

Agência de Desenvolvimento Turístico do Tocantins - ADTUR/TO
Esplanada das Secretarias Praça dos Girassóis AANE, Centro, Palmas, 77001-002
tel 63 3218 2385/2357
www.to.gov.br

TOURIST OFFICES OUTSIDE BRAZIL

The Brazilian ministry of tourism website www.embratur.gov.br is available in Portuguese, English, Spanish, French, German and Italian.

Germany ☎ + 49 69 9623 8733
France ☎ +33 1 5353 6962
Italy ☎ +39 02 8633 7791
Japan ☎ +81 3 5565 7591
Portugal ☎ +351 21 340 4668
Spain ☎ +34 91 503 0687
UK ☎ +44 20 7396 5551
US East Coast ☎ +1 646 378 2126
US West Coast ☎ +1 310 341 8394

USEFUL WEBSITES

BACKPACKERS

www.hostelbookers.com
An excellent site for the booking of hostels.

DOCUMENTATION

www.fco.gov.uk
Advice from the British government on how to get help abroad.

www.travel.state.gov
US Department of the State Bureau of Consular Affairs.

MUSIC

www.redebma.ning.com
Excellent site for information on Brazilian music with blogs, information and downloads.

HEALTH

www.netdoctor.co.uk
NetDoctor, a general health advice site with a useful forum.

www.who.int
World Health Organization (WHO) with news of the latest outbreaks and vaccination recommendations.

INDIGENOUS PEOPLE

www.wrm.org.uy
World Rainforest Movement works with the United Nations to support indigenous people and their homelands.

www.socioambiental.org
Instituto Socioambiental is the leading Brazilian NGO campaigning for rights for traditional and indigenous peoples.

www.survivalinternational.org
Survival International is an NGO which campaigns for indigenous people's rights in Brazil and worldwide.

NATURAL HISTORY AND CONSERVATION

www.birdlife.org
Birdlife International is an organization devoted to bird conservation.

www.conservation.org
Conservation International works in all the key Brazilian biomes.

www.greenpeace.org
Greenpeace International campaigns to prevent the exportation of mahogany and other hardwoods from Brazil.

RESPONSIBLE TOURISM

www.ecotourism.org
The International Ecotourism Society (TIES) campaigns for eco-tourism best practice.

VOLUNTARY TOURISM

www.earthwatch.org
Earthwatch has conservational research placements in countries worldwide including Brazil.

GAY AND LESBIAN TRAVEL

www.ggb.org.br
Information on gay and lesbian travel in Brazil.

SHOPPING

Brazilians like to shop, and in the larger cities they like best to shop in malls. There are also wonderful markets and little specialist boutiques throughout the country. Retail sales have more in common with Europe or North America than Andean South America, with a few notable exceptions. Brazil has a strong arts and crafts tradition, but unusual and beautifully crafted traditional souvenirs are thin on the ground in so large a country.

MARKETS

Brazil has very few large arts and crafts markets *(mercados).* Exceptions are the Feira Hippie in Rio de Janeiro (▷ 92–93), the markets of Caruaru (▷ 246), the Mercado Modelo in Salvador (▷ 230) and the weekend market in the Praça da República in Belém (▷ 314). However, most cities have a *mercado municipal* (food market), which is worth visiting in its own right. The best are in São Paulo and Belém (Ver o Peso). Prices are fixed.

OPENING HOURS

There are no set opening hours in Brazil or even within individual cities. Small shops tend to open at 10am and close at 6pm. Big shops and malls generally open at 8am and close at 8pm. In the larger cities they stay open far later. Larger shops and boutiques usually open from 8am to 6pm.

PAYMENT

Prices in Brazil are almost invariably fixed. Personal cheques are not accepted without two forms of Brazilian identification, a social security number (CPF) and an ID card (RG/RNE). Credit cards are widely accepted, but purchases may also require presentation of ID.

SHOPPING MALLS

Brazilian shopping malls are called *shoppings* (pronounced 'shoor-paings'). They are filled with local (and a handful of international) brand shops selling fashion, jewellery, home wares, books, CDs and suchlike. Most *shoppings* have a large food court comprising chain restaurants, and many of the malls also have multiplex cinemas.

WHAT TO BUY

Art

Brazilian artists like Carlos Vergara, Siron Franco, Tunga and Adriana Varejão demand increasingly high prices at international auctions and fairs. Work by them and other up-and-coming Brazilian artists is sold at galleries in São Paulo and Rio de Janeiro.

Ceramics

Excavations in the Amazon have shown that Brazilians have been making high-quality ceramics for thousands of years. Replica Marajó civilization vases and pots can be bought on the Ilha de Marajó and in Belém. Northeastern towns—in particular Caruaru—sell naïve clay figurines by traditional artists like Zé Caboclo, which are becoming increasingly collectable on the international folk art market.

Fashion

Brazil is South America's fashion capital with its most important fashion show (the twice-yearly São Paulo fashion week) and boutique labels stocked in the world's finest department stores including Barneys and Harvey Nichols. São Paulo and Rio are the principal fashion centres in the country.

Hammocks

Hammocks were invented by American indigenous people and they are used instead of beds by many northern Brazilians. Cotton hammocks can be bought cheaply in Amazon towns.

Jewellery

Almost two-thirds of the world's coloured gemstones are produced in Brazil and Brazil has some of the world's finest jewellers. They include the largest national brand, H.Stern, celebrity favourite Jack Vartanian and Antônio Bernardo. Brazil also produces unique bead and seed jewellery made from plants from the Amazon and *cerrado*. Belém and Bahia are good places to buy this.

Lace

Fine lace *(renda)* is produced in Brazil's northeast (and particularly Ceará). Fatima Rendas, a shop found in most of Brazil's airports, sells clothing and lace spreads, although they can be bought far more cheaply in local shops and street stalls.

Leather

Brazil produces very fine leather shoes, jackets, bags and belts. The quality is high, with some beautiful soft fabric, and items are sold virtually everywhere.

Music

Brazil is one of the world's major music producers. All of the principal labels have Brazilian divisions entirely devoted to national artists; Brazil has its own MTV station and many smaller national labels. The choice of available CDs by Brazilian artists is staggering. A number of music shops throughout Brazil will let you listen before you buy.

Musical Instruments

The country has dozens of its own unique musical instruments, most of them percussive. These include the *berimbau* (a bow with a gourd sound-box used in *capoeira)*; the *cuíca* friction drum, which produces squeaks and squeals like a human voice and which is used in samba; hand drums including the big samba bass drum, the *surdo*; and other samba drums including the tambor. Brazil gave the world the tambourine *(pandeiro)*. A variation, the *tamborim,* comes without bells. There are also many stringed instruments including the *rabeca* fiddle, the Portuguese ancestor of the ukulele—the *cavaquinho*, and the pear-shaped Portuguese *bandolim*. Companies such as Gianini produce excellent nylon-strung guitars of the kind used for *bossa nova*.

ENTERTAINMENT AND NIGHTLIFE

There is no shortage of entertainment in Brazil—from live music to cinema, dance and theatre. While samba is known to non-Brazilians as the quintessential Brazilian sound, it is one of literally hundreds, all of which are worth tracking down and many of which are associated with the country's lively festival circuit. Brazilian nightlife is the best in Latin America. This is a country which enjoys partying and which can create a celebration out of the most unlikely event with the most meagre of resources. Rio de Janeiro, São Paulo, Belém, Salvador and Recife have the most vibrant scenes. Brasília and São Paulo have orchestras of international standing and excellent concert halls.

BARS

Brazil's bars usually serve food, often entire meals and almost invariably *petiscos*—bars snacks or tapas (▷ 364). There are bars in every area—reflecting the fact that Brazil's cities usually have distinct neighborhoods or *bairros*, with their own communities. In Rio, bars are often *botequims* (also known as *botecos)*. These are small, informal establishments which lie somewhere between pubs, restaurants and bars. They usually have little decoration beyond wall tiles and beer posters, and simple plastic or fold-up metal tables. But herein lie their charm and their uniquely Brazilian feel—there is no ceremony to going to a bar in Brazil, *botequims* are places to meet and chat over a bottle of beer and a bowl of *petiscos*. Many *botequims* have low-key, live music.

CINEMA

Brazilians are avid cinema fans. Multiplexes in the larger cities show Hollywood fare, often with subtitles *(legendas)*. Smaller movie theatres show world cinema and the country has one of the largest film festival circuits in the world. There are scores of festivals. The biggest and best are in São Paulo (www.mostra.org), Rio (www.festivaldorio.com.br), Gramado (www.festivaldegramado.net), Brasília (www.festbrasilia.com.br) and Curitiba (www.festivaldecinema.pr.gov.br).

CLASSICAL MUSIC

Brazil and Argentina are the leading producers of classical music in South America. In Rio, Brasília and São Paulo there is usually a good selection of classical music concerts, often with unusual repertoires.

The country has a large number of internationally recognized orchestras. The most famous is the São Paulo State Symphony (www.osesp.art.br), currently under the French conductor Yan Pascal Tortelier, which performs in one of the finest concert halls on the continent. The Orquestra Sinfônica Brasileira (www.iralevin.net) under American conductor Ira Levin has one of the largest and most unusual annual concert programmes in the world and performs in a striking Modernist auditorium in the capital. Other important orchestras include the Petrobras Sinfônica (www.petrobrasinfonica.com.br), supported by Brazilian state oil company Petrobras.

The state of São Paulo also hosts the Winter Festival in the city of Campos do Jordão (www.festivalcamposdojordao.org.br), one of the largest classical music festivals in the southern hemisphere.

CLUBS

Only São Paulo and Rio states have big dance clubs. Going out at night to a venue where you have to shout to communicate is a new phenomenon in Brazil and not a popular one. Even the huge, state-of-the-art São Paulo clubs like Disco or The Week in São Paulo have plenty of sitting and chatting space, with really loud music only in certain areas.

CONTEMPORARY LIVE MUSIC

A major concert happens somewhere every night in Brazil's largest cities and music of some kind is being performed in any city at any time. All the state capitals have excellent large concert theatres and dozens of smaller venues. The most commercial acts play in huge arenas like Pacaembu in São Paulo, which also plays host to international artists.

Regional music is performed all over Brazil with a richness and diversity unrivalled in any country. Important centres are Rio Grande do Sul (for *gaucho* music and avant garde rock), Rio de Janeiro (for *choro* samba and its variants including *bossa nova)*, Belo Horizonte (for its own distinctive regional music, *musica mineira)*, Salvador (for drum orchestras and carnival *axé* music), Recife (for an astonishing variety of rhythms and sounds including cutting-edge mangue beat rock), Belém (for distinctive *carimbó* and calypso-infused rock) and São Paulo where everything meets.

Some of the best places to hear the smaller, quality Brazilian acts are the SESC cultural centres (www.sesc.com.br), especially in São Paulo and Rio.

DANCE

Like music, Brazilian dance is unique to the country and has little, if nothing, in common with other Latin American countries: There is no salsa or tango in Brazil. However, there are more than 50 regional dance styles. The most famous internationally is samba, which was developed in Rio from Bahian roots. It is danced at Carnaval and can be danced either with a partner or alone. The other popular dances are *pagode*, a derivation of samba; *forró,* a kind of jig from the northeast; the swirling-skirt dances of *carimbó* from Belém; *cacuriá* from São Luís (from which lambada is derived); and coco in Pernambuco.

Brazil is an important centre for performance dance. The country has produced international ballet dancers, including Marcelo Gomes (a principal dancer with the American Ballet Theatre) and Thiago Soares (a principal dancer of London's Royal Ballet). Performance dance includes *capoeira*, a dance mixed with martial arts, performed most spectacularly in Bahia.

THEATRE

Unless you are a Portuguese speaker then Brazil's lively drama scene is unlikely to be of interest. São Paulo, Rio and Recife are the most important local centres.

LISTINGS AND TICKETS

Tickets should be purchased through the venues themselves. The website www.guiadasemana.com.br provides listings of what's on nightly in São Paulo, Rio, Aracaju, Salvador, Belo Horizonte, João Pessoa, Florianópolis, Brasília, Maceió, Natal, Fortaleza, Recife, São Luís, Belém, Porto Alegre, Curitiba and Vitória.

GAY AND LESBIAN SCENE

Brazil's cities have an active gay and lesbian scene, especially Rio, São Paulo and Salvador. In Rio de Janeiro the scene is focused on Rua Farme de Amoedo in Ipanema. Information can be obtained from the Rio Gay Guide (www.riogayguide.com) and in Salvador from Centro Cultura, Rua do Sodre 45, close to the Museu de Arte Sacra da Bahia, which publishes a guide to the gay scene. São Paulo's scene can be accessed through Rota Gay Brasil (www.rotagaybrasil.com.br). The city's Pride march (usually in May) is one of the biggest in the world, with more than 3 million people taking part.

SPORTS AND ACTIVITIES

Brazil is an outdoor country and Brazilians enjoy a range of sports and outdoor activities. The most popular is football, which is more important to Brazilians than pretty much anything else. Brazil also offers a broad range of other outdoor activities, many beach-based. Some of the world's best volleyball teams are found in Brazil—the game was perfected on the beaches of Rio, which also have the world's best kite-surfing and superb windsurfing. Large hotels outside the big cities often have a decent swimming pool, but in the cities hotel pools are usually tiny. There is some great hiking, kayaking on wild rivers, jungle trekking and wildlife watching, especially for birds—a fifth of all the birds on Earth live within Brazil.

BIRD WATCHING

Brazil has the third greatest number of bird species in the world (behind Colombia and Peru), with 1,750 species. It has more endemic species than any country in the world (218) and new species are discovered every week (recent additions include cryptic forest-falcon, bald-headed parrot, sulphur-breasted parakeet, Pernambuco pygmy owl, Sincorá antwren and pink-legged graveteiro). Brazil also has more globally threatened birds than any other country: 127 of the world total of 1,240, including two species very recently extinct in the wild, the Alagoas curassow and the Spix's macaw (▷ 13).

The country has a number of distinct biomes with their own endemic and migratory species: the Mata Atlântica coastal rainforests, the *cerrado* in the Central West, *caatinga xeric* scrubland in the *sertão* of the northeast, the Amazonian forests and the seashore and oceanic islands. Each Brazilian biome offers wonderful bird watching as does the huge Pantanal wetland.

Bird-watching tourism in Brazil is in its infancy, but there are a number of good guides and a handful of properly equipped lodges. Guides include Ciro Albano (▷ 226), Edson Endrigo (▷ 155 and 196) and Pantanal Nature (▷ 337). Lodges with state-of-the-art facilities include Cristalino (▷ 304) and Mamirauá (▷ 308) in the Amazon. World-class birding areas in Brazil are too numerous to mention.

FISHING

The Amazon has superb catch-and-release fishing, especially for Peacock Bass *(tucunare)*, one of the world's most spectacular fighting fish. You will need a permit to fish in Brazil, obtainable through Instituto Chico Mendes de Conservação da Biodiversidade (ICMBio; www.icmbio.gov.br), a division of the Ministry of the Environment, which administers many of the protected areas. However, it is far easier to leave the paperwork to a tour company. One of the best companies and one of the few with any fishing infrastructure is Amazon Clipper (▷ 315). Most US operators such as Peacock trips use them.

FOOTBALL

Football *(futebol)* is not only Brazil's most popular spectator sport, it is one of the most important pillars of cultural identity in the country. This is so much so that Brazilians commonly refer to their country as *'o pais do futebol'* (the football country) and as general elections coincide with World Cup year, politicians can appeal to nationalism during the patriotic wave which sweeps across the country. The national team has won the FIFA World Cup five times and is the only football team to have qualified for every competition. Football is played all year round in Brazil.

The most successful and popular teams are from the south and southeast of the country. In São Paulo, Corinthians are the first and the most popular team, and the second most popular in Brazil after Flamengo. They have been World Club Champions, national champions and have won the Brazilian cup three times. Ronaldo was their star player until he announced his retirement in February 2011. São Paulo have been World Club Champions twice and play in the largest private stadium in Brazil. Santos were Pele's team during his golden years. They have been national champions.

In Rio de Janeiro, Flamengo are the most popular team in Brazil. They were Brazilian champions in 2009. Vasco da Gama is the second most popular team in Rio. They have won the national championships four times. Botafogo had their golden age in the 1960s when Garrincha was playing, and have been national champions five times.

Other important teams with very strong followings are Cruzeiro and Atletico from Minas, and Gremio from Rio Grande do Sul.

NATIONAL PARKS

Brazil has more than 40 national parks, many of them spectacular and the highlight of any trip. However, several are not open to the public or have no infrastructure for visits. A number of others are too remote to visit without mounting an expedition. Highlights are listed below.

ACRE

Serra do Divisor
Remote rugged mountains on the border with Peru close to many indigenous villages (▷ 316).

BAHIA

Chapada Diamantina (▷ 206–207)
Hulking table-top mountains with fast-flowing waterfalls and wonderful hiking.

Marinho dos Abrolhos (▷ 210)
Some of the best diving and snorkelling in Brazil, and the chance to see humpback whales.

CEARÁ

Ubajara (▷ 277)
Good for hiking and a spectacular cave system.

GOIÁS

Chapada dos Veadeiros (▷ 332)
Beautiful stands of *cerrado*, abundant wildlife and fantastic waterfalls.

Emas (▷ 329)
Extensive areas of savannah grasslands roamed by maned wolves and giant anteaters.

MARANHÃO

Lençóis Maranhenses (▷ 280–281)
Huge coastal desert of shifting dunes pocked with lakes..

MATO GROSSO

Chapada dos Guimarães (▷ 329)
Table-top mountains with good walking and great views.

Pantanal Matogrossense (▷ 330–331)
World's largest wetland and the best location in South America for seeing wildlife.

MINAS GERAIS

Serra da Canastra (▷ 185)
Remote park in rugged highlands protecting *cerrado* and savannahs and with some of the best bird watching in Brazil.

Serra do Cipó (▷ 185)
Good light walking and horse-riding in *cerrado* forest.

PARANÁ

Iguaçu (▷ 167)
Preserved rainforest around what are, arguably, the most impressive waterfalls on the planet.

Superagüi (▷ 170)
Islands, beaches and mangroves in the middle of the largest stretch of coastal rainforest in Brazil.

PERNAMBUCO

Fernando de Noronha (▷ 247)
Beautiful oceanic islands fringed with coral reef.

PIAUÍ

Serra da Capivara (▷ 282)
Beehive dome mountains with some of the oldest rock art in the Americas.

Sete Cidades (▷ 277)
Strange, eroded rocks and pristine *caatinga*.

RIO GRANDE DO SUL

Lagoa do Peixe (▷ 169)
Enormous shallow saltwater lake with abundant migratory water birds.

RIO DE JANERIO

Itatiaia (▷ 145)
Wonderful mountain walks and good wildlife watching.

Serra dos Órgãos (▷ 148–149)
Named after its bizarre rock formations; good hiking and bird watching.

Tijuca (▷ 81)
Rainforests, waterfalls and hiking in the middle of the country's second largest city.

RORAIMA

Monte Roraima
Huge table-top mountain on the frontier with Guyana and Venezuela with wonderful trekking (▷ 315).

SANTA CATARINA

Aparados da Serra (▷ 169)
Superb hiking in deep gorges and canyons.

HEALTH AND BEAUTY

Spas in Brazil are relatively few and far between. At present they tend to be limited to prestige hotels in São Paulo, Bahia and Rio Grande do Sul states. However, most hotels can usually organize a massage given a visiting masseuse in your hotel room *(massagem terapeutica).*

FOR CHILDREN

Travel with children in Brazil is easy and children are welcome pretty much everywhere. Larger resort hotels often have a designated play area for children and many establishments organize children's activities. However, outside São Paulo, Rio and southern Bahia, Brazil has few designated children's attractions or theme parks.

Brazilian attitudes to children are very different to those in the UK or North America, and children are not segregated from adults. You will find them everywhere—including places that would be reserved for grown-ups back home, like *botequim* bars. Children stay up late in Brazil and, as a result, not all hotels offer babysitting services.

FESTIVALS AND EVENTS

Brazil has some of the biggest and liveliest festivals in the world with dozens of *festas*, rooted in Europe, Africa or the country's indigenous heritage. Many are a fusion of all three. There are the huge festivals like Carnaval and the Festas Juninas which attract millions, and smaller village festivals many of which are celebrated with equal vigour and verve. Even festivals which are celebrated internationally, like Christmas and New Year, are rendered uniquely Brazilian.

Each festival is different but most are connected to an event in the Christian calendar. Carnaval takes place on the weekend before Mardi Gras (Shrove Tuesday), the Festas Juninas are based around the Festa do São João (St. John's Day), the Círio de Nazaré celebrates the appearance of the Virgin at Aparecida in Brazil. Others celebrate the patron saint of a town or city.

There are also many arts, fashion, architecture and cinema festivals in Brazil. Embratur (the international Brazilian tourist office, ▷ 355) can supply details of all the festivals, and state tourist office websites (▷ 354–355) list festival dates.

DECEMBER/JANUARY

Reveillon

Brazil's huge New Year's Eve party sees the largest crowds of any Brazilian festival. The biggest party is on the beach in Copacabana, Rio de Janeiro, with firework displays, dancing and music from the city's most popular bands on huge sound stages. There are similar celebrations in São Paulo on Avenida Paulista.

FEBRUARY

Carnaval

Taking place in almost every city, town and village in Brazil on the weekend before Shrove Tuesday, Carnaval is an excuse for a huge party before the privations of Lent. It is infused with pageantry from African-Brazilian parades which commemorated tribal identity during the slavery era, when African nations were mixed together in Brazil. The biggest carnivals are in Rio (with samba music), Salvador (with *axé* and *afoxé* music) and Recife/Olinda (with *maracatu* and *frevo*).

JUNE

Boi Bumba

An Amazonian variation of Bumba Meu Boi (▷ below) takes place at the same time as that festival on an island in the Amazon river at the town of Parintins.

Bumba-Meu-Boi

The pageant which takes place in Maranhão (and in particular in São Luís) tells the story of a farm worker, Francisco, who kills an ox to satisfy his wife's craving to eat the animal's tongue. The landowner gives him until dawn the next day to resurrect the animal and he enlists the help of an indigenous shaman, who brings the beast back to life. Francisco is forgiven and everyone celebrates.

Festas Juninas

These rural festivals take place all over Brazil throughout June, especially in the northeastern towns of Caruaru and Campina Grande. There is *forró* dancing in traditional *sertão* clothes.

OCTOBER

Círio de Nazaré

One of the world's largest celebrations honouring the Virgin occurs in Belém. The Virgin of Nazaré is the patron saint of Pará. The festival takes place over 15 days and the second Sunday of October sees the arrival of around one million pilgrims for a candlelit procession.

Influences from dozens of European countries, indigenous America, Japan and Africa come together in the kitchen to create a continent of cooking in Brazil. There are many different regional cuisines and a few national dishes and cooking styles. The national dish, *feijoada,* is heavy and meaty, and this could be said of Brazilian cooking in general. Vegetarians are well catered for throughout Brazil. Brazilian cooking evolved from simple roots—the campfires of the *bandeirantes* and slaves, and the simple wood-fired stoves of the big Portuguese houses. It has been helped by some of the most delicious fruits and vegetables, fish and meats in the world.

NATIONAL DISHES

Brazil's national dish, *feijoada*, is made of black beans, off-cuts of meat, jerked beef, smoked sausage and salt pork, thrown together in a pot and cooked for many hours. It is said to have evolved from the scraps left for slaves on the *senzalas* (slave quarters). It is served with greens, rice, *farofa* flour and slices of orange and washed down with *cachaça* sugar cane spirit. Many restaurants serve *feijoada* for Saturday lunch. The other national dish is spit-grilled meat or *churrasco*, accompanied by a buffet of salads, beans and mashed vegetables. *Churrascaria* restaurants can be found in cities throughout the country.

Brazil is also the world's largest consumer of North Atlantic cod, eaten in fillets or in little balls *(bolinhos)* as *bacalhau*.

The Brazilian staple meal served as a cheap *almoço* or *prato feito* in many restaurants comprises fried or barbecued beef, chicken or fish accompanied by rice, boiled rose coco beans and unseasoned salad.

PETISCOS

Brazil's equivalent of Spanish tapas, *pesticos* are available in most bars and *botequims*. Traditional *petiscos* are deep-fried and include *empadas* (baked puff-pastry patties with prawns, chicken, heart of palm or meat), *coxinha* (deep-fried chicken or meat in dough), *madioca* (deep-fried manioc), *casquinhas de siri* (mud-crab served in its shell) and *tortas* (little pies filled with the same ingredients).

REGIONAL COOKING

Bahia

Bahian cooking is strongly influenced by Africa, with seafood cooked in palm oil and coconut milk. The most famous Bahian dish is *moqueca*, sea fish or prawns cooked on low heat in palm oil, coconut milk with garlic, tomatoes, herbs and very mild chillies. A variety served in Espírito Santo, the state south of Bahia, is seasoned with blood-red urucum berry and served in a clay pot. Other Bahian dishes include *vatapá* and *caruru* (pastes made from prawns, nuts, bread, coconut milk and *dendê* oil), and *acarajé* (black-eyed peas or beans squashed into a ball, deep-fried in *dendê* oil and served split in half, stuffed with *vatapá* or *caruru* and seasoned with chilli).

Minas Gerias and Goiás
Minas and Goiás cuisine is made up of hearty stews cooked and kept warm over a wood-fired stove. Dishes are prepared from a variety of meats and *cerrado* fruits and vegetables. Specialities include *frango com quiabo* (chicken cooked in a rich sauce with okra, garlic and onion) and *tutu á Mineira* (bacon, egg and refried and puréed rose coco beans).

Pará
This state in the Amazon has some of the most unusual cooking in Brazil. Alongside delicious river fish like tambaqui and paca are dishes like *tacacá no tucupi* (prawn soup cooked in manioc juice and jambo leaf—the leaf releases an alkaloid which numbs the mouth), and *pato com cupuaçu* (duck breast with pungent, sautéed *cupuaçu* fruit).

The South
Southern Brazilian cooking is strongly influenced by the dishes of Bavaria in Germany, with many varieties of sausage *(chorizos)* and spit-roasted meats. Other dishes include *barreado* (slow broiled beef cooked in distinctive pots and served with rice and vegetables).

MEALS AND MEALTIMES

Mealtimes vary enormously in Brazil, which is not a country preoccupied with the clock.

In hotels, breakfast *(café de manhã)* is served between 6am and 10am. It usually comprises bread rolls, cold meats and cheeses, fruit, very sweet cereals, fruit juices and coffee. Coffee is often served with sugar and milk already added.

Lunch *(almoço)* is served between noon and 2pm. It is traditionally the largest meal of the day and consists of two courses—a main course and a very sweet dessert. Desserts vary by region but may include *pudim de leite* (crème caramel), *goiabada* (guava cheese) served with mild Minas Gerais cheese and sweet mousses made from exotic fruit.

Supper *(janta)* is for very many Brazilians a light meal—perhaps a cooked sandwich *(lanche)* or a soup *(sopa)*.

WHERE TO EAT

Padarias (bakeries) and *lanchonetes* (snack bars) offer *prato feitos, petiscos* and *lanches* as well as good coffee, juices and snacks. The best *padarias* are in São Paulo. Cafés serve coffee and snacks.

Restaurantes (restaurants) are more formal and vary from a la carte to buffet. *Rodizio* restaurants (which are usually *churrascarias*) have waiting staff bring prepared food to the table. The best *restaurantes* are of the highest international quality, and the best of the best are in São Paulo and Rio.

DRINKS

The national alcoholic drink is a sugar cane spirit *(cachaça*, also known as *pinga)*. When mixed with pulped limes (or other fruits), sugar and crushed ice the result is a *caipirinha*, and when weaker, a *batida*.

Brazilian beer is blonde, weak and similar to lager. Draught beer is called *chope* or *chopp* (after the German *Schoppen*, and pronounced 'shoppi'). There are various national brands, which include Bohemia, Brahma, Skol and Antartica. The best beer is from the German breweries in Rio Grande do Sul.

Fruit juices or *sucos* come in many exotic flavours. They include *açai* (a palm berry from the Amazon), *caju* (cashew fruit) and *cacau* (cocoa fruit).

Brazilian food and drink are diverse with a regional aspect. The dishes in the south, southeast and central west are clearly influenced by European tradition, mainly Portuguese, Italian and German. The indigenous north gained exotic ingredients and endemic fish from the Amazon. The northeast cuisine, the most unusual of all, inherited its hot flavour from Africa. It can be a bit of a gamble to chose your dish if you don't read Portuguese. Here is some basic vocabulary to get you started.

MEALS *(REFEIÇÃO)*
café da manhã .... breakfast
almoço .... lunch
jantar .... dinner
lanche .... snack

COURSES *(PRATOS)*
entradas .... starters
prato principal .... main course
sobremesa .... dessert

DRINKS *(BEBIDAS)*
agua com gás .... sparkling water
agua mineral .... mineral water
café .... coffee
cerveja .... beer
chá .... tea
gelo .... ice
leite .... milk
refrigerante .... fizzy soft drink
suco .... fruit juice
vinho .... wine

CONDIMENTS *(CONDIMENTOS)*
açúcar .... sugar
açúcar mascavo .... brown sugar
azeite .... oil
geleia .... jam
manteiga .... butter
mel .... honey
sal .... salt
pão .... bread
pimenta .... chilli
pimenta do reino .... black pepper
vinagre .... vinegar

MEAT *(CARNE)*
bacon/toucinho .... bacon
bife .... steak
cabrito .... kid
porco .... pork
carne seca/carne de sol .... jerky
carne de vaca .... beef
carneiro .... mutton
churrasco .... barbecue
cordeiro .... lamb
costeleta .... cutlets
coxa de frango .... chicken leg
frango .... chicken
linguiça .... pork sausage
peito de frango .... chicken breast
peru .... turkey
picanha .... sirloin
presunto .... ham
salsicha .... sausage

FISH *(PEIXE)*
atum .... tuna
bacalhau .... cod
garopa .... grouper
pescada .... hake
pintado .... catfish
robalo .... bass
salmão .... salmon
sardinhas .... sardines
surubim .... tiger catfish
truta .... trout
tucunaré .... peacock bass

SEAFOOD *(FRUTAS DO MAR)*

camarão .... shrimps/prawns
carangueijo .... crab
lagosta .... lobster
lagostim .... crayfish
lula .... squid
mexilhões .... mussels
moluscos .... clams
ostra .... oyster
polvo .... octopus
siri .... soft shell crab
vieiras .... scallops
vôngole .... clams

VEGETABLES *(LEGUMES/ VERDURAS)*

abacate .... avocado
abóbora .... pumpkin
abobrinha .... courgette/zucchini
aeringela .... aubergine/eggplant
aipo .... celery
alface .... lettuce
aspargos .... asparagus
azeitonas .... olives
batata .... potato
beterreba .... beetroot
brócules .... broccoli
cenoura .... carrot
couve .... spring greens
ervilhas .... peas
nabos .... turnip
pepino .... cucumber
pimentão .... capsicum/pepper
repolho .... cabbage
salada .... salad
tomate .... tomato

FRUITS *(FRUTAS)*

abacaxí .... pineapple
cacau .... cocoa
caju .... cashew fruit
caqui .... persimmon
goiaba .... guava
laranja .... orange
limão .... lime
mamão papaya .... papaya
manga .... mango
maracujá .... passion fruit
melão .... melon
uva .... grape

GRAINS *(GRÃOS)*

arroz .... rice
feijão .... beans
feijão preto .... black beans
grão de bico .... chickpeas
lentilha .... lentils

COOKING METHODS

assado .... roasted
bem passado .... well done
crú .... raw
frito .... fried
na brasa .... flame grilled
na chapa .... grilled on a griddle
no forno .... baked
pochê .... poached
recheado .... stuffed/filled

SNACKS

batata frita .... crisps/chips
empada/empanada/torta .... baked pastries
pão-de-queijo .... cheese bread
pastel/coxinha .... fried pastries
queijo .... cheese
sanduíche .... sandwich
sopa .... soup

CUTLERY

colher .... spoon
faca .... knife
garfo .... fork

STAYING

Brazil does not have the choice and range of accommodation of other popular destinations around the world, especially outside the major tourist centres. Small, luxury accommodation, spas and the boutique hotel are relatively new to Brazil. Brazilians like their resorts big and brash, and it can be difficult to find accommodation that doesn't feel old-fashioned by European or North American standards. Large Portuguese, Spanish and North American chains are well represented in Brazil and there are many Brazilian hotel chains of various sizes too; they include Blue Tree and Othon.

TAXES

Taxes for rooms in Brazil vary from state to state and hotel to hotel. They can be as much as 17 per cent or as low as 5 per cent, or they can be a flat fee of R$10 per room. There is sometimes an additional service tax (*Imposto Sobre Serviços* or ISS)—5 per cent of the total room charges.

ALBERGUES

Albergues are the Brazilian version of hostels. Many are affiliated to the International Youth Hostel Association (IYHA). *Albergues* have the cheapest accommodation for tourists willing to share a dormitory room *(dormitório)* with their own group or with strangers. Many also have double and single rooms. These are often more expensive than double rooms in guest houses. *Albergues* usually have internet, lockers, tour information and luggage storage, and they sometimes have WiFi (free or for a small fee).

PENSÕES

Pensões are Brazil's equivalent of guest houses. They are the simplest hotels after *albergues* and usually fall outside Brazil's categorization system, which is based on stars. They vary hugely. Rooms are usually small by US standards but generous by European and, while some hotels have a handful of cheap rooms with shared bathrooms, they generally have private bathrooms, fans, a writing table and a wardrobe. Some have refrigerators and air-conditioning.

POUSADAS

Pousadas offer a range of accommodation—from simple guest houses to bed and breakfasts, and all the way to plush small luxury establishments. They often offer the best value mid-range types of accommodation and standards are generally unclassified.

HOTELS

Hotels operate according to the international star system—although 5-star hotels are not price controlled and hotels in any category are not always of the standard of their star equivalent in North America or Europe. They vary enormously in quality. Standard hotels in the less touristy cities tend to be basic with little to no decoration. Many haven't

been refurbished since the 1980s. Older hotels often offer double rooms which are cheaper than those in hostels.

Boutique hotels are relatively new to Brazil and tend to be found in the more chic beach resorts in states like Bahia, which has some of South America's finest. The majority of them are clustered around Itacaré and Trancoso.

APARTMENTS

A number of companies offer private home beach rentals and apartments. These include Paradise Properties (www.pp-bahia.com) in Bahia, Cama e Café (www.camaecafe.com.br) in Rio and Recife, and Casas Charmosas (www.casascharmosas.com.br) and Matueté (www.matuete.com) throughout Brazil.

FINDING ACCOMMODATION

Online travel agents and booking services (OTAs) often give the cheapest deals. While the reviews featured are often penned by the resort staff or their rivals, Tripadvisor offers a one-click price listing for a number of the larger OTAs, including Expedia.com, LateRooms.com, Hotels.com, venere.com and Splendia.com. It is also possible to search through the websites of those companies.

Hotel rooms come in various categories. *Apartamentos* are apartments with a separate living and sleeping area and sometimes cooking facilities. A *quarto* is a standard room; *com banheiro* is with a private bathroom and *sem banheiro* is with a shared bathroom.

Finding a room is only usually a problem in high season—a week before and after Shrove Tuesday and a week before Christmas until the weekend after New Year. During this period hotel prices can increase by as much as four times, especially in the places popular with tourists. However, it is always a good idea to book ahead, as the best rates are often available only in advance. Rack rates (displayed in the hotel) can be as much as twice the real price. It is always worth bargaining.

Rooms with a fan *(ventilador)* are usually about 25 per cent cheaper than the same rooms with air-conditioning *(ar condicionado)*.

Hotel rooms at the front of the building can be very noisy, so always ask for the best *(o melhor)* when booking ahead. When arriving at a hotel without a booking, ask to look at several rooms as the first shown to guests is usually the worst.

Many city hotels are housed in tall tower blocks. The upper-floor rooms often have good views and come at no extra cost.

At the budget end of the market www.hostelbookers.com, www.hostels.com and www.hostelworld.com offer an online booking service. Many Bahian hostels are part of the IYHA chain (www.iyha.org), but again be circumspect about the reviews.

Couchsurfing (www.couchsurfing.org) and Servas (http://joomla.servas.org) offer the latest alternative to hostelling or camping—a homeshare exchange service whereby members offer their homes to other members visiting their city.

CAMPING

Camping Clube do Brasil, the Brazilian Camping Club, (www.campingclube.com.br) has sites throughout Brazil and comprehensive listings can be found on their website, but the club does not offer a booking service.

The website www.campingo.com offers an online booking service for campsites, although their Brazil options were limited in 2010.

Camping outside designated areas is not safe and not recommended.

The differences between Brazilian and European Portuguese are analogous to those between British and American English. While literary Portuguese is similar, discrepancies are far more acute within the spoken form of the language, where Brazilian Portuguese is less formal than its European counterpart and makes use of different and often uniquely Brazilian terminology and grammatical forms. These include the use of *você* for 'you', rather than *tu*, which is regarded as grammatically incorrect and uncultured in Portugal.

Even if you are far from fluent, it is always a good idea to try to speak a few words of Brazilian Portuguese. The words and phrases on the following pages should help you with the basics, from ordering a meal to dealing with emergencies.

Tip on pronunciation: If a word has an accent this is where the stress falls.

(´) on a vowel gives it an open tone: coffee = ca**fé** (car-**fay**)

(^) on a vowel gives it a deep tone: flight = **vô**o (**vo**-o)

(˜) on a vowel gives it a deep nasal tone (combine the letter stressed with a half 'm'—don't close your lips at the end of 'm'): no = **não** (**nah**m-oo)

CONVERSATION

Hello, pleased to meet you.
Olá, prazer em conhecê-lo(a).

My name is...
Meu nome é...

I don't speak Portuguese.
Não falo português.

Do you speak English?
Fala inglês?

I don't understand.
Não compreendo.

I'm on holiday.
Estou de férias.

I live in...
Vívo em...

Good morning
Bom dia

Good afternoon
Boa tarde

Good evening/night
Boa noite
Goodbye
Tchau

See you later
Até logo

May I/Can I?
Posso?

How are you?
Tudo bom?

I'm sorry
Desculpe

Excuse me
Com licença

USEFUL WORDS

yes .... sim
no .... não
there .... ali
here .... aqui
where .... onde
who .... quem
when .... quando
why .... porquê
how .... como
later .... mais tarde
now .... agora
open .... aberto
closed .... fechado
please .... por favor
thank you .... obrigado(a)
big .... grande
small .... pequeno
full .... cheio
empty .... vazio
bad .... mau
good .... bom
enough .... suficiente

SHOPPING

Could you help me, please?
Pode me ajudar, por favor?

How much is this?
Quanto custa?

I'm looking for...
Preciso de...

This isn't what I want.
Não é isto que eu queria.

When does the store open/close?
Quando é que a loja abre/fecha?

I'm just looking, thank you.
Só estou olhando, obrigado(a).

Do you accept credit cards?
Aceitam cartões de crédito?

This is the right size.
Este é o tamanho certo.

Do you have anything less expensive/smaller/larger?
Tem algo mais barato/mais pequeno/ maior?

I'll take this.
Levo este(a).

This one
Este(a)

Do you have a bag for this?
Tem um sacola para isto?

I'd like...grams please.
Queria...gramas, por favor.

I'd like a kilo of...
Queria um quilo de...

What does this contain?
O que é que isto contém?

I'd like...slices of that.
Queria...fatias disto.

bakery.................................. padaria
bookshop.............................. livraria
chemist.............................. farmácia
clothes.................................... roupa
expensive................................. caro
market.............................. mercado
supermarket .... supermercado

NUMBERS

1 .... um
2 .... dois
3 .... três
4 .... quatro
5 .... cinco
6 .... seis
7 .... sete
8 .... oito
9 .... nove
10 .... dez
11 .... onze
12 .... doze
13 .... treze
14 .... catorze
15 .... quinze
16 .... dezasseis
17 .... dezassete
18 .... dezoito
19 .... dezanove
20 .... vinte
21 .... vinte e um
30 .... trinta
40 .... quarenta
50 .... cinquenta
60 .... sessenta
70 .... setenta
80 .... oitenta
90 .... noventa
100 .... cem
1000 .... mil

HOTELS

Do you have a room?
Tem um quarto?

I have made a reservation for... nights.
Fiz uma reserva para...noites.

How much each night?
Quanto é por noite?

double room
quarto de casal

twin room
quarto duplo

single room
quarto individual

bathroom/toilet
banheiro/toalete

with bath/shower
com banheiro/choveiro

Is there a lift in the hotel?
O hotel tem elevador?

Is the room air-conditioned/ heated?
O quarto tem ar condicionado/ aquecimento?

Is breakfast/lunch/dinner included in the cost?
O café da manhã/ almoço/jantar está incluído no preço?

Is room service available?
Tem serviço de quarto?

When do you serve breakfast?
Quando servem o café da manhã?

May I have breakfast in my room?
Posso tomar o café da manhã no quarto?

Do you serve evening meals?
Servem jantar?

The room is too hot/cold.
O quarto está muito quente/frio.

May I see the room?
Posso ver o quarto?

May I have my room key?
Pode me dar a chave do quarto?

Where can I park my car?
Onde posso estacionar o carro?

Please can I pay my bill?
Posso pagar a conta?

swimming pool .... piscina
boutique hotel....... hotel de charme
bed and breakfast ...... cama e café

guest house...................... pousada
hostel.................................. albergue

RESTAURANTS

I'd like to reserve a table for... people at...
Gostaria de reservar uma mesa para...pessoas às....

A table for..., please.
Uma mesa para..., por favor.

We have/haven't reserved.
Temos reserva/não temos reserva.

Is this table taken?
Esta mesa está ocupada?

Could we see the menu/wine list?
Pode nos trazer um cardápio/lista dos vinhos?

Are there tables outside?
Há mesas lá fora?

Where are the toilets?
Onde ficam os banheiros?

We'd like something to drink.
Gostaríamos de tomar uma bebida.

Could I have bottled still/ sparkling water, please?
Pode me trazer uma garrafa de água sem gás/com gás, por favor?

I can't eat wheat/sugar/salt/pork/ beef/dairy.
Não posso comer trigo/açúcar/sal/ porco/carne de vaca/lacticínios.

I am a vegetarian.
Sou vegetariano(a).

The bill, please.
A conta por favor.

Is service included?
A taxa de serviço está incluída?

FOOD AND DRINK

barbecue .... churrasco
beans .... feijão
beer .... cerveja
black pepper .... pimenta do reino
bread .... pão
breakfast .... café da manhã
canned drink .... refrigerante
cheese .... queijo
chicken .... frango
chilli .... pimenta
coffee .... café
dessert .... sobremesa
dinner .... jantar
drink .... bebida
fish .... peixe
fork .... garfo
fries .... batata frita
fruit .... fruta
fruit juice .... suco
knife .... faca
lunch .... almoço
main course .... prato principal
milk .... leite
oil .... azeite
rice .... arroz
salt .... sal
salt cod .... bacalhau
sandwich .... sanduíche
sardines .... sardinhas
snack .... lanche
soup .... sopa
spoon .... colher
starter .... entrada
steak .... bife
sugar .... açúcar
tea .... chá
well done .... bem passado
wine .... vinho

GETTING AROUND

Where is the information desk?
Onde é o balcão de informações?

Where is the timetable?
Onde está o horário?

Does this train/bus go to...?
Este trem/ônibus vai para...?

Do you have a metro/bus map?
Tem um mapa do metrô/dos ônibus?

train/bus/metro station
estação de trem/terminal de ônibus/ estação de metrô

Where can I buy a ticket?
Onde posso comprar um bilhete/ passagem?

Where can I reserve a seat?
Onde posso reservar um lugar?

Please can I have a single/round-trip ticket to...?
Pode dar-me um bilhete/bilhete de ida e volta para...?

Where can I find a taxi?
Onde posso encontrar um táxi?

How much is the journey?
Quanto é a viagem?

I'd like to rent a car.
Gostaria de alugar um carro.

I'm lost.
Estou perdido(a).

Is this the way to...?
É este o caminho para...?

Go straight on.
Vá sempre em frente.

Turn left.
Vire à esquerda.

Turn right.
Vire à direita.

traffic lights .... semáforos/ farol
intersection .... cruzamento
corner .... esquina
no parking .... estacionamento proibido
art gallery .... galeria de arte
cathedral .... catedral
church .... igreja
guide .... guia
museum .... museu
national park .... parque nacional
ticket .... bilhete
tourist information .... informaçoes turisticas

MONEY

Is there a bank/currency exchange office nearby?
Há um banco/uma agência de câmbio aqui perto?

Can I cash this here?
Posso tirar isto aqui?

I'd like to change sterling/dollars into euros.
Gostaria de cambiar libras/dólares para euros.

Can I use my credit card to withdraw cash?
Posso usar o meu cartão de crédito para tirar dinheiro?

What is the exchange rate today?
Qual é a taxa de câmbio hoje?

HEALTH/EMERGENCIES

Help! .... Socorro!
accident .... acidente
dangerous .... perigoso
dehydration .... desidratação
diarrhoea .... diarréia
emergency .... emergência
medicine .... remédio
police .... polícia
stop .... pare
Keep out .... Mantenha distância.

I don't feel well.
Não me sinto bem.

I've got a fever.
Tenho febre.

Can you call a doctor?
Pode chamar um médico?

Where is the nearest hospital?
Onde é o hospital mais proximo?

I have been robbed.
Fui assaltado.

DAYS OF THE WEEK

Monday .... segunda-feira
Tuesday .... terça-feira
Wednesday .... quarta-feira
Thursday .... quinta-feira
Friday .... sexta-feira
Saturday .... sábado
Sunday .... domingo

MONTHS
January .... janeiro
February .... fevereiro
March .... março
April .... abril
May .... maio
June .... junho
July .... julho
August .... agosto
September .... setembro
October .... outubro
November .... novembro
December .... dezembro

SEASONS
spring .... primavera
summer .... verão
autumn .... outono
winter .... inverno

TIME
morning .... manhã
afternoon .... tarde
evening .... fim da tarde
night .... noite
today .... hoje
yesterday .... ontem
tomorrow .... amanhã
day .... dia
month .... mês
year .... ano

HOLIDAYS
New Year's Day .... Ano Novo
Carnival .... Carnaval
Good Friday .... Paixão de Cristo
Easter Sunday .... Páscoa
Christmas .... Natal
New Year's Eve .... Reveillon

COLOURS
black .... preto
blue .... azul
brown .... marron
golden .... dourado
green .... verde
grey .... cinza
light blue .... azul claro
metallic .... metálico
orange .... laranja
pink .... rosa
purple .... roxo
red .... vermelho

silvery .... prateado
violet .... lilás
white .... branco
yellow .... amarelo

ANIMALS
amphibian .... anfibio
bird .... ave
butterfly .... borboleta
insect .... inseto
mammal .... mamífero
reptile .... réptil
Amazonian river dolphin .... boto
anaconda .... sucuri
anteater .... tamanduá
armadillo .... tatu
caiman .... jacaré
giant otter .... ariranha
jaguar .... onça-pintada
parrot .... papagaio
macaw .... arara
monkey .... macaco
tapir .... anta

WEATHER
cloud .... nuvem
cloudy .... nublado
cold .... frio
fog .... neblina
hot .... quente
humid .... húmido
humidity .... humidade
lighting .... raio
rain .... chuva
rainy day .... dia chuvoso
rainy season .... estação chuvosa
sultry .... mormaço
sun .... sol
sunburn .... queimadura de sol
sunny .... ensolarado
sunscreen .... protetor solar
thunder .... trovão
thunderstorm .... tempesdade
weather forecast .... previsão do
.... tempo
wind .... vento

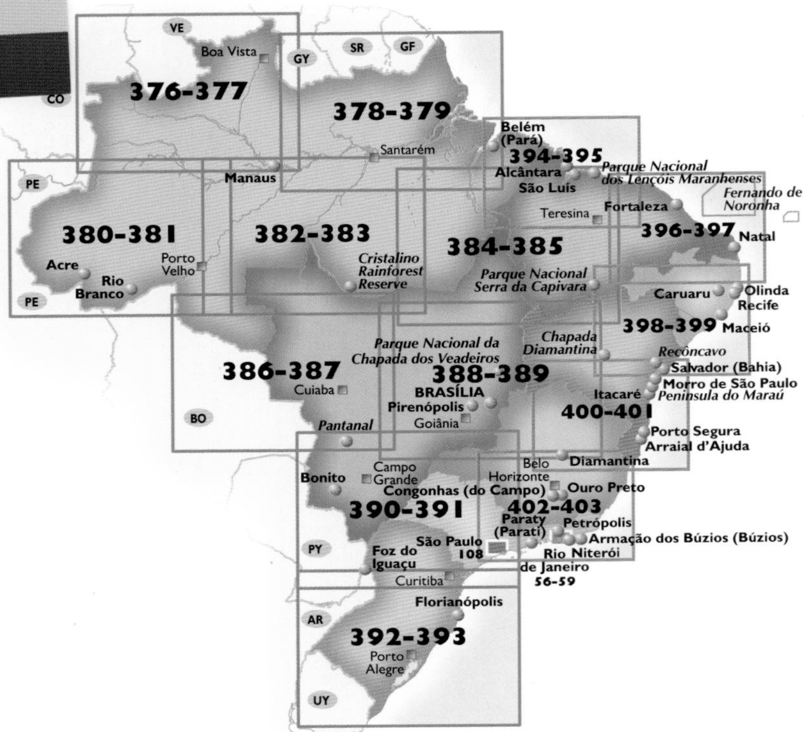

VE
CO
PE
PE
PE
GY
SR
GF
BO
PY
AR
UY
Boa Vista
376-377
378-379
Santarém
Manaus
Belém
(Pará)
394-395
Alcântara
São Luís
Parque Nacional
dos Lençóis Maranhenses
Fernando de
Noronha
Fortaleza
Teresina
396-397
Natal
380-381
382-383
384-385
Acre
Rio
Branco
Porto
Velho
Cristalino
Rainforest
Reserve
Parque Nacional
Serra da Capivara
Caruaru
Olinda
Recife
398-399
Maceió
Chapada
Diamantina
Recôncavo
Salvador (Bahia)
Morro de São Paulo
Peninsula do Maraú
Itacaré
Parque Nacional da
Chapada dos Veadeiros
386-387
Cuiaba
388-389
BRASÍLIA
Pirenópolis
Goiânia
Pantanal
400-401
Porto Segura
Arraial d'Ajuda
Belo
Horizonte
Diamantina
Campo
Grande
Bonito
Congonhas (do Campo)
Ouro Preto
390-391
402-403
Paraty
(Parati)
Petrópolis
Armação dos Búzios (Búzios)
São Paulo
108
Foz do
Iguaçu
Rio
de Janeiro
56-59
Niterói
Curitiba
Florianópolis
392-393
Porto
Alegre

376-393
0
100 km
0
60 miles
394-403
0
60 km
0
40 miles
397
0
3 km
0
2 miles

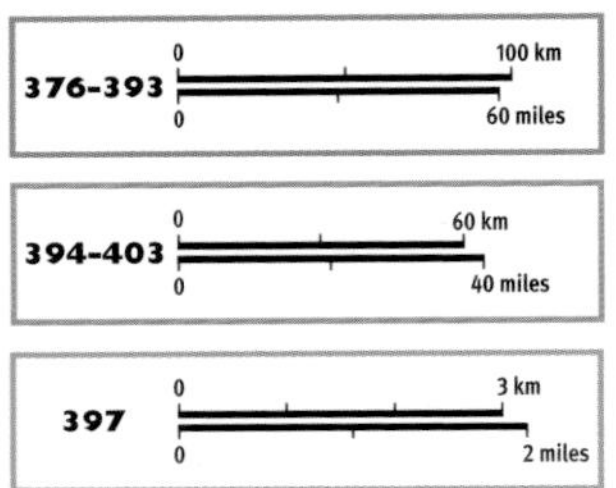

- Motorway
- National road
- Regional road
- Local road
- Railway
- International boundary
- Disputed International boundary
- State boundary
- Featured place of interest
- City / Town / Village
- National park / Protected area
- Marsh
- Waterfall
- Airport
- 621 Height in metres
- Equator

MAPS

Map references for the sights refer to the atlas pages within this section or to the individual town plans within the regions. For example, Salvador has the reference 401 T10, indicating the page on which the map is found (401) and the grid square in which Salvador sits (T10).

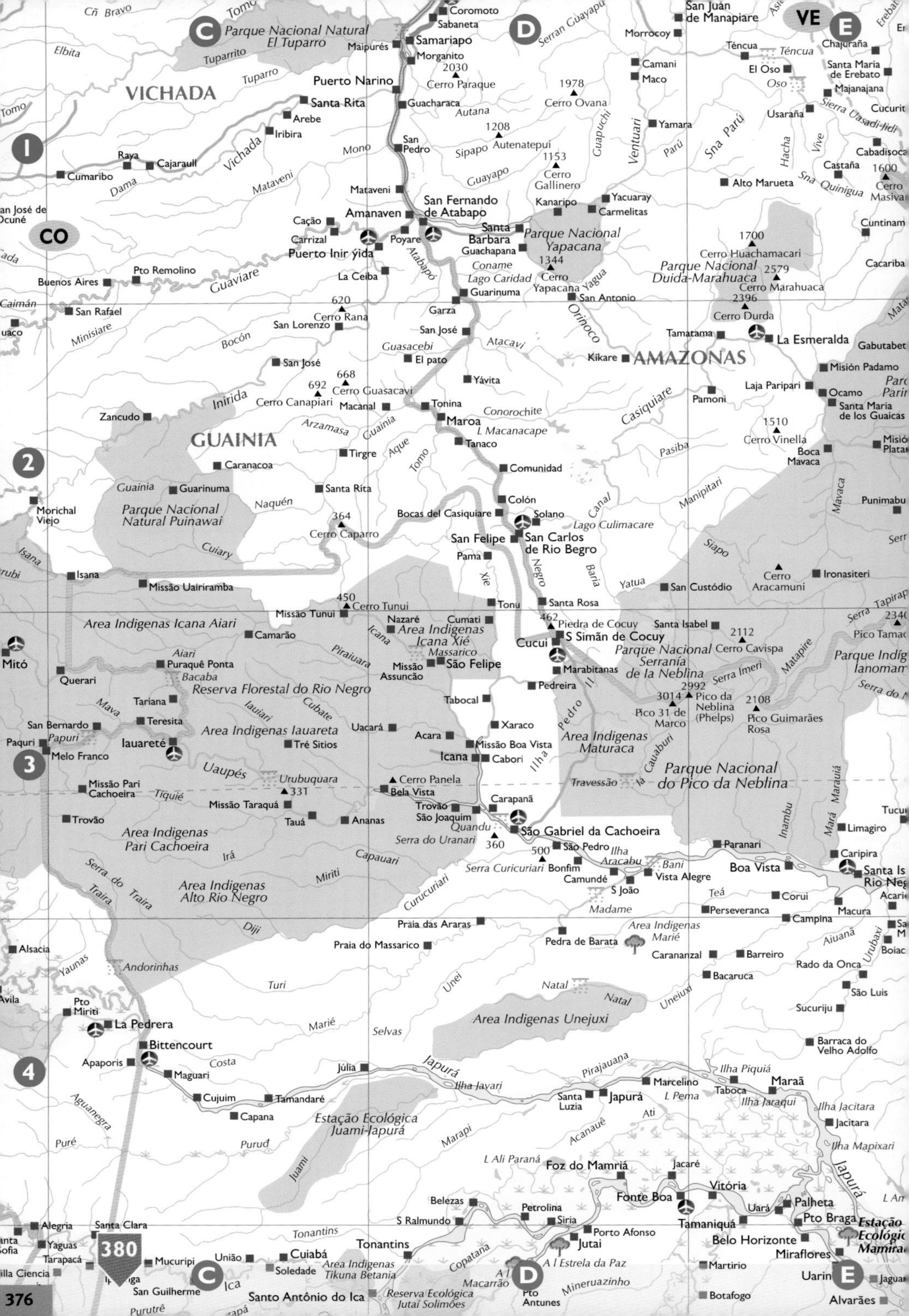
C
D
E
VE
I
2
3
4
CO
Cñ Bravo
Tomo
Parque Nacional Natural
El Tuparro
Tuparrito
Tuparro
Elbita
VICHADA
Coromoto
Sabaneta
Maipurés
Samariapo
Morganito
2030
Cerro Paraque
Puerto Narino
Santa Rita
Arebe
Iribira
Guacharaca
Autana
Serran Guayapu
San Juán
de Manapiare
Morrocoy
Camani
Maco
1978
Cerro Ovana
Yamara
Ventuari
Guapuchi
Parú
Sna Parú
Téncua
El Oso
Oso
Chajuraña
Santa Maria
de Erebato
Majanajana
Sierra Uasadi-Jidi
Usaraña
Cucurit
Cabadisoca
Castaña
1600
Cerro
Masiva
Hacha
Vive
Sna Quinigua
Alto Marueta
Tomo
Raya
Cajaraull
Cumaribo
Dama
Vichada
Mono
San
Pedro
1208
Autenatepui
Sipapo
1153
Cerro
Gallinero
Guayapo
Mataveni
Mataveni
San Fernando
de Atabapo
Amanaven
Kanaripo
Yacuaray
Carmelitas
Cuntinam
San José de
Ocuné
Cação
Carrizal
Poyare
Puerto Inir ýida
Atabapo
Santa
Barbara
Guachapana
Parque Nacional
Yapacana
1700
Cerro Huachamacari
Parque Nacional
Duida-Marahuaca
2579
Cerro Marahuaca
Cacariba
Pto Remolino
Buenos Aires
Guaviare
La Ceiba
Coname
Lago Caridad
1344
Cerro
Yapacana
Yagua
San Antonio
Guarinuma
2396
Cerro Durda
Caimán
San Rafael
620
Cerro Rana
San Lorenzo
Minisiare
Bocón
Garza
San José
Orinoco
Tamatama
La Esmeralda
Gabutabe
Guasacebi
El pato
Atacavi
Kikare
AMAZONAS
Misión Padamo
San José
668
692
Cerro Guasacavi
Cerro Canapiari
Yávita
Laja Paripari
Ocamo
Santa Maria
de los Guaicas
Inirida
Zancudo
Macanal
Tonina
Maroa
Conorochite
L Macanacape
Casiquiare
Pamoni
Arzamasa
Guainia
GUAINIA
Aque
Tomo
Tanaco
1510
Cerro Vinella
Pasiba
Boca
Mavaca
Misió
Plata
Tirgre
Caranacoa
Comunidad
Guainia
Guarinuma
Santa Rita
Parque Nacional
Natural Puinawai
Naquén
Morichal
Viejo
Colón
Manipitari
Mavaca
Punimabu
Bocas del Casiquiare
364
Cerro Caparro
Solano
Canal
Lago Culimacare
San Felipe
San Carlos
de Rio Begro
Siapo
Cuiary
Isana
Pama
Negro
Baria
Cerro
Aracamuni
Ironasiteri
Isana
Missão Uairiramba
Xie
Yatua
San Custódio
450
Cerro Tunui
Missão Tunui
Tonu
Santa Rosa
Tapirapé
Serra
2340
Area Indigenas Icana Aiari
Camarão
Nazaré
Cumati
Area Indigenas
Icana Xié
Icana
462
Piedra de Cocuy
Santa Isabel
S Simãn de Cocuy
Cucui
2112
Pico Tamac
Mitó
Aiari
Puraquê Ponta
Bacaba
Piraiuara
Massarico
Missão
Assuncão
São Felipe
Parque Nacional
Serranía
de la Neblina
Cerro Cavispa
Matapire
Parque Indíg
Ianomam
Querari
Marabitanas
Pedreira
Serra Imeri
Serra do
Reserva Florestal do Rio Negro
Cubate
Tariana
Tabocal
2992
3014
Pico da
Neblina
(Phelps)
2108
Pico 31 de
Marco
Pico Guimarães
Rosa
Mava
Iauiari
Teresita
Area Indigenas Iauareta
Uacará
Acara
Xaraco
Pedro II
San Bernardo
Papuri
Paquri
Iauareté
Tré Sitios
Missão Boa Vista
Area Indigenas
Maturaca
Cauaburi
Melo Franco
Icana
Cabori
Ilha
Parque Nacional
do Pico da Neblina
Uaupés
Urubuquara
Cerro Panela
Travessão
Maraulá
Missão Pari
Cachoeira
Tiquié
331
Bela Vista
Carapanã
Missão Taraquá
Trovão
São Joaquim
Trovão
Tauá
Ananas
Quandu
Inambu
Tucu
Area Indigenas
Pari Cachoeira
360
São Gabriel da Cachoeira
Serra do Uranari
Limagiro
Irá
Capauari
500
São Pedro
Ilha
Aracabu
Paranari
Bani
Caripira
Serra do
Traira
Miriti
Serra Curicuriari
Bonfim
Camundé
Vista Alegre
Boa Vista
Santa Is
Rio Neg
Area Indigenas
Alto Rio Negro
Curucuriari
S João
Teá
Corui
Acari
Diji
Madame
Perseveranca
Macura
Campina
Praia das Araras
Area Indigenas
Marié
Alsacia
Praia do Massarico
Pedra de Barata
Caranazal
Barreiro
Aiuanã
Urubaxi
Yaunas
Andorinhas
Rado da Onca
Bacaruca
Turi
Unei
Natal
Natal
Uneiuxi
São Luis
Avila
Pto
Miriti
La Pedrera
Area Indigenas Unejuxi
Sucuriju
Marié
Selvas
Bittencourt
Barraca do
Velho Adolfo
Apaporis
Costa
Júlia
Japurá
Pirajauana
Ilha Piquiá
Maguari
Ilha Javari
Marcelino
Taboca
Maraã
Cujuim
Tamandaré
Santa
Luzia
Japurá
L Pema
Ilha Jaraqui
Ilha Jacitara
Aguanegra
Capana
Estação Ecológica
Juami-Japurá
Ati
Jacitara
Puré
Puruê
Marapi
Acanauê
Ilha Mapixari
Juami
L Ali Paraná
Foz do Mamriá
Jacaré
Japurá
Vitória
Fonte Boa
L Am
Belezas
Petrolina
Palheta
Tamaniquá
Uará
Pto Braga
Estação
Ecológic
Mamira
Alegria
Santa Clara
Tonantins
S Ralmundo
Siria
Porto Afonso
Yaguas
Tarapacá
380
Cuiabá
Tonantins
Jutai
Belo Horizonte
Miraflores
Mucuripi
União
Soledade
Area Indigenas
Tikuna Betania
Copatana
A I Estrela da Paz
Martirio
Macarrão
Mineruazinho
Uarin
Jaguar
Ica
Ipiranga
San Guilherme
Santo Antônio do Ica
Reserva Ecológica
Jutaí Solimões
Pto
Antunes
Botafogo
Alvarães
Purutrê

F
G
H
BOLIVAR
Guaina
Urimán
Apradarepui
Puricama
2713
1810
Weitepui
Ilutepui
Sabana
Mte Kukenam
(Mata Hui)
2680
Paikwa
Opadai
Pakaraima Mtns
1456
2036
Mt Ayanganna
Garraway Stream
Kangaruma
Parque Nacional Jáua-Sarisariñama
Antavari
Acopantepui
2320
Akopántepui
Chimtatepui
Apónguao
Arabanmeru
Monte Roraima
2810
Parque Nacional de Monte Roraima
2370
Ueitepui
Potaro
Parque Nacional Kaieteur
Mandia
426
Arabelo
Curutu
Sierra del Zamuro
Won-Kén
San Fco de Yuruani
Arabapó
Peraitepui
Kopinang Mission
Glendor Mtns
Guanacoco-jidi
Paragua
Carun
San Ignacio de Yuruani
Reserva Indigenas Ingricó
Orinduik
Jáua-jidi
Meseta del Cerro Jáua
Sansariñama-jidi
Caroni
Misión Divina Pastora
Cuquenán
Piolho
Buritizal
Kurukabaru
Kato
1555
Icabarú
Yumaribó
Puraitepui
Santa Ana
Santa Elena de Uairén
Serra Imerari
Siparuni
I
Maracuni
Caura
Ichún
Malhia
1860
Cotingo
Xiriqui
Mutum
Takutu
Burro Burro
Icabarú
Los Caribes
Mau (Ireng)
Kata
Merevari
Guanajuña
Sierra de Pacaraima
Asiasito
Milagre
A I Santa Inês
Acari
Derpásito
Area Indigenas Raposa Serra do Sul
Col I São Marcos
Karasabai
Uauaris
(Auari)
Surubai
Pacu
A I Ananãs
Parimé
Cantão
Surumu
Annai
Serra Tepequem
Tepequém
Copacabana
Consolação
Area Indigenas Araca
A I Ponta da Serra
Normandia
Good Hope
Bellavista
Pununi
A I Uraricoera
Uaicas
Conceição do Maú
Amuku
Kanarambo
Parima
Serra Parima
Uraricoera
Pirara
Yupukarri
Area Indigenas Palimiu
Puruaa
Ilha da Maracá
Colonia Taiano
Manari
Marakanata
Nappi
Reserva Florestal Parima
Bonfim
Lethem
A I Cutiaba
Uraricoera
Estação Ecológica do Maracá
A I Serra da Moça
A I Jaboti
Area Indigenas Parima
Parque Indígena Ianomaml
Feira
A I Boqueirão
BR-174
Tacutu
St Ignatius Mission
Kanuku Mtns
Serra das Surucucus
Mucajai
Cauamé
Santa Fe
Warumia
Mariwa
Parque Nacional Serra Parapecó
Missão Surucucu
Funil
Mucajai
Alto Alegre
Boa Vista
Macusi
Sand Creek
Shea
Pasobequiteri
Area Indigenas Surucucu
Reserva Biológica de Mucajaí
A I Raimundão
Wichabai
Dadanawa
1000
Pico Redondo
Apiaú
Serra do Apilaú
Serrinha
Caubi
1150 Serra Grande (Carauná)
F Machidpawa
Sawariwau
Awaruwa
Wariwau
1047
Serra do Mucajai
Mucajai
A I Muriru
Rupununi
Orinoco
Cerro Delgado Chalbaud
Ugueto
Catrimani
RORAIMA
Col Agricola de Preta
Antonio Andrade
Serra Dalua
Urubu
Aishalt
Lumidpau
2
Achiwiub
Cusubuateri
Va Nova
Maloca Camaleão
Marudi Mtns
Area Indigenas Tootototbi
Serras do Demini
Area Indigenas Jundiá
Estação Ecológica de Caracaraí
Caracaraí
Serra Balata
Area Indigenas Jacamim
Kuyuwini Lodge
Aratabiteri
Missão Tootototbi
Missão Catrimani
Caracarai
Vista Alegre
Barauna
Serra Baruana
527
Katit
Sna Urucuzeiro
1189
Pico Rondon
Anta
Serra da Mocidade
Itá
Serra Anauá
Kamoa Mtns
Konashen
Serra Gurupira
Demini
Raul
Bacabal
Anauá
1009
Sipu
Pico Tabatinga
Reserva Biológica Uatuma
Viruna
Novo Paraiso
Novo
Area Indigenas Uai-Uai
Serra A
A I Gurupira
Serra Tabatinga
Ressaca do Bacaba
Moderna
A I Ajuricaba
Jaqueira
José de Anauá
Ilha Onofre
Paca
Anauá
São Luis
São João da Baliza
Jandia
Serrinha
Uberlândia
Bea Branca
Cordazal
Branco
BR-174
Padauari
Demini
Xeriuini
Ilha Catrimani
Catrimani
Buraco
Jatapuzinho
Terra Vermelha
3
Curuduri
Ilha Curuá
Redenção
Jatapu
Bela Vista
Arara Vermelha
378
Telheiro
Carimau
Juiguara
Pretinho
Ilha Silva
Tapera
Curupira
Santa Rosa
Jatacuá
Negro
Tomar
Romão
Flechal
Jauaperi
Santana
Boiacu
Posto FUNAI
Serra do Urupi
Novo Pensamento
Preto
Pote
Ilha Matada
Itaubal
Alalaú
Criminosa
São João
Jufari
Posto FUNAI
Taboca
Barcelos
Campinho
S José
Area Indigenas Waimiri Atroari
Pitinga
Cumaru
Atauba
Caurés
Marova
Manacauaca
Bom Futuro
Posto FUNAI
S Paulo
Tapera
S Antônio do Abunari
Carvoeiro
Carunã
Moura
Serra Dourada
Represa de Balbina
Preta
Vila Nova
Faz Tropicália
Arraia
Unini
Prosperanca
Faz Boa Esperanca
4
Panema
Samaúma
Curiuaú
Arara
Pombas
Foz do Jaú
Faz Rio Branco
Pauini
Maranhoto
Ad Vila Batista
Balbina
Macaco
Faz Igrejinha
Presidente Figueiredo
Miriti
Parque Nacional do Jaú
Tambor
Repartimento
Faz Martel
Uatumã
Negro
Morena
Oncas
Faz Nova Esperanca
Faz Maringá
Faz Monte Rosa
Nonato
Jaú
Paratuba
Santo Antônio
BR-174
Preto
Mucura
Taboca
Bobrado
Estação Ecológica de Anavilhanas
da Eva
R F Walter Egler
Lindóla
Caju
Carabinani
Boa Vista
Codeagro
Novo Airão
Piorini
Morcego
Arquipélago Anavilhanas
Quartel
Rio Preto da Eva
L Grande de Manacapuru
382
Mucura
Eva
Faz Carijós
Manacapuru
F Adolfo Ducke
AMAZONAS
Faz Mucuim
Cigarro
Manacapuru
MANAUS
Amatari
Vila Nazaré
Badajós
L Badajós
Iranduba
Ilha do Careiro
Careiro da Várzea
Bonsucesso

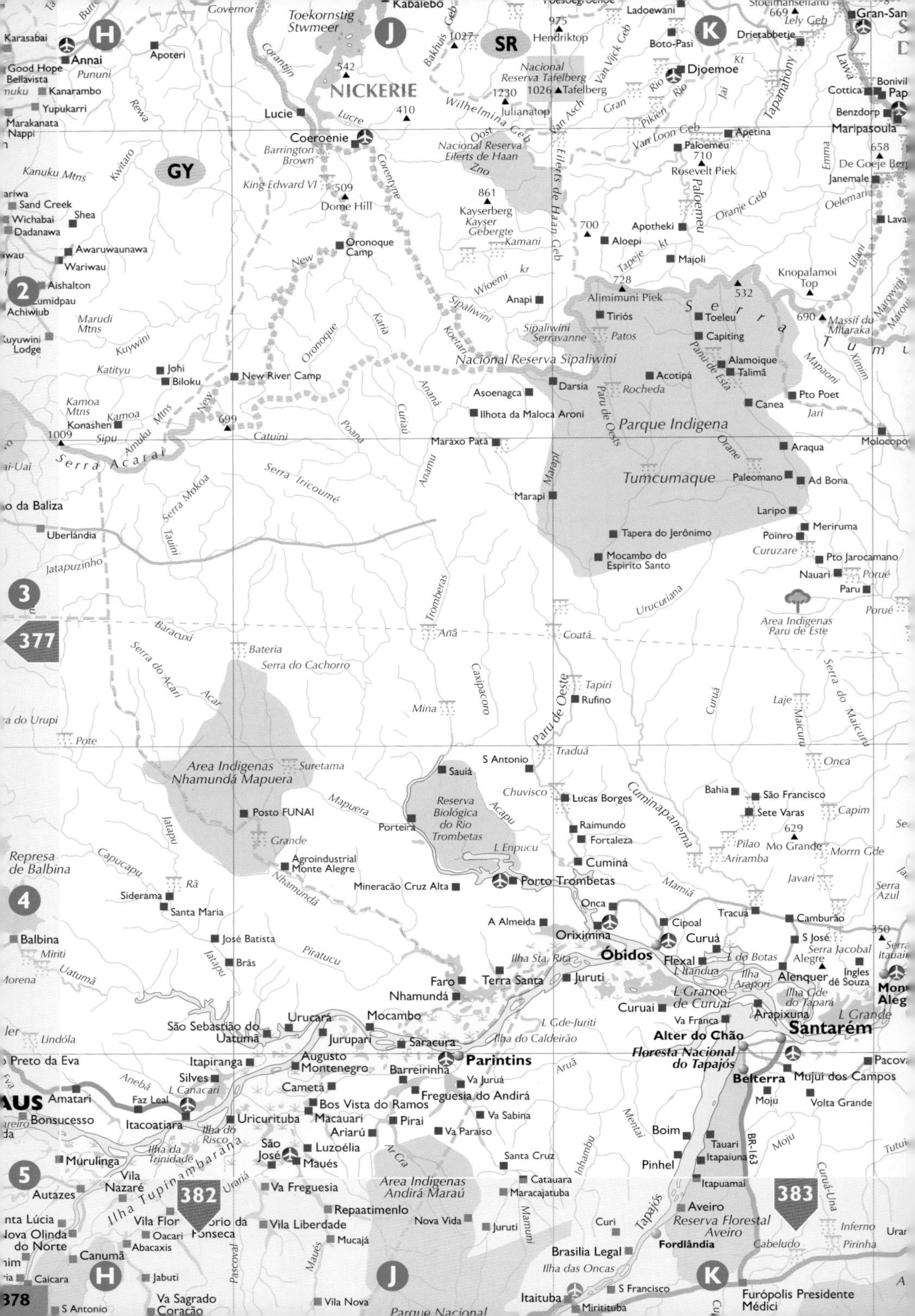
H
J
K
SR
GY
NICKERIE
2
3
4
5
377
382
383
Karasabai
Annai
Apoteri
Governor
Toekornstig Stwmeer
Kabalebo
Good Hope
Bellavista
Pununi
Kanarambo
Yupukarri
Marakanata
Nappi
Rewa
Corantijn
542
410
Lucie
Lucre
Coeroenie
Barrington Brown
Kwitaro
Kanuku Mtns
King Edward VI
509
Dome Hill
Corentyne
Sand Creek
Shea
Wichabai
Dadanawa
Awaruwaunawa
Wariwau
Oronoque Camp
New
Aishalton
Achiwiub
Marudi Mtns
Kuyuwini Lodge
Kuywini
Oronoque
Karia
Katityu
Johi
Biloku
New River Camp
Kamoa Mtns
Kamoa
Konashen
Amuku Mtns
699
1009
Sipu
Catuini
Serra Acarai
Poana
Curiaú
Ananá
Bakhuis Geb
1027
975
Hendriktop
Nacional Reserva Tafelberg
1230
1026
Tafelberg
Julianatop
Wilhelmina Geb
Oost
Nacional Reserva Eilerts de Haan
Zno
Van Asch
Eilerts de Haan Geb
861
Kayserberg
Kayser Gebergte
Kamani
Wioemi
kr
Sipaliwini
Koetari
Anapi
Van Vijck Geb
Ladoewani
Boto-Pasi
Djoemoe
Gran Rio
Pikien Rio
Jai
Kt
Tapanahony
Drietabbetje
669
Lely Geb
Gran-San
Lawa
Bonivil
Cottica
Pap
Benzdorp
Maripasoula
Van Loon Geb
Apetina
Paloemeu
710
Rosevelt Piek
Emma
658
De Goeje Berg
Janemale
Oelemari
Oranje Geb
700
Apotheki
Aloepi
Majoli
Tapeje
Lava
Lilani
Knopalamoi Top
728
Alimimuni Piek
532
Tiriós
Serra Tumuc
Toeleu
690
Massif du Mitaraka
Marowini
Sipaliwini Serravanne
Patos
Capiting
Nacional Reserva Sipaliwini
Alamoique
Talimã
Mapaoni
Ximim
Paru de Este
Acotipá
Darsia
Asoenagca
Rocheda
Pto Poet
Canea
Jari
Ilhota da Maloca Aroni
Paru de Oeste
Parque Indigena
Tumcumaque
Molocopo
Maraxo Patá
Anamu
Serra Iricoumé
Serra Mokoa
Marapi
Orane
Araqua
Paleomano
Ad Bona
Laripo
Meriruma
Poinro
Curuzare
Tapera do Jerônimo
Mocambo do Espirito Santo
Pto Jarocamano
Nauari
Porué
Paru
Area Indigenas Paru de Este
Urucuriana
o da Baliza
Uberlândia
Tauini
Jatapuzinho
Trombetas
Anã
Coatá
Baracuxi
Bateria
Serra do Cachorro
Serra do Acari
Acar
Caxipacoro
Tapiri
Rufino
Curuá
Laje
Maicuru
Serra do Maicuru
Mina
a do Urupi
Pote
Traduá
S Antonio
Sauiá
Onca
Area Indigenas Nhamundá Mapuera
Suretama
Mapuera
Posto FUNAI
Jatapu
Grande
Porteira
Reserva Biológica do Rio Trombetas
Acapu
Chuvisco
Lucas Borges
Cuminapanema
Bahia
São Francisco
Sete Varas
Capim
629
Raimundo
Fortaleza
Pilao
Mo Grande
Arirramba
Morrn Gde
Represa de Balbina
Capucapu
Agroindustrial Monte Alegre
L Enpucu
Cuminá
Javari
Serra Azul
Nhamundá
Rã
Siderama
Santa Maria
Mineracão Cruz Alta
Porto Trombetas
Mamiá
Onca
Tracua
Camburão
A Almeida
Cipoal
350
Balbina
José Batista
Oriximiná
Curuá
S José
Miriti
Uatumã
Piratucu
Brás
Ilha Sta. Rita
Óbidos
Flexal
L do Botas
Serra Jacobal
Alegre
Serra Itauai
Morena
Juruti
L Itandua
Ilha Arapori
Alenquer
Ingles dê Souza
Faro
Terra Santa
L Granoe de Curuai
Ilha Gde do Tapará
Monte Alegre
Nhamundá
Curuai
Arapixuna
L Grande
São Sebastião do Uatumã
Urucará
Mocambo
L Gde-Juriti
Va Franca
Lindóla
Jurupari
Saracura
Ilha do Caldeirão
Alter do Chão
Santarém
Preto da Eva
Itapiranga
Augusto Montenegro
Parintins
Floresta Nacional do Tapajós
Pacoval
Silves
Anebá
L Canacari
Barreirinha
Aruã
Va Juruá
Belterra
Mujui dos Campos
AUS
Amatari
Faz Leal
Cametá
Freguesia do Andirá
Moju
Volta Grande
Bonsucesso
Itacoatiara
Uricurituba
Bos Vista do Ramos
Macauari
Va Sabina
Mentai
Boim
Pirai
Ariarú
Va Paraíso
Ilha do Risco
Ilha da Trinidade
São José
Luzoélia
Maués
Ar Cra
Inhambu
Tauari
BR-163
Tutui
Murulinga
Santa Cruz
Pinhel
Itapaiuna
Vila Nazaré
Ilha Tupinambarana
Uraria
Va Freguesia
Area Indigenas Andirá Maraú
Cataurara
Maracajatuba
Itapuamai
Curuá-Una
Autazes
Repaatimenlo
Tapajós
Aveiro
Reserva Florestal Aveiro
Santa Lúcia
Vila Flor
Fonseca
Vila Liberdade
Nova Vida
Juruti
Mamuri
Curi
Inferno
Nova Olinda do Norte
Oacari
Abacaxis
Mucajá
Fordlândia
Cabeludo
Pirinha
Canumã
Maués
Brasilia Legal
Pascoval
Ilha das Oncas
Caicara
Jabuti
Itaituba
S Francisco
Furópolis Presidente Médici
S Antonio
Va Sagrado Coracão
Vila Nova
Parque Nacional
Miritituba

Régina
Kaw
Baie d'Oyapock
Belizon
Guillaume
Coco
Ouanary
Approuague
Cabo Orange
Parque Nacional de Cabo Orange
Sophie
Mana
Arataye
St-Georges de l'Oyapock
Oiapoque
Certitude
760
Belvédere
Popote
ROURA
Cabo Caciporé
Mt Bellevue de l'Inini
Saül
GF
Saut Grand Canori
Clevlandia do Norte
Mte Tipac
851
Bicade
Degrad Roche
Maïpouri
Oyapock
S João do Caciporé
Area Indigenas Uaca
Cainopi
Oiapoque
BR-156
Vila Velha
845
Massif Tabulaire
Inipi
St-Pierre
Ponta Grande
Oscar
Marupi
Anotaié
Cunani
476
Yaroupi
Cacipora
Serra Lombarda
Alice
Almeriana
635
Mt St Marcel
Regina
Calcoene
Trois Sauts
Lourenco
562
Mte Itu
541
Ponta da Pescada
Estação Ecológica de Maracá-Jipioca
Ilha de Maracá
Amapa
Piquiá
Ilha Jipioca
250
Cabo Norte
Sucuriju
Amapari
L Garera Novo
Reserva Biológica do Lago Piratuba
AMAPÁ
Area Indigenas Waiãpi
Anta
Tartarugal Grande
Ilha Juruá
Angelim
L Mutuco
Aporema
Sete Ilhas
S Miguel
Desespero
Serra do Curunuri
Ponta Grossa
Santa Cruz
Serra do Navio
Cotias
Bailique
Serra de Irarapuru
Araguari
Ilha Bailique
Pedra Branca
Ferreira Gomes
Ilha do Brique
Cachorrinho
Buritizal
Ilha Curuá
Porto Grande
S Luzia do Pacui
Oupixi
Cupixi
Ponta do Santarém
Jari
Flechal
Canmo
Gaivota
Ilha Januacu
Aurucuopatari
Vila Nova
S Antonio
Canal do Norte
S Sebastiao da Vicosa
Pto Arari
Abacate
Matapi
Ilha Vicosa
Ilha Nova
Amaipi
Ilha S Bento
Ilha Caviana
Porto Santana
Macapá
Arquipélago Jurupari
Carecuru
Angelim
Ilha Caras
Canal Perigoso
Estação Ecológica do Jari
Ilha Queimada
B do Vieira
Ilha Mexicana
Mazagão Velho
Mazagao
Afuá
Ilha Ganhoão
Planalto Maracanaquará
Chaves
Canal do Sul
Ilha Camaleão
Ilha dos Porcos
Ilha dos Cavalos
Agua Branca
Baturité
Ilha Charapucu
Cabo Maguarinh
Santa Clara
Ilha Gde Vieira
Cajuuna
Itatupã
S Cruz do Arari
228
Santónio
Beiradão
Ilha Anajás
Monte Dourado
Ilha Mututi
São Luis
Cajari
Ilha Capinal
Anajás
Mocães
L Arari
Soure
Mungaba
Ilha Japichaua
Salvaterra
Parnagua
Jari
Vida Nova
Ilha de Marajó
Arari
Camara do Marajó
Vigia
Curumu
Anajás
Colares
228
Tueré
Serra do Almeirim
Boca do Jari
Ilha Urutai
Ilha Grande de Gurupá
Cach do Arari
Baia de Marajó
Areias
359
Jutai
Arumanduba
S Miguel dos Macacos
Reserva Biológica do Marajó
Anabiú
Paranaquará
Ilha do Comandai
Gurupá
Mosqueiro
Amazonas
Almeirim
Ilha Urucuricaia
Antônio Lemos
Benevides
Pta de Pedras
Prainha
Vilarinho do Monte
Carrazedo
Laguna
Muana
Ilha Futurosa
Barcarena
Porto de Moz
Breves
Piria
BELÉM (PARÁ)
S Sebastião da Boa Vista
Reserva Florestal Caxiuana
B de Caxiuna
Melgaco
Curralinho
Pará
Ilha Sirituba
Limoeiro do Ajuru
Abaetetuba
Portel
Bagre
Joana Coeli
Veiros
Moju
Acará
Prdreira
Oeiras do Para
Igarape-Miri
Caju
Xingu
Cametá
Curucambabe
Pombal
394
Acarai
Pacajá
Camaraipi
Juaba
Carapajó
S Pedro de Viseu
Moiraba
Moju
Tomé-Acu
Anapu
Senador José Porfirio
Manjeiro
Jurupari
Mocajuba
Acará
Quatro Boca
Independencia
Vira e Volta
Baião
Area Indigenas Anambe
Quia
Vitória
Ilha de Bacuri
Altamira
Serra do Tapará
Belo Monte
Cairari
Acará-Mirim
Penatecaua
Favânia
Serra da Piranga
Tocantins
BR-230
229
Tubarão
Uriuaná
Aratu
Ilha Grande de Jutai
Tailândia
Joana Peres
Caima
RODOVIA
384
Acarirema
Pindobal
Nazaré dos Patos
Pedra Alta
Area Indigenas Trocará
Capim
Alto Pacalá
42
Reserva Indigenas Cararao
Camaleão
Pacajá
Goianésia
Tucuruý
Sport
Caião
Mana
Tampoc
Cricou
Marupi
Iaué
Mururé
Araguari
Tajaui
Mutum
Falsine
Maraca
Irataparuru
Moucouro
Ipitinga
Paru
Uruará
Guajará
Jaraucu
Pracupi
Pacajá
Jacundá
Bacajá
2
3
4
5
L
M
N

A
B
C
PE
5
6
7
8
Estrecho
Esperanza
Chorrera
Vidal
Algodón
Yaguas
Alegria
Santa Clara
Santa Sofia
Tonanti
Cuiabá
Soledade
Napo
Bellavista
Negro Urco
Tutapisco
Oro Blanco
Yarina
Francisco de Orellana
Ipora
Tbo Anguilla
Pucaurquillo
Pebas
Tarma
Ampiyacu
Tarapacá
Villa Ciencia
Mucuripi
Ipiranga
San Guilherme
Ica
Santo Antônio
Cotuhé
Buenos Aires
Parque Nacional Natural Amacayacu
Puruté
Purutrê
Jacurapá
Ilha Caturia
Amataura
Santa Rita do Weil
Area Indigenas Vui-Uata
S Paulo de Olivenca
Nova Italia
Area Indigenas Tikuna Evare II
Area Indigenas Tikuna Evare I
Momón
Mazán
Indiana
Amazonas
Apayacu
Huata
Atacuari
Aguirre
Santa Maria de Nanay
Ilha Padre
Ilha Iquitos
Iquitos
Pto Soledad
Orosa
Pichana
Peruaté
Pto España
Atacuari
Loreto
Calderón
Caballococha
Lupana
Timareo
Ilha Tarapoto
126
Munichis
Ungurahue
San Pablo de Loreto
Leticia
Boa Esperanca
Peña Blanca
Tbo Tello
Area Indigenas Aldeia Lameirão
Ramón Castilla
Tabatinga
Feijoal
Area Indigenas Tikuna de Feijoal
Desengaño
Bela Vista
Amelia
Atalaia do Norte
Benjamin Constant
Itaya
Bosmediano
Puritania
San Fernando
Iracema
Tembladera
Javari
Area Indigenas Lauro Sodré
Bóia
Vista
Colonia Barrosa
Mirim
Yavari
Nauta
Yarapa
Santa Ana
Santa Fé
Estirão do Equador
Boca do Itui
Area Indigenas Tikuna São Leopoldo
Boa
Cajueiro
S Bento
Botafogo
Quixito
Curuca
Itui
Jandiatuba
Bagazán
Paz Engano
S Antonio
Boa Vista
Eureka
Palmeiras do Javari
Argemiro
Genaro Herrera
Requena
120
Canamã
Santa Cruz
Colonia Angamos
Posto Indig Marubo
90
Curuena
Bom Futuro
Zapote
Gálvez
Pardo
Nova Vida
Pajurá
Blanco
Santa Sofia
Toledo
Area Indigenas do Vale do Javari
AMAZONAS
Mutumzinho
Mutum
Nova Alejandria
Progreso
Santa Elena
Tarpacá
Bom Jesus
Jutaí
Cubiu
Remanso
Juruá
Gaviãozinho
Liquidación
Arojo
Itaquai
Eirunepé
Três Unidos
Punga
Bolognesi
Psto Indig Curuca
Itui
Seringal Condor
Deixa-Falar
Seringal da Foz
Rodrihues
Alto Yavari
Nova Lorque
Penedo
Tambaqui
Torre da Lua
Vila Martins
Area Indigenas Kanamari do Rio Juruá
Conta
Reconquista
Juruá
Serraria Sacado do Humaitá
Ipixuna
Boca do Conceicão
Buretama
Envira
Ana-Maria
Tapiara
Escondido
Area Indigenas Kulina do Medio Juruá
Faz Santa Maria
Santa Maria
Queimada
Negro
S João
Ipixuna
Estirão do Robojo
Estrema
Bom Intento
Itucuma
Céu Aberto
A I Nucuni
609
A I Poianava
S José
Curu
Gregório
Atalaia
Envira
S Vicente
Cajueiro
Moa
Faz Trombetas
Mochila
S Antônio
Serra
Gibraltar
S Bárbara
Tarauacá
Faz Pederval
Guajará
Lorena
Macucauá
Novo Mundo
Pauini
Rio Branco
Azul
Iapim
Cruzeiro do Sul
Havre
Boco do Rio Preto
Saúde
Pólo Norte
Atucatiquini
Mancio Lima
Lagoinha
Santa Fé
Seringal Macatatuba
Ilusão
Sierra
Três Bocas
Moura
Nova Cintra
Area Indigenas Campinas
Bom Futuro
Acuruauá
Caica
Boch
Area Indigenas Jaminauá
A I Feijó
A I Igarapé Paroá
Boqueirão
Liberdade
Jurupari
Seringal Reforma
Jroquinea
878
Leôncio Rodrigues
Tarauacá
Feijó
Abujao
Chico Mana
São Luis
Juruá
Mirim
Porto Walter
Cocameira
Ouro
A I Igarapé Gaúcho
Pto Santos
Cuntamana
do
Divisor
Natal
Area Indigenas Arara-Ig Humaitá
Area Indigenas Rio Gregório
BR-364
Abujao
Ouro Preto
Joaci
Veneza
Humaitá
do
Juriti
Macapá
Flora
Sta Helena
Santa Fé
Masisea
Parque Nacional da Serra do Divisor
Grajaú
Muru
Aliança
Pto Alegre
Juruá
Seringal Canadá
Manuel Urbano
Chauya Cocha
Triunfo
Area Indigenas Jaminauá-Arara
Guajará
Paraná
ACRE
Mamoeiro
Sena Madureira
138
L Inuria
Tamaya
Pto Putaya
Marechal Taumaturgo
Purus
A I Fronteira
Platanal
Pto Silva
Tejo
Area Indigenas Kaxinawá do Rio Humaitá
Area Indigenas Kaxinawá Nova Olinda
A I Alto Rio Purus
Seringal Granja
Boca do Macauã
Amônia
A I Igarapé do Pau
Caeté
Seringal Barracãozinho
Area Indigenas Kampa do Rio Amônia
Santa Rosa
San Luis
La Copa
Foz do Breu
Foz do Jordão
Seringal Triunfo
Area Indigenas Kaxinawá do Rio Jordão
Jaminauá
Santa Rosa
Sheshea
Breu
Envira
Pto Calay
Vista Alegre
Yapara
Puerto Portillo
431
Esperanza
Hugo Carneiro
Cumaria
Dimpolis
Cochicha
Chandless
Macauá
Iaco
Irruya
Area Indigenas Kampa do Rio Envira
Curanja
Seringal Belo Horizonte
Celtiberia
San Gregorio
Liberdade
Toroyuc
Balta
Faz Canamari
Bolognesi
UCAYALI
Curanja
Sindrichal
Purus
Avelino Chaves
Mapinguari
Tahuania
Floresta
Espalha
San Pedro
Faz São José
Mapuya
Faz Petrópolis
Cocama
338
Xapuri
Alto
Area Indigenas Mamoadate
Sai Cinza
Xapuri
Mapuya
Inuya
Puesto Varadero
Ucayali
280
Pto Inuya
Alerta
Chandless
Acre
Assis Brasil
Atalaya
Colonia Penal del Sepa
Yaco
Estação Ecológica do Rio Acre
Iñapari
Bolpebra
Cobija
Brasiléia
Unine
Cujar
Noaya
Sepa
Shepahua
Tahuamanú
Vespas
Nazareth
Tahua
Shepahua
Pto Ceticayo
Pto Chiclayo
Porvenir

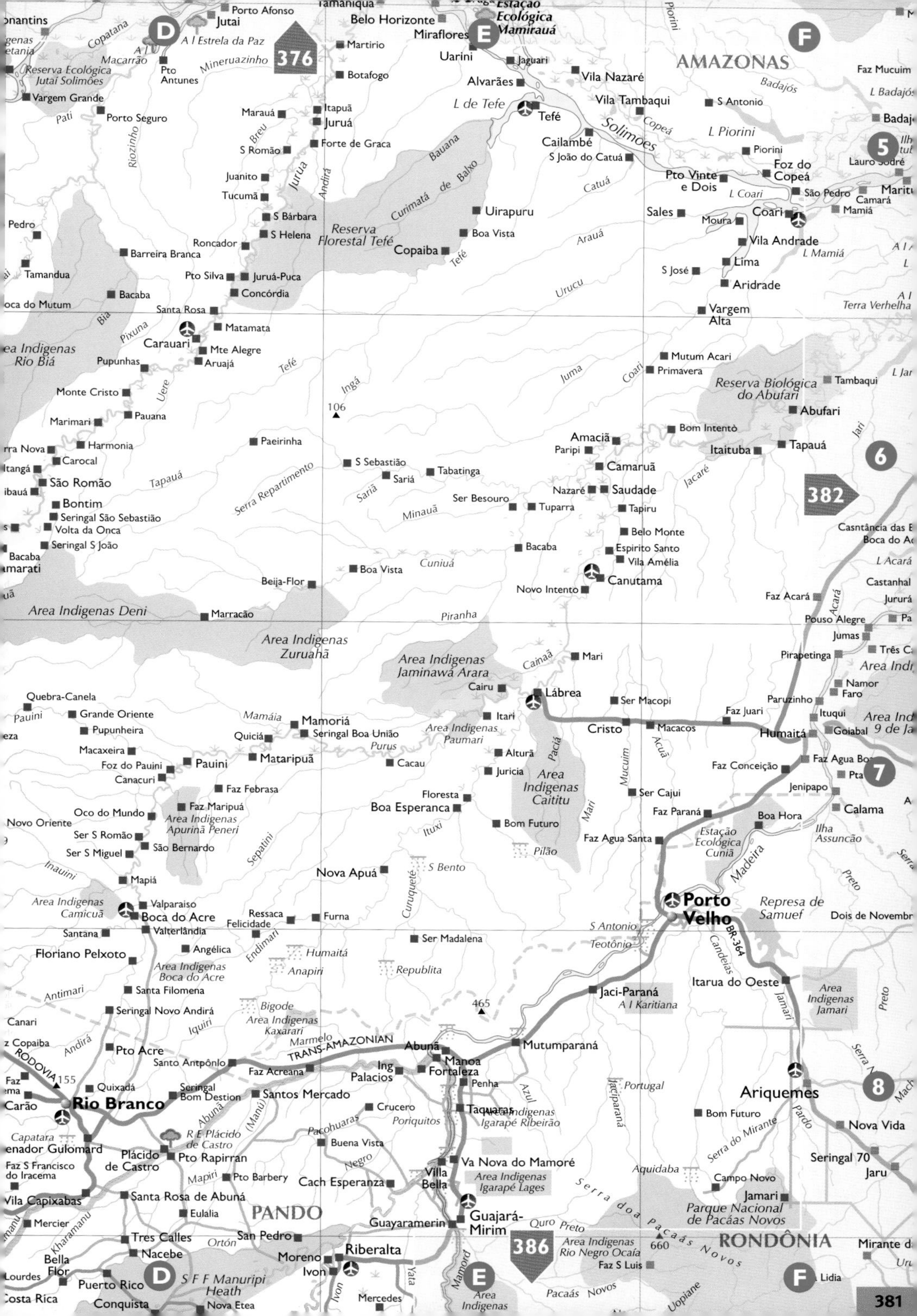

Porto Afonso
Jutai
Belo Horizonte
Estação Ecológica Mamirauá
Miraflores
Uarini
D
E
F
A I Estrela da Paz
Copatana
Macarrão
376
Martirio
Jaguari
AMAZONAS
Faz Mucuim
Reserva Ecológica Jutaí Solimões
Pto Antunes
Mineruazinho
Botafogo
Alvarães
Vila Nazaré
Badajós
L Badajós
Vargem Grande
Pati
Porto Seguro
Maraué
Itapuã
Juruá
L de Tefe
Tefé
Vila Tambaqui
S Antonio
Badajós
Riozinho
Breu
S Romão
Forte de Graca
Bauana
Cailambé
Solimoes
Copeá
L Piorini
S João do Catuá
Piorini
5
Juanito
Tucumã
Jurua
Andirá
Curimatá de Balxo
Catuá
Pto Vinte e Dois
Foz do Copeá
Lauro Sodré
São Pedro
Camará
Maritu
L Coari
Coari
Mamiá
Pedro
S Bárbara
S Helena
Reserva Florestal Tefé
Uirapuru
Sales
Moura
Boa Vista
Arauá
Vila Andrade
Roncador
Barreira Branca
Copaiba
Tefé
L Mamiá
Tamandua
Pto Silva
Juruá-Puca
Lima
S José
Aridrade
Bacaba
Concórdia
Urucu
Terra Verhelha
oca do Mutum
Santa Rosa
Vargem Alta
Bia
Pixuna
Matamata
Carauari
Mte Alegre
Area Indigenas Rio Biá
Pupunhas
Aruajá
Tefé
Mutum Acari
Primavera
Juma
Coari
Reserva Biológica do Abufari
Tambaqui
L Jari
Monte Cristo
Uere
Ingá
106
Abufari
Marimari
Pauana
Bom Intento
Amaciã
Harmonia
Paeirinha
Paripi
Itaituba
Tapauá
Jari
6
rra Nova
Carocal
S Sebastião
Camaruã
Tapauá
Sariá
Tabatinga
Jacaré
São Romão
Serra Repartimento
Sariã
Nazaré
Saudade
382
Bontim
Ser Besouro
Tuparra
Tapiru
Seringal São Sebastião
Minauã
Volta da Onca
Belo Monte
Casntância das B
Boca do Ac
Seringal S João
Bacaba
Espirito Santo
Vila Amélia
Bacaba
L Acará
Cuniuá
Boa Vista
Canutama
Beija-Flor
Novo Intento
Castanhal
Faz Acará
Juruá
Acará
Area Indigenas Deni
Marracão
Piranha
Pouso Alegre
Jumas
Area Indigenas Zuruahã
Mari
Area Indigenas Jaminawá Arara
Cainaã
Pirapetinga
Três C
Area Indi
Cairu
Lábrea
Namor
Faro
Quebra-Canela
Paruzinho
Pauini
Grande Oriente
Mamáia
Ser Macopi
Itari
Faz Juari
Ituqui
Area Ind
9 de Ja
Pupunheira
Mamoriá
Seringal Boa União
Area Indigenas Paumari
Cristo
Macacos
Humaitá
Goiabal
Quiciá
Purus
Macaxeira
Acuã
Pacia
Mucuim
Alturã
Faz Agua Bo
Foz do Pauini
Pauini
Matariputã
Cacau
Juricia
Faz Conceição
Pta
7
Canacuri
Area Indigenas Caititu
Ser Cajui
Jenipapo
Faz Febrasa
Floresta
Faz Maripuá
Boa Esperanca
Calama
Oco do Mundo
Area Indigenas Apurinã Peneri
Faz Paraná
Boa Hora
Novo Oriente
Ituxi
Mari
Bom Futuro
Ser S Romão
Estação Ecológica Cuniã
Ilha Assuncão
São Bernardo
Faz Agua Santa
Ser S Miguel
Sepatini
Pilão
Madeira
Inauini
S Bento
Mapiá
Nova Apuá
Preto
Curuquetê
Area Indigenas Camicuã
Valparaiso
Porto Velho
Represa de Samuef
Boca do Acre
Ressaca
Felicidade
Furna
Dois de Novembr
Santana
Valterlândia
S Antonio
BR-364
Endimari
Teotônio
Ser Madalena
Angélica
Candeias
Humaitá
Floriano Pelxoto
Anapiri
Republita
Area Indigenas Boca do Acre
Itarua do Oeste
Antimari
Area Indigenas Jamari
Santa Filomena
Jaci-Paraná
Jamari
Preto
A I Karitiana
Bigode
Seringal Novo Andirá
465
Canari
Area Indigenas Kaxarari
Iquiri
z Copaiba
Marmelo
Mutumparaná
Andirá
TRANS-AMAZONIAN
Abunã
Pto Acre
RODOVIA
Manoa
Santo Antpônlo
Faz Acreana
Ing
Fortaleza
Palacios
Penha
Portugal
8
155
Quixadá
Seringal Bom Destion
Ariquemes
Carão
Santos Mercado
Azul
Rio Branco
Crucero
Taquaras
Area Indigenas Igarapé Ribeirão
Bom Futuro
Pardo
Nova Vida
Poriquitos
Jaciparanã
Capatara
Abunã
Pacohuaras
R E Plácido de Castro
Serra do Mirante
enador Gulomard
Buena Vista
Plácido de Castro
(Manú)
Seringal 70
Faz S Francisco do Iracema
Pto Rapirran
Negro
Va Nova do Mamoré
Jaru
Aquidaba
Mapiri
Pto Barbery
Villa Bella
Area Indigenas Igarapé Lages
Campo Novo
Cach Esperanza
Vila Capixabas
Serra dos Pacaás Novos
Santa Rosa de Abuná
Jamari
Parque Nacional de Pacáas Novos
Mercier
PANDO
Eulalia
Kharamanu
Guayaramerin
Guajará-Mirim
Ouro Preto
Tres Calles
Ortón
San Pedro
386
Area Indigenas Rio Negro Ocaía
660
RONDÔNIA
Mirante d
Bella Flor
Nacebe
Riberalta
Moreno
Faz S Luis
Lourdes
Ivon
Yata
Mamoré
Puerto Rico
S F F Manuripi Heath
Lidia
Costa Rica
Conquista
Ivon
Mercedes
Nova Etea
Area Indigenas
Pacaás Novos
Uopiane

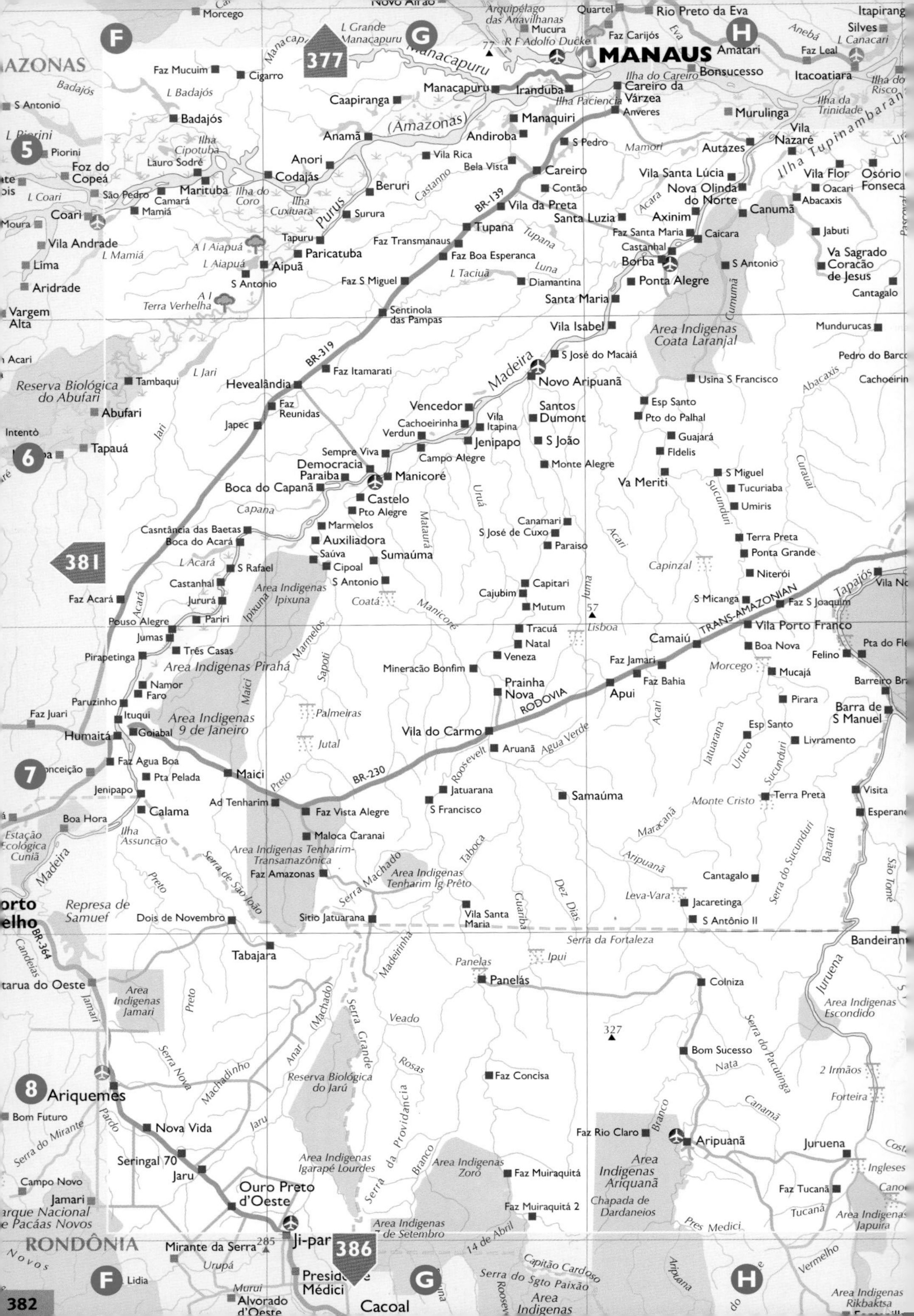
MANAUS
AMAZONAS
RONDÔNIA
377
381
386
F
G
H
5
6
7
8
Morcego
Arquipélago das Anavilhanas
Quartel
Rio Preto da Eva
Itapiranga
Silves
L Grande Manacapuru
Mucura
R F Adolfo Ducke
Faz Carijós
Anebá
L Canacari
Manacapuru
Eva
Amatari
Faz Leal
Faz Mucuim
Cigarro
Ilha do Careiro
Bonsucesso
Itacoatiara
Ilha do Risco
Badajós
L Badajós
Manacapuru
Iranduba
Careiro da Várzea
S Antonio
Caapiranga
Ilha Paciencia
Murulinga
Ilha da Trinidade
Badajós
(Amazonas)
Manaquiri
Anveres
Ilha Tupinambarana
L Piorini
Ilha Cipotuba
Anamã
Andiroba
S Pedro
Mamori
Autazes
Vila Nazaré
Piorini
Lauro Sodré
Anori
Vila Rica
Foz do Copeá
Codajás
Bela Vista
Careiro
Vila Santa Lúcia
Vila Flor
Osório Fonseca
Maritubá
Ilha do Coro
Beruri
Contão
Nova Olinda do Norte
Oacari
L Coari
São Pedro
Camará
Purus
Castanho
BR-139
Vila da Preta
Acara
Abacaxis
Mamiá
Ilha Cuxiuara
Surura
Santa Luzia
Axinim
Canumã
Coari
Moura
Tupana
Faz Santa Maria
Caicara
Jabuti
Vila Andrade
A I Aiapuá
Tapuru
Faz Transmanaus
Tupana
Castanhal
Va Sagrado Coração de Jesus
L Mamiá
Paricatuba
Faz Boa Esperanca
Borba
S Antonio
Lima
L Aiapuá
Aipuã
Luna
Ponta Alegre
L Taciuã
Faz S Miguel
Diamantina
Cantagalo
Aridrade
S Antonio
A I Terra Verhelha
Santa Maria
Cumumã
Vargem Alta
Sentinola das Pampas
Vila Isabel
Area Indigenas Coata Laranjal
Mundurucas
BR-319
Acari
L Jari
Faz Itamarati
S José do Macaiá
Pedro do Barco
Madeira
Reserva Biológica do Abufari
Tambaqui
Hevealândia
Novo Aripuanã
Usina S Francisco
Cachoeirinha
Abacaxis
Faz Reunidas
Vencedor
Santos Dumont
Esp Santo
Abufari
Japec
Cachoeirinha
Vila Itapina
Pto do Palhal
Intentò
Jari
Verdun
Jenipapo
S João
Guajará
Tapauá
Sempre Viva
Campo Alegre
Fidelis
Democracia
Monte Alegre
S Miguel
Curuaí
Paraiba
Manicoré
Va Meriti
Tucuriaba
Boca do Capanã
Castelo
Sucunduri
Umiris
Capana
Pto Alegre
Uruá
Marmelos
Mataurá
Canamari
Casntância das Baetas
S José de Cuxo
Boca do Acará
Auxiliadora
Acari
Terra Preta
Saúva
Sumaúma
Paraiso
Ponta Grande
L Acará
S Rafael
Cipoal
Capinzal
Tapajós
Area Indigenas Ipixuna
S Antonio
Capitari
Niterói
Castanhal
Vila Nova
Ipixuna
Cajubim
Juma
Jururá
Coatá
Manicoré
57
S Micanga
Faz S Joaquim
Faz Acará
Acará
Mutum
TRANS-AMAZONIAN
Pariri
Pouso Alegre
Tracuá
Lisboa
Camaiú
Vila Porto Franco
Jumas
Marmelos
Natal
Boa Nova
Pta do Fle
Três Casas
Pirapetinga
Sapoti
Veneza
Faz Jamari
Felino
Area Indigenas Pirahã
Mineracão Bonfim
Morcego
Mucajá
Namor
Maici
Faz Bahia
Prainha Nova
Barreiro Bra
Faro
RODOVIA
Apui
Paruzinho
Pirara
Barra de S Manuel
Palmeiras
Acari
Ituqui
Esp Santo
Faz Juari
Area Indigenas 9 de Janeiro
Humaitá
Goiabal
Jutal
Vila do Carmo
Jatuarana
Uruco
Livramento
Roosevelt
Aruanã
Agua Verde
Sucunduri
Conceição
Faz Agua Boa
Maici
Pta Pelada
Preto
BR-230
Jenipapo
Jatuarana
Samaúma
Monte Cristo
Terra Preta
Visita
Ad Tenharim
S Francisco
Calama
Faz Vista Alegre
Maracanã
Boa Hora
Esperança
Ilha Assuncão
Barararti
Estação Ecológica Cuniã
Maloca Caranai
Taboca
Area Indigenas Tenharim-Transamazônica
Aripuanã
Serra do Sucunduri
Madeira
São Tomé
Serra de São João
Preto
Faz Amazonas
Serra Machado
Area Indigenas Tenharim Ig Prêto
Dez Dias
Cantagalo
Guariba
Leva-Vara
Jacaretinga
Porto Velho
Represa de Samuel
Dois de Novembro
Sitio Jatuarana
Vila Santa Maria
S Antônio II
BR-364
Serra da Fortaleza
Bandeirant
Candeias
Tabajara
Madeirinha
Ipui
Panelas
Jamari
Panelás
Colniza
Juruena
Ariquemes
Area Indigenas Jamari
Preto
(Machado)
Serra Grande
Veado
Area Indigenas Escondido
327
Anar
Serra do Pacutinga
Serra Nova
Machadinho
Reserva Biológica do Jarú
Rosas
Bom Sucesso
Nata
2 Irmãos
Faz Concisa
Forteira
Bom Futuro
Pardo
Serra da Providancia
Canamã
Serra do Mirante
Nova Vida
Jaru
Branco
Faz Rio Claro
Aripuanã
Juruena
Costa
Area Indigenas Igarapé Lourdes
Area Indigenas Zoró
Area Indigenas Ariquanã
Seringal 70
Branco
Faz Muiraquitá
Ingleses
Campo Novo
Jaru
Ouro Preto d'Oeste
Faz Tucanã
Canoa
Jamari
Chapada de Dardaneios
Serra da
Faz Muiraquitá 2
Tucanã
Area Indigenas Japura
Parque Nacional de Pacaás Novos
Area Indigenas 7 de Setembro
Pres Medici
Mirante da Serra
285
Ji-paraná
14 de Abril
Vermelho
Novos
Urupá
Capitão Cardoso
Aripuana
Lidia
Presidente Médici
Serra do Sgto Paixão
Muruí
Roosevelt
Alvorado d'Oeste
Cacoal
Area Indigenas
Area Indigenas Rikbaktsa

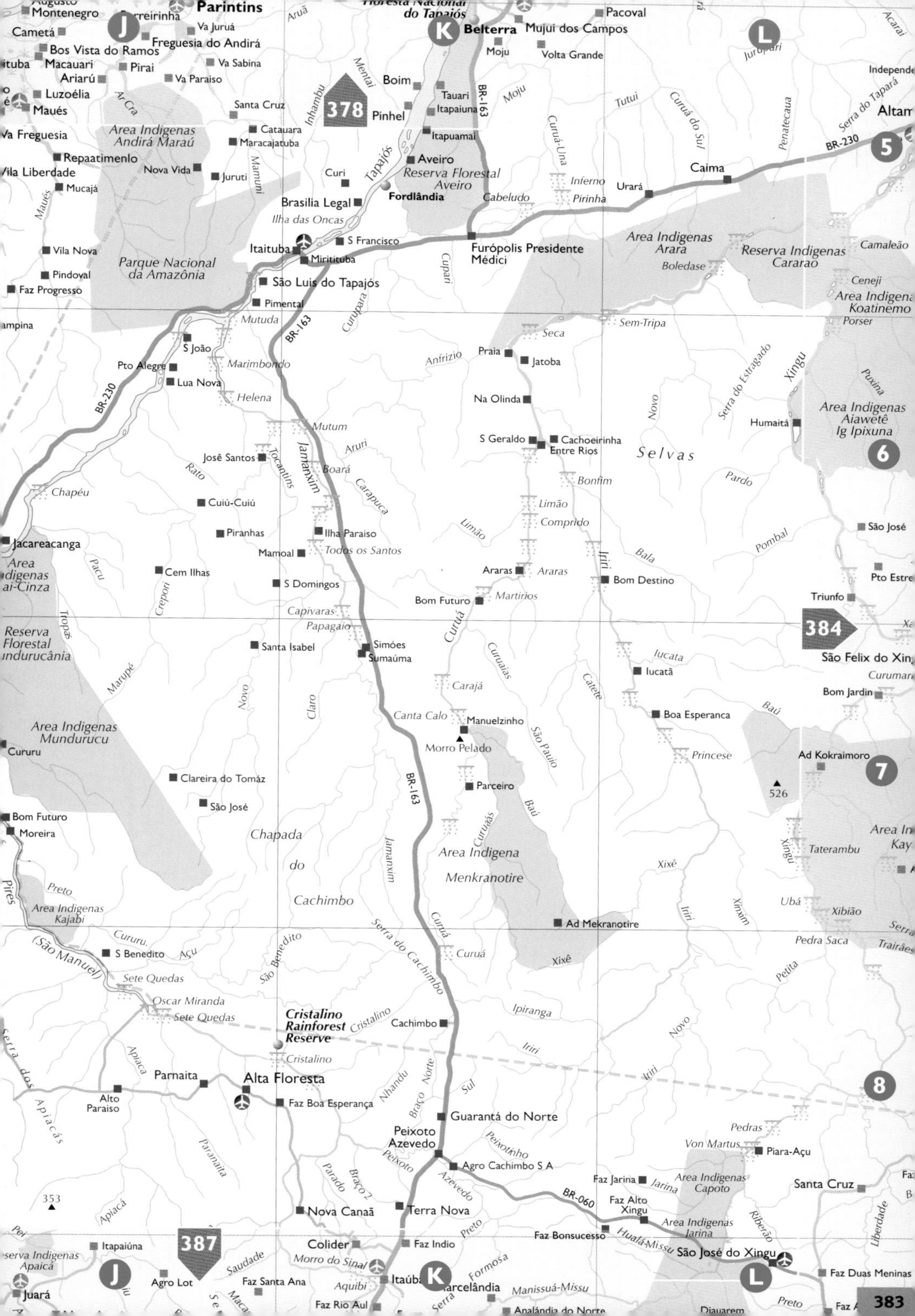

Montenegro
Parintins
Floresta Nacional do Tapajós
Pacoval
Cametá
J
Va Juruá
K
Belterra
Mujui dos Campos
L
Acarai
Freguesia do Andirá
Moju
Volta Grande
Bos Vista do Ramos
Aruã
Jurupari
Macauari
Pirai
Va Sabina
Mentai
Ariarú
Va Paraiso
Boim
Independe
Luzoélia
Tauari
BR-163
Moju
Tutui
Curuá do Sul
Serra do Tapará
Maués
Santa Cruz
378
Itapaiuna
Pinhel
Altam
Va Freguesia
Area Indigenas Andirá Maraú
Inhambu
Cataurara
Itapuamai
Curuá-Una
Penatecaua
BR-230
Maracajatuba
5
Repaatimenlo
Aveiro
Vila Liberdade
Nova Vida
Juruti
Mamuni
Curi
Tapajós
Reserva Florestal Aveiro
Caima
Mucajá
Inferno
Urará
Fordlândia
Cabeludo
Pirinha
Maués
Brasilia Legal
Ilha das Oncas
Itaituba
S Francisco
Furópolis Presidente Médici
Area Indigenas Arara
Reserva Indigenas Cararao
Camaleão
Vila Nova
Miritituba
Cupari
Boledase
Parque Nacional da Amazônia
Pindoval
São Luis do Tapajós
Ceneji
Faz Progresso
Area Indigena Koatinemo
Pimental
Curupara
Mutuda
Sem-Tripa
Porser
ampina
BR-163
Seca
S João
Praia
Jatoba
Serra do Estragado
Xingu
Pto Alegre
Marimbondo
Anfrizio
Lua Nova
Puxina
BR-230
Helena
Na Olinda
Novo
Area Indigenas Aiawetê Ig Ipixuna
Mutum
Humaitá
Aruri
S Geraldo
Cachoeirinha
Entre Rios
Jamanxim
Selvas
6
Josê Santos
Tocantins
Rato
Boará
Bonfim
Pardo
Carapuca
Chapéu
Limão
Cuiú-Cuiú
Comprido
Limão
São José
Piranhas
Ilha Paraiso
Jacareacanga
Iriri
Pombal
Todos os Santos
Mamoal
Bala
Area Indigenas ai-Cinza
Pacu
Cem Ilhas
Araras
Araras
Pto Estre
Crepori
S Domingos
Bom Destino
Martirios
Bom Futuro
Triunfo
Tropas
Capivaras
384
Reserva Florestal Mundurucânia
Papagaio
Simões
Sumaúma
Santa Isabel
Curuá
Curuaias
Iucata
São Felix do Xing
Iucatã
Curumar
Marupé
Carajá
Catete
Bom Jardin
Novo
Claro
Baú
Canta Calo
Manuelzinho
Boa Esperanca
Area Indigenas Mundurucu
São Pauio
Morro Pelado
Cururu
Princese
Ad Kokraimoro
7
BR-163
Clareira do Tomáz
Parceiro
526
Baú
São José
Bom Futuro
Curuaás
Area In Kay
Moreira
Chapada do Cachimbo
Area Indigena Menkranotire
Jamanxim
Xixê
Xingu
Taterambu
Pires
Preto
Area Indigenas Kajabi
Iriri
Xinxim
Ubá
Xibião
Serra do Cachimbo
Curuá
Ad Mekranotire
Serra
Cururu
São Benedito
Pedra Saca
Trairães
(São Manuel)
S Benedito
Açu
Curuá
Xixê
Petita
Sete Quedas
Oscar Miranda
Ipiranga
Sete Quedas
Cristalino Rainforest Reserve
Cristalino
Cachimbo
Novo
Serra dos
Iriri
Apiaca
Cristalino
Iriri
Parnaita
Alta Floresta
Norte
Sul
8
Alto Paraiso
Apiacás
Nhandu
Braço
Faz Boa Esperança
Guarantá do Norte
Paranaita
Peixoto Azevedo
Peixotinho
Pedras
Von Martus
Piara-Açu
Parado
Peixoto
Agro Cachimbo S A
Braço 2
Azevedo
Faz Jarina
Jarina
Area Indigenas Capoto
Santa Cruz
353
Apiacá
Nova Canaã
Terra Nova
BR-060
Faz Alto Xingu
Riberão
Liberdade
Pei
387
Preto
Faz Bonsucesso
Area Indigenas Jarina
Itapaiúna
Colider
Faz Indio
Huaiá-Missu
Reserva Indigenas Apiacá
Morro do Sinal
São José do Xingu
J
Saudade
K
Formosa
L
Faz Duas Meninas
Agro Lot
Faz Santa Ana
Aquibi
Itaúba
Marcelândia
Juará
Serra
Manissuá-Missu
Faz Rio Aul
Preto
Analândia do Norte
Diauarem

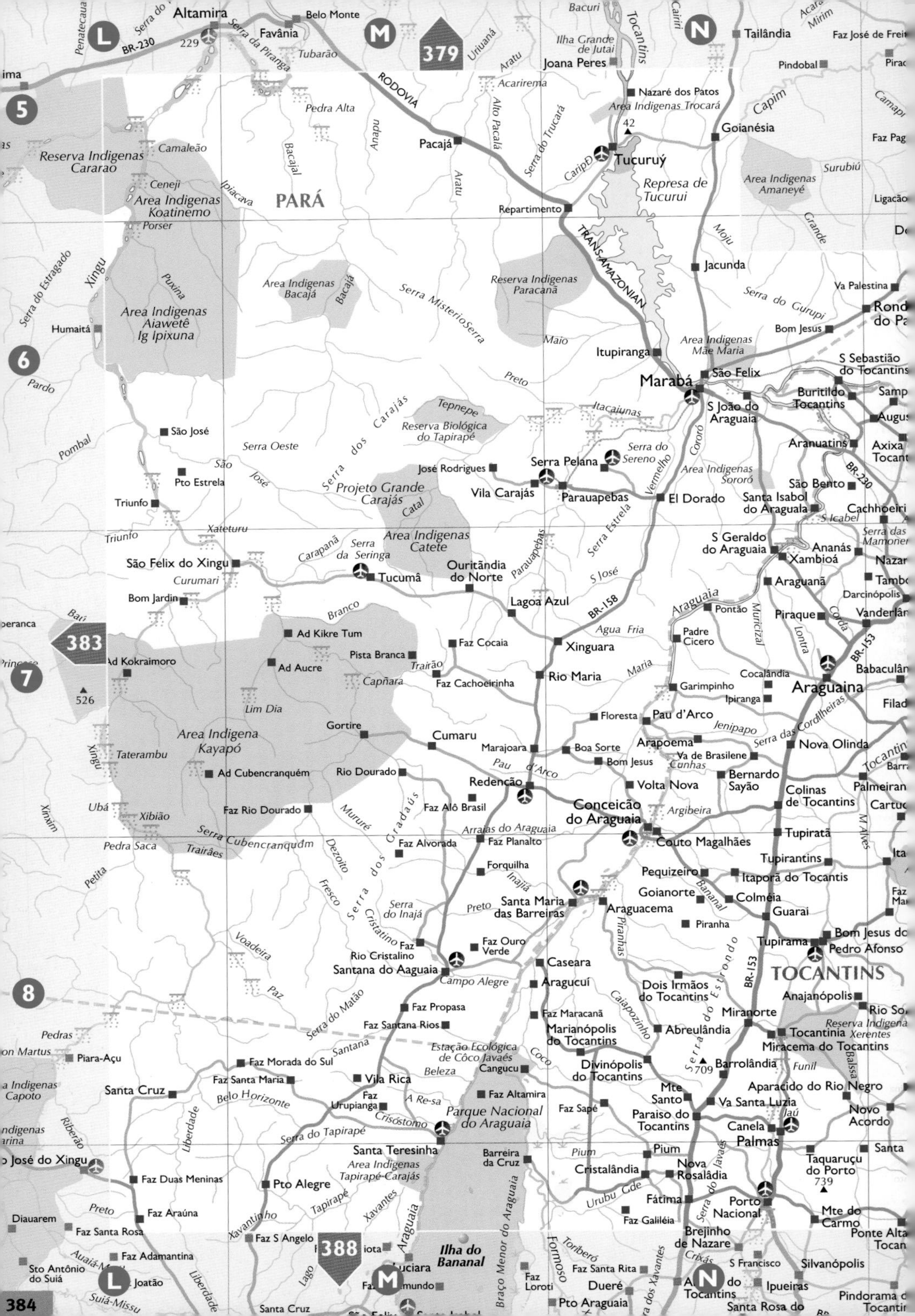

Altamira
Belo Monte
Favânia
Tubarão
BR-230
229
L
M
N
379
383
388
5
6
7
8
RODOVIA
Pacajá
Joana Peres
Ilha Grande de Jutai
Tocantins
Tailândia
Pindobal
Nazaré dos Patos
Area Indigenas Trocará
Tucuruý
Goianésia
Represa de Tucurui
Reserva Indigenas Cararao
Camaleão
Ceneji
Area Indigenas Koatinemo
Porser
PARÁ
Repartimento
TRANSAMAZONIAN
Jacunda
Area Indigenas Amaneyé
Area Indigenas Bacajá
Reserva Indigenas Paracanã
Serra Misterio Serra
Area Indigenas Aiawetê Ig Ipixuna
Humaitá
Xingu
Itupiranga
Area Indigenas Mãe Maria
Marabá
São Felix
S João do Araguaia
Bom Jesus
Va Palestina
S Sebastião do Tocantins
Buritildo Tocantins
Tepnepe
Reserva Biológica do Tapirapé
São José
Serra Oeste
Serra dos Carajás
Serra Pelana
Serra do Sereno
José Rodrigues
Vila Carajás
Parauapebas
Projeto Grande Carajás
El Dorado
Pto Estrela
Triunfo
Area Indigenas Sororó
Aranuatins
São Bento
Santa Isabol do Araguala
BR-230
Area Indigenas Catete
São Felix do Xingu
Tucumâ
Ouritândia do Norte
S Geraldo do Araguaia
Ananás
Xambioá
Araguanã
Bom Jardin
Lagoa Azul
BR-158
Pontão
Padre Cicero
Piraque
Ad Kikre Tum
Pista Branca
Faz Cocaia
Xinguara
Ad Kokraimoro
Ad Aucre
Capñara
Faz Cachoeirinha
Rio Maria
526
Cocalândia
Araguaina
BR-153
Garimpinho
Ipiranga
Babaculândia
Lim Dia
Floresta
Pau d'Arco
Area Indigena Kayapó
Taterambu
Gortire
Cumaru
Marajoara
Boa Sorte
Arapoema
Va de Brasilene
Bom Jesus
Nova Olinda
Ad Cubencranquém
Rio Dourado
Redenção
Volta Nova
Bernardo Sayão
Colinas de Tocantins
Faz Rio Dourado
Faz Alô Brasil
Conceicão do Araguaia
Xibião
Serra Cubencranqudm
Faz Alvorada
Faz Planalto
Couto Magalhães
Tupiratã
Tupirantins
Forquilha
Pequizeiro
Itaporã do Tocantis
Goianorte
Colméia
Santa Maria das Barreiras
Araguacema
Guarai
Piranha
Bom Jesus do
Tupirama
Pedro Afonso
Faz
Rio Cristalino
Faz Ouro Verde
Santana do Aaguaia
Campo Alegre
Caseara
TOCANTINS
Araguacuí
Dois Irmãos do Tocantins
Anajanópolis
Faz Propasa
Faz Maracanã
Miranorte
Faz Santana Rios
Marianópolis do Tocantins
Abreulândia
Tocantinia
Miracema do Tocantins
Reserva Indigena Xerentes
Pedras
Piara-Açu
Estação Ecológica de Côco Javaés
Faz Morada do Sul
Divinópolis do Tocantins
709
Barrolândia
Santa Cruz
Faz Santa Maria
Vila Rica
Cangucu
Faz Altamira
Mte Santo
Aparacido do Rio Negro
Faz Urupianga
Parque Nacional do Araguaia
Faz Sapé
Paraiso do Tocantins
Va Santa Luzia
Novo Acordo
Canela
Palmas
Serra do Tapirapé
Santa Teresinha
Barreira da Cruz
Pium
Taquaruçu do Porto
739
Area Indigenas Tapirapé-Carajás
José do Xingu
Faz Duas Meninas
Pto Alegre
Cristalândia
Nova Rosalâdia
Fátima
Porto Nacional
Faz Araúna
Faz Galiléia
Mte do Carmo
Diauarem
Faz Santa Rosa
Faz S Angelo
Brejinho de Nazare
Ponte Alta Tocan
Faz Adamantina
Ilha do Bananal
Sto Antônio do Suiá
Joatão
Faz Santa Rita
S Francisco
Silvanópolis
Luciara
Faz Loroti
Dueré
Tocantins
Ipueiras
Pto Araguaia
Santa Rosa do
Santa Cruz
Pindorama
Araguaia
Braço Menor do Araguaia

P
Q
R
Paragominas
Uraim
Area Indigenas Alto Turiacu
BR-316
Pto de Itaúna
SÃO LUÍS
Bento
St-Vicente Ferrar
Cajapio
S João Barista
Bacabeira
Ribamar
Anil
Icatu
Axixá
Morros
Rosário
Primeira Cruz
Humberto de Campos
Parque Nacional dos Lençóis Maranhenses
Ilha Caj
Delta
Barreirinhas
Tutoia
5
Croantã
Colcalzinho
Penalva
Matinha
Viana
Santa Rita
Anajatuba
Serra da Desordem
Reserva Biológica do Gurupi
Gurupizinho
Gurupi Mirim
Caru
Area Indigenas Caru
Bom Jardim
Vitória do Mearim
Pindaré-Mirim
BR-222
Arari
Itapecuru
Itapecuru-Mirim
Miranda
Urbano Santos
São Benedito
Cana Brava
Piranji
Magalhães de Almeida
Santa Quiteria
Vargem Gde
Preto
Anapurás
Luzilândia
Santa Inês
Cantanhede
Andirobal
Mearim
Gurupi
Pindare
Santa Luzia
Pio XII
Olho d Agua das Cunhãs
Pirapemas
Chapadinha
Breio
394
395
Serra do Tiracambu
Vitorino Freire
BR-135
S Mateus do Maranhão
Porto
Esperantina
Buriticupu
Paulo Ramos
Coroatá
Munim
Parnaíba
Batanha
Barras
BR-222
296
Lago da Preta
Bacabal
BR-316
Timbiras
Peritoró
Miguel Alves
Piripiri
Arame
Igarpé-Grande
Lima Campos
Codó
Coelho Neto
Poção de Pedras
Pedreiras
Santa Rita
Cabaceiras
Marianópolis
Cameleira
União
Olinda
6
Tocaia
Area Indigenas Arariboia
Esperantinópolis
Codozinho
João Lisboa
Area Indigenas Ceraldo e Toco Preto
S Antonio dos Lopes
Caxias
José de Freitas
MARANHAO
Gov Archer
Campo Maior
Area Indigenas Lagoa Comprida
BR-316
BR-343
Imperatriz
Buritirana
Area Indigenas Governador
Naru
Tuntum
Pres Dulra
Gov Eugenio Barros
TERESINA
Altos
S N de Tocantins
Amarante do Maranhão
Area Indigenas Jurua Urucu
Barra do Corda
Graca Aranha
Pedreiras
Alto Longa
Area Indigenas Cricati
Area Indigenas Cana Brava e Guajajara
A I Roncador
S Domingos do Maranhao
Demerval Loão
Montes Allos
Crajaú
Arranca
Serra Valentim
Sitio Novo
A I Morro Branco
Area Indigenas Bacurizinho
Roncador
Fortuna
Mons Gil
Beneditinos
Lageado
Santana
Papagaios
Matoes
PIAUÝ
396
Tocantinópolis
Serra Branca
Leandro
Buriti Branvo
Palmeirais
Barro Duro
Porto Franco
Colinas
Agua Branca
Serra das Alpercatas
Area Indigenas Canela
S Pedrodo Piauj
S Félix do Piaui
Estreito
Serra Negra
Area Indigenas Porquinhos
549
640
Serra da Cinta
Mirador
Passagem Franca
490
S Francisco do Maranhão
Amarante
Elesbão Veloso
Regeneracão
Sucupira do Note
Paraibano
Serra do Itapicuru
Rocado
Pastos Bons
Riachão
Parque Nacional Chapada das Mesas
Serra da Croeira
Santa Teresa
Novo Iorque
S João dos Patos
BR-230
BR-343
Várzea Gde
Farinha
Fotalza dos Nogueiras
S Raimundo das Mangabeiras
S Domingos
Represa de Boa Esperanca
Guadalupe
Barao de Grajaú
Floriano
7
Serra das Araras
Carolina
Loreto
São Felix de Balsas
Nazare do Piaui
Santa Rosa
Inhuma
Riachão
Sambaiba
Benedito Leite
Jerumenha
Serra Boqueirão
Oeiras
Cocal
Urucui
Antônio Almeida
Landrri Sales
Balsas
Coqueiro
Maravilha
BR-140
Goiatins
Ribeiro Goncalves
Parelha
Sereno
Alve Grande
Bertolinia
495
S José do Peixe
Mte Lindo
Craolândia
Itaueira
Formosa
550
Manuel Emidio
Flores do Piaui
Socomo do Piaul
678
525
Simplicio Mendes
Novo Retiro
Tasso Fragoso
Eliseu Martins
Canto do Buriti
Tem Medo
BR-234
Conceicão do Canindé
Colônia
Engano
Sertão
L do Boi
Amaro Leite
Inhumas
516
Estação Ecológica de Uruçui-Una
BR-135
S João do Piaui
Palmeira do Piaui
Boa Esperança
Salina
Cristino Castro
Gameleira
8
Alto Parnaiba
Santa Filomena
Santa Luz
Parque Nacional Serra da Capivara
Falha
Fação
Bom Jesus
660
S Raimun do Nonato
398
Mansinha
Pedro de Amolar
Serra Bom Jesus da Gurguéia
Estiva
730
Lizarda
Serra do Uruçui
Tabua
L Tabua
Anisio de Abreu
Chapada das Mangabeiras
Pausa
Redenção do Gurguéia
Caraco
406
Serra da Cruz
Mte Alegre do Piaui
Campo Alegre de Lourdes
Queimadas
Serra do Piaui
Curupá
Gilbués
Serra Vermelha
BR-235
Faz S Félix
Barreiras do Piaui
Remanso
Tocantis
L Pau d'Arco
Pilão Arcado
Soninho
780
Curimatá
Barra da Prata
Fundo
Cruz
Arcado
Sobradinho
Barragem de Sobradinho
Sento Sé
Jalapão
807
Mateiros
Galhão
Corrente
L de Parnagua
Parnaguá
Avelino Lopes
727
Faz Gaihão
Faz Cedro
389
Cristalândia do Piaui
Serra da Tabatinga
Mansidão
Amaniú
São Marceio
Buritirama
1123
Formosa do Rio Preto
Santa Rita de Cássia
Ibiraba
Rio da
Ilha do Gado Bravo
Xique-

Aquidaba
Campo Novo
Jaru
Ouro Preto d'Oeste
Zoró
Faz Muiraquitá
Faz Muiraquitá 2
Igarapé
E
F
G
381
382
Serra dos Caás Novos
Jamari
Parque Nacional de Pacáas Novos
Guajará-Mirim
Quro Preto
Area Indigenas 7 de Setembro
14 de Abril
660
RONDÔNIA
Area Indigenas Rio Negro Ocaía
Faz S Luis
Mirante da Serra
285
Ji-paraná
Mamoré
Urupá
Presidente Médici
Fortuna
Capitão Cardoso
Serra do Sgto Paixão
Area Indigenas Pacãas Novos
Pacaás Novos
Alta Lidia
Murui
Alvorado d'Oeste
Cacoal
Roosevelt
Area Indigenas Roosevelt
Novo
Serra do Uopiane
Area Indigenas Uru-Eu-Wau-Wau Cautário
Lomba das Cutapines
Polonês
Riozinho
Espigão d'Oeste
Marques
Santa Rosa
Rolim de Moura
Pimenta Bueno
Navaité
Parque Indigenas do Aripuanã
Villanueva
592
Santa Fe
S Lalza do Oeste
9
Area Indigenas Rio Guaporé
Alta Floreta do Oeste
Comemoração
Duvida
Alejandria
São Miguel
Area Indigenas Rio Branco
Branco
Arara
Marco Rondon
BR-364
Sto Domingos
Principe da Beira
Porto Murtinho
Pto Lirio
Costa Marques
Limoeiro
Guaporé
Ilha Monte Castelo
Reserva Biológica do Guaporé
Area Indigenas Rio Mequens
José Bonitácio
Majetú
La Horquilla
Curiche
Eliza
San Ramón
Colorado
Mequens
Barracão Liberato
663
Las Marias
Nuevo Berlin
Versalles
Area Indigenas Tuberão Latunde
Vilhena
Aldeia Nambiquara
Puerto Siles
Pedras Negras
Verde
Area Indigenas Ig Omera
Pto Triunfo
Las Pampitas
Mateguá
Colorado do Oeste
San Joaquin
Bella Vista
Pto Rubio
Corumbiara
Chapada
El Cerro
San Ramón
Magdalena
Cerejeiras
Exaltación
Laranjeiras
Pimenteiras
Patrocito
Huahuatiri
San Martin
Villazón
Cabixi
Va Jatai
Lucuma
Huacaraje
Branca
BENI
Baures
Pto Rico
Saucedo
Peñas
Piso Firme
Iténez (Guaporé)
Piolho
Rogaguado
Nova Alvorada
Santa Ana de Yacuma
L San Luis
Negro
10 de Abril
Santa Antta
Buena Hora
Pto Cármen
El Carmen
Pto Saucedo
Paredón
Evora
10
Mamoré
Sna Negra
Porvenir
Area Indigenas Vale do Guaporé
La Esperanza
Pto Menacho
Petania
San Pedro
L Huachi
Tre Personas
San Cármen
Nazareth
Huachi
L Negra
Serrania Huanchacá
Verde
Guapold
San Nicolás
San Pedro Burtón
Dosconcierto
Reserva Florestal Bajo Paraguá
Faz Guapore
Pto Leigue
L Concepción
Curiche Liverpool
Paraguá
Candelaria
Blotin Quemado
San Miguel
San Francisco
Blanco
Codicia
259
Parque Nacional Noel Kempft Mercado
Ibo
Pto Fray
Serra Ricardo Franco
Serra São Vic
Loma Suárez
Chapacura
El Pensamiento
Cristo
San Javier
Perseverancia
Monte Cristo
Tarvo
248
Trinidad
S F F Rios Blanco y Negro
Area Indig
Pto Almacén
Casarebe
La Cruz
Pto Cañada
1995
Vila Bela
Peroto
Va Banzer
Guarayos
Sachojere
El Mutua
Puerto Arturo
San Andrés
L Cueva
Pto Alegre
Llanos de Mojos
Loreto
(Moxos)
San Pedro de Cururó
L Kaaupa
San Martin
Casalvasco
San Lorenzo
La Unión
La Laja
Camirco
L Alberto
San Martin
Alegre
Securé
Santa Maria
Caimanes
Baia Grande
Destacamento Casalvasco
Jesús
San Pablo
La Desgracia
Negro
Agro C
Santa Lucia
San Rafaelito
Buena Hora
San Miguelito
Todos Santos
Carmen
San Miguel
San Ramón
Destacamento S Simão
11
Las Lajas
El Tunas
Grande
Santa Rosa de la Roca
San Diego
Reserva Florestal Guarayos
BO
Faz S Bento
California
San Rafael
Concepción
Isiboró
San Pablo
San Javier
San Ignacio de Velasco
Pinto
Zapocas
Ichilo
Yapacani
Urucu
San Lucas
Chipiri
Chaparé
Santa Rosa de Lima
Pto Mamoré
Colonia Hardemari
Santa Ana
Monte
San Ramón
Tunas
Pto Villarroel
San Julián
San Miguel
Choro
Trinidad
San Rafael
Todos Santos
4 Ojos
Chimoré
Palometas
Grande
Colonia San Juán
Piray
Chané
El Plato
Tunari
Mataco
San Juán
San Miguelito
Pto Grether
Va Sucre
Santa Rosa del Sara
Fn Libertad
Santa Maria
SANTA CRUZ
Vandiola
Salta
Gral Saavedra
802
Okinawa I
Cordillera de Tiraque
Portachuelo
Yapacani
San Carlos
Montero
Quimome
Nuevo Horizonte
Montepuncu
Buena Vista
El Cerro
L Concepción
Pozo del Tigre
Warnes
Epizana
Canada Larga
Motacucito
Quituquiña
Parque Nacional Amboró
Pojo
3202
Cerro Bravo
Tres Cruces
El Tunas
Quimome
Lupe
Totora
Real
Ayacucho
SANTA CRUZ DE LA SIERRA
Piococa
San Juan
Mizque
San Juán del Potrero
Serra Santa Cruz
La Guardia
Curiches
Llanos de Chiquitos
Natividad
San José de Chiquitos
Taperas
Tucavaca
Comarapa
12
Palmar del Oratorio
Sna de Santiago
San Isidro
Mairana
Mizque
Grande (Guapay)
396
Poa Grande
Samaipata
Yupe
Aiquile
Pasorapa
Quirucillas
Roboré
Trigal
Quiroga
Rostrer Valle
Pto Izozog
Los Ciros
Vallegrande
Ing Mora
Banados del Izozog
Poroma
Grande
Toborochi
Sapsi
Pucará
El Curiche
San
Fn Suárez Arana
Mojocoya
Cabezas
Zudañes
San Miguel
Masicuri
Abapo
Higuera
Tomina
Presto
Pto Camcho
Puesto S José
Miguel

H
J
K
383
388
390
9
10
11
12
Faz Tucanã
Ingleses
Canoeiros
Tucanã
Area Indigenas Japuira
353
Apiacá
Nova Canaã
Terra Nova
Agro Cachimbo S A
Faz Jarina
BR-060
Pres Medici
Vermelho
Serra do Norte
Reserva Indigenas Apiacá
Itapaiúna
Tapaiuna
Colider
Faz Indio
Faz Bonsucesso
Morro do Sinal
Itaúba
Marcelândia
Manissuá-Missu
Area Indigenas Rikbaktsa
Juará
Fontanillas
Juina
Agro Lot
Faz Santa Ana
Aquibi
Saudade
Faz Rio Aul
Faz São Luis
Faz São José
Analândia do Norte
Faz Barra Azul
Novo Horizonte
Arinos
Catua
Porto dos Gaúchos
Juina - Mirim
Faz Cortez
Preto
Iporanga
Serra dos Caiabis
(São Manuel)
Faz Renata
Claudia
São Francisco
Ilha do Uatapite
Faz Centro Oeste
Sinop
Faz Vale do Arraias
Faz Rio Negro
ação Ecológica ouê Juruena
R E Sema
Brásnorte
S Miguel
Faz Igoranga
Faz Fanorte
S Carmen
Area Indigenas Menqui
Sangue
Venceslau
Faz São Paulo
Verde
Teles Pires
Vera
Faz Consul
Parque I. do X
genas Saluma
rea Indigenas Nambikwara
Faz Mataporã
Faz S Paulo do Cravari
Faz Soledade
Faz S Anastácia
Sorriso
Alvorado do Norte
Steinen
Faz Paraiso
Faz Membeca
Agro Guimarães
Tapurah
5 de Maio
Ferro
Faz Terra Nova
Reserva Indigenas Irantxé
Faz Marapé
Agro Iberé
Itiariti
Faz Continental
Faz Divisão
Claro
BR-163
Primavera
Agro Agrovensa
Faz Ubiratan
Agro Jatobá
Area Indigenas Tirecatinga
Faz Londrina
Jardim da Amazonia
Cosme e Damião
Lucas do Rio Verde
Pto Artur
Faz Itaguaçu
Faz J Olive
Faz Agua Quente
Buriti
Faz Graciosa
S José do Rio Claro
Piuva
Piuvinha
MATO GROSSO
Parecis
Faz Agromar
Patos
Colônia São Manuel
Serra Daniel
Faz Reivilo
Area Indigenas Utiariti
Faz São José
Agro Flamingo
Nova Mutum
Faz Paratininga
345
Boca da Mata
Faz Formiga
Faz Mutum
Ranchão
Faz Leyton
Santa Rita
Faz Palmito
Sumidouro
Faz Lagoa Rica
BR-364
Faz Barrinha
Pascoval
Area Indigenas Batovi
Area Indigenas Paresi
Faz Sulca
Sacuriuiná
Faz União
Serra do Cuiabá
Faz Rio Novo
Faz Fecho de Ouro
Faz Carajá Grande
Jirapuru
669
Rio Verde
Marilândia
Arenópolis
Arenápolis
Diamantino
A I Santana
673
Area Indigenas Bakairi
Parantinga
A I Estivadinho
Tangara da Serra
Afonso
Nortelândia
Simóes Lópes
São Jorge
Progresso
S Joaquim
Alto Paraquai
Posto Gil
Cuiabá
Rancheria
Faz Laranjal
Marzagão
Paranatinga
Nova Olimpia
Denise
Nobres
Perosópolis
Serra Azul
Culuene
Faz 3 Coracoes
A I Figueiras
Tapirapuã
Serra do Tombador
Rosario Oeste
Praia Ria
Faz Nova Esperança
Va Progfesso
Area Indigenas Umutina
Arruda
Manso
Fica
792
Lucialva
Salto do Céu
Barra do Bugres
Engenho
Faz Caiana
Nova Brasilândia
Planalto do Mato Grosso
Rio Branco
Cristianópolis
Bauxi
Acorizal
Parque Nacional da Chapada dos Guimarães
893
Cumbuco
Serra Sta Bárbara
Jauru
Lambari
Boa União
Jangada
Pto Estrela
Buriti
Faz da Fé
Figueirópolis
Araputanga
Cabaçal
Guia
Mortes
Faz Primavera
Quatro Marcos
Coxipo do Ouro
Ponte Alta
Chapada dos Guimarães
Aguapel
Mirassol d'Oeste
Monjolinho
CUIABÁ
Cnl Ponce
Primavera
Area Indigenas Sangradouro
Cruzeiro d'Oeste
BR-174
Estação Ecológica Serra de Araras
Várzea Grande
Coxipó
São Vicente
Latobá
Pres Murtinho
N Sra do Livramento
Engenho Velho
Dom Aquino
Alto Coité
Jaurú
Faz das Conchas
Serra das Araras
BR-070
S Antônio do Leverger
Palmeiras
BR-364
Jaciara
Poxoréu
Serra da Saudade
Batovi
Cáceres
Cangas
S Pedro da Cipa
Juscimeirra
Aparecida do Leste
Santa Rita
San Matias
Faz Onça
Jacobina
Poconé
Barão de Melgaço
776
Paraiso do Leste
Las Petas
Dest de Corixa
Faz Chapadão
Sangradouro
B Chacorore
Mimoso
S Elvira
Boa Vista
Jarudoré
Area Indigenas Perigara
S Lourenço de Fátima
Vale Rico
Guiratinga
Faz São Carlos
Faz Descalvacos
Bento Gomes
Joselândia
Rondonópolis
S José do Povo
Candelaria
137
Claro
Colónia S Isabel
Area Indigenas Gomes Carneiro
Serra do Jurique
Tigrecito
E E Taiamã
Pousada Pixaim
Serra São Jerônimo
Ponte de Pedra
Pedra Preta
Serra da Petrolina
Faz Boa Vista
Faz Beira Rio
Alegre
Faz Santa Luzia
L Orión (Providencia)
130
Pindaival
Jurigão
Anhumas
Alto Garças
Faz Pindaival
Peixe
S José do Planalto
Faz Aguacerito
Alegre
São Lourenço
724
Itiquira
Pto Jofre
Piquiri
Itiquira
San Fernando
L Uberaba
Parque Nacional do Pantanal Matogrossense
Pantanal de São Lourenço
Sozinho
Alto Araguaia
Paraiso
Turupaqui
L Gaiba
La Gaiba
Pto Caracará Novo
Faz S Joé
Pto Badeco
Sonora
Correntes
Sto Corazón
Serra Amolar
640
San Juan
Amolar
Pantanal
L Mandiré
Taquari
La Cal
Pto Isabel
Faz São Sebastião
Pedro Gómes
Buriti
Matogrossense
Promissão
BR-163
B de Castelo
Corixão
Taquari
Pólvora
Alcinópolis
Naranjos
Sna Tapia
Paiaguas
Faz Bor Branco
Taquan
Serra do Taquari
Espejo
Pantanal do Taquari
Faz Buritizal
Coxim
olândia
Jauru
El Cármen
Faz Alegria
Jauru
Figueirão
Pto Suárez
Corumbá
Taquari
Faz Imaculada

São José do Xingu
Faz Duas Meninas
Pto Alegre
Santa Teresinha
Barreira da Cruz
Cristalândia
Fátima
Porto Nacional
384
Ilha do Bananal
Luciara
Faz Araúna
Diauarem
Faz Santa Rosa
Faz S Angelo
Faz da Gaviota
Faz Adamantina
Sto Antônio do Suiá
Faz Joatão
Ilha dos Uatapités
Xingu
Rio Negro
Faz S Raimundo
Faz Loroti
Faz Santa Rita
Brejinho de Nazare
Duerê
Aliança do Tocantins
Santa Cruz
São Felix do Araguaia
Santa Isabel do Morro
Pto Araguaia
Liquilâdia
Agro Amoreiras
Parque Indigenas do Araguaia
Formoso do Araguaia
Gurupi
Cariri
Parque Indigena do Xingu
Posto Leonardo Vilas Boas
Faz Tamacaá
Faz Lago Preto
Canuanã
Barreira do Pequi
Alo Brasil
Sto Antônio
Serra do Ador
Carchunu
Faz Presidente
Figueirópolis
Peixe
Dorilândia
S Helena
Pto dos Meinacos
Faz Bete
BR-158
Barreira Amarela
217
Faz Cocal
Landico
Faz Almeida Prado
Faz Caracol
Sandolândia
Alvorada
Jatobá
265
Faz J Oliveira
Gaúcho do Norte
Faz Cristo Rei
Ribeirão Cascalheira
Talismã
Araguaçu
Chapéu de Palha
Garapu
Faz Pinheral
São João Mirapuxi
Reserva Indigenas Pimental Barbosa
Luis Alves
658
Palmeirópolis
670
Faz Catetinho
São Miguel do Araguaia
Nova Planalto
BR-153
Boca da Mata
Matinha
Area Indigenas Karajá-Aruanã
Canarana
Montividiu
Porangatu
Faz Sa Dourada
Bandeirantes
Mundo Novo
Santa Telesa
396
Mutunópolis
Formoso
Indigenas Batovi
Faz Carajá Grande
Água Boa
Faz Planalto
Rima
Xixá
Estrela do Norte
1145
Campinaçu
387
Reserva Indigenas Parabubure
Reserva Indigenas Areães
Cocalinho
Peixe
Nova Crixás
Mara Rosa
Pau Terra
Colinas
Campinópolis
Aregas
Santa Terezinha de Goiás
Campinorte
Nova Esperança
Faz Bacaba
Nova Xavantina
Tupiracaba
Niquelândia
792
Nova S Joaquim
Faz Cristina
Crixás
Hidrrolina
Uruacu
Agro Independencia S A
Faz Júlia Branca
Mozarrlândia
Faz Santa Cruz
Aruanã
Pilar de Goias
820
Mato Grosso
Pindaiba
Reserva Indigenas São Marcos
Itapaci
Toricuelje
863
Araguapaz
Nova América
Rubiataba
1341
Barro Alto
Area Indigenas Sangradouro
Brilânia
Carmo do Rio Verde
Juscelândia
Jeroaquara
Ceres
Dois Irmãos
Pres Murtinho
BR-070
Reserva Indigenas Merure
Rialma
Faina
Gral Carneiro
330
Uruanã
Goianésia
Tesouro
Araguaiana
Registro do Araguala
Jacilândia
Rianánolis
861
1240
Brazlândia
Barragem do Descoberto
Bara do Garças
Santa Fe
São João
Itapuranga
Jaraguá
Aragarças
Aparecida do Rio Claro
Jucara
Itapirapuã
Itaguari
Pirenópolis
Taguatinga
Baliza
Uva
Golás
Guiratinga
Torixoréu
Bo Jaldim de Goiás
Novo Brasil
Mocamedes
Itaberaí
S Fco de Goias
Cd Ecléctica
Fazenda Nova
730
Petrolina de Goias
Alexânia
Diamantino
1010
Diorama
Israelândia
Sancerlâdia
Itaucu
BR-060
Luziânia
Cafelândia do Leste
Piranhas
Iporã
GOIÁS
Inhumas
Damolândia
Nerópolis
Abadiânia
Arenápolis
São Luis de Montes Belos
Anicuns
Anâpolis
745
Ponte Branca
Amorinópolis
Trinidade
Goianira
Chapada de Covas
Araguainha
396
Doverlândia
Cach de Goiás
Firminópolis
Goianápolis
Garças
Palestina
Aurilândia
GOIÂNIA
Leopoldo de Bulhões
724
Caiapônia
Guapó
Silvânia
Faz Sa Caiapó
Palminópolis
Aparecida de Goiânia
Vianópolis
Santa Rita do Araguaia
Serra do Caiapó
1010
Paraúna
Palmeiras de Goiás
Hidrrolândia
Alto Araguaia
Portelândia
Serra das Divisões
Aragoiânia
Orizona
Indiara
Montividiu
Acreuna
Edéia
Mairipotaba
Cristianópolis
863
Mte Alegre
Mineiros
Perolândia
759
Piracanjuba
181
Palmelo
879
Pires do Rio
551
Pontalina
Taquari
BR-364
Jatai
BR-060
Vicentinópolis
Rancho Alegre
Urutai
Buriti
Plaça de Mineiros
Rio Verde
Santa Helena de Goiás
Joviânia
Aloânia
Morrinhos
Parque Nacional das Emas
Caldas Novas
Alcinópolis
Naveslândia
Maurilândia
S Domingos
Ipameri
Plaça
Serra da Mombuca
Marzagão
Capela
Baús
Castelândia
Goiatuba
Nova Aurora
Costa Rica
Serranópolis
Aparecida do Rio Doce
Bom Jesus de Goiás
Buriti Alegre
Corumbaiba
Pouso Frio
811
552
Inaciol
391
Sarandi
Cumari
Catalão
Itumbiara
Barr Itumbiara
Anhangüera
Chapadão do Sul
Itumirim
Itarumã
Cacu
Quirinópolis
Cach Dourada
Centralina
Piracaiba
Barragem de S Simão
Cach Alta
Aporé
Ipiacu
Capinópolis
Tupaciguara
Paraiso
Indalá do Sul
Paranalguara
Mte Alegre de Minas
Estrela do Sul
Cassilândia
Itajá
São Simão
Santa Vitória
Ituiutaba
Serra das Araras
9
10
11
12
L
M
N

Santa Teresa do Tocantis
Taquaruçu do Porto
739
P
Soninho
780
Vermelho
Faz S Bento
Jalapão
Mateiros
Galhão 807
das Mangabeiras
do Piaui
Barra da Prata
Fundo
L Pau d'Arco
Curimatá
Cruz
Q
385
Parnaguá
Curimata
Corrente
Faz Gaihão
Arcado
R
Pilão Arcado
Avelino Lopes
727
Poço
Mte do Carmo
Ponte Alta
Preto
Novo
Ponte Alta do Tocantins
Faz Cedro
Cristalândia do Piaui
Serra da Tabatinga
Mansidão
Serra do Estrelto
Silvanópolis
Baisas
Serra Geral
Sapão
864
São Marceio
Buritirama
Pindorama do Tocantins
Serra Negra
Preto
Formosa do Rio Preto
Santa Rita de Cássia
Ibiraba
9
Xique-Xique
BR-010
Rio da Conceição
Ilha do Gado Bravo
Chapada
Peixe
Almas
Ouro
705
BR-135
Barra
Pto Alegre do Tocantins
Dianópolis
Chapada Redonda
Boqueirão
Natividade
777
Serra das Figuras
Cambueiro
Verde
Capixaba
Itajubaquara
ão Valério Natividade
Alves
Faz São Luis
Palmeiras
Cabeceirinha
Prata
Branca
Janeiro
Riachão das Neves
Grande
Boqueirão
Igarité
Morpará
1065
Gentio do Our
Serranópolis
Ibitunane
Ponte Alta do Bom Jesus
Taipas
Mimoso d'Oeste
Cotejipe
1263
Conceição do Tocantins
Conceição
Pedras
Angical
Quixaba
Bom Jardin
Faz Onça
Ondas
Barreiras
BR-242
Vanderlei
Ipupiara
398
Paranã
Palma
Taguatinga
São Desidério
Cristópolis
Limoeiro
Brotas
Paramirim
Pirajiba
Ibotirama
857
Sobrado
Fémeas
Sitio Gde
Várzeas
Baianópolis
553
Oliveira dos Brejinhos
Aurora do Tocantins
Roda Velha
São Desidério
BR-242
Cana-Brava
Arraias
Combinado
Roda Velha
Galheiro
Brejolândia
Brejo Velho
Novo Alegre
Grande
Serra Dourada
Pernambuco
Paratinga
Campo Alegre
Campos Belos
BR-020
Porcos
691
Santana
Boquira
10
Mte Alegre de Goiás
Manso
Guara
Inhaúmas
Gameleira da Lapa
Santa Rita
Serra da Garapa
Sto Onofre
Ibipitanga
1340
Galheiros
Meio
Sitio do Mato
Macaúbas
São Domingos
Açudina
608
Ibiajara
São Domingos
631
Correntina
Cavalcante
Éguas
Santa Maria da Vitória
Bom Jesus da Lapa
Gaturama
Teresina de Goiás
Goiás
Arrojado
Formoso
Parque Nacional da Chapada dos Veadeiros
Nova Roma
1129
Botuporã
Alto Peraíso de Goiás
Pratudão
Coribe
Riacho de Santana
Paramirim
Iaciara
Posse
Serra do Ramalho
Pitubas
Igaporã
Paranã
676
São Francisco
Alvorada do Norie
Cocos
Maniaçu
Carnaíba
Carinhanha
Mambai
Formoso
881
Itaguari
Cachá
Caetilé
Flores de Goiás
Malhada
S João da Aliança
Damianópolis
Coxá
Montalvânia
Guanambi
Ibiassucé
Serra Geral do Paraná
1678
Paraim
Candiba
Sitio d'Abadia
Nhandutiba
Serra de Monte Alto
Pindal
Rio do Antôn
Santa Rosa
Santa Maria
Serra de Sta Maria
Serra da Capivara
Serra Paratodos
Carinhanha
Manga
Verde Pequeno
Caculé
BR-020
Formoso
809
Verde
11
S Gabriel
Serra Bonita
Piratinga
Serra São Domingos
Parque Nacional de Grande Sertão Veredas
Serra dos Tropeiros
Matias Cardoso
Licinio de Almeida
Urandi
1061
S Domingos
1500
Condeúba
Formosa
Chapadão de Sta Maria
Itacarambi
Serra de Jaiba
Corotuba
Espinosa
Serra Geral
Mortugaba
Planaltina
Buritis
Levinópolis
Monte Azul
BRASÍLIA
Serra da Paraná
Serra das Araras
Pardo
Januária
Jaiba
Salinas
S João do Paraiso
Caberceiras
S Miguel
Areiras
Pedras de Santa Maria da Cruz
Serra de São Felipe
Mato Verde
400
Arinos
Acari
São Francisco
Lontra
Janaúba
685
Porteirinha
Pardo
Taiobeiras
Guarapuavã
Serra Rio Preto
Urucuia
Morro
S João da Ponte
Conceição
Urucuia
Unai
Chapada do Tapiocanga
Luislândia
Ubai
Brasilia de Minas
Caveira
Ferreirópolis
Cristais
Cangalha
São Romão
Mirabela
830
Vacaria
Cristalina
Preto
Bomfinópolis
Campo Azul
Cap Enéas
Salinas
Fermino
Ponte dos Ciganos
Miraita
Barrocão
BR-040
Inhumas
Cach do Manteiga
Pacui
Nova Esperanca
BR-251
Francisco Sá
Itinga
Boqueirão
São Francisco
Coracão de Jesus
S João
Paracatu
Montes Claros
Cnel Murta
Paracatu
BR-365
Brasilândia
Planalto
12
Marcos
Claro dos Pocães
Juramento
Escurinho
Caatinga
Guaicui
Bocaiúva
Virem da Lapa
Iting
954
Serra do Catuni
Aracuari
Araçuai
Canabrava
Jaquitinhonha
o Alegre Goias
Sono
Buritzeiro
Pirapora
Jequitai
Fco Bedaró
Serra dos Pilães
696
Terra Branca
Minas Novas
Padre Paraíse
Guarda Mor
Sto. Antônio
Chapada dos Gerais
Várzea da Palma
Serra do Cabral
Espinhaço
Eng Scohoor
Carai
Belo
Verde
Claro de Minas
Paracatu
Prata
João Pinheifo
1300
Carbonita
Chifre
Serra do
Vazante
Velhas
Fanado
Nova Cruzeiro
Ponte Firme
Joaquim Felicio
Capelinha
Ladainha
Lagamar
Canoeiras
Lassance
Buenópofis
Pres Olegário
BR-365
Abaeté
Trés Marias
402
Augusto de Lima
Setubinha
Serra da Carcaça
Itamarandiba
Poté
Coromandel
S Gonçalo do Abaeté
Andrequice
Contria
Serra Negra
Malacache
R
P
Q
Patos de Minas
Galena
Morada Nova
Represa Três Marias
Corinto
Guinda
Diamantina
Santa Maria
Agua Boa

Pantanal
387
J
K
L
Amolar
L Mandiré
Pto Isabel
B de Castelo
Corixão
Sna Tapia
Paiaguas
Faz Bor Branco
Pantanal do Taquari
Matogrossen
Sebastião
Promissão
Taquari
Taquan
BR-163
Pedro Gómes
Pólvora
Alcinópolis
Buriti
Plaça de Mineiro
Parque Nacional das Emas
Serra do Taquari
Plaça
Capela
Formoso
Baús
Costa Rica
Pouso Frio
Aporé
Chapadão do Sul
Faz Buritizal
Coxim
Silvolândia
Jauru
Figueirão
Faz Alegria
Espejo
Cármen
Pto Suárez
Corumbá
Yacuses
Quijarro
Ladário
Guachalla
Mutún
1067
161
Pto Manga
Serra Albuquerque
Faz Imaculada
Pantanal do Rio Nego
Faz Cocais
Rio Verde de Mato Grosso
Faz Ribeirão Brejão
Serra das Araras
Paraiso
Grande
138
Negro
Vila Areado
417
Alto Sucuriú
Indaiá Grand
617
S Domingos
Quijarro
Albuquerque
Morinho
Passo da Lontra
Buraco das Piranhas
Faz S Roque
Faz Tupanceretã
Bara Mansa
Rio Negro
S Gabriel do Oeste
Porto Esperança
Ponte Vermelha
Taboco
Camapuã
Verde
Paraguai
Carandázal
Bodoquena
MATO GROSSO DO SUL
Forte Coimbra
13
Capim Verde
Ponte de Rio Verde
Sertão
Pto Busch
Cabello
Guaicurus
BR-262
São Simão
Miranda
Faz Taboco
Tabaco
Cipolândia
Rochedo
Bandeirante
Bomfim
Jaraguari
Rochedinho
Pardo
Prata
Taunay
Nabileque
Bodoquena
Aquidauana
Paxixi
Anastácio
Palmeiras
Terenos
649
Bálsamo
Ribas do Rio Pardo
Mutum
CAMPO GRANDE
389
Agua Clara
Pto Esperanza
Mihanovich
Campo dos Indios
Morraria
Naitaca
Lalima
Parque Nacional da Serra da Bodoquena
Pto Lidia
Pto Braga
Aquidabã
708
290
Trés Barras
Bolicho
Sidrolândia
Faz Transparana
Faz Mateira
Fuerte Olimpo
Yacaré
Baia das Garcas
Bonito
Miranda
Nioaque
Nioaque
606
Anhandui
Capão Seco
Vacaria
Ribeirão Claro
Faz Firme
Branco
Reserva Ecologica Baia Bonita
Reserva Ecologica Bala Bonita
Anhandui
Anhanduizinho
Lontra
Agro São Victor
Santa Rita do Pardo
Pto Guarani
545
Pão de Açúcar
Guia Lo Pes da Laguna
Serra de Maracaju
S Luzia
Nova Alvorada
Porto Murtinho
Margarida
Jardim
Maracaju
Prudéncio Thomaz
Zuzu
BR-267
Taquaraçu
Pto 3 Palmas
Boqueirão
Caracol
Vista Alegre
Brilhante
Vacaria
Serra de Santa Bárbara
Pardo
Bataguas
14
665
Santa Maria
Carumbé
Destilarie Rio Briharite
Vitor
Rio Brilhante
Casa Verde
Pto XV de Nov
Pres Epitáci
Pto Esperanza
San Lázaro
Pto Valle Mi
Pto La Victonia
S Carlos
Caracol
Apá
Bela Vista
Cabeceira do Apá
Itaum
Itaporã
Douradina
Continental
182
San Carlos
Campestre
Antônio João
Inezal
Angélica
Dourados
Deodápolis
Nova Andradina
Anaurilândia
Paraná
Cerro Galván
Pto Fonciere
Colonia San Jose
Fatima de Sul
Ivinhema
Presiden
Pto Calera Cue
Parque Nacional Serranías San Luís
Parque Nacional del Cerro Cora
Ponta Porã
Nova America
Vicentina
Glória de Dourados
Bataiporã
Pto Pinasco
Paraguay
Pedro Juan Caballero
Sanga Puita
L Caarapá
Vila Rica
Jatei
447
Area de Proteção Ambrental Varzeas do Rio de Parana
Pto Itapucu Mi
Cáceres-Cué
Ea Garay Cué
Ea Va Sana
Cruce Bella Vista
Col co Memby
Serra de Amambay
Aral Moreira
Bocaja
Caarapó
BR-163
Rosana
Terra Rica
Teodoro Sampaio
Sete Placas
Guarei
Pto São José
San Carlos
Pto Cooper
Col Yby Yaú
Paso Mbutú
Aquidabán
Cagatá
Secador
Campanário
Juti
Laranjal
Porto Peroba
Nova Londrina
Paranaci
Retiro Lota
Pto San Juán
Granja Tres Maria
Amambai
Pto Felicidade
Amambai
Navirai
Querencia do Norte
Loanda
Serra do Lagarto
Verde
Pto Colón
Loreto
Toldo Cué
Arroyito
Ypané
AMAMBAY
460
Ivai
Santa Isabel do Ivai
Paranavai
Concepciãn
Capitán Bado
Cnl Sapucaia
Pto Caiua
Paraiso de Norte
Florai
Negro
Belén
Tacuati
Torin
Inhopi
Iguira
Pto Morotim
Faz Brencha Azul
Icaraima
Od Gaúcha
Maring
Ea Yukyry
Pto Ybapopó
Ea Aguaray-Mi
Morotim
Puntas
Pto Tacurú Pytá
Colonia Rio Verde
Tacuru
Itaquirai
Nova Olimpia
Paicandu
Celada Cué
L Blanco
Ea S Júan
Iguatemi
S Jorge do Patrosinio
Cianorte
15
Psto
SAN PEDRO
Santa Rosa
Itanara
Sete Quedos
Iguatemi
Eldorado
Umuarama
Dr Camar
Monte Lindo
Nova Germania
Lima
Ypé-Jhú
Jacarei
Pérola
Cruzeiro do Oeste
Hotel Rio Negro
Antequera
San Pedro
Jejui-Guazú
S F F de Mbaracayú
Paranhos
Mundo Novo
Altônia
Perobal
Terra Boa
215
Serra de Maracajú
Salto del Guaira
Pto Crl Renato
Iporã
Manluz
Peabir
Ygatimi
Carapá
Francisco Talvez
Araruna
Camp Mourã
Ea S Antonio
Pto San Vicente
Guaira
Moreira Sales
Janiópolis
Pto Carlos Pfannl
CANINDEYU
Formosa do Oeste
Pilaga
Ea Adela
Rosario
Capiibari
Col Y Jhiby
Alvar Nunez Cabeza de Vaca
Palotina
Goiô-Erê
Mamborê
Guazú
Itacurubi del Rosario
Curuguaty
Assis
Serra do Cantú
Ea Alina
Ea Villa Rey
Ybyra Pyta
Pto Adela
Chateaubnand
Pto Piquiri
Iretama
L Verá
San Estanislao
Snas de San Joaquin
ALTO
Ytambey
Mal Cândido Rondon
Sarandi
Ubiratá
25 de Diciembre
Felipe Matiauda
Colondrina
Pto
Marangatú
Tupassi
Ciarvos
Benjamin Aceval
Union
Juán de Mena
Capiibary
Pto Santa Teresa
Campina
Nova Cantu
Roncad
Toledo
Villa Hayes
CORDILLERA
Santa Rosa
San Joaquin
Mingapora
Itaquyry
Santa Helena
Corbélia
Cantu
Chaco-i
Luque
Arroyos y Esteros
Rep de Itaipu
Reserva Biológica Santa Elena
Braganey
Palmital
Pto Faicón
Clorinda
ASUNCIÓN
Dr Cecilio Baéz
PARANA
802
Cascavel
Parque Nacional Ypacarai
Carayao
CAAGUAZÓ
Acaray
Veracrus d'Oeste
Santa Teresa
Guaraniacu
Piquí
Capiata
San Lorenzo
Hugo Stroessner
Represa de Caray
Santa Inês
Matelândia
Cantanduvas
Faxinal S João
Inglés
Ambare
Caacupe
Coronel Oviedo
Res Biológica Tati Yupi
São Miguel do Iquacu
Boa Vista Apavecida
Tres Barras
Quedas do Iguacu
Goiox
Ita
Pinbebuy
Paraguari
San Jose
Caaguazú
Jose O Ocampos
Hernandanas
R B Itaipú
Medianeira
Parque Nacional do Iguacu
Cantaga
16
CENTRAL
Carapeguá
Mbocayaty
N Talavera
Cordillera de Caaguazú
Cuidad del Este
Foz do Iguaçu
Cap L Marques
Espigão Alto
Laranjeiras do Sul
Dalmacia
La Coimena
GUAIRA
Pto Franco
Capanema
Nova Prata
Carro
EMBUCU
Acahay
Villarrica
Res Nacional Kuri'y
Pto Iguazu
Parque Nacional d Iguazú
Rep de
Salto Santiago
630
Gral E Garay
Parque Nacional Ybytyruzú
Realza
Va Oliva
Parque Nacional Ybycui
Iturbe
P N
San Cristobal
Wanda
Valerio Deste
São
Dois Vizinhos
S Francisco
Paz
Alberdi
L Verá
Mbuyyapey
Sarandi
Pranchita
Francisco Beltrão
Passa Qualro
Caapucú
Quyquyó
Caazapa
Caaguazú
A Juan Nepomuceno
Tavai
392
Punta Esperanza
Sto Antônio do Sudoeste
Mangu
PARAGUARI
365
Bertoni
ITAPU
Salgado Filho
Marmeleiro
Coronel Vivida
Chopin
Tebicua
Cerrito
Va Flonda
CAAZAPÁ
Dolores
Pto Mayor Otaño
Bern de Irigove
Barração
Yegros

Jatai
BR-060
Rio Verde
Serra do Verdinho
Vicentinópolis
Pontalina
Rancho Alegre
Urutai
Joviânia
Aloânia
Morrinhos
Cpo Alegre de Goias
Caldas Novas
Ipameri
Naveslândia
Maurilândia
S Domingos
Marzagão
Castelândia
388
Goiatuba
Guarda Mor
Claro de Minas
Aparecida do Rio Doce
Buriti Alegre
Nova Aurora
BR-050
Pires Belo
Serranópolis
de Goiás
Corumbaiba
Goiandira
Vazante
552
Sarandi
Cumari
Catalão
Inaciolândia
Itumbiara
Itumirim
Itarumã
Cacu
Quirinópolis
Cach Dourada
Barr Itumbiara
Anhangüera
Represa de Emborcação
Lagamar
Centralina
Piracaiba
Pres Olegário
Barragé de S Simão
Serra da Carcaça
Aporé
Cach Alta
Ipiacu
Tupaciguara
Araguari
Coromandel
Capinópolis
Estrela do Sul
Abadia
Patos de Minas
Paranalguara
Santa Vitória
Ituiutaba
Mte Alegre de Minas
Itajá
São Simão
Chaveslândia
Romaria
Monte Carmelo
Arvore Gde
Uberlândia
Lagoa Formosa
Raimundo
Indianópolis
Guimarânia
BR-153
Patrocínio
Gurinhatã
Irai de Minas
Jardinésia
Nova Ponte
Carmo do Paranaiba
735
515
Campina Verde
Miraporanga
Prata
13
Paranaiba
Pto Alencastro
Honorópolis
Santa Juliana
Comendador Gomes
778
Rio Paranaiba
Alexandrina
Iturama
Patrimônio
Perdizes
1147
Cupins
Zelândia
Ibiá
São Pedro
Populina
Barragem Agua Vermelha
S Francisco de Sales
Campo Florido
Araxá
Santa Albertina
Aparecida do Taboado
Itapajipe
Pirajuba
Uberaba
Campos Altos
Ouroeste
Mira Estrela
Riolândia
Conceição das Alagoas
Ilha Soltera
Santa Fé do Sul
Cardoso
Fruta
Delta
Sacramento
Pratinha
Fernandópolis
Plariura
Conquista
Selvíria
Jales
Igarapava
Tapira
Tapiraí
Marinópolis
Valentim Gentil
BR-153
Colômbia
Rifaina
Ilha Solteira
Pontalinda
Fronteira
Parque Nacional da Serra da Canastra
Icém
Guaira
Estreito
Bambuí
Represa Jupia
Pereira Barreto
Votuporanga
Nova Granada
Guaraci
1047
Ituverava
Delfinópolis
271
Castilho
Tanabi
Barretos
S Joaquim da Barra
Franca
Lagoas
Auriflama
Major Prado
Nhandeara
M Aprazivel
Olímpia
558
Morro Agudo
Represa Peixoto
Andradina
Colina
Cassia
Ilha Comprida
Piumhi
Murutinga do Sul
Mirandópolis
Vicentópolis
Mirassol
S José do Rio Preto
Terra Roxa
Orlândia
Passos
Pto João Andre
Buritama
José Bonifácio
Viradouro
Itaú de Minas
Valparaiso
Araçatuba
Ibirá
Bebedouro
Pitanguairas
Pontan
Batatais
S Sebastião do Paraiso
Guapé
Tupi Paulista
Represa Nova Avanhandava
Catanduva
Jardinópolis
Alpinópolis
Junqueirópolis
Guararapes
Barbosa
Urupés
Sertãozinho
Nova Rezende
Dracena
Birigüi
Novo Horizonte
Monte Alto
RIBEIRÃO PRÊTO
Serrana
M S de Minas
14
Pacaembu
Brauna
Penápolis
Jaboticabal
Pres Venceslau
Adamantina
Lucelia
Taquaritinga
Guariba
Cravinhos
Guaxupé
Campos Gerais
Rinópolis
Prormssão
Borborema
Muzambinho
Osvaldo Cruz
Parapuã
Lins
Itápolis
Matão
Mococa
Sto Anastácio
Bastos
Getulina
Americo Brasilense
Santa Rosa de Viterbo
402
Areado
Alfenas
Alvares Machado
Tupã
Calelândia
Ibitinga
Pres
Herculândia
SÃO PAULO
Guarantã
Araraquara
Tambaú
Machado
Martinópolis
Pompeia
Pirajui
Iacanga
Campestre
Regente Feijó
Rancheria
Vera Cruz
Bariri
Descalvado
Pto Ferreira
Poços de Caldas
Quatá
Marilia
Garca
Dourado
Ibate
Pirassununga
Anhumas
Paraguacu Paulista
Galia
Bauru
São Carlos
Narandiba
Capivara
Echaporã
Jaú
Brotas
Leme
Aquai
Andradas
Itororó
Nantes
Duartina
Pederneiras
Esp Santo do Pinhal
Maracai
RIO CLARO
Araras
Iepê
Assis
Ubirajara
Agudós
Moji-guaçu
Porecatu
Represa Capivara
Florinia
Santa Cruz do Rio Pardo
Barra Bonita
São Pedro
Limeira
Moji-mirim
Pouso Alegre
Bela Vista do Paraiso
Palmital
Clarinia
Lençóis Paulista
Itapira
Corhelio Procópio
Piracicaba
Cosmpolis
Socorro
Sertanópolis
São Manoel
Americana
Astorga
Ourinhos
S Bárb' d'Oeste
Cambui
Campos do Jordão
Cambe
Cambará
Ipauçu
Botucatu
Sumaré
Rolândia
LONDRINA
Jacarezinho
CAMPINAS
Valinhos
Bragança Paulista
Arapongas
Assai
Sto Antônio da Platina
Piraju
Avaré
Itatinga
Padista
Indaiatuba
Itatiba
Res Armando
Cerquilho
Tietê
Jundiai
Taubaté
Apucarana
Ribeiro do Pinhal
Fartura
Paranapanema
Atibaia
Carlópolis
Pto Feliz
Salto
Bom Sucesso
Tamarana
Congonhinhas
Itai
Guarei
Itu
Francisco Morato
15
S Pedro do Ivai
S Jerônimo da Serra
Represã de Xavantes
Taquantuba
Angatuba
Tatui
SOROCABA
Borrazópolis
Figueira
Ibaiti
Tomazina
Itaporanga
Itapetininga
Jacarei
Sapopema
Votorantim
OSASCO
GUARULHOS
Faxinal
Riversul
Grandes Rios
Natingui
Venceslau Bras
Itaberá
649
Buri
SÃO PAULO
STO ANDRÉ
Curuiva
Itapeva
Capão Bonito
S Miguel Arcanjo
Pilar do Sul
Itapecerica da Cerra
Em Guaçu
S BERNARDO
Ivaiporã
Ortigueira
Ventania
Arapoti
Itararé
BR-151
Cubacão
BR-376
Telémaco Borba
Jaguariaiva
SANTOS
Manuel Ribas
Candido de Abreu
Praia Grande
Imbaú
1260
Rio Branco
Guapiara
Parque Intervals
Juquiá
Bigua
BR-116
Guarujá
Tibaji
Itanhaém
Pitanga
Pirai do Sul
Sete Barras
Apiai
Varzeão
Itariri
Peruibe
Ilha de Alcatrazes
Reserva
Eldorado
PARANÁ
S Damas
Castro
Adrianópolis
Ribeira
Registro
Estação Ecológica Juréia
Vitor
Iporanga
Juquiá
Boa Ventura
Jacupiranga
Barra do Ribeira
Ponta Grossa
Cerro Azul
Ivai
Cajati
Barra do Turvo
Iguape
Ipiranga
R F Açungui
Prudentópolis
Imbiluva
Rio Branco do Sul
Ilha Comprida
BR-376
Cananéia
Morro Alto
Relógio
Estação Ecológica Guaraqueçaba
Ilha do Cardoso
16
Guarapuava
Teixeira Soares
Almte Tamandaré
Colombo
Ponta Camboriú
Palmeira
Compaina Grande de Sul
Guaraqueçaba
Reserva Florestal Irati
Irati
Parque Nacional de Superagüi
Jordão
855
Guaiaca
CURITIBA
Piraquara
Ilha do Mel
Pinhão
Araucana
Rebouças
Rio Azul
Faz Rio Grande
393
Paranaguá
Cruz Machado
S Mateus do Sul
BR-476
Lapa
Serra da Graciosa
Pontal do Sul
Areia
Paulo Frontin
Agua Amarela
Campo do Tenente
Matinhos
Negro
Garuva
Guaratuba

390
J
K
L
16
17
18
19
20
PY
AR
UY
CENTRAL
Carapeguá
Dalmacia
EEMBUCU
Va Oliva
Mbocayaty
La Colmena
Acahay
630
Iturbe
GUAIRA
Parque Nacional Ybycui
Parque Na Ybytyruzú
Res Nacional Kuri'y
Cuidad del Este
Pto Franco
Pto Iguazu
Parque Nac d Iguazu
Foz do Iguacu
Cap L Marques
Capanema
São
Valerio Deste
Espigão Alto
Nova Prata
Realza
Sarandi
Laranjeiras
Rep de do Sul
Salto Santiago
Dois Vizinhos
S Francisco
Wanda
San Cristobal
Caaguazú
Nacunday
Tavai
Alberdi
L Verá
Caapucú
Quyquyó
Mbuyyapey
Caazapa
A Juan Nepomuceno
365
PARAGUARI
Moises Bertoni
ITAPUA
Punta Esperanza
Pto Delicia
Sto Antônio do Sudoeste
Pranchita
Francisco Beltrão
Passa Qualro
Coronel Vivida
Salgado Filho
Marmeleiro
Chopin
Cerrito
Va Flonda
CAAZAPA
Dolores
Tebicuary
Pto Mayor Otaño
Bern de Irigove
Barração
S Juán Neembucú
Yegros
Arquitecto Tomas Romero Pereira
Eldorado
Piray-guazú
Dionisio Cerqueira
Campo Eré
Pato Branco
S Miguel
S Juan Bautista
Yuty
São Lourenco de Oeste
Palmas
MISIONES
Santa Maria
Salitre Cué
850
Colonia Pirapo
Edelira
Montecarlo
S Miguel d'Oeste
Anchieta
Tacuaras
San Ingacio
S Pedro de Paraná
Cerro Chatá
Serra Alta
Abelardo Lu
Quilombo
Neembucu
Ea Santa Elisa
Gral Artigas
Jesús
Cap Meza
Pto Rico
MISIONES
Maravilha
Desmochado
S Patricio
Capiovi
Pto Mineral
Bom Jesus
Coronel Freitas
Faximal d
Villalbin
Cnl Bogado
Bella Vista
Jardin América
San Vicente
Iporã
Modelo
Palmitos
S Carlos
Xanxeré
Xaxim
Laureles
Yabebyry
Santiago
Yababyry
2 de Mayo
Itapitanga
Tte Portela
Mondia
Aguas de Chapecó
Chapecó
Cerrito
Ilha Entre Rios
Encarnación
Posadas
S Ignacio
Campo Grande
Campo Viera
Três Passos
Irai
Frederico Westphalen
Concórdia
Itá Ibaté
Ilha Apipé Grande
Barranqueras
Ilha Talavera
Candelaria
Xapecó
Presidente C Branco
B de Estrada
Ituzaingó
Oberá
Crissiumal
Seberi
Aratiba
Sra del Rosario de Caa-Cati
Horizontina
Erval Seco
Campinas do Sul
Erechim
Leandro N Alem
Alecrim
3 de Maio
Campo Novo
Loreto
San José
Tucunduva
Várzea
Constantina
Esteros de Iberá
Po Concepción
Apostoles
S Javier
Pto Lucena
Santa Rosa
Santo Augusto
S Miguel
Laguna de Luna
Gobernador Agr Valentin Virasoro
Inhacora
Ronda Alta
Getúlio Varg
Colonia Madariaga
Concepción de la Sierra
Pto Xavier
Candido Godi
Giruá
Palmeira das Missões
Sarandi
Sertão
Santa Lucia
Azara
Salvador das Missões
Guarani das Missões
Chapada
Santa Rosa
L Galaza
Aguapey
Cerro Largo
Ijui
Catuípe
Ajuricaba
Carazinho
Tapejara
Concepción
S Luis Gonzaga
Santo Angelo
Panambi
Santa Bárbara do Sul
Passo Fundo
Reserva Florestal Passo Fundo
L Trin
Santo Tomé
São José
Sto Antonio das Misães
S Miguel
Ijui
A Pestana
Nao-Me-Toque
Marau
David
Corrientes
Uruguay
Cuay Grande
São Borja
Piratini
Missões Jesuíticas
Cruz Alta
Barr Ernestina
CORRIENTES
Po Mesa
Torrent
Nhu Porã
Icamaquã
Bororoca
Joia
Tapera
Casca
Qunze de Novembro
Nova Alvorada
Buriti
Espumoso
S Gabriél
Uruguai
Encruzilhada
Itacurubi
Capao do Cipo
Fortaleza dos Valos
Alto Alegre
Soledade
Mercedes
Alvear
Itaqui
Tupanciretã
Salto de Jaçuí
Arvorezinha
Guapo
Sobradinho
Santiago
Represa de Passo Real
Veranópolis
La Cruz
Itao
Mirinay
Mariano Loza
Itu
Serra do Iguariaça
Flórida
Júlio de Castilhos
Barro Cassal
Guaviravi
Mariano Pinto
429
Quevedos
Gramado Xavier
Bento Gonçalves
Yaguari
S Francisco de Assis
Jacuí
Tapebicuá
João Arregui
Ibicuí
Jaguari
Toropi
Coxilha
Cera
Velha
Encantado
Baibiene
S Marcos
Manuel Viana
S Pedro do Sul
Nova Palma
Sobradinho
Garibald
Paso de los Libres
S Vicente do Sul
Mata
Teutonia
Passo Novo
Lajeado
Bonpland
Uruguaiana
Plano Alto
Santa Maria
Candelaria
Étrela
Venâncio Aires
São Rafael
Dilermando de Agiar
Agudo
Quaral
Alegrete
Cacequi
Umbu
Montenegro
Monte Caseros
Vertentes
Catimbau
Santa Cruz do Sul
São Leop
Barra do Quarai
Harmonia
Cavera
RIO GRANDE DO SUL
Bernabé Rivera
Ibirapuitã
Saiçã
Azevado Sodré
Formigueira
Rio Pardo
Bella Unión
Coxilha del Santana
Cavera
Lajeado Grande
Bexiga
Topador
Tiaracu
São Sepé
Cachoeira do Sul
Jacui
Quarai
Rosário do Sul
Guaib
Mocoretá
Passo da Guarda
Area de Proteção Ambiental Ibirapuita
Barro Vermelho
Itacumbu
Artigas
São Gabriel
Pantano Grande
Butiá
PO ALE
Embalse Salto Grande
ARTIGAS
206
313
Vila Nova do Sul
Forminho
Vacacai
Campo Seco
Caçapava do Sui
Quiteria
Baltasar Brum
Cuch de Belén
Cuareim
247
S José
Encruzilhada do Sul
Belén
Supiro
Maria
420
Cerro Grande de Sul
Santa Ana
Campamento
Santana do Livramento
Ibaré
Termas de Arapey
Sarandi del Arapey
Serra das Encantadas
Lavras do Sul
Aguas Brancas
Lavalleja
Olivera
Rivera
Torquato Severo
Santana da Boa Vista
Constitución
Arapey
Ferreira
Masoller
Dom Pedrito
Pedro Antunes
Minas de Camaqua
Amaral Ferrador
Camaq
Concordia
SALTO
Cayetano
Mataojo
338
Camaqua
Cristal
Salto
Biassini
Tranqueras
Tres Vendas
Bagé
Arambi
Quintana
Cuch del Daymán
Silveira
Maqrio Qubio
La Calera
José Otávio
Esperenca
Boqueirão
Santa Rita
Daymán
Herreria
Paso del Cerro
Berruti
Pirai
Hulha Negra
Serra do Canguçu
Boa Vista
148
Carumbe
Paso de las Carretas
Manuel Diaz
Seival
Santa Clara
Chapicuy
Minas de Carrales
Pirantini
Canguaçu
S Lourenço do Sul
Patos
Daymán
Hospital
Rivas
Cuchilla de Haedo
Tacuarembó
RIVERA
Negro
Candiota
Pinheiro Machado
Freie
Arthur Lange
Vichadero
Colonia Nova
Turuçu
Pelotas
Co Chato
El Eucalipto
Tambores
Martinote
Ansina
Coronilla
Zania Honda
Pedrras Altas
Basílio
Dunas
PAYSANDU
Federación
Piedra Sola
Los Novillos
Picada de Cuello
Aceguá
Capão do Leão
Pedro Osorio
Varzea
Estreito
Queguay Gde
Curtina
Buene Vista
Conde Matarazzo
Ilha dos Marinheiros
Guichón
Pinera
Morato
Pampa
Clara
Cuchilla Cuaraguate
Nando
Erval
S José do Norte
Algorta
Achar
TACUAREMBÓ
C LARGO
Centurión
Santa Isbel do Sul
Quinta
Rio Grande
Orvenir
Represe del Rio Negro
Km 329
Paso Pareira
Melo
Jaguarão
Arroio Gde
Cassino
R NEGRO
Rolon
Lago Artificial de Baygorria
Chamberlain
San Gregório de Polanco
Negro
3 Islas
La Pedrera
Lagoa Mirim
Grande
L Caiubá
Young
Fraile Muerto
Uruguay
Paso de los Toros
Arevalo
Rio Branco
Taim
L Formosa
Tres Bocas
Grecco
San Jorge
Cerro Zuelo
Cerro de las Cuentas
Arbolito
Plácido Rosas
Lago Merin
Baygorria
Tupambaé
Tacuari
Ponta dos Latinos
Negro
DURAZNO
Rincon
Estação Ecológica do Taim
Lago Artificial Paso del Palmar
Carlos Reyes
Santa Clara de Olimar
TREINTA Y TRES
Vergara
Mercedes
Yarbalito
Cural Alto
Va del Carmen
Cerro Chato
Cuchilla Grande
Treinta Y Tres
Julio Maria Sanz
Arrozal '33'
SORIANO
Yi
Valentines
Olimar
Arvore So
Palmitas
Santa Bernardina
Sarandi del Yi
Cebollati
Lag Mangabeira
Trinidad
Durazno
Capilla del Sauce
José Batlle Y Ordóñez
Picade de Techera
Joan J Castro
Marcie
Santo Luis al Medio
José E-Rodó
FLORIDA
Zapicán
José P Varela
Salvador
Sarandi Grande
Hernandarias
Pirarajá
Lascano
La Corronilla
Santa Vitória do Palmar
Cardona
Cuch Grande Interior
Balneário Hermenegildo
Ombúes de Lavalle
La Cruz
Cerro Colorado
Cebollati
Emb India Muerta
Chui (Chuy)
SAN JOSÉ
LAVALLEJA
Casupa
377
Velásquez
ROCHA
La Coronilla
Nva Helvecia
Florioa
Fray Marcos
Mariscala
L Negra

Guarapuava
Teixeira Soares
Almte Tamandaré
Colombo
Ecológica Guaraqueçaba
Ilha do Cardoso
Ponta Camboriú
Palmeira
Reserva Florestal Irati
Jordão
Irati
855
Guaiaca
CURITIBA
Compaina Grande de Sul
Guaraqueçaba
Parque Nacional de Superagüi
391
Pinhão
Rebouças
Araucana
Piraquara
Ilha do Mel
M
N
Rio Azul
Cruz Machado
S Mateus do Sul
Faz Rio Grande
S José dos Pinhais
Paranaguá
BR-476
Lapa
Serra da Graciosa
Pontal do Sul
Paulo Frontin
Agua Amarela
Campo do Tenente
Matinhos
Iguaçu
Garuva
Guaratuba
da Vitória
S Cristovão
Três Baras
Rio Negro
Negro
Pto União
Canoinhas
Mafra
S Bento do Sul
Estação Ecológica de Babitonga
Reserva Biológica Irineópolis
Rio Negrinho
Ubatuba
Monte Castelo
Paparuva
JOINVILLE
S Francisco do Sul
Serra do Espigão
Araquari
Caçador
1340
Timbo Grande
BR-116
Jaraguá do Sul
Guaramirim
SANTA CATARINA
Caçaranduba
Itapocu
Barra Velha
Caçador
Lebon Régis
Santa Cecília
1220
Rio dos Cedros
Pomerode
Videira
Salete
Blumenau
890
Picarras
Tangará
Indaial
Timbó
Itajaí
Peixe
Fraiburgo
Rio do Campo
BR-101
Erval d'Oeste
Curitibanos
Taio
Pres Getúlio
Gaspar
Baineário Camboriú
Trombudo Central
Rio do Sul
Brusque
Campos Novos
BR-470
Porto Belo
Tupitinga
São Jose do Cerrito
Otacilio Costa
S João Batista
Tijucas
Ilha dos Macucos
Celso Ramos
Ituporanga
E E de Carijós
Gvo Celso Ramos
Pelotas
Correla Pinto
Biguaçu
Anita Garibaldi
BR-116
Ilha de Santa Catarina
Alfredo Wagner
São José
Florianópolis
Campo Belo do Sul
Lages
Bom Retiro
Palhoça
Estação Ecológica Aracuri-Esmeralda
1853
Canoas
Pântano do Sul
Urubici
Santa Rosa de Lima
São Bonifácio
Parque Nacional São Joaquim
1808
Garopaba
BR-285
S Joaquim
Grao-Para
Praia do Rosa
São Sebastiao do Arvoredo
São Ludgero
Gravatal
Imbituba
Lauro Muller
Orleães
Imarui
Vacaria
1055
Uruçanga
Tubarão
Siderópolis
Bom Jesus
Laguna
Nova Veneza
Criciúma
Cabo de Santa Marta
Antônio Prando
Antas
Jaquirana
Içara
Farol de Santa Marta
Alziro Ramos
Meleiro
Vila Nova
853
Jacinto Machado
Araranguá
Caxias do Sul
Arr do Silva
P N Aparados da Serra
Praia Gde
Sombrio
L do Sombrio
Cai
Canela
Tainhas
Santa Rose de Sul
1250
Itao
Torres
Gramado
Terra Areia
Cachoeiras
Sapiranga
L Itapeví
Taquará
Arroio do Sal
Campo Bom
L dos Quadros
Sapucaia do Sul
Capão da Canoa
Gravatai
Osorio
L de Fora
Alvorada
Tramandai
Viamao
Capivari
Itapua
Cidreira
Palmares do Sul
Pinhal
L do Quintão
Guiba
Quintão
Dr E Pereira
Bacopari
Doutor Edgardo Pereira Velho
S Simão
Parque Nacional Lagoa do Peixe
Mostardas
Tavares
16
17
18
19
20
M
N

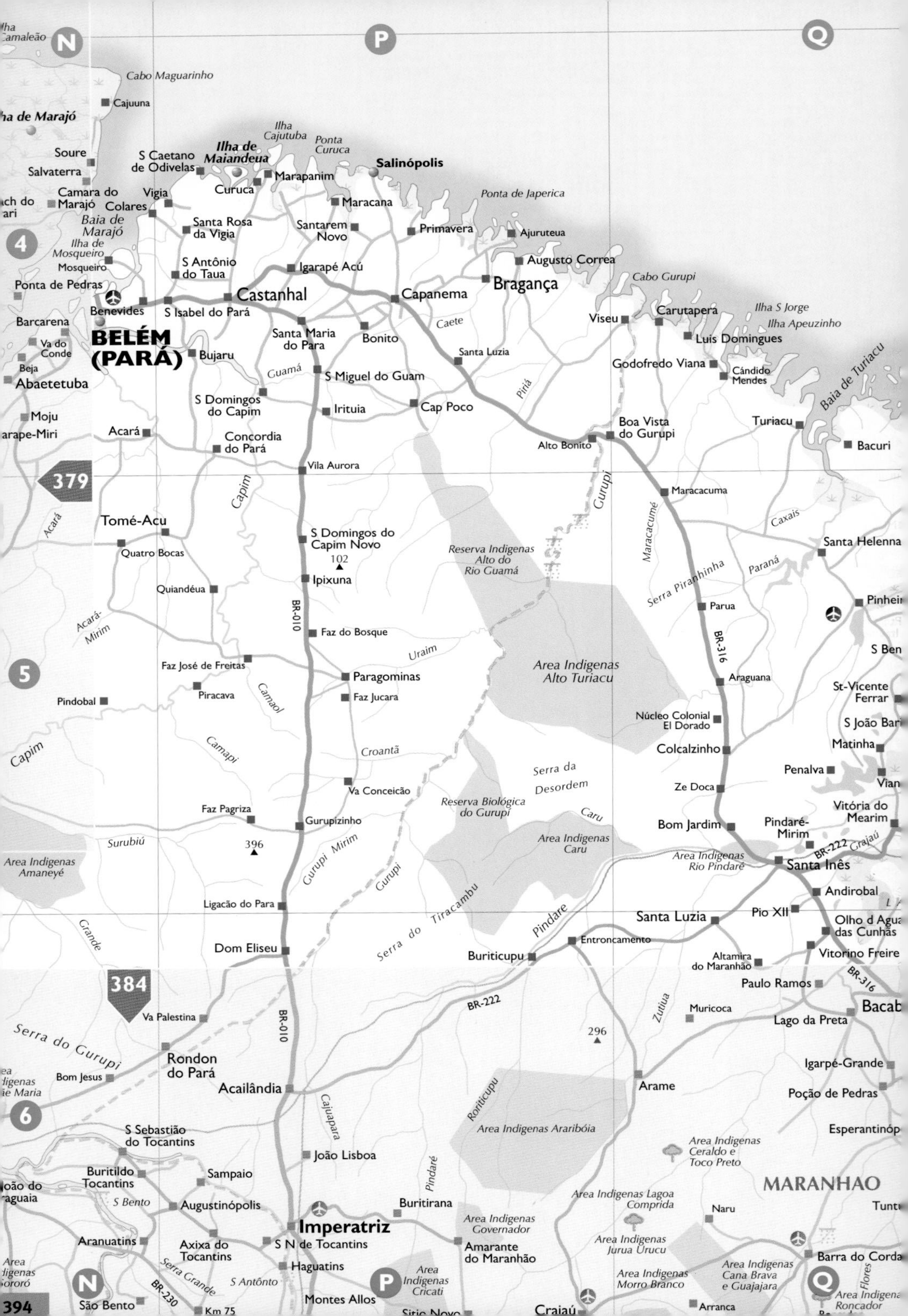

N
P
Q
Cabo Maguarinho
Cajuuna
Ilha de Marajó
Ilha Cajutuba
Ponta Curuca
Soure
S Caetano de Odivelas
Ilha de Maiandeua
Salinópolis
Salvaterra
Marapanim
Camara do Marajó
Vigia
Curuca
Colares
Maracana
Ponta de Japerica
Baia de Marajó
Santa Rosa da Vigia
Santarem Novo
Primavera
Ajuruteua
4
Ilha de Mosqueiro
Mosqueiro
S Antônio do Taua
Igarapé Acú
Augusto Correa
Ponta de Pedras
Castanhal
Capanema
Bragança
Cabo Gurupi
Benevides
S Isabel do Pará
Barcarena
Santa Maria do Para
Caete
Viseu
Carutapera
Ilha S Jorge
Ilha Apeuzinho
Va do Conde
BELÉM (PARÁ)
Bonito
Luís Domingues
Beja
Bujaru
Santa Luzia
Baia de Turiacu
Godofredo Viana
Cándido Mendes
Abaetetuba
Guamá
S Miguel do Guam
Piriá
S Domingos do Capim
Irituia
Cap Poco
Moju
Boa Vista do Gurupi
Turiacu
Acará
Concordia do Pará
Alto Bonito
Bacuri
Vila Aurora
379
Capim
Gurupi
Maracacuma
Tomé-Acu
Acará
Maracacumé
Caxais
S Domingos do Capim Novo
Quatro Bocas
102
Reserva Indigenas Alto do Rio Guamá
Santa Helenna
Ipixuna
Paraná
Quiandéua
Serra Piranhinha
Pinheiro
Parua
BR-010
Acará-Mirim
Faz do Bosque
BR-316
S Ben
Uraim
Faz José de Freitas
Area Indigenas Alto Turiacu
5
Paragominas
Araguana
St-Vicente Ferrar
Pindobal
Piracava
Camaol
Faz Jucara
Núcleo Colonial El Dorado
S João Bari
Camapi
Colcalzinho
Matinha
Capim
Croantã
Serra da Desordem
Penalva
Va Conceicão
Ze Doca
Vian
Faz Pagriza
Reserva Biológica do Gurupi
Caru
Vitória do Mearim
Gurupizinho
Bom Jardim
Pindaré-Mirim
Surubiú
396
Gurupi Mirim
Area Indigenas Caru
BR-222
Grajaú
Area Indigenas Amaneyé
Gurupi
Area Indigenas Rio Pindaré
Santa Inês
Andirobal
Ligacão do Para
Serra do Tiracambu
Pio XII
Grande
Pindare
Santa Luzia
Olho d Agua das Cunhas
Entroncamento
Dom Eliseu
Buriticupu
Altamira do Maranhão
Vitorino Freire
384
BR-316
Paulo Ramos
BR-222
Zutiua
Va Palestina
Muricoca
Bacab
BR-010
Lago da Preta
Serra do Gurupi
296
Rondon do Pará
Igarpé-Grande
Bom Jesus
Acailândia
Arame
Poção de Pedras
6
Cajuapara
Roriticupu
Area Indigenas Araribóia
Esperantinóp
S Sebastião do Tocantins
Area Indigenas Ceraldo e Toco Preto
João Lisboa
Buritildo Tocantins
Sampaio
Pindaré
MARANHAO
S Bento
Augustinópolis
Buritirana
Area Indigenas Lagoa Comprida
Naru
Imperatriz
Area Indigenas Governador
Aranuatins
Axixa do Tocantins
S N de Tocantins
Amarante do Maranhão
Area Indigenas Jurua Urucu
Barra do Corda
Haguatins
Serra Grande
Area Indigenas Cricati
Area Indigenas Morro Branco
Area Indigenas Cana Brava e Guajajara
S Antônto
BR-230
Flores
Area Indigenas Roncador
São Bento
Km 75
Montes Allos
Grajaú
Arranca

R
S
4
5
6
São João
Marizal
Ponta do Zumbi
Ilha Cacacueira
Ilha Mangunca
Ponta do Faval
Ponta Guajuru
Cedrai
Mirinzal
Guimarães
R de Cumã
Ponta Itacolomi
Ilha Santana
Alcântara
Ilha Carrapatal
Pto de Itaúna
Baia de São Marcos
Ribamar
Baia de São José
Primeira Cruz
SÃO LUÍS
Anil
Parque Nacional dos Lençóis Maranhenses
Santo Amaro
Humberto de Campos
Icatu
Axixá
Morros
Cajapio
Bacabeira
Rosário
Barreirinhas
Paulino Cruz
Tutoia
Ilha Caju
Delta do Parnaiba
Ilha Gde de Santa Isabel
Santa Rita
Anajatuba
Itapicuru
Urbano Santos
Cocal
Fome
Cana Brava
Parnaiba
Luis Correia
Camocim
Magu
Chaval
Itapecuru-Mirim
São Benedito
Bacuri
Buriti dos Lopes
Granj
Nina Rodrigues
Piranji
Miranda
Vargem Gde
Magalhães de Almeida
Cantanhede
Preto
Santa Quiteria
Luzilândia
Longa
Cocal
Martinópolis
Anapuras
L do Cajueiro
Joaquim Pires
Timonha
BR-135
Pirapemas
Chapadinha
Breio
Matias Olimpio
Vicosa do Ceara
Coreaú
Pirapemas
Iguará
Barra
Deserto
S Mateus do Maranhão
Porto
Tlanguá
Parque Nacional de Ubajara
Munim
Parnaíba
Piranji
385
Coroatá
Buriti
Esperantina
Piracuruca
Duque Bacela
N S dos Remédios
Alto Alegre
BR-222
Ubajara
Peritoró
Timbiras
Mocambo
Batanha
Atonso Cunna
Miguel Alves
Parque Nacional de Sete Cidades
Barras
Serra da Ibiapaba
Pacu
Lima Campos
Coelho Neto
396
Guaraciaba do Norte
Inhucu
Codó
Piripiri
SantaRita
Cameleira
Cabaceiras
Marianópolis
Itapicuru
União
Pedro
Capitao de Campos
Codozinho
Olinda
Serra do Pedro II
Tocaia
S Antonio dos Lopes
José de Freitas
Caxias
Gov Archer
Campo Maior
Poranga
BR-316
BR-343
Pres Dulra
Altos
Capivara
Gov Eugenio Barros
Onga
TERESINA
Sucesso
Graca Aranha
Poti
Oiticaca
S Domingos do Maranhao
Pedreiras
Serra Valentim
Alto Longa
Demerval Loão
BR-116
Beneditinos
Castelo do Piaui

Ilha Caju
S
T
Delta do Parnaiba
Ilha Gde de Santa Isabel
Parnaiba
Luis Correia
Jericoacoara
Camocim
Arana
Acaraú
5
Chaval
L Grande
Ponta de Itapajé
Buriti dos Lopes
Granja
Bela Cruz
Marco
Ponta dos Patos
Patos
Icarai
Martinópolis
Uruoca
Morrinhos
Longa
Cocal
Ponta de Mundaú
Joaquim Pires
Timonha
Mundaú
Sapo
Amantada
Train
Vicosa do Ceara
Coreaú
Massapé
Acaraú
Santana do Acaraú
Itapipoca
Paracuru
Barra
Deserto
Coreau
Ponta Corumiquara
Pirajá
Tlanguá
Parque Nacional de Ubajara
Sobral
Uruburetama
S Luis
L Talos
Piracuruca
Pecém
Alto Alegre
BR-222
Ubajara
Iraucuba
Itapaje
Cruata
Batanha
Pacujá
BR-222
Pentecostes
Caucaia
FORTALEZA
Parque Nacional de Sete Cidades
Serra da Ibiapaba
Cariré
Acude Aracatiacu
Acude Pentecostes
Mondubim
Parangaba
Piripiri
395
Inhucu
Guaraciaba do Norte
Taperauaba
Gral Sampaio
Maranguape
Mecejana
776
Pacatuba
6
Capitao de Campos
Pedro
Serra do Pedro II
Acude Santa Maria
Acude Gral Sampaio
Guaiuba
Capor
Ipu
Acude Araras
Sta Quiteria
Pacajus
Cascavel
Canindé
BR-020
Redencão
Sucatir
Ioueiras
Hidrolancia
Baturité
Serra do Machado
Beber
Poranga
Aracoiaba
Chorozinho
ampo Maior
Nova Russas
Itallra
Serra de Baturité
Capistrano
Cristais
Capivara
Tamborin
Serra das Matas
Choró
Monsenhor Tabosa
Piranji
BR-116
Sucesso
Madalena
Poti
Oiticaca
Boa Agua
Acude Choro
Pedra
Crateús
Quixadá
Castelo do Piaui
Ematuba
Boa Viagem
Russas
Gracas
CEARÁ
Morada Nova
S João da Serra
Quixeramobim
S Miguel do Tapuio
Serra Grande
Independencia
Limoeiro do Norte
Banabuiú
Novo Oriente
Riachao do Banabuiú
Mineirolandia
Acude Banabuiu
Tabuleiro do Norte
São Nicolau
São Francisco
Senador Pompeu
Serra da Joaninha
Acude Varzea do Boi
Mombaca
Jaguaretama
Brejo da Onca
Alto Santo
660
Trici
Carrapateiras
Piquiet Carneiro
Solonopole
Tauá
BR-116
Iracema
Sambito
Nova Floresta
Jaguanbe
BR-316
Pimenteiras
Parambu
Valenca do Piaui
Serra dos Cariris Novos
Catarina
Acopiara
Erere
7
Serra da Batista
Cocotá
Pau dos Ferros
Acude Orós
Orós
Inhuma
Jaguaribe
Saboeiro
Jucas
Iguatu
São Miguel
Icó
385
506
Guaribas
BR-020
Barra
683
Estação Ecológica de Aiuaba
Alexandria
Santo Antônio de Lisboa
Pio IX
Antonina do Norte
Cedro
Uiraúna
Mons Hipolito
Conceição
Assaré
Várzea Alegre
Lavras
Piox
Picos
Carmelópolis
Ipaumirim
Sousa
Fronteiras
Farias Brito
Saigado
Itaim
Campos Sales
Aratema
Nova Olinda
Cariríaçu
Aurora
Cajazeiros
Marizópolis
Jaicós
Araripe
Iara
BR-230
Itainópolis
Reserva Florestal Araripe
Crato
Juazeiro do Norte
Açude Piranhas
Barro
BR-316
Marcolândia
Chapada do Araripe
S José de Piranhas
Simães
Serrolândia
Barbalha
Missão Velha
Milagres
Açude Core
Araripina
Bonito de Santa Fé
Ipubi
Exú
Brejo Santo
Mauriti
Itaporanga
impliclo Mendes
Morais
Jardim
Umburanas
Conceicão do Canindé
Bodocó
Trinidade
Granito
BR-407
Gentio
Pianco
8
398
São Pedro
Ouricuri
Gameleira
Princesa Isabel
Canindé
Serra Dois Irmãos
Vidéu
Serrita
S José do Belmonte
1056
Paulistana
Munduri
Parnamirim
Triunfo
Flores
Volta
BR-316
Cruz de Malta
Umás
Salgueiro
Serra Talhada
Sitio

PN Marinho de Fernando de Noronha
Fernando de Noronha
Ponta da Macaxeira
Ilha do Lucena
Ponta Oeste
Ilha Rata
Ens da Ressurreta
Ilha de Meio
Ilha de São José
Ilha Sela Gineta
Ilha de Fora
Ilha Rasa
Ponta de Santo Antônio
Baía de Sto Antônio
Ilha da Conceição
Ens da Caieira
Baía do Pico
Vila dos Remedios
321
Pico
Ilha Dois Irmãos
195
Pontinha
Morro do Meio
Morro do Francês
Baía do Sancho
Ponta da Pedra Alta
223
Saco da Atalata
Ens do Carreiro da Pedra
Morro do Espinhaço
Ilha do Frade
Ponta do Espinhaço
Morro Branco
172
Morro do Medeira
Ilha Ovos
Ens do Portão
Morro da Quixabinha
Ilha Cabeluda
Poonta da Sapata
Alto da Floresta
Baía de Sudeste
Ilha Mo do Leão
Ponta das Caracas
Ponta do Barro Vermelho
Ponta do Cupim-Açu
RIO GRANDE DO NORTE
PARAÝBA
NATAL
João Pessoa
Campina Grande
Mossoró
Caicó
Paripueira
Ponta de Maceió
Canoa Quebrada
Aracati
Ponta Grossa
Ibicuitaba
BR-304
Jaguaruana
Tibaú
Recife João Dias
Grossos
Areia Branca
Recife do Tubarão
Recife Minhoto
Barauna
Ponta Redonda
Recife Conceição
Jucuri
Macaú
Caicara
Gov Dix
Pendências
Guamaré
Reduto
Ponta Santo Cristo
Apodi
Carmo
Parazinho
Touros
Ponta do Calcanhar
Rio do Fogo
Acu
Afonso Bezerra
Upanema
Caraúbas
Angicos
João Câmara
Cabo de São Roque
Ceará Mirim
Maxaranguape
Augusto Severo
S Rafael
Lajes
Ceara-Mirim
Ponta de Santa Rita
Janduis
Santana do Matos
Riachueto
Redinha
Patu
S Paulo do Potenji
Jucurutu
Macaiba
Catole do Rocha
Piranhas
Florania
Cerro Corá
São Tomé
Eduardo Gomes
Ponta Flamingo
Brejo da Cruz
Pres Juscelino
Buzios
Currais Novos
Santa Cruz
BR-427
Tangará
S José de Mipibu
Trairi
Ponta da Conceição
S José do Campestre
Tibau do Sul
Serra Negra
Açude Itãs
Acari
Picui
Goianinha
Parque Estadual Mata da Pipa
Jardim do Seridó
Japi
BR-101
Canguaretama
Açuda Saboji
Cuité
Baia Formosa
Bento
Parelhas
Araruna
Nova Cruz
Estação Ecológica de Serido
Malta
Santa Luzia
Jacu
Curimatau
Belém
Cubati
Jacarau
Solânea
Reserva Biológica Guirabas
Patos
BR-230
Baia da Traição
Rio Tinto
Estação Ecológica Mamanguape
Juazeirinho
Guarabira
Mamanguape
Teixeira
Soledade
1090
Esperanca
Miriri
Taperoã
S José do Egito
Cabedelo
Bayeux
Santa Rita
Planalto da Borborema
Queimadas
Ingá
Ponta do Seixas
Cariri
Itabaiana
Tuparetama
Pajeú
Boqueirão
Itambé
Sumé
Açude Boqueirão
Jacumã
Açude Sumé
Alhandra
Jabitacá
Timbaúba
Caraúbas
Paraiba
Goiana
Aliança
Pitimbu
Monteiro
399

Socomo do Piaul
R
Simpliclo Mendes
Simães
S
Serrolândia
Araripina
Ipubi
Exú
Barbalha
Velha
Brejo Santo
T
Jardim
Umburanas
Morais
Bodocó
396
Granito
Conceição do Canindé
BR-407
Gentio
Trinidade
São Pedro
Ouricuri
Gameleira
Fidalgo
Canindé
Serra Dois Irmãos
Vidéu
Serrita
S José do Belmonte
Munduri
Parnamirim
BR-316
S João do Piaui
Paulistana
Volta
Salgueiro
Piaui
Cruz de Malta
Umás
Mirandi
Boa Esperança
Gameleira
Dórmentes
Terra Nova
8
Parque Nacional da Serra da Capivara
Lagoa
Urimama
PERNAMBUCO
Afrânio
São Bento
Garças
BR-116
Vargem Grande
Itaqualiara
Jutai
BR-428
Cabrobó
Barro da Silv
Raimun do Nonato
Curral Novo
Orocó
Ouricuri
Rajada
Cnstália
Santa Maria da Boa Vista
Ibó
Ibó
Floresta
385
730
Serra das Marrecas
Belén de S Francisco
Nova Barra do Tarrachil
BR-234
Dirceu Arcoverde
406
Lagoa Grande
Serra do Piaui
Casa Nova
Curaçá
Nva Rodelas
ueimadas
Serra de Itiúba
Macururé
Francisco
BR-235
Vargem
São
Curaçá
Petrolina
Macurure
Sobradinho
Remanso
Juazeiro
Sobradinho
Barro Vermelho
Barragem de
Carnaiba do Sertão
Sento Sé
Ião Arcado
Formosa
Brejinho
Juremal
Comprido
Raso da Catarina
Estaçao Ecológica do Raso da Catarina
Salitre
Glóri
Caraiba
Maçaroca
Uauá
Açude Codorobó
Serra São Francisco
1229
Canudos
Barrinha
Amaniú
Canché
Laje
Juacema
1123
Delfino
BR-116
Jaguarari
Andorinha
Canaça
9
Picada
Senhor do Bonfim
Serra
Campo Formoso
Igara
Monte Santo
Umburanas
António Concalves
Açude Jacurici
Anta
da
Tiririca
Euclides da Cunha
Serra Jacobina
Carnaiba
Itiuba
Cicero Dantas
Serra da Batista
Salitre
Pindobaçu
Gansanção
Central
Jucara
Canastra
Verde
Mirangaba
Saúde
Gabriel
BR-324
Caldeirão Gde
Ribeira do Pombal
Uibai
BR-407
Queimadas
Irecê
Jacaré
Sentio o Ouro
Várzea Nova
Tucano
Lapão
Jacobina
Pedra
Açude Peixe
Cipo
Miguel Calmon
Ibitilà
BAHIA
Junco
Caldas do Jorro
Serra do Tombador
Serrolândia
Santaluz
Ibipiba
Morro do Chaéu
Nova Soure
Cafarnaum
Várzea do Poco
BR-116
Olind
389
1275
Jacuipe
Valente
Barra do Mendes
Piritiba
Araci
314
Olhos d'Agua do Seco
Mairi
Vila Fátima
Conceição do Coté
Mulungu
Serrinha
BR-110
1036
BR-407
Inhambupe
Mundo Novo
Baixa Gde
Riachão do Jacuipe
Chapada Diamantina
ocal
Utingá
1138
Capivari
Peixe
Iraquara
Wagner
Tanquinha
BR-242
Macajuba
Inhamb
Seabra
Saracura
Ipirá
Bravo
Ibitlara
Rui Barbosa
Irará
Aramari
1098
Palmeiras
BR-242
Feira de Santana
Lençóis
Serra do Orobo
BR-324
Alagoinhas
10
Parque Nacional da Chapada Diamantina
Tubim
Patarai
S Goncalo dos Campos
Conceicão do Jauipe
Santo Estêvão
Boa Vista do Tupim
Abara
Itaberaba
Paraguaçu
Santo Amaro
Pojuca
Catu
Andarai
234
BR-116
Barragem Podro do Cavalo
Muritiba
Ibiajara
Paraguaça
Mata de São João
Cruz das Almas
Cachoeira
Iaçu
Itaeré
Recôncavo
Candeias
Mucujé
Milagres
Castro Alves
Maragojipe
Camaç
Serra do
Baía de Todos os Santos
Cascavel
Marcionilio Souza
401
Santo Antônio de Jesus
Simães Filh
970
Itaparica
aramirim
Planaltino
Tramaia
S Mig das Matas
Lauro Freitas
Sincorá
Serra Geral
Chapada de Maracás
S
Nazaré
1850
R
Mutuipe
T
Jussiape
SALVADO
BR-101
Maracás
Santa Inês
Jiquiriça
Jaguaripe
Ilha Itaparica

PARAYBA
Campina Grande
João Pessoa
Caruaru
Olinda
RECIFE
ALAGOAS
MACEIÓ
SERGIPE
Aracaju
BAHIA)
397
8
9
10
U
V

Meio
Correntina
631
Q
Açudina
Pto Novo
Sitio do Mato
Bom Jesus da Lapa
Santa Rira
Serra da Garapa
Santo Onofre
Macaúbas
608
R
Ibiajara
Cascavel
Santa Maria da Vitória
Arrojado
Formoso
Gaturama
Botuporã
Paramirim
1129
1850
Pico das Almas
Jussiape
Pratudão
Coribe
Serra do Ramalho
São Francisco
Riacho de Santana
Pitubas
676
Igaporã
Livramento do Brumado
Brumado
Coltas
Cocos
Maniaçu
Carnaíba
Itaguari
Carinhanha
Caetité
Pitarana
Cachá
Malhada
Itaquari
Montalvânia
Coxá
Guanambi
Brumado
Serra da Capivara
S Seb dos Poções
Candiba
Ibiassucé
Serra de Monte Alto
Nhandutiba
Pindal
Rio do Antônio
Carinhanha
Serra Paratodos
Miravânia
Manga
Caculé
Verde
Verde Pequeno
Aracatu
11
Serra dos Tropeiros
Missães
Matias Cardoso
Urandi
Licinio de Almeida
Serra Linda
1500
Morro do Chapéu
Itacarambi
Grande
Condeúba
Gameleiras
Espinosa
Mortugaba
Palmeira
Cónego Marinho
Serra Geral
Montezuma
Belo Campo
Serra das Araras
Pandeiros
Levinópolis
Jaiba
Serra de Jaiba
Gorutuba
Monte Azul
Pardo
Salinas
Januária
S João do Paraiso
1013
Pedras de Santa Maria da Cruz
Serra de São Felipe
Mato Verde
Campo Redondo
Indaiabira
Salitre
Acari
Cândido Sales
389
Rio Pardo de Minas
São Franciscó
Lontra
Janaúba
685
Porteirinha
Berizal
Morro
S João da Ponte
Pardo
Luislândia
Taiobeiras
Aguas Vermelhas
Divisa Alegre
Ubai
Gameleira
Brasilia de Minas
Caçarema
Caveira
1053
o Romão
Mirabela
Ferreirópolis
BR-251
Francisco
São
Campo Azul
Fernão Dias
Cap Enéas
Vacaria
830
Salinas
Pedra Azul
Ponte dos Ciganos
Barrocão
Cach do Manteiga
Miraita
BR-251
Padre Carvalho
Medina
Paracatu
Pacuí
Francisco Sá
Itinga
Comercinho
Coracão de Jesus
Nova Esperanca
Grão Mogol
São Francisco
S João
Montes Claros
Ibiai
Cnel Murta
Itaobim
12
Juramento
Planalto
Itinga
BR-365
Claro dos Pocães
Virem da Lapa
Guaicui
954
Serra do Catuni
Bocaiúva
Araçuai
Santana do Arac
Aracuai
Buritzeiro
Jequitai
Itacambira
Pirapora
Fco Bedaró
Antas
Minas Novas
BR-116
Terra Branca
Jequitai
Jaquitinhonha
Padre Paraiso
Chifre
Serra do Cabral
Eng Scohoor
Várzea da Palma
Velhas
Caraí
Águ Formos
Veredinha
1300
Setúbal
Serra do
Crisólit
Espinhaço
Carbonita
Fanado
Joaquim Felicio
Novilhona
Nova Cruzeiro
Pavão
Lassance
Planalto de Minas
Buenópofis
Capelinha
Setubinha
Ladainha
Itamarandiba
Poté
Malacacheta
Andrequice
Contria
Augusto de Lima
Serra Negra
Teófilo Otoni
Agua Boa
Guinda
Diamantina
Santa Maria do Suacui
Corinto
1340
Brasil
Itambacuri
Velhas
13
2033
Senhora da Glória
Pico de Itambé
Rio Vermelho
Ataléia
Gouvea
Campanamo
30
BR-040
S João Evangelista
Virgolândia
403
Curvelo
Pres Juscelino
Serro
Marilac
BR-116
Pescador
Felixlândia
Inimutaba
Sabinópolis
Pecanha
Serra das Safiras
Ecopora
Serra
Guanhães
Coroaci
Frei Inocêncio
R
Itabirinha de Mantena
Q
Santana
765
Central de Minas
Angueretá
Dom Joaquim
Governador Valadares
Mantena

Andaraí
Itaeré
Marcionílio Souza
Tramaia
970
Serra Geral
Chapada de Maracás
Planaltino
Maracás
Pe da Serra
Barra da Estiva
Contendas do Sincorá
Itiruçu
Itaquara
Jaguaquara
BR-116
Jequié
Contas
Peixe
Suçuarana
Manuel Victoriano
Mirante
Jitiaúna
Gandu
Ipiaú
Ibirapitanga
Ubatá
Jibóia
Dario Mera
Gongoji
Ubaitaba
Aurelino Real
Poções
Anajé
Planalto
Gongoji
Vitória da Conquista
1004
Serra da Ouricana
Iguaí
Coaraci
Uruçuca
Itajuípe
Floresta Azul
Itabuna
Ibicara
Ilhéus
Buerarema
Olivença
Ponta Itapuã
BR-116
Itambé
Ilororó
Colônia
Itaju do Colônia
Pardo
Itapetinga
Itatingui
Reserva Biológica Mico Leão de Una
Una
Encruzilhada
Macarani
Pau Brasil
Camaçari
Maiquinique
Potiraguá
Mascote
Divisópolis
Itarantim
Pardo
BR-101
Canavieiras
Bandeira
Jordânia
Jequitinhonha
Salto da Divisa
Itapebi
Belmonte
Almenara
Jacinto
Itajimirim
Boca do Córrego
Barrolândia
Santa Sto Antônio
Rubim
Eunápolis
Sul
Santa Cruz Cabrália
Rio de Prado
Santo Antônio do Jacinto
Buranhém
N Sra da Ajuda
Porto Seguro
Arraial d'Ajuda
Guaratinga
Cajuíta
Frade
Trancoso
2 de Abril
Caraíva
Caraíva
Bertópolis
Jucuruçu
536
Monte Pascoal
Ponta Corumbaú
Parque Nacional de Monte Pascoal
Machacalis
Itanhém
Itamaraju
Medeiro Neto
Serra dos Aimorés
Pampo
Itanhém
BR-101
Prado
Nova Lidice
Carlos Chagas
Teixeira de Freitas
Recifes de Guaratibas
Alcobaça
Ibarapuã
Nanuque
Sa dos Aimorés
Ponta da Baleia
Caravelas
Helvécia
Melo
Ilha Caravelas
Mucuri
Montanha
250
Nova Viçosa
Parque Nacional Marinho dos Abrolhos
Mucuri
S João do Sobrado
Reserva Biológica de Córrego Grande
Ilha Sta Bárbara
Pinheiros
Reserva Biológica do Córrego do Veado
Itaúnas
São Mateus
234
BR-116
Barragem Pedro do Cavalo
Muritiba
Santo Amaro
Catu
Subaúma
BA-099
Pto Suipé
Mata de São João
Cruz das Almas
Cachoeira
Iaçu
Milagres
398
Castro Alves
Recôncavo
Maragojipe
Candeias
Camaçari
Praia do Forte
Ponta Açu da Torre
Baía de Todos os Santos
Santo Antônio de Jesus
S Mig das Matas
Simões Filho
Itaparica
Lauro Freitas
Nazaré
Mutuípe
BR-101
Santa Inês
Jiquiriça
Jaguaripe
Ilha Itaparica
SALVADOR (BAHIA)
Guaibim
Valença
Morro de São Paulo
Gamboa
Taperoá
Ilha de Tinharé
Pardo
Ituberá
Ilha de Boipeba
Camamu
Ponta de Apaga Fogo
Ponta do Mutá
Península do Maraú
Ilha Cruz
Maraú
Itacaré
Ponta Sa Grande
11
12
13

Araguari
Abadia
Coromandel
Serra da Carcaça
Pres Olegário
Patos de Minas
Galena
BR-365
S Gonçalo do Abaeté
Abaeté
Três Marias
389
Estação Ecológica Parapitinga
Represa Três Marias
Andrequice
Contria
Augusto de Lima
Estrela do Sul
Monte Carmelo
Romaria
Uberlândia
Guimarânia
Lagoa Formosa
Morada Nova de Minas
Paineiras
Corinto
Senhora da Glória
Velhas
Patrocínio
Quintinos
530
BR-040
Curvelo
Indianópolis
Irai de Minas
Frei Oriando
Felixlândia
Inimutaba
Pres Juscelino
Nova Ponte
Carmo do Paranaiba
Serra da Mata da Corda
Tiros
Indaiá
Serra da Saudade
MINAS GERAIS
Quebra-Aznol
Santa Juliana
Perdizes
Rio Paranaiba
Abaete
Anguerетá
Santana
São Gotardo
Pompeu
1147
Zelândia
Ibiá
S Francisco
Martinho Campos
Paraopeba
Jequitibá
BR-050
Araxá
Estrela do Indaiá
Dores do Indaiá
Papagaios
775
Caetanópolis
Uberaba
Pratinha
Campos Altos
Pará
Sête Lagoas
Delta
Sacramento
Bom Despacho
Ribeirão das Neves
Matozinhos
Conquista
Tapira
Tapirai
Serra da Canastra
Luz
BR-262
Pitangui
Pedro Leopoldo
Igarapava
Moema
Esmeraldas
Rifaina
Pará de Minas
CONTAGEM
Miguelópolis
Buritizal
Estreito
Bambui
Lagoa da Prata
Parque Nacional da Serra da Canastra
Ipuã
Ituverava
Pedregulho
Sto Antônio do Monte
Betim
Guará
1047
Igualama
Ribeirao Corrente
Delfinópolis
S Roque de Minas
Itaúna
Ibirite
Represa Peixoto
Vargem Bonite
Doresópolis
Arcos
Divinópolis
Brumadinho
Morro Agudo
S Joaquim da Barra
Franca
Ponte Alta
Pains
Pedra de Indaia
Itatiaucu
Itabirito
Cassia
Babilônia
Piumhi
Itamembe
Itapederica
Itaguara
Orlândia
Itirapuã
São João Batista de Gloria
Passos
Corrego Fundo
Formiga
Carmo da Mata
Cláudio
Crucilandia
Capitólio
Furnas
Represa de Furnas
Carmópolis de Minas
Congonhas (do Campo)
BR-040
Serra da Moeda
Batatais
Sapuca
Itaú de Minas
391
S Sebastião do Paraiso
Alpinópolis
Guapé
Bamacho
Oliveira
Pontal
Brodowski
Cristais
Candeias
Passa Tempo
Ouro Branco
Jardinópolis
Altinópolis
Jacu
Carmo do R Claro
Ilicinea
Campo Belo
Entre Rios de Minas
Itamoji
Serra das Vertentes
Sertãozinho
RIBEIRÃO PRÊTO
São Pedro da Uniao
Campo do Meio
Aguanil
BR-381
São Tiago
Christiano Otoni
Serrana
Cajuru
M Sto de Minas
Nova Rezende
Boa Esperança
Bom Sucesso
Resende Costa
Lagoa Dourada
Cravinhos
Cassia dos Coqueiros
Guaranesia
Alterosa
Perdões
São João del Rei
Serra Azul
Pardo
Guaxupé
Muzambinho
Campos Gerais
Neponnuceno
Ijaci
Prados
Tiradentes
São Simao
Santana da Vargem
Nazareno
Luis Antonio
Santa Rosa de Viterbo
Mococa
Tapiratiba
Areado
Lavras
Barroso
860
Caconde
Alfenas
Três Pontas
Represa Camargo
Barbacena
Santa Rita do Passa Quatro
Tambaú
S José do R Pardo
Divisa Nova
Serrania
Paraguacu
Carmo la Cochoeira
Itutinge
Mogi-Guaçu
Casa Branca
Botelhos
Campestre
Carrancas
Antônio Carlos
Represa Graminha
Varginha
Luminarias
1089
Madre de Deus de Minas
Descalvado
Ibate
Pto Ferreira
Vargem Grande do Sul
Machado
Eloi Mendes
Três Corações
Santana do Garambeu
Poços de Caldas
Monsenhor Paulo
Minduri
Grande
São Carlos
Pirassununga
S João da Boa Vista
Caldas
S Gonçalo do Sapucai
Cambuquira
Cruzilia
Parque Estação de Ibitipoca
Pedro Teixeira
Aquai
Santa Rita de Caldas
Andrrelândia
Leme
Guaçu
Andradas
Careaçu
Lambari
Baependi
Itirapina
Esp Santo do Pinhal
1500
Ipuiúna
Congonhal
Caxambu
Carvalhos
Bom Jardim de Minas
Lima Duarte
RIO CLARO
Araras
Jacutinga
Ouro Fino
Pouso Alegre
Berda da Mata
Carmo de Minas
Parque Estação da Serra do Papagaio
Serra da Mantiqueira
Moji-mirim
Moji-Guaçu
São Lourenço
S Seb do R Verde
Santa Rita de Jacutinge
Rio Preto
Santa Barbara de Monte Verde
São Pedro
Limeira
Itapira
Monte Siao
Santa Rita do Sapucaí
Maria da Fé
Itamonte
Preto
Nogueita
Aguas de Lindóia
2781
Virginia
Pico das Agulhas Negras
Piracicaba
Cosmpoiis
Serra Negra
Evista
BR-381
Brasópolis
Itajubá
Parque Nacional do Itatiaia
Conservatoria
Valença
Americana
Socorro
Paraisópolis
2422
S Barbara d'Oeste
Paulinia
Amparo
Cambui
Cruzeiro
Itatias
Resende
Volta Redonda
Vassouras
Miguel Pereira
Sumaré
Mte Alegre
Campos do Jordão
Piquete
BR-116
Barra Mansa
Barra do Pirai
Tietê
Itapeva
Cach Paulista
Capivari
CAMPINAS
Extrema
Macaco
Bananal
Paracambi
Japeri
Valinhos
Bragança Paulista
Apatecida
Lorena
Rio Claro
Pirai
BELFORD ROXO
Indaiatuba
Itatiba
Res Jaguari
Guaratinguetá
Seropédica
Tietê
Vinhedo
Piracaia
Roseira
Estação Ecológica de Piral
Pto Feliz
Salto
Jundiai
Atibaia
Taubaté
Pindamonhangaba
2085
N IGUAÇU
Verzea Paulista
Lagoinha
Cunhembebe
Mangaratiba
NITÓPOLIS
Boituva
Itu
Francisco Morato
Caçapava
Cunha
P N de Serra da Bocaina
Franco da Rocha
Santa Isabel
SAN JUAN DOS CAMPOS
Angra dos Reis
Santa Cruz
Campo Grande
SOROCABA
Jacarei
Redenção da Serra
Catucaba
Paraty (Parati)
Estação Ecológica de Tamoios
990
Ilha Grande
644
Restinga de Marambala
B de Sepetiba
OSASCO
GUARULHOS
Santa Branca
Votorantim
San Miguel Paulista
Natividade da Serra
Trinidade
Baia de Ilha Grande
Ilha Jorge Greco
SÃO PAULO
STO ANDRE
Ubatuba
Picinguaba
Ponta de Juatinga
Piedade
Embu
S BERNARDO
Salesópolis
Ilha Achieta
Pilar do Sul
1083
Itapecerica da Cerra
Diadema
Caraguatatuba
Em Guaçu
Cubacão
Bertioga
Marasias
Pto Novo
Serra do Paranapiacaba
São Vicente
SANTOS
S Sebastião
Ilhabela
Ilha da Vitória
1379
Ilha dos Búzios
Mongagua
Vicente de Carvalho
Cambanquara
Pedro Barros
Praia Grande
Guarujá
Ens das Enchovas
Ilhabela (Ilha de São Sebastião)
Juquiá
Ana Dias
Itanhaém
Itariri
Peruibe
Ilha de Alcatrazes
Estação Ecológica de Tupinambás

Q
R
400
Malacacheta
Teófilo Otoni
Carlos Chagras
Aimorés
Ibarapuã
Diamantina
Serra Negra
Agua Boa
Santa Maria do Suacui
Itambacuri
Nanuque
Sa dos Aimorés
Helvécia
2033
Pico de Itambé
Rio Vermelho
B r a s i l
Campanamo
Ataléia
Mucurici
Montanha
Mucuri
Serro
S João Evangelista
Virgolândia
Marilac
BR-116
Pescador
250
S João do Sobrado
Reserva de Côrre
Sabinópolis
Pecanha
Serra das Safiras
Ecoporanga
Guanhães
Coroaci
Frei Inocêncio
Itabirinha de Mantena
Pinhelros
Reserva Biológica do Corrego do Veado
Serra
765
Dom Joaquim
Governador Valadares
Central de Minas
São Mateus
Itaúnas
13
Conceição do Mato Dentro
Correntes
São Vitór
Mantena
Barra do São Francisco
Nova Venécia
Conceição da Barra
1304
Acucena
Doce
Mantenópolis
Ferros
Santo Antônio
Tumiritinga
Jaguaré
São Mateus
Parque Nacional da Serra do Cipó
Itanhorni
Galileia
S José
São Gabriel
Seca
Naque
Conselheiro Pena
Valério
Santa Maria de Itabira
Barra Alegre
Ipatinga
Sobrália
Culeté
S Domingos
Reserva Biológica de Sooretama
Dom Cavat
Pancas
ESPÍRITO SANTO
BR-381
Cnl Fabriciano
Angelo Resplendor
Itabira
Timóteo
Alvaranga
Frechiani
Bananal
João Monlevade
Reserva Florestal do Rio Doce
Inhabin
Aimorés
Baixo Guandu
Juparanã
Caete
BR-116
Caratinga
Pocrane
Colatina
Linhares
Santa Barbara
Rio Piracicaba
São Domingos do Prata
Ipanema
Ibituba
Itapina
L Monsaráz
Bom Jesus de Galho
R B Augusto Ruschi
Guandu
Guaraná
Povoação
Aguas Ferreas
Mutun
Itaguaçu
Doce
Alvinópolis
Santa Bárbara
Estação Biologica de Caratinga
Regência
Rio Casca
Laranja de Terra
João Neiva
Ponta do Mansaraz
Camargos
Dom Correa
Itarana
Ibiracu
Barra do Riacho
D Silverio
Doce
Raul Soares
Chale
729
Aracruz
Mariana
Rio Doce
BR-262
Afonso Cláudio
Santa Teresa
Fundão
Manhuaçu
Martins Soares
Santa Maria de Jetiba
Santa Cruz
Jequeri
Lajinha
Brejetuba
Ponte Nova
Sta Margarida
Manhumirim
Ibatiba
Santa Leopoldina
Nova Almeida
2890
Venda Nova do Imigrante
Serra
Piranga
Sericita
Pico da Bandetra
Lúna
BR-262
Carapina
Jacaraipe
Parque Nacional da Capraó
Muniz Freire
Cariacica
Canaa
Araponga
1098
Domingos Martins
Jacu
Vitória
Viçosa
Serra do Caparaó
Divino
Parque Estadual Pedra Azul
Vila Velha
14
Sen Firmino
Coimbra
Ervália
Glória
Espera Feliz
Ibitirama
Viana
Rio Espera
Anutiba
Castelo
Alfredo Chaves
Sagrada Familia
Jucu
Carangola
BR-116
Itapemirim
Parque Estadual Paulo Cesar Vinha
Alto R Doce
Divinesia
Visconde do R Branco
Miradouro
Guaçui
Cachoeiro do Itapemirim
Guarapari
Porciúncula
Alegre
Marces
Ubá
Muriaé
Eugenópolis
Varre-Sai
Muqui
Anchieta
Natividade
Mimoso do Sul
Rio Novo do Sul
Piuma
Iteipava
Tabulero
Rio Pomba
Mirai
Patrocinio do Muriae
Itaperuna
Bom Jesus
Itapemirim
Anu
Maratalzes
Guarani
Cataguases
São Jose das Torres
Pres Kennedy
Novo
S João Nepomuceno
Palma
726
Pedra do Baú
Ponte de Itabapoana
Neves
Pomba
Miracema
Cnl Pacheco
Leopoldina
Italva
Itabapoana
BR-101
JUIZ DE FORA
S Antônio de Padua
Cardoso Moreira
Muriaé
Cons Josino
Ponta do Retiro
Barra Seca
Bicas
Aperibe
Matias Barbosa
Volte Grande
Itaocara
Travessão
Guaxindiba
Mar de Espanha
Sul
L do Campero
Gargau
São Fidelis
Euclidelandia
Grande
1576
S João da Bara
Lago Cima
Alem Paraiba
Paraiba do
P São Mateus
Campos
Ibitiana
Rios
Sapucaia
Cantagalo
Santa Maria Madalena
São Sebastiao de Campos
RIO DE JANEIRO
Cordeiro
Tocos
Duas Barras
Conceição de Macabu
Cabo de São Tomé
Lago Feia
Sul
Cons Paulino
1429
Posse
São Tomé (Farlo)
Carapebus
Quiçamã
Cabionas
Cascatinha
Serra dos Orgãos
Nova Friburgo
Barra do Pires
Teresópolis
Lumiar
Parque Nacional da Restinga de Jurubatiba
Petrópolis
Cachoeiras de Macacu
Casimiro de Abreu
Barra de Macaé
R B do Tingua
Macaé
806
Majé
Japuiba
Ilha de Santana
RB do Poco das Antas
Rio das Ostras
UQUE DE CAXAIS
Neves
Itabora
Rio Bonito
Barra de São João
Ipijba
Araruama
São Vicente de Paula
Cabo dos Búzios
NITERÓI
São Pedro
Armação dos Búzios (Búzios)
IO DE ANEIRO
Ponta Negra
Saquarema
Cabo Frio
Lago de Araruama
Arraial do Cabo
Ilha do Cabo Frio
15
Q
R

MAPS | INDEX

MAPS INDEX

MAPS | INDEX

MAPS | INDEX

MAPS INDEX

G

H

I

J

K

L

M

N

S

PICTURES

The Automobile Association wishes to thank the following photographers and organizations for their assistance in the preparation of this book.

Abbreviations for the picture credits are as follows – (t) top; (b) bottom; (l) left; (r) right; (c) centre; (AA) AA World Travel Library

2 AA/Julian Love;
3t AA/Paulo Fridman;
3ct AA/Alex Robinson;
3cb AA/Karl Blackwell;
3b AA/Julian Love;
4 AA/James Tims;
5 AA/Karl Blackwell;
6 AA/Karl Blackwell;
7bl Clive Sawyer;
7br AA/Karl Blackwell;
9bl AA/Julian Love;
9tr AA/Karl Blackwell;
10 AA/Julian Love;
11t AA/Karl Blackwell;
11b AA/Julian Love;
12b AA/Karl Blackwell;
13 AA/Yadid Levy;
14 Luiz C. Marigo/Photolibrary;
15tl Edward Parker/Alamy;
15br AA/Alex Robinson;
16 AA/Julian Love;
17bl AA/Karl Blackwell;
17br Lunae Parracho/LatinContent/Getty Images;
18 AA/Karl Blackwell;
19bl AA/Julian Love;
19tr Alexandre Meneghini/AP/Press Association Images;
20 AA/Yadid Levy;
21t Marcos Issa/Argosfoto;
21b Cesar Duarte/Argosfoto;
22tl AA/Julian Love;
22tr AA/Karl Blackwell;
23 Bibliotheque Nationale, Paris, France/Giraudon/The Bridgeman Art Library;
24 Service Historique de la Marine, Vincennes, France/Giraudon/The Bridgeman Art Library;
25bl Tony Morrison/South American Pictures;
25tr Private Collection/Index/The Bridgeman Art Library;
26 Museum Paulista/USP Collection/Helio Nobre;
27bl Private Collection/The Stapleton Collection/The Bridgeman Art Library;
27br BrazilPhotos.com/Alamy;
28 Tony Morrison/South American Pictures;
29bl AA/Karl Blackwell;
29tr Private Collection/Michael Graham-Stewart/The Bridgeman Art Library;
30 Duravitski/Alamy;
31bl AA/Julian Love;
31tr Interfoto/Alamy;
32 BrazilPhotos.com/Alamy;
33bl Stefano Bianchetti/Corbis;
33br Museu Historico Nacional, Rio de Janeiro, Brazil/Giraudon/The Bridgeman Art Library;
34 Juca Martins/argosfoto;
35bl O. Reitz/Royal Geographical Society;
35tr Paul Schutzer//Time Life Pictures/Getty Images;
36 Alexandre Guzanshe/FotoArena/LatinContent/Getty Images;
37 AA/Julian Love;
38 AA/Julian Love;
41 AA/Alex Robinson;
42 AA/Karl Blackwell;
44t AA/Alex Robinson;
44b AA/Alex Robinson;
45 AA/Paulo Fridman;
47 AA/Julian Love;
49 AA/Julian Love;
50 AA/Alex Robinson;
51 AA/Alex Robinson;
52 AA/Julian Love;
53 AA/Julian Love;
54 AA/Julian Love;
62 AA/Julian Love;
63bl AA/Julian Love;
63br AA/Julian Love;
64 AA/Julian Love;
65 AA/Julian Love;
66 Michele Falzone/Alamy;
67 AA/Julian Love;
68tl AA/Julian Love;
68tr AA/Julian Love;
69 AA/Julian Love;
70 AA/Julian Love;
71bl AA/Julian Love;
71br AA/Julian Love;
72 AA/Julian Love;
73 AA/Julian Love;
74 AA/Julian Love;
75 AA/Julian Love;
76 AA/Julian Love;
77bl AA/Julian Love;
77br AA/Julian Love;
78 AA/Julian Love;
79bl AA/Julian Love;
79br AA/Julian Love;
80bl AA/Julian Love;
80br AA/Julian Love;
81 AA/Julian Love;
82 AA/Julian Love;
83bl AA/Julian Love;
83br AA/Julian Love;
84 AA/Julian Love;
85tl AA/Julian Love;
85tr AA/Julian Love;
86 AA/Julian Love;
87 AA/Julian Love;
88 AA/Julian Love;
89 AA/Julian Love;
90 AA/Julian Love;
91 Mike Lane/NHPA/Photoshot;
92 AA/Julian Love;
95 AA/Julian Love;
98 AA/Julian Love;
100 AA/Julian Love;
101 AA/Julian Love;
102 AA/Julian Love;
104bl AA/Julian Love;
104br AA/Julian Love;
105 AA/Julian Love;
106 AA/Alex Robinson;
110 David R. Frazier Photolibrary, Inc./Alamy;
111 AA/Alex Robinson;
112tl AA/Alex Robinson;
112tr AA/Alex Robinson;
113 AA/Alex Robinson;
114 AA/Alex Robinson;
115bl AA/Alex Robinson;
115br AA/Alex Robinson;
116 AA/Alex Robinson;
117 AA/Alex Robinson;
118 JTB Photo Communications, Inc./Alamy;
119 AA/Alex Robinson;
120tl AA/Alex Robinson;
120tr AA/Alex Robinson;
121 Tibor Bognar/Alamy;
122 AA/Alex Robinson;
123bl AA/Alex Robinson;
123br AA/Alex Robinson;
124 AA/Alex Robinson;
125bl AA/Alex Robinson;

125br AA/Alex Robinson;
126 AA/Alex Robinson;
127 AA/Alex Robinson;
128 AA/Alex Robinson;
131tl AA/Alex Robinson;
131tr AA/Alex Robinson;
132 Sipa Press/Rex Features;
134 AA/Alex Robinson;
136 AA/Alex Robinson;
138 AA/Julian Love;
140 AA/Julian Love;
141 StockBrazil/Alamy;
142 AA/Julian Love;
143 Cristiano Burmester/Alamy;
144tl AA/Julian Love;
144tr AA/Julian Love;
145 AA/Julian Love;
146 AA/Julian Love;
147 AA/Julian Love;
148 AA/Julian Love;
149 AA/Julian Love;
150 AA/Julian Love;
151 Arco Images GmbH/Alamy;
152 Mark Bowler/Nature Picture Library;
153tl AA/Julian Love;
153tr AA/Julian Love;
154 AA/Julian Love;
156 AA/Julian Love;
158 AA/Julian Love;
160 AA/Paulo Fridman;
162 AA/Paulo Fridman;
163 AA/Paulo Fridman;
164 AA/Paulo Fridman;
165 AA/Paulo Fridman;
166 AA/James Tims;
167bl AA/James Tims;
167br AA/James Tims;
168 StockBrazil/Alamy;
169 Sue Cunningham Photographic/Alamy;
170 Peter Arnold, Inc./Alamy;
171bl Justin Wastnage/Alamy;
171br AA/Paulo Fridman;
172 AA/Paulo Fridman;
173 AA/Paulo Fridman;
174 AA/James Tims;
176 AA/Paulo Fridman;
178 AA/James Tims;
180 AA/Yadid Levy;
182 Andre Seale/Alamy;
183 AA/Yadid Levy;
184 AA/Yadid Levy;
185tl GM Photo Images/Alamy;
185tr BrazilPhotos.com/Alamy;
186 GTW GTW/www.photolibrary.com;
187 GTW GTW/www.photolibrary.com;
188 AA/Yadid Levy;
189bl AA/Yadid Levy;
189br AA/Yadid Levy;
190 Arco Images GmbH/Alamy;
191 Andre Seale/Alamy;
192 AA/Yadid Levy;
194 Ingolf Pompe 25/Alamy;
195 Haroldo Palo JR/NHPA/Photoshot;
196bl AA/Yadid Levy;
196br Genevieve Vallee/Alamy;
198 AA/Yadid Levy;
200 AA/Yadid Levy;
202 AA/Karl Blackwell;
204 AA/Yadid Levy;
205 Pete Oxford/Nature Picture Library;
206 AA/Karl Blackwell;
207bl AA/Karl Blackwell;
207br AA/Karl Blackwell;
208 Steven Poe/Alamy;
209 AA/Karl Blackwell;
210tl AA/Yadid Levy;
210tr A.N.T. Photo Library/NHPA/Photoshot;
211 AA/Yadid Levy;
212 AA/Karl Blackwell;
213 AA/Karl Blackwell;
214 AA/Karl Blackwell;
215 Edward Parker/Alamy;
216bl AA/Karl Blackwell;
216br AA/Karl Blackwell;
217 AA/Karl Blackwell;
218 AA/Karl Blackwell;
219 AA/Karl Blackwell;
220 AA/Karl Blackwell;
221tl AA/Karl Blackwell;
221tr AA/Karl Blackwell;
222 AA/Karl Blackwell;
223 AA/Karl Blackwell;
224 AA/Karl Blackwell;
225tl AA/Karl Blackwell;
225tr AA/Karl Blackwell;
226 AA/Karl Blackwell;
227 AA/Karl Blackwell;
229 AA/Yadid Levy;
230 AA/Karl Blackwell;
232 AA/Yadid Levy;
234 AA/Karl Blackwell;
235 AA/Karl Blackwell;
236 AA/Yadid Levy;
239 AA/Karl Blackwell;
240 AA/Karl Blackwell;
242 AA/Karl Blackwell;
244 AA/Karl Blackwell;
245 Stefano Paterna/Alamy;
246 Agencia Argosfoto;
247 AA/Karl Blackwell;
248 Lonely Planet Images/Alamy;
249 Robert Harding Picture Library Ltd/Alamy;
250 AA/Karl Blackwell;
251bl AA/Karl Blackwell;
251br AA/Karl Blackwell;
252bl Stefano Paterna/Alamy;
252br Thomas Cockrem/Alamy;
253 Marka/Alamy;
254 AA/Karl Blackwell;
256 AA/Karl Blackwell;
257tl AA/Karl Blackwell;
257tr AA/Karl Blackwell;
258 AA/Karl Blackwell;
259bl AA/Karl Blackwell;
259br AA/Karl Blackwell;
260 AA/Karl Blackwell;
262 AA/Karl Blackwell;
264 AA/Karl Blackwell;
266 AA/Karl Blackwell;
268 AA/Karl Blackwell;
270 Balthasar Thomass/Alamy;
271 BrazilPhotos.com/Alamy;
272tl Franck Camhi/Alamy;
272tr Hemis/Alamy;
273 Franck Camhi/Alamy;
274 AA/Karl Blackwell;
275 AA/Karl Blackwell;
276 Mike Lane/NHPA/Photoshot;
277tl Sergio Tafner Jorge/www.photolibrary.com;
277tr Gary Cook/Alamy;
278 AA/Karl Blackwell;
279 AA/Karl Blackwell;
280 Genevieve Vallee/Alamy;
281bl Robert Harding Picture Library Ltd/Alamy;
281br Balthasar Thomass/Alamy;
282 BrazilPhotos.com/Alamy;
283 AA/Karl Blackwell;
284 AA/Karl Blackwell;
285bl AA/Karl Blackwell;
285br AA/Karl Blackwell;
286 Genevieve Vallee/Alamy;
287tl Genevieve Vallee/Alamy;
287tr Balthasar Thomass/Alamy;
288 AA/Karl Blackwell;
290 AA/Karl Blackwell;
292 AA/Karl Blackwell;
294 Edson Endrigo/Cristalino Jungle Lodge;
296 AA/Alex Robinson;
297 Robert Harding Picture Library Ltd/Alamy;

298 AA/Alex Robinson;
299bl AA/Alex Robinson;
299br AA/Alex Robinson;
300 AA/Karl Blackwell;
302-303 AA/Karl Blackwell;
304 Cecile Dubois/Cristalino Jungle Lodge;
305 Balthasar Thomass/Alamy;
306 AA/Alex Robinson;
307bl AA/Alex Robinson;
307br AA/Alex Robinson;
308 Travel Pix/Alamy;
309 BrazilPhotos.com/Alamy;
310 Edward Parker/www.photolibrary.com;
311 Danita Delimont/Alamy;
312 AA/Karl Blackwell;
313 AA/Karl Blackwell;
314 AA/Karl Blackwell;
315 AA/Karl Blackwell;
316 AA/Alex Robinson;
317 AA/Karl Blackwell;
319 Katia Kuwabara/Cristalino Jungle Lodge;
320 AA/Alex Robinson;
322 Hemis/Alamy;
324 Travel Pix/Alamy;
325 Roberto Machado/www.photolibrary.com;
326 Alan Weintraub/Arcaid;
327 Galit Seligmann/Arcaid;
328 AA/Paulo Fridman;
330 AA/Paulo Fridman;
331 AA/Paulo Fridman;
332 Fabio Pili/Alamy;
333 Travel Ink/Alamy;
334 AA/Paulo Fridman;
335bl AA/James Tims;
335br AA/Paulo Fridman;
336 AA/Paulo Fridman;
338 AA/Julian Love;
340 Royal Tulip Alvorada;
342 AA/Paulo Fridman;
343 AA/Karl Blackwell;
346 AA/Julian Love;
349 AA/Karl Blackwell;
350 AA/Julian Love;
351 AA/Julian Love;
352 AA/Julian Love;
356 AA/Julian Love;
357 AA/Karl Blackwell;
358 AA/Julian Love;
359 AA/Julian Love;
360 AA/Paulo Fridman;
362 AA/Yadid Levy;
363 AA/Yadid Levy;
364 AA/Karl Blackwell;
365bl AA/Julian Love;
365br AA/Julian Love;
366 AA/Karl Blackwell;
367 AA/Julian Love;
368 AA/Karl Blackwell;
369tl AA/Karl Blackwell;
369tr AA/Yadid Levy;
375 AA/Paulo Fridman.

Every effort has been made to trace the copyright holders, and we apologize in advance for any unintentional omissions or errors. We would be pleased to apply any corrections in a following edition of this publication.

CREDITS

Series editor
Sheila Hawkins

Title editor
Marie-Claire Jefferies

Project editor
Lodestone Publishing Ltd

Copy editor
Jennifer Wood

Design
Low Sky Design Ltd

Cover design
Chie Ushio

Picture research
Alice Earle

Image retouching and repro
Sarah Montgomery

Mapping
Maps produced by the Mapping Services Department of AA Publishing

Author
Alex Robinson

Verifier
Jane Egginton

Indexer
Marie Lorimer

Production
Lorraine Taylor

See It Brazil
ISBN 978-0-87637-147-3
First Edition

Published in the United States by Fodor's Travel and simultaneously in Canada by Random House of Canada Limited, Toronto.
Published in the United Kingdom by AA Publishing.
Fodor's is a registered trademark of Random House, Inc., and Fodor's See It is a trademark of Random House, Inc.
Fodor's Travel is a division of Random House, Inc.

Color separation by AA Digital Department
Printed and bound by Leo Paper Products, China
10 9 8 7 6 5 4 3 2 1

Special Sales: This book is available for special discounts for bulk purchases for sales promotions or premiums. Special editions, including personalized covers, excerpts of existing books, and corporate imprints, can be created in large quantities for special needs.
For more information, write to Special Markets/Premium Sales, 1745 Broadway, New York, NY 10019
or e-mail specialmarkets@randomhouse.com
Important Note: Time inevitably brings changes, so always confirm prices, travel facts, and other perishable information when it matters. Although Fodor's cannot accept responsibility for errors, you can use this guide in the confidence that we have taken every care to ensure its accuracy.

A04922
Mapping in this title produced from map data supplied by Global Mapping, Brackley, UK. Copyright © Global Mapping/ITMB
Additional data from Mountain High Maps © Copyright © 1993 Digital Wisdom, Inc.
Transport maps © Communicarta Ltd, UK
Weather chart statistics supplied by Weatherbase © Copyright 2011 Canty and Associates, LLC.